Top 100 CAREERS

Without a Four-Year Degree™

Your Complete Guidebook to Major Jobs in Many Fields

P9-DIE-084

NINTH EDITION

Michael Farr

JIST Works
America's Career Publisher®

Top 100 Careers Without a Four-Year Degree, Ninth Edition
Your Complete Guidebook to Major Jobs in Many Fields

© 2009 by JIST Publishing

Published by JIST Works, an imprint of JIST Publishing
7321 Shadeland Station, Suite 200
Indianapolis, IN 46256-3923
Phone: 800-648-JIST   Fax: 877-454-7839
E-mail: info@jist.com   Web site: www.jist.com

Some books by Michael Farr:
Best Jobs for the 21st Century
Overnight Career Choice
Same-Day Resume
Next-Day Job Interview
The Quick Resume & Cover Letter Book
The Very Quick Job Search

JIST's Top Careers™ Series:
Top 300 Careers
Top 100 Health-Care Careers
100 Fastest-Growing Jobs
Top 100 Careers Without a Four-Year Degree
Top 100 Careers for College Graduates
Top 100 Computer and Technical Careers

Visit www.jist.com for free job search information, tables of contents, sample pages, and ordering information on our many products.

Quantity discounts are available for JIST products. Have future editions of JIST books automatically delivered to you on publication through our convenient standing order program. Please call 800-648-JIST or visit www.jist.com for a free catalog and more information.

Acquisitions Editor: Susan Pines
Development Editor: Stephanie Koutek
Database Work: Laurence Shatkin
Cover Photo: Frank Walker, Ton studio 8, iStock
Cover Layout: Alan Evans
Interior Design and Layout: Marie Kristine Parial-Leonardo, Aleata Halbig
Proofreaders: Linda Seifert, Jeanne Clark

Printed in the United States of America

13 12 11 10 09 08   9 8 7 6 5 4 3 2 1

Library of Congress Cataloging-in-Publication Data

Farr, J. Michael.
   Top 100 careers without a four-year degree : your complete guidebook to
   major jobs in many fields / Michael Farr. -- 9th ed.
        p. cm. -- (JIST's top careers series)
   Includes index.
   ISBN 978-1-59357-600-4 (alk. paper)
   1. Vocational guidance--United States. 2. Occupations--United States. 3.
   Job hunting--United States. 4. Employment forecasting--United States. 5.
   Résumés (Employment) 6. Vocational qualifications. I. Title. II. Title:
   Top one hundred careers without a four-year degree.
   HF5382.5.U5F375 2008
   331.702--dc22

                                        2008038777

All rights reserved. No part of this book may be reproduced in any form or by any means, or stored in a database or retrieval system, without prior permission of the publisher except in the case of brief quotations embodied in articles or reviews. Making copies of any part of this book for any purpose other than your own personal use is a violation of United States copyright laws. For permission requests, please contact the Copyright Clearance Center at www.copyright.com or (978) 750-8400.

We have been careful to provide accurate information throughout this book, but it is possible that errors and omissions have been introduced. Please consider this in making any career plans or other important decisions. Trust your own judgment above all else and in all things.

Trademarks: All brand names and product names used in this book are trade names, service marks, trademarks, or registered trademarks of their respective owners.

ISBN 978-1-59357-600-4

Relax. You Don't Have to Read This Whole Book!

You don't need to read this entire book. I've organized it into easy-to-use sections so you can get just the information you want. You will find everything you need to

★ Learn about the 100 top careers that don't require a four-year college degree, including their daily tasks, pay, outlook, and required education and skills.

★ Match your personal skills to the careers.

★ Take seven steps to land a good job in less time.

To get started, simply scan the table of contents to learn more about these sections and to see a list of the jobs described in this book. Really, this book is easy to use, and I hope it helps you.

Who Should Use This Book?

This is more than a book of job descriptions. I've spent quite a bit of time thinking about how to make its contents useful for a variety of situations, including

★ **Exploring career options.** The job descriptions in Part II give a wealth of information on many of the most desirable jobs in the labor market. The assessment in Part I can help you focus your career options.

★ **Considering more education or training.** The information helps you avoid costly mistakes in choosing a career or deciding on additional training or education—and it increases your chances of planning a bright future.

★ **Job seeking.** This book helps you identify new job targets, prepare for interviews, and write targeted resumes. The advice in Part III has been proven to cut job search time in half.

★ **Career planning.** The job descriptions help you explore your options, and Parts III and IV provide career planning advice and other useful information.

Source of Information

The job descriptions come from the good people at the U.S. Department of Labor, as published in the most recent edition of the *Occupational Outlook Handbook*. The *OOH* is the best source of career information available, and the descriptions include the most current, accurate data on jobs. Thank you to all the people at the Department of Labor who gather, compile, analyze, and make sense of this information. It's good stuff, and I hope you can make good use of it.

Mike Farr

Mike Farr

Contents

Summary of Major Sections

Introduction. Provides an explanation of the job descriptions, how best to use the book, and other details. *Begins on page 1.*

Part I: Using the Job-Match Grid to Choose a Career. Match your skills and preferences to the jobs in this book. *Begins on page 15.*

Part II: Descriptions of the Top 100 Careers Without a Four-Year Degree. Presents thorough descriptions of the top 100 careers that don't require a four-year degree. Education and training requirements for these jobs vary from on-the-job training to less than a four-year degree. Each description gives information on the nature of the work, working conditions, employment, training, other qualifications, advancement, job outlook, earnings, related occupations, and sources of additional information. The jobs are presented in alphabetical order. The page numbers where specific descriptions begin are listed in the detailed contents. *Begins on page 31.*

Part III: *Quick Job Search—Seven Steps to Getting a Good Job in Less Time.* This relatively brief but important section offers results-oriented career planning and job search techniques. It includes tips on identifying your key skills, defining your ideal job, using effective job search methods, writing resumes, organizing your time, improving your interviewing skills, and following up on leads. The last part of this section features professionally written and designed resumes for some of the top jobs that don't require a four-year degree. *Begins on page 303.*

Part IV: Important Trends in Jobs and Industries. This section includes three well-written articles on labor market trends. The articles are worth your time. Titles of the articles are "Tomorrow's Jobs," "Employment Trends in Major Industries," and "Job Outlook for People Who Don't Have a Bachelor's Degree." *Begins on page 349.*

Detailed Contents

Part III: Quick Job Search—Seven Steps to Getting a Good Job in Less Time 303

Part IV: Important Trends in Jobs and Industries 359

Index 393

Introduction

This book is about improving your life, not just about selecting a job. The career you choose will have an enormous impact on how you live your life.

A huge amount of information is available on occupations, but most people don't know where to find accurate, reliable facts to help them make good career decisions—or they don't take the time to look. Important choices such as what to do with your career or whether to get additional training or education deserve your time.

If you are considering more training or education—whether additional coursework, an apprenticeship, or a two-year degree—this book will help with solid information. Training or education beyond high school is now typically required to get better jobs, and the education and training needed for the jobs in this book vary enormously. This book is designed to give you facts to help you explore your options.

A certain type of work or workplace may interest you as much as a certain type of job. If your interests and values lead you to work in health care, for example, you can do this in a variety of work environments, in a variety of industries, and in a variety of jobs. For this reason, I suggest you begin exploring alternatives by following your interests and finding a career path that allows you to use your talents doing something you enjoy.

Also, remember that money is not everything. The time you spend in career planning can pay off in higher earnings, but being satisfied with your work—and your life—is often more important than how much you earn. This book can help you find the work that suits you best.

Keep in Mind That Your Situation Is *Not* "Average"

Projected employment growth and earnings trends are quite positive for many occupations and industries. Keep in mind, however, that the averages in this book will not be true for many individuals. Within any field, many people earn more and many earn less than the average.

My point is that *your* situation is probably not average. Some people do better than others, and some are willing to accept less pay for a more desirable work environment. Earnings vary enormously in different parts of the country, in different occupations, and in different industries. But this book's solid information is a great place to start. Good information will give you a strong foundation for good decisions.

Four Important Labor Market Trends That Will Affect Your Career

Our economy has changed in dramatic ways over the past 10 years, with profound effects on how we work and live. Part IV of this book provides more information on labor market trends, but in case you don't read it, here are four trends that you simply *must* consider.

1. Education Pays

I'm sure you won't be surprised to learn that people with higher levels of education and training have higher average earnings. The data that follows comes from the U.S. Department of Labor. I've selected data to show you the median earnings for people with various levels of education. (The median is the point where half earn more and half earn less.) Based on this information, I computed the earnings advantage of people at various education levels over those who did not graduate from high school. I've also included information showing the average percentage of people at that educational level who are unemployed.

Earnings for Year-Round, Full-Time Workers Age 25 and Over, by Educational Attainment

Level of Education	Median Annual Earnings	Premium Over High School Dropouts	Unemployment Rate
Professional degree	$76,648	$54,860	1.1%
Doctoral degree	$74,932	$53,144	1.4%
Master's degree	$59,280	$37,492	1.7%
Bachelor's degree	$50,024	$28,236	2.3%
Associate degree	$37,492	$15,704	3.0%
Some college, no degree	$35,048	$13,260	3.9%
High-school graduate	$30,940	$9,152	4.3%
High school dropout	$21,788	—	6.8%

Source: Bureau of Labor Statistics

As you can see in the table, the earnings difference between someone who holds an associate degree and someone with a high school education is $6,552 a year, money that could be used toward a car, a down payment on a house, or even a vacation. As you see, over a lifetime, this earnings difference will make an enormous difference in lifestyle.

The table makes it very clear that those with more training and education earn more than those with less and experience lower levels of unemployment. Jobs that require education and training beyond high school are projected to grow significantly faster than jobs that do not. People with higher levels of education and training are less likely to be unemployed, and when they are, they remain unemployed for shorter periods of time. There are always exceptions, but it is quite clear that more education results in higher earnings and lower rates of unemployment.

2. Knowledge of Computer and Other Technologies Is Increasingly Important

As you look over the list of jobs in the table of contents, you may notice that many require computer or technical skills. Even jobs that do not appear to be technical often call for computer literacy. Agricultural managers, for example, are often expected to understand and use scheduling and estimating software.

In all fields, those without job-related technical and computer skills will have a more difficult time finding good opportunities because they are competing with those who have these skills. Older workers, by the way, often do not have the computer skills that younger workers do. Employers tend to hire people who have the skills they need, and people without these abilities won't get the best jobs. So, whatever your age, consider upgrading your job-related computer and technology skills if you need to—and plan to stay up to date on your current and future jobs.

3. Ongoing Education and Training Are Essential

School and work once were separate activities, and most people did not go back to school after they began working. But with rapid changes in technology, most people are now required to learn throughout their work lives. Jobs are constantly upgraded, and today's jobs often cannot be handled by people who have only the knowledge and skills that were adequate for workers a few years ago.

To remain competitive, you will need to constantly upgrade your technology and other job-related skills. This may include taking formal courses, reading work-related magazines at home, signing up for on-the-job training, or participating in other forms of education. Upgrading your work-related skills on an ongoing basis is no longer optional for most jobs, and you ignore doing so at your peril.

4. Good Career Planning Is More Important Than Ever

Most people spend more time watching TV in a week than they spend on career planning during an entire year. Yet most people will change their jobs many times and make major career changes five to seven times. For this reason, it is important for you to spend time considering your career options and preparing to advance.

While you probably picked up this book for its information on jobs, it also provides a great deal of information on career planning. For example, Part III gives good career and job search advice, and Part IV has useful information on labor market trends. I urge you to read these and related materials because career-planning and job-seeking skills are the keys to surviving in this new economy.

Tips on Using This Book

This book is based on information from a variety of government sources and includes the most up-to-date and accurate data available. The entries are well written and pack a lot of information into short descriptions. *Top 100 Careers Without a Four-Year Degree* can be used in many ways, and I've provided tips for these four major uses:

★ For people exploring career, education, or training alternatives

★ For job seekers

★ For employers and business people

★ For counselors, instructors, and other career specialists

Tips for People Exploring Career, Education, or Training Alternatives

Top 100 Careers Without a Four-Year Degree is an excellent resource for anyone exploring career, education, or training alternatives. Many people do not have a good idea of what they want to do in their careers. They may be considering additional training or education but may not know what sort they should get. If you are one of these people, this book can help in several ways. Here are a few pointers.

Review the list of jobs. Trust yourself. Research studies indicate that most people have a good sense of their interests. Your interests can be used to guide you to career options you should consider in more detail.

Begin by looking over the occupations listed in the table of contents. Look at all the jobs, because you may identify previously overlooked possibilities. If other people will be using this book, please don't mark in it. Instead, on a separate sheet of paper, list the jobs that interest you. Or make a photocopy of the table of contents and use it to mark the jobs that interest you.

Next, look up and carefully read the descriptions of the jobs that most interest you in Part II. A quick review will often eliminate one or more of these jobs based on pay, working conditions, education required, or other considerations. After you have identified the three or four jobs that seem most interesting, research each one more thoroughly before making any important decisions.

Match your skills to the jobs in this book using the Job-Match Grid. Another way to identify possible job options is to answer questions about your skills and job preferences in Part I, "Using the Job-Match Grid to Choose a Career." This section will help you focus your job options and concentrate your research on a handful of job descriptions.

Study the jobs and their training and education requirements. Too many people decide to obtain additional training or education without knowing much about the jobs the training will lead to. Reviewing the descriptions in this book is one way to learn more about an occupation before you enroll in an education or training program. If you are currently a student, the job descriptions in this book can also help you decide on a major course of study or learn more about the jobs for which your studies are preparing you.

Do not be too quick to eliminate a job that interests you. If a job requires more education or training than you currently have, you can obtain this training in many ways.

Don't abandon your past experience and education too quickly. If you have significant work experience, training, or education, these should not be abandoned too quickly. Many times, after people carefully consider what they want to do, they change careers and find that the skills they have can still be used.

Top 100 Careers Without a Four-Year Degree can help you explore career options in several ways. First, carefully review descriptions for jobs you have held in the past. On a separate sheet of paper, list the skills needed in those jobs. Then do the same for jobs that interest you now. By comparing the lists, you will be able to identify skills you used in previous jobs that you could also use in jobs that interest you for the future. These "transferable" skills form the basis for moving to a new career.

You can also identify skills you have developed or used in nonwork activities, such as hobbies, family responsibilities, volunteer work, school, military, and extracurricular interests. If you want to stay with your current employer, the job descriptions can also help. For example, you may identify jobs within your organization that offer more rewarding work, higher pay, or other advantages over your present job. Read the descriptions related to these jobs, as you may be able to transfer into another job rather than leave the organization.

Tips for Job Seekers

You can use the job descriptions in this book to give you an edge in finding job openings and in getting job offers—even when you are competing with people who have better credentials. Here are some ways *Top 100 Careers Without a Four-Year Degree* can help you in the job search.

Identify related job targets. You may be limiting your job search to a small number of jobs for which you feel qualified, but by doing so you eliminate many jobs you could do and enjoy. Your search for a new job should be broadened to include more possibilities.

Go through the entire list of jobs in the table of contents and check any that require skills similar to those you have. Look at all the jobs, as doing so sometimes helps you identify targets you would otherwise overlook.

You may want to answer questions about your skills and job preferences in Part I, "Using the Job-Match Grid to Choose a Career." Your results can help you identify career options that may suit you.

© JIST Works

Many people are not aware of the many specialized jobs related to their training or experience. The descriptions in *Top 100 Careers Without a Four-Year Degree* are for major job titles, but a variety of more-specialized jobs may require similar skills. The "Other Major Career Information Sources" section later in this introduction lists sources you can use to find out about more-specialized jobs.

The descriptions can also point out jobs that interest you but that have higher responsibility or compensation levels. While you may not consider yourself qualified for such jobs now, you should think about seeking jobs that are above your previous levels but within your ability to handle.

Prepare for interviews. This book's job descriptions are an essential source of information to help you prepare for interviews. If you carefully review the description of a job before an interview, you will be much better prepared to emphasize your key skills. You should also review descriptions for past jobs and identify skills needed in the new job.

Negotiate pay. The job descriptions in this book will help you know what pay range to expect. Note that local pay and other details can differ substantially from the national averages in the descriptions.

Tips for Employers and Business People

Employers, human resource professionals, and other business users can use this book's information to write job descriptions, study pay ranges, and set criteria for new employees. The information can also help you conduct more-effective interviews by providing a list of key skills needed by new hires.

Tips for Counselors, Instructors, and Other Career Specialists

Counselors, instructors, and other career specialists will find this book helpful for their clients or students exploring career options or job targets. My best suggestion to professionals is to get this book off the shelf and into the hands of the people who need it. Leave it on a table or desk and show people how the information can help them. Wear this book out—its real value is as a tool used often and well.

Additional Information About the Projections

For more information about employment change, job openings, earnings, unemployment rates, and training requirements by occupation, consult *Occupational Projections and Training Data,* published by the Bureau of Labor Statistics. For occupational information from an industry perspective, including some occupations and career paths that *Top 100 Careers Without a Four-Year Degree* does not cover, consult another BLS publication, *Career Guide to Industries.* This book is also available from JIST with enhanced content under the title *40 Best Fields for Your Career.*

Information on the Major Parts of This Book

This book was designed to be easy to use. The table of contents provides brief comments on each section, and that may be all you need. If not, here are some additional details you may find useful in getting the most out of this book.

Part I: Using the Job-Match Grid to Choose a Career

Part I features an assessment with checklists and questions to match your skills and preferences to the jobs in this book. The seven skills covered in the assessment are artistic, communication, interpersonal, managerial, mathematics, mechanical, and science. The five job characteristics covered in the assessment are economically sensitive, geographically concentrated, hazardous conditions, outdoor work, and physically demanding.

Part II: Descriptions of the 100 Top Careers Without a Four-Year Degree

Part II is the main part of the book and probably the reason you picked it up. It contains brief, well-written descriptions for 100 major jobs typically held by people without a four-year degree. A list of the jobs is provided in the table of contents. The content for each of these job descriptions comes from the U.S. Department of Labor and is considered by many to be the most accurate and up-to-date data available. These jobs are presented in alphabetical order.

Together, the jobs in Part II provide enormous variety at all levels of earnings and interest. One way to explore career options is to go to the table of contents and identify those jobs that seem interesting. If you are interested in medical jobs, for example, you can quickly spot those you will want to learn more about. You may also see other jobs that look interesting, and you should consider these as well.

Next, read the descriptions for the jobs that interest you and, based on what you learn, identify those that *most* interest you. These are the jobs you should consider, and Parts III and IV will give you additional information on how you might best do so.

How the 100 Jobs Were Selected

The jobs included in this book are selected from the 270 jobs covered in detail by the *Occupational Outlook Handbook,* published by the U.S. Department of Labor. They are jobs that normally require less education than a bachelor's degree and that had a workforce of more than 200,000 people in 2006. (The largest had a workforce of over 10 million.) Any job that employs at least one-fifth of a million people is going to account for a lot of job openings and therefore is worth your consideration. Even if overall employment in the job is shrinking, you can expect many job opportunities because of retirements and turnover.

Details on Each Section of the Job Descriptions

Each occupational description in this book follows a standard format, making it easier for you to compare jobs. The following overview describes the kinds of information found in each part of a description and offers tips on how to interpret the information.

Job Title

This is the title used for the job in the *Occupational Outlook Handbook.*

*O*NET Codes*

The numbers that appear just below the title of every job description are from the Occupational Information Network (O*NET), a major occupational information system created by the U.S. Department of Labor and used by state employment service offices to classify applicants and job openings and by some career information centers and libraries to file occupational information.

Through the O*NET at www.online.onetcenter.org, you can search for occupations that match your skills, or you may search by keyword or O*NET code. For each occupation, O*NET reports information about tasks performed, knowledge, skills, abilities, and work activities. It also lists interests; work styles, such as independence; and work values, such as achievement, that are well suited to the occupation. The O*NET is also available as a book titled the *O*NET Dictionary of Occupational Titles* (JIST).

Significant Points

The bullet points in this part of a description highlight key characteristics for each job, such as recent trends or education and training requirements.

Nature of the Work

What workers do on the job, what tools and equipment they use, and how closely they are supervised is discussed in this section. Some descriptions mention alterative job titles or occupational specialties.

Work environment. This subsection discuses the workplace, physical activities, and typical hours of workers in the occupation. It describes opportunities for part-time work, the extent of travel required, special equipment that is used, and the risk of injury that workers may face.

Information on various worker characteristics, such as the average number of hours worked per week, is obtained from the Current Population Survey (CPS), a survey of households conducted by the U.S. Census Bureau for the Bureau of Labor Statistics (BLS). Other sources include articles as well as the Web sites of professional associations, unions, and trade groups. Information found on the Internet or in periodicals is verified through interviews with workers; professional associations; unions; and others with occupational knowledge, such as university professors and career counselors.

Training, Other Qualifications, and Advancement

After gathering your initial impressions of what a job is all about, it is important to understand how to prepare for it. The Training, Other Qualifications, and Advancement section explains the steps necessary to enter and advance in an occupation.

Education and training. This subsection describes the most significant sources of education and training, the type of education or training preferred by employers, and the typical length of training.

Licensure. The kinds of mandatory licenses or certifications associated with an occupation are described in this subsection. To be certified or licensed, a worker usually is required to complete one or more training courses and pass one or more examinations. Most occupations do not have mandatory licensure or certification requirements. Some occupations have professional credentials granted by different organizations, in which case the most widely recognized organizations are listed.

Other qualifications. Additional qualifications that are not included in the previous subsections, such as the desirable skills, aptitudes, and personal characteristics that employers look for, are discussed in this section.

Advancement. This subsection details advancement opportunities after gaining experience in an occupation. Advancement can come in several forms, including advancement within the occupation, such as promotion to a management position; advancement into other occupations; and advancement to self-employment. Certain types of certification can serve as a form of advancement. Voluntary certification often demonstrates a level of competency to employers and can result in more responsibility, higher pay, or a new job.

Information in the Training, Other Qualifications, and Advancement section comes from interviews with workers; Web sites; training materials; and interviews with the organizations that grant degrees, certifications, or licenses or are otherwise associated with the occupation.

© **JIST Works**

Employment

This section reports the number of jobs the occupation recently provided, the key industries where these jobs are found, and the number or proportion of self-employed workers in the occupation, if significant. Information in this section comes from various surveys by the BLS.

When significant, the geographic distribution of jobs and the proportion of part-time (less than 35 hours a week) workers in the occupation are mentioned.

Job Outlook

In planning for the future, you need to consider potential job opportunities. This section describes the factors that will result in employment growth or decline.

Employment change. This subsection reflects the occupational projections in the National Employment Matrix. Each occupation is assigned a descriptive phrase based on its projected percent change in employment over the 2006–2016 period. This phrase describes the occupation's projected employment change relative to the projected average employment change for all occupations combined.

Many factors are examined in projecting the employment change for each occupation. One such factor is changes in technology. New technology can either create new job opportunities or eliminate jobs by making workers obsolete. Another factor that influences employment trends is demographic change. By affecting the services demanded, demographic change can influence occupational growth or decline.

Another factor affecting job growth or decline is changes in business practices, such as restructuring businesses or outsourcing (contracting out) work. Corporate restructuring has made many organizations "flatter," resulting in fewer middle management positions. Also, in the past few years, jobs in some occupations have been "off-shored"—moved to low-wage foreign countries. The substitution of one product or service for another can also affect employment projections. Competition from foreign trade usually has a negative affect on employment. Often, foreign manufacturers can produce goods more cheaply than they can be produced in the United States, and the cost savings can be passed on in the form of lower prices with which U.S. manufacturers cannot compete. Another factor is job growth or decline in key industries. If an occupation is concentrated in an industry that is growing rapidly, it is likely that that occupation will grow rapidly as well.

Job prospects. In some cases, this book mentions that an occupation is likely to provide numerous or relatively few job openings. This information reflects the projected change in employment, as well as replacement needs. Large occupations in which workers frequently enter and leave generally provide the most job openings—reflecting the need to replace workers who transfer to other occupations or who stop working.

Key Phrases Used in the Job Descriptions

This table explains how to interpret the key phrases that describe projected changes in employment. It also explains the terms for the relationship between the number of job openings and the number of job seekers.

Changing Employment Between 2006 and 2016

If the statement reads	Employment is projected to
Grow much faster than average	Increase 21 percent or more
Grow faster than average	Increase 14 to 20 percent
Grow about as fast as average	Increase 7 to 13 percent
Grow more slowly than average	Increase 3 to 6 percent
Little or no change	Decrease 2 percent to increase 2 percent
Decline slowly or moderately	Decrease 3 to 9 percent
Decline rapidly	Decrease 10 percent or more

Opportunities and Competition for Jobs

If the statement reads	Job openings compared to job seekers may be
Very good to excellent opportunities	More numerous
Good or favorable opportunities	In rough balance
May face or can expect keen competition	Fewer

Projections Data

The employment projections table lists employment statistics from the National Employment Matrix. It includes 2006 employment, projected 2016 employment, and the 2006-2016 change in employment in both numerical and percentage terms. Numbers below 10,000 are rounded to the nearest hundred, numbers above 10,000 are rounded to the nearest thousand, and percentages are rounded to the nearest whole number. Numerical and percentage changes are calculated using non-rounded 2006 and 2016 employment figures and then are rounded for presentation in the employment projections table.

Earnings

This section discusses typical earnings and how workers are compensated—by means of annual salaries, hourly wages, commissions, piece rates, tips, or bonuses. Within every occupation, earnings vary by experience, responsibility, performance, tenure, and geographic area. Information on earnings in the major industries in which the occupation is employed may be given. Some statements contain additional earnings data from non-BLS sources. Starting and average salaries of federal workers are based on 2007 data from the U.S. Office of Personnel Management. The National Association of Colleges and Employers supplies information on average salary offers in 2007 for students graduating with a bachelor's, master's, or Ph.D. degree in certain fields. A few statements contain additional earnings information from other sources, such as unions, professional associations, and private companies. These data sources are cited in the text.

Benefits account for a significant portion of total compensation costs to employers. Benefits such as paid vacation, health insurance, and sick leave may not be mentioned because they are so widespread. Although not as common as traditional benefits, flexible hours and profit-sharing plans may be offered to attract and retain highly qualified workers. Less-common benefits also include childcare, tuition for dependents, housing assistance, summers off, and free or discounted merchandise or services. For certain occupations, the percentage of workers affiliated with a union is listed.

Related Occupations

Occupations involving similar duties, skills, interests, education, and training are listed here. This allows you to look up these jobs if they also interest you.

Sources of Additional Information

No single publication can describe all aspects of an occupation. Thus, this section lists the mailing addresses of associations, government agencies, unions, and other organizations that can provide occupational information. In some cases, toll-free telephone numbers and Internet addresses also are listed. Free or relatively inexpensive publications offering more information may be mentioned; some of these publications also may be available in libraries, in school career centers, in guidance offices, or on the Internet.

Part III: *Quick Job Search—Seven Steps to Getting a Good Job in Less Time*

For more than 25 years, I've been helping people find better jobs in less time. If you have ever experienced unemployment, you know it is not pleasant. Unemployment is something most people want to get over quickly—in fact, the quicker the better. Part III will give you some techniques to help.

I know that most of you who read this book want to improve yourselves. You want to consider career and training options that lead to a better job and life in whatever way you define this—better pay, more flexibility, work that is more enjoyable or more meaningful, proving to your mom that you really can do anything you set your mind to, and other reasons. That is why I include advice on career planning and job search in Part III. It's a short section, but it includes the basics that are most important in planning your career and in reducing the time it takes to get a job. I hope it will make you think about what is important to you in the long run.

The second section of Part III showcases professionally written resumes for some of America's top jobs for people without a four-year degree. Use these as examples when creating your own resume.

I know you will resist completing the activities in Part III, but consider this: It is often not the best person who gets the job, but the best job seeker. People who do their career planning and job search homework often get jobs over those with better credentials, because they have these distinct advantages:

1. **They get more interviews,** including many for jobs that will never be advertised.

2. **They do better in interviews.**

People who understand what they want and what they have to offer employers present their skills more convincingly and are much better at answering problem questions. And, because they have learned more about job search techniques, they are likely to get more interviews with employers who need the skills they have.

Doing better in interviews often makes the difference between getting a job offer and sitting at home. And spending time planning your career can make an enormous difference to your happiness and lifestyle over time. So please consider reading Part III and completing its activities. I suggest you schedule a time right now to at least read Part III. An hour or so spent there can help you do just enough better in your career planning, job seeking, and interviewing to make the difference.

Part IV: Important Trends in Jobs and Industries

This section is made up of three very good articles on labor market trends. These articles come directly from U.S. Department of Labor sources and are interesting, well written, and short. One is on overall trends, with an emphasis on occupational groups; another is on trends in major industry groups; and the third discusses the job outlook for people without a bachelor's degree. I know they sound boring, but the articles are quick reads and will give you a good idea of factors that will impact your career in the years to come.

The first article is titled "Tomorrow's Jobs." It highlights many important trends in employment and includes information on the fastest-growing jobs, jobs with high pay at various levels of education, and other details.

The second article is titled "Employment Trends in Major Industries." I included this information because you may find that you can use your skills or training in industries you have not considered. The article provides a good review of major trends with an emphasis on helping you make good employment decisions. This information can help you seek jobs in industries that offer higher pay or that are more likely to interest you. Many people overlook one important fact—the industry you work in is as important as the occupation you choose.

The third article is called "Job Outlook for People Who Don't Have a Bachelor's Degree." It identifies high-paying and high-growth career options for people who don't complete four years of college. It includes tables with facts about specific careers, including the typical entry route—which may be as quick as short-term on-the-job training or as long as an associate degree program.

Some Additional Jobs to Consider

Here is a list of additional jobs that may not require a four-year degree that you may want to consider. Their descriptions are not included in this book, but you can find them in the *Occupational Outlook Handbook*, *Top 300 Careers*, or the *Enhanced Occupational Outlook Handbook* or online at www.bls.gov.

★ Agricultural Workers

★ Air Traffic Controllers

★ Animal Care and Service Workers

★ Announcers

★ Assemblers and Fabricators

★ Billing and Posting Clerks and Machine Operators

★ Bookbinders and Bindery Workers

★ Bus Drivers

★ Carpet, Floor, and Tile Installers and Finishers

★ Cashiers

★ Coin, Vending, and Amusement Machine Servicers and Repairers

★ Communications Equipment Operators

★ Computer Control Programmers and Operators

★ Computer Operators

★ Computer, Automated Teller, and Office Machine Repairers

★ Couriers and Messengers

★ Credit Authorizers, Checkers, and Clerks

★ Dancers and Choreographers

★ Data Entry and Information Processing Workers

★ Demonstrators, Product Promoters, and Models

★ Desktop Publishers

★ Dispatchers

★ Electrical and Electronics Installers and Repairers

★ Electronic Home Entertainment Equipment Installers and Repairers

★ Elevator Installers and Repairers

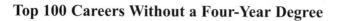

- ★ Fashion Designers
- ★ File Clerks
- ★ Fishers and Fishing Vessel Operators
- ★ Floral Designers
- ★ Food Processing Occupations
- ★ Forest, Conservation, and Logging Workers
- ★ Gaming Cage Workers
- ★ Gaming Services Occupations
- ★ Glaziers
- ★ Hazardous Materials Removal Workers
- ★ Heavy Vehicle and Mobile Equipment Service Technicians and Mechanics
- ★ Home Appliance Repairers
- ★ Hotel, Motel, and Resort Desk Clerks
- ★ Human Resources Assistants, Except Payroll and Timekeeping
- ★ Industrial Production Managers
- ★ Inspectors, Testers, Sorters, Samplers, and Weighers
- ★ Insulation Workers
- ★ Interviewers
- ★ Jewelers, and Precious Stone and Metal Workers
- ★ Library Assistants, Clerical
- ★ Library Technicians
- ★ Lodging Managers
- ★ Machine Setters, Operators and Tender— Metal and Plastic
- ★ Machinists
- ★ Material Moving Occupations
- ★ Medical Transcriptionists
- ★ Medical, Dental, and Ophthalmic Laboratory Technicians

- ★ Meter Readers, Utilities
- ★ Millwrights
- ★ Opticians, Dispensing
- ★ Order Clerks
- ★ Painting and Coating Workers, except Construction and Maintenance
- ★ Payroll and Timekeeping Clerks
- ★ Pest Control Workers
- ★ Pharmacy Aides
- ★ Photographers
- ★ Photographic Process Workers and Processing Machine Operators
- ★ Plasterers and Stucco Masons
- ★ Postal Service Workers
- ★ Power Plant Operators, Distributors, and Dispatchers
- ★ Precision Instrument and Equipment Repairers
- ★ Prepress Technicians and Workers
- ★ Printing Machine Operators
- ★ Private Detectives and Investigators
- ★ Procurement Clerks
- ★ Radio and Telecommunications Equipment Installers and Repairers
- ★ Rail Transportation Occupations
- ★ Recreation Workers
- ★ Reservation and Transportation Ticket Agents and Travel Clerks
- ★ Semiconductor Processors
- ★ Shipping and Receiving, and Traffic Clerks
- ★ Small Engine Mechanics
- ★ Stationary Engineers and Boiler Operators
- ★ Stock Clerks and Order Fillers

★ Structural and Reinforcing Iron and Metal Workers

★ Taxi Drivers and Chauffeurs

★ Teacher Assistants

★ Television, Video, and Motion Picture Camera Operators and Editors

★ Textile, Apparel, and Furnishings Occupations

★ Tool and Die Makers

★ Travel Agents

★ Weighers, Measurers, Checkers, and Samplers, Recordkeeping

★ Welding, Soldering and Brazing Workers

★ Woodworkers

Other Major Career Information Sources

The information in this book will be very useful, but you may want or need additional information. Keep in mind that the job descriptions here cover major jobs and not the many more-specialized jobs that are often related to them. Each job description in this book provides some sources of information related to that job, but here are additional resources to consider.

Occupational Outlook Handbook (or the *OOH*): Updated every two years by the U.S. Department of Labor, this book provides descriptions for 270 major jobs covering more than 85 percent of the workforce. The *OOH* is the source of the job descriptions used in this book, and the book *Top 300 Careers* includes all the *OOH* content plus additional information.

The *Enhanced Occupational Outlook Handbook:* Includes all descriptions in the *OOH* plus descriptions of more than 5,800 more-specialized jobs that are related to them.

The *O*NET Dictionary of Occupational Titles:* The only printed source of the more than 900 jobs described in the U.S. Department of Labor's Occupational Information Network database (O*NET).

The *New Guide for Occupational Exploration:* An important career reference that allows you to explore all major O*NET jobs based on your interests.

Best Jobs for the 21st Century: Includes descriptions for the 500 jobs (out of more than 900) with the best combination of earnings, growth, and number of openings. Useful lists make jobs easy to explore (examples: highest-paying jobs by level of education or training; best jobs overall; and best jobs for different ages, personality types, interests, and many more).

Exploring Careers—A Young Person's Guide to 1,000 Jobs: For youth exploring career and education opportunities, this book covers 1,000 job options in an interesting and useful format.

Using the Job-Match Grid to Choose a Career

By the Editors at JIST

This book describes so many occupations—how can you choose the best job for you? This section is your answer! It can help you to identify the jobs where your abilities will be valued, and you can rule out jobs that have certain characteristics you'd rather avoid. You will respond to a series of statements and use the Job-Match Grid to match your skills and preferences to the most appropriate jobs in this book.

So grab a pencil and get ready to mark up the following sections. Or, if someone else will be using this book, find a sheet of paper and get ready to take notes.

Thinking About Your Skills

Everybody knows that skills are important for getting and keeping a job. Employers expect you to list relevant skills on your resume. They ask about your skills in interviews. And they expect you to develop skills on the job so that you will remain productive as new technologies and new work situations emerge.

But maybe you haven't thought about how closely skills are related to job satisfaction. For example, let's say you have enough communication skills to hold a certain job where these skills are used heavily, but you wouldn't really *enjoy* using them. In that case, this job probably would be a bad choice for you. You need to identify a job that will use the skills that you *do* enjoy using.

That's why you need to take a few minutes to think about your skills: the ones you're good at and the ones you like using. The checklists that follow can help you do this. On each of the seven skills checklists that follow, use numbers to indicate how much you agree with each statement:

3 = I strongly agree

2 = I agree

1 = There's some truth to this

0 = This doesn't apply to me

Artistic Skills

_____ I am an amateur artist.

_____ I have musical talent.

(continued)

(continued)

_____ I enjoy planning home makeovers.

_____ I am good at performing onstage.

_____ I enjoy taking photos or shooting videos.

_____ I am good at writing stories, poems, articles, or essays.

_____ I have enjoyed taking ballet or other dance lessons.

_____ I like to cook and plan meals.

_____ I can sketch a good likeness of something or somebody.

_____ Playing music or singing is a hobby of mine.

_____ I have a good sense of visual style.

_____ I have participated in amateur theater.

_____ I like to express myself through writing.

_____ I can prepare tasty meals better than most people.

_____ I have a flair for creating attractive designs.

_____ I learn new dance steps or routines easily.

_____ **Total for Artistic Skills**

A note for those determined to work in the arts: Before you move on to the next skill, take a moment to decide whether working in some form of art is essential to you. Some people have exceptional talent and interest in a certain art form and are unhappy unless they are working in that art form—or until they have given their best shot at trying to break into it. If you are that kind of person, the total score shown above doesn't really matter. In fact, you may have given a 3 to just *one* of the statements above, but if you care passionately about your art form, you should toss out ordinary arithmetic and change the total to 100.

Communication Skills

_____ I am good at explaining complicated things to people.

_____ I like to take notes and write up minutes for meetings.

_____ I have a flair for public speaking.

_____ I am good at writing directions for using a computer or machine.

_____ I enjoy investigating facts and showing other people what they indicate.

_____ People consider me a good listener.

_____ I like to write letters to newspaper editors or political representatives.

_____ I have been an effective debater.

_____ I like developing publicity fliers for a school or community event.

_____ I am good at making diagrams that break down complex processes.

_____ I like teaching people how to drive a car or play a sport.

_____ I have been successful as the secretary of a club.

_____ I enjoy speaking at group meetings or worship services.

_____ I have a knack for choosing the most effective word.

_____ I enjoy tutoring young people.

_____ Technical manuals are not hard for me to understand.

_____ **Total for Communication Skills**

Interpersonal Skills

_____ I am able to make people feel that I understand their point of view.

_____ I enjoy working collaboratively.

_____ I often can make suggestions to people without sounding critical of them.

_____ I enjoy soliciting clothes, food, and other supplies for needy people.

_____ I am good at "reading" people to tell what's on their minds.

_____ I have a lot of patience with people who are doing something for the first time.

_____ People consider me outgoing.

_____ I enjoy taking care of sick relatives, friends, or neighbors.

_____ I am good at working out conflicts between friends or family members.

_____ I enjoy serving as a host or hostess for houseguests.

_____ People consider me a team player.

_____ I enjoy meeting new people and finding common interests.

_____ I am good at fundraising for school groups, teams, or community organizations.

_____ I like to train or care for animals.

_____ I often know what to say to defuse a tense situation.

_____ I have enjoyed being an officer or advisor for a youth group.

_____ **Total for Interpersonal Skills**

Managerial Skills

_____ I am good at inspiring people to work together toward a goal.

_____ I tend to use time wisely and not procrastinate.

_____ I usually know when I have enough information to make a decision.

_____ I enjoy planning and arranging programs for school or a community organization.

_____ I am not reluctant to take responsibility when things turn out wrong.

_____ I have enjoyed being a leader of a scout troop or other such group.

_____ I often can figure out what motivates somebody.

_____ People trust me to speak on their behalf and represent them fairly.

_____ I like to help organize things at home, such as shopping lists and budgets.

(continued)

© JIST Works

(continued)

_____ I have been successful at recruiting members for a club or other organization.

_____ I have enjoyed helping run a school or community fair or carnival.

_____ People find me persuasive.

_____ I enjoy buying large quantities of food or other products for an organization.

_____ I have a knack for identifying abilities in other people.

_____ I am able to get past details and look at the big picture.

_____ I am good at delegating authority rather than trying to do everything myself.

_____ **Total for Managerial Skills**

Mathematics Skills

_____ I have always done well in math classes.

_____ I enjoy balancing checkbooks for family members.

_____ I can make mental calculations quickly.

_____ I enjoy calculating sports statistics or keeping score.

_____ Preparing family income tax returns is not hard for me.

_____ I like to tutor young people in math.

_____ I have taken or plan to take courses in statistics or calculus.

_____ I enjoy budgeting the family expenditures.

_____ **Subtotal for Mathematics Skills**

x 2   **Multiply by 2**

_____ **Total for Mathematics Skills**

Mechanical Skills

_____ I have a good sense of how mechanical devices work.

_____ I like to tinker with my car or motorcycle.

_____ I can understand diagrams of machinery or electrical wiring.

_____ I enjoy installing and repairing home stereo or computer equipment.

_____ I like looking at the merchandise in a building-supply warehouse store.

_____ I can sometimes fix household appliances when they break down.

_____ I have enjoyed building model airplanes, automobiles, or boats.

_____ I can do minor plumbing and electrical installations in the home.

_____ **Subtotal for Mechanical Skills**

x 2   **Multiply by 2**

_____ **Total for Mechanical Skills**

Science Skills

_____ Some of my best grades have been in science classes.

_____ I enjoy tweaking my computer's settings to make it run better.

_____ I have a good understanding of the systems and organs of the human body.

_____ I have enjoyed performing experiments for a science fair.

_____ I have taken or plan to take college-level courses in science.

_____ I like to read about new breakthroughs in science and technology.

_____ I know how to write programs in a computer language.

_____ I enjoy reading medical or scientific magazines.

_____ **Subtotal for Science Skills**

x 2   **Multiply by 2**

_____ **Total for Science Skills**

Finding Your Skills on the Job-Match Grid

Okay, you've made a lot of progress so far. Now it's time to review what you've said about skills so you can use these insights to sort through the jobs listed on the Job-Match Grid.

Look at your totals for the seven skills listed previously. Enter your totals in the left column on this scorecard:

Total	Skill	Rank
_____	Artistic	_____
_____	Communication	_____
_____	Interpersonal	_____
_____	Managerial	_____
_____	Mathematics	_____
_____	Mechanical	_____
_____	Science	_____

Next, enter the rank of each skill in the right column—that is, the highest-scored skill gets ranked #1, the next-highest #2, and so forth. **Important:** Keep in mind that *the numbers in the Total column are only a rough guideline.* If you feel that a skill should be ranked higher or lower than its numerical total would suggest, *go by your impressions rather than just by the numbers.*

Now turn to the Job-Match Grid and find the columns for your #1-ranked and #2-ranked skills. Move down through the grid, going from page to page, and notice what symbols appear in those columns. If a row of the grid has a black circle (●) in *both* columns, circle the occupation name—or, if someone else will be using this book, jot down the name on a piece of paper. These occupations use a high level of both skills, or the skills are essential to these jobs.

Go through the Job-Match Grid a second time, looking at the column for your #3-ranked skill. If a *job you have already circled* has a black circle (●) or a bull's-eye (◉) in the column for your #3-ranked skill, put a check mark next to the occupation name. If none of your selected jobs has a black circle or a bull's-eye in this column, look for a white circle (○) and mark these jobs with check marks.

A second note for those determined to work in the arts: If a *particular* art form is essential for you to work in, you almost certainly know which occupations involve that art form and which don't. So not every job that has a black circle (●) in the "Artistic" column is going to interest you. Circle only the jobs that have a black circle in this column that *are* related to your art form (if you're not sure, look at the description of the occupation in this book) and that also have a symbol of some kind (●, ◐, or ○) in the column for your #2-ranked skill. As you circle each job, also give it a check mark, because there will be so few of them that you won't need to go through the Job-Match Grid a second time. If you have a more general interest in the arts, follow the general instructions.

Your Hot List of Possible Career Matches

Now that you have made a first and second cut of the jobs on the Job-Match Grid, you can focus on the occupations that look most promising at this point. Write the names of the occupations that are both *circled* and *checked:*

_____	_____
_____	_____
_____	_____
_____	_____
_____	_____
_____	_____

This is your Hot List of occupations that you are going to explore in detail *if* they are not eliminated by certain important job-related factors that you'll consider next.

Thinking About Other Job-Related Factors

Next, you need to consider four other job-related factors:

- ★ Economic sensitivity
- ★ Outdoor work
- ★ Physically demanding work
- ★ Hazardous conditions

Economic Sensitivity

You've read about how our nation's economy has gone up and down over the years. When the economy is on an upswing, there are more job openings, but when it veers downward toward recession, jobs are harder to find.

Are you aware that these trends affect some occupations more than others? For example, during an economic upswing, people do more vacation traveling and businesses send more workers on business trips. This keeps travel agencies very busy, so they need to hire more travel agents. When the economy is going down, people cut back on their vacation travel, businesses tell their workers to use teleconferencing instead of business trips, and travel agents are not in demand. Some may be laid off, and people who want to enter this field may find very few openings. By contrast, most jobs in the health-care field are not sensitive to the economy, and automotive mechanics are just as busy as ever during economic slowdowns because people want to keep their old cars running.

So this issue of economic sensitivity (and its opposite, job security) is one that may affect which occupation you choose. Some people want to avoid economically sensitive occupations because they don't want to risk losing their job (or having difficulty finding a job) during times of recession. Other people are willing to risk being in an

© **JIST Works**

economically sensitive occupation because they want to profit from the periods when both the economy and the occupation are booming.

How important is it to you to be in an occupation that *doesn't* go through periods of boom and bust along with the nation's economy? Check one:

_____ It doesn't matter to me.

_____ It's not important, but I'd consider it.

_____ It's somewhat important to me.

_____ It's very important to me.

If you answered "It doesn't matter to me," skip to the next section, "Outdoor Work." Otherwise, turn back to the Job-Match Grid and find the column for "Economically Sensitive."

If you answered "It's not important, but I'd consider it," see whether any of the jobs on your Hot List have a black circle (●) in this column. If so, cross them off and write an "E" next to them.

If you answered "It's somewhat important to me," see whether any of the jobs on your Hot List have a black circle (●) or a bull's-eye (◉) in this column. If so, cross them off and write an "E" next to them.

If you answered "It's very important to me," see whether any of the jobs on your Hot List have *any* symbol (●, ◉, or ○) in this column. If so, cross them off and write an "E" next to them.

Outdoor Work

Some people prefer to work indoors in a climate-controlled setting, such as an office, a classroom, a factory floor, a laboratory, or a hospital room. Other people would rather work primarily in an outdoor setting, such as a forest, an athletic field, or a city street. And some would enjoy a job that alternates between indoor and outdoor activities.

What is *your* preference for working indoors or outdoors? Check one:

_____ It's very important to me to work **indoors.**

_____ I'd prefer to work mostly **indoors.**

_____ Either indoors or outdoors is okay with me.

_____ I'd prefer to work mostly **outdoors.**

_____ It's very important to me to work **outdoors.**

If you answered "Either indoors or outdoors is okay with me," skip to the next section, "Physically Demanding Work." Otherwise, turn to the Job-Match Grid and find the column for "Outdoor Work."

If you answered "It's very important to me to work **indoors,**" see whether any of the jobs on your Hot List have *any* symbol (●, ◉, or ○) in this column. If so, cross them off and write an "O" next to them.

If you answered "I'd prefer to work mostly **indoors,**" see whether any of the jobs on your Hot List have a black circle (●) in this column. If so, cross them off and write an "O" next to them.

If you answered "I'd prefer to work mostly **outdoors,**" see whether any of the jobs on your Hot List have *no* symbol—just a blank—in this column. If so, cross them off and write an "O" next to them. All the jobs remaining on your Hot List should have some kind of symbol (●, ◉, or ○) in this column.

If you answered "It's very important to me to work **outdoors,**" see whether any of the jobs on your Hot List have either *no* symbol or just a white circle (○) in this column. If so, cross them off and write an "O" next to them. All the jobs remaining on your Hot List should have either a black circle (●) or a bull's-eye (◉) in this column.

Physically Demanding Work

Jobs vary by how much muscle power they require you to use. Some jobs require a lot of lifting heavy loads, standing for long times, climbing, or stooping. On other jobs, the heaviest thing you lift is a notebook or telephone handset, and most of the time you are sitting. Still other jobs require only a moderate amount of physical exertion.

> What is *your* preference for the physical demands of work? Check one:
>
> _____ I don't care whether my work requires heavy or light physical exertion.
>
> _____ I want my work to require only light physical exertion.
>
> _____ I want my work to require no more than occasional moderate physical exertion.
>
> _____ I want my work to require moderate physical exertion, with occasional heavy exertion.
>
> _____ I want my work to require a lot of heavy physical exertion.

If you answered "I don't care whether my work requires heavy or light physical exertion," skip to the next section, "Hazardous Conditions." Otherwise, turn to the Job-Match Grid and find the column for "Physically Demanding Work."

If you answered "I want my work to require only light physical exertion," see whether any of the jobs on your Hot List have *any* symbol (●, ◉, or ○) in this column. If so, cross them off and write a "P" next to them.

If you answered "I want my work to require no more than occasional moderate physical exertion," see whether any of the jobs on your Hot List have either a black circle (●) or a bull's-eye (◉) in this column. If so, cross them off and write a "P" next to them.

If you answered "I want my work to require moderate physical exertion, with occasional heavy exertion," see whether any of the jobs on your Hot List have either a black circle (●), a white circle (○), or *no* symbol in this column. If so, cross them off and write a "P" next to them. All the jobs remaining on your Hot List should have a bull's-eye (◉) in this column.

If you answered "I want my work to require a lot of heavy physical exertion," see whether any of the jobs on your Hot List have either *no* symbol or just a white circle (○) or a bull's-eye (◉) in this column. If so, cross them off and write a "P" next to them. All the jobs remaining on your Hot List should have a black circle (●) in this column.

Hazardous Conditions

Every day about 9,000 Americans sustain a disabling injury on the job. Many workers have jobs that require them to deal with hazardous conditions, such as heat, noise, radiation, germs, toxins, or dangerous machinery. These workers need to wear protective clothing or follow safety procedures to avoid injury.

> What is *your* preference regarding hazardous conditions on the job? Check one:
>
> _____ I want hazardous workplace conditions to be very unlikely.
>
> _____ I want hazardous conditions to be unlikely or minor.
>
> _____ I am willing to accept some major workplace hazards.

If you answered "I am willing to accept some major workplace hazards," skip to the section "Geographically Concentrated Jobs." Otherwise, turn to the Job-Match Grid and find the column for "Hazardous Conditions."

If you answered "I want hazardous workplace conditions to be very unlikely," see whether any of the jobs on your Hot List have *any* symbol (●, ◒, or ○) in this column. If so, cross them off and write an "H" next to them.

If you answered "I want hazardous conditions to be unlikely or minor," see whether any of the jobs on your Hot List have a black circle (●) in this column. If so, cross them off and write an "H" next to them.

If Every Job on Your Hot List Is Now Crossed Off

It's possible that you have crossed off *all* the occupations on your Hot List. If so, consider these two options:

★ You may want to relax some of your requirements. Maybe you were too hasty in crossing off some of the jobs. Take another look at the four job-related factors and decide whether you could accept work that doesn't meet the requirements you set previously—for example, work that is not as much indoors or outdoors as you specified. If you change your mind now, you can tell by the letters in the margin which jobs you crossed off for which reasons.

★ You may want to add to your Hot List by considering additional skills. So far you have considered only occupations that involve your top three skills. You may want to add jobs that have a black circle (●) or a bull's-eye (◒) in the column for your #4-ranked skill and possibly for your #5-ranked skill. If you do add any jobs, be sure to repeat your review of the four job-related factors.

Evaluating Occupations Described in This Book

You are now ready to make the jump from the checklists to the detailed information about jobs in this book. The first detailed issue you need to consider is whether you will be able to find work in your area or have to relocate.

Geographically Concentrated Jobs

Turn to the Job-Match Grid one more time and find the column for "Geographically Concentrated." Look at all the occupations on your Hot List that haven't been crossed off. If there is a symbol in this column, especially a bull's-eye (◒) or a black circle (●), it means that employment for this occupation tends to be concentrated in certain geographic areas. For example, most acting jobs are found in big cities because that's where you'll find most theaters, TV studios, and movie studios. Most water transportation jobs are found on the coasts and beside major lakes and rivers.

If a symbol shows that a Hot List occupation *is* geographically concentrated, the location of the jobs may be obvious, as in the examples of acting and water transportation. If it's not clear to you where the jobs may be found, find the occupation in "The Job Descriptions" section and look for the facts under the heading "Employment" in the description. Once you understand where most of the jobs are, you have to make some decisions:

★ **Are most of the job openings in a geographic location where I am now or would enjoy living?** If you answered "yes" to this question, repeat this exercise for all the other occupations still on your Hot List. Then jump to the next heading, "Nature of the Work." If you answered "no," proceed to the next bulleted question.

★ **If most of the job openings are in a distant place where I don't want to relocate, am I willing to take a chance and hope to be one of the few workers who get hired in an *uncommon* location?** If you answered "yes," take a good look at the Job Outlook information in the job description. If the outlook for the occupation is very good and if you expect to have some of the advantages mentioned there (such as the right training, in some cases), taking a chance on being hired in an unusual location may be a reasonable decision. On the other hand, if the outlook is only so-so or not good and if you have no special qualifications, you probably are setting yourself up for disappointment. You should seriously consider changing your mind about this decision. At least speak to people in your area who are knowledgeable about the occupation to determine whether you have any chance of success. If you answered "no"—you are not willing to take a chance—cross off this occupation and write a "G" next to it. (If you now have no jobs left on your Hot List, see the previous section titled "If Every Job on Your Hot List Is Now Crossed Off.")

Nature of the Work

When you read the job description for an occupation on your Hot List, you will see that the "Nature of the Work" section discusses what workers do on the job, what tools and equipment they use, and how closely they are supervised. Keep in mind that this is an overview of a diverse collection of workers, and in fact few workers perform the full set of tasks itemized here. In fact, in many cases the work force covered by the job description is so diverse that it actually divides into several occupational specialties, which are italicized.

Here are some things to think about as you read this section:

★ Note the kinds of problems, materials, and tools you will encounter on the job. Are these a good match for your interests?

★ Also note the work activities mentioned here. Do you think they will be rewarding? Are there many that stand out as unpleasant or boring?

The Work Environment subsection identifies the typical hours worked, the workplace environment (both physical and psychological), physical activities and susceptibility to injury, special equipment, and the extent of travel required. If conditions vary between the occupational specialties, that is mentioned here. Here are some things to look for in the Work Environment subsection:

★ If you have a disability, note the physical requirements that are mentioned here and consider whether you can meet these requirements with or without suitable accommodations.

★ If you're bothered by conditions such as heights, stress, or a cramped workspace, see whether this section mentions any conditions that would discourage you.

★ Note what this section says about the work schedule and the need for travel, if any. This information may be good to know if you have pressing family responsibilities or, on the other hand, a desire for unusual hours or travel.

★ If you find a working condition that bothers you, be sure to check the wording to see whether it *always* applies to the occupation or whether it only *may* apply. Even if it seems to be a condition that you cannot avoid, find out for sure by talking to people in the occupation or educators who teach related courses. Maybe you can carve out a niche that avoids the unappealing working condition.

Training, Other Qualifications, and Advancement

In the "Training, Other Qualifications, and Advancement" section, you can see how to prepare for the occupation and how to advance in it. It identifies the significant entry routes—those that are most popular and that are preferred by employers. It mentions any licensure or certification that may be necessary for entry or advancement. It also identifies the particular skills, aptitudes, and work habits that employers value. Look for these topics in this section:

★ Compare the entry requirements to your background and to the educational and training opportunities that are available to you. Be sure to consider nontraditional and informal entry routes, if any are possible, as well as the formal routes. Ask yourself, Am I willing to get the additional education or training that will be necessary? Do I have the time, money, ability, interest, and commitment?

★ Maybe you're already partway down the road to job entry. In general, you should try to use your previous education, training, and work experience rather than abandon it. Look for specifics that are already on your resume—educational accomplishments, skills, work habits—that will meet employers' expectations. If you have some of these qualifications already, this occupation may be a better career choice than some others.

Employment

The "Employment" section in the job description reports how many jobs the occupation currently provides, the industries that provide the most jobs, and the number or proportion of self-employed or part-time workers in the occupation, if significant. In this section, you'll want to pay attention to these facts:

★ Note the industries that provide most of the employment for the occupation. This knowledge can help you identify contacts who can tell you more about the work, and later it can help in your job hunting.

★ If you're interested in self-employment or part-time work, see whether these work arrangements are mentioned here.

Job Outlook

The "Job Outlook" section describes the economic forces that will affect future employment in the occupation. Here are some things to look for in this section:

★ The information here can help you identify occupations with a good job outlook so that you will have a better-than-average chance of finding work. Be alert for any mention of an advantage that you may have over other job seekers (for example, a college degree) or any other factor that might make your chances better or worse.

★ If you are highly motivated and highly qualified for a particular occupation, don't be discouraged by a bad employment outlook. Job openings occur even in shrinking or overcrowded occupations, and with exceptional talent or good personal connections, you may go on to great success.

★ These projections are the most definitive ones available, but they are not foolproof and apply only to a 10-year time span. No matter what occupation you choose, you will need to adapt to changes.

Projections Data

This section consists of a table of numerical data. It shows how many people were employed in the occupation in 2006, how many are projected to be employed in 2016, and the difference between these two figures in both numerical and percentage terms. These figures form the basis of some information in the "Job Outlook" section, but they add to the previous information in several ways that you may find useful:

★ The figures indicate whether the occupation has a large or small workforce. A large occupation can provide many job openings—even if it is shrinking in size—because of job turnover. Conversely, a small occupation may provide few job openings even though it is growing rapidly.

★ Often the table consists of more than one row because the occupation covers several specializations. In such cases, you can see which specializations have the largest workforces and which have the most promising projections for employment growth.

Earnings

The "Earnings" section discusses the wages for the occupation. Here are some things to keep in mind:

★ The wage figures are national averages. Actual wages in your geographic region may be considerably higher or lower. Also, an average figure means that half of the workers earn more and half earn less, and the actual salary any one worker earns can vary greatly from that average.

★ Remember to consider *all* the pluses and minuses of the job. Not every day of the work week is payday, so make your choice based on the whole occupation, not just the paycheck.

Related Occupations

The "Related Occupations" section identifies occupations that are similar to the one featured in the job description in terms of tasks, interests, skills, education, or training. You may find this section interesting for these reasons:

★ If you're interested in an occupation but not strongly committed to pursuing it, this section may suggest another occupation with similar rewards that may turn out to be a better fit. Try to research these related occupations, but keep in mind that they may not all be included in this book.

★ You may want to choose one of these occupations as your Plan B goal if your original goal should not work out. In that case, it helps to identify an occupation that involves similar kinds of problems and work settings but requires *less* education or training.

Sources of Additional Information

This section in each job description lists several sources and resources you can turn to for more information about the occupation. Try to consult at least some of these sources. This book should be only the beginning of your career decision-making process. You need more detailed information from several viewpoints to make an informed decision.

Don't rely entirely on the Web sites listed here. You especially need to talk to and observe individual workers to learn what their workdays are like, what the workers enjoy and dislike about the job, how they got hired, and what effects the job has had on other aspects of their lives. Maybe you can make contact with local workers through the local chapter of an organization listed here.

Narrowing Down Your Choices

The information in the job descriptions should help you cross more jobs off your Hot List. And what you learn by turning to other resources should help you narrow down your Hot List jobs to a few promising choices and maybe one best bet. Here are some final considerations: Have I talked to people who are actually doing this work? Am I fully aware of the pluses and minuses of this job? If there are aspects of the job that I don't like, how do I expect to avoid them or overcome them? If the odds of finding a job opening are not good, why do I expect to beat the odds? What is my Plan B goal if I lose interest in my original goal or don't succeed at it?

© JIST Works

The Job-Match Grid

The grid on the following pages provides information about the personal skills and job characteristics for occupations covered in this book. Use the directions and questions that start at the beginning of this section to help you get the most from this grid.

Below is what the symbols on the grid represent. If a job has no symbol in a column, it means that the skill or job characteristic is not important or relevant to the job.

Personal Skills

● Essential or high skill level

◉ Somewhat essential or moderate skill level

○ Basic skill level

Job Characteristics

● Highly likely

◉ Somewhat likely

○ A little likely

© **JIST Works**

Job-Match Grid

	Personal Skills							Job Characteristics				
	Artistic	Communication	Interpersonal	Managerial	Mathematics	Mechanical	Science	Economically Sensitive	Outdoor Work	Physically Demanding Work	Hazardous Conditions	Geographically Concentrated
Actors, producers, and directors	●	●	●	◉		●	○	○	○	●		●
Advertising sales agents	◉	●	●		○			●				
Aircraft and avionics equipment mechanics and service technicians		○	○		◉	●	◉	◉	●	◉	○	◉
Aircraft pilots and flight engineers		●	●	●	●	◉	●	●	○	◉	●	○
Armed forces		◉	◉	◉	○	○	○			◉	●	●
Artists and related workers	●	○	○	○	○	◉	○	◉	○	○		
Athletes, coaches, umpires, and related workers	◉	◉	◉	●		○	○			●	●	○
Automotive body and related repairers	○	○	○		○	●	○		○	◉	○	
Automotive service technicians and mechanics		○	○		○	●	◉		○	◉	○	
Barbers, cosmetologists, and other personal appearance workers	●	◉	○		○	◉	○	◉		○	○	
Bill and account collectors		○	●		●			◉				
Boilermakers	○	○	○		○	●	○	●		●	●	◉
Bookkeeping, accounting, and auditing clerks		○	○		●			○				
Brickmasons, blockmasons, and stonemasons	◉	○	○		○	●	○	●	◉	●	○	
Brokerage clerks		○	○		◉			○				●
Building cleaning workers	○	○			○	●		○		●	○	
Cardiovascular technologists and technicians		◉	○	○	●	●	●			○		
Cargo and freight agents		○	○	○	◉		○	○	◉	○		◉
Carpenters	◉	○	○		◉	●	○	●	◉	●	●	
Cement masons, concrete finishers, segmental pavers, and terrazzo workers	◉	○	○		○	●	○	●	◉	●	○	
Chefs, cooks, and food preparation workers	●	◉	◉	●	○	◉	○	●		◉	○	
Child care workers	○	◉	●	○	○		○		○	◉		
Claims adjusters, appraisers, examiners, and investigators		◉	○	◉	◉	◉	○		◉			
Clinical laboratory technologists and technicians		◉	○	○	●	●	●				○	○
Communications equipment operators		◉	◉		◉	◉	○	◉				
Computer scientists and database administrators		◉	○	○	●		●	○				
Computer support specialists and systems administrators		◉	◉	○	◉	●	◉	○				
Construction and building inspectors		○	○	○	○	●	◉	○	◉	○	○	
Construction equipment operators		○	○		○	●	○	●	●	●	●	
Construction laborers	○	○	○		○	●	○	●	◉	●	●	
Correctional officers		●	○	○	○		○			◉	●	
Counter and rental clerks		○	◉		◉			◉		◉		

Personal Skills: ●—Essential or high skill level; ◉—Somewhat essential or moderate skill level; ○—Basic skill level
Job Characteristics: ●—Highly likely; ◉—Somewhat likely; ○—A little likely

© JIST Works

	Personal Skills							Job Characteristics				
	Artistic	Communication	Interpersonal	Managerial	Mathematics	Mechanical	Science	Economically Sensitive	Outdoor Work	Physically Demanding Work	Hazardous Conditions	Geographically Concentrated
Court reporters		◐	○			●				○		
Customer service representatives		●	●		◐		○	○				
Dental assistants		◐	◐	○	○	●	◐			◐	◐	
Diesel service technicians and mechanics		○	○		○	●	◐	○	○	◐	○	
Drafters	●	◐	○		◐	●	○	◐				
Drywall installers, ceiling tile installers, and tapers	○	○	○		○	●	○	●	○	●	○	
Electricians		○	○		◐	●	◐	●	○	◐	●	
Emergency medical technicians and paramedics		●	●	●	○	●	●			●	●	●
Engineering technicians	○	◐	○		●	●	●	○	○	○	○	
Farmers, ranchers, and agricultural managers		●	●	●	◐	●	◐	○	●	◐	◐	●
Fire fighting occupations		●	○	○	○	●	○			●	●	
Fitness workers	○	●	●	○	○	○	○	◐	◐	●		
Flight attendants		●	●	○	○	○		●		●	○	◐
Food and beverage serving and related workers	○	◐	●		○			●	○	●		
Food processing occupations		○			○	●				●	●	
Food service managers	◐	●	●	●	◐	◐	○	◐		○		
Funeral directors	○	●	●	◐	◐	○	○			○		
Grounds maintenance workers	◐	○			○	●	○	○	●	●	◐	
Heating, air conditioning, and refrigeration mechanics and installers		○	○		○	●	○	◐	○	◐	○	
Industrial machinery mechanics and maintenance workers		○			○	●	○	○		◐	◐	○
Interior designers	●	○	○	◐	●		◐	●		○		○
Interpreters and translators	●	●	○									
Licensed practical and licensed vocational nurses		◐	●	○	○	●	●			◐	◐	
Line installers and repairers		○			◐	●	○	○	●	◐	◐	
Maintenance and repair workers, general		○	○		○	●	○			◐	◐	◐
Massage therapists			○							◐		
Medical assistants		◐	◐	○	◐	●	●			◐	◐	
Medical records and health information technicians		◐	○	○	◐		◐					
Musicians, singers, and related workers	●	◐	◐	○		○	○			○		○
Nuclear medicine technologists		◐	○	○	●	●	●				◐	
Nursing, psychiatric, and home health aides		◐	◐	○	○	◐	○			●	●	
Occupational therapist assistants and aides		◐	●	○	○	●	◐			◐	◐	
Office and administrative support worker supervisors and managers		●	●	●	◐	○		○				
Office clerks, general		○	◐		○			◐				

(continued)

Personal Skills: ●—Essential or high skill level; ◐—Somewhat essential or moderate skill level; ○—Basic skill level
Job Characteristics: ●—Highly likely; ◐—Somewhat likely; ○—A little likely

(continued)

	Personal Skills							Job Characteristics				
	Artistic	Communication	Interpersonal	Managerial	Mathematics	Mechanical	Science	Economically Sensitive	Outdoor Work	Physically Demanding Work	Hazardous Conditions	Geographically Concentrated
Painters and paperhangers	◐	○	○		○	●	○	●	●	●	○	
Paralegals and legal assistants		●	●	○	○		○	◐				
Personal and home care aides		◐	●	○	○		○			●	◐	
Pharmacy technicians		◐	◐	○	◐	◐	◐			○		
Physical therapist assistants and aides		◐	◐	○	○	◐	◐			●	◐	
Pipelayers, plumbers, pipefitters, and steamfitters		○	○		○	●	◐	●	○	●	○	
Police and detectives		●	○	◐	○	●	○			●	●	●
Production, planning, and expediting clerks		◐	○	○	◐		○	○				
Purchasing managers, buyers, and purchasing agents		●	●	●	◐		○	○				
Radiation therapists		●	◐	●	◐	◐	●			●		
Radiologic technologists and technicians		◐	◐	○	●	●	◐			◐	◐	
Real estate brokers and sales agents	○	●	●	◐	◐			◐	○			
Receptionists and information clerks		●	●		◐	◐		○				
Registered nurses		●	●	◐	●	●	●			◐	◐	
Respiratory therapists		●	●	○	●	●	●			○	◐	
Retail salespersons	○	◐	●		○			◐				
Roofers	○	○	○		○	●	○	○	●	●	●	
Sales representatives, wholesale and manufacturing	○	●	●		◐		○	●				
Sales worker supervisors	○	●	●	●	◐	○	○	●				
Science technicians	○	◐	○		●	●	●	◐	○	○	○	
Secretaries and administrative assistants	○	●	●	○	○			○				
Security guards and gaming surveillance officers		○	○	○		○		○	◐	○	●	
Sheet metal workers	○	○	○		○	●	○	●		●	●	
Social and human service assistants		◐	●				○					
Surgical technologists		◐	◐	○	●	●	●			◐	◐	
Surveyors, cartographers, photogrammetrists, and surveying and mapping technicians	◐	◐	◐	○	◐	◐	◐	◐	◐	◐		
Teachers—preschool, kindergarten, elementary, middle, and secondary	◐	●	●	●	◐	○	◐					
Teachers—self-enrichment education	◐	●	●	●	◐		◐					
Tellers		◐	●		●			○				
Truck drivers and driver/sales workers		○				○		●	○	●	●	
Veterinary technologists and technicians		◐	◐	◐	◐	●	◐	○	○	●	●	
Water and liquid waste treatment plant and system operators		○	○	○	◐	●	◐			◐	◐	●
Water transportation occupations		◐	○	●	◐	●	◐	●	◐	◐	●	●

Personal Skills: ●—Essential or high skill level; ◐—Somewhat essential or moderate skill level; ○—Basic skill level
Job Characteristics: ●—Highly likely; ◐—Somewhat likely; ○—A little likely

© JIST Works

Descriptions of the Top 100 Careers Without a Four-Year Degree

This is the book's main section. It contains helpful descriptions of the 100 major occupations that don't require a four-year college degree. To learn a job's ranking, see the introduction.

The jobs are arranged in alphabetical order. Refer to the table of contents for a list of the jobs and the page numbers where their descriptions begin. Review the table of contents to discover occupations that interest you and then find out more about them in this section. If you are interested in medical careers, for example, you can go through the list and quickly pinpoint those you want to learn more about. Or use the assessment in Part I to identify several possible career matches.

While the job descriptions in this part are easy to understand, the introduction provides additional information for interpreting them. Keep in mind that the descriptions present information that is average for the country. Conditions in your area and with specific employers may be quite different.

Also, you may come across jobs that sound interesting but require more education and training than you have or are considering. Don't eliminate them too soon. There are many ways to obtain education and training, and most people change careers many times. You probably have more skills than you realize that can transfer to new jobs. People often have more opportunities than barriers. Use the descriptions to learn more about possible jobs and look into the suggested resources to help you take the next step.

Actors, Producers, and Directors

(O*NET 27-2011.00, 27-2012.00, 27-2012.01, 27-2012.02, 27-2012.03, 27-2012.04, and 27-2012.05)

Significant Points

■ Actors endure long periods of unemployment, intense competition for roles, and frequent rejections in auditions.

■ Formal training through a university or acting conservatory is typical; however, many actors, producers, and directors find work on the basis of their experience and talent alone.

■ Because earnings may be erratic, many supplement their incomes by holding jobs in other fields; however, the most successful actors, producers, and directors may have extraordinarily high earnings.

Nature of the Work

Actors, producers, and directors express ideas and create images in theater, film, radio, television, and other performing arts media. They interpret a writer's script to entertain, inform, or instruct an audience. Although many actors, producers, and directors work in New York or Los Angeles, far more work in other places. They perform, direct, and produce in local or regional television studios, theaters, or film production companies, often creating advertising or training films or small-scale independent movies.

Actors perform in stage, radio, television, video, or motion picture productions. They also work in cabarets, nightclubs, and theme parks. Actors portray characters, and, for more complex roles, they research their character's traits and circumstances so that they can better understand a script.

Most actors struggle to find steady work and only a few achieve recognition as stars. Some well-known, experienced performers may be cast in supporting roles or make brief, cameo appearances, speaking only one or two lines. Others work as "extras," with no lines to deliver. Some actors do voiceover and narration work for advertisements, animated features, books on tape, and other electronic media. They also teach in high school or university drama departments, acting conservatories, or public programs.

Producers are entrepreneurs who make the business and financial decisions involving a motion picture, made-for-television feature, or stage production. They select scripts, approve the development of ideas, arrange financing, and determine the size and cost of the endeavor. Producers hire or approve directors, principal cast members, and key production staff members. They also negotiate contracts with artistic and design personnel in accordance with collective bargaining agreements. They guarantee payment of salaries, rent, and other expenses.

Television and radio producers determine which programs, episodes, or news segments get aired. They may research material, write scripts, and oversee the production of individual pieces. Producers in any medium coordinate the activities of writers, directors, managers, and agents to ensure that each project stays on schedule and within budget.

Directors are responsible for the creative decisions of a production. They interpret scripts, audition and select cast members, conduct rehearsals, and direct the work of cast and crew. They approve the design elements of a production, including the sets, costumes, choreography, and music. Assistant directors cue the performers and technicians, telling them when to make entrances or light, sound, or set changes.

Work environment. Actors, producers, and directors work under constant pressure. Many face stress from the continual need to find their next job. To succeed, actors, producers, and directors need patience and commitment to their craft. Actors strive to deliver flawless performances, often while working under undesirable and unpleasant conditions. Producers and directors organize rehearsals and meet with writers, designers, financial backers, and production technicians. They experience stress not only from these activities, but also from the need to adhere to budgets, union work rules, and production schedules.

Acting assignments typically are short term—ranging from 1 day to a few months—which means that actors frequently experience long periods of unemployment between jobs. The uncertain nature of the work results in unpredictable earnings and intense competition for jobs. Often, actors, producers, and directors must hold other jobs in order to sustain a living.

When performing, actors typically work long, irregular hours. For example, stage actors may perform one show at night while rehearsing another during the day. They also might travel with a show when it tours the country. Movie actors may work on location, sometimes under adverse weather conditions, and may spend considerable time waiting to perform their scenes. Actors who perform in a television series often appear on camera with little preparation time, because scripts tend to be revised frequently or even written moments before taping. Those who appear live or before a studio audience must be able to handle impromptu situations and calmly ad lib, or substitute, lines when necessary.

Evening and weekend work is a regular part of a stage actor's life. On weekends, more than one performance may be held per day. Actors and directors working on movies or television programs, especially those who shoot on location, may work in the early morning or late evening hours to film night scenes or tape scenes inside public facilities outside of normal business hours.

Actors should be in good physical condition and have the necessary stamina and coordination to move about theater stages and large movie and television studio lots. They also need to maneuver about complex technical sets while staying in character and projecting their voices audibly. Actors must be fit to endure heat from stage or studio lights and the weight of heavy costumes. Producers and directors ensure the safety of actors by conducting extra rehearsals on the set so that the actors can learn the layout of set pieces and props, by allowing time for warmups and stretching exercises to guard against physical and vocal injuries, and by providing an adequate number of breaks to prevent heat exhaustion and dehydration.

Training, Other Qualifications, and Advancement

People who become actors, producers, and directors follow many paths to employment. The most important qualities employers look for are creative instincts, innate talent, and the intellectual capacity to perform. The best way to prepare for a career as an actor, especially in the theater, is through formal dramatic training, preferably obtained as part of a bachelor's degree program. Producers and especially directors need experience in the field, either as actors or in other related jobs.

Education and training. Formal dramatic training, either through an acting conservatory or a university program, generally is necessary for these jobs, but some people successfully enter the field without it. Most people studying for a bachelor's degree take courses in radio and television broadcasting, communications, film, theater, drama, or dramatic literature. Many stage actors continue their academic training and receive a Master of Fine Arts (MFA) degree. Advanced curricula may include courses in stage speech and movement, directing, playwriting, and design, as well as intensive acting workshops. The National Association of Schools of Theatre accredits 150 programs in theater arts.

Most aspiring actors participate in high school and college plays, work in college radio or television stations, or perform with local community theater groups. Local and regional theater experience and work in summer stock, on cruise lines, or in theme parks helps many young actors hone their skills. Membership in one of the actors' unions and work experience in smaller communities may lead to work in larger cities, notably New York, Chicago, or Los Angeles. In television and film, actors and directors typically start in smaller television markets or with independent movie production companies and then work their way up to larger media markets and major studio productions. A few people go into acting after successful careers in other fields, such as broadcasting or announcing.

Actors, regardless of experience level, may pursue workshop training through acting conservatories or mentoring by a drama coach. Sometimes actors learn a foreign language or train with a dialect coach to develop an accent to make their characters more realistic.

There are no specific training requirements for producers. They come from many different backgrounds. Actors, writers, film editors, and business managers commonly enter the field. Producers often start in a theatrical management office, working for a press agent, managing director, or business manager. Some start in a performing arts union or service organization. Others work behind the scenes with successful directors, serve on the boards of art companies, or promote their own projects. Although there are no formal training programs for producers, a number of colleges and universities offer degree programs in arts management and in managing nonprofit organizations.

Directors often start out as actors. Many also have formal training in directing. The Directors Guild of America and the Alliance of Motion Picture and Television Producers jointly sponsor the Assistant Directors Training Program. To be accepted to this highly competitive program, an individual must have either a bachelor's or associate degree or two years of experience and must complete a written exam and other assessments. Program graduates are eligible to become a member of the Directors Guild and typically find employment as a second assistant director.

Other qualifications. Actors need talent and creativity that will enable them to portray different characters. Because competition for parts is fierce, versatility and a wide range of related performance skills, such as singing, dancing, skating, juggling, acrobatics, or miming are especially useful. Experience in horseback riding, fencing, linguistics, or stage combat also can lift some actors above the average and get them noticed by producers and directors. Actors must have poise, stage presence, the ability to affect an audience, and the ability to follow direction. Modeling experience also may be helpful. Physical appearance, such as having certain features and being the specified size and weight, often is a deciding factor in who gets a particular role.

Many professional actors rely on agents or managers to find work, negotiate contracts, and plan their careers. Agents generally earn a percentage of the pay specified in an actor's contract. Other actors rely solely on attending open auditions for parts. Trade publications list the times, dates, and locations of these auditions.

Some actors begin as movie extras. To become an extra, one usually must be listed by casting agencies that supply extras to the major movie studios in Hollywood. Applicants are accepted only when the numbers of people of a particular type on the list, for example, athletic young women, old men, or small children, falls below what is needed. In recent years, only a very small proportion of applicants have succeeded in being listed.

Like actors, directors and producers need talent and creativity. They also need business acumen.

Advancement. As the reputations and box-office draw of actors, producers, and directors grow, they might work on bigger budget productions, on network or syndicated broadcasts, or in more prestigious theaters. Actors may advance to lead roles and receive star billing. A few actors move into acting-related jobs, such as drama coaches or directors of stage, television, radio, or motion picture productions. Some teach drama privately or in colleges and universities.

Employment

In May 2006, actors, producers, and directors held about 163,000 jobs, primarily in motion picture and video, performing arts, and broadcast industries. Because many others were between jobs, the total number of actors, producers, and directors available for work was higher. Employment in the theater, and other performing arts companies, is cyclical—higher in the fall and spring seasons—and concentrated in New York and other major cities with large commercial houses for musicals and touring productions. Also, many cities support established professional regional theaters that operate on a seasonal or year-round basis. About 28 percent of actors, producers, and directors were self-employed.

Actors, producers, and directors may find work in summer festivals, on cruise lines, and in theme parks. Many smaller, nonprofit professional companies, such as repertory companies, dinner theaters, and theaters affiliated with drama schools, acting conservatories, and universities, provide employment opportunities for local amateur talent and professional entertainers. Auditions typically are held in New York for many productions across the country and for shows that go on the road.

Employment in motion pictures and in films for television is centered in New York and Los Angeles. However, small studios exist throughout the country. Many films are shot on location and may employ local professional and nonprofessional actors. In television, opportunities are concentrated in the network centers of New York and Los Angeles, but cable television services and local television stations around the country also employ many actors, producers, and directors.

Job Outlook

Employment of actors, producers, and directors is expected to grow about as fast as the average for all occupations. Competition for jobs will be keen. Although a growing number of people aspire to enter

Projections data from the National Employment Matrix

Occupational Title	SOC Code	Employment, 2006	Projected employment, 2016	Change, 2006-2016	
				Number	Percent
Actors, producers, and directors	27-2010	163,000	182,000	18,000	11
Actors	27-2011	70,000	78,000	8,100	12
Producers and directors	27-2012	93,000	103,000	10,000	11

NOTE: Data in this table are rounded.

these professions, many will leave the field early because the work—when it is available—is hard, the hours are long, and the pay may be low.

Employment change. Employment in these occupations is expected to grow 11 percent during the 2006–2016 decade, about as fast as the average for all occupations. Expanding cable and satellite television operations, increasing production and distribution of major studio and independent films, and rising demand for films in other countries should create more employment opportunities for actors, producers, and directors. Also fueling job growth is the continued development of interactive media, direct-for-Web movies, and mobile content, produced for cell phones or other portable electronic devices. However, greater emphasis on national, rather than local, entertainment productions may restrict employment opportunities in the broadcasting industry.

Job prospects. Competition for jobs will be stiff. The large number of highly trained and talented actors auditioning for roles generally exceeds the number of parts that become available. Only performers with the most stamina and talent will find regular employment.

Venues for live entertainment, such as Broadway and Off-Broadway theaters, touring productions, and repertory theaters in many major metropolitan areas, as well as theme parks and resorts, are expected to offer many job opportunities. However, prospects in these venues are variable because they fluctuate with economic conditions.

Earnings

The most successful actors, producers, and directors may have extraordinarily high earnings but for others, because earnings may be erratic, many supplement their income by holding jobs in other fields.

Median hourly earnings of actors were $11.61 in May 2006. The middle 50 percent earned between $8.47 and $22.51. The lowest 10 percent earned less than $7.31, and the highest 10 percent earned more than $51.02. Median hourly earnings were $16.82 in performing arts companies and $10.69 in the motion picture and video industry. Annual earnings data for actors were not available because of the wide variation in the number of hours worked by actors and the short-term nature of many jobs, which may last for 1 day or 1 week; it is extremely rare for actors to have guaranteed employment that exceeded 3 to 6 months.

Median annual earnings of salaried producers and directors were $56,310 in 2006. The middle 50 percent earned between $37,980 and $88,700. Median annual earnings were $70,750 in the motion picture and video industry and $47,530 in radio and television broadcasting.

Minimum salaries, hours of work, and other conditions of employment are often covered in collective bargaining agreements between the producers and the unions representing workers. The Actors' Equity Association (AEA) represents stage actors; the Screen Actors Guild (SAG) covers actors in motion pictures, including television, commercials, and film; and the American Federation of Television and Radio Artists (AFTRA) represents television and radio studio performers. Some actors who regularly work in several media find it advantageous to join multiple unions, while SAG and AFTRA may share jurisdiction for work in additional areas, such as the production of training or educational films not slated for broadcast, television commercial work, and interactive media. While these unions generally determine minimum salaries, any actor or director may negotiate for a salary higher than the minimum.

Under terms of a joint SAG and AFTRA contract covering all unionized workers, motion picture and television actors with speaking parts earned a minimum daily rate of $759 or $2,634 for a 5-day week as of July 1, 2007. Actors also receive contributions to their health and pension plans and additional compensation for reruns and foreign telecasts of the productions in which they appear.

According to AEA, the minimum weekly salary for actors in Broadway productions as of June 2007 was $1,509. Actors in Off-Broadway theaters received minimums ranging from $516 to $976 a week as of October 29, 2007, depending on the seating capacity of the theater. Regional theaters that operate under an Equity agreement pay actors $544 to $840 per week. For touring productions, actors receive an additional $113 per day for living expenses ($119 per day in higher cost cities). New terms were negotiated under an "experimental touring program" provision for lower budget musicals that tour to smaller cities or that perform for fewer performances at each stop. In an effort to increase the number of paid work weeks while on tour, actors may be paid less than the full production rate for touring shows in exchange for higher per diems and profit participation.

Some well-known actors—stars—earn well above the minimum; their salaries are many times the figures cited, creating the false impression that all actors are highly paid. For example, of the nearly 100,000 SAG members, only about 50 might be considered stars. The average income that SAG members earn from acting, less than $5,000 a year, is low because employment is sporadic. Therefore, most actors must supplement their incomes by holding jobs in other occupations.

Many actors who work more than a qualifying number of days, or weeks per year or earn over a set minimum pay, are covered by a union health, welfare, and pension fund, which includes hospitalization insurance to which employers contribute. Under some employment conditions, Equity and AFTRA members receive paid vacations and sick leave.

Many stage directors belong to the Society of Stage Directors and Choreographers (SSDC), and film and television directors belong to the Directors Guild of America. Earnings of stage directors vary greatly. The SSDC usually negotiates salary contracts which include royalties (additional income based on the number of performances) with smaller theaters. Directing a production at a dinner theater generally will pay less than directing one at a summer theater, but has more potential for generating income from royalties. Regional theaters may hire directors for longer periods, increasing compensation accordingly. The highest-paid directors work on Broadway and commonly earn over $50,000 per show. However, they also receive payment in the form of royalties—a negotiated percentage of gross box office receipts—that can exceed their contract fee for long-running box office successes.

Stage producers seldom get a set fee; instead, they get a percentage of a show's earnings or ticket sales.

Related Occupations

People who work in performing arts occupations that may require acting skills include announcers; dancers and choreographers; and musicians, singers, and related workers. Others working in occupations related to film and theater include makeup artists, theatrical and performance; fashion designers; and set and exhibit designers. Producers share many responsibilities with those who work as top executives.

Sources of Additional Information

For general information about theater arts and a list of accredited college-level programs, contact

▸ National Association of Schools of Theater, 11250 Roger Bacon Dr., Suite 21, Reston, VA 20190. Internet: http://nast.arts-accredit.org

For general information on actors, producers, and directors, contact any of the following organizations:

▸ Actors' Equity Association, 165 West 46th St., New York, NY 10036. Internet: http://www.actorsequity.org

▸ Screen Actors Guild, 5757 Wilshire Blvd., Los Angeles, CA 90036-3600. Internet: http://www.sag.org

▸ American Federation of Television and Radio Artists, 4340 East-West Hwy., Suite 204, Bethesda, MD 20814-4411. Internet: http://www.aftra.org

Advertising Sales Agents

(O*NET 41-3011.00)

Significant Points

■ Overall earnings are higher than average but vary considerably because they usually are based on a salary plus performance-based commissions and bonuses.

■ Pressure to meet monthly sales quotas can be stressful.

Nature of the Work

Advertising sales agents—often referred to as *account executives* or *advertising sales representatives*—sell or solicit advertising primarily for newspapers and periodicals, television and radio, websites, telephone directories, and direct mail and outdoor advertisers. Because such a large share of revenue for many of these media outlets is generated from advertising, advertising sales agents play an important role in their success.

More than half of all advertising sales agents work in the information sector, mostly for media firms including television and radio broadcasters, print and Internet publishers, and cable program distributors. Firms that are regionally based often need the help of two types of advertising sales agents, one to handle local clients and one to solicit advertising from national advertisers. Print publications and radio and television stations employ local sales agents who are responsible for sales in an immediate territory, while separate companies known as media representative firms sell advertising space or time for media owners at the national level with their own teams of advertising sales agents. Sales agents employed in media representation work exclusively through executives at advertising agencies, called media buyers, who purchase advertising space for their clients that want to initiate national advertising campaigns. When a local television broadcaster, radio station, print, or online publisher is working with a media representative firm, the media company normally employs a national sales manager to coordinate efforts with the media representative.

Local sales agents are often referred to as outside sales agents or inside sales agents. *Outside sales agents* call on clients and prospects at their places of business. They may have an appointment, or they may practice cold calling—arriving without an appointment. For these sales agents, obtaining new accounts is an important part of the job, and they may spend much of their time traveling to and visiting prospective advertisers and current clients. *Inside sales agents* work on their employer's premises and handle sales for customers who walk in or telephone the firm to inquire about advertising. Some may also make telephone sales calls—calling prospects, attempting to sell the media firm's advertising space or time, and arranging follow-up appointments between interested prospects and outside sales agents.

A critical part of building a relationship with a client is to find out as much as possible about the client. Before the first meeting with a client, sales agents gather background information on the client's products, current customers, prospective customers, and the geographic area of the target market. They then meet with the clients to explain how specific types of advertising will help promote the client's products or services most effectively. If a client wishes to proceed, the advertising sales agent prepares an advertising proposal to present to the client. This entails determining the advertising medium to be used, preparing sample advertisements, and providing clients with cost estimates for the proposal. Because consolidation among media industries has brought the sales of different types of advertising under one roof, advertising sales are increasingly in the form of integrated packages. This means that advertising sales agents may sell packages that include print and online ad space and time slots with a broadcast subsidiary.

After a contract has been established, advertising sales agents serve as the main contact between the advertiser or ad agency and the media firm. They handle communication between the parties and assist in developing sample artwork or radio and television spots, if needed. For radio and television advertisements, they may also arrange for commercial taping sessions and accompany clients to these sessions.

In addition to maintaining sales and overseeing clients' accounts, advertising sales agents' other duties include analyzing sales statistics and audience demographics, preparing reports on client's accounts, and scheduling and keeping their appointments and work hours. They read about new and existing products and monitor the sales, prices, and products of their competitors. In many firms, the advertising sales agent handles the drafting of contracts specifying the advertising work to be performed and its cost, and may undertake customer service responsibilities such as answering questions or addressing any problems the client may have with the proposal.

Sales agents are also responsible for developing sales tools, promotional plans, and media kits, which they use to help make the sale.

Work environment. Selling can be stressful work because income and job security depend directly on the agent's ability to maintain and expand clientele. Companies generally set monthly sales quotas and place considerable pressure on advertising sales agents to meet those quotas. The added stress of rejection places more pressure on the agent.

Although agents work long and often irregular hours, most have the freedom to determine their own schedule. The Internet and other electronic tools allow agents to do more work from home or while on the road, enabling them to send messages and documents to clients and coworkers, keep up with industry news, and access databases that help them target potential customers. Advertising sales agents use e-mail to conduct much of the business with their clients.

Many advertising sales agents work more than 40 hours per week. This frequently involves irregular hours and may also include working on weekends and holidays. However, most advertising sales agents are able to set their own schedule. Eleven percent of advertising sales agents were employed part time in 2006.

Training, Other Qualifications, and Advancement

For sales positions that require meeting with clients, large employers prefer applicants with a college degree. Smaller companies generally are more willing to hire individuals with a high school degree. Successful sales experience and the ability to communicate effectively become more important than educational attainment once hired. Most training for advertising sales agents takes place informally on the job.

Education and training. Some employers, large companies in particular, prefer applicants with a college degree, particularly for sales positions that require meeting with clients. Courses in marketing, leadership, communication, business, and advertising are helpful. For those who sell over the telephone or who have a proven record of successfully selling other products, a high school degree may be sufficient. In 2006, the highest level of educational attainment for advertising sales agents was as follows.

High school graduate or less 20

Some college, no degree...19

Associate's degree 10

Bachelor's degree or higher.......................................52

Most training, however, takes place on the job, and can be formal or informal in nature. In most cases, an experienced sales manager instructs a newly hired advertising sales agent who lacks sales experience. In this one-on-one environment, supervisors typically coach new hires and observe as they make sales calls and contact clients. Supervisors then advise new hires on ways to improve their interaction with clients. Employers may bring in consultants to lead formal training sessions when agents sell to a specialized market segment. This practice is common when advertising sales agents sell space to automotive dealers and real estate professionals.

Other qualifications. Employers look for applicants who are honest and possess a pleasant personality and neat professional appearance. After gaining entry into the occupation, successful sales experience

and the ability to communicate effectively become more important than educational attainment. In fact, when selling or soliciting ad space, personality traits are equally, if not more, important than academic background. In general, smaller companies are more willing to hire unproven individuals.

Because they represent their employers to the executives of client organizations, advertising sales agents must have excellent interpersonal and written communication skills. Being multi-lingual, particularly in English and Spanish, is another trait that will benefit prospective advertising agents as media increasingly seek to market to Hispanics and other foreign-born persons. Self-motivation, organization, persistence, independence, and the ability to multitask are required because advertising sales agents set their own schedules and perform their duties without much supervision.

Advancement. Advancement in the occupation means taking on bigger, more important clients. Agents with proven leadership ability and a strong sales record may advance to supervisory and managerial positions such as sales supervisor, sales manager, or vice president of sales. Frequent contact with managers of other departments and people in other firms provides sales agents with leads about job openings, enhancing advancement opportunities. In small firms, where the number of supervisory and management positions is limited, advancement may come slowly. Promotion may occur more quickly in larger media firms and in media representative firms.

Employment

Advertising sales agents held over 170,000 jobs in 2006. Workers were concentrated in three industries: More than 3 in 10 jobs were in newspaper, periodical, book, and directory publishers; 3 in 10 in advertising and related services; and nearly 2 in 10 in radio and television broadcasting. Media representative firms are in the advertising and related services industry. A relatively small number of jobs were found in specialized design services, including industrial and graphic designers; printing and related support activities; computer systems design and related services; business support services; and cable and other program distribution.

Employment is spread around the country, but jobs in radio and television stations and large, well-known publications are concentrated in big metropolitan areas. Media representative firms are also concentrated in large cities with many advertising agencies, such as New York City.

Job Outlook

Employment growth of advertising sales agents is expected to grow faster than average for all occupations for the 2006–2016 period. Because of growth in new media outlets, such as the Internet, advertising agents with an ability to sell, should see good job opportunities.

Employment change. Employment of advertising sales agents is expected to increase by 20 percent from 2006 to 2016, which is faster than the average for all occupations. Fast growth in the number of cable channels, online advertisers, and other advertising mediums will create many new opportunities for advertisers. These opportunities, along with increased efforts by media outlets to market to the growing Hispanic population, will lead to the growth of advertising sales agents.

Projections data from the National Employment Matrix

Occupational Title	SOC Code	Employment, 2006	Projected employment, 2016	Change, 2006-16	
				Number	Percent
Advertising sales agents..	41-3011	170,000	205,000	35,000	20

NOTE: Data in this table are rounded.

The industries employing advertising sales agents, particularly the newspaper, periodical, radio, and television industries, have experienced considerable consolidation in recent years, which created efficiencies in the sale of advertising and reduced the need for more sales agents. While this trend is expected to continue over the next decade, it should do so at a slower pace and not affect employment of advertising sales agents significantly.

While advances in technology have made advertising sales agents more productive, allowing agents to take on additional duties and improve the quality of the services they provide, technological advances have not substantially decreased overall demand for these workers. Productivity gains have had the largest effect on miscellaneous services that workers provide, such as accounting, proposal creation, and customer service responsibilities, allowing them to provide faster, improved services to their clients. For example, the use of e-mail has considerably shortened the time it takes to negotiate a sale and place an ad. Sales agents may accomplish more in less time, but many work more hours than in the past, spending additional time on follow-up and service calls. Thus, while productivity gains will temper the growth of advertising sales agents, who can now manage more accounts, the increasing growth in advertising across all industries will ensure that new advertising sales agents will continue to be needed in the future.

Job prospects. Those interested in ad sales positions can expect good job opportunities. This is particularly true for sales people with experience and those with a college degree. For those with a proven sales record in advertising sales, opportunities should be excellent. In addition to the job openings generated by employment growth, openings will occur each year because of the need to replace sales representatives who transfer to other occupations or leave the labor force. Each year, many advertising sales agents discover they are unable to earn enough money and leave the occupation.

Advertising revenues are sensitive to economic downturns, which cause the industries and companies that advertise to reduce both the frequency of campaigns and the overall level of spending on advertising. Advertising sales agents must work hard to get the most out of every dollar spent on advertising under these conditions. Therefore, the number of opportunities for advertising sales agents fluctuates with the business cycle. So while advertising sales candidates can expect good opportunities, applicants can expect keen competition for job openings during downturns in advertising spending.

Earnings

Including commissions, median annual earnings for all advertising sales agents were $42,750 in May 2006. The middle 50 percent earned between $29,450 and $63,120 a year. The lowest 10 percent earned less than $21,460, and the highest 10 percent earned more than $91,280 a year. Median annual earnings for sales agents in the industries in which they were concentrated were

Motion picture and video industries $55,340

Cable and other subscription programming 50,260

Advertising and related services 47,640

Radio and television broadcasting 41,110

Newspaper, periodical, book, and
   directory publishers...36,880

Performance-based pay, including bonuses and commissions, can make up a large portion of advertising sales agents' earnings. Most employers pay some combination of salaries, commissions, and bonuses. Commissions are usually based on individual sales numbers, whereas bonuses may depend on individual performance, on the performance of all sales workers in a group or district, or on the performance of the entire company. For agents covering multiple areas or regions, commissions also may be based on the difficulty in making a sale in that particular area. Sales revenue is affected by the economic conditions and business expectations facing the industries that tend to advertise. Earnings from commissions are likely to be high when these industries are doing well and low when companies decide not to advertise as frequently.

In addition to their earnings, advertising sales agents are usually reimbursed for entertaining clients and for other business expenses such as transportation costs, meals, and hotel stays. They often receive benefits such as health and life insurance, pension plans, vacation and sick leave, personal use of a company car, and frequent flier mileage. Some companies offer incentives such as free vacation trips or gifts for outstanding sales workers.

Related Occupations

Advertising sales agents must have sales ability and knowledge of their clients' business and personal needs. Workers in other occupations requiring these skills include telemarketers; advertising, marketing, promotions, public relations, and sales managers; insurance sales agents; purchasing managers, buyers, and purchasing agents; real estate brokers and sales agents; sales engineers; sales representatives, wholesale and manufacturing; and securities, commodities, and financial services sales agents.

Sources of Additional Information

To learn about opportunities for employment as an advertising sales agent, contact local broadcasters, radio stations, and publishers for advertising sales representative positions, or look for media representative firms in your area.

For information about advertising sales careers in newspaper publishing, contact

▸ The Newspaper Association of America, 1921 Gallows Rd., Suite 600, Vienna, VA 22182. Internet: http://www.naa.org

Aircraft and Avionics Equipment Mechanics and Service Technicians

(O*NET 49-2091.00 and 49-3011.00)

Significant Points

■ Most workers learn their jobs in 1 of about 170 schools certified by the Federal Aviation Administration (FAA).

■ Job opportunities should be favorable for persons who have completed an aircraft mechanic training program, but keen competition is likely for jobs at major airlines, which offer the best pay and benefits.

■ Job opportunities are likely to continue to be best at small commuter and regional airlines, at FAA repair stations, and in general aviation.

Nature of the Work

To keep aircraft in peak operating condition, aircraft and avionics equipment mechanics and service technicians perform scheduled maintenance, make repairs, and complete inspections required by the Federal Aviation Administration (FAA).

Many aircraft mechanics, also called airframe mechanics, power plant mechanics, and avionics technicians, specialize in preventive maintenance. They inspect aircraft engines, landing gear, instruments, pressurized sections, accessories—brakes, valves, pumps, and air-conditioning systems, for example—and other parts of the aircraft, and do the necessary maintenance and replacement of parts. They also keep records related to the maintenance performed on the aircraft. Mechanics and technicians conduct inspections following a schedule based on the number of hours the aircraft has flown, calendar days since the last inspection, cycles of operation, or a combination of these factors. In large, sophisticated planes equipped with aircraft monitoring systems, mechanics can gather valuable diagnostic information from electronic boxes and consoles that monitor the aircraft's basic operations. In planes of all sorts, aircraft mechanics examine engines by working through specially designed openings while standing on ladders or scaffolds or by using hoists or lifts to remove the entire engine from the craft. After taking an engine apart, mechanics use precision instruments to measure parts for wear and use x-ray and magnetic inspection equipment to check for invisible cracks. They repair or replace worn or defective parts. Mechanics also may repair sheet metal or composite surfaces; measure the tension of control cables; and check for corrosion, distortion, and cracks in the fuselage, wings, and tail. After completing all repairs, they must test the equipment to ensure that it works properly.

Other mechanics specialize in repair work rather than inspection. They find and fix problems that pilot's describe. For example, during a preflight check, a pilot may discover that the aircraft's fuel gauge does not work. To solve the problem, mechanics may troubleshoot the electrical system, using electrical test equipment to make sure that no wires are broken or shorted out, and replace any defective electrical or electronic components. Mechanics work as fast as safety permits so that the aircraft can be put back into service quickly.

Some mechanics work on one or many different types of aircraft, such as jets, propeller-driven airplanes, and helicopters. Others specialize in one section of a particular type of aircraft, such as the engine, hydraulics, or electrical system. *Airframe mechanics* are authorized to work on any part of the aircraft except the instruments, power plants, and propellers. *Powerplant mechanics* are authorized to work on engines and do limited work on propellers. *Combination airframe-and-powerplant mechanics*—called A&P mechanics—work on all parts of the plane except the instruments. Most mechanics working on civilian aircraft today are A&P mechanics. In small, independent repair shops, mechanics usually inspect and repair many different types of aircraft.

Avionics systems—components used for aircraft navigation and radio communications, weather radar systems, and other instruments and computers that control flight, engine, and other primary functions—are now an integral part of aircraft design and have vastly increased aircraft capability. *Avionics technicians* repair and maintain these systems. Their duties may require additional licenses, such as a radiotelephone license issued by the U.S. Federal Communications Commission (FCC). Because of the increasing use of technology, more time is spent repairing electronic systems, such as computerized controls. Technicians also may be required to analyze and develop solutions to complex electronic problems.

Work environment. Mechanics usually work in hangars or in other indoor areas. When hangars are full or when repairs must be made quickly, they may work outdoors, sometimes in unpleasant weather. Mechanics often work under time pressure to maintain flight schedules or, in general aviation, to keep from inconveniencing customers. At the same time, mechanics have a tremendous responsibility to maintain safety standards, and this can cause the job to be stressful.

Frequently, mechanics must lift or pull objects weighing more than 70 pounds. They often stand, lie, or kneel in awkward positions and occasionally must work in precarious positions, such as on scaffolds or ladders. Noise and vibration are common when engines are being tested, so ear protection is necessary.

Aircraft mechanics usually work 40 hours a week on 8-hour shifts around the clock. Overtime and weekend work is frequent.

Training, Other Qualifications, and Advancement

Most workers learn their jobs in one of about 170 trade schools certified by the FAA. Most mechanics who work on civilian aircraft are certified by the FAA as an "airframe mechanic" or a "powerplant mechanic."

Education and training. Although a few people become mechanics through on-the-job training, most learn their jobs in one of about the 170 schools certified by the FAA. About one-third of these schools award two-year and four-year degrees in avionics, aviation technology, or aviation maintenance management.

FAA standards established by law require that certified mechanic schools offer students a minimum of 1,900 class hours. Coursework in schools normally lasts from 18 to 24 months and provides training with the tools and equipment used on the job. Aircraft trade schools are placing more emphasis on technologies such as turbine engines, composite materials—including graphite, fiberglass, and boron—and aviation electronics, which are increasingly being used in the construction of new aircraft.

Courses in mathematics, physics, chemistry, electronics, computer science, and mechanical drawing are helpful because they demonstrate many of the principles involved in the operation of aircraft, and knowledge of these principles is often necessary to make repairs. Recent technological advances in aircraft maintenance require mechanics to have an especially strong background in electronics to get or keep jobs in this field.

Courses that develop writing skills also are important because mechanics are often required to submit reports. Mechanics must be able to read, write, and understand English.

A few mechanics are trained on the job by experienced mechanics. They must be supervised by certified mechanics until they have FAA certificates.

Licensure. The FAA requires at least 18 months of work experience for an airframe or powerplant certificate, although completion of a program at an FAA-certified mechanic school can be substituted for the work experience requirement. Mechanics and technicians also must pass an exam for certification and take at least 16 hours of training every 24 months to keep their certificate current. Many mechanics take training courses offered by manufacturers or employers, usually through outside contractors.

The FAA also offers a combined certificate that allows for certification as both an airframe and a powerplant mechanic, the A&P certificate. For a combined A&P certificate, mechanics must acquire at least 30 months of experience working with both engines and airframes, or experience combined with the completion of an FAA-certified mechanic school program. FAA regulations also require current work experience to keep the A&P certificate valid. Applicants must have at least 1,000 hours of work experience in the previous 24 months or take a refresher course. Most airlines require that mechanics have a high school diploma and an A&P certificate. Applicants for all certificates must pass written and oral tests and demonstrate that they can do the work authorized by the certificate.

Avionics technicians need an FAA mechanics' certificate. They also must be trained and qualified and have the proper tools to work on avionics equipment. Many have avionics repair experience from the military or from working for avionics manufacturers.

Other qualifications. Applicants must be at least 18 years of age. Some aircraft mechanics in the Armed Forces acquire enough general experience to satisfy the work experience requirements for the FAA certificate. With additional study, they may pass the certifying exam. In general, however, jobs in the military services are too specialized to provide the broad experience required by the FAA. Most Armed Forces mechanics have to complete the entire FAA training program, although a few receive some credit for the material they learned in the service. In any case, military experience is a great advantage when seeking employment; employers consider applicants with formal training to be the most desirable applicants.

Aircraft mechanics must do careful and thorough work that requires a high degree of mechanical aptitude. Employers seek applicants who are self-motivated, hard working, enthusiastic, and able to diagnose and solve complex mechanical problems. Additionally, employers prefer mechanics who can perform a variety of tasks. Agility is important for the reaching and climbing necessary to do the job. Because they may work on the tops of wings and fuselages on large jet planes, aircraft mechanics must not be afraid of heights.

Advances in computer technology, aircraft systems, and the materials used to manufacture airplanes have made mechanics' jobs more highly technical. Aircraft mechanics must possess the skills necessary to troubleshoot and diagnose complex aircraft systems. They also must continually update their skills with and knowledge of new technology and advances in aircraft technology

Advancement. As aircraft mechanics gain experience, they may advance to lead mechanic (or crew chief), inspector, lead inspector, or shop supervisor positions. Opportunities are best for those who have an aircraft inspector's authorization. To obtain an inspector's authorization, a mechanic must have held an A&P certificate for at least three years, with 24 months of hands-on experience.

In the airlines, where promotion often is determined by examination, supervisors sometimes advance to executive positions. Those with broad experience in maintenance and overhaul might become inspectors with the FAA. With additional business and management training, some open their own aircraft maintenance facilities. Mechanics with the necessary pilot licenses and flying experience may take the FAA examination for the position of flight engineer, with opportunities to become pilots.

Mechanics and technicians learn many different skills in their training that can be applied to other jobs, and some transfer to other skilled repairer occupations or electronics technician jobs. For example, some avionics technicians continue their education and become aviation engineers, electrical engineers (specializing in circuit design and testing), or communication engineers. Others become repair consultants, in-house electronics designers, or join research groups that test and develop products.

Employment

Aircraft and avionics equipment mechanics and service technicians held about 138,000 jobs in 2006; about 5 in 6 of these workers was an aircraft mechanic and service technician.

Employment of aircraft and avionics equipment mechanics and service technicians primarily is concentrated in a small number of industries. More than half of aircraft and avionics equipment mechanics and service technicians worked in air transportation and support activities for air transportation. Around 18 percent worked in aerospace product and parts manufacturing and about 16 percent worked for the federal government. Most of the rest worked for companies that operate their own planes to transport executives and cargo.

Most airline mechanics and service technicians work at major airports near large cities. Civilian mechanics employed by the U.S. Armed Forces work at military installations. Mechanics who work for aerospace manufacturing firms typically are located in California or in Washington state. Others work for the FAA, many at the facilities in Oklahoma City, Atlantic City, Wichita, or Washington, DC. Mechanics for independent repair shops work at airports in every part of the country.

Job Outlook

Job growth for these mechanics and technicians is expected to be about as fast as the average for all occupations. Job opportunities should be favorable for people who have completed an aircraft mechanic training program, but keen competition is likely for jobs at major airlines.

Employment change. Employment is expected to increase by 10 percent during the 2006–2016 period, about as fast as the average for all occupations. Passenger traffic is expected to increase as the

Projections data from the National Employment Matrix

Occupational Title	SOC Code	Employment, 2006	Projected employment, 2016	Change, 2006-16	
				Number	Percent
Aircraft and avionics equipment mechanics and service technicians..	—	138,000	152,000	14,000	10
Avionics technicians	49-2091	16,000	17,000	1,300	8
Aircraft mechanics and service technicians................................	49-3011	122,000	135,000	13,000	11

NOTE: Data in this table are rounded.

result of an expanding economy and a growing population, and the need for aircraft mechanics and service technicians will grow accordingly.

Job prospects. Most job openings for aircraft mechanics through the year 2016 will stem from the need to replace the many mechanics expected to retire over the next decade. In addition, some mechanics will leave to work in related fields, such as automobile repair, as their skills are largely transferable to other maintenance and repair occupations.

Also contributing to favorable future job opportunities for mechanics is the long-term trend toward fewer students entering technical schools to learn skilled maintenance and repair trades. Many of the students who have the ability and aptitude to work on planes are choosing to go to college, work in computer-related fields, or go into other repair and maintenance occupations with better working conditions. If this trend continues, the supply of trained aviation mechanics may not keep up with the needs of the air transportation industry.

Job opportunities will continue to be the best at small commuter and regional airlines, at FAA repair stations, and in general aviation. Commuter and regional airlines is the fastest growing segment of the air transportation industry, but wages in these airlines tend to be lower than those in the major airlines, so they attract fewer job applicants. Also, some jobs will become available as experienced mechanics leave for higher paying jobs with the major airlines or transfer to other occupations. At the same time, general aviation aircraft are becoming increasingly sophisticated, boosting the demand for qualified mechanics. Mechanics will face more competition for jobs with large airlines because the high wages and travel benefits that these jobs offer generally attract more qualified applicants than there are openings. Also, there is an increasing trend for large airlines to outsource aircraft and avionics equipment mechanic jobs overseas; however, most airline companies prefer that aircraft maintenance be performed in the U.S. because overseas contractors may not comply with more stringent U.S. safety regulations.

In spite of these factors, job opportunities with the airlines are expected to be better than they have been in the past. But, in general, prospects will be best for applicants with experience. Mechanics who keep abreast of technological advances in electronics, composite materials, and other areas will be in greatest demand. Also, mechanics who are mobile and willing to relocate to smaller rural areas will have better job opportunities. The number of job openings for aircraft mechanics in the federal government should decline as the Government increasingly contracts out service and repair functions to private repair companies.

Avionics technicians who do not have FAA certification, but who are prepared to master the intricacies of the aircraft while working with certified A&P mechanics, should have good opportunities.

However, certified technicians who are trained to work with complex aircraft systems, performing some duties normally performed by certified A&P mechanics, should have the best job prospects. Additionally, technicians with licensing that enables them to work on the airplane, either removing or reinstalling equipment, are expected to be in especially high demand.

Earnings

Median hourly earnings of aircraft mechanics and service technicians were about $22.95 in May 2006. The middle 50 percent earned between $18.96 and $28.12. The lowest 10 percent earned less than $14.94, and the highest 10 percent earned more than $34.51. Median hourly earnings in the industries employing the largest numbers of aircraft mechanics and service technicians in May 2006 were

Scheduled air transportation $27.46

Nonscheduled air transportation 23.33

Federal government 23.19

Aerospace product and parts manufacturing 21.58

Support activities for air transportation 19.57

Median hourly earnings of avionics technicians were about $22.57 in May 2006. The middle 50 percent earned between $19.02 and $26.65. The lowest 10 percent earned less than $15.65, and the highest 10 percent earned more than $30.33.

Mechanics who work on jets for the major airlines generally earn more than those working on other aircraft. Those who graduate from an aviation maintenance technician school often earn higher starting salaries than individuals who receive training in the Armed Forces or on the job. Airline mechanics and their immediate families receive reduced-fare transportation on their own and most other airlines.

About 3 in 10 aircraft and avionics equipment mechanics and service technicians are members of unions or covered by union agreements. The principal unions are the International Association of Machinists and Aerospace Workers, and the Transport Workers Union of America. Some mechanics are represented by the International Brotherhood of Teamsters.

Related Occupations

Workers in some other occupations that involve similar mechanical and electrical work are electricians, electrical and electronics installers and repairers, and elevator installers and repairers.

Sources of Additional Information

Information about jobs with a particular airline can be obtained by writing to the personnel manager of the company.

For general information about aircraft and avionics equipment mechanics and service technicians, contact

▶ Professional Aviation Maintenance Association, 400 Commonwealth Dr., Warrendale, PA 15096. Internet: http://www.pama.org

For information on jobs in a particular area, contact employers at local airports or local offices of the state employment service.

Information on obtaining positions as aircraft and avionics equipment mechanics and service technicians with the federal government is available from the Office of Personnel Management through USAJOBS, the federal government's official employment information system. This resource for locating and applying for job opportunities can be accessed through the Internet at http://www.usajobs.opm.gov or through an interactive voice response telephone system at (703) 724-1850 or TDD (978) 461-8404. These numbers are not toll free, and charges may result.

Aircraft Pilots and Flight Engineers

(O*NET 53-2011.00 and 53-2012.00)

Significant Points

■ Regional and low-cost airlines offer the best opportunities; pilots attempting to get jobs at the major airlines will face strong competition.

■ Pilots usually start with smaller commuter and regional airlines to acquire the experience needed to qualify for higher paying jobs with national or major airlines.

■ Many pilots have learned to fly in the military, but growing numbers have college degrees with flight training from civilian flying schools that are certified by the Federal Aviation Administration (FAA).

■ Earnings of airline pilots are among the highest in the nation.

Nature of the Work

Pilots are highly trained professionals who either fly airplanes or helicopters to carry out a wide variety of tasks. Most are *airline pilots, copilots*, and *flight engineers* who transport passengers and cargo. However, 1 out of 5 pilots is a commercial pilot involved in dusting crops, spreading seed for reforestation, testing aircraft, flying passengers and cargo to areas not served by regular airlines, directing firefighting efforts, tracking criminals, monitoring traffic, and rescuing and evacuating injured persons.

Before departure, pilots plan their flights carefully. They thoroughly check their aircraft to make sure that the engines, controls, instruments, and other systems are functioning properly. They also make sure that baggage or cargo has been loaded correctly. They confer with flight dispatchers and aviation weather forecasters to find out about weather conditions en route and at their destination. Based on this information, they choose a route, altitude, and speed that will provide the safest, most economical, and smoothest flight. When flying under instrument flight rules—procedures governing the operation of the aircraft when there is poor visibility—the pilot in command, or the company dispatcher, normally files an instrument flight plan with air traffic control so that the flight can be coordinated with other air traffic.

Takeoff and landing are the most difficult parts of the flight, and require close coordination between the two pilots. For example, as the plane accelerates for takeoff, the pilot who is flying the take off concentrates on the runway while the other pilot scans the instrument panel. To calculate the speed they must attain to become airborne, pilots consider the altitude of the airport, outside temperature, weight of the plane, and speed and direction of the wind. The moment the plane reaches takeoff speed, the nonflying pilot informs the flying pilot, who then pulls back on the controls to raise the nose of the plane. Captains and first officers usually alternate flying each leg from takeoff to landing.

Unless the weather is bad, the flight itself is relatively routine. Airplane pilots, with the assistance of autopilot and the flight management computer, steer the plane along their planned route and are monitored by the air traffic control stations they pass along the way. They regularly scan the instrument panel to check their fuel supply; the condition of their engines; and the air-conditioning, hydraulic, and other systems. Pilots may request a change in altitude or route if circumstances dictate. For example, if the ride is rougher than expected, pilots may ask air traffic control if pilots flying at other altitudes have reported better conditions; if so, they may request an altitude change. This procedure also may be used to find a stronger tailwind or a weaker headwind to save fuel and increase speed. In contrast, because helicopters are used for short trips at relatively low altitude, helicopter pilots must be constantly on the lookout for trees, bridges, power lines, transmission towers, and other dangerous obstacles as well as low-flying general aviation aircraft. Regardless of the type of aircraft, all pilots must monitor warning devices designed to help detect sudden shifts in wind conditions that can cause crashes.

Pilots must rely completely on their instruments when visibility is poor. On the basis of altimeter readings, they know how high above ground they are and whether they can fly safely over mountains and other obstacles. Special navigation radios give pilots precise information that, with the help of special charts, tells them their exact position. Other very sophisticated equipment provides directions to a point just above the end of a runway and enables pilots to land completely without an outside visual reference. Once on the ground, pilots must complete records on their flight and the aircraft maintenance status for their company and the FAA.

The number of nonflying duties that pilots have depends on the employment setting. Airline pilots have the services of large support staffs and, consequently, perform few nonflying duties. However, because of the large numbers of passengers, airline pilots may be called upon to coordinate handling of disgruntled or disruptive passengers. Also, under the Federal Flight Deck Officer program airline pilots who undergo rigorous training and screening are deputized as federal law enforcement officers and are issued firearms to protect the cockpit against intruders and hijackers. Pilots employed by other organizations, such as charter operators or businesses, have many other duties. They may load the aircraft, handle all passenger luggage to ensure a balanced load, and supervise refueling; other nonflying responsibilities include keeping records, scheduling flights, arranging for major maintenance, and performing minor aircraft maintenance and repairs.

Except on small aircraft, two pilots usually make up the cockpit crew. Generally, the most experienced pilot, the *captain*, is in command and supervises all other crew members. The pilot and the copilot, often called the first officer, share flying and other duties, such as communicating with air traffic controllers and monitoring the instruments. Some large aircraft have a third crewmember, the flight engineer, who assists the pilots by monitoring and operating many of the instruments and systems, making minor in-flight repairs, and watching for other aircraft. The flight engineer also assists the pilots with the company, air traffic control, and cabin crew communications. New technology can perform many flight tasks, however, and virtually all new aircraft now fly with only two pilots, who rely more heavily on computerized controls.

Some pilots are flight instructors. They teach their students in ground-school classes, in simulators, and in dual-controlled planes and helicopters. A few specially trained pilots are examiners or check pilots. They periodically fly with other pilots or pilot's license applicants to make sure that they are proficient.

Work environment. Most pilots spend a considerable amount of time away from home because the majority of flights involve overnight layovers. When pilots are away from home, the airlines provide hotel accommodations, transportation between the hotel and airport, and an allowance for meals and other expenses.

Airline pilots, especially those on international routes, often experience jet lag—fatigue caused by many hours of flying through different time zones. To guard against pilot fatigue, which could result in unsafe flying conditions, the FAA requires airlines to allow pilots at least 8 hours of uninterrupted rest in the 24 hours before finishing their flight duty.

Commercial pilots face other types of job hazards. The work of test pilots, who check the flight performance of new and experimental planes, may be dangerous. Pilots who are crop-dusters may be exposed to toxic chemicals and seldom have the benefit of a regular landing strip. Helicopter pilots involved in rescue and police work may be subject to personal injury.

Although flying does not involve much physical effort, the mental stress of being responsible for a safe flight, regardless of the weather, can be tiring. Pilots must be alert and quick to react if something goes wrong, particularly during takeoff and landing.

FAA regulations limit flying time of airline pilots of large aircraft to a maximum of 100 hours a month or 1,000 hours a year. Most airline pilots fly an average of 65 to 75 hours a month and work at least an additional 65 to 75 hours a month performing nonflying duties. Most pilots have variable work schedules, working several days on, then several days off. Airlines operate flights at all hours of the day and night, so work schedules often are irregular. Flight assignments are based on seniority; the sooner pilots are hired, the stronger their bidding power is for preferred assignments.

Commercial pilots also may have irregular schedules, flying 30 hours one month and 90 hours the next. Because these pilots frequently have many nonflying responsibilities, they have much less free time than do airline pilots. Except for corporate flight department pilots, most commercial pilots do not remain away from home overnight. But, they may work odd hours. However, if the company owns a fleet of planes, pilots may fly a regular schedule.

Flight instructors may have irregular and seasonal work schedules, depending on their students' available time and the weather. Instructors frequently work in the evening or on weekends.

Training, Other Qualifications, and Advancement

All pilots who are paid to transport passengers or cargo must have a commercial pilot's license with an instrument rating issued by the FAA. Helicopter pilots also must hold a commercial pilot's license with a helicopter rating.

Education and training. Although some small airlines hire high school graduates, most airlines require at least two years of college and prefer to hire college graduates. In fact, most entrants to this occupation have a college degree. Because the number of college-educated applicants continues to increase, many employers are making a college degree an educational requirement. For example, test pilots often are required to have an engineering degree.

Pilots also need flight experience to qualify for a license. Completing classes at a flight school approved by the FAA can reduce the amount of flight experience required for a pilot's license. In 2006, the FAA certified about 600 civilian flying schools, including some colleges and universities that offer degree credit for pilot training. Initial training for airline pilots typically includes a week of company indoctrination; three to six weeks of ground school and simulator training; and 25 hours of initial operating experience, including a check-ride with an FAA aviation safety inspector. Once trained, pilots are required to attend recurrent training and simulator checks once or twice a year throughout their career.

Licensure. To qualify for FAA licensure, applicants must be at least 18 years old and have at least 250 hours of flight experience.

The U.S. Armed Forces have always been an important source of experienced pilots because of the extensive flying time and experience on jet aircraft and helicopters. Those without Armed Forces training may become pilots by attending flight schools or by taking lessons from FAA-certified flight instructors. Applicants also must pass a strict physical examination to make sure that they are in good health and have 20/20 vision with or without glasses, good hearing, and no physical handicaps that could impair their performance. They must pass a written test that includes questions on the principles of safe flight, navigation techniques, and FAA regulations, and must demonstrate their flying ability to FAA or designated examiners.

To fly during periods of low visibility, pilots must be rated by the FAA to fly by instruments. Pilots may qualify for this rating by having the required hours of flight experience, including 40 hours of experience in flying by instruments; they also must pass a written examination on procedures and FAA regulations covering instrument flying and demonstrate to an examiner their ability to fly by instruments. Requirements for the instrument rating vary depending on the certification level of flight school.

Airline pilots must fulfill additional requirements. Captains must have an airline transport pilot's license. Applicants for this license must be at least 23 years old and have a minimum of 1,500 hours of flying experience, including night and instrument flying, and must pass FAA written and flight examinations. Usually, they also have one or more advanced ratings depending on the requirements of their particular job. Because pilots must be able to make quick decisions and accurate judgments under pressure, many airline companies reject applicants who do not pass required psychological and aptitude tests. All licenses are valid so long as a pilot can pass the periodic physical and eye examinations and tests of flying skills required by the FAA and company regulations.

© JIST Works

Projections data from the National Employment Matrix

Occupational Title	SOC Code	Employment, 2006	Projected employment, 2016	Change, 2006-16	
				Number	Percent
Aircraft pilots and flight engineers	53-2010	107,000	121,000	14,000	13
Airline pilots, copilots, and flight engineers	53-2011	79,000	90,000	10,000	13
Commercial pilots	53-2012	28,000	31,000	3,600	13

NOTE: Data in this table are rounded.

Other qualifications. Depending on the type of aircraft, new airline pilots start as first officers or flight engineers. Although some airlines favor applicants who already have a flight engineer's license, they may provide flight engineer training for those who have only the commercial license. Many pilots begin with smaller regional or commuter airlines, where they obtain experience flying passengers on scheduled flights into busy airports in all weather conditions. These jobs often lead to higher paying jobs with bigger, national or major airlines.

Companies other than airlines usually require less flying experience. However, a commercial pilot's license is a minimum requirement, and employers prefer applicants who have experience in the type of craft they will be flying. New employees usually start as first officers, or fly less sophisticated equipment.

Advancement. Advancement for pilots usually is limited to other flying jobs. Many pilots start as flight instructors, building up their flying hours while they earn money teaching. As they become more experienced, these pilots occasionally fly charter planes or perhaps get jobs with small air transportation firms, such as air-taxi companies. Some advance to flying corporate planes. A small number get flight engineer jobs with the airlines.

In the airlines, advancement usually depends on seniority provisions of union contracts. After one to five years, flight engineers advance according to seniority to first officer and, after 5 to 15 years, to captain. Seniority also determines which pilots get the more desirable routes. In a nonairline job, a first officer may advance to captain and, in large companies, to chief pilot or director of aviation in charge of aircraft scheduling, maintenance, and flight procedures.

Employment

Civilian aircraft pilots and flight engineers held about 107,000 jobs in 2006. About 79,000 worked as airline pilots, copilots, and flight engineers. The rest were commercial pilots who worked as flight instructors at local airports or for large businesses that fly company cargo and executives in their own airplanes or helicopters. Some commercial pilots flew small planes for air-taxi companies, usually to or from lightly traveled airports not served by major airlines. Others worked for a variety of businesses, performing tasks such as dusting crops, inspecting pipelines, or conducting sightseeing trips.

Pilots are located across the country, but airline pilots usually are based near major metropolitan airports or airports operating as hubs for the major airlines.

Federal, state, and local governments employed pilots. A few pilots were self-employed.

Job Outlook

Regional airlines and low-cost carriers will present the best opportunities; pilots attempting to get jobs at the major airlines will face strong competition.

Employment change. Employment of aircraft pilots and flight engineers is projected to grow 13 percent from 2006 to 2016, about as fast as the average for all occupations. Population growth and an expanding economy are expected to boost the demand for air travel, contributing to job growth. New jobs will be created as airlines expand their capacity to meet this rising demand by increasing the number of planes in operation. However, employment growth will be limited by productivity improvements as airlines switch to larger planes and adopt the low-cost carrier model that emphasizes faster turnaround times for flights, keeping more pilots in the air rather than waiting on the ground. Also, fewer flight engineers will be needed as new planes requiring only two pilots replace older planes that require flight engineers.

Job prospects. Job opportunities are expected to continue to be better with the regional airlines and low-cost carriers, which are growing faster than the major airlines. Opportunities with air cargo carriers also should arise because of increasing security requirements for shipping freight on passenger airlines, growth in electronic commerce, and increased demand for global freight. Business, corporate, and on-demand air taxi travel also should provide some new jobs for pilots.

Pilots attempting to get jobs at the major airlines will face strong competition, as those firms tend to attract many more applicants than the number of job openings. Applicants also will have to compete with laid-off pilots for any available jobs. Pilots who have logged the greatest number of flying hours using sophisticated equipment typically have the best prospects. For this reason, military pilots often have an advantage over other applicants.

In the long run, demand for air travel is expected to grow along with the population and the economy. In the short run, however, employment opportunities of pilots generally are sensitive to cyclical swings in the economy. During recessions, when a decline in the demand for air travel forces airlines to curtail the number of flights, airlines may temporarily furlough some pilots.

Earnings

Earnings of aircraft pilots and flight engineers vary greatly depending whether they work as airline or commercial pilots. Earnings of airline pilots are among the highest in the nation, and depend on factors such as the type, size, and maximum speed of the plane and the number of hours and miles flown. For example, pilots who fly jet aircraft usually earn higher salaries than pilots who fly turboprops. Airline pilots and flight engineers may earn extra pay for night and international flights. In May 2006, median annual earnings of airline pilots, copilots, and flight engineers were $141,090.

Median annual earnings of commercial pilots were $57,480 in May 2006. The middle 50 percent earned between $40,780 and $83,760. The lowest 10 percent earned less than $28,450, and the highest 10 percent earned more than $115,220.

Airline pilots usually are eligible for life and health insurance plans. They also receive retirement benefits and, if they fail the FAA physical examination at some point in their careers, they get disability payments. In addition, pilots receive an expense allowance, or "per diem," for every hour they are away from home. Some airlines also provide allowances to pilots for purchasing and cleaning their uniforms. As an additional benefit, pilots and their immediate families usually are entitled to free or reduced-fare transportation on their own and other airlines.

More than half of all aircraft pilots are members of unions. Most of the pilots who fly for the major airlines are members of the Air Line Pilots Association, International, but those employed by one major airline are members of the Allied Pilots Association.

Related Occupations

Although they are not in the cockpit, air traffic controllers and airfield operations specialists also play an important role in making sure flights are safe and on schedule, and participate in many of the decisions that pilots must make.

Sources of Additional Information

For information about job opportunities, salaries, and qualifications, write to the personnel manager of the particular airline.

For information on airline pilots, contact

▸ Air Line Pilots Association, International, 1625 Massachusetts Ave. NW, Washington, DC 20036.

▸ Air Transport Association of America, Inc., 1301 Pennsylvania Ave. NW, Suite 1100, Washington, DC 20004.

▸ Federal Aviation Administration, 800 Independence Ave. SW, Washington, DC 20591. Internet: http://www.faa.gov

For information on helicopter pilots, contact

▸ Helicopter Association International, 1635 Prince St., Alexandria, VA 22314.

For information about job opportunities in companies other than airlines, consult the classified section of aviation trade magazines and apply to companies that operate aircraft at local airports.

Armed Forces

(O*NET 55-1011.00, 55-1012.00, 55-1013.00, 55-1014.00, 55-1015.00, 55-1016.00, 55-1017.00, 55-1019.99, 55-2011.00, 55-2012.00, 55-2013.00, 55-3011.00, 55-3012.00, 55-3013.00, 55-3014.00, 55-3015.00, 55-3016.00, 55-3017.00, 55-3018.00, and 55-3019.99)

Significant Points

■ Some training and duty assignments are hazardous, even in peacetime; hours and working conditions can be arduous and vary substantially, and personnel must strictly conform to military rules at all times.

■ Enlisted personnel need at least a high school diploma or its equivalent while officers need a bachelor's or graduate degree.

■ Opportunities should be excellent in all branches of the Armed Forces for applicants who meet designated standards.

■ Military personnel are eligible for retirement after 20 years of service.

Nature of the Work

Maintaining a strong national defense requires workers who can do such diverse tasks as run a hospital, command a tank, program a computer system, operate a nuclear reactor, or repair and maintain a helicopter. The military provides training and work experience in these and many other fields for more than 2.6 million people. More than 1.4 million people serve in the active Army, Navy, Marine Corps, and Air Force, and more than 1.2 million serve in their Reserve components and the Air and Army National Guard. The Coast Guard, which is also discussed in this job profile, is part of the Department of Homeland Security.

The military distinguishes between enlisted and officer careers. Enlisted personnel, who make up about 84 percent of the Armed Forces, carry out the fundamental operations of the military in combat, administration, construction, engineering, health care, human services, and other areas. Officers, who make up the remaining 16 percent of the Armed Forces, are the leaders of the military, supervising and managing activities in every occupational specialty.

The sections that follow discuss the major occupational groups for enlisted personnel and officers.

Enlisted occupational groups. *Administrative careers* include a wide variety of positions. The military must keep accurate information for planning and managing its operations. Both paper and electronic records are kept on personnel and on equipment, funds, supplies, and all other aspects of the military. Administrative personnel record information, prepare reports, maintain files, and review information to assist military officers. Personnel may work in a specialized area such as finance, accounting, legal affairs, maintenance, supply, or transportation.

Combat specialty occupations include enlisted specialties such as infantry, artillery, and Special Forces, whose members operate weapons or execute special missions during combat. People in these occupations normally specialize by type of weapon system or combat operation. These personnel maneuver against enemy forces and position and fire artillery, guns, mortars, and missiles to destroy enemy positions. They also may operate tanks and amphibious assault vehicles in combat or scouting missions. When the military has especially difficult or specialized missions to perform, they call upon Special Forces teams. These elite combat forces maintain a constant state of readiness to strike anywhere in the world on a moment's notice. Team members from the Special Forces conduct offensive raids, demolitions, intelligence, search-and-rescue missions, and other operations from aboard aircraft, helicopters, ships, or submarines.

Construction occupations in the military include personnel who build or repair buildings, airfields, bridges, foundations, dams, bunkers, and the electrical and plumbing components of these structures. Personnel in construction occupations operate bulldozers, cranes, graders, and other heavy equipment. Construction specialists also may work with engineers and other building specialists as part of military construction teams. Some personnel specialize in areas such as plumbing or electrical wiring. Plumbers and pipefitters install and repair the plumbing and pipe systems needed in buildings and on aircraft and ships. Building electricians install and repair electrical-wiring systems in offices, airplane hangars, and other buildings on military bases.

Electronic and electrical equipment repair personnel repair and maintain electronic and electrical equipment used in the military.

Repairers normally specialize by type of equipment, such as avionics, computer, optical, communications, or weapons systems. For example, electronic instrument repairers install, test, maintain, and repair a wide variety of electronic systems, including navigational controls and biomedical instruments. Weapons maintenance technicians maintain and repair weapons used by combat forces; most of these weapons have electronic components and systems that assist in locating targets and in aiming and firing the weapon.

Engineering, science, and technical personnel in the military require specific knowledge to operate technical equipment, solve complex problems, or provide and interpret information. Personnel normally specialize in one area, such as space operations, information technology, environmental health and safety, or intelligence. Space operations specialists use and repair ground-control command equipment related to spacecraft, including electronic systems that track the location and operation of a craft. Information technology specialists develop software programs and operate computer systems. Environmental health and safety specialists inspect military facilities and food supplies for the presence of disease, germs, or other conditions hazardous to health and the environment. Intelligence specialists gather and study aerial photographs and various types of radar and surveillance systems to discover information needed by the military.

Health care personnel assist medical professionals in treating and providing services for men and women in the military. They may work as part of a patient-service team in close contact with doctors, dentists, nurses, and physical therapists. Some specialize in emergency medical treatment, the operation of diagnostic tools such as x-ray and ultrasound equipment, laboratory testing of tissue and blood samples, maintaining pharmacy supplies or patients' records, constructing and repairing dental equipment or eyeglasses, or some other health care task.

Human resources development specialists recruit and place qualified personnel and provide training programs. Personnel in this career area normally specialize by activity. For example, recruiting specialists provide information about military careers to young people, parents, schools, and local communities and explain the Armed Service's employment and training opportunities, pay and benefits, and service life. Personnel specialists collect and store information about the people in the military, including information on their previous and current training, job assignments, promotions, and health. Training specialists and instructors teach classes, give demonstrations, and teach military personnel how to perform their jobs.

Machine operator and production personnel operate industrial equipment, machinery, and tools to fabricate and repair parts for a variety of items and structures. They may operate engines, turbines, nuclear reactors, and water pumps. Often, they specialize by type of work performed. Welders and metalworkers, for instance, work with various types of metals to repair or form the structural parts of ships, submarines, buildings, or other equipment. Survival equipment specialists inspect, maintain, and repair survival equipment such as parachutes and aircraft life support equipment.

Media and public affairs personnel assist with the public presentation and interpretation of military information and events. They take and develop photographs; film, record, and edit audio and video programs; present news and music programs; and produce artwork, drawings, and other visual displays. Other public affairs specialists act as interpreters and translators to convert written or spoken foreign languages into English or other languages.

Protective service personnel include those who enforce military laws and regulations and provide emergency response to natural and human-made disasters. For example, military police control traffic, prevent crime, and respond to emergencies. Other law enforcement and security specialists investigate crimes committed on military property and guard inmates in military correctional facilities. Firefighters put out, control, and help prevent fires in buildings, on aircraft, and aboard ships.

Support service personnel provide subsistence services and support the morale and well-being of military personnel and their families. Food service specialists prepare all types of food in dining halls, hospitals, and ships. Counselors help military personnel and their families deal with personal issues. They work as part of a team that may include social workers, psychologists, medical officers, chaplains, personnel specialists, and commanders. Religious program specialists assist chaplains with religious services, religious education programs, and related administrative duties.

Transportation and material handling specialists ensure the safe transport of people and cargo. Most personnel within this occupational group are classified according to mode of transportation, such as aircraft, motor vehicle, or ship. Aircrew members operate equipment on aircraft. Vehicle drivers operate all types of heavy military vehicles, including fuel or water tank trucks, semi-trailers, heavy troop transports, and passenger buses. Quartermasters and boat operators navigate and pilot many types of small watercraft, including tugboats, gunboats, and barges. Cargo specialists load and unload military supplies, using equipment such as forklifts and cranes.

Vehicle and machinery mechanics conduct preventive and corrective maintenance on aircraft, automotive and heavy equipment, heating and cooling systems, marine engines, and powerhouse station equipment. These workers typically specialize by the type of equipment that they maintain. For example, aircraft mechanics inspect, service, and repair helicopters, airplanes, and drones. Automotive and heavy equipment mechanics maintain and repair vehicles such as humvees, trucks, tanks, self-propelled missile launchers, and other combat vehicles. They also repair bulldozers, power shovels, and other construction equipment. Heating and cooling mechanics install and repair air-conditioning, refrigeration, and heating equipment. Marine engine mechanics repair and maintain gasoline and diesel engines on ships, boats, and other watercraft. They also repair shipboard mechanical and electrical equipment. Powerhouse mechanics install, maintain, and repair electrical and mechanical equipment in power-generating stations.

Officer occupational groups. *Combat specialty officers* plan and direct military operations, oversee combat activities, and serve as combat leaders. This category includes officers in charge of tanks and other armored assault vehicles, artillery systems, Special Forces, and infantry. Combat specialty officers normally specialize by the type of unit that they lead. Within the unit, they may specialize by type of weapon system. Artillery and missile system officers, for example, direct personnel as they target, launch, test, and maintain various types of missiles and artillery. Special operations officers lead their units in offensive raids, demolitions, intelligence gathering, and search-and-rescue missions.

Engineering, science, and technical officers have a wide range of responsibilities based on their area of expertise. They lead or perform activities in areas such as space operations, environmental health and safety, and engineering. These officers may direct the operations of communications centers or the development of complex computer systems. Environmental health and safety officers study the air, ground, and water to identify and analyze sources of pollution and its effects. They also direct programs to control safety and health hazards in the workplace. Other personnel work as aerospace engineers to design and direct the development of military aircraft, missiles, and spacecraft.

Executive, administrative, and managerial officers oversee and direct military activities in key functional areas such as finance, accounting, health administration, international relations, and supply. Health services administrators, for instance, are responsible for the overall quality of care provided at the hospitals and clinics they operate. They must ensure that each department works together. As another example, purchasing and contracting managers negotiate and monitor contracts for the purchase of the billions of dollars worth of equipment, supplies, and services that the military buys from private industry each year.

Health care officers provide health services at military facilities, on the basis of their area of specialization. Officers who examine, diagnose, and treat patients with illness, injury, or disease include physicians, registered nurses, and dentists. Other health care officers provide therapy, rehabilitative treatment, and additional services for patients. Physical and occupational therapists plan and administer therapy to help patients adjust to disabilities, regain independence, and return to work. Speech therapists evaluate and treat patients with hearing and speech problems. Dietitians manage food service facilities and plan meals for hospital patients and for outpatients who need special diets. Pharmacists manage the purchase, storage, and dispensing of drugs and medicines. Physicians and surgeons in this occupational group provide the majority of medical services to the military and their families. dentists treat diseases, disorders, and injuries of the mouth. Optometrists treat vision problems by prescribing eyeglasses or contact lenses. Psychologists provide mental health care and also conduct research on behavior and emotions.

Human resource development officers manage recruitment, placement, and training strategies and programs in the military. Recruiting managers direct recruiting efforts and provide information about military careers to young people, parents, schools, and local communities. Personnel managers direct military personnel functions such as job assignment, staff promotion, and career counseling. Training and education directors identify training needs and develop and manage educational programs designed to keep military personnel current in the skills they need.

Media and public affairs officers oversee the development, production, and presentation of information or events for the public. These officers may produce and direct motion pictures, videos, and television and radio broadcasts that are used for training, news, and entertainment. Some plan, develop, and direct the activities of military bands. Public information officers respond to inquiries about military activities and prepare news releases and reports to keep the public informed.

Protective service officers are responsible for the safety and protection of individuals and property on military bases and vessels. Emergency management officers plan and prepare for all types of natural and human-made disasters. They develop warning, control, and evacuation plans to be used in the event of a disaster. Law enforcement and security officers enforce all applicable laws on military bases and investigate crimes when the law has been broken.

Support services officers manage food service activities and perform services in support of the morale and well-being of military personnel and their families. Food services managers oversee the preparation and delivery of food services within dining facilities located on military installations and vessels. Social workers focus on improving conditions that cause social problems such as drug and alcohol abuse, racism, and sexism. Chaplains conduct worship services for military personnel and perform other spiritual duties according to the beliefs and practices of all religious faiths.

Transportation officers manage and perform activities related to the safe transport of military personnel and material by air and water. These officers normally specialize by mode of transportation or area of expertise because, in many cases, they must meet licensing and certification requirements. Pilots in the military fly various types of specialized airplanes and helicopters to carry troops and equipment and to execute combat missions. Navigators use radar, radio, and other navigation equipment to determine their position and plan their route of travel. Officers on ships and submarines work as a team to manage the various departments aboard their vessels. Ship engineers direct engineering departments aboard ships and submarines, including engine operations, maintenance, repair, heating, and power generation.

Work environment. Most military personnel live and work on or near military bases and facilities throughout the United States and the world. These bases and facilities usually offer comfortable housing and amenities, such as stores and recreation centers. Service members move regularly to complete their training or to meet the needs of their branch of service. Some are deployed to defend national interests. Military personnel must be physically fit, mentally stable, and ready to participate in or support combat missions that maybe difficult and dangerous and involve time away from family. Some, however, are never deployed near combat areas. Specific work environments and conditions depend on branch of service, occupational specialty, and other factors.

In many circumstances, military personnel work standard hours, but personnel must be prepared to work long hours to fulfill missions, and they must conform to strict military rules at all times. Work hours depend on occupational specialty and mission.

Training, Other Qualifications, and Advancement

To join the military, people must meet age, educational, aptitude, physical, and character requirements. These requirements vary by branch of service and vary between officers, who usually have a college degree, and enlisted personnel, who often do not. People are assigned an occupational specialty based on their aptitude, former training, and the needs of the military. All service members must sign a contract and commit to a minimum term of service. After joining the military, all receive general and occupation-specific training.

People thinking about enlisting in the military should learn as much as they can about military life before making a decision. Doing so is especially important if you are thinking about making the military a career. Speaking to friends and relatives with military experience is a good idea. Find out what the military can offer you and what it will expect in return. Then, talk to a recruiter, who can determine whether you qualify for enlistment, explain the various enlistment options, and tell you which military occupational specialties currently have openings. Bear in mind that the recruiter's job is to recruit promising applicants into his or her branch of military service, so the information that the recruiter gives you is likely to stress the positive aspects of military life in the branch in which he or she serves.

Ask the recruiter for the branch you have chosen to assess your chances of being accepted for training in the occupation of your choice, or, better still, take the aptitude exam to see how well you score. The military uses this exam as a placement exam, and test scores largely determine an individual's chances of being accepted into a particular training program. Selection for a particular type of training depends on the needs of the service, your general and technical aptitudes, and your personal preference. Because all prospective recruits are required to take the exam, those who do so before committing themselves to enlist have the advantage of knowing in advance whether they stand a good chance of being accepted for training in a particular specialty. The recruiter can schedule you for the Armed Services Vocational Aptitude Battery without any obligation. Many high schools offer the exam as an easy way for students to explore the possibility of a military career, and the test also affords an insight into career areas in which the student has demonstrated aptitudes and interests. The exam is not part of the process of joining the military as an officer.

If you decide to join the military, the next step is to pass the physical examination and sign an enlistment contract. Negotiating the contract involves choosing, qualifying for, and agreeing on a number of enlistment options, such as the length of active-duty time, which may vary according to the option. Most active-duty programs have first-term enlistments of four years, although there are some two-year, three-year, and six-year programs. The contract also will state the date of enlistment and other options—for example, bonuses and the types of training to be received. If the service is unable to fulfill any of its obligations under the contract, such as providing a certain kind of training, the contract may become null and void.

All branches of the Armed Services offer a delayed entry program (DEP) by which an individual can delay entry into active duty for up to one year after enlisting. High school students can enlist during their senior year and enter a service after graduation. Others choose this program because the job training they desire is not currently available, but will be within the coming year, or because they need time to arrange their personal affairs.

The process of joining the military as an officer is different. Officers must meet educational, physical, and character requirements, but they do not take an aptitude test, for example. The education and training section that follows includes more information.

Education and training. All branches of the Armed Forces usually require their members to be high school graduates or have equivalent credentials, such as a GED. In 2006, more than 98 percent of recruits were high school graduates. Officers usually need a bachelor's or graduate degree. Training varies for enlisted and officer personnel and varies by occupational specialty.

Enlisted personnel training. Following enlistment, new members of the Armed Forces undergo initial-entry training, better known as "basic training" or "boot camp." Through courses in military skills and protocol recruit training provides a six- to 13-week introduction to military life. Days and nights are carefully structured and include rigorous physical exercise designed to improve strength and endurance and build each unit's cohesion.

Following basic training, most recruits take additional training at technical schools that prepare them for a particular military occupational specialty. The formal training period generally lasts from 10 to 20 weeks, although training for certain occupations—nuclear power plant operator, for example—may take as long as a year. Recruits not assigned to classroom instruction receive on-the-job training at their first duty assignment.

Many service people get college credit for the technical training they receive on duty, which, combined with off-duty courses, can lead to an associate degree through programs in community colleges such as the Community College of the Air Force. In addition to on-duty training, military personnel may choose from a variety of educational programs. Most military installations have tuition assistance programs for people wishing to take courses during off-duty hours. The courses may be correspondence courses or courses in degree programs offered by local colleges or universities. Tuition assistance pays up to 100 percent of college costs up to a credit-hour and annual limit. Each branch of the service provides opportunities for full-time study to a limited number of exceptional applicants. Military personnel accepted into these highly competitive programs receive full pay, allowances, tuition, and related fees. In return, they must agree to serve an additional amount of time in the service. Other highly selective programs enable enlisted personnel to qualify as commissioned officers through additional military training.

Warrant officer training. Warrant officers are technical and tactical leaders who specialize in a specific technical area; for example, Army aviators make up one group of warrant officers. The Army Warrant Officer Corps constitutes less than 5 percent of the total Army. Although the Corps is small in size, its level of responsibility is high. Its members receive extended career opportunities, worldwide leadership assignments, and increased pay and retirement benefits. Selection to attend the Warrant Officer Candidate School is highly competitive and restricted to those who meet rank and length-of-service requirements. The only exception is the Army aviator warrant officer, which has no prior military service requirements.

Officer training. Officer training in the Armed Forces is provided through the federal service academies (Military, Naval, Air Force, and Coast Guard); the Reserve Officers Training Corps (ROTC) program offered at many colleges and universities; Officer Candidate School (OCS) or Officer Training School (OTS); the National Guard (State Officer Candidate School programs); the Uniformed Services University of Health Sciences; and other programs. All are highly selective and are good options for those wishing to make the military a career. Some are directly appointed. People interested in obtaining training through the federal service academies must be unmarried and without dependants to enter and graduate, while those seeking training through OCS, OTS, or ROTC need not be single.

Federal service academies provide a four-year college program leading to a Bachelor of Science (B.S.) degree. Midshipmen or cadets are provided free room and board, tuition, medical and dental care, and a monthly allowance. Graduates receive regular or reserve commissions and have a five-year active-duty obligation or more if they are entering flight training.

To become a candidate for appointment as a cadet or midshipman in one of the service academies, applicants are required to obtain a nomination from an authorized source, usually a member of Congress. Candidates do not need to know a member of Congress personally to request a nomination. Nominees must have an academic record of the requisite quality, college aptitude test scores above an established minimum, and recommendations from teachers or school officials; they also must pass a medical examination. Appointments are made from the list of eligible nominees. Appointments to the Coast Guard Academy, however, are based strictly on merit and do not require a nomination.

ROTC programs train students in 273 Army, 130 Navy and Marine Corps, and 144 Air Force units at participating colleges and universities. Trainees take three to five hours of military instruction a week, in addition to regular college courses. After graduation, they may serve as officers on active duty for a stipulated period. Some may serve their obligation in the Reserves or National Guard. In the last two years of an ROTC program, students typically receive a monthly allowance while attending school, as well as additional pay for summer training. ROTC scholarships for two, three, and four years are available on a competitive basis. All scholarships pay for tuition and have allowances for textbooks, supplies, and other costs.

College graduates can earn a commission in the Armed Forces through OCS or OTS programs in the Army, Navy, Air Force, Marine Corps, Coast Guard, and National Guard. These programs consist of several weeks of intensive academic, physical, and leadership training. These officers generally must serve their obligation on active duty.

Those with training in certain health professions may qualify for direct appointment as officers. In the case of people studying for the health professions, financial assistance and internship opportunities are available from the military in return for specified periods of military service. Prospective medical students can apply to the

Uniformed Services University of Health Sciences, which offers a salary and free tuition in a program leading to a Doctor of Medicine (M.D.) degree. In return, graduates must serve for seven years in either the military or the Public Health Service. Direct appointments also are available for those qualified to serve in other specialty areas, such as the judge advocate general (legal) or chaplain corps. Flight training is available to commissioned officers in each branch of the Armed Forces. In addition, the Army has a direct enlistment option to become a warrant officer aviator.

Other qualifications. In order to join the services, enlisted personnel must sign a legal agreement called an enlistment contract, which usually involves a commitment of up to eight years of service. Depending on the terms of the contract, two to six years are spent on active duty, and the balance is spent in the National Guard or Reserves. The enlistment contract obligates the service to provide the agreed-upon job, rating, pay, cash bonuses for enlistment in certain occupations, medical and other benefits, occupational training, and continuing education. In return, enlisted personnel must serve satisfactorily for the period specified.

Requirements for each service vary, but certain qualifications for enlistment are common to all branches. In order to enlist, usually one must be at least 17 years old, be a U.S. citizen or an alien holding permanent resident status, not have a felony record, and possess a birth certificate. Applicants who are 17 years old must have the consent of a parent or legal guardian before entering the service. For active service in the Army, the maximum age is 42; for the Navy and

Table 1. Military rank and employment for active duty personnel, January 2007

Grade	Rank and title				
	Army	Navy	Air Force	Marine Corps	Total Employment
Commissioned officers:					
O-10	General	Admiral	General	General	40
O-9	Lieutenant General	Vice Admiral	Lieutenant General	Lieutenant General	136
O-8	Major General	Rear Admiral (U)	Major General	Major General	285
O-7	Brigadier General	Rear Admiral (L)	Brigadier General	Brigadier General	449
O-6	Colonel	Captain	Colonel	Colonel	11,345
O-5	Lieutenant Colonel	Commander	Lieutenant Colonel	Lieutenant Colonel	28,566
O-4	Major	Lieutenant Commander	Major	Major	44,908
O-3	Captain	Lieutenant	Captain	Captain	70,131
O-2	1st Lieutenant	Lieutenant (JG)	1st Lieutenant	1st Lieutenant	26,894
O-1	2nd Lieutenant	Ensign	2nd Lieutenant	2nd Lieutenant	23,331
Warrant officers:					
W-5	Chief Warrant Officer	Chief Warrant Officer	—	Chief Warrant Officer	591
W-4	Chief Warrant Officer	Chief Warrant Officer	—	Chief Warrant Officer	2,661
W-3	Chief Warrant Officer	Chief Warrant Officer	—	Chief Warrant Officer	4,676
W-2	Chief Warrant Officer	Chief Warrant Officer	—	Chief Warrant Officer	5,627
W-1	Warrant Officer	Warrant Officer	—	Warrant Officer	3,084
Enlisted personnel:					
E-9	Sergeant Major	Master Chief Petty Officer	Chief Master Sergeant	Sergeant Major/ Master Gunnery Sergeant	10,596
E-8	1st Sergeant/Master Sergeant	Senior Chief Petty Officer	Senior Master Sergeant	1st Sergeant/Master Sergeant	26,987
E-7	Sergeant First Class	Chief Petty Officer	Master Sergeant	Gunnery Sergeant	98,497
E-6	Staff Sergeant	Petty Officer 1st Class	Technical Sergeant	Staff Sergeant	169,725
E-5	Sergeant	Petty Officer 2nd Class	Staff Sergeant	Sergeant	248,226
E-4	Corporal	Petty Officer 3rd Class	Senior Airman	Corporal	257,974
E-3	Private First Class	Seaman	Airman 1st Class	Lance Corporal	186,830
E-2	Private	Seaman Apprentice	Airman	Private 1st Class	83,987
E-1	Private	Seaman Recruit	Airman Basic	Private	57,644

SOURCE: U.S. Department of Defense, Defense Manpower Data Center

Table 2. Military enlisted personnel by broad occupational category and branch of military service, January 2007

Occupational Group - Enlisted	Army	Air Force	Coast Guard	Marine Corps	Navy	Total, all services
Administrative occupations	8,912	23,366	1,683	9,460	22,512	65,933
Combat specialty occupations	120,297	427	856	47,250	5,508	174,338
Construction occupations	16,848	4,979	—	5,597	5,927	33,351
Electronic and electrical repair occupations	35,932	37,722	4,351	14,656	51,424	144,085
Engineering, science, and technical occupations	36,451	46,304	1,110	22,915	38,853	145,633
Health care occupations	29,242	16,805	821	—	24,950	71,818
Human resource development occupations	16,464	12,741	1	6,113	6,756	42,075
Machine operator and precision work occupations	5,727	7,134	1,583	2,301	7,913	24,658
Media and public affairs occupations	6,541	7,574	136	2,340	4,726	21,317
Protective service occupations	25,455	31,483	3,050	5,872	13,122	78,982
Support services occupations	12,014	1,608	1,268	2,289	9,930	27,109
Transportation and material handling occupations	58,237	32,464	11,479	22,344	43,026	167,550
Vehicle machinery mechanic occupations	49,679	44,025	5,821	19,340	49,166	168,031
Total, by service (1)	421,855	271,009	32,477	160,484	287,118	1,172,913

Air Force the maximum age is 35. Coast Guard enlisted personnel must enter active duty before their 28th birthday, whereas Marine Corps enlisted personnel must not be over the age of 29 when entering. Applicants must pass a written examination—the Armed Services Vocational Aptitude Battery—and meet certain minimum physical standards, such as height, weight, vision, and overall health. Officers must meet different age and physical standards depending on their branch of service.

Women are eligible to enter most military specialties; for example, they may become mechanics, missile maintenance technicians, heavy equipment operators, and fighter pilots, or they may enter into medical care, administrative support, and intelligence specialties. Generally, only occupations involving direct exposure to combat are excluded.

Advancement. Each service has different criteria for promoting personnel. Generally, the first few promotions for both enlisted and officer personnel come easily; subsequent promotions are much more competitive. Criteria for promotion may include time in service and in grade, job performance, a fitness report (supervisor's recommendation), and passing scores on written examinations. Table 1 shows the officer, warrant officer, and enlisted ranks by service.

People planning to apply the skills gained through military training to a civilian career should first determine how good the prospects are for civilian employment in jobs related to the military specialty that interests them. Second, they should know the prerequisites for the related civilian job. Because many civilian occupations require a license, certification, or minimum level of education, it is important to determine whether military training is sufficient for a person to enter the civilian equivalent occupation or, if not, what additional training will be required. Occupational descriptions in this book discuss the job outlook, training requirements, and other aspects of civilian occupations for which military training and experience are helpful. Additional information often can be obtained from school counselors.

Employment

In 2007, more than 2.6 million people served in the Armed Forces. More than 1.4 million were on active duty—about 505,000 in the Army, 339,000 in the Navy, 340,000 in the Air Force, and 179,000 in the Marine Corps. In addition, more than 1.2 million people served in their Reserve components and the Air and Army National Guard, and 40,000 individuals served in the Coast Guard, which is now part of the Department of Homeland Security. Table 2 shows the occupational composition of the active-duty enlisted personnel in January 2007; table 3 presents similar information for active-duty officers, including noncommissioned warrant officers.

Military personnel are stationed throughout the United States and in many countries around the world. About half of all military jobs in the U.S. are located in California, Texas, North Carolina, Virginia, Florida, and Georgia. Approximately 250,000 service members were deployed in support of Operations Enduring Freedom and Iraqi Freedom as of April 30, 2007. An additional 363,000 individuals

Table 3. Military officer personnel by broad occupational category and branch of service, January 2007

Occupational Group - Officer	Army	Air Force	Coast Guard	Marine Corps	Navy	Total, all services
Combat specialty occupations	19,421	2,861	81	4,684	1,260	28,307
Engineering, science, and technical occupations	20,189	19,852	1,057	3,639	7,873	52,610
Executive, administrative, and managerial occupations	11,262	9,013	231	2,572	5,437	28,515
Health care occupations	9,953	8,970	5	—	7,737	26,665
Human resource development occupations	2,151	2,275	184	293	643	5,546
Media and public affairs occupations	237	408	19	170	265	1,099
Protective service occupations	2,611	1,229	96	327	275	4,538
Support services occupations	1,596	768	—	38	884	3,286
Transportation occupations	13,112	23,540	1,736	7,188	27,049	72,625
Total, by service (1)	82,884	69,284	7,853	18,998	51,558	230,577

(1) Occupational employment does not sum to totals because occupational information is not available for all personnel.
SOURCE: U.S. Department of Defense, Defense Manpower Data Center

were stationed outside the United States, including 168,000 assigned to ships at sea. About 105,000 were stationed in Europe, mainly in Germany, and another 70,000 were assigned to East Asia and the Pacific area, mostly in Japan and the Republic of Korea.

Job Outlook

Opportunities should be excellent for qualified individuals in all branches of the Armed Forces through 2016.

Employment change. The United States spends a significant portion of its overall budget on national defense. Despite reductions in personnel due to the elimination of the threats of the Cold War, the number of active-duty personnel is expected to remain roughly constant through 2016. However, recent conflicts and the resulting strain on the military may lead to an increase in the number of active-duty personnel. The current goal of the Armed Forces is to maintain a force sufficient to fight and win two major regional conflicts at the same time. Political events, however, could lead to a significant restructuring with or without an increase in size.

Job prospects. Opportunities should be excellent for qualified individuals in all branches of the Armed Forces through 2016. Many military personnel retire with a pension after 20 years of service, while they still are young enough to start a new career. About 168,000 personnel must be recruited each year to replace those who complete their commitment or retire. Since the end of the draft in 1973, the military has met its personnel requirements with volunteers. When the economy is good and civilian employment opportunities generally are more favorable, it is more difficult for all the services to meet their recruitment quotas. It is also more difficult to meet these goals during times of war, when recruitment goals typically rise.

Educational requirements will continue to rise as military jobs become more technical and complex. High school graduates and applicants with a college background will be sought to fill the ranks of enlisted personnel, while virtually all officers will need at least a bachelor's degree and, in some cases, a graduate degree as well.

Earnings

The earnings structure for military personnel is shown in table 4. Most enlisted personnel started as recruits at Grade E-1 in 2007; however, those with special skills or above-average education started as high as Grade E-4. Most warrant officers had started at Grade W-1 or W-2, depending upon their occupational and academic qualifications and the branch of service of which they were a member, but warrant officer typically is not an entry-level occupation and, consequently, most of these individuals had previous military service. Most commissioned officers started at Grade O-1; some with advanced education started at Grade O-2, and some highly trained officers—for example, physicians and dentists—started as high as Grade O-3. Pay varies by total years of service as well as rank. Because it usually takes many years to reach the higher ranks, most personnel in higher ranks receive the higher pay rates awarded to those with many years of service.

In addition to receiving their basic pay, military personnel are provided with free room and board (or a tax-free housing and subsistence allowance), free medical and dental care, a military clothing allowance, military supermarket and department store shopping privileges, 30 days of paid vacation a year (referred to as leave), and travel opportunities. In many duty stations, military personnel may receive a housing allowance that can be used for off-base housing. This allowance can be substantial, but varies greatly by rank and

Table 4. Military basic monthly pay by grade for active duty personnel, April 2007

Grade	Less than 2	Over 4	Over 8	Over 12	Over 16	Over 20
O-10	—	—	—	—	—	$13,659.00
O-9	—	—	—	—	—	11,946.60
O-8	$8,453.10	$8,964.90	$9,577.20	$10,030.20	$10,447.80	11,319.00
O-7	7,023.90	7,621.20	8,052.90	8,548.80	9,577.20	10,236.00
O-6	5,206.20	6,094.50	6,380.10	6,414.60	7,423.80	8,180.10
O-5	4,339.80	5,291.10	5,628.60	6,110.10	6,776.40	7,158.00
O-4	3,744.60	4,688.40	5,244.60	5,882.40	6,187.50	6,252.30
O-3	3,292.20	4,392.00	4,833.00	5,228.40	5,355.90	5,355.90
O-2	2,844.30	3,857.40	3,936.60	3,936.60	3,936.60	3,936.60
O-1	2,469.30	3,106.50	3,106.50	3,106.50	3,106.50	3,106.50
W-5	—	—	—	—	—	5,845.80
W-4	3,402.00	3,868.50	4,222.20	4,574.10	5,035.50	5,392.20
W-3	3,106.80	3,412.80	3,711.30	4,129.20	4,515.60	4,751.40
W-2	2,732.70	3,124.50	3,443.70	3,755.10	3,973.80	4,191.00
W-1	2,413.20	2,828.40	3,193.50	3,451.20	3,622.80	3,856.20
E-9	—	—	—	4,203.90	4,459.50	4,821.60
E-8	—	—	3,364.80	3,606.00	3,835.80	4,161.30
E-7	2,339.10	2,780.70	3,055.20	3,250.20	3,511.20	3,644.10
E-6	2,023.20	2,419.80	2,744.10	2,928.30	3,043.50	3,064.50
E-5	1,854.00	2,171.40	2,454.90	2,582.10	2,582.10	2,582.10
E-4	1,699.50	1,978.50	2,062.80	2,062.80	2,062.80	2,062.80
E-3	1,534.20	1,729.20	1,729.20	1,729.20	1,729.20	1,729.20
E-2	1,458.90	1,458.90	1,458.90	1,458.90	1,458.90	1,458.90
E-1 4 months of more	1,301.40	1,301.40	1,301.40	1,301.40	1,301.40	1,301.40
E-1 Less than 4 months	1,203.90	—	—	—	—	—

SOURCE: U.S. Department of Defense—Defense Finance and Accounting Service

duty station. For example, in fiscal year 2007, the average housing allowance for an E-4 with dependents was $1,151.24 per month; for a comparable individual without dependents, it was $910.66. The allowance for an O-4 with dependents was $1,856.97 per month; for a comparable individual without dependents, it was $1,611.69. Other allowances are paid for foreign duty, hazardous duty, submarine and flight duty, and employment as a medical officer. Athletic and other facilities—such as gymnasiums, tennis courts, golf courses, bowling centers, libraries, and movie theaters—are available on many military installations. Military personnel are eligible for retirement benefits after 20 years of service.

The Veterans Administration (VA) provides numerous benefits to those who have served at least 24 months of continuous active duty in the Armed Forces. Veterans are eligible for free care in VA hospitals for all service-related disabilities, regardless of time served; those with other medical problems are eligible for free VA care if they are unable to pay the cost of hospitalization elsewhere. Admission to a VA medical center depends on the availability of beds, however. Veterans also are eligible for certain loans, including loans to purchase a home. Veterans, regardless of health, can convert a military life insurance policy to an individual policy with any participating company upon separation from the military. In addition, job counseling, testing, and placement services are available.

Veterans who participate in the Montgomery GI Bill Program receive education benefits. Under this program, Armed Forces personnel may elect to deduct up to $100 a month from their pay during the first 12 months of active duty, putting the money toward their future education. In fiscal year 2007, veterans who served on active duty for 3 or more years or who spent 2 years in active duty plus 4 years in the Selected Reserve received $1,075 a month in basic benefits for 36 months of full-time institutional training. Those who enlisted and serve less than 3 years received $873 a month for 36 months for the same. In addition, each service provides its own contributions to the enlistee's future education. The sum of the amounts from all these sources becomes the service member's educational fund. Upon separation from active duty, the fund can be used to finance educational costs at any VA-approved institution. Among those institutions which are approved by the VA are many vocational, correspondence, certification, business, technical, and flight training schools; community and junior colleges; and colleges and universities.

Sources of Additional Information

Each of the military services publishes handbooks, fact sheets, and pamphlets describing entrance requirements, training and advancement opportunities, and other aspects of military careers. These publications are widely available at all recruiting stations, at most state employment service offices, and in high schools, colleges, and public libraries. Information on educational and other veterans' benefits is available from VA offices located throughout the country.

In addition, the Defense Manpower Data Center, an agency of the Department of Defense, publishes *Military Career Guide Online*, a compendium of military occupational, training, and career information designed for use by students and jobseekers. This information is available on the Internet: http://www.todaysmilitary.com.

The *Occupational Outlook Quarterly* also provides information about military careers and training in its spring 2007 article "Military training for civilian careers (Or: How to gain practical experience while serving your country)," available online at http://www.bls.gov/opub/ooq/2007/spring/art02.pdf.

Artists and Related Workers

(O*NET 27-1011.00, 27-1012.00, 27-1013.00, 27-1014.00, and 27-1019.99)

Significant Points

■ About 62 percent of artists and related workers are self employed.

■ Keen competition is expected for both salaried jobs and freelance work because the arts attract many talented people with creative ability.

■ Artists usually develop their skills through a bachelor's degree program or other postsecondary training in art or design.

■ Earnings for self-employed artists vary widely; some well-established artists earn more than salaried artists, while others find it difficult to rely solely on income earned from selling art.

Nature of the Work

Artists create art to communicate ideas, thoughts, or feelings. They use a variety of methods—painting, sculpting, or illustration—and an assortment of materials, including oils, watercolors, acrylics, pastels, pencils, pen and ink, plaster, clay, and computers. Artists' works may be realistic, stylized, or abstract and may depict objects, people, nature, or events.

Artists generally fall into one of four categories. Art directors formulate design concepts and presentation approaches for visual communications. Craft artists create or reproduce handmade objects for sale or exhibition. Fine artists, including painters, sculptors, and illustrators, create original artwork, using a variety of media and techniques. Multi-media artists and animators create special effects, animation, or other visual images on film, on video, or with computers or other electronic media.

Art directors develop design concepts and review material that is to appear in periodicals, newspapers, and other printed or digital media. They decide how best to present information visually, so that it is eye catching, appealing, and organized. Art directors decide which photographs or artwork to use and oversee the design, layout, and production of material to be published. They may direct workers engaged in artwork, design, layout, and copywriting.

Craft artists make a wide variety of objects, mostly by hand, that are sold either in their own studios, in retail outlets, or at arts-and-crafts shows. Some craft artists display their works in galleries and museums. Craft artists work with many different materials, including ceramics, glass, textiles, wood, metal, and paper, to create unique pieces of art, such as pottery, stained glass, quilts, tapestries, lace, candles, and clothing. Many craft artists also use fine-art techniques—for example, painting, sketching, and printing—to add finishing touches to their art.

Fine artists typically display their work in museums, commercial art galleries, corporate collections, and private homes. Some of their artwork may be commissioned (done on request from clients), but most is sold by the artist or through private art galleries or dealers. The gallery and the artist predetermine how much each will earn from the sale. Only the most successful fine artists are able to support themselves solely through the sale of their works. Most fine artists have at least one other job to support their art careers. Some work in museums or art galleries as fine-arts directors or as curators, planning and setting up art exhibits. A few artists work as art critics for newspapers or magazines or as consultants to foundations or institutional collectors. Other artists teach art classes or conduct workshops in schools or in their own studios. Some artists also hold full-time or part-time jobs unrelated to art and pursue fine art as a hobby or second career.

Usually, fine artists specialize in one or two art forms, such as painting, illustrating, sketching, sculpting, printmaking, and restoring. Painters, illustrators, cartoonists, and sketch artists work with two-dimensional art forms, using shading, perspective, and color to produce realistic scenes or abstractions.

Illustrators usually create pictures for books, magazines, and other publications and for commercial products such as textiles, wrapping paper, stationery, greeting cards, and calendars. Increasingly, illustrators are working in digital format, preparing work directly on a computer. This has created new opportunities for illustrators to work with animators and in broadcast media.

Medical and *scientific illustrators* combine drawing skills with knowledge of biology or other sciences. Medical illustrators work digitally or traditionally to create images of human anatomy and surgical procedures as well as 3-dimensional models and animations. Scientific illustrators draw animal and plant life, atomic and molecular structures, and geologic and planetary formations. These illustrations are used in medical and scientific publications and in audiovisual presentations for teaching purposes. Illustrators also work for lawyers, producing exhibits for court cases.

Cartoonists draw political, advertising, social, and sports cartoons. Some cartoonists work with others who create the idea or story and write captions. Some cartoonists write captions themselves. Most cartoonists have comic, critical, or dramatic talents in addition to drawing skills.

Sketch artists create likenesses of subjects with pencil, charcoal, or pastels. Sketches are used by law enforcement agencies to assist in identifying suspects, by the news media to depict courtroom scenes, and by individual patrons for their own enjoyment.

Sculptors design three-dimensional artworks, either by molding and joining materials such as clay, glass, wire, plastic, fabric, or metal or by cutting and carving forms from a block of plaster, wood, or stone. Some sculptors combine various materials to create mixed-media installations. Some incorporate light, sound, and motion into their works.

Printmakers create printed images from designs cut or etched into wood, stone, or metal. After creating the design, the artist inks the surface of the woodblock, stone, or plate and uses a printing press to roll the image onto paper or fabric. Some make prints by pressing the inked surface onto paper by hand or by graphically encoding and processing data, using a computer. The digitized images are then printed on paper with the use of a computer printer.

Painting restorers preserve and restore damaged and faded paintings. They apply solvents and cleaning agents to clean the surfaces of the paintings, they reconstruct or retouch damaged areas, and they apply preservatives to protect the paintings. Restoration is highly detailed work and usually is reserved for experts in the field.

Multi-media artists and animators work primarily in motion picture and video industries, advertising, and computer systems design services. They draw by hand and use computers to create the series of pictures that form the animated images or special effects seen in movies, television programs, and computer games. Some draw storyboards for television commercials, movies, and animated features. Storyboards present television commercials in a series of scenes similar to a comic strip and allow an advertising agency to evaluate commercials proposed by advertising companies. Storyboards also serve as guides to placing actors and cameras on the television or motion picture set and to other production details. Many multi-media artists model objects in three dimensions by computer and work with programmers to make those images move.

Work environment. Many artists work in fine art or commercial art studios located in office buildings, warehouses, or lofts. Others work in private studios in their homes. Some fine artists share studio space, where they also may exhibit their work. Studio surroundings usually are well lighted and ventilated; however, fine artists may be exposed to fumes from glue, paint, ink, and other materials and to dust or other residue from filings, splattered paint, or spilled cleaners and other fluids. Artists who sit at drafting tables or who use computers for extended periods may experience back pain, eyestrain, or fatigue.

Artists employed by publishing companies, advertising agencies, and design firms generally work a standard work week. During busy periods, they may work overtime to meet deadlines. Self-employed artists can set their own hours. They may spend much time and effort selling their artwork to potential customers or clients and building a reputation.

Training, Other Qualifications, and Advancement

Artists usually develop their skills through a bachelor's degree program or other postsecondary training in art or design. Although formal schooling is not strictly required for craft and fine artists, it is very difficult to become skilled enough to make a living without some training. Art directors usually have years of work experience and generally need at least a bachelor's degree. Due to the level of technical expertise demanded, multimedia artists and animators generally also need a bachelor's degree.

Education and training. Many colleges and universities offer programs leading to a bachelor's or master's degree in fine arts. Courses usually include core subjects such as English, social science, and natural science, in addition to art history and studio art. Independent schools of art and design also offer postsecondary studio training in the craft, fine, and multi-media arts leading to certificates in the specialties or to an associate or bachelor's degree in fine arts. Typically, these programs focus more intensively on studio work than do the academic programs in a university setting. In 2007 the National Association of Schools of Art and Design accredited 282 postsecondary institutions with programs in art and design; most of these schools award a degree in art.

Many educational programs in art also provide training in computer techniques. Computers are used widely in the visual arts, and knowledge and training in computer graphics and other visual display software are critical elements of many jobs in these fields.

Medical illustrators must have both a demonstrated artistic ability and a detailed knowledge of living organisms, surgical and medical procedures, and human and animal anatomy. A bachelor's degree combining art and premedical courses usually is required. However, most medical illustrators also choose to pursue a master's degree in medical illustration. This degree is offered in four accredited schools in the United States.

Art directors usually begin as entry-level artists in advertising, publishing, design, and motion picture production firms. Artists are promoted to art director after demonstrating artistic and leadership abilities. Some art schools offer coursework in art direction as part of their curricula. Depending on the scope of their responsibilities, some art directors also may pursue a degree in art administration, which teaches non-artistic skills such as project management and finance.

Those who want to teach fine arts at public elementary or secondary schools usually must have a teaching certificate in addition to a bachelor's degree. An advanced degree in fine arts or arts administration is usually necessary for management or administrative positions in government or in foundations or for teaching in colleges and universities.

Other qualifications. Evidence of appropriate talent and skill, displayed in an artist's portfolio, is an important factor used by art directors, clients, and others in deciding whether to hire an individual or contract for their work. A portfolio is a collection of handmade, computer-generated, photographic, or printed samples of the artist's best work. Assembling a successful portfolio requires skills usually developed through postsecondary training in art or visual communications. Internships also provide excellent opportunities for artists to develop and enhance their portfolios.

Advancement. Artists hired by firms often start with relatively routine work. While doing this work, however, they may observe other artists and practice their own skills.

Craft and fine artists advance professionally as their work circulates and as they establish a reputation for a particular style. Many of the most successful artists continually develop new ideas, and their work often evolves over time.

Many artists freelance part-time while continuing to hold a full-time job until they are established. Others freelance part time while still in school, to develop experience and to build a portfolio of published work.

Freelance artists try to develop a set of clients who regularly contract for work. Some freelance artists are widely recognized for their skill in specialties such as cartooning or children's book illustration. These artists may earn high incomes and can choose the type of work they do.

Employment

Artists held about 218,000 jobs in 2006. About 62 percent were self-employed. Employment was distributed as follows:

Multimedia artists and animators	87,000
Art directors	78,000
Fine artists, including painters, sculptors and illustrators	30,000
Craft artists	8,800
Artists and related workers, all other	14,000

Of the artists who were not self-employed, many worked for advertising and related services; newspaper, periodical, book, and software publishers; motion picture and video industries; specialized design services; and computer systems design and related services. Some self-employed artists offered their services to advertising agencies, design firms, publishing houses, and other businesses.

Job Outlook

Employment of artists is projected to grow faster than average. Competition for jobs is expected to be keen for both salaried and freelance jobs in all specialties because the number of people with creative ability and an interest in this career is expected to continue to exceed the number of available openings. Despite the competition, employers and individual clients are always on the lookout for talented and creative artists.

Employment change. Employment of artists and related workers is expected to grow 16 percent through 2016, faster than the average for all occupations.

Demand for illustrators who work on a computer will increase as Web sites use more detailed images and backgrounds in their designs. Many cartoonists, in particular, opt to post their work on political Web sites and online publications. Cartoonists often create animated or interactive images to satisfy readers' demands for more sophisticated images. The small number of medical illustrators will also be in greater demand as medical research continues to grow.

Demand for multimedia artists and animators will increase as consumers continue to demand more realistic video games, movie and television special effects, and 3D animated movies. Additional job openings will arise from an increasing demand for Web site development and for computer graphics adaptation from the growing number of mobile technologies. Animators are also increasingly finding work in alternative areas such as scientific research or design services.

Job prospects. Competition for jobs as artists and related workers will be keen because there are more qualified candidates than available jobs. Employers in all industries should be able to choose from among the most qualified candidates.

Despite the competition, studios, galleries, and individual clients are always on the lookout for artists who display outstanding talent, creativity, and style. Among craft and fine artists, talented individuals who have developed a mastery of artistic techniques and skills will have the best job prospects. Multi-media artists and animators should have better job opportunities than other artists, but still will experience competition. Job opportunities for animators of lower-technology cartoons could be hampered as these jobs continue to be outsourced overseas.

Despite an expanding number of opportunities, art directors should experience keen competition for the available openings. Craft and fine artists work mostly on a freelance or commission basis and may find it difficult to earn a living solely by selling their artwork. Only the most successful craft and fine artists receive major commissions for their work. Competition among artists for the privilege of being shown in galleries is expected to remain acute, as will competition for grants from sponsors such as private foundations, state and local arts councils, and the National Endowment for the Arts.

The growth in computer graphics packages and stock art Web sites is making it easier for writers, publishers, and art directors to create their own illustrations. As the use of this technology grows, there will be fewer opportunities for illustrators. However, it also has opened up new opportunities for illustrators who prefer to work digitally. Salaried cartoonists will have fewer job opportunities because many newspapers and magazines increasingly rely on freelance work.

Projections data from the National Employment Matrix

Occupational Title	SOC Code	Employment, 2006	Projected employment, 2016	Change, 2006-2016	
				Number	Percent
Artists and related workers	27-1010	218,000	253,000	34,000	16
Art directors	27-1011	78,000	85,000	7,000	9
Craft artists...	27-1012	8,800	9,500	700	8
Fine artists, including painters, sculptors, and illustrators............	27-1013	30,000	33,000	3,000	10
Multi-media artists and animators	27-1014	87,000	110,000	23,000	26
Artists and related workers, all other	27-1019	14,000	15,000	1,200	8

NOTE: Data in this table are rounded.

Earnings

Median annual earnings of salaried art directors were $68,100 in May 2006. The middle 50 percent earned between $49,480 and $94,920. The lowest 10 percent earned less than $37,920, and the highest 10 percent earned more than $135,090. Median annual earnings were $70,630 in advertising and related services.

Median annual earnings of salaried craft artists were $24,090. The middle 50 percent earned between $18,860 and $35,840. The lowest 10 percent earned less than $14,130, and the highest 10 percent earned more than $46,700. Earnings data for the many self-employed craft artists were not available.

Median annual earnings of salaried fine artists, including painters, sculptors, and illustrators were $41,970. The middle 50 percent earned between $28,500 and $58,550. The lowest 10 percent earned less than $18,350, and the highest 10 percent earned more than $79,390. Earnings data for the many self-employed fine artists were not available.

Median annual earnings of salaried multi-media artists and animators were $51,350, not including the earnings of the self-employed. The middle 50 percent earned between $38,980 and $70,050. The lowest 10 percent earned less than $30,390, and the highest 10 percent earned more than $92,720. Median annual earnings were $57,310 in motion picture and video industries and $48,860 in advertising and related services.

Earnings for self-employed artists vary widely. Some charge only a nominal fee while they gain experience and build a reputation for their work. Others, such as well-established freelance fine artists and illustrators, can earn more than salaried artists. Many, however, find it difficult to rely solely on income earned from selling paintings or other works of art. Like other self-employed workers, freelance artists must provide their own benefits.

Related Occupations

Other workers who apply artistic skills include architects, except landscape and naval; archivists, curators, and museum technicians; commercial and industrial designers; fashion designers; floral designers; graphic designers; interior designers; jewelers and precious stone and metal workers; landscape architects; photographers; and woodworkers. Some workers who use computers extensively, including computer software engineers and desktop publishers, may require art skills.

Sources of Additional Information

For general information about art and design and a list of accredited college-level programs, contact

▸ National Association of Schools of Art and Design, 11250 Roger Bacon Dr., Suite 21, Reston, VA 20190. Internet: http://nasad.arts-accredit.org

For information on careers in the craft arts and for a list of schools and workshops, contact

▸ American Craft Council Library, 72 Spring St., 6th Floor, New York, NY 10012. Internet: http://www.craftcouncil.org

For information on careers in illustration, contact

▸ Society of Illustrators, 128 E. 63rd St., New York, NY 10021. Internet: http://www.societyillustrators.org

For information on careers in medical illustration, contact

▸ Association of Medical Illustrators, 245 First St., Suite 1800, Cambridge, MA 02142. Internet: http://www.ami.org

For information on workshops, scholarships, internships, and competitions for art students interested in advertising careers, contact

▸ Art Directors Club, 106 W. 29th St., New York, NY 10001. Internet: http://www.adcglobal.org

Athletes, Coaches, Umpires, and Related Workers

(O*NET 27-2021.00, 27-2022.00, and 27-2023.00)

Significant Points

- Work hours are often irregular and extensive travel may be required.
- Career-ending injuries are always a risk for athletes.
- Job opportunities will be best for part-time coaches, sports instructors, umpires, referees, and sports officials in high schools, sports clubs, and other settings.
- Competition to become a professional athlete will continue to be extremely intense; athletes who seek to compete professionally must have extraordinary talent, desire, and dedication to training.

Nature of the Work

We are a nation of sports fans and sports players. Some of those who participate in amateur sports dream of becoming paid professional athletes, coaches, or sports officials, but very few beat the long and daunting odds of making a full-time living from professional athletics. Those athletes who make it to the professional level find that careers are short and jobs are insecure. Even though the chances of employment as a professional athlete are slim, there are many opportunities for at least a part-time job as a coach, instructor, referee, or umpire in amateur athletics or in high school, college, or university sports.

Athletes and *sports competitors* compete in organized, officiated sports events to entertain spectators. When playing a game, athletes are required to understand the strategies of their game while obeying the rules and regulations of the sport. The events in which they compete include both team sports, such as baseball, basketball, football, hockey, and soccer, and individual sports, such as golf, tennis, and bowling. The level of play varies from unpaid high school athletics to professional sports, in which the best from around the world compete in events broadcast on international television.

Being an athlete involves more than competing in athletic events. Athletes spend many hours each day practicing skills and improving teamwork under the guidance of a coach or a sports instructor. They view videotapes to critique their own performances and techniques and to learn their opponents' tendencies and weaknesses to gain a competitive advantage. Some athletes work regularly with strength trainers to gain muscle and stamina and to prevent injury. Many athletes push their bodies to the limit during both practice and play, so career-ending injury always is a risk; even minor injuries may put a player at risk of replacement. Because competition at all levels is extremely intense and job security is always precarious, many athletes train year round to maintain excellent form and technique and peak physical condition. Very little downtime from the sport exists at the professional level. Athletes also must conform to regimented diets during their sports season to supplement any physical training program.

Coaches organize amateur and professional athletes and teach them the fundamentals of individual and team sports. (In individual sports, *instructors* sometimes may fill this role.) Coaches train athletes for competition by holding practice sessions to perform drills that improve the athletes' form, technique, skills, and stamina. Along with refining athletes' individual skills, coaches are responsible for instilling good sportsmanship, a competitive spirit, and teamwork and for managing their teams during both practice sessions and competitions. Before competition, coaches evaluate or scout the opposing team to determine game strategies and practice specific plays. During competition, coaches may call specific plays intended to surprise or overpower the opponent, and they may substitute players for optimum team chemistry and success. Coaches' additional tasks may include selecting, storing, issuing, and taking inventory of equipment, materials, and supplies.

Many coaches in high schools are primarily teachers of academic subjects who supplement their income by coaching part time. College coaches consider coaching a full-time discipline and may be away from home frequently as they travel to scout and recruit prospective players.

Sports instructors teach professional and nonprofessional athletes individually. They organize, instruct, train, and lead athletes in indoor and outdoor sports such as bowling, tennis, golf, and swimming. Because activities are as diverse as weight lifting, gymnastics, scuba diving, and karate, instructors tend to specialize in one or a few activities. Like coaches, sports instructors also may hold daily practice sessions and be responsible for any needed equipment and supplies. Using their knowledge of their sport and of physiology, they determine the type and level of difficulty of exercises, prescribe specific drills, and correct athletes' techniques. Some instructors also teach and demonstrate the use of training apparatus, such as

trampolines or weights, for correcting athletes' weaknesses and enhancing their conditioning. Like coaches, sports instructors evaluate the athlete and the athlete's opponents to devise a competitive game strategy.

Coaches and sports instructors sometimes differ in their approaches to athletes because of the focus of their work. For example, while coaches manage the team during a game to optimize its chance for victory, sports instructors—such as those who work for professional tennis players—often are not permitted to instruct their athletes during competition. Sports instructors spend more of their time with athletes working one-on-one, which permits them to design customized training programs for each individual. Motivating athletes to play hard challenges most coaches and sports instructors but is vital for the athlete's success. Many coaches and instructors derive great satisfaction working with children or young adults, helping them to learn new physical and social skills, improve their physical condition, and achieve success in their sport.

Umpires, referees, and other sports officials officiate at competitive athletic and sporting events. They observe the play, detect infractions of rules, and impose penalties established by the rules and regulations of the various sports. Umpires, referees, and sports officials anticipate play and position themselves to best see the action, assess the situation, and determine any violations. Some sports officials, such as boxing referees, may work independently, while others such as umpires work in groups. Regardless of the sport, the job is highly stressful because officials are often required to make a decision in a split second, sometimes resulting in strong disagreement among competitors, coaches, and spectators.

Professional *scouts* evaluate the skills of both amateur and professional athletes to determine talent and potential. As a sports intelligence agent, the scout's primary duty is to seek out top athletic candidates for the team he or she represents. At the professional level, scouts typically work for scouting organizations or as freelance scouts. In locating new talent, scouts perform their work in secrecy so as not to "tip off" their opponents about their interest in certain players. At the college level, the head scout often is an assistant coach, although freelance scouts may aid colleges by reporting to coaches about exceptional players. Scouts at this level seek talented high school athletes by reading newspapers, contacting high school coaches and alumni, attending high school games, and studying videotapes of prospects' performances. They also evaluate potential players' background and personal characteristics, such as motivation and discipline, by talking to the players' coaches, parents, and teachers.

Work environment. Irregular work hours are the trademark of the athlete. They also are common for coaches, umpires, referees, and other sports officials. Athletes and others in sports related occupations often work Saturdays, Sundays, evenings, and holidays. Athletes and full-time coaches usually work more than 40 hours a week for several months during the sports season, if not most of the year. Some coaches in educational institutions may coach more than one sport, particularly in high schools.

Athletes, coaches, and sports officials who participate in competitions that are held outdoors may be exposed to all weather conditions of the season. Those involved in events that are held indoors tend to work in climate-controlled comfort, often in arenas, enclosed stadiums, or gymnasiums. Athletes, coaches, and some sports officials frequently travel to sporting events by bus or airplane. Scouts also travel extensively in locating talent, often by automobile.

Umpires, referees, and other sports officials regularly encounter verbal abuse by fans, coaches, and athletes. The officials also face possible physical assault and, increasingly, lawsuits from injured athletes based on their officiating decisions.

Training, Other Qualifications, and Advancement

Education and training requirements for athletes, coaches, umpires, and related workers vary greatly by the level and type of sport. Regardless of the sport or occupation, these jobs require immense overall knowledge of the game, usually acquired through years of experience at lower levels.

Education and training. Becoming a professional athlete is the culmination of years of effort. Athletes usually begin competing in their sports while in elementary or middle school, and continue through high school and sometimes college. They play in amateur tournaments and on high school and college teams, where the best attract the attention of professional scouts. Most schools require that participating athletes maintain specific academic standards to remain eligible to play. Athletes who seek to compete professionally must have extraordinary talent, desire, and dedication to training.

Head coaches at public secondary schools and sports instructors at all levels usually must have a bachelor's degree. For high school coaching and sports instructor jobs, schools usually prefer to hire teachers willing to take on the jobs part time. If no suitable teacher is found, schools hire someone from outside. Some entry-level positions for coaches or instructors require only experience derived as a participant in the sport or activity. Those who are not teachers must meet state requirements for certification to become a head coach. Certification, however, may not be required for coaching and sports instructor jobs in private schools. Degree programs specifically related to coaching include exercise and sports science, physiology, kinesiology, nutrition and fitness, physical education, and sports medicine.

Each sport has specific requirements for umpires, referees, and other sports officials. Umpires, referees, and other sports officials often begin their careers by volunteering for intramural, community, and recreational league competitions.

Scouting jobs require experience playing a sport at the college or professional level that makes it possible to spot young players who possess extraordinary athletic ability and skills. Most beginning scouting jobs are as part-time talent spotters in a particular area or region. Hard work and a record of success often lead to full-time jobs responsible for bigger territories. Some scouts advance to scouting director jobs or various administrative positions in sports.

Certification and other qualifications. Athletes, coaches, umpires, and related workers must relate well to others and possess good communication and leadership skills. Coaches also must be resourceful and flexible to successfully instruct and motivate individuals and groups of athletes.

To officiate at high school athletic events, officials must register with the state agency that oversees high school athletics and pass an exam on the rules of the particular game. For college refereeing, candidates must be certified by an officiating school and be evaluated during a probationary period. Some larger college sports conferences require officials to have certification and other qualifications, such as residence in or near the conference boundaries, along with several years of experience officiating at high school, community college, or other college conference games.

For those interested in becoming a tennis, golf, karate, or other kind of instructor, certification is highly desirable. Often, one must be at least 18 years old and certified in cardiopulmonary resuscitation (CPR). There are many certifying organizations specific to the various sports, and their training requirements vary. Participation in a clinic, camp, or school usually is required for certification. Part-time workers and those in smaller facilities are less likely to need formal education or training.

Standards for officials become more stringent as the level of competition advances. Whereas umpires for high school baseball need a high school diploma or its equivalent, 20/20 vision, and quick reflexes, those seeking to officiate at minor or major league games must attend professional umpire training school. Top graduates are selected for further evaluation while officiating in a rookie minor league. Umpires then usually need seven to 10 years of experience in various minor leagues before being considered for major league jobs. Becoming an official for professional football also is competitive, as candidates must have at least 10 years of officiating experience, with five of them at a collegiate varsity or minor professional level. For the National Football League (NFL), prospective trainees are interviewed by clinical psychologists to determine levels of intelligence and ability to handle extremely stressful situations. In addition, the NFL's security department conducts thorough background checks. Potential candidates are likely to be interviewed by a panel from the NFL officiating department and are given a comprehensive examination on the rules of the sport.

Advancement. Many coaches begin their careers as assistant coaches to gain the knowledge and experience needed to become a head coach. Head coaches at large schools that strive to compete at the highest levels of a sport require substantial experience as a head coach at another school or as an assistant coach. To reach the ranks of professional coaching, a person usually needs years of coaching experience and a winning record in the lower ranks.

Employment

Athletes, coaches, umpires, and related workers held about 253,000 jobs in 2006. Coaches and scouts held 217,000 jobs; athletes, 18,000; and umpires, referees, and other sports officials, 19,000. Nearly 42 percent of athletes, coaches, umpires, and related workers worked part time, while 15 percent maintained variable schedules. Many sports officials and coaches receive such small and irregular payments for their services—occasional officiating at club games, for example—that they may not consider themselves employed in these occupations, even part time.

Among those employed in wage and salary jobs, 47 percent held jobs in public and private educational services. About 13 percent worked in amusement, gambling, and recreation industries, including golf and tennis clubs, gymnasiums, health clubs, judo and karate schools, riding stables, swim clubs, and other sports and recreation facilities. Another six percent worked in the spectator sports industry.

About 1 out of 5 workers in this occupation was self-employed, earning prize money or fees for lessons, scouting, or officiating assignments. Many other coaches and sports officials, although technically not self-employed, have such irregular or tenuous working arrangements that their working conditions resemble those of self-employment.

Projections data from the National Employment Matrix

Occupational Title	SOC Code	Employment, 2006	Projected employment, 2016	Change, 2006-2016	
				Number	Percent
Athletes, coaches, umpires, and related workers	27-2020	253,000	291,000	38,000	15
Athletes and sports competitors	27-2021	18,000	21,000	3,400	19
Coaches and scouts	27-2022	217,000	249,000	32,000	15
Umpires, referees, and other sports officials...............................	27-2023	19,000	22,000	3,000	16

NOTE: Data in this table are rounded.

Job Outlook

Employment of athletes, coaches, umpires, and related workers is expected to grow faster than the average for all occupations through 2016. Very keen competition is expected for jobs at the highest levels of sports.

Employment change. Employment of athletes, coaches, umpires, and related workers is expected to increase by 15 percent from 2006 to 2016, which is faster than the average for all occupations. Employment will grow as the general public continues to participate in organized sports for entertainment, recreation, and physical conditioning. Increasing participation in organized sports by girls and women will boost demand for coaches, umpires, and related workers. Job growth also will be driven by the increasing number of baby boomers approaching retirement, during which they are expected to participate more in leisure activities such as golf and tennis which require instruction.

Employment of coaches and instructors also will increase with expansion of school and college athletic programs and growing demand for private sports instruction. Sports-related job growth within education also will be driven by the decisions of local school boards. Population growth dictates the construction of additional schools, particularly in the expanding suburbs, but funding for athletic programs often is cut first when budgets become tight. Still, the popularity of team sports often enables shortfalls to be offset somewhat by assistance from fundraisers, booster clubs, and parents.

Job prospects. Persons who are state-certified to teach academic subjects in addition to physical education are likely to have the best prospects for obtaining coaching and instructor jobs. The need to replace the many high school coaches who change occupations or leave the labor force entirely also will provide some coaching opportunities.

Competition for professional athlete jobs will continue to be extremely intense. Opportunities to make a living as a professional in individual sports such as golf or tennis may grow as new tournaments are established and as prize money distributed to participants increases. Because most professional athletes' careers last only a few years due to debilitating injuries and age, annual replacement needs for these jobs is high, creating some job opportunities. However, the talented young men and women who dream of becoming sports superstars greatly outnumber the number of openings.

Opportunities should be best for persons seeking part-time umpire, referee, and other sports official jobs at the high school level. Competition is expected for higher paying jobs at the college level and will be even greater for jobs in professional sports. Competition should be keen for jobs as scouts, particularly for professional teams, because the number of available positions is limited.

Earnings

Median annual wage and salary earnings of athletes were $41,060 in May 2006. However, the highest paid professional athletes earn much more.

Median annual wage and salary earnings of umpires and related workers were $22,880 in May 2006. The middle 50 percent earned between $17,090 and $33,840. The lowest-paid 10 percent earned less than $14,120, and the highest-paid 10 percent earned more than $45,430.

In May 2006, median annual wage and salary earnings of coaches and scouts were $26,950. The middle 50 percent earned between $17,510 and $40,850. The lowest-paid 10 percent earned less than $13,990, and the highest-paid 10 percent earned more than $58,890. However, the highest paid professional coaches earn much more. Median annual earnings in the industries employing the largest numbers of coaches and scouts in May 2006 are shown below:

Colleges, universities, and professional schools $37,530

Other amusement and recreation industries 27,180

Fitness and recreational sports centers 26,150

Other schools and instruction 23,840

Elementary and secondary schools 21,960

Earnings vary by level of education, certification, and geographic region. Some instructors and coaches are paid a salary, while others may be paid by the hour, per session, or based on the number of participants.

Related Occupations

Athletes and coaches use their extensive knowledge of physiology and sports to instruct, inform, and encourage sports participants. Other workers with similar duties include dietitians and nutritionists; physical therapists; recreation workers; fitness workers; recreational therapists; and teachers—preschool, kindergarten, elementary, middle, and secondary.

Sources of Additional Information

For information about sports officiating for team and individual sports, contact

▸ National Association of Sports Officials, 2017 Lathrop Ave., Racine, WI 53405. Internet: http://www.naso.org

For more information about certification of tennis instructors and coaches, contact

▸ Professional Tennis Registry, P.O. Box 4739, Hilton Head Island, SC 29938. Internet: http://www.ptrtennis.org

▸ U. S. Professional Tennis Association, 3535 Briarpark Dr., Suite One, Houston, TX 77042. Internet: http://www.uspta.org

Automotive Body and Related Repairers

(O*NET 49-3021.00 and 49-3022.00)

Significant Points

■ To become a fully skilled automotive body repairer, formal training followed by on-the-job instruction is recommended because fixing newer automobiles requires advanced skills.

■ Excellent job opportunities are projected because of the large number of older workers who are expected to retire in the next 10 to 15 years.

■ Repairers need good reading ability and basic mathematics and computer skills to use print and digital technical manuals.

Nature of the Work

Most of the damage resulting from everyday vehicle collisions can be repaired, and vehicles can be refinished to look and drive like new. *Automotive body repairers*, often called collision repair technicians, straighten bent bodies, remove dents, and replace crumpled parts that cannot be fixed. They repair all types of vehicles, and although some work on large trucks, buses, or tractor-trailers, most work on cars and small trucks. They can work alone, with only general direction from supervisors, or as specialists on a repair team. In some shops, helpers or apprentices assist experienced repairers.

Each damaged vehicle presents different challenges for repairers. Using their broad knowledge of automotive construction and repair techniques, automotive body repairers must decide how to handle each job based on what the vehicle is made of and what needs to be fixed. They must first determine the extent of the damage and order any needed parts.

If the car is heavily damaged, an automotive body repairer might start by realigning the frame of the vehicle. Repairers chain or clamp frames and sections to alignment machines that use hydraulic pressure to align damaged components. "Unibody" vehicles—designs built without frames—must be restored to precise factory specifications for the vehicle to operate correctly. For these vehicles, repairers use benchmark systems to accurately measure how much each section is out of alignment, and hydraulic machinery to return the vehicle to its original shape.

Once the frame is aligned, repairers can begin to fix or replace damaged body parts. If the vehicle or part is made of metal, body repairers will use a pneumatic metal-cutting gun or other tools to remove badly damaged sections of body panels and then weld in replacement sections. Less serious dents are pulled out with a hydraulic jack or hand prying bar or knocked out with handtools or pneumatic hammers. Small dents and creases in the metal are smoothed by holding a small anvil against one side of the damaged area while hammering the opposite side. Repairers also remove very small pits and dimples with pick hammers and punches in a process called metal finishing. Body repairers use plastic or solder to fill small dents that cannot be worked out of plastic or metal panels. On metal panels, they file or grind the hardened filler to the original shape and clean the surface with a media blaster—similar to a sand blaster—before repainting the damaged portion of the vehicle.

Body repairers also repair or replace the plastic body parts that are increasingly used on new vehicles. They remove damaged panels and identify the type and properties of the plastic used. With most types of plastic, repairers can apply heat from a hot-air welding gun or immerse the panel in hot water and press the softened section back into shape by hand. Repairers replace plastic parts that are badly damaged or very difficult to fix. A few body repairers specialize in fixing fiberglass car bodies.

Some body repairers specialize in installing and repairing glass in automobiles and other vehicles. *Automotive glass installers and repairers* remove broken, cracked, or pitted windshields and window glass. Glass installers apply a moisture-proofing compound along the edges of the glass, place the glass in the vehicle, and install rubber strips around the sides of the windshield or window to make it secure and weatherproof.

Many large shops make repairs using an assembly-line approach where vehicles are fixed by a team of repairers who each specialize in one type of repair. One worker might straighten frames while another repairs doors and fenders, for example. In most shops, automotive painters do the painting and refinishing, but in small shops, workers often do both body repairing and painting.

Work environment. Repairers work indoors in body shops that are noisy with the clatter of hammers against metal and the whine of power tools. Most shops are well ventilated to disperse dust and paint fumes. Body repairers often work in awkward or cramped positions, and much of their work is strenuous and dirty. Hazards include cuts from sharp metal edges, burns from torches and heated metal, injuries from power tools, and fumes from paint. However, serious accidents usually are avoided when the shop is kept clean and orderly and safety practices are observed. Automotive repair and maintenance shops averaged 4 cases of work-related injuries and illnesses per 100 full-time workers in 2005, compared to 4.6 per 100 workers in all private industry.

Most automotive body repairers work a standard 40-hour week. More than 40 hours a week may be required when there is a backlog of repair work to be completed. This may include working on weekends.

Training, Other Qualifications, and Advancement

Automotive technology is rapidly becoming more sophisticated, and most employers prefer applicants who have completed a formal training program in automotive body repair or refinishing. Most new repairers complete at least part of this training on the job. Many repairers, particularly in urban areas, need a national certification to advance past entry-level work.

Education and training. A high school diploma or GED is often all that is required to enter this occupation, but more specific education and training is needed to learn how to repair newer automobiles. Collision repair programs may be offered in high school or in postsecondary vocational schools and community colleges. Courses in electronics, physics, chemistry, English, computers, and mathematics provide a good background for a career as an automotive body repairer. Most training programs combine classroom instruction and hands-on practice.

Trade and technical school programs typically award certificates to graduates after six months to a year of collision repair study. Some community colleges offer two-year programs in collision repair.

Many of these schools also offer certificates for individual courses, so that students are able to take classes incrementally or as needed.

New repairers begin by assisting experienced body repairers in tasks such as removing damaged parts, sanding body panels, and installing repaired parts. Novices learn to remove small dents and make other minor repairs. They then progress to more difficult tasks, such as straightening body parts and returning them to their correct alignment. Generally, it takes three to four years of hands-on training to become skilled in all aspects of body repair, some of which may be completed as part of a formal education program. Basic automotive glass installation and repair can be learned in as little as six months, but becoming fully qualified can take several years.

Continuing education and training are needed throughout a career in automotive body repair. Automotive parts, body materials, and electronics continue to change and to become more complex. To keep up with these technological advances, repairers must continue to gain new skills by reading technical manuals and furthering their education with classes and seminars. Many companies within the automotive body repair industry send employees to advanced training programs to brush up on skills or to learn new techniques.

Other qualifications. Fully skilled automotive body repairers must have good reading ability and basic mathematics and computer skills. Restoring unibody automobiles to their original form requires repairers to follow instructions and diagrams in technical manuals and to make precise three-dimensional measurements of the position of one body section relative to another. In addition, repairers should enjoy working with their hands and be able to pay attention to detail while they work.

Certification and advancement. Certification by the National Institute for Automotive Service Excellence (ASE), although voluntary, is the pervasive industry credential for non entry-level automotive body repairers. This is especially true in large, urban areas. Repairers may take up to four ASE Master Collision Repair and Refinish Exams. Repairers who pass at least one exam and have two years of hands-on work experience earn ASE certification. The completion of a postsecondary program in automotive body repair may be substituted for one year of work experience. Those who pass all four exams become ASE Master Collision Repair and Refinish Technicians. Automotive body repairers must retake the examination at least every five years to retain their certification. Many vehicle manufacturers and paint manufacturers also have product certification programs that can advance a repairer's career.

As beginners increase their skills, learn new techniques, earn certifications, and complete work more rapidly, their pay increases. An experienced automotive body repairer with managerial ability may advance to shop supervisor, and some workers open their own body repair shops. Other repairers become automobile damage appraisers for insurance companies.

Employment

Automotive body and related repairers held about 206,000 jobs in 2006; about 13 percent specialized in automotive glass installation and repair. Fifty-eight percent of repairers worked for automotive repair and maintenance shops in 2006, while 20 percent worked for automobile dealers. Others worked for organizations, such as trucking companies, that maintain their own motor vehicles. A small number of repairers worked for wholesalers of motor vehicles, parts, and supplies. More than 15 percent of automotive body repairers were self-employed, roughly double the number for all installation, maintenance, and repair occupations.

Job Outlook

Employment of automotive body and related repairers is expected to grow about as fast as average through the year 2016, and job opportunities are projected to be excellent due to a growing number of retirements in this occupation.

Employment change. Employment of automotive body repairers is expected to grow 12 percent over the 2006–2016 decade, as compared to 10 percent for all occupations. Demand for qualified body repairers will increase as the number of vehicles on the road continues to grow. With more motor vehicles in use, more vehicles will be damaged in accidents. In addition, new automotive designs of lighter weight are prone to greater collision damage than are older, heavier designs, so more repairs are needed. Employment growth will continue to be concentrated in automotive body, paint, interior, and glass repair shops, with little or no change in automotive dealerships.

Despite the anticipated increase in the number of auto accidents, the increasing demand for automotive body repairers will be tempered by improvements in the quality of vehicles. Also, technological innovations that enhance safety will reduce the likelihood of accidents.

Demand for automotive body repair services will similarly be constrained as more vehicles are declared a total loss after accidents. In many such cases, the vehicles are not repaired because of the high cost of replacing the increasingly complex parts and electronic components and because of the extensive damage that results when airbags deploy. Also, higher insurance premiums and deductibles mean that minor damage is more often going unrepaired. Larger shops are instituting productivity enhancements, such as employing a team approach to repairs, which may limit employment growth by reducing the time it takes to make repairs.

Job prospects. Employment growth will create some opportunities, but the need to replace experienced repairers who transfer to other occupations or who retire or stop working for other reasons will account for the majority of job openings over the next 10 years. Opportunities will be excellent for people with formal training in automotive body repair and refinishing. Those without any training

Projections data from the National Employment Matrix

Occupational Title	SOC Code	Employment, 2006	Projected employment, 2016	Change, 2006-16	
				Number	Percent
Automotive body and related repairers	—	206,000	232,000	26,000	12
Automotive body and related repairers	49-3021	183,000	204,000	21,000	12
Automotive glass installers and repairers	49-3022	24,000	28,000	4,400	19

NOTE: Data in this table are rounded.

or experience in automotive body refinishing or collision repair—before or after high school—will face competition for these jobs.

Experienced body repairers are rarely laid off during a general slowdown in the economy as the automotive repair business is not very sensitive to changes in economic conditions. Although repair of minor dents and crumpled fenders is often put off when drivers have less money, major body damage must be repaired before a vehicle can be driven safely.

Earnings

Median hourly wage-and-salary earnings of automotive body and related repairers, including incentive pay, were $16.92 in May 2006. The middle 50 percent earned between $13.00 and $22.33 an hour. The lowest 10 percent earned less than $10.10, and the highest 10 percent earned more than $28.71 an hour. Median hourly earnings of automotive body and related repairers were $17.85 in automobile dealers and $16.66 in automotive repair and maintenance.

Median hourly wage-and-salary earnings of automotive glass installers and repairers, including incentive pay, were $14.77. The middle 50 percent earned between $11.44 and $18.42 an hour. The lowest 10 percent earned less than $9.19, and the highest 10 percent earned more than $22.22 an hour. Median hourly earnings in automotive repair and maintenance shops, the industry employing most automotive glass installers and repairers, were $14.80.

The majority of body repairers employed by independent repair shops and automotive dealers are paid on an incentive basis. Under this system, body repairers are paid a set amount for various tasks, and earnings depend on both the amount of work assigned and how fast it is completed. Employers frequently guarantee workers a minimum weekly salary. Body repairers who work for trucking companies, buslines, and other organizations that maintain their own vehicles usually receive an hourly wage.

Helpers and trainees typically earn between 30 percent and 60 percent of the earnings of skilled workers. They are paid by the hour until they are skilled enough to be paid on an incentive basis.

Employee benefits vary widely from business to business. However, industry sources report that benefits such as paid leave, health insurance, and retirement assistance are increasingly common in the collision repair industry. Automotive dealerships are the most likely to offer such incentives.

Related Occupations

Repairing damaged motor vehicles often involves working on mechanical components, as well as vehicle bodies. Automotive body repairers often work closely with individuals in several related occupations, including automotive service technicians and mechanics, diesel service technicians and mechanics, auto damage appraisers, and painting and coating workers, except construction and maintenance. Automotive glass installers and repairers complete tasks very similar to those of glaziers.

Sources of Additional Information

Additional details about work opportunities may be obtained from automotive body repair shops, automobile dealers, or local offices of your state employment service. state employment service offices also are a source of information about training programs.

For general information about automotive body repairer careers, contact any of the following sources:

▸ Automotive Careers Today, 8400 Westpark Dr., MS #2, McLean, VA 22102. Internet: http://www.autocareerstoday.org

▸ Automotive Service Association, P.O. Box 929, Bedford, Texas 76095. Internet: http://www.asashop.org

▸ Inter-Industry Conference On Auto Collision Repair Education Foundation (I-CAR), 5125 Trillium Blvd., Hoffman Estates, IL 60192. Internet: http://www.collisioncareers.org

▸ National Automobile Dealers Association, 8400 Westpark Dr., McLean, VA 22102. Internet: http://www.nada.org

For general information about careers in automotive glass installation and repair, contact

▸ National Glass Association. 8200 Greensboro Dr., Suite 302, McLean, VA 22102. Internet: http://www.glass.org

For information on how to become a certified automotive body repairer, write to

▸ National Institute for Automotive Service Excellence (ASE), 101 Blue Seal Dr. SE, Suite 101, Leesburg, VA 20175. Internet: http://www.asecert.org

For a directory of certified automotive body repairer programs, contact

▸ National Automotive Technician Education Foundation, 101 Blue Seal Dr., SE, Suite 101, Leesburg, VA 20175. Internet: http://www.natef.org

For a directory of accredited private trade and technical schools that offer training programs in automotive body repair, contact

▸ Accrediting Commission of Career Schools and Colleges of Technology, 2101 Wilson Blvd., Suite 302, Arlington, VA 22201. Internet: http://www.accsct.org

Automotive Service Technicians and Mechanics

(O*NET 49-3023.00, 49-3023.01, and 49-3023.02)

Significant Points

■ Automotive service technicians and mechanics must continually adapt to changing technology and repair techniques as vehicle components and systems become increasingly sophisticated.

■ Formal automotive technician training is the best preparation for these challenging technology-based jobs.

■ Opportunities should be very good for automotive service technicians and mechanics with diagnostic and problem-solving skills, knowledge of electronics and mathematics, and mechanical aptitude.

Nature of the Work

Automotive service technicians inspect, maintain, and repair automobiles and light trucks that run on gasoline, electricity, or alternative fuels such as ethanol. Automotive service technicians' and mechanics' responsibilities have evolved from simple mechanical repairs to high-level technology-related work. The increasing sophistication of automobiles requires workers who can use computerized shop equipment and work with electronic components while maintaining their skills with traditional handtools. As a result, automotive service workers are now usually called technicians rather than mechanics. (Service technicians who work on diesel-powered trucks, buses, and equipment are discussed in the job profile on diesel service technicians and mechanics elsewhere in this book.)

Today, integrated electronic systems and complex computers regulate vehicles and their performance while on the road. Technicians must have an increasingly broad knowledge of how vehicles' complex components work and interact. They also must be able to work with electronic diagnostic equipment and digital manuals and reference materials.

When mechanical or electrical troubles occur, technicians first get a description of the problem from the owner or, in a large shop, from the repair service estimator or service advisor who wrote the repair order. To locate the problem, technicians use a diagnostic approach. First, they test to see whether components and systems are secure and working properly. Then, they isolate the components or systems that might be the cause of the problem. For example, if an air-conditioner malfunctions, the technician might check for a simple problem, such as a low coolant level, or a more complex issue, such as a bad drive-train connection that has shorted out the air conditioner. As part of their investigation, technicians may test drive the vehicle or use a variety of testing equipment, including onboard and hand-held diagnostic computers or compression gauges. These tests may indicate whether a component is salvageable or whether a new one is required.

During routine service inspections, technicians test and lubricate engines and other major components. Sometimes technicians repair or replace worn parts before they cause breakdowns or damage the vehicle. Technicians usually follow a checklist to ensure that they examine every critical part. Belts, hoses, plugs, brake and fuel systems, and other potentially troublesome items are watched closely.

Service technicians use a variety of tools in their work. They use power tools, such as pneumatic wrenches to remove bolts quickly; machine tools like lathes and grinding machines to rebuild brakes; welding and flame-cutting equipment to remove and repair exhaust systems, and jacks and hoists to lift cars and engines. They also use common handtools, such as screwdrivers, pliers, and wrenches, to work on small parts and in hard-to-reach places. Technicians usually provide their own handtools, and many experienced workers have thousands of dollars invested in them. Employers furnish expensive power tools, engine analyzers, and other diagnostic equipment.

Computers are also commonplace in modern repair shops. Service technicians compare the readouts from computerized diagnostic testing devices with benchmarked standards given by the manufacturer. Deviations outside of acceptable levels tell the technician to investigate that part of the vehicle more closely. Through the Internet or from software packages, most shops receive automatic updates to technical manuals and access to manufacturers' service information, technical service bulletins, and other databases that allow technicians to keep up with common problems and learn new procedures.

High technology tools are needed to fix the computer equipment that operates everything from the engine to the radio in many cars. In fact, today most automotive systems, such as braking, transmission, and steering systems, are controlled primarily by computers and electronic components. Additionally, luxury vehicles often have integrated global positioning systems, Internet access, and other new features with which technicians will need to become familiar. Also, as more alternate-fuel vehicles are purchased, more automotive service technicians will need to learn the science behind these automobiles and how to repair them.

Automotive service technicians in large shops often specialize in certain types of repairs. For example, *transmission technicians and rebuilders* work on gear trains, couplings, hydraulic pumps, and other parts of transmissions. Extensive knowledge of computer controls, the ability to diagnose electrical and hydraulic problems, and other specialized skills are needed to work on these complex components, which employ some of the most sophisticated technology used in vehicles. *Tune-up technicians* adjust ignition timing and valves and adjust or replace spark plugs and other parts to ensure efficient engine performance. They often use electronic testing equipment to isolate and adjust malfunctions in fuel, ignition, and emissions control systems.

Automotive air-conditioning repairers install and repair air-conditioners and service their components, such as compressors, condensers, and controls. These workers require special training in federal and state regulations governing the handling and disposal of refrigerants. *Front-end mechanics* align and balance wheels and repair steering mechanisms and suspension systems. They frequently use special alignment equipment and wheel-balancing machines. *Brake repairers* adjust brakes, replace brake linings and pads, and make other repairs on brake systems. Some technicians specialize in both brake and front-end work.

Work environment. While most automotive service technicians worked a standard 40 hour week in 2006, 30 percent worked longer hours. Some may work evenings and weekends to satisfy customer service needs. Generally, service technicians work indoors in well-ventilated and -lighted repair shops. However, some shops are drafty and noisy. Although many problems can be fixed with simple computerized adjustments, technicians frequently work with dirty and greasy parts, and in awkward positions. They often lift heavy parts and tools. Minor cuts, burns, and bruises are common, but technicians can usually avoid serious accidents if safe practices are observed.

Training, Other Qualifications, and Advancement

Automotive technology is rapidly increasing in sophistication, and most training authorities strongly recommend that people seeking work in automotive service complete a formal training program in high school or in a postsecondary vocational school or community college. However, some service technicians still learn the trade solely by assisting and learning from experienced workers. Acquiring National Institute for Automotive Service Excellence (ASE) certification is important for those seeking work in large, urban areas.

Education and training. Most employers regard the successful completion of a vocational training program in automotive service technology as the best preparation for trainee positions. High school programs, while an asset, vary greatly in scope. Graduates of these programs may need further training to become qualified. Some of the more extensive high school programs participate in Automotive Youth Education Service (AYES), a partnership between high school automotive repair programs, automotive manufacturers, and franchised automotive dealers. All AYES high school programs are certified by the National Institute for Automotive Service Excellence. Students who complete these programs are well prepared to enter entry-level technician positions or to advance their technical education. Courses in automotive repair, electronics, physics, chemistry, English, computers, and mathematics provide a good educational background for a career as a service technician.

Postsecondary automotive technician training programs usually provide intensive career preparation through a combination of classroom instruction and hands-on practice. Schools update their curriculums frequently to reflect changing technology and equipment. Some trade and technical school programs provide concentrated training for six months to a year, depending on how many hours the student attends each week, and award a certificate. Community college programs usually award a certificate or an associate degree. Some students earn repair certificates in a particular skill and leave to begin their careers. Associate degree programs, however, usually take two years to complete and include classes in English, basic mathematics, computers, and other subjects, as well as automotive repair. Recently, some programs have added classes on customer service, stress management, and other employability skills. Some formal training programs have alliances with tool manufacturers that help entry-level technicians accumulate tools during their training period.

Various automobile manufacturers and participating franchised dealers also sponsor two-year associate degree programs at postsecondary schools across the nation. Students in these programs typically spend alternate six- to 12-week periods attending classes full time and working full time in the service departments of sponsoring dealers. At these dealerships, students work with an experienced worker who provides hands-on instruction and timesaving tips.

Those new to automotive service usually start as trainee technicians, technicians' helpers, or lubrication workers, and gradually acquire and practice their skills by working with experienced mechanics and technicians. In many cases, on-the-job training may be a part of a formal education program. With a few months' experience, beginners perform many routine service tasks and make simple repairs. While some graduates of postsecondary automotive training programs are often able to earn promotion to the journey level after only a few months on the job, it typically takes two to five years of experience to become a fully qualified service technician, who is expected to quickly perform the more difficult types of routine service and repairs. An additional one to two years of experience familiarizes technicians with all types of repairs. Complex specialties, such as transmission repair, require another year or two of training and experience. In contrast, brake specialists may learn their jobs in considerably less time because they do not need complete knowledge of automotive repair.

Employers increasingly send experienced automotive service technicians to manufacturer training centers to learn to repair new models or to receive special training in the repair of components, such as electronic fuel injection or air-conditioners. Motor vehicle dealers and other automotive service providers may send promising beginners or experienced technicians to manufacturer-sponsored technician training programs to upgrade or maintain employees' skills. Factory representatives also visit many shops to conduct short training sessions.

Other qualifications. The ability to diagnose the source of a problem quickly and accurately requires good reasoning ability and a thorough knowledge of automobiles. Many technicians consider diagnosing hard-to-find troubles one of their most challenging and satisfying duties. For trainee automotive service technician jobs, employers look for people with strong communication and analytical skills. Technicians need good reading, mathematics, and computer skills to study technical manuals. They must also read to keep up with new technology and learn new service and repair procedures and specifications.

Training in electronics is vital because electrical components, or a series of related components, account for nearly all malfunctions in modern vehicles. Trainees must possess mechanical aptitude and knowledge of how automobiles work. Experience working on motor vehicles in the Armed Forces or as a hobby can be very valuable.

Certification and advancement. ASE certification has become a standard credential for automotive service technicians. While not mandatory for work in automotive service, certification is common for all non entry-level technicians in large, urban areas. Certification is available in one or more of eight different areas of automotive service, such as electrical systems, engine repair, brake systems, suspension and steering, and heating and air-conditioning. For certification in each area, technicians must have at least two years of experience and pass the examination. Completion of an automotive training program in high school, vocational or trade school, or community or junior college may be substituted for one year of experience. For ASE certification as a Master Automobile Technician, technicians must be certified in all eight areas.

By becoming skilled in multiple auto repair services, technicians can increase their value to their employer and their pay. Experienced technicians who have administrative ability sometimes advance to shop supervisor or service manager. Those with sufficient funds many times open independent automotive repair shops. Technicians who work well with customers may become automotive repair service estimators.

Employment

Automotive service technicians and mechanics held about 773,000 jobs in 2006. Automotive repair and maintenance shops and automotive dealers employed the majority of these workers—29 percent each. In addition, automotive parts, accessories, and tire stores employed 7 percent of automotive service technicians. Others worked in gasoline stations; general merchandise stores; automotive equipment rental and leasing companies; federal, state, and local governments; and other organizations. Almost 17 percent of service technicians were self-employed, more than twice the proportion for all installation, maintenance, and repair occupations.

Job Outlook

The number of jobs for automotive service technicians and mechanics is projected to grow faster than average for all occupations over the next decade. Employment growth will create many new jobs, but total job openings will be significantly larger because many skilled technicians are expected to retire and will need to be replaced.

Employment change. Employment of automotive service technicians and mechanics is expected to increase 14 percent between 2006 and 2016, compared to 10 percent for all occupations. It will add a large number of new jobs, about 110,000, over the decade. Demand for technicians will grow as the number of vehicles in operation increases, reflecting continued growth in the driving age population

Projections data from the National Employment Matrix

Occupational Title	SOC Code	Employment, 2006	Projected employment, 2016	Change, 2006-16	
				Number	Percent
Automotive service technicians and mechanics...............................	49-3023	773,000	883,000	110,000	14

NOTE: Data in this table are rounded.

and in the number of multi-car families. Growth in demand will be offset somewhat by continuing improvements in the quality and durability of automobiles, which will require less frequent service.

Employment growth will continue to be concentrated in automobile dealerships and independent automotive repair shops. Many new jobs also will be created in small retail operations that offer after-warranty repairs, such as oil changes, brake repair, air-conditioner service, and other minor repairs generally taking less than 4 hours to complete. Employment of automotive service technicians and mechanics in gasoline service stations will continue to decline, as fewer stations offer repair services.

Job prospects. In addition to openings from growth, many job openings will be created by the need to replace a growing number of retiring technicians. Job opportunities in this occupation are expected to be very good for those who complete high school or postsecondary automotive training programs and who earn ASE certification. Some employers report difficulty in finding workers with the right skills. People with good diagnostic and problem-solving abilities, and training in basic electronics and computer courses are expected to have the best opportunities. Those without formal automotive training are likely to face competition for entry-level jobs.

Most people who enter the occupation can expect steady work, even during downturns in the economy. Although car owners tend to postpone maintenance and repair on their vehicles when their budgets are strained, employers usually cut back on hiring new workers during economic downturns instead of letting experienced workers go.

Earnings

Median hourly wage-and-salary earnings of automotive service technicians and mechanics, including commission, were $16.24 in May 2006. The middle 50 percent earned between $11.96 and $21.56 per hour. The lowest 10 percent earned less than $9.17, and the highest 10 percent earned more than $27.22 per hour. Median annual earnings in the industries employing the largest numbers of service technicians were as follows:

Local government, excluding schools	$19.07
Automobile dealers	18.85
Automotive repair and maintenance	14.55
Gasoline stations	14.51
Automotive parts, accessories, and tire stores	14.38

Many experienced technicians employed by automobile dealers and independent repair shops receive a commission related to the labor cost charged to the customer. Under this system, weekly earnings depend on the amount of work completed. Employers frequently guarantee commissioned technicians a minimum weekly salary.

Automotive service technicians who are members of labor unions, such as the International Association of Machinists and Aerospace Workers; the International Union, United Automobile, Aerospace, and Agricultural Implement Workers of America; the Sheet Metal Workers' International Association; and the International Brotherhood of Teamsters, may enjoy more benefits than non-union workers do.

Related Occupations

Other workers who repair and service motor vehicles include automotive body and related repairers, diesel service technicians and mechanics, and small engine mechanics.

Sources of Additional Information

For more details about work opportunities, contact local automobile dealers and repair shops or local offices of the state employment service. The state employment service also may have information about training programs.

For general information about a career as an automotive service technician, contact

▸ Automotive Careers Today, 8400 Westpark Dr., MS #2, McLean, VA 22102. Internet: http://www.autocareerstoday.org

▸ Career Voyages, U.S. Department of Labor, 200 Constitution Ave., NW, Washington, DC 20210. Internet: http://www.careervoyages.gov/automotive-main.cfm

▸ National Automobile Dealers Association, 8400 Westpark Dr., McLean, VA 22102. Internet: http://www.nada.org

A list of certified automotive service technician training programs can be obtained from

▸ National Automotive Technicians Education Foundation, 101 Blue Seal Dr., SE, Suite 101, Leesburg, VA 20175. Internet: http://www.natef.org

For a directory of accredited private trade and technical schools that offer programs in automotive service technician training, contact

▸ Accrediting Commission of Career Schools and Colleges of Technology, 2101 Wilson Blvd., Suite 302, Arlington, VA 22201. Internet: http://www.accsct.org

Information on automobile manufacturer-sponsored programs in automotive service technology can be obtained from

▸ Automotive Youth Educational Systems (AYES), 100 W. Big Beaver, Suite 300, Troy, MI 48084. Internet: http://www.ayes.org

Information on how to become a certified automotive service technician is available from

▸ National Institute for Automotive Service Excellence (ASE), 101 Blue Seal Dr. SE, Suite 101, Leesburg, VA 20175. Internet: http://www.asecert.org

Barbers, Cosmetologists, and Other Personal Appearance Workers

(O*NET 39-5011.00, 39-5012.00, 39-5091.00, 39-5092.00, 39-5093.00, and 39-5094.00)

Significant Points

■ A state license is required for barbers, cosmetologists, and most other personal appearance workers, although qualifications vary by state.

■ About 46 percent of workers are self employed; many also work flexible schedules.

Nature of the Work

Barbers and cosmetologists focus on providing hair care services to enhance the appearance of consumers. Other personal appearance workers, such as manicurists and pedicurists, shampooers, theatrical and performance makeup artists, and skin care specialists provide specialized beauty services that help clients look and feel their best.

Barbers cut, trim, shampoo, and style hair mostly for male clients. They also may fit hairpieces and offer scalp treatments and facial shaving. In many states, barbers are licensed to color, bleach, or highlight hair and to offer permanent-wave services. Barbers also may provide skin care and nail treatments.

Hairdressers, hairstylists, and cosmetologists offer a wide range of beauty services, such as shampooing, cutting, coloring, and styling of hair. They may advise clients on how to care for their hair at home. In addition, cosmetologists may be trained to give manicures, pedicures, and scalp and facial treatments; provide makeup analysis; and clean and style wigs and hairpieces.

A number of workers offer specialized services. *Manicurists and pedicurists,* called *nail technicians* in some states, work exclusively on nails and provide manicures, pedicures, polishing, and nail extensions to clients. Another group of specialists is *skin care specialists*, or *estheticians*, who cleanse and beautify the skin by giving facials, full-body treatments, and head and neck massages as well as apply makeup. They also may remove hair through waxing or, if properly trained, laser treatments. *Theatrical and performance makeup artists*, apply makeup to enhance performing artists' appearance for movie, television, or stage performances. Finally, in larger salons, *shampooers* specialize in shampooing and conditioning hair.

In addition to working with clients, personal appearance workers may keep records of hair color or skin care regimens used by their regular clients. A growing number actively sell hair, skin, and nail care products. Barbers, cosmetologists, and other personal appearance workers who operate their own salons have managerial duties that may include hiring, supervising, and firing workers, as well as keeping business and inventory records, ordering supplies, and arranging for advertising.

Work environment. Most full-time barbers, cosmetologists, and other personal appearance workers put in a 40-hour week, but longer hours are common, especially among self-employed workers. Work schedules may include evenings and weekends, the times when beauty salons and barbershops are busiest. In 2006, about 31 percent

of cosmetologists and 19 percent of barbers worked part time, and 16 percent of cosmetologists and 11 percent of barbers had variable schedules.

Barbers, cosmetologists, and other personal appearance workers usually work in clean, pleasant surroundings with good lighting and ventilation. Good health and stamina are important, because these workers are on their feet for most of their shift. Prolonged exposure to some hair and nail chemicals may cause irritation, so protective clothing, such as plastic gloves or aprons, may be worn.

Training, Other Qualifications, and Advancement

All states require barbers, cosmetologists, and other personal appearance workers to be licensed, with the exceptions of shampooers and makeup artists. To qualify for a license, most job seekers are required to graduate from a state-licensed barber or cosmetology school.

Education and training. A high school diploma or GED is required for some personal appearance workers in some states. In addition, most states require that barbers and cosmetologists complete a program in a state-licensed barber or cosmetology school. Programs in hairstyling, skin care, and other personal appearance services can be found in both high schools and in public or private postsecondary vocational schools.

Full-time programs in barbering and cosmetology usually last nine months and may lead to an associate degree, but training for manicurists and pedicurists and skin care specialists requires significantly less time. Makeup artists can attend schools that specialize in this subject, but it is not required. Shampooers generally do not need formal training. Most professionals take advanced courses in hairstyling or other personal appearance services to keep up with the latest trends. They also may take courses in sales and marketing.

During their first weeks on the job, new workers may be given relatively simple tasks. Once they have demonstrated their skills, they are gradually permitted to perform more complicated procedures, such as coloring hair. As they continue to work in the field, more training usually is required to help workers learn the techniques particular to each salon and to build on the basics learned in cosmetology school. Personal appearance workers attend training at salons, cosmetology schools, or industry trade shows throughout their careers.

Licensure. All states require barbers, cosmetologists, and other personal appearance workers to be licensed, with the exceptions of shampooers and makeup artists. Qualifications for a license vary by state, but generally a person must have a high school diploma or GED, be at least 16 years old, and have graduated from a state-licensed barber or cosmetology school. After graduating from a state approved training program, students take a state licensing examination. The exam consists of a written test and, in some cases, a practical test of styling skills or an oral examination. In many states, cosmetology training may be credited toward a barbering license, and vice versa, and a few states combine the two licenses. Most states require separate licensing examinations for manicurists, pedicurists, and skin care specialists.

Some states have reciprocity agreements that allow licensed barbers and cosmetologists to obtain a license in a different state without additional formal training, but such agreements are uncommon.

Consequently, persons who wish to work in a particular state should review the laws of that state before entering a training program.

Other qualifications. Successful personal appearance workers should have an understanding of fashion, art, and technical design. They also must keep a neat personal appearance and a clean work area. Interpersonal skills, image, and attitude play an important role in career success. As client retention and retail sales become an increasingly important part of salons' revenue, the ability to be an effective salesperson becomes ever more vital for salon workers. Some cosmetology schools consider "people skills" to be such an integral part of the job that they require coursework in that area. Business skills are important for those who plan to operate their own salons.

Advancement. Advancement usually takes the form of higher earnings as barbers and cosmetologists gain experience and build a steady clientele. Some barbers and cosmetologists manage salons, lease booth space in salons, or open their own salons after several years of experience. Others teach in barber or cosmetology schools or provide training through vocational schools. Still others advance to become sales representatives, image or fashion consultants, or examiners for state licensing boards.

Employment

Barbers, cosmetologists, and other personal appearance workers held about 825,000 jobs in 2006. Of these, barbers and cosmetologists held 677,000 jobs, manicurists and pedicurists 78,000, skin care specialists 38,000, and shampooers 29,000. Theatrical and performance makeup artists held 2,100 jobs.

Most of these workers are employed in beauty salons or barber shops, but they also are found in nail salons, day and resort spas, and nursing and other residential care homes. Nearly every town has a barbershop or beauty salon, but employment in this occupation is concentrated in the most populous cities and states. Theatrical and performance makeup artists work for movie and television studios, performing arts companies, and event promoters. Some apply makeup in retail stores.

About 46 percent of all barbers, cosmetologists, and other personal appearance workers are self-employed. Many of these workers own their own salon, but a growing number of the self-employed lease booth space or a chair from the salon's owner.

Job Outlook

Overall employment of barbers, cosmetologists, and other personal appearance workers is projected to grow slightly faster than the average for all occupations. Opportunities for entry level workers should be favorable, while job candidates at high-end establishments will face keen competition.

Employment change. Personal appearance workers will grow by 14 percent from 2006 to 2016, which is faster than the average for all occupations. This growth primarily will be a result of an increasing population and from the growing demand for personal appearance services, particularly skin care services.

Employment trends are expected to vary among the different occupational specialties. Employment of hairdressers, hairstylists, and cosmetologists should increase by 12 percent because many now cut and style both men's and women's hair and because the demand for hair treatment by teens and aging baby boomers is expected to remain steady or even grow. As a result, fewer people are expected to go to barber shops and employment of barbers is expected to see relatively little change in employment.

Continued growth in the number of nail salons and full-service day spas will generate numerous job openings for manicurists, pedicurists, and skin care specialists. Employment of manicurists and pedicurists will grow by 28 percent, while employment of shampooers will increase by 13 percent. Estheticians and other skin care specialists will see large gains in employment, and are expected to grow 34 percent as more facial procedures to improve one's complexion become available and become more popular in spas and some medical settings. Makeup artists are expected to grow by 40 percent, but because of its relatively small size, the occupation will only add a few hundred jobs over the decade.

Job prospects. Job opportunities generally should be good. However, competition is expected for jobs and clients at higher paying salons as applicants compete with a large pool of licensed and experienced cosmetologists for these positions. More numerous than those arising from job growth, an abundance of job openings will come about from the need to replace workers who transfer to other occupations, retire, or leave the labor force for other reasons. Opportunities will be best for those with previous experience and for those licensed to provide a broad range of services.

Earnings

Median hourly earnings in May 2006 for salaried hairdressers, hairstylists, and cosmetologists, including tips and commission, were $10.25. The middle 50 percent earned between $7.92 and $13.75. The lowest 10 percent earned less than $6.68, and the highest 10 percent earned more than $18.78.

Median hourly earnings in May 2006 for salaried barbers, including tips, were $11.13. The middle 50 percent earned between $8.71 and

Projections data from the National Employment Matrix

Occupational Title	SOC Code	Employment, 2006	Projected employment, 2016	Change, 2006-16	
				Number	Percent
Personal appearance workers	39-5000	825,000	942,000	117,000	14
Barbers and cosmetologists..	39-5010	677,000	755,000	77,000	11
Barbers	39-5011	60,000	61,000	600	1
Hairdressers, hairstylists, and cosmetologists..........................	39-5012	617,000	694,000	77,000	12
Miscellaneous personal appearance workers	39-5090	148,000	187,000	39,000	27
Makeup artists, theatrical and performance	39-5091	2,100	3,000	900	40
Manicurists and pedicurists..	39-5092	78,000	100,000	22,000	28
Shampooers	39-5093	29,000	33,000	3,900	13
Skin care specialists	39-5094	38,000	51,000	13,000	34

NOTE: Data in this table are rounded.

© JIST Works

$14.25. The lowest 10 percent earned less than $7.12, and the highest 10 percent earned more than $20.56.

Among skin care specialists, median hourly earnings, including tips, were $12.58, for manicurists and pedicurists $9.23, and for shampooers $7.78.

While earnings for entry-level workers usually are low, earnings can be considerably higher for those with experience. A number of factors, such as the size and location of the salon, determine the total income of personal appearance workers. They may receive commissions based on the price of the service, or a salary based on the number of hours worked, and many receive commissions on the products they sell. In addition, some salons pay bonuses to employees who bring in new business. For many personal appearance workers the ability to attract and hold regular clients are key factors in determining earnings.

Although some salons offer paid vacations and medical benefits, many self-employed and part-time workers in this occupation do not enjoy such benefits. Some personal appearance workers receive free trail products from manufacturers in the hope that they will recommend the products to clients.

Related Occupations

Other workers who provide a personal service to clients and are usually professionally licensed or certified include massage therapists and fitness workers.

Sources of Additional Information

For details on state licensing requirements and approved barber or cosmetology schools, contact your state boards of barber or cosmetology examiners.

State licensing board requirements and a list of licensed training schools for cosmetologists may be obtained from

▸ National Accrediting Commission of Cosmetology Arts and Sciences, 4401 Ford Ave., Suite 1300, Alexandria, VA 22302. Internet: http://www.naccas.org

Information about a career in cosmetology is available from

▸ National Cosmetology Association, 401 N. Michigan Ave., 22nd floor, Chicago, IL 60611. Internet: http://www.ncacares.org

For information on a career as a barber, contact

▸ National Association of Barber Boards of America, 2703 Pine Street, Arkadelphia, AR 71923. Internet: http://www.nationalbarberboards.com

An additional list of private schools for several different types of personal appearance workers is available from

▸ Beauty Schools Directory. Internet: http://www.beautyschoolsdirectory.com

Bill and Account Collectors

(O*NET 43-3011.00)

Significant Points

■ Almost 1 in 4 collectors works for a collection agency; others work in banks, retail stores, government, physicians' offices, hospitals, and other institutions that lend money and extend credit.

■ Most jobs in this occupation require only a high school diploma, though many employers prefer workers with some postsecondary training.

■ Much faster than average employment growth is expected as companies focus more efforts on collecting unpaid debts.

Nature of the Work

Bill and account collectors, often called simply *collectors*, keep track of accounts that are overdue and attempt to collect payment on them. Some are employed by third-party collection agencies, while others—known as "in-house collectors"—work directly for the original creditors, such as department stores, hospitals, or banks.

The duties of bill and account collectors are similar across the many different organizations in which they work. First, collectors are called upon to locate and notify customers of delinquent accounts, usually over the telephone, but sometimes by letter. When customers move without leaving a forwarding address, collectors may check with the post office, telephone companies, credit bureaus, or former neighbors to obtain the new address. The attempt to find the new address is called "skip tracing." New computer systems assist in tracing by automatically tracking when customers change their address or contact information on any of their open accounts.

Once collectors find the debtor, they inform him or her of the overdue account and solicit payment. If necessary, they review the terms of the sale, service, or credit contract with the customer. Collectors also may attempt to learn the cause of the delay in payment. Where feasible, they offer the customer advice on how to pay off the debts, such as taking out a bill consolidation loan. However, the collector's prime objective is always to ensure that the customer pays the debt in question.

If a customer agrees to pay, collectors record this commitment and check later to verify that the payment was made. Collectors may have authority to grant an extension of time if customers ask for one. If a customer fails to pay, collectors prepare a statement indicating the customer's action for the credit department of the establishment. In more extreme cases, collectors may initiate repossession proceedings, disconnect the customer's service, or hand the account over to an attorney for legal action. Most collectors handle other administrative functions for the accounts assigned to them, including recording changes of address and purging the records of the deceased.

Collectors use computers and a variety of automated systems to keep track of overdue accounts. In sophisticated predictive dialer systems, a computer dials the telephone automatically, and the collector speaks only when a connection has been made. Such systems eliminate time spent calling busy or nonanswering numbers. Many collectors use regular telephones, but others wear headsets like those used by telephone operators.

Work environment. In-house bill and account collectors typically are employed in an office environment, and those who work for third-party collection agencies may work in a call-center environment. Workers spend most of their time on the phone tracking down and contacting people with debts. The work can be stressful as some customers are confrontational when pressed about their debts. Still, some appreciate assistance in resolving their outstanding debt. Collectors may also feel pressured to meet targets for debt recovered in a certain period.

Bill and account collectors often have to work evenings and weekends, when it is easier to reach people. Many collectors work

Projections data from the National Employment Matrix

Occupational Title	SOC Code	Employment, 2006	Projected employment, 2016	Change, 2006-16	
				Number	Percent
Bill and account collectors..	43-3011	434,000	534,000	99,000	23

NOTE: Data in this table are rounded.

part time or on flexible work schedules, though the majority work 40 hours per week.

Training, Other Qualifications, and Advancement

Most employers require collectors to have at a least a high school diploma and prefer some customer service experience. Employers usually provide on-the-job training to new employees.

Education and training. Most bill and account collectors are required to have at least a high school diploma. However, employers prefer workers who have completed some college or who have experience in other occupations that involve contact with the public.

Once hired, workers usually receive on-the-job training. Under the guidance of a supervisor or some other senior worker, new employees learn company procedures. Some formal classroom training also may be necessary, such as training in specific computer software. Additional training topics usually include telephone techniques and negotiation skills. Workers are also instructed in the laws governing the collection of debt as mandated by the Fair Debt Collection Practices Act, which applies to all third party and some in-house collectors.

Other qualifications. Workers should have good communication and people skills because they need to speak to customers daily, some of whom may be in stressful financial situations. In addition, collectors should be computer literate, and experience with advanced telecommunications equipment is also useful.

Advancement. Collectors most often advance by taking on more complex cases. Some might become team leaders or supervisors. Workers who acquire additional skills, experience, and training improve their advancement opportunities.

Employment

Bill and account collectors held about 434,000 jobs in 2006. About 24 percent of collectors work in the business support services industries, which includes collection agencies. Many others work in banks, retail stores, government, physician's offices, hospitals, and other institutions that lend money and extend credit.

Job Outlook

Employment of bill and account collectors is expected to grow much faster than the average for all occupations through 2016. Job prospects are expected to be favorable because growth in the occupation and the many people who leave the occupation are expected to create plentiful openings.

Employment change. Over the 2006–2016 decade, employment of bill and account collectors is expected to grow by 23 percent, which is much faster than the average for all occupations. Cash flow is becoming increasingly important to companies, which are now placing greater emphasis on collecting unpaid debts sooner. Thus, the workload for collectors is expected to continue to increase as they seek to collect not only debts that are relatively old, but also ones that are more recent. In addition, as more companies in a wide range of industries get involved in lending money and issuing credit cards, they will need to hire collectors because debt levels will likely continue to rise.

Hospitals and physicians' offices are two of the fastest growing industries requiring collectors. With insurance reimbursements not keeping up with cost increases, the health care industry is seeking to recover more money from patients. Government agencies also are making more use of collectors to collect on everything from parking tickets to child-support payments and past-due taxes. In addition, the Internal Revenue Service (IRS) has begun outsourcing the collection of overdue federal taxes to third-party collection agencies, adding to the need for workers in this occupation.

Despite the increasing demand for bill collectors, employment growth may be somewhat constrained by the increased use of third-party debt collectors, who are generally more efficient than in-house collectors. Also, some firms are beginning to use offshore collection agencies, whose lower cost structures allow them to collect debts that are too small for domestic collection agencies.

Job prospects. Job openings will not be created from employment growth alone. A significant number of openings will result from the many people who leave the occupation and must be replaced. As a result, job opportunities should be favorable.

Contrary to the pattern in most occupations, employment of bill and account collectors tends to rise during recessions, reflecting the difficulty that many people have in meeting their financial obligations. However, collectors usually have more success at getting people to repay their debts when the economy is good.

Earnings

Median hourly earnings of bill and account collectors were $13.97 in May 2006. The middle 50 percent earned between $11.49 and $17.14. The lowest 10 percent earned less than $9.61, and the highest 10 percent earned more than $21.12. Many bill and account collectors earn commissions based on the amount of debt they recover.

Related Occupations

Bill and account collectors review and collect information on accounts. Other occupations with similar responsibilities include credit authorizers, checkers, and clerks; loan officers; and interviewers.

Sources of Additional Information

Career information on bill and account collectors is available from

▸ ACA International, The Association of Credit and Collection Professionals, P.O. Box 390106, Minneapolis, MN 55439. Internet: http://www.acainternational.org

© JIST Works

Boilermakers

(O*NET 47-2011.00)

Significant Points

- Boilermakers use potentially dangerous equipment and the work is physically demanding.

- Most boilermakers learn through a formal apprenticeship; people with a welding certification or other welding training get priority in selection to apprenticeship programs.

- Excellent employment opportunities are expected.

Nature of the Work

Boilermakers and *boilermaker mechanics* make, install, and repair boilers, closed vats, and other large vessels or containers that hold liquids and gases. Boilers heat water or other fluids under extreme pressure for use in generating electric power and to provide heat and power in buildings, factories, and ships. Chemicals, oil, beer, and hundreds of other products are processed and stored in the tanks and vats made by the nation's boilermakers.

In addition to installing and maintaining boilers and other vessels, boilermakers also help erect and repair air pollution equipment, blast furnaces, water treatment plants, storage and process tanks, and smoke stacks. Boilermakers also install refractory brick and other heat-resistant materials in fireboxes or pressure vessels. Some install and maintain the huge pipes used in dams to send water to and from hydroelectric power generation turbines.

Electric power plants harness highly pressurized steam in a boiler to spin the blades of a turbine, which is attached to an electric generator. In most plants, coal burned in a firebox is the dominant fuel used to generate steam in the boiler.

Because boilers last a long time—sometimes 50 years or more—boilermakers regularly maintain them and upgrade components, such as boiler tubes, heating elements, and ductwork, to increase efficiency. They regularly inspect fittings, feed pumps, safety and check valves, water and pressure gauges, boiler controls, and auxiliary machinery. For closed vats and other large vessels, boilermakers clean or supervise cleaning using scrapers, wire brushes, and cleaning solvents. They repair or replace defective parts using hand and power tools, gas torches, and welding equipment, and may operate metalworking machinery to repair or make parts. They also dismantle leaky boilers, patch weak spots with metal stock, replace defective sections, and strengthen joints.

Boilers and other high-pressure vessels used to hold liquids and gases usually are made in sections by casting each piece out of steel, iron, copper, or stainless steel. Manufacturers are increasingly automating this process to improve the quality of these vessels. Boiler sections are then welded together, often using robotic welding systems or automated orbital welding machines, which make more consistent welds than are possible by hand and eliminates some of the monotony of the task. Small boilers may be assembled in the manufacturing plant; larger boilers usually are prefabricated in numerous pieces and assembled on site, although they may be temporarily assembled in a fabrication shop to ensure a proper fit before final assembly on the permanent site.

Before making or repairing a fabricated metal product, a boilermaker studies design drawings and creates full size patterns or templates, using straightedges, squares, transits, and tape measures. After the various sized shapes and pieces are marked out on metal, boilermakers use hand and power tools or flame cutting torches to make the cuts. The sections of metal are then bent into shape and accurately lined up before they are welded together. If the plate sections are very large, heavy cranes are used to lift the parts into place. Boilermakers align sections using plumb bobs, levels, wedges, and turnbuckles. They use hammers, files, grinders, and cutting torches to remove irregular edges so that metal pieces fit together properly. They then join them by bolting, welding, or riveting. Boilermakers also align and attach water tubes, stacks and liners, safety and check valves, water and pressure gauges, and other parts and test complete vessels for leaks or other defects.

Work environment. Boilermakers often use potentially dangerous equipment, such as acetylene torches and power grinders; handle heavy parts and tools; and work on ladders or on top of large vessels. Dams, boilers, storage tanks, and pressure vessels are usually of substantial size, thus a major portion of boilermaker work is performed at great heights, sometimes hundreds of feet above the ground in the case of dams. The work is physically demanding and may be done in cramped quarters inside boilers, vats, or tanks that are often dark, damp, and poorly ventilated. Field construction work is performed outside so exposure to all types of weather conditions, including extreme heat and cold, is common. To reduce the chance of injuries, boilermakers often wear hardhats, harnesses, protective clothing, ear plugs, safety glasses and shoes, and respirators.

Boilermakers may experience extended periods of overtime when equipment is shut down for maintenance. Overtime work also may be necessary to meet construction or production deadlines. However, since most field construction and repair work is contract work, there may be periods of unemployment when a contract is complete. Many boilermakers must travel to a project and live away from home for long periods of time.

Training, Other Qualifications, and Advancement

Most boilermakers learn this trade through a formal apprenticeship. A few become boilermakers through a combination of trade or technical school training and employer-provided training.

Education and training. Most boilermakers train in both boilermaking and structural fabrication. Apprenticeship programs usually consist of 6,000 hours or four years of paid on-the-job training, supplemented by a minimum of 144 hours of classroom instruction each year in subjects such as set-up and assembly rigging, plate and pressure welding, blueprint reading, and layout. Those who finish registered apprenticeships are certified as fully qualified journeyworkers.

Most apprentices must be high school graduates or have a GED or its equivalent. Those with welding training or a welding certification will have priority in applying for apprenticeship programs. Experienced boilermakers often attend apprenticeship classes or seminars to learn about new equipment, procedures, and technology. When an apprenticeship becomes available, the local union publicizes the opportunity by notifying local vocational schools and high school vocational programs.

Other qualifications. The work of boilermakers requires a high degree of technical skill, knowledge, and dedication. Because the tools and equipment used by boilermakers are typically heavier and

Projections data from the National Employment Matrix

Occupational Title	SOC Code	Employment, 2006	Projected employment, 2016	Change, 2006-16	
				Number	Percent
Boilermakers	47-2011	18,000	20,000	2,500	14

NOTE: Data in this table are rounded.

more cumbersome than those in other construction trades, having physical strength and stamina is important. Good manual dexterity is also important. Most apprentices must be at least 18 years old.

Advancement. Some boilermakers advance to supervisory positions. Because of their extensive training, those trained through apprenticeships usually have an advantage in getting promoted over those who have not gone through the full program.

Employment

Boilermakers held about 18,000 jobs in 2006. About 63 percent worked in the construction industry, assembling and erecting boilers and other vessels. Around 18 percent worked in manufacturing, primarily in boiler manufacturing shops, iron and steel plants, petroleum refineries, chemical plants, and shipyards. Some also worked for boiler repair firms or railroads.

Job Outlook

Employment of boilermakers is expected to grow faster than average. Excellent employment opportunities are expected.

Employment change. Overall employment of boilermakers is expected to grow by 14 percent between 2006 and 2016, faster than the average for all occupations. Growth will be driven by the need to maintain and upgrade, rather than replace, the many existing boilers that are getting older, and by the need to meet the growing population's demand for electric power. While boilers historically have lasted over 50 years, the need to replace components, such as boiler tubes, heating elements, and ductwork, is an ongoing process that will continue to spur demand for boilermakers. To meet the requirements of the Clean Air Act, utility companies also will need to upgrade many of their boiler systems in the next few years.

The Energy Policy Act of 2005 is expected to lead to the construction of many new clean-burning coal power plants, spurring demand for boilermakers. The law, designed to promote conservation and use of cleaner technologies in energy production through tax credits and higher efficiency standards, is expected to positively affect the occupation and the energy industry throughout the 2006–2016 projection period.

Installation of new boilers and pressure vessels, air pollution equipment, blast furnaces, water treatment plants, storage and process tanks, electric static precipitators, and stacks and liners, will further drive growth of boilermakers, although to a slightly lesser extent than repairs will.

Job prospects. Job prospects should be excellent because of job growth and because the work of a boilermaker remains hazardous and physically demanding, leading some new apprentices to seek other types of work. An even greater number of openings will arise from the numerous boilermakers expected to retire over the projection decade.

People who have welding training or a welding certificate should have the best opportunities for being selected for boilermaker apprenticeship programs.

Most industries that purchase boilers are sensitive to economic conditions. Therefore, during economic downturns, boilermakers in the construction industry may be laid off. However, maintenance and repairs of boilers must continue even during economic downturns so boilermaker mechanics in manufacturing and other industries generally have more stable employment.

Earnings

In May 2006, the median annual earnings of wage and salary boilermakers were about $46,960. The middle 50 percent earned between $37,300 and $59,710. The lowest 10 percent earned less than $30,410, and the highest 10 percent earned more than $71,170. Apprentices generally start at about half of journey-level wages, with wages gradually increasing to the journey wage as workers gain skills.

Many boilermakers belong to labor unions, most to the International Brotherhood of Boilermakers. Other boilermakers are members of the International Association of machinists, the United Automobile Workers, or the United Steelworkers of America.

Related Occupations

Workers in a number of other occupations assemble, install, or repair metal equipment or machines. These occupations include assemblers and fabricators; machinists; industrial machinery mechanics and maintenance workers; millwrights; pipelayers, plumbers, pipefitters, and steamfitters; sheet metal workers; tool and die makers; and welding, soldering, and brazing workers.

Sources of Additional Information

For more information about boilermaking apprenticeships or other training opportunities, contact local offices of the unions previously mentioned, local construction companies and boiler manufacturers, or the local office of your state employment service. You can also find information on the registered apprenticeships together with links to state apprenticeship programs on the U.S. Department of Labor's Web site: http://www.doleta.gov/atels_bat. Apprenticeship information is also available from the U.S. Department of Labor's toll free helpline: 1 (877) 872-5627.

For information on apprenticeships and the boilermaking occupation, contact

▸ International Brotherhood of Boilermakers, Iron Ship Builders, Blacksmiths, Forgers, and Helpers, 753 State Ave., Suite 570, Kansas City, KS 66101. Internet: http://www.boilermakers.org

For general information on apprenticeships and how to get them, see the *Occupational Outlook Quarterly* article "Apprenticeships: Career training, credentials—and a paycheck in your pocket," online at http://www.bls.gov/opub/ooq/2002/summer/art01.pdf and in print at many libraries and career centers.

Bookkeeping, Accounting, and Auditing Clerks

(O*NET 43-3031.00)

Significant Points

- Bookkeeping, accounting, and auditing clerks held more than 2.1 million jobs in 2006 and are employed in every industry.

- Employment is projected to grow as fast as the average due to a growing economy.

- The large size of this occupation ensures plentiful job openings, including many opportunities for temporary and part-time work.

Nature of the Work

Bookkeeping, accounting, and auditing clerks are financial record-keepers. They update and maintain accounting records, including those which calculate expenditures, receipts, accounts payable and receivable, and profit and loss. These workers have a wide range of skills from full-charge bookkeepers who can maintain an entire company's books to accounting clerks who handle specific tasks. All of these clerks make numerous computations each day and increasingly must be comfortable using computers to calculate and record data.

In small businesses, *bookkeepers and bookkeeping clerks* often have responsibility for some or all of the accounts, known as the general ledger. They record all transactions and post debits (costs) and credits (income). They also produce financial statements and prepare reports and summaries for supervisors and managers. Bookkeepers also prepare bank deposits by compiling data from cashiers, verifying and balancing receipts, and sending cash, checks, or other forms of payment to the bank. They also may handle payroll, make purchases, prepare invoices, and keep track of overdue accounts.

In large-companies' accounting departments, *accounting clerks* have more specialized tasks. Their titles, such as accounts payable clerk or accounts receivable clerk, often reflect the type of accounting they do. In addition, their responsibilities vary by level of experience. Entry-level accounting clerks post details of transactions, total accounts, and compute interest charges. They also may monitor loans and accounts to ensure that payments are up to date. More advanced accounting clerks may total, balance, and reconcile billing vouchers; ensure the completeness and accuracy of data on accounts; and code documents according to company procedures.

Accounting clerks post transactions in journals and on computer files and update the files when needed. Senior clerks also review computer printouts against regularly maintained journals and make necessary corrections. They may review invoices and statements to ensure that all the information appearing on them is accurate and complete, and they may reconcile computer reports with operating reports.

Auditing clerks verify records of transactions posted by other workers. They check figures, postings, and documents to ensure that they are correct, mathematically accurate, and properly coded. They also correct or note errors for accountants or other workers to fix.

As organizations continue to computerize their financial records, many bookkeeping, accounting, and auditing clerks use specialized accounting software, spreadsheets, and databases. Most clerks now enter information from receipts or bills into computers, and the information is then stored either electronically or as computer printouts, or both. The widespread use of computers also has enabled bookkeeping, accounting, and auditing clerks to take on additional responsibilities, such as payroll, procurement, and billing. Many of these functions require these clerks to write letters and make phone calls to customers or clients.

Work environment. Bookkeeping, accounting, and auditing clerks work in an office environment. They may experience eye and muscle strain, backaches, headaches, and repetitive motion injuries from using computers on a daily basis. Clerks may have to sit for extended periods while reviewing detailed data.

Many bookkeeping, accounting, and auditing clerks work regular business hours and a standard 40-hour week, although some may work occasional evenings and weekends. About 24 percent of these clerks worked part time in 2006.

Bookkeeping, accounting, and auditing clerks may work longer hours to meet deadlines at the end of the fiscal year, during tax time, or when monthly or yearly accounting audits are performed. Additionally, those who work in hotels, restaurants, and stores may put in overtime during peak holiday and vacation seasons.

Training, Other Qualifications, and Advancement

Employers usually prefer bookkeeping, accounting, and auditing clerks to have at least a high school diploma and some accounting coursework or relevant work experience. Clerks should also have good communication skills, be detail-oriented, and trustworthy.

Education and training. Most bookkeeping, accounting, and auditing clerks are required to have a high school degree at a minimum. However, having some college is increasingly important and an associate degree in business or accounting is required for some positions. Although a bachelor's degree is rarely required, graduates may accept bookkeeping, accounting, and auditing clerk positions to get into a particular company or to enter the accounting or finance field with the hope of eventually being promoted.

Once hired, bookkeeping, accounting, and auditing clerks usually receive on-the-job training. Under the guidance of a supervisor or another more experienced employee, new clerks learn company procedures. Some formal classroom training also may be necessary, such as training in specialized computer software.

Other qualifications. Experience in a related job and working in an office environment also is recommended. Employers prefer workers who can use computers; knowledge of word processing and spreadsheet software is especially valuable.

Bookkeeping, accounting, and auditing clerks must be careful, orderly, and detail-oriented in order to avoid making errors and to recognize errors made by others. These workers also should be discreet and trustworthy because they frequently come in contact with confidential material. They should also have good communication skills because they increasingly work with customers. In addition, all bookkeeping, accounting, and auditing clerks should have a strong aptitude for numbers.

Certification and advancement. Bookkeeping, accounting, and auditing clerks, particularly those who handle all the recordkeeping for a company, may find it beneficial to become certified. The

Projections data from the National Employment Matrix

Occupational Title	SOC Code	Employment, 2006	Projected employment, 2016	Change, 2006-16	
				Number	Percent
Bookkeeping, accounting, and auditing clerks	43-3031	2,114,000	2,377,000	264,000	12

NOTE: Data in this table are rounded.

Certified Bookkeeper (CB) designation, awarded by the American Institute of Professional Bookkeepers, demonstrates that individuals have the skills and knowledge needed to carry out all bookkeeping functions, including overseeing payroll and balancing accounts according to accepted accounting procedures. For certification, candidates must have at least two years of bookkeeping experience, pass a four-part examination, and adhere to a code of ethics. Several colleges and universities offer a preparatory course for certification; some offer courses online.

Bookkeeping, accounting, and auditing clerks usually advance by taking on more duties for higher pay or by transferring to a closely related occupation. Most companies fill office and administrative support supervisory and managerial positions by promoting individuals from within their organizations, so clerks who acquire additional skills, experience, and training improve their advancement opportunities. With appropriate experience and education, some bookkeeping, accounting, and auditing clerks may become accountants or auditors.

Employment

Bookkeeping, accounting, and auditing clerks held more than 2.1 million jobs in 2006. They work in all industries and at all levels of government. Local government and the accounting, tax preparation, bookkeeping, and payroll services industry are among the individual industries employing the largest numbers of these clerks.

Job Outlook

Job growth is projected to be average through 2016, and job prospects should be good as a large number of bookkeeping, accounting, and auditing clerks are expected to retire or transfer to other occupations.

Employment change. Employment of bookkeeping, accounting, and auditing clerks is projected to grow by 12 percent during the 2006–2016 decade, which is as fast as the average for all occupations. Due its size, this occupation will have among the largest numbers of new jobs arise, about 264,000 over the projections decade.

A growing economy will result in more financial transactions and other activities that require recordkeeping by these workers. Additionally, the Sarbanes-Oxley Act of 2002 calls for more accuracy and transparency in the reporting of financial data for public companies, which will increase the demand for these workers. Moreover, companies will continue to outsource their bookkeeping and accounting departments to independent accounting, tax preparation, bookkeeping, and payroll services firms. However, at the same time, the increasing use of tax preparation software in place of the services of tax professionals will hinder growth somewhat.

Clerks who can carry out a wider range of bookkeeping and accounting activities will be in greater demand than specialized clerks. Demand for full-charge bookkeepers is expected to increase, for example, because they do much of the work of accountants and perform a wider variety of financial transactions, from payroll to billing. Technological advances will continue to change the way these workers perform their daily tasks, such as using computer software programs to maintain records, but will not decrease the demand for these workers, especially in smaller establishments.

Job prospects. Some job openings are expected to result from job growth, but even more openings will stem from the need to replace existing workers who leave. Each year, numerous jobs will become available as clerks transfer to other occupations or leave the labor force. The large size of this occupation ensures plentiful job openings, including many opportunities for temporary and part-time work. Certified Bookkeepers (CBs) and those with several years of accounting or bookkeeping experience will have the best job prospects.

Earnings

In May 2006, the median wage and salary earnings of bookkeeping, accounting, and auditing clerks were $30,560. The middle half of the occupation earned between $24,540 and $37,780. The top 10 percent of bookkeeping, accounting, and auditing clerks more than $46,020, and the bottom 10 percent earned less than $19,760.

Benefits offered by employers may vary by the type and size of establishment, but health insurance and paid leave are common.

Related Occupations

Bookkeeping, accounting, and auditing clerks work with financial records. Other workers who perform similar duties include accountants and auditors; bill and account collectors; billing and posting clerks and machine operators; brokerage clerks; credit authorizers, checkers, and clerks; payroll and timekeeping clerks; procurement clerks; and tellers.

Sources of Additional Information

For information on the Certified Bookkeeper designation, contact

▸ American Institute of Professional Bookkeepers, 6001 Montrose Rd., Suite 500, Rockville, MD 20852. Internet: http://www.aipb.org

Brickmasons, Blockmasons, and Stonemasons

(O*NET 47-2021.00 and 47-2022.00)

Significant Points

■ Job prospects are expected to be very good, especially for workers with restoration skills.

■ Most entrants learn informally on the job, but apprenticeship programs provide the most thorough training.

■ The work is usually outdoors and involves lifting heavy materials and working on scaffolds.

■ About 24 percent are self employed.

Nature of the Work

Brickmasons, blockmasons, and stonemasons create attractive, durable surfaces and structures. For thousands of years, these workers have built buildings, fences, roads, walkways, and walls using bricks, concrete blocks, and natural stone. The structures that they build will continue to be in demand for years to come.

The work varies in complexity, from laying a simple masonry walkway to installing an ornate exterior on a highrise building. Workers cut or break the materials used to create walls, floors, and other structures. Once their building materials are properly sized, they are laid with or without a binding material. These workers use their own perceptions and a variety of tools to ensure that the structure meets the desired standards. After finishing laying the bricks, blocks, or stone, these workers clean the finished product with a variety of cleaning agents.

Brickmasons and *blockmasons*—who often are called simply *bricklayers*—build and repair walls, floors, partitions, fireplaces, chimneys, and other structures with brick, precast masonry panels, concrete block, and other masonry materials. Some brickmasons specialize in installing firebrick linings in industrial furnaces.

When building a structure, brickmasons use one of two methods, either the corner lead or the corner pole. Using the corner lead method, they begin by constructing a pyramid of bricks at each corner—called a lead. After the corner leads are complete, less experienced brickmasons fill in the wall between the corners using a line from corner to corner to guide each course, or layer, of brick. Due to the precision needed, corner leads are time-consuming to erect and require the skills of experienced bricklayers.

Because of the expense associated with building corner leads, some brickmasons use corner poles, also called masonry guides, which enable them to build an entire wall at the same time. They fasten the corner poles (posts) in a plumb position to define the wall line and stretch a line between them. This line serves as a guide for each course of brick. Brickmasons then spread a bed of mortar (a cement, lime, sand, and water mixture) with a trowel (a flat, bladed metal tool with a handle), place the brick on the mortar bed, and press and tap the brick into place. Depending on blueprint specifications, brickmasons either cut bricks with a hammer and chisel or saw them to fit around windows, doors, and other openings. Mortar joints are then finished with jointing tools for a sealed, neat, uniform appearance. Although brickmasons typically use steel supports, or lintels, at window and door openings, they sometimes build brick arches, which support and enhance the beauty of the brickwork.

Refractory masons are brickmasons who specialize in installing firebrick and refractory tile in high-temperature boilers, furnaces, cupolas, ladles, and soaking pits in industrial establishments. Most of these workers are employed in steel mills, where molten materials flow on refractory beds from furnaces to rolling machines. They also are employed at oil refineries, glass furnaces, incinerators, and other locations requiring high temperatures during the manufacturing process.

After a structure is completed there is still work that often needs to be done. *Pointing, cleaning, and caulking* workers can be the final workers on a job or the primary workers on a restoration project. These workers use chemicals to clean the laid materials to give the structure a finished appearance. Older structures also need to be refurbished as the mortar or binding agents break down. In many cases a grinder or blade is used to carefully remove the old mortar.

Special care is taken to not damage the main structural integrity or the bricks, blocks, or stone. New mortar is then inserted. Depending on how much mortar is being replaced and how, it may take several applications to allow the new mortar to cure properly. These same masons replace and repair damaged masonry materials as part of the building's restoration process.

Stonemasons build stone walls, as well as set stone exteriors and floors. They work with two types of stone—natural cut stone, such as marble, granite, and limestone and artificial stone made from concrete, marble chips, or other masonry materials. Stonemasons usually work on nonresidential structures, such as houses of worship, hotels, and office buildings, but they also work on residences.

Stonemasons often work from a set of drawings, in which each stone has been numbered for identification. Helpers may locate and carry these prenumbered stones to the masons. A derrick operator using a hoist may be needed to lift large stone pieces into place.

When building a stone wall, masons set the first course of stones into a shallow bed of mortar. They then align the stones with wedges, plumb lines, and levels, and work them into position with various tools. Masons continue to build the wall by alternating layers of mortar and courses of stone. As the work progresses, masons remove the wedges, fill the joints between stones, and use a pointed metal tool, called a tuck pointer, to smooth the mortar to an attractive finish. To hold large stones in place, stonemasons attach brackets to the stone and weld or bolt these brackets to anchors in the wall. Finally, masons wash the stone with a cleansing solution to remove stains and dry mortar.

When setting stone floors, which often consist of large and heavy pieces of stone, masons first use a trowel to spread a layer of damp mortar over the surface to be covered. Using crowbars and hard rubber mallets for aligning and leveling, they then set the stone in the mortar bed. To finish, workers fill the joints and clean the stone slabs.

Masons use a special hammer and chisel to cut stone. They cut stone along the grain to make various shapes and sizes, and valuable pieces often are cut with a saw that has a diamond blade. Some masons specialize in setting marble which, in many respects, is similar to setting large pieces of stone. Brickmasons and stonemasons also repair imperfections and cracks, and replace broken or missing masonry units in walls and floors.

Most nonresidential buildings now are built with walls made of concrete block, brick veneer, stone, granite, marble, tile, or glass. In the past, masons doing nonresidential interior work mainly built block partition walls and elevator shafts, but because many types of masonry and stone are used in the interiors of today's nonresidential structures, these workers now must be more versatile. For example, some brickmasons and blockmasons now install structural insulated concrete units and wall panels. They also install a variety of masonry anchors and other masonry-associated accessories used in many highrise buildings.

Work environment. Brickmasons, blockmasons, and stonemasons usually work outdoors, but in contrast to the past when work slowed down in the winter months, new processes and materials are allowing these masons to work in a greater variety of weather conditions. Masons stand, kneel, and bend for long periods and often have to lift heavy materials. Common hazards include injuries from tools and falls from scaffolds, but these can often be avoided when proper safety equipment is used and safety practices are followed.

Most workers work a standard 40-hour week. Earnings for workers in these trades can be reduced on occasion because poor weather and slowdowns in construction activity limit the time they can work.

Training, Other Qualifications, and Advancement

Most brickmasons, blockmasons, and stonemasons pick up their skills informally, observing and learning from experienced workers. Many others receive initial training in vocational education schools or from industry-based programs common throughout the country. Others complete an apprenticeship, which generally provides the most thorough training.

Education and training. Individuals who learn the trade on the job usually start as helpers, laborers, or mason tenders. These workers carry materials, move or assemble scaffolds, and mix mortar. When the opportunity arises, they learn from experienced craftworkers how to mix and spread mortar, lay brick and block, or set stone. They also may learn restoration skills such as cleaning, pointing, and repointing. As they gain experience, they learn more difficult tasks and make the transition to full-fledged craftworkers. The learning period on the job may last longer than if trained in an apprenticeship program. Industry-based training programs offered through construction companies usually last between two and four years.

Apprenticeships for brickmasons, blockmasons, and stonemasons usually are sponsored by local contractors, trade associations, or local union-management committees. Apprenticeship programs usually require three years of on-the-job training, in addition to a minimum of 144 hours of classroom instruction each year in blueprint reading, mathematics, layout work, sketching, and other subjects. Applicants for apprenticeships must be at least 17 years old and in good physical condition. A high school education is preferable with courses in mathematics, mechanical drawing, and general shop.

Apprentices often start by working with laborers, carrying materials, mixing mortar, and building scaffolds for about a month. Next, apprentices learn to lay, align, and join brick and block. They may also learn on the job to work with stone and concrete, which enables them to work with more than one masonry material.

Bricklayers who work in nonresidential construction usually work for large contractors and receive well-rounded training—normally through apprenticeship in all phases of brick or stone work. Those who work in residential construction usually work primarily for small contractors and specialize in only one or two aspects of the job.

Some workers learn at technical schools that offer masonry courses. Entrance requirements and fees vary depending on the school and who is funding the program. Some people take courses before being hired, and some take them later as part of the on-the-job training.

Other qualifications. The most desired quality in workers is dependability and a strong work ethic. Knowledge of basic math including measurement, volume, mixing proportions, algebra, plane geometry, and mechanical drawing are important in this trade.

Advancement. With additional training and experience, brickmasons, blockmasons, and stonemasons may become supervisors for masonry contractors. Some eventually become owners of businesses employing many workers and may spend most of their time as managers. Others move into closely related areas such as construction management or building inspection. Many unionized Joint Apprenticeship and Training Committees offer continual "life long learning" through continuing education courses that help those members who want to advance their technical knowledge and their careers.

Employment

Brickmasons, blockmasons, and stonemasons held 182,000 jobs in 2006. The vast majority were brickmasons. Workers in these crafts are employed primarily by building, specialty trade, or general contractors.

About 24 percent of brickmasons, blockmasons, and stonemasons were self-employed. Many of the self-employed are contractors who work on small jobs, such as patios, walkways, and fireplaces.

Job Outlook

Average employment growth is expected. Job prospects should be very good, especially for workers with restoration skills.

Employment change. Jobs for brickmasons, blockmasons, and stonemasons are expected to increase 10 percent over the 2006–2016 decade, about as fast as the average for all occupations, as population and business growth create a need for new houses, industrial facilities, schools, hospitals, offices, and other structures. Also stimulating demand for workers will be the need to restore a growing number of old brick buildings. Moreover, the use of brick and stone for decorative work on building fronts, sidewalks, and in lobbies and foyers is increasing. Brick exteriors should remain very popular, reflecting a growing preference for durable exterior materials requiring little maintenance. Increased construction on hillsides also will spur the demand for new masons as designers create attractive areas that need retaining walls to hold soil in place. There is also an increased demand for durable homes that incorporate brick or stone in hurricane-prone areas.

Job prospects. Job opportunities for brickmasons, blockmasons, and stonemasons are expected to be very good through 2016. A large number of masons are expected to retire over the next decade. The large number of aging masonry buildings will increase opportunities for workers with restoration skills. Also, workers able to install new synthetic materials will have improved opportunities. Applicants who take masonry-related courses at technical schools will have better opportunities than those without these courses.

Employment of brickmasons, blockmasons, and stonemasons, like that of many other construction workers, is sensitive to changes in

Projections data from the National Employment Matrix

Occupational Title	SOC Code	Employment, 2006	Projected employment, 2016	Change, 2006-16	
				Number	Percent
Brickmasons, blockmasons, and stonemasons...................................	47-2020	182,000	200,000	18,000	10
Brickmasons and blockmasons..	47-2021	158,000	174,000	15,000	10
Stonemasons	47-2022	24,000	26,000	2,400	10

NOTE: Data in this table are rounded.

the economy. When the level of construction activity falls, workers in these trades can experience periods of unemployment. On the other hand, shortages of these workers may occur in some areas during peak periods of building activity.

Earnings

Median hourly earnings of wage and salary brickmasons and blockmasons in May 2006 were $20.66. The middle 50 percent earned between $15.96 and $26.26. The lowest 10 percent earned less than $12.24, and the highest 10 percent earned more than $32.43. Median hourly earnings in the two industries employing the largest number of brickmasons in May 2006 were $20.57 in the foundation, structure, and building exterior contractors industry and $20.67 in the masonry contractors industry.

Median hourly earnings of wage and salary stonemasons in May 2006 were $17.29. The middle 50 percent earned between $13.12 and $22.04. The lowest 10 percent earned less than $10.36, and the highest 10 percent earned more than $28.46.

Apprentices or helpers usually start at about 50 percent of the wage rate paid to experienced workers. Pay increases as apprentices gain experience and learn new skills. Employers usually increase apprentices' wages about every 6 months based on specific advancement criteria.

Some brickmasons, blockmasons, and stonemasons are members of the International Union of Bricklayers and Allied Craftsworkers.

Related Occupations

Brickmasons, blockmasons, and stonemasons combine a thorough knowledge of brick, concrete block, stone, and marble with manual skill to erect attractive, yet highly durable, structures. Workers in other occupations with similar skills include carpet, floor, and tile installers and finishers; cement masons, concrete finishers, segmental pavers, and terrazzo workers; and plasterers and stucco masons.

Sources of Additional Information

For details about apprenticeships or other work opportunities in these trades, contact local bricklaying, stonemasonry, or marble-setting contractors; the Associated Builders and Contractors; a local office of the International Union of Bricklayers and Allied Craftsworkers; a local joint union-management apprenticeship committee; or the nearest office of the state employment service or apprenticeship agency. Apprenticeship information is also available from the U.S. Department of Labor's toll free helpline: 1 (877) 872-5627 and online at: http://www.doleta.gov/atels_bat.

For general information on apprenticeships and how to get them, see the *Occupational Outlook Quarterly* article "Apprenticeships: Career training, credentials—and a paycheck in your pocket," online at http://www.bls.gov/opub/ooq/2002/summer/art01.pdf and in print in many libraries and career centers.

For information on training for brickmasons, blockmasons, and stonemasons, contact

- Associated Builders and Contractors, Workforce Development Division, 4250 North Fairfax Dr., 9th Floor, Arlington, VA 22203. Internet: http://www.trytools.org
- International Union of Bricklayers and Allied Craftworkers, International Masonry Institute National Training Center, 17101 Science Dr., Bowie, MD 20715. Internet: http://www.imiweb.org

- Mason Contractors Association of America, 33 South Roselle Rd., Schaumburg, IL 60193. Internet: http://www.masoncontractors.org
- National Association of Home Builders, Home Builders Institute, 1201 15th St. NW, Washington, DC 20005. Internet: http://www.hbi.org
- National Center for Construction Education and Research, 3600 NW 43rd St., Bldg. G, Gainesville, FL 32606. Internet: http://www.nccer.org

For general information about the work of bricklayers, contact

- Associated General Contractors of America, Inc., 2300 Wilson Blvd., Suite 400, Arlington, VA 22201. Internet: http://www.agc.org
- Brick Industry Association, 11490 Commerce Park Dr., Reston, VA 22091-1525. Internet: http://www.brickinfo.org
- National Concrete Masonry Association, 13750 Sunrise Valley Dr., Herndon, VA 20171-3499. Internet: http://www.ncma.org

Broadcast and Sound Engineering Technicians and Radio Operators

(O*NET 27-4011.00, 27-4012.00, 27-4013.00, and 27-4014.00)

Significant Points

- Job applicants will face keen competition for jobs in major metropolitan areas, where pay generally is higher; prospects are expected to be better in small cities and towns.

- Technical school, community college, or college training in broadcast technology, electronics, or computer networking provides the best preparation.

- About 30 percent of these workers are in broadcasting, mainly in radio and television stations, and 17 percent work in the motion picture, video, and sound recording industries.

- Evening, weekend, and holiday work is common.

Nature of the Work

Broadcast and sound engineering technicians and radio operators set up, operate, and maintain a wide variety of electrical and electronic equipment used in almost any radio or television broadcast, concert, play, musical recording, television show, or movie. With such a range of work, there are many specialized occupations within the field.

Audio and video equipment technicians set up and operate audio and video equipment, including microphones, sound speakers, video screens, projectors, video monitors, and recording equipment. They also connect wires and cables and set up and operate sound and mixing boards and related electronic equipment for concerts, sports events, meetings and conventions, presentations, and news conferences. They may set up and operate associated spotlights and other custom lighting systems.

Broadcast technicians set up, operate, and maintain equipment that regulates the signal strength, clarity, and the range of sounds and colors of radio or television broadcasts. These technicians also operate control panels to select the source of the material. Technicians

may switch from one camera or studio to another, from film to live programming, or from network to local programming.

Sound engineering technicians operate machines and equipment to record, synchronize, mix, or reproduce music, voices, or sound effects in recording studios, sporting arenas, theater productions, or movie and video productions.

Radio operators mainly receive and transmit communications using a variety of tools. These workers also repair equipment, using such devices as electronic testing equipment, handtools, and power tools. One of their major duties is to help to maintain communication systems in good condition.

The transition to digital recording, editing, and broadcasting has greatly changed the work of broadcast and sound engineering technicians and radio operators. Software on desktop computers has replaced specialized electronic equipment in many recording and editing functions. Most radio and television stations have replaced videotapes and audiotapes with computer hard drives and other computer data storage systems. Computer networks linked to specialized equipment dominate modern broadcasting. This transition has forced technicians to learn computer networking and software skills. (See the job profile on computer support specialists and systems administrators elsewhere in this book.)

Broadcast and sound engineering technicians and radio operators perform a variety of duties in small stations. In large stations and at the networks, technicians are more specialized, although job assignments may change from day to day. The terms "operator," "engineer," and "technician" often are used interchangeably to describe these jobs. Workers in these positions may monitor and log outgoing signals and operate transmitters; set up, adjust, service, and repair electronic broadcasting equipment; and regulate fidelity, brightness, contrast, volume, and sound quality of television broadcasts.

Technicians also work in program production. *Recording Engineers* operate and maintain video and sound recording equipment. They may operate equipment designed to produce special effects, such as the illusions of a bolt of lightning or a police siren. *Sound mixers* or *re-recording mixers* produce soundtracks for movies or television programs. After filming or recording is complete, these workers may use a process called "dubbing" to insert sounds. *Field technicians* set up and operate portable transmission equipment outside the studio. Because television news coverage requires so much electronic equipment and the technology is changing so rapidly, many stations assign technicians exclusively to news.

Chief Engineers, transmission engineers, and *broadcast field supervisors* oversee other technicians and maintain broadcasting equipment.

Work environment. Broadcast and sound engineering technicians and radio operators generally work indoors in pleasant surroundings. However, those who broadcast news and other programs from locations outside the studio may work outdoors in all types of weather or in other dangerous conditions. Technicians doing maintenance may climb poles or antenna towers, while those setting up equipment do heavy lifting.

Technicians at large stations and the networks usually work a 40-hour week under great pressure to meet broadcast deadlines, and may occasionally work overtime. Technicians at small stations routinely work more than 40 hours a week. Evening, weekend, and holiday work is usual because most stations are on the air 18 to 24 hours

a day, 7 days a week. Even though a technician may not be on duty when the station is broadcasting, some technicians may be on call during nonwork hours; these workers must handle any problems that occur when they are on call.

Technicians who work on motion pictures may be on a tight schedule and may work long hours to meet contractual deadlines.

Training, Other Qualifications, and Advancement

Both broadcast and sound engineering technicians usually receive some kind of formal training prior to beginning work. Audio and video technicians usually learn the skills they need through a year or more of on-the-job training, but some have formal education after high school. Radio operators usually train for several months on the job

Education and training. The best way to prepare for a broadcast and sound engineering technician job is to obtain technical school, community college, or college training in broadcast technology, electronics, or computer networking. For broadcast technicians, an associate degree is recommended. Sound engineering technicians usually complete vocational programs, which usually takes about a year, although there are shorter programs. Prospective technicians should take high school courses in math, physics, and electronics.

When starting out, broadcast and sound engineering technicians learn skills on the job from experienced technicians and supervisors. These beginners often start their careers in small stations and, once experienced, transfer to larger ones. Large stations usually hire only technicians with experience. Many employers pay tuition and expenses for courses or seminars to help technicians keep abreast of developments in the field.

Audio and video equipment technicians generally need a high school diploma. Many recent entrants have a community college degree or other forms of postsecondary degrees, although they are not always required. These technicians may substitute on-the-job training for formal education requirements. Many audio and video technicians learn through long-term on-the-job training, lasting from one to several years, depending on the specifics of their job. Working in a studio as an assistant is a good way of gaining experience and knowledge.

Radio operators usually are not required to complete any formal training. This is an entry-level position that generally requires on-the-job training.

In the motion picture industry, people are hired as apprentice editorial assistants and work their way up to more skilled jobs. Employers in the motion picture industry usually hire experienced freelance technicians on a picture-by-picture basis. Reputation and determination are important in getting jobs.

Continuing education to become familiar with emerging technologies is recommended for all broadcast and sound engineering technicians and radio operators.

Other qualifications. Building electronic equipment from hobby kits and operating a "ham," or amateur, radio are good ways to prepare for these careers, as is working in college radio and television stations. Information technology skills also are valuable because digital recording, editing, and broadcasting are now the norm. Broadcast and sound engineering technicians and radio operators must have manual dexterity and an aptitude for working with electrical, electronic, and mechanical systems and equipment.

Certification and advancement. Licensing is not required for broadcast technicians. However, certification by the Society of Broadcast Engineers is a mark of competence and experience. The certificate is issued to experienced technicians who pass an examination.

Experienced technicians can become supervisory technicians or chief engineers. A college degree in engineering is needed to become chief engineer at a large television station.

Employment

Broadcast and sound engineering technicians and radio operators held about 105,000 jobs in 2006. Their employment was distributed among the following detailed occupations:

Audio and video equipment technicians 50,000

Broadcast technicians 38,000

Sound engineering technicians 16,000

Radio operators 1,500

About 30 percent worked in broadcasting (except Internet) and 17 percent worked in the motion picture, video, and sound recording industries. About 13 percent were self-employed. Television stations employ, on average, many more technicians than radio stations. Some technicians are employed in other industries, producing employee communications, sales, and training programs. Technician jobs in television and radio are located in virtually all cities; jobs in radio also are found in many small towns. The highest paying and most specialized jobs are concentrated in New York City, Los Angeles, Chicago, and Washington, DC—the originating centers for most network or news programs. Motion picture production jobs are concentrated in Los Angeles and New York City.

Job Outlook

Employment is expected to grow faster than average through 2016. But people seeking entry-level jobs as technicians in broadcasting are expected to face keen competition in major metropolitan areas. Prospects are expected to be better in small cities and towns.

Employment change. Overall employment of broadcast and sound engineering technicians and radio operators is expected to grow 17 percent over the 2006–2016 decade, which is faster than the average for all occupations. Job growth in radio and television broadcasting will be limited by consolidation of ownership of radio and television stations and by labor-saving technical advances, such as computer-controlled programming and remotely controlled transmitters. Stations often are consolidated and operated from a single location, reducing employment because one or a few technicians can provide

support to multiple stations. Offsetting these trends, however, is a move toward digital broadcasting that will increase employment opportunities. As of February 2009, television stations will only be allowed to broadcast digital signals and, by law, will be forced to turn off their analog signals. Technicians who can install and operate digital transmitters will be in demand as stations attempt to meet this deadline. Radio stations are beginning to broadcast digital signals as well, but there is no law that will require them to do so.

Projected job growth varies among detailed occupations in this field. Employment of audio and video equipment technicians is expected to grow 24 percent through 2016, which is much faster than the average for all occupations. Not only will these workers have to set up audio and video equipment, but they will have to maintain and repair it as well. Employment of broadcast technicians and sound engineering technicians is expected to grow 12 percent and 9 percent respectively, through 2016, about as fast as the average for all occupations. Advancements in technology will enhance the capabilities of technicians to produce higher quality radio and television programming. Employment of radio operators, on the other hand, is projected to decline rapidly by 16 percent through 2016 as more stations control programming and operate transmitters remotely.

Employment of broadcast and sound engineering technicians in the cable and pay television portion of the broadcasting industry is expected to grow as the range of products and services expands, including cable Internet access and video-on-demand. Employment of these workers in the motion picture industry is expected to grow rapidly. However, this job market is expected to remain competitive because of the large number of people who are attracted by the glamour of working in motion pictures.

Job prospects. People seeking entry-level jobs as technicians in broadcasting are expected to face keen competition in major metropolitan areas, where pay generally is higher and the number of qualified jobseekers typically exceeds the number of openings. Prospects for entry-level positions are expected to be better in small cities and towns for beginners with appropriate training.

In addition to employment growth, job openings will result from the need to replace experienced technicians who leave this field. Some of these workers leave for other jobs that require knowledge of electronics, such as computer repairer or industrial machinery repairer.

Earnings

Television stations usually pay higher salaries than radio stations; commercial broadcasting usually pays more than public broadcasting; and stations in large markets pay more than those in small markets.

Median annual earnings of audio and video equipment technicians in May 2006 were $34,840. The middle 50 percent earned between $26,090 and $46,320. The lowest 10 percent earned less than

Projections data from the National Employment Matrix

Occupational Title	SOC Code	Employment, 2006	Projected employment, 2016	Change, 2006-2016	
				Number	Percent
Broadcast and sound engineering technicians and radio operators ..	27-4010	105,000	123,000	18,000	17
Audio and video equipment technicians	27-4011	50,000	62,000	12,000	24
Broadcast technicians...	27-4012	38,000	42,000	4,600	12
Radio operators	27-4013	1,500	1,300	-300	-16
Sound engineering technicians	27-4014	16,000	18,000	1,500	9

NOTE: Data in this table are rounded.

$19,980, and the highest 10 percent earned more than $62,550. Median annual earnings in motion picture and video industries, which employed the largest number of audio and video equipment technicians, were $34,530.

Median annual earnings of broadcast technicians in May 2006 were $30,690. The middle 50 percent earned between $20,880 and $45,310. The lowest 10 percent earned less than $15,680, and the highest 10 percent earned more than $64,860. Median annual earnings in radio and television broadcasting, which employed the largest number of broadcast technicians, were $27,380.

Median annual earnings of sound engineering technicians in May 2006 were $43,010. The middle 50 percent earned between $29,270 and $65,590. The lowest 10 percent earned less than $21,050, and the highest 10 percent earned more than $90,770.

Median annual earnings of radio operators in May 2006 were $37,890. The middle 50 percent earned between $28,860 and $48,280. The lowest 10 percent earned less than $20,790, and the highest 10 percent earned more than $57,920.

Related Occupations

Broadcast and sound engineering technicians and radio operators need the electronics training necessary to operate technical equipment, and they generally complete specialized postsecondary programs. Occupations with similar characteristics include engineering technicians, science technicians, and electrical and electronics installers and repairers. Broadcast and sound engineering technicians also may operate computer networks, as do computer support specialists and systems administrators. Broadcast technicians on some live radio and television programs screen incoming calls; these workers have responsibilities similar to those of communications equipment operators.

Sources of Additional Information

For career information and links to employment resources, contact

▶ National Association of Broadcasters, 1771 N St. NW, Washington, DC 20036. Internet: http://www.nab.org

For information on certification, contact

▶ Society of Broadcast Engineers, 9182 North Meridian St., Suite 150, Indianapolis, IN 46260. Internet: http://www.sbe.org

For information on audio and video equipment technicians, contact

▶ InfoComm International, 11242 Waples Mill Rd., Suite 200, Fairfax, VA 22030. Internet: http://www.infocomm.org

Brokerage Clerks

(O*NET 43-4011.00)

Significant Points

■ More than 9 out of 10 brokerage clerks work for securities and commodities firms, banks, and other establishments in the financial services industry.

■ High school graduates qualify for many of these positions, but many workers now hold associate or bachelor's degrees.

■ Good prospects are expected for qualified jobseekers as employment grows and as existing brokerage clerks advance to other occupations.

Nature of the Work

For a typical investor, buying and selling stock is a simple process. Often, it is as easy as calling a broker on the phone or entering the trade into a computer. Behind the scenes, however, buying and selling stock is more complicated, involving trade execution and a fair amount of paperwork. While brokers do some of this work themselves, much of it is delegated to brokerage clerks.

Brokerage clerks perform a number of different tasks with a wide range of responsibilities. Most involve computing and recording data pertaining to securities transactions. Brokerage clerks may also contact customers, take orders, and inform clients of changes to their accounts. Brokerage clerks work in the operations departments of securities firms, on trading floors, and in branch offices. Technology has had a major impact on these positions over the last several years. A significant and growing number of brokerage clerks use custom-designed software programs to process transactions more quickly. Only a few customized accounts are still handled manually.

A *broker's assistant*, also called a *sales assistant*, is the most common type of brokerage clerk. These clerks typically assist a small number of brokers, for whom they take client calls, write up order tickets, process the paperwork for opening and closing accounts, record a client's purchases and sales, and inform clients of changes to their accounts. All broker's assistants must be knowledgeable about investment products so that they can communicate clearly with clients. Those who are licensed by the Financial Industry Regulatory Authority (FINRA) can make recommendations to clients at the instruction of the broker.

Brokerage clerks in the operations areas of securities firms perform many duties to help the sale and purchase of stocks, bonds, commodities, and other kinds of investments. They also produce the necessary records of all transactions that occur in their area of the business. *Purchase-and-sale clerks* match orders to buy with orders to sell. They balance and verify trades of stock by comparing the records of the selling firm with those of the buying firm. *Dividend clerks* ensure timely payments of stock or cash dividends to clients of a particular brokerage firm. *Transfer clerks* execute customer requests for changes to security registration and examine stock certificates to make sure that they adhere to banking regulations. *Receive-and-deliver clerks* handle the receipt and delivery of securities among firms and institutions. *Margin clerks* record and monitor activity in customers' accounts to ensure that clients make payments and stay within legal boundaries concerning their purchases of stock.

Work environment. Brokerage clerks work in offices and on trading floors, areas that are clean and well lit but which may be noisy at times. The workload is generally manageable but can become very heavy when the market fluctuates rapidly. Brokerage clerks generally work a standard 40-hour week, but they may work overtime during particularly busy periods.

Training, Other Qualifications, and Advancement

Most brokerage clerks learn their jobs through a few months of on-the-job training and experience. Once they have worked in the firm for a few years, many clerks advance to sales representative or broker positions.

Education and training. Some brokerage clerk positions require only a high school diploma, but graduates from two- and four-year

Projections data from the National Employment Matrix

Occupational Title	SOC Code	Employment, 2006	Projected employment, 2016	Change, 2006-16	
				Number	Percent
Brokerage clerks	43-4011	73,000	88,000	15,000	20

NOTE: Data in this table are rounded.

college degree programs are increasingly preferred. Positions dealing with the public, such as broker's or sales assistant, and those dealing with more complicated financial records are especially likely to require a college degree.

Most new employees are trained on the job, working under the close supervision of more experienced employees. Some firms offer formal training that may include courses in telephone etiquette, computer use, and customer service skills. They may also offer training programs to help clerks study for the broker licensing exams.

Licensure. Licenses are not strictly required for most brokerage clerk positions, but a Series seven brokerage license can make a clerk more valuable to the broker. This license gives the holder the ability to act as a registered representative of the firm. A registered representative has the right to answer more of a client's questions and to pass along securities recommendations from the broker. In order to receive this license, a clerk must pass the General Securities Registered Representative Examination (Series seven exam), administered by FINRA, and be an employee of a registered firm for at least four months.

Other qualifications. Brokerage clerk jobs require good organizational and communication skills, as well as attention to detail. Computer skills are extremely important, as most of the work is done by computer. An aptitude for working with numbers is also very helpful, as is a basic knowledge of accounting.

Advancement. Clerks may be promoted to sales representative positions or other professional positions within the securities industry. Employment as a brokerage clerk may also be a stepping-stone into a position as a broker.

Employment

Brokerage clerks held about 73,000 jobs in 2006. More than 9 out of 10 worked for securities and commodities, banking, and other financial industries.

Job Outlook

The job outlook for prospective brokerage clerks is good. As the securities industry grows, the number of clerks will increase. Opportunities will be abundant relative to other securities industry occupations, due to advancement of other clerks and job growth.

Employment change. Employment of brokerage clerks is expected to grow by 20 percent during the 2006–2016 decade, which is faster than the average for all occupations. With more people investing in securities, brokerage clerks will be required to process larger volumes of transactions. Moreover, regulatory changes have resulted in more legal documentation and recordkeeping requirements. Demand will be tempered, however, by continually improving technologies that allow increased automation of many tasks. Further, clerks are often seen as reducing profits, since they do not bring in customers, making them particularly prone to layoffs. Because of

intense competition, especially among discount brokerages, companies must continually focus on cutting costs, meaning that many responsibilities formerly handled by clerks are now handled by the brokers themselves.

Job prospects. Because brokerage clerks are often entry-level workers, many opportunities will result from the advancement of other clerks. Prospects will be good for qualified workers. New entrants who have strong sales skills and an aptitude for understanding numbers will have the best opportunities. While not required, a 4-year degree can also be very helpful.

Earnings

Median annual earnings of brokerage clerks were $36,390 in May 2006. The middle 50 percent earned between $29,480 and $46,030. The lowest 10 percent earned less than $24,590 and the highest 10 percent earned more than $57,600.

Related Occupations

Brokerage clerks compute and record data. Other workers who perform calculations and record data include bill and account collectors; billing and posting clerks and machine operators; bookkeeping, accounting, and auditing clerks; and tellers.

Sources of Additional Information

For more information on employment in the securities industry, contact

▸ Securities Industry and Financial Markets Association, 120 Broadway, 35th Floor, New York, NY 10271. Internet: http://www.sifma.org

For information on licensing, contact

▸ Financial Industry Regulatory Authority (FINRA), 1735 K St. NW, Washington, DC 20006. Internet: http://www.finra.org

Building Cleaning Workers

(O*NET 37-1011.00, 37-2011.00, 37-2012.00, and 37-2019.99)

Significant Points

■ This very large occupation requires few skills to enter and each year has one of the largest numbers of job openings of any occupation.

■ Most job openings result from the need to replace the many workers who leave these jobs because they provide low pay and few benefits, limited opportunities for training or advancement, and often only part-time or temporary work.

■ Most new jobs will occur in businesses providing janitorial and cleaning services on a contract basis.

© JIST Works

Nature of the Work

Building cleaning workers—including janitors, maids, housekeeping cleaners, window washers, and rug shampooers—keep office buildings, hospitals, stores, apartment houses, hotels, and residences clean, sanitary, and in good condition. Some do only cleaning, while others have a wide range of duties.

Janitors and cleaners perform a variety of heavy cleaning duties, such as cleaning floors, shampooing rugs, washing walls and glass, and removing rubbish. They may fix leaky faucets, empty trash cans, do painting and carpentry, replenish bathroom supplies, mow lawns, and see that heating and air-conditioning equipment works properly. On a typical day, janitors may wet- or dry-mop floors, clean bathrooms, vacuum carpets, dust furniture, make minor repairs, and exterminate insects and rodents. They may also clean snow or debris from sidewalks in front of buildings and notify management of the need for major repairs. While janitors typically perform most of the duties mentioned, cleaners tend to work for companies that specialize in one type of cleaning activity, such as washing windows.

Maids and housekeeping cleaners perform any combination of light cleaning duties to keep private households or commercial establishments, such as hotels, restaurants, hospitals, and nursing homes, clean and orderly. In hotels, aside from cleaning and maintaining the premises, maids and housekeeping cleaners may deliver ironing boards, cribs, and rollaway beds to guests' rooms. In hospitals, they also may wash bed frames, make beds, and disinfect and sanitize equipment and supplies with germicides. Janitors, maids, and cleaners use many kinds of equipment, tools, and cleaning materials. For one job they may need standard cleaning implements; another may require an electric floor polishing machine and a special cleaning solution. Improved building materials, chemical cleaners, and power equipment have made many tasks easier and less time consuming, but cleaning workers must learn the proper use of equipment and cleaners to avoid harming floors, fixtures, building occupants, and themselves.

Cleaning supervisors coordinate, schedule, and supervise the activities of janitors and cleaners. They assign tasks and inspect building areas to see that work has been done properly; they also issue supplies and equipment and inventory stocks to ensure that supplies on hand are adequate. They may be expected to screen and hire job applicants; train new and experienced employees; and recommend promotions, transfers, or dismissals. Supervisors may prepare reports concerning the occupancy of rooms, hours worked, and department expenses. Some also perform cleaning duties.

Cleaners and servants in private households dust and polish furniture; sweep, mop, and wax floors; vacuum; and clean ovens, refrigerators, and bathrooms. They also may wash dishes, polish silver, and change and make beds. Some wash, fold, and iron clothes; a few wash windows. General houseworkers also may take clothes and laundry to the cleaners, buy groceries, and perform many other errands.

Building cleaning workers in large office and residential buildings, and more recently in large hotels, often work in teams consisting of workers who specialize in vacuuming, picking up trash, and cleaning restrooms, among other things. Supervisors conduct inspections to ensure that the building is cleaned properly and the team is functioning efficiently. In hotels, one member of the team is responsible for reporting electronically to the supervisor when rooms are cleaned.

Work environment. Because most office buildings are cleaned while they are empty, many cleaning workers work evening hours. Some, however, such as school and hospital custodians, work in the daytime. When there is a need for 24-hour maintenance, janitors may be assigned to shifts. Most full-time building cleaners work about 40 hours a week. Part-time cleaners usually work in the evenings and on weekends.

Most building cleaning workers work indoors, but some work outdoors part of the time, sweeping walkways, mowing lawns, or shoveling snow. Working with machines can be noisy, and some tasks, such as cleaning bathrooms and trash rooms, can be dirty and unpleasant. Janitors may suffer cuts, bruises, and burns from machines, handtools, and chemicals. They spend most of their time on their feet, sometimes lifting or pushing heavy furniture or equipment. Many tasks, such as dusting or sweeping, require constant bending, stooping, and stretching. Lifting the increasingly heavier mattresses at nicer hotels in order to change the linens can cause back injuries and sprains.

Training, Other Qualifications, and Advancement

Most building cleaning workers, except supervisors, have a high school degree or less and mainly learn their skills on the job or in informal training sessions sponsored by their employers. Supervisors, though, generally have at least a high school diploma and often some college.

Education and training. No special education is required for most entry-level janitorial or cleaning jobs, but workers should be able to perform simple arithmetic and follow instructions. High school shop courses are helpful for jobs involving repair work. Most building cleaners learn their skills on the job. Beginners usually work with an experienced cleaner, doing routine cleaning. As they gain more experience, they are assigned more complicated tasks. In some cities, programs run by unions, government agencies, or employers teach janitorial skills. Students learn how to clean buildings thoroughly and efficiently; how to select and safely use various cleansing agents; and how to operate and maintain machines, such as wet and dry vacuums, buffers, and polishers. Students learn to plan their work, to follow safety and health regulations, to interact positively with people in the buildings they clean, and to work without supervision. Instruction in minor electrical, plumbing, and other repairs also may be given.

Supervisors of building cleaning workers usually need at least a high school diploma, but many have some college or more, especially those who work at places where clean rooms and well-functioning buildings are a necessity, such as in hospitals and hotels.

Other qualifications. Those who come in contact with the public should have good communication skills. Employers usually look for dependable, hard-working individuals who are in good health, follow directions well, and get along with other people.

Certification and advancement. A small number of cleaning supervisors and managers are members of the International Executive Housekeepers Association, which offers two kinds of certification programs for cleaning supervisors and managers: Certified Executive Housekeeper (CEH) and Registered Executive Housekeeper (REH). The CEH designation is offered to those with a high school education, while the REH designation is offered to those who have a four-year college degree. Both designations are earned by attending courses and passing exams and both must be renewed every three years to ensure that workers keep abreast of new cleaning methods. Those with the REH designation usually oversee the cleaning services of hotels, hospitals, casinos, and other large institutions that rely on well-trained experts for their cleaning needs.

Advancement opportunities for workers usually are limited in organizations where they are the only maintenance worker. Where there is a large maintenance staff, however, cleaning workers can be promoted to supervisor or to area supervisor or manager. In many establishments, they are required to take some in-service training to improve their housekeeping techniques and procedures and to enhance their supervisory skills. A high school diploma improves the chances for advancement. Some janitors set up their own maintenance or cleaning businesses.

Employment

Building cleaning workers held about 4.2 million jobs in 2006. More than 7 percent were self-employed.

Janitors and cleaners worked in nearly every type of establishment and held about 2.4 million jobs. They accounted for more than 57 percent of all building cleaning workers. More than 31 percent worked for firms supplying building maintenance services on a contract basis, about 20 percent were employed in public or private educational services, and 2 percent worked in hotels or motels. Other employers included hospitals; restaurants; religious institutions; manufacturing firms; government agencies; and operators of apartment buildings, office buildings, and other types of real estate.

First-line supervisors of housekeeping and janitorial workers held more than 282,000 jobs. Approximately 20 percent worked in firms supplying building maintenance services on a contract basis, while approximately 11 percent were employed in hotels or motels. About 4 percent worked for state and local governments, primarily at schools and colleges. Others worked for hospitals, nursing homes and other residential care facilities.

Maids and housekeepers held about 1.5 million jobs. Private households employed the most maids and housekeepers—almost 29 percent—while hotels, motels, and other traveler accommodations employed about the same percentage, almost 29 percent. Hospitals, nursing homes, and other residential care facilities employed large numbers, also. Although cleaning jobs can be found in all cities and towns, most are located in highly populated areas where there are many office buildings, schools, apartment houses, nursing homes, and hospitals.

Job Outlook

Overall employment of building cleaning workers is expected to grow faster than average for all occupations through 2016, as more office complexes, apartment houses, schools, factories, hospitals, and other buildings requiring cleaning are built to accommodate a growing population and economy.

Employment change. The number of building cleaning workers is expected to grow 14 percent between 2006 and 2016, which is faster than the average for all occupations. This occupation will have, in fact, one of the largest numbers of new jobs arise, about 570,000 over the 2006–2016 period.

Much of the growth in these occupations will come from cleaning residential properties. As families become more pressed for time, they increasingly hire cleaning and handyman services to perform a variety of tasks in their homes. Also, as the population ages, older people will need to hire cleaners to help maintain their houses. In addition, housekeeping cleaners will be needed to clean the growing number of residential care facilities for the elderly. These facilities, including assisted-living residences, generally provide housekeeping services as part of the rent. Although there have been some improvements in productivity in the way buildings are cleaned and maintained—using teams of cleaners, for example, and better cleaning supplies—cleaning still is very much a labor-intensive job.

As many firms reduce costs by contracting out the cleaning and maintenance of buildings, businesses providing janitorial and cleaning services on a contract basis are expected to have the greatest number of new jobs in this field.

Job prospects. In addition to job openings arising due to growth, numerous openings should result from the need to replace those who leave this very large occupation each year. Limited promotion potential, low pay, and the fact that many jobs are part-time and temporary, induce many to leave the occupation, thereby contributing to the number of job openings and the need to replace these workers.

Building cleaners usually find work by answering newspaper advertisements, applying directly to organizations where they would like to work, contacting local labor unions, or contacting state employment service offices.

Earnings

Median annual earnings of janitors and cleaners, except maids and housekeeping cleaners, were $19,930 in May 2006. The middle 50 percent earned between $16,220 and $25,640. The lowest 10 percent earned less than $14,010 and the highest 10 percent earned more than $33,060. Median annual earnings in 2006 in the industries

Projections data from the National Employment Matrix

Occupational Title	SOC Code	Employment, 2006	Projected employment, 2016	Change, 2006-16 Number	Change, 2006-16 Percent
Building cleaning workers	—	4,154,000	4,723,000	569,000	14
First-line supervisors/managers of housekeeping and janitorial workers	37-1011	282,000	318,000	36,000	13
Building cleaning workers	37-2010	3,872,000	4,405,000	533,000	14
Janitors and cleaners, except maids and housekeeping cleaners	37-2011	2,387,000	2,732,000	345,000	14
Maids and housekeeping cleaners	37-2012	1,470,000	1,656,000	186,000	13
Building cleaning workers, all other	37-2019	16,000	18,000	2,400	15

NOTE: Data in this table are rounded.

employing the largest numbers of janitors and cleaners, except maids and housekeeping cleaners, were as follows:

Elementary and secondary schools	$24,010
Local government	23,930
Colleges, universities, and professional schools	23,170
General medical and surgical hospitals	21,670
Services to buildings and dwellings	17,870

Median annual earnings of maids and housekeepers were $17,580 in May 2006. The middle 50 percent earned between $15,060 and $21,440. The lowest 10 percent earned less than $13,140, and the highest 10 percent earned more than $26,390. Median annual earnings in 2006 in the industries employing the largest numbers of maids and housekeepers were as follows:

General medical and surgical hospitals	$20,080
Community care facilities for the elderly	17,900
Nursing care facilities	17,690
Services to buildings and dwellings	17,540
Traveler accommodation	16,790

Median annual earnings of first-line supervisors and managers of housekeeping and janitorial workers were $31,290 in May 2006. The middle 50 percent earned between $24,230 and $40,670. The lowest 10 percent earned less than $19,620, and the highest 10 percent earned more than $51,490. Median annual earnings in May 2006 in the industries employing the largest numbers of first-line supervisors and managers of housekeeping and janitorial workers were as follows:

Local government	$38,170
Elementary and secondary schools	35,660
Nursing care facilities	30,570
Services to buildings and dwellings	29,730
Traveler accommodation	26,730

Related Occupations

Workers who specialize in one of the many job functions of janitors and cleaners include pest control workers; general maintenance and repair workers; and grounds maintenance workers.

Sources of Additional Information

Information about janitorial jobs may be obtained from state employment service offices.

For information on certification in executive housekeeping, contact

▸ International Executive Housekeepers Association, Inc., 1001 Eastwind Dr., Suite 301, Westerville, OH 43081-3361. Internet: http://www.ieha.org

Cardiovascular Technologists and Technicians

(O*NET 29-2031.00)

Significant Points

■ Employment is expected to grow much faster than average; technologists and technicians trained to perform certain procedures will be in particular demand.

■ About 3 out of 4 jobs are in hospitals.

■ The vast majority of workers complete a 2-year junior or community college program.

Nature of the Work

Cardiovascular technologists and technicians assist physicians in diagnosing and treating cardiac (heart) and peripheral vascular (blood vessel) ailments.

Cardiovascular technologists and technicians schedule appointments perform ultrasound or cardiovascular procedures, review doctors' interpretations and patient files, and monitor patients' heart rates. They also operate and care for testing equipment, explain test procedures, and compare findings to a standard to identify problems. Other day-to-day activities vary significantly between specialties.

Cardiovascular technologists may specialize in any of three areas of practice: invasive cardiology, echocardiography, or vascular technology.

Invasive cardiology. Cardiovascular technologists specializing in invasive procedures are called *cardiology technologists*. They assist physicians with cardiac catheterization procedures in which a small tube, or catheter, is threaded through a patient's artery from a spot on the patient's groin to the heart. The procedure can determine whether a blockage exists in the blood vessels that supply the heart muscle. The procedure also can help to diagnose other problems. Part of the procedure may involve balloon angioplasty, which can be used to treat blockages of blood vessels or heart valves without the need for heart surgery. Cardiology technologists assist physicians as they insert a catheter with a balloon on the end to the point of the obstruction. Another procedure using the catheter is electrophysiology test, which help locate the specific areas of heart tissue that give rise to the abnormal electrical impulses that cause arrhythmias.

Technologists prepare patients for cardiac catheterization by first positioning them on an examining table and then shaving, cleaning, and administering anesthesia to the top of their leg near the groin. During the procedures, they monitor patients' blood pressure and heart rate with EKG equipment and notify the physician if something appears to be wrong. Technologists also may prepare and monitor patients during open-heart surgery and during the insertion of pacemakers and stents that open up blockages in arteries to the heart and major blood vessels.

Noninvasive technology. Technologists who specialize in vascular technology or echocardiography perform noninvasive tests using. Tests are called "noninvasive" if they do not require the insertion of probes or other instruments into the patient's body. For example, procedures such as Doppler ultrasound transmit high-frequency sound waves into areas of the patient's body and then processes reflected echoes of the sound waves to form an image. Technologists view the ultrasound image on a screen and may record the image on videotape or photograph it for interpretation and diagnosis by a physician. As the technologist uses the instrument to perform scans and record images, technologists check the image on the screen for subtle differences between healthy and diseased areas, decide which images to include in the report to the physician, and judge whether the images are satisfactory for diagnostic purposes. They also explain the procedure to patients, record any additional medical history the patient relates, select appropriate equipment settings, and change the patient's position as necessary. (See the job profile of diagnostic medical sonographers elsewhere in the this book to learn more about other sonographers.)

Vascular technology. Technicians who assist physicians in the diagnosis of disorders affecting the circulation are known as *vascular technologists* or *vascular sonographers*. Vascular technologists complete patients' medical history, evaluate pulses and assess blood flow in arteries and veins by listening to the vascular flow sounds for abnormalities, and assure the appropriate vascular test has been ordered. Then they perform a noninvasive procedure using ultrasound instruments to record vascular information such as vascular blood flow, blood pressure, oxygen saturation, cerebral circulation, peripheral circulation, and abdominal circulation. Many of these tests are performed during or immediately after surgery. Vascular technologists then provide a summary of findings to the physician to aid in patient diagnosis and management.

Echocardiography. This area of practice includes giving electrocardiograms (EKGs) and sonograms of the heart. Cardiovascular technicians who specialize in EKGs, stress testing, and those who perform Holter monitor procedures are known as cardiographic or *electrocardiograph* (or *EKG) technicians*.

To take a basic EKG, which traces electrical impulses transmitted by the heart, technicians attach electrodes to the patient's chest, arms, and legs, and then manipulate switches on an EKG machine to obtain a reading. An EKG is printed out for interpretation by the physician. This test is done before most kinds of surgery or as part of a routine physical examination, especially on persons who have reached middle age or who have a history of cardiovascular problems.

EKG technicians with advanced training perform Holter monitor and stress testing. For Holter monitoring, technicians place electrodes on the patient's chest and attach a portable EKG monitor to the patient's belt. Following 24 or more hours of normal activity by the patient, the technician removes a tape from the monitor and places it in a scanner. After checking the quality of the recorded impulses on an electronic screen, the technician usually prints the information from the tape for analysis by a physician. Physicians use the output from the scanner to diagnose heart ailments, such as heart rhythm abnormalities or problems with pacemakers.

For a treadmill stress test, EKG technicians document the patient's medical history, explain the procedure, connect the patient to an EKG monitor, and obtain a baseline reading and resting blood pressure. Next, they monitor the heart's performance while the patient is walking on a treadmill, gradually increasing the treadmill's speed to observe the effect of increased exertion. Like vascular technologists and cardiac sonographers, cardiographic technicians who perform EKG, Holter monitor, and stress tests are known as "noninvasive" technicians.

Technologists who use ultrasound to examine the heart chambers, valves, and vessels are referred to as *cardiac sonographers*, or *echocardiographers*. They use ultrasound instrumentation to create images called echocardiograms. An echocardiogram may be performed while the patient is either resting or physically active. Technologists may administer medication to physically active patients to assess their heart function. Cardiac sonographers also may assist physicians who perform transesophageal echocardiography, which involves placing a tube in the patient's esophagus to obtain ultrasound images.

Work environment. Cardiovascular technologists and technicians spend a lot of time walking and standing. Heavy lifting may be involved to move equipment or transfer patients. These workers wear heavy protective aprons while conducting some procedures. Those who work in catheterization laboratories may face stressful working conditions because they are in close contact with patients with serious heart ailments. For example, some patients may encounter complications that have life-or-death implications.

Some cardiovascular technologists and technicians may have the potential for radiation exposure, which is kept to a minimum by strict adherence to radiation safety guidelines. In addition, those who use sonography can be at an increased risk for musculoskeletal disorders such as carpel tunnel syndrome, neck and back strain, and eye strain. However, greater use of ergonomic equipment and an increasing awareness will continue to minimize such risks.

Technologists and technicians generally work a 5-day, 40-hour week that may include weekends. Those in catheterization laboratories tend to work longer hours and may work evenings. They also may be on call during the night and on weekends.

Training, Other Qualifications, and Advancement

The most common level of education completed by cardiovascular technologists and technicians is an associate degree. Certification, although not required in all cases, is available.

Education and training. Although a few cardiovascular technologists, vascular technologists, and cardiac sonographers are currently trained on the job, most receive training in two- to four-year programs. The majority of technologists complete a two-year junior or community college program, but four-year programs are increasingly available. The first year is dedicated to core courses and is followed by a year of specialized instruction in either invasive, noninvasive cardiovascular, or noninvasive vascular technology. Those who are qualified in an allied health profession need to complete only the year of specialized instruction.

The Joint Review Committee on Education in Cardiovascular Technology reviews education programs seeking accreditation. The Commission on Accreditation of Allied Health Professionals (CAAHEP) accredits these education programs; as of 2006, there were 31 programs accredited in cardiovascular technology in the United States. Similarly, those who want to study echocardiography or vascular sonography may also attend CAAHEP accredited programs in diagnostic medical sonography. In 2006, there were 147 diagnostic medical sonography programs accredited by CAAHEP. Those who attend these accredited programs are eligible to obtain professional certification.

Unlike most other cardiovascular technologists and technicians, most EKG technicians are trained on the job by an EKG supervisor

Projections data from the National Employment Matrix

Occupational Title	SOC Code	Employment, 2006	Projected employment, 2016	Change, 2006-2016	
				Number	Percent
Cardiovascular technologists and technicians...................................	29-2031	45,000	57,000	12,000	26

NOTE: Data in this table are rounded.

or a cardiologist. On-the-job training usually lasts about eight to 16 weeks. Most employers prefer to train people already in the health care field—nursing aides, for example. Some EKG technicians are students enrolled in two-year programs to become technologists, working part time to gain experience and make contact with employers. One-year certification programs exist for basic EKGs, Holter monitoring, and stress testing.

Licensure and certification. Some states require workers in this occupation to be licensed. For information on a particular state, contact that state's medical board. Certification is available from two organizations: Cardiovascular Credentialing International (CCI) and the American Registry of Diagnostic Medical Sonographers (ARDMS). The CCI offers four certifications—Certified Cardiographic Technician (CCT), Registered Cardiac Sonographer (RCS), Registered Vascular Specialist (RVS), and Registered Cardiovascular Invasive Specialist (RCIS). The ARDMS offers Registered Diagnostic Cardiac Sonographer (RDCS) and Registered Vascular Technologist (RVT) credentials. Some states require certification as part of licensure. In other states, certification is not required but many employers prefer it.

Other qualifications. Cardiovascular technologists and technicians must be reliable, have mechanical aptitude, and be able to follow detailed instructions. A pleasant, relaxed manner for putting patients at ease is an asset. They must be articulate as they must communicate technically with physicians and also explain procedures simply to patients.

Advancement. Technologists and technicians can advance to higher levels of the profession as many institutions structure the occupation with multiple levels, each having an increasing amount of responsibility. Technologists and technicians also can advance into supervisory or management positions. Other common possibilities include working in an educational setting or conducting laboratory work.

Employment

Cardiovascular technologists and technicians held about 45,000 jobs in 2006. About 3 out of 4 jobs were in hospitals (public and private), primarily in cardiology departments. The remaining jobs were mostly in offices of physicians, including cardiologists, or in medical and diagnostic laboratories, including diagnostic imaging centers.

Job Outlook

Employment is expected to grow much faster than average; technologists and technicians trained to perform certain procedures will be in particular demand.

Employment change. Employment of cardiovascular technologists and technicians is expected to increase by 26 percent through the year 2016, much faster than the average for all occupations. Growth will occur as the population ages, because older people have a higher incidence of heart disease and other complications of the heart and vascular system. Procedures such as ultrasound are being performed more often as a replacement for more expensive and more invasive procedures. Due to advances in medicine and greater public awareness, signs of vascular disease can be detected earlier, creating demand for cardiovascular technologists and technicians to perform various procedures.

Employment of vascular technologists and echocardiographers will grow as advances in vascular technology and sonography reduce the need for more costly and invasive procedures. Electrophysiology is also becoming a rapidly growing specialty. However, fewer EKG technicians will be needed, as hospitals train nursing aides and others to perform basic EKG procedures. Individuals trained in Holter monitoring and stress testing are expected to have more favorable job prospects than those who can perform only a basic EKG.

Medicaid has relaxed some of the rules governing reimbursement for vascular exams, which is resulting in vascular studies becoming a more routine practice. As a result of increased use of these procedures, individuals with training in vascular studies should have more favorable employment opportunities.

Job prospects. Some additional job openings for cardiovascular technologists and technicians will arise from replacement needs as individuals transfer to other jobs or leave the labor force. Although growing awareness of musculoskeletal disorders has made prevention easier, some cardiovascular technologists and technicians have been forced to leave the occupation early because of this disorder.

It is not uncommon for cardiovascular technologists and technicians to move between the specialties within the occupation by obtaining certification in more than one specialty.

Earnings

Median annual earnings of cardiovascular technologists and technicians were $42,300 in May 2006. The middle 50 percent earned between $29,900 and $55,670. The lowest 10 percent earned less than $23,670, and the highest 10 percent earned more than $67,410. Median annual earnings of cardiovascular technologists and technicians in 2006 were $41,960 in offices of physicians and $41,950 in general medical and surgical hospitals.

Related Occupations

Cardiovascular technologists and technicians operate sophisticated equipment that helps physicians and other health practitioners to diagnose and treat patients. So do diagnostic medical sonographers, nuclear medicine technologists, radiation therapists, radiologic technologists and technicians, and respiratory therapists.

Sources of Additional Information

For general information about a career in cardiovascular technology, contact

▸ Alliance of Cardiovascular Professionals, Thalia Landing Offices, Bldg. 2, 4356 Bonney Rd., Suite 103, Virginia Beach, VA 23452-1200. Internet: http://www.acp-online.org

For a list of accredited programs in cardiovascular technology, contact

▶ Committee on Accreditation for Allied Health Education Programs, 1361 Park St, Clearwater, FL 33756. Internet: http://www.caahep.org

▶ Society for Vascular Ultrasound, 4601 Presidents Dr., Suite 260, Lanham, MD 20706-4381. Internet: http://www.svunet.org

For information on echocardiography, contact

▶ American Society of Echocardiography, 1500 Sunday Dr., Suite 102, Raleigh, NC 27607. Internet: http://www.asecho.org

For information regarding registration and certification, contact

▶ Cardiovascular Credentialing International, 1500 Sunday Dr., Suite 102, Raleigh, NC 27607. Internet: http://www.cci-online.org

▶ American Registry of Diagnostic Medical Sonographers, 51 Monroe St., Plaza East One, Rockville, MD 20850-2400. Internet: http://www.ardms.org

Cargo and Freight Agents

(O*NET 43-5011.00)

Significant Points

■ Cargo and freight agents need no more than a high school diploma and learn their duties informally on the job.

■ Faster than average employment growth is expected.

Nature of the Work

Cargo and freight agents arrange for and track incoming and outgoing shipments in airline, train, or trucking terminals or on shipping docks. They expedite shipments by determining the route that shipments will take and by preparing all necessary documents. Agents take orders from customers and arrange for the pickup of freight or cargo and its delivery to loading platforms. Cargo and freight agents may keep records of the cargo, including its amount, type, weight, dimensions, destination, and time of shipment. They keep a tally of missing items and record the condition of damaged items.

Cargo and freight agents arrange cargo according to its destination. They also determine any shipping rates and other charges that usually apply to freight. For imported or exported freight, they verify that the proper customs paperwork is in order. Cargo and freight agents often track shipments electronically, using bar codes, and answer customers' questions about the status of their shipments.

Work environment. Cargo and freight agents work in a wide variety of businesses, institutions, and industries. Some work in warehouses, stockrooms, or shipping and receiving rooms that may not be temperature controlled. Others may spend time in cold storage rooms or outside on loading platforms, where they are exposed to the weather.

Most jobs for cargo and freight agents involve frequent standing, bending, walking, and stretching. Some lifting and carrying of small items may be involved. Although automated devices have lessened the physical demands of this occupation, not every employer has these devices. The work still can be strenuous, even though mechanical material-handling equipment is used to move heavy items.

The typical work week is Monday through Friday. However, evening and weekend hours are common in jobs involving large shipments.

Training, Other Qualifications, and Advancement

Cargo and freight agents need no more than a high school diploma and learn their duties informally on the job.

Education and training. Many jobs are entry level and require only a high school diploma. Cargo and freight agents undergo informal on-the-job training. They start out by checking items to be shipped, attaching labels to them, and making sure that addresses are correct. As this occupation becomes more automated, workers may need longer periods of training to master the use of equipment.

Other qualifications. Employers prefer to hire people who can use computers. Typing, filing, recordkeeping, and other clerical skills also are important.

Advancement. Advancement opportunities for cargo and freight agents are usually limited, but some agents may become team leaders or use their hands-on experience to switch to other clerical occupations in the businesses where they work.

Employment

Cargo and freight agents held about 86,000 jobs in 2006. Most agents were employed in transportation. Approximately 44 percent worked for firms engaged in support activities for the transportation industry, 23 percent were in the air transportation industry, 9 percent worked for courier businesses, and 7 percent were in the truck transportation industry.

Job Outlook

Employment is expected to grow faster than average.

Employment change. Employment of cargo and freight agents is expected to increase by 16 percent during the 2006–2016 decade, faster than the average for all occupations. A growing number of agents will be needed to handle the increasing number of shipments resulting from increases in cargo traffic. Additional demand will stem from the growing popularity of online shopping and same-day delivery.

Job prospects. In addition to new job growth, openings will be created by the need to replace cargo and freight agents who leave the occupation.

Projections data from the National Employment Matrix

Occupational Title	SOC Code	Employment, 2006	Projected employment, 2016	Change, 2006-16	
				Number	Percent
Cargo and freight agents	43-5011	86,000	100,000	14,000	16

NOTE: Data in this table are rounded.

Earnings

Median annual earnings of cargo and freight agents in May 2006 were $37,110. The middle 50 percent earned between $27,750 and $46,440. The lowest 10 percent earned less than $22,470, and the highest 10 percent earned more than $57,440. Median annual earnings in the industries employing the largest numbers of cargo and freight agents in May 2006 were

Scheduled air transportation $38,340

Freight transportation arrangement 37,130

Couriers 36,750

General freight trucking 34,010

Support activities for air transportation 23,770

These workers usually receive the same benefits as most other workers. If uniforms are required, employers generally provide them or offer an allowance to purchase them.

Related Occupations

Cargo and freight agents plan and coordinate shipments of cargo by airlines, trains, and trucks. They also arrange freight pickup with customers. Others who do similar work are couriers and messengers; shipping, receiving, and traffic clerks; weighers, measurers, checkers, and samplers, recordkeeping; truck drivers and driver/sales workers; and Postal Service workers.

Sources of Additional Information

Information about job opportunities may be obtained from local employers and local offices of the state employment service.

Carpenters

(O*NET 47-2031.00, 47-2031.01, and 47-2031.02)

Significant Points

■ About 32 percent of all carpenters—the largest construction trade—are self employed.

■ Job opportunities should be best for those with the most training and skills.

■ Between 3 and 4 years of both on-the-job training and classroom instruction usually is needed to become a skilled carpenter.

Nature of the Work

Carpenters are involved in many different kinds of construction, from the building of highways and bridges to the installation of kitchen cabinets. Carpenters construct, erect, install, and repair structures and fixtures made from wood and other materials.

Each carpentry task is somewhat different, but most involve the same basic steps. Working from blueprints or instructions from supervisors, carpenters first do the layout—measuring, marking, and arranging materials—in accordance with local building codes. They cut and shape wood, plastic, fiberglass, or drywall using hand and power tools, such as chisels, planes, saws, drills, and sanders. They then join the materials with nails, screws, staples, or adhesives. In the last step, carpenters do a final check of the accuracy of their

work with levels, rules, plumb bobs, framing squares, and surveying equipment, and make any necessary adjustments.

When working with prefabricated components, such as stairs or wall panels, the carpenter's task is somewhat simpler because it does not require as much layout work or the cutting and assembly of as many pieces. Prefabricated components are designed for easy and fast installation and generally can be installed in a single operation.

Some carpenters do many different carpentry tasks, while others specialize in one or two. Carpenters who remodel homes and other structures, for example, need a broad range of carpentry skills. As part of a single job, for example, they might frame walls and partitions, put in doors and windows, build stairs, install cabinets and molding, and complete many other tasks. Because these carpenters are so well-trained, they often can switch from residential building to commercial construction or remodeling work, depending on which offers the best work opportunities.

Carpenters who work for large construction contractors or specialty contractors may perform only a few regular tasks, such as constructing wooden forms for pouring concrete, or erecting scaffolding. Some carpenters build tunnel bracing, or brattices, in underground passageways and mines to control the circulation of air through the passageways and to worksites. Others build concrete forms for tunnel, bridge, or sewer construction projects.

Carpenters employed outside the construction industry perform a variety of installation and maintenance work. They may replace panes of glass, ceiling tiles, and doors, as well as repair desks, cabinets, and other furniture. Depending on the employer, carpenters install partitions, doors, and windows; change locks; and repair broken furniture. In manufacturing firms, carpenters may assist in moving or installing machinery. (For more information on workers who install machinery, see the discussion of industrial machinery mechanics and maintenance workers elsewhere in this book.)

Work environment. As is true of other building trades, carpentry work is sometimes strenuous. Prolonged standing, climbing, bending, and kneeling often are necessary. Carpenters risk injury working with sharp or rough materials, using sharp tools and power equipment, and working in situations where they might slip or fall. Although many carpenters work indoors, those that work outdoors are subject to variable weather conditions.

Most carpenters work a standard 40 hour week. Hours may be longer during busy periods.

Training, Other Qualifications, and Advancement

Carpenters learn their trade through formal and informal training programs. Between three and four years of both on-the-job training and classroom instruction usually is needed to become a skilled carpenter. There are a number of ways to train, but a more formal training program often improves job opportunities.

Education and training. Learning to be a carpenter can start in high school. Classes in English, algebra, geometry, physics, mechanical drawing, blueprint reading, and general shop will prepare students for the further training they will need.

After high school, there are a number of different ways to obtain the necessary training. Some people get a job as a carpenter's helper, assisting more experienced workers. At the same time, the helper might attend a trade or vocational school, or community college to receive further trade-related training and eventually become a carpenter.

Some employers offer employees formal apprenticeships. These programs combine on-the-job training with related classroom instruction. Apprentices usually must be at least 18 years old and meet local requirements. Apprenticeship programs usually last three to four years, but length varies with the apprentice's skill.

On the job, apprentices learn elementary structural design and become familiar with common carpentry jobs, such as layout, form building, rough framing, and outside and inside finishing. They also learn to use the tools, machines, equipment, and materials of the trade. In the classroom, apprentices learn safety, first aid, blueprint reading, freehand sketching, basic mathematics, and various carpentry techniques. Both in the classroom and on the job, they learn the relationship between carpentry and the other building trades.

The number of apprenticeship programs is limited, however, so only a small proportion of carpenters learn their trade through these programs. Most apprenticeships are offered by commercial and industrial building contractors with union membership.

Some people who are interested in carpentry careers choose to get their classroom training before seeking a job. There are a number of public and private vocational-technical schools and training academies affiliated with unions and contractors that offer training to become a carpenter. Employers often look favorably upon these students and usually start them at a higher level than those without the training.

Other qualifications. Carpenters need manual dexterity, eye-hand coordination, physical fitness, and a good sense of balance. The ability to solve arithmetic problems quickly and accurately also is required. In addition, military service or a good work history is viewed favorably by employers.

Certification and advancement. Carpenters who complete formal apprenticeship programs receive certification as journeypersons. Some carpenters earn other certifications in scaffold building, high torque bolting, or pump work. These certifications prove that carpenters are able to perform these tasks, which can lead to additional responsibilities.

Carpenters usually have more opportunities than most other construction workers to become general construction supervisors because carpenters are exposed to the entire construction process. For those who would like to advance, it is increasingly important to be able to communicate in both English and Spanish in order to relay instructions and safety precautions to workers; Spanish-speaking workers make up a large part of the construction workforce in many areas. Carpenters may advance to carpentry supervisor or general construction supervisor positions. Others may become independent contractors. Supervisors and contractors need good communication skills to deal with clients and subcontractors. They should be able to identify and estimate the quantity of materials needed to complete a job and accurately estimate how long a job will take to complete and what it will cost.

Employment

Carpenters are employed throughout the country in almost every community and make up the largest building trades occupation. They held about 1.5 million jobs in 2006.

About 32 percent worked in construction of buildings and about 23 percent worked for specialty trade contractors. Most of the rest of the wage and salary workers worked for manufacturing firms, government agencies, retail establishments, and a wide variety of other industries. About 32 percent of all carpenters were self-employed. Some carpenters change employers each time they finish a construction job. Others alternate between working for a contractor and working as contractors themselves on small jobs, depending on where the work is available.

Job Outlook

Average job growth, coupled with replacement needs, create a large number of openings each year. Job opportunities should be best for those with the most training and skills.

Employment change. Employment of carpenters is expected to increase by 10 percent during the 2006–2016 decade, about as fast as the average for all occupations. The need for carpenters should grow as construction activity increases in response to demand for new housing and office and retail space, and for modernizing and expanding schools and industrial plants. A strong home remodeling market also will create demand for carpenters. Moreover, construction of roads and bridges as well as restaurants, hotels, and other businesses will increase the demand for carpenters in the coming decade.

Some of the demand for carpenters, however, will be offset by expected productivity gains resulting from the increasing use of prefabricated components and improved fasteners and tools. Prefabricated wall panels, roof assemblies, and stairs, as well as prehung doors and windows can be installed very quickly. Instead of having to be built on the worksite, prefabricated walls, partitions, and stairs can be lifted into place in one operation; beams and, in some cases, entire roof assemblies, are lifted into place using a crane. As prefabricated components become more standardized, builders will use them more often. In addition, improved adhesives are reducing the time needed to join materials, and lightweight, cordless, and pneumatic tools—such as nailers and drills—will all continue to make carpenters more productive. New and improved tools, equipment, techniques, and materials also have made carpenters more versatile, allowing them to perform more carpentry tasks.

Job prospects. Job opportunities should be best for those with the most training and skills. Job growth and replacement needs for those who leave the occupation create a large number of openings each year. Many people with limited skills take jobs as carpenters but eventually leave the occupation because they dislike the work or cannot find steady employment.

Carpenters with all-around skills will have better opportunities for steady work than carpenters who can perform only a few relatively simple, routine tasks. Carpenters can experience periods of unemployment because of the short-term nature of many construction projects, winter slowdowns in construction activity in northern areas, and the cyclical nature of the construction industry.

Employment of carpenters, like that of many other construction workers, is sensitive to the fluctuations of the economy. Workers in these trades may experience periods of unemployment when the overall level of construction falls. On the other hand, shortages of these workers may occur in some areas during peak periods of building activity.

Job opportunities for carpenters also vary by geographic area. Construction activity parallels the movement of people and businesses and reflects differences in local economic conditions. The areas with

© JIST Works

Projections data from the National Employment Matrix

Occupational Title	SOC Code	Employment, 2006	Projected employment, 2016	Change, 2006-16	
				Number	Percent
Carpenters	47-2031	1,462,000	1,612,000	150,000	10

NOTE: Data in this table are rounded.

the largest population increases will also provide the best opportunities for jobs as carpenters and for apprenticeships for people seeking to become carpenters.

Earnings

In May 2006, median hourly earnings of wage and salary carpenters were $17.57. The middle 50 percent earned between $13.55 and $23.85. The lowest 10 percent earned less than $10.87, and the highest 10 percent earned more than $30.45. Median hourly earnings in the industries employing the largest numbers of carpenters were as follows:

Residential building construction	$17.39
Foundation, structure, and building exterior contractors	17.03
Nonresidential building construction	15.12
Building finishing contractors	13.76
Employment services	10.88

Earnings can be reduced on occasion, because carpenters lose work time in bad weather and during recessions when jobs are unavailable. Earnings may be increased by overtime during busy periods.

Some carpenters are members of the United Brotherhood of Carpenters and Joiners of America.

Related Occupations

Carpenters are skilled construction workers. Other skilled construction occupations include brickmasons, blockmasons, and stonemasons; cement masons, concrete finishers, segmental pavers, and terrazzo workers; drywall installers, ceiling tile installers, and tapers; electricians; pipelayers, plumbers, pipefitters, and steamfitters; and plasterers and stucco masons.

Sources of Additional Information

For information about carpentry apprenticeships or other work opportunities in this trade, contact local carpentry contractors, locals of the union mentioned above, local joint union-contractor apprenticeship committees, or the nearest office of the state employment service or apprenticeship agency. You can also find information on the registered apprenticeship system with links to state apprenticeship programs on the U.S. Department of Labor's Web site: http://www.doleta.gov/atels_bat. Apprenticeship information is also available from the U.S. Department of Labor's toll free helpline: 1 (877) 872-5627.

For information on training opportunities and carpentry in general, contact

▸ Associated Builders and Contractors, 4250 North Fairfax Dr., 9th Floor, Arlington, VA 22203. Internet: http://www.trytools.org

▸ Associated General Contractors of America, Inc., 2300 Wilson Blvd., Suite 400, Arlington, VA 22201. Internet: http://www.agc.org

▸ National Center for Construction Education and Research, 3600 NW 43rd St., Bldg. G, Gainesville, FL, 32606. Internet: http://www.nccer.org

▸ National Association of Home Builders, Home Builders Institute, 1201 15th St. NW, Washington, DC 20005. Internet: http://www.hbi.org

▸ United Brotherhood of Carpenters and Joiners of America, Carpenters Training Fund, 6801 Placid St., Las Vegas, NV 89119. Internet: http://www.carpenters.org

For general information on apprenticeships and how to get them, see the *Occupational Outlook Quarterly* article "Apprenticeships: Career training, credentials—and a paycheck in your pocket," online at http://www.bls.gov/opub/ooq/2002/summer/art01.pdf and in print at many libraries and career centers.

Cement Masons, Concrete Finishers, Segmental Pavers, and Terrazzo Workers

(O*NET 47-2051.00, 47-2053.00, and 47-4091.00)

Significant Points

■ Job opportunities are expected to be good, especially for those with the most experience and skills.

■ Most learn on the job or though a combination of classroom and on-the-job training that can take 3 to 4 years.

■ Cement masons often work overtime, with premium pay, because once concrete has been placed, the job must be completed.

Nature of the Work

Cement masons, concrete finishers, and terrazzo workers all work with concrete, one of the most common and durable materials used in construction. Once set, concrete—a mixture of Portland cement, sand, gravel, and water—becomes the foundation for everything from decorative patios and floors to huge dams or miles of roadways.

Cement masons and *concrete finishers* place and finish concrete. They also may color concrete surfaces, expose aggregate (small stones) in walls and sidewalks, or fabricate concrete beams, columns, and panels. In preparing a site to place concrete, cement masons first set the forms for holding the concrete and properly align them. They then direct the casting of the concrete and supervise laborers who use shovels or special tools to spread it. Masons then guide a straightedge back and forth across the top of the forms to "screed," or level, the freshly placed concrete. Immediately after leveling the concrete, masons carefully float it—smooth the concrete surface with a "bull float," a long-handled tool about 8 by 48 inches that covers the coarser materials in the concrete and brings a rich mixture of fine cement paste to the surface.

After the concrete has been leveled and floated, concrete finishers press an edger between the forms and the concrete and guide it along the edge and the surface. This produces slightly rounded edges and helps prevent chipping or cracking. Concrete finishers use a special tool called a "groover" to make joints or grooves at specific intervals that help control cracking. Next, they smooth the surface using either a powered or hand trowel, a small, smooth, rectangular metal tool.

Sometimes, cement masons perform all the steps of laying concrete, including the finishing. As the final step, they retrowel the concrete surface back and forth with powered or hand trowels to create a smooth finish. For a coarse, nonskid finish, masons brush the surface with a broom or stiff-bristled brush. For a pebble finish, they embed small gravel chips into the surface. They then wash any excess cement from the exposed chips with a mild acid solution. For color, they use colored premixed concrete. On concrete surfaces that will remain exposed after the forms are stripped, such as columns, ceilings, and wall panels, cement masons cut away high spots and loose concrete with hammer and chisel, fill any large indentations with a Portland cement paste, and smooth the surface with a carborundum stone. Finally, they coat the exposed area with a rich Portland cement mixture, using either a special tool or a coarse cloth to rub the concrete to a uniform finish.

Throughout the entire process, cement masons must monitor how the wind, heat, or cold affects the curing of the concrete. They must have a thorough knowledge of concrete characteristics so that, by using sight and touch, they can determine what is happening to the concrete and take measures to prevent defects.

Segmental pavers lay out, cut, and install pavers—flat pieces of masonry made from compacted concrete or brick. This masonry is typically installed in patios, sidewalks, plazas, streets, crosswalks, parking lots, and driveways. Installers usually begin their work on a previously prepared base that has been graded to the proper depth, although some projects may include the base preparation. A typical segmental paver installation begins with leveling a layer of sand, followed by placement of the pavers, normally by hand but sometimes by machine. Usually the work includes constructing edges to prevent horizontal movement of the pavers. Sand is then added to fill the joints between the pavers.

Terrazzo workers create attractive walkways, floors, patios, and panels by exposing marble chips and other fine aggregates on the surface of finished concrete. Much of the preliminary work of terrazzo workers is similar to that of cement masons. There are six different types of terrazzo, but the focus of this description is on the most common standard terrazzo, marble-chip terrazzo, which requires three layers of materials. First, cement masons or terrazzo workers build a solid, level concrete foundation that is 3 to 4 inches deep. Second, after the forms are removed from the foundation, workers add a 1-inch layer of sandy concrete. Terrazzo workers partially embed, or attach with adhesive, metal divider strips in the concrete wherever there is to be a joint or change of color in the terrazzo. For the third and final layer, terrazzo workers blend and place into each of the panels a fine marble chip mixture that may be color-pigmented. While the mixture is still wet, workers add additional marble chips of various colors into each panel and roll a lightweight roller over the entire surface.

When the terrazzo is thoroughly set, helpers grind it with a terrazzo grinder, which is somewhat like a floor polisher, only much heavier. Any depressions left by the grinding are filled with a matching grout material and hand-troweled for a smooth, uniform surface. Terrazzo workers then clean, polish, and seal the dry surface for a lustrous finish.

Work environment. Concrete, segmental paving, or terrazzo work is fast-paced and strenuous and requires continuous physical effort. Because most finishing is done at floor level, workers must bend and kneel often. Many jobs are outdoors, and work is generally halted during inclement weather. The work, either indoors or outdoors, may be in areas that are muddy, dusty, or dirty. To avoid chemical burns from uncured concrete and sore knees from frequent kneeling, many workers wear kneepads. Workers usually also wear water-repellent boots while working in wet concrete.

Most workers work 40 hours a week, although the number of hours can be increased or decreased by outside factors. Earnings for workers in these trades can be reduced on occasion because poor weather and slowdowns in construction activity limit the time they can work.

Training, Other Qualifications, and Advancement

Most cement masons, concrete finishers, segmental pavers, and terrazzo workers learn their trades through on-the-job training, either as helpers or in apprenticeship programs. Some workers also learn their jobs by attending trade or vocational-technical schools.

Education and training. Many masons and finishers first gain experience as construction laborers. (See the section on construction laborers elsewhere in this book.) Most on-the-job training programs consist of informal instruction, in which experienced workers teach helpers to use the tools, equipment, machines, and materials of the trade. Trainees begin with tasks such as edging, jointing, and using a straightedge on freshly placed concrete. As training progresses, assignments become more complex, and trainees can usually do finishing work within a short time.

Other workers train in formal apprenticeship programs usually sponsored by local contractors, trade associations, or local union-management committees. These earn while you learn programs provide on-the-job training and the recommended minimum of 144 hours of classroom instruction each year. In the classroom, apprentices learn applied mathematics, blueprint reading, and safety. Apprentices generally receive special instruction in layout work and cost estimation. Apprenticeships may take three to four years to complete. Applying for an apprenticeship may require a written test and a physical exam.

Many states have technical schools that offer courses in masonry which improve employment and advancement opportunities. Entrance requirements and fees vary depending on the school and who is funding the program. These schools may offer courses before hiring or after hiring as part of the on-the-job training.

Other qualifications. The most important quality employers look for is dependability and a strong work ethic. When hiring helpers and apprentices, employers prefer high school graduates who are at least 18 years old, possess a driver's license, and are in good physical condition. The ability to get along with others is also important because cement masons frequently work in teams. High school courses in general science, mathematics, and vocational-technical subjects, such as blueprint reading and mechanical drawing provide a helpful background. Cement masons, concrete finishers, segmental pavers, and terrazzo workers should enjoy doing demanding work. They should take pride in craftsmanship and be able to work without close supervision.

Advancement. With additional training, cement masons, concrete finishers, segmental pavers, or terrazzo workers may become supervisors for masonry contractors or move into construction management, building inspection, or contract estimation. Some eventually become owners of businesses, where they may spend most of their time managing rather than practicing their original trade. For those who want to own their own business, taking business classes will help them prepare.

Employment

Cement masons, concrete finishers, segmental pavers, and terrazzo workers held about 229,000 jobs in 2006; segmental pavers and terrazzo workers accounted for only a small portion of the total. Most cement masons and concrete finishers worked for specialty trade contractors, primarily foundation, structure, and building exterior contractors. They also worked for contractors in residential and nonresidential building construction and in heavy and civil engineering construction on projects such as highways; bridges; shopping malls; or large buildings such as factories, schools, and hospitals. A small number were employed by firms that manufacture concrete products. Most segmental pavers and terrazzo workers worked for specialty trade contractors who install decorative floors and wall panels.

Only about 2 percent of cement masons, concrete finishers, segmental pavers, and terrazzo workers were self-employed, a smaller proportion than in other building trades. Most self-employed masons specialized in small jobs, such as driveways, sidewalks, and patios.

Job Outlook

Average employment growth is expected, and job prospects are expected to be good, especially for those with the most experience and skills.

Employment change. Employment of cement masons, concrete finishers, segmental pavers, and terrazzo workers is expected to grow 11 percent over the 2006–2016 decade, about as fast as the average for all occupations. More workers will be needed to build new highways, bridges, factories, and other residential and nonresidential structures to meet the demands of a growing population. Additionally, cement masons will be needed to repair and renovate existing highways and bridges and other aging structures.

The use of concrete for buildings is increasing. For example, residential construction in Florida is using more concrete as building requirements are changed in reaction to the increased frequency and intensity of hurricanes. Concrete use is likely to expand into other hurricane-prone areas as the durability of the Florida homes is demonstrated.

Job prospects. Opportunities for cement masons, concrete finishers, segmental pavers, and terrazzo workers are expected to be good, particularly for those with the most experience and skills. Employers report difficulty in finding workers with the right skills, as many qualified jobseekers often prefer work that is less strenuous and has more comfortable working conditions. There are expected to be a significant number of retirements over the next decade, which will create more job openings. Applicants who take masonry-related courses at technical schools will have better opportunities than those without these courses.

Employment of cement masons, concrete finishers, segmental pavers, and terrazzo workers, like that of many other construction workers, is sensitive to the fluctuations of the economy. Workers in these trades may experience periods of unemployment when the overall level of construction falls. On the other hand, shortages of these workers may occur in some areas during peak periods of building activity.

Earnings

In May 2006, the median hourly earnings of wage and salary cement masons and concrete finishers were $15.70. The middle 50 percent earned between $12.38 and $20.70. The bottom 10 percent earned less than $10.02, and the top 10 percent earned more than $27.07. Median hourly earnings in the industries employing the largest numbers of cement masons and concrete finishers were as follows:

Masonry contractors	$17.05
Nonresidential building construction	16.34
Highway, street, and bridge construction	16.20
Other specialty trade contractors	16.15
Poured concrete foundation and structure contractors	15.38

In May 2006, the median hourly earnings of wage and salary terrazzo workers and finishers were $15.21. The middle 50 percent earned between $12.01 and $20.50. The bottom 10 percent earned less than $9.31, and the top 10 percent earned more than $27.22.

In May 2006, the median hourly earnings of wage and salary segmental pavers were $13.80. The middle 50 percent earned between $10.47 and $17.05. The bottom 10 percent earned less than $8.41, and the top 10 percent earned more than $19.11.

Like other construction trades workers, earnings of cement masons, concrete finishers, segmental pavers, and terrazzo workers may be reduced on occasion because poor weather and slowdowns in

Projections data from the National Employment Matrix

Occupational Title	SOC Code	Employment, 2006	Projected employment, 2016	Change, 2006-16	
				Number	Percent
Cement masons, concrete finishers, segmental pavers, and terrazzo workers	—	229,000	255,000	26,000	11
Cement masons, concrete finishers, and terrazzo workers	47-2050	228,000	254,000	26,000	11
Cement masons and concrete finishers	47-2051	222,000	247,000	25,000	11
Terrazzo workers and finishers	47-2053	6,800	7,500	700	11
Segmental pavers	47-4091	1,000	1,100	100	10

NOTE: Data in this table are rounded.

construction activity limit the amount of time they can work. Nonunion workers generally have lower wage rates than union workers. Apprentices usually start at 50 to 60 percent of the rate paid to experienced workers, and increases are generally achieved by meeting specified advancement requirements every 6 months. Cement masons often work overtime, with premium pay, because once concrete has been placed, the job must be completed.

Some cement masons, concrete finishers, segmental pavers, and terrazzo workers belong to unions, mainly the Operative Plasterers' and Cement Masons' International Association of the United States and Canada, and the International Union of Bricklayers and Allied Craftworkers. A few terrazzo workers belong to the United Brotherhood of Carpenters and Joiners of the United States.

Related Occupations

Cement masons, concrete finishers, segmental pavers, and terrazzo workers combine skill with knowledge of building materials to construct buildings, highways, and other structures. Other occupations involving similar skills and knowledge include brickmasons, blockmasons, and stonemasons; carpet, floor, and tile installers and finishers; drywall installers, ceiling tile installers, and tapers; and plasterers and stucco masons.

Sources of Additional Information

For information about apprenticeships and work opportunities, contact local concrete or terrazzo contractors, locals of unions previously mentioned, a local joint union-management apprenticeship committee, or the nearest office of the state employment service or apprenticeship agency. Apprenticeship information is also available from the U.S. Department of Labor's toll free helpline: (877) 872-5627. You may also check the U.S. Department of Labor's Web site for information on apprenticeships and links to state apprenticeship programs. Internet: http://www.doleta.gov/atels_bat

For general information about cement masons, concrete finishers, segmental pavers, and terrazzo workers, contact

▶ Associated Builders and Contractors, Workforce Development Division, 4250 North Fairfax Dr., 9th Floor, Arlington, VA 22203. Internet: http://www.trytools.org

▶ Associated General Contractors of America, Inc., 2300 Wilson Blvd., Suite 400, Arlington, VA 22201. Internet: http://www.agc.org

▶ International Union of Bricklayers and Allied Craftworkers, International Masonry Institute, The James Brice House, 42 East St., Annapolis, MD 21401. Internet: http://www.imiweb.org

▶ National Center for Construction Education and Research, 3600 NW 43rd St., Bldg. G, Gainesville, FL 32606. Internet: http://www.nccer.org

▶ National Concrete Masonry Association, 13750 Sunrise Valley Dr., Herndon, VA 20171-3499. Internet: http://www.ncma.org

▶ National Terrazzo and Mosaic Association, 201 North Maple, Suite 208, Purcellville, VA 20132.

▶ Operative Plasterers' and Cement Masons' International Association of the United States and Canada, 11720 Beltsville Dr., Suite 700, Beltsville, MD 20705. Internet: http://www.opcmia.org

▶ Portland Cement Association, 5420 Old Orchard Rd., Skokie, IL 60077. Internet: http://www.cement.org

▶ United Brotherhood of Carpenters and Joiners, 50 F St. NW, Washington, DC 20001. Internet: http://www.carpenters.org

For more information about careers and training as a mason, contact

▶ Mason Contractors Association of America, 33 South Roselle Rd., Schaumburg, IL 60193. Internet: http://www.masoncontractors.org

For general information on apprenticeships and how to get them, see the *Occupational Outlook Quarterly* article "Apprenticeships: Career training, credentials—and a paycheck in your pocket," online at http://www.bls.gov/opub/ooq/2002/summer/art01.pdf and in print at many libraries and career centers.

Chefs, Cooks, and Food Preparation Workers

(O*NET 35-1011.00, 35-2011.00, 35-2012.00, 35-2013.00, 35-2014.00, 35-2015.00, 35-2019.99, and 35-2021.00)

Significant Points

■ Many cooks and food preparation workers are young—37 percent are below the age of 24.

■ One-third of these workers are employed part time.

■ Job openings are expected to be plentiful because many of these workers will leave the occupation for full-time employment or better wages.

Nature of the Work

Chefs, cooks, and food preparation workers prepare, season, and cook a wide range of foods—from soups, snacks, and salads to entrees, side dishes, and desserts. They work in a variety of restaurants and other food services establishments. Chefs and cooks create recipes and prepare meals, while food preparation workers peel and cut vegetables, trim meat, prepare poultry, and perform other duties, such as keeping work areas clean and monitoring temperatures of ovens and stovetops.

Specifically, *chefs* and *cooks* measure, mix, and cook ingredients according to recipes, using a variety of equipment, including pots, pans, cutlery, ovens, broilers, grills, slicers, grinders, and blenders. Chefs and head cooks also are responsible for directing the work of other kitchen workers, estimating food requirements, and ordering food supplies.

Food preparation workers perform routine, repetitive tasks under the direction of chefs and cooks. These workers ready the ingredients for complex dishes by slicing and dicing vegetables, and composing salads and cold items. They weigh and measure ingredients, go after pots and pans, and stir and strain soups and sauces. Food preparation workers may cut and grind meats, poultry, and seafood in preparation for cooking. They also clean work areas, equipment, utensils, dishes, and silverware.

Larger restaurants and food services establishments tend to have varied menus and larger kitchen staffs. Staffs often include several chefs and cooks, sometimes called assistant or line cooks. Each chef or cook works an assigned station that is equipped with the types of stoves, grills, pans, and ingredients needed for the foods prepared at that station. Job titles often reflect the principal ingredient prepared or the type of cooking performed—vegetable cook, fry cook, or grill cook, for example. These cooks also may direct or work with other food preparation workers.

Executive chefs and *head cooks* coordinate the work of the kitchen staff and direct the preparation of meals. They determine serving sizes, plan menus, order food supplies, and oversee kitchen operations to ensure uniform quality and presentation of meals. An executive chef, for example, is in charge of all food service operations and also may supervise the many kitchens of a hotel, restaurant group, or corporate dining operation. A *chef de cuisine* reports to an executive chef and is responsible for the daily operations of a single kitchen. A *sous chef*, or sub chef, is the second-in-command and runs the kitchen in the absence of the chef. Many chefs earn fame both for themselves and for their kitchens because of the quality and distinctive nature of the food they serve.

Responsibilities depend on where cooks work. *Institution and cafeteria cooks*, for example, work in the kitchens of schools, cafeterias, businesses, hospitals, and other institutions. For each meal, they prepare a large quantity of a limited number of entrees, vegetables, and desserts according to preset menus. Meals generally are prepared in advance so diners seldom get the opportunity to special order a meal. *Restaurant cooks* usually prepare a wider selection of dishes, cooking most orders individually. *Short-order cooks* prepare foods in restaurants and coffee shops that emphasize fast service and quick food preparation. They grill and garnish hamburgers, prepare sandwiches, fry eggs, and cook French fries, often working on several orders at the same time. *Fast-food cooks* prepare a limited selection of menu items in fast-food restaurants. They cook and package batches of food, such as hamburgers and fried chicken, to be kept warm until served. (Combined food preparation and service workers, who both prepare and serve items in fast-food restaurants, are included with the material on food and beverage serving and related workers elsewhere in this book.)

The number and types of workers employed in kitchens also depends on the type of establishment. Small, full-service restaurants offering casual dining often feature a limited number of easy-to-prepare items supplemented by short-order specialties and ready-made desserts. Typically, one cook prepares all the food with the help of a short-order cook and one or two other kitchen workers.

Grocery and specialty food stores employ chefs, cooks, and food preparation workers to develop recipes and prepare meals for customers to carry out. Typically, entrees, side dishes, salads, or other items are prepared in large quantities and stored at an appropriate temperature. Counter assistants portion and package items according to customer orders for serving at home.

Some cooks, called *research chefs*, combine culinary skills with knowledge of food science to develop recipes for chain restaurants and food processors and manufacturers. They test new formulas and flavors for prepared foods and determine the most efficient and safest way to prepare new foods.

Some cooks work for individuals rather than for restaurants, cafeterias, or food manufacturers. These *private household cooks* plan and prepare meals in private homes according to the client's tastes or dietary needs. They order groceries and supplies, clean the kitchen, and wash dishes and utensils. They also may serve meals. Private chefs are employed directly by a single individual or family or sometimes by corporations or institutions, such as universities and embassies, to perform cooking and entertaining tasks. These chefs usually live in and may travel with their employer. Because of the sensitive nature of their employment, they are usually required to sign confidentiality agreements. As part of the job, private chefs

often perform additional services, such as paying bills, coordinating schedules, and planning events.

Another type of private household cooks, called personal chefs, usually prepare a week's worth of meals in the client's home for the client to heat and serve according to directions throughout the week. Personal chefs are self-employed or employed by a company that provides this service.

Work environment. Many restaurant and institutional kitchens have modern equipment, convenient work areas, and air conditioning, but kitchens in older and smaller eating places are often not as well designed. Kitchen staffs invariably work in small quarters against hot stoves and ovens. They are under constant pressure to prepare meals quickly, while ensuring quality is maintained and safety and sanitation guidelines are observed. Because the pace can be hectic during peak dining times, workers must be able to communicate clearly so that food orders are completed correctly.

Working conditions vary with the type and quantity of food prepared and the local laws governing food service operations. Workers usually must stand for hours at a time, lifting heavy pots and kettles, and working near hot ovens and grills. Job hazards include slips and falls, cuts, and burns, but injuries are seldom serious.

Work hours in restaurants may include early mornings, late evenings, holidays, and weekends. Work schedules of chefs, cooks and other kitchen workers in factory and school cafeterias may be more regular. In 2006, about 29 percent of cooks and 44 percent of food preparation workers had part-time schedules, compared to 15 percent of workers throughout the economy. Work schedules in fine-dining restaurants, however, tend to be longer because of the time required to prepare ingredients in advance. Many executive chefs regularly work 12-hour days because they oversee the delivery of foodstuffs early in the day, plan the menu, and prepare those menu items that take the most skill.

The wide range in dining hours and the need for fully-staffed kitchens during all open hours creates work opportunities for students, youth, and other individuals seeking supplemental income, flexible work hours, or variable schedules. Eighteen percent of cooks and food preparation workers were 16 to 19 years old in 2006; nineteen percent were age 20 to 24. Ten percent had variable schedules. Kitchen workers employed by schools may work during the school year only, usually for 9 or 10 months. Similarly, resort establishments usually only offer seasonal employment.

Training, Other Qualifications, and Advancement

On-the-job training is most common for fast-food cooks, short-order cooks, and food preparation workers. Chefs and others with more advanced cooking duties often attend cooking school. Vocational training programs are available to many high school students, but advanced positions usually require training after high school. Experience, an ability to develop and enhance cooking skills, and a strong desire to cook are the most common requirements for advancement.

Education and training. A high school diploma is not required for beginning jobs, but it is recommended for those planning a career as a cook or chef. Most fast-food or short-order cooks and food preparation workers require little education or training to start because most skills are learned on the job. Training generally starts with basic sanitation and workplace safety and continues with instruction on food handling, preparation, and cooking procedures. Training in food handling, sanitation, and health and safety procedures are mandatory in most jurisdictions for all workers. Those who become proficient and who show an interest in learning complicated cooking techniques may advance to more demanding cooking positions or into supervisory positions.

Some high school or vocational school programs offer courses in basic food safety and handling procedures, cooking, and general business and computer classes that can be helpful for those who might someday want to be a chef or to open their own restaurant. Many school districts, in cooperation with state departments of education, provide on-the-job training and summer workshops for cafeteria kitchen workers who aspire to become cooks. Food service management companies or hotel and restaurant chains, also offer paid internships and summer jobs to those starting out in the field. Internships provide valuable experience and can lead to placement in more formal chef training programs.

When hiring chefs and others in advanced cooking positions, however, employers usually prefer applicants who have training after high school. These training programs range from a few months to two years or more. Vocational or trade-school programs typically offer basic training in food handling and sanitation procedures, nutrition, slicing and dicing methods for various kinds of meats and vegetables, and basic cooking methods, such as baking, broiling, and grilling. Longer programs leading to a certificate or a two- or four-year degree train chefs for fine-dining or upscale restaurants. They offer a wider array of training specialties, such as advanced cooking techniques; cooking for banquets, buffets, or parties; and cuisines and cooking styles from around the world.

A growing number of chefs participate in these longer training programs through independent cooking schools, professional culinary institutes, two- or four-year college degree programs in hospitality or culinary arts, or in the armed forces. Some large hotels and restaurants also operate their own training and job-placement programs for chefs and cooks. Executive chefs and head cooks who work in fine-dining restaurants require many years of training and experience and an intense desire to cook.

Although curricula may vary, students in culinary training programs spend most of their time in kitchens learning to prepare meals by practicing cooking skills. They learn good knife techniques and proper use and care of kitchen equipment. Training programs also include courses in nutrition, menu planning, portion control, purchasing and inventory methods, proper food storage procedures, and use of leftover food to minimize waste. Students also learn sanitation and public health rules for handling food. Training in food service management, computer accounting and inventory software, and banquet service are featured in some training programs. Most formal training programs also require students to get experience in a commercial kitchen through an internship, apprenticeship, or out-placement program.

Many chefs are trained on the job, receiving real work experience and training from chef-mentors in the restaurants where they work. Professional culinary institutes, industry associations, and trade unions sponsor formal apprenticeship programs in coordination with the U.S. Department of Labor.

The American Culinary Federation accredits more than 200 formal academic training programs and sponsors apprenticeship programs around the country. Typical apprenticeships last two years and combine classroom training and work experience. Accreditation is an indication that a culinary program meets recognized standards regarding course content, facilities, and quality of instruction.

Other qualifications. Chefs, cooks, and food preparation workers must be efficient, quick, and work well as part of a team. Manual dexterity is helpful for cutting, chopping, and plating. These workers also need creativity and a keen sense of taste and smell. Personal cleanliness is essential because most states require health certificates indicating that workers are free from communicable diseases. Knowledge of a foreign language can be an asset because it may improve communication with other restaurant staff, vendors, and the restaurant's clientele.

Certification and advancement. The American Culinary Federation certifies pastry professionals, personal chefs, and culinary educators in addition to various levels of chefs. Certification standards are based primarily on experience and formal training. Although certification is not required, it can help to prove accomplishment and lead to advancement and higher-paying positions.

Advancement opportunities for chefs, cooks, and food preparation workers depend on their training, work experience, and ability to perform more responsible and sophisticated tasks. Many food preparation workers, for example, may move into assistant or line cook positions. Chefs and cooks who demonstrate an eagerness to learn new cooking skills and to accept greater responsibility may also move up and be asked to train or supervise lesser skilled kitchen staff. Others may move to larger or more prestigious kitchens and restaurants.

Some chefs and cooks go into business as caterers or personal chefs or open their own restaurant. Others become instructors in culinary training programs. A number of cooks and chefs advance to executive chef positions or food service management positions, particularly in hotels, clubs, or larger, more elegant restaurants. (See the section on food service managers elsewhere in this book.)

Employment

Chefs, cooks, and food preparation workers held 3.1 million jobs in 2006. The distribution of jobs among the various types of chefs, cooks, and food preparation workers was as follows:

Food preparation workers	902,000
Cooks, restaurant	850,000
Cooks, fast food	629,000
Cooks, institution and cafeteria	401,000
Cooks, short order	195,000
Chefs and head cooks	115,000
Cooks, private household	4,900
Cooks, all other	16,000

Two-thirds of all chefs, cooks, and food preparation workers were employed in restaurants and other food services and drinking places. About 15 percent worked in institutions such as schools, universities, hospitals, and nursing care facilities. Grocery stores, hotels, and gasoline stations with convenience stores employed most of the remainder.

Job Outlook

Job opportunities for chefs, cooks, and food preparation workers are expected to be plentiful because of the continued growth and expansion of food services outlets, resulting in average employment

Projections data from the National Employment Matrix

Occupational Title	SOC Code	Employment, 2006	Projected employment, 2016	Change, 2006-16	
				Number	Percent
Chefs, cooks, and food preparation workers................................	—	3,113,000	3,464,000	351,000	11
Chefs and head cooks...	35-1011	115,000	124,000	8,700	8
Cooks and food preparation workers	35-2000	2,998,000	3,340,000	342,000	11
Cooks	35-2010	2,097,000	2,301,000	204,000	10
Cooks, fast food	35-2011	629,000	681,000	52,000	8
Cooks, institution and cafeteria..........................	35-2012	401,000	445,000	43,000	11
Cooks, private household..	35-2013	4,900	5,400	400	9
Cooks, restaurant..	35-2014	850,000	948,000	98,000	12
Cooks, short order..	35-2015	195,000	205,000	9,500	5
Cooks, all other	35-2019	16,000	16,000	500	3
Food preparation workers	35-2021	902,000	1,040,000	138,000	15

NOTE: Data in this table are rounded.

growth, and because of the large numbers of workers who leave these occupations and need to be replaced. However, those seeking the highest-paying positions will face keen competition.

Employment change. Employment of chefs, cooks, and food preparation workers is expected to increase by 11 percent over the 2006–2016 decade, which is about as fast as the average for all occupations. This occupation will have among the largest numbers of new jobs arise, about 351,000 over the period. Growth will be spurred by increases in population, household income, and demand for convenience that will lead to more people dining out and taking vacations that include hotel stays and restaurant visits. In addition, employment of chefs, cooks, and food preparation workers who prepare meals-to-go, such as those who work in the prepared foods sections of grocery or specialty food stores, should grow faster than average as these stores compete with restaurants for people's food dollars. Also, there is a growing consumer desire for convenient, healthier, made-from-scratch meals.

Projected employment growth varies by detailed occupation. The number of higher-skilled chefs and cooks working in full-service restaurants—those that offer table service and more varied menus—is expected to increase about as fast as the average for all occupations. Much of this increase will come from job growth in more casual dining settings, rather than in up-scale full-service restaurants. Dining trends suggest that an increasing number of meals are eaten away from home, which creates growth in family dining restaurants, but greater limits on expense-account meals is expected to generate slower growth for up-scale restaurants.

Employment of food preparation workers is expected to grow faster than the average for all occupations, reflecting diners' desires for convenience as they shop for carryout meals in a greater variety of places, including full-service restaurants, limited-service eating places, and grocery stores.

Employment of fast-food cooks is expected to grow about as fast as the average for all occupations. Duties of cooks in fast-food restaurants are limited; most workers are likely to be combined food preparation and serving workers, rather than fast-food cooks. Employment of short-order cooks is expected to increase more slowly than average.

Employment of institution and cafeteria chefs and cooks will show growth about as fast as the average. Their employment will not keep pace with the rapid growth in the educational and health services industries—where their employment is concentrated. Offices,

schools, and hospitals increasingly contract out their food services in an effort to make "institutional food" more attractive to office workers, students, staff, visitors, and patients. Much of the growth of these workers will be in contract food service establishments that provide catering services or food management and staff for employee dining rooms, sports complexes, convention centers, and educational or health care facilities.

Employment of private household cooks is projected to grow by 9 percent, about as fast as the average. While the employment of personal chefs is expected to increase—reflecting the growing popularity and convenience of eating restaurant-quality meals at home—the number of private chefs will not grow as fast, reflecting slower growth in private household service employment.

Job prospects. Job openings for chefs, cooks, and food preparation workers are expected to be plentiful through 2016; however, competition should be keen for jobs in the top kitchens of higher end restaurants. Although job growth will create many new positions, the overwhelming majority of job openings will stem from the need to replace workers who leave this large occupational group. Many chef, cook, and food preparation worker jobs are attractive to people seeking first-time or short-term employment, additional income, or a flexible schedule. Employers typically hire a large number of part-time workers, but many of these workers soon transfer to other occupations or stop working, creating numerous openings for those entering the field. At higher end restaurants, the fast pace, long hours, and high energy levels required to succeed also cause some top chefs and cooks to leave for other jobs, creating job openings.

Earnings

Earnings of chefs, cooks, and food preparation workers vary greatly by region and the type of employer. Earnings usually are highest in elegant restaurants and hotels, where many executive chefs are employed, and in major metropolitan and resort areas.

Median annual wage-and-salary earnings of chefs and head cooks were $34,370 in May 2006. The middle 50 percent earned between $25,910 and $46,040. The lowest 10 percent earned less than $20,160, and the highest 10 percent earned more than $60,730. Median annual earnings in the industries employing the largest number of chefs and head cooks were

Other amusement and recreations industries $46,460

Traveler accommodation 40,020

Special food services 36,450

Full-service restaurants...32,360

Limited-service eating places 27,560

Median annual wage-and-salary earnings of cooks, private household were $22,870 in May 2006. The middle 50 percent earned between $17,960 and $31,050. The lowest 10 percent earned less than $14,690, and the highest 10 percent earned more than $55,040.

Median annual wage-and-and salary earnings of institution and cafeteria cooks were $20,410 in May 2006. The middle 50 percent earned between $16,280 and $25,280. The lowest 10 percent earned less than $13,450, and the highest 10 percent earned more than $30,770. Median annual earnings in the industries employing the largest numbers of institution and cafeteria cooks were

General medical and surgical hospitals $22,980

Special food services 21,650

Community care facilities for the elderly...............20,910

Nursing care facilities 20,470

Elementary and secondary schools 18,770

Median annual wage-and-salary earnings of restaurant cooks were $20,340 in May 2006. The middle 50 percent earned between $16,860 and $24,260. The lowest 10 percent earned less than $14,370, and the highest 10 percent earned more than $28,850. Median annual earnings in the industries employing the largest numbers of restaurant cooks were

Traveler accommodations $23,400

Full-service restaurants...20,100

Limited-service eating places 18,200

Median annual wage-and-salary earnings of short-order cooks were $17,880 in May 2006. The middle 50 percent earned between $14,960 and $21,820. The lowest 10 percent earned less than $12,930, and the highest 10 percent earned more than $26,110. Median annual earnings in full-service restaurants were $18,340.

Median annual wage-and-salary earnings of food preparation workers were $17,410 in May 2006. The middle 50 percent earned between $14,920 and $21,230. The lowest 10 percent earned less than $13,190, and the highest 10 percent earned more than $25,940. Median annual earnings in the industries employing the largest number of food preparation workers were

Grocery stores $18,920

Full-service restaurants...17,390

Limited-service eating places 15,550

Median annual wage-and-salary earnings of fast-food cooks were $15,410 in May 2006. The middle 50 percent earned between $13,730 and $17,700. The lowest 10 percent earned less than $12,170, and the highest 10 percent earned more than $20,770. Median annual earnings were $15,360 in full-service restaurants and $15,350 in limited-service eating places.

Some employers provide employees with uniforms and free meals, but federal law permits employers to deduct from their employees' wages the cost or fair value of any meals or lodging provided, and some employers do so. Chefs, cooks, and food preparation workers who work full time often receive typical benefits, but part-time and hourly workers usually do not.

In some large hotels and restaurants, kitchen workers belong to unions. The principal unions are the Hotel Employees and Restaurant Employees International Union and the Service Employees International Union.

Related Occupations

People who perform tasks similar to those of chefs, cooks, and food preparation workers include those in food processing occupations, such as butchers and meat cutters, and bakers. Others who work closely with these workers include food service managers and food and beverage serving and related workers.

Sources of Additional Information

Information about job opportunities may be obtained from local employers and local offices of the state employment service.

Career information about chefs, cooks, and other kitchen workers, including a directory of two- and four-year colleges that offer courses or training programs is available from

▸ National Restaurant Association, 1200 17th St. NW, Washington, DC 20036. Internet: http://www.restaurant.org

Information on the American Culinary Federation's apprenticeship and certification programs for cooks and a list of accredited culinary programs is available from

▸ American Culinary Federation, 180 Center Place Way, St. Augustine, FL 32095. Internet: http://www.acfchefs.org

For information about becoming a personal or private chef, contact

▸ American Personal & Private Chef Association, 4572 Delaware St., San Diego, CA 92116. Internet: http://www.personalchef.com

For information about culinary apprenticeship programs registered with the U.S. Department of Labor, contact the local office of your state employment service agency, check the department's apprenticeship Web site: http://www.doleta.gov/atels_bat, or call the toll free helpline: (877) 872-5627.

Child Care Workers

(O*NET 39-9011.00 and 39-9011.01)

Significant Points

■ About 35 percent of child care workers are self employed, most of whom provided child care in their homes.

■ Training requirements range from a high school diploma to a college degree, although a high school diploma and a little experience are adequate for many jobs.

■ Many workers leave these jobs every year, creating good job opportunities.

Nature of the Work

Child care workers nurture and care for children who have not yet entered formal schooling. They also supervise older children before and after school. These workers play an important role in children's development by caring for them when parents are at work or away for other reasons. In addition to attending to children's basic needs, child care workers organize activities and implement curricula that stimulate children's physical, emotional, intellectual, and social growth. They help children explore individual interests, develop talents and independence, build self-esteem, and learn how to get along with others.

Child care workers generally are classified into three different groups based on where they work: private household workers, who care for children at the children's home; family child care providers, who care for children in the provider's own home; and child care workers who work at separate child care centers.

Private household workers who are employed on an hourly basis usually are called *babysitters*. These child care workers bathe, dress, and feed children; supervise their play; wash their clothes; and clean their rooms. Babysitters also may put children to bed and wake them, read to them, involve them in educational games, take them for doctors' visits, and discipline them. Those who are in charge of infants, sometimes called *infant nurses*, also prepare bottles and change diapers. *Nannies* work for a single family. They generally take care of children from birth to age 12, tending to the child's early education, nutrition, health, and other needs. They also may perform the duties of a housekeeper, including cleaning and laundry.

Family child care providers often work alone with a small group of children, though some work in larger settings with multiple adults. Child care centers generally have more than one adult per group of children; in groups of older children, a child care worker may assist a more experienced preschool teacher.

Most child care workers perform a combination of basic care and teaching duties, but the majority of their time is spent on care giving activities. Workers whose primary responsibility is teaching are classified as preschool teachers. However, many basic care activities also are opportunities for children to learn. For example, a worker who shows a child how to tie a shoelace teaches the child while also providing for that child's basic needs.

Child care workers spend most of their day working with children. However, they do maintain contact with parents or guardians through informal meetings or scheduled conferences to discuss each child's progress and needs. Many child care workers keep records of each child's progress and suggest ways in which parents can stimulate their child's learning and development at home. Some child care centers and before- and after-school programs actively recruit parent volunteers to work with the children and participate in administrative decisions and program planning.

Young children learn mainly through play. Child care workers recognize this and capitalize on children's play to further language development (storytelling and acting games), improve social skills (working together to build a neighborhood in a sandbox), and introduce scientific and mathematical concepts (balancing and counting blocks when building a bridge or mixing colors when painting). Often a less structured approach is used to teach young children, including small-group lessons; one-on-one instruction; and creative activities such as art, dance, and music. Child care workers play a vital role in preparing children to build the skills they will need in school.

Child care workers in child care centers or family child care homes greet young children as they arrive, help them with their jackets, and select an activity of interest. When caring for infants, they feed and change them. To ensure a well-balanced program, child care workers prepare daily and long-term schedules of activities. Each day's activities balance individual and group play, as well as quiet and active time. Children are given some freedom to participate in activities in which they are interested. As children age, child care work-

ers may provide more guided learning opportunities, particularly in the areas of math and reading.

Concern over school-aged children being home alone before and after school has spurred many parents to seek alternative ways for their children to constructively spend their time. The purpose of before- and after-school programs is to watch over school-aged children during the gap between school hours and the end of their parents' daily work hours. These programs also may operate during the summer and on weekends. Workers in before- and after-school programs may help students with their homework or engage them in other extracurricular activities. These activities may include field trips, sports, or learning about computers, painting, photography, or other fun subjects. Some child care workers are responsible for taking children to school in the morning and picking them up from school in the afternoon. Before- and after-school programs may be operated by public school systems, local community centers, or other private organizations.

Helping to keep children healthy is another important part of the job. Child care workers serve nutritious meals and snacks and teach good eating habits and personal hygiene. They ensure that children have proper rest periods. They identify children who may not feel well and, in some cases, may help parents locate programs that will provide basic health services. Child care workers also watch for children who show signs of emotional or developmental problems and discuss these matters with their supervisor and the child's parents. Early identification of children with special needs—such as those with behavioral, emotional, physical, or learning disabilities—is important to improve their future learning ability. Special education teachers often work with preschool children to provide the individual attention they need.

Work environment. Helping children grow, learn, and gain new skills can be very rewarding. The work is sometimes routine but new activities and challenges mark each day. Child care can be physically and emotionally taxing, as workers constantly stand, walk, bend, stoop, and lift to attend to each child's interests and problems.

States regulate child care facilities, the number of children per child care worker, staff qualifications, and the health and safety of the children. State regulations in all of these areas vary. To ensure that children in child care centers receive proper supervision, state or local regulations may require a certain ratio of workers to children. The ratio varies with the age of the children. Child development experts generally recommend that a single caregiver be responsible for no more than 3 or 4 infants (less than 1 year old) and toddler's (1 to 2 years old) or 6 or 7 preschool-aged children (between 2 and 5 years old). In before- and after-school programs, workers may be responsible for many school-aged children at a time.

Family child care providers work out of their own homes. While this arrangement provides convenience, it also requires that their homes be accommodating to young children. Private household workers usually work in the homes or apartments of their employers. Most live in their own homes and travel to work, though some live in the home of their employer and generally are provided with their own room and bath. They often come to feel like part of their employer's family.

The work hours of child care workers vary widely. Child care centers usually are open year round, with long hours so that parents can drop off and pick up their children before and after work. Some centers employ full-time and part-time staff with staggered shifts to cover the entire day. Some workers are unable to take regular breaks during the day due to limited staffing. Public and many private pre-school programs operate during the typical 9- or 10-month school year, employing both full-time and part-time workers. Family child care providers have flexible hours and daily routines, but they may work long or unusual hours to fit parents' work schedules. Live-in nannies usually work longer hours than do those who have their own homes. However, although nannies may work evenings or week-ends, they usually get other time off.

Training, Other Qualifications, and Advancement

Licensure and training requirements vary greatly by state, but many jobs require little more than a high school diploma.

Education and training. The training and qualifications required of child care workers vary widely. Each state has its own licensing requirements that regulate caregiver training. These requirements range from a high school diploma, a national Child Development Associate (CDA) credential to community college courses or a col-lege degree in child development or early childhood education. State requirements are generally higher for workers at child care centers than for family child care providers. Child care workers in private settings who care for only a few children often are not regulated by states at all. Child care workers generally can obtain some form of employment with a high school diploma and little or no experience, but certain private firms and publicly funded programs have more demanding training and education requirements. Some employers may prefer workers who have taken secondary or postsecondary courses in child development and early childhood education or who have work experience in a child care setting. Other employers require their own specialized training. An increasing number of employers require an associate degree in early childhood education.

Licensure. Many states require child care centers, including those in private homes, to be licensed if they care for more than a few chil-dren. In order to obtain their license, child care centers may require child care workers to pass a background check and get immuniza-tions. Furthermore, child care workers may need to be trained in first aid and CPR and receive continuous training on topics of health and safety.

Other qualifications. Child care workers must anticipate and pre-vent problems, deal with disruptive children, provide fair but firm discipline, and be enthusiastic and constantly alert. They must com-municate effectively with the children and their parents, as well as with teachers and other child care workers. Workers should be mature, patient, understanding, and articulate and have energy and physical stamina. Skills in music, art, drama, and storytelling also are important. Self-employed child care workers must have business sense and management abilities.

Certification and advancement. Some employers prefer to hire child care workers who have earned a nationally recognized Child Development Associate (CDA) credential or the Certified Childcare Professional (CCP) designation from the Council for Professional Recognition and the National Child Care Association, respectively. Requirements include child care experience and coursework, such as college courses or employer-provided seminars.

Opportunities for advancement are limited. However, as child care workers gain experience, some may advance to supervisory or administrative positions in large child care centers or preschools. Often, these positions require additional training, such as a

bachelor's or master's degree. Other workers move on to work in resource and referral agencies, consulting with parents on available child services. A few workers become involved in policy or advo-cacy work related to child care and early childhood education. With a bachelor's degree, workers may become preschool teachers or become certified to teach in public or private schools. Some work-ers set up their own child care businesses.

Employment

Child care workers held about 1.4 million jobs in 2006. Many worked part time. About 35 percent of child care workers were self-employed; most of these were family child care providers.

Child day care services employed about 18 percent of all child care workers and about 20 percent work for private households. The remainder worked primarily in educational services; nursing and residential care facilities; religious organizations; amusement and recreation industries; civic and social organizations; individual and family services; and local government, excluding education and hospitals. Some child care programs are for-profit centers, which may be affiliated with a local or national company. Religious insti-tutions, community agencies, school systems, and state and local governments operate nonprofit programs. A very small percentage of private industry establishments operate onsite child care centers for the children of their employees.

Job Outlook

Child care workers are expected to experience job growth that is faster than the average for all occupations. Job prospects will be excellent because of the many workers who leave and need to be replaced.

Employment change. Employment of child care workers is pro-jected to increase by 18 percent between 2006 and 2016, which is faster than the average for all occupations. Child care workers will have a very large number of new jobs arise, almost 248,000 over the projections decade. The proportion of children being cared for exclusively by parents or other relatives is likely to continue to decline, spurring demand for additional child care workers. Concern about the safety and supervision of school-aged children during non-school hours also should increase demand for before- and after-school programs and the child care workers who staff them.

The growth in demand for child care workers will be moderated, however, by an increasing emphasis on early childhood education programs, which hire mostly preschool workers instead of child care workers. While only a few states currently provide targeted or uni-versal preschool programs, many more are considering or starting such programs. A rise in enrollment in private preschools is likely as the value of formal education before kindergarten becomes more widely accepted. Since the majority of workers in these programs are classified as preschool teachers, this growth in preschool enroll-ment will mean less growth among child care workers.

Job prospects. High replacement needs should create good job opportunities for child care workers. Qualified persons who are interested in this work should have little trouble finding and keeping a job. Many child care workers must be replaced each year as they leave the occupation to fulfill family responsibilities, to study, or for other reasons. Others leave because they are interested in pursuing other occupations or because of low wages.

Projections data from the National Employment Matrix

Occupational Title	SOC Code	Employment, 2006	Projected employment, 2016	Change, 2006-16	
				Number	Percent
Child care workers	39-9011	1,388,000	1,636,000	248,000	18

NOTE: Data in this table are rounded.

Earnings

Pay depends on the educational attainment of the worker and the type of establishment. Although the pay generally is very low, more education usually means higher earnings. Median annual earnings of wage-and-salary child care workers were $17,630 in May 2006. The middle 50 percent earned between $14,790 and $21,930. The lowest 10 percent earned less than $12,910, and the highest 10 percent earned more than $27,050. Median annual earnings in the industries employing the largest numbers of child care workers in 2006 were as follows:

Other residential care facilities	$20,770
Elementary and secondary schools	20,220
Civic and social organizations	16,460
Child day care services	16,320
Other amusement and recreation industries	16,300

Earnings of self-employed child care workers vary depending on the number of hours worked, the number and ages of the children, and the location.

Benefits vary but are minimal for most child care workers. Many employers offer free or discounted child care to employees. Some offer a full benefits package, including health insurance and paid vacations, but others offer no benefits at all. Some employers offer seminars and workshops to help workers learn new skills. A few are willing to cover the cost of courses taken at community colleges or technical schools. Live-in nannies receive free room and board.

Related Occupations

Child care work requires patience; creativity; an ability to nurture, motivate, teach, and influence children; and leadership, organizational, and administrative skills. Others who work with children and need these qualities and skills include teacher assistants; teachers—preschool, kindergarten, elementary, middle, and secondary; and teachers—special education.

Sources of Additional Information

For an electronic question-and-answer service on child care, information on becoming a child care provider, and other resources, contact

▸ National Child Care Information Center, 243 Church St. NW, 2nd Floor, Vienna, VA 22180. Internet: http://www.nccic.org

For eligibility requirements and a description of the Child Development Associate credential, contact

▸ Council for Professional Recognition, 2460 16th St. NW, Washington, DC 20009-3575. Internet: http://www.cdacouncil.org

For eligibility requirements and a description of the Certified Childcare Professional designation, contact

▸ National Child Care Association, 2025 M St. NW, Suite 800, Washington, DC 20036. Internet: http://www.nccanet.org

For information about a career as a nanny, contact

▸ International Nanny Association, 191 Clarksville Rd., Princeton Junction, NJ 08550-3111. Telephone (toll free): 888-878-1477. Internet: http://www.nanny.org

State departments of human services or social services can supply state regulations and training requirements for child care workers.

Claims Adjusters, Appraisers, Examiners, and Investigators

(O*NET 13-1031.00, 13-1031.01, 13-1031.02, and 13-1032.00)

Significant Points

■ Employment is expected to increase moderately, but many job openings will arise from the need to replace workers who retire or leave for other reasons.

■ Licensing and continuing education requirements vary by state.

■ College graduates have the best opportunities; competition will be keen for jobs as investigators because this occupation attracts many qualified people.

Nature of the Work

Individuals and businesses purchase insurance policies to protect against monetary losses. In the event of a loss, policyholders submit claims, or requests for payment, seeking compensation for their loss. Adjusters, appraisers, examiners, and investigators deal with those claims. They work primarily for property and casualty insurance companies, for whom they handle a wide variety of claims alleging property damage, liability, or bodily injury. Their main role is to investigate the claims, negotiate settlements, and authorize payments to claimants, all the while mindful not to violate the claimant's rights under federal and state privacy laws. They must determine whether the customer's insurance policy covers the loss and how much of the loss should be paid to the claimant. Although many adjusters, appraisers, examiners, and investigators have overlapping functions and may even perform the same tasks, the insurance industry generally assigns specific roles to each of these claims workers.

Adjusters plan and schedule the work required to process a claim. They might, for example, handle the claim filed after an automobile accident or after a storm damages a customer's home. Adjusters investigate claims by interviewing the claimant and witnesses, consulting police and hospital records, and inspecting property damage to determine the extent of the company's liability. Adjusters may consult with other professionals, such as accountants, architects, construction workers, engineers, lawyers, and physicians, who can offer a more expert evaluation of a claim. The information gathered—including photographs and statements, either written, audio, or on videotape—is set down in a report that is then used to evaluate the associated claim. When the policyholder's claim is legitimate, the claims adjuster negotiates with the claimant and settles the claim. When claims are contested, adjusters will work with attorneys and expert witnesses to defend the insurer's position.

Many companies centralize claims adjustment in a claims center, where the cost of repair is estimated and a check is issued immediately. More complex cases, usually involving bodily injury, are referred to senior adjusters. Some adjusters work with multiple types of insurance, but most specialize in homeowner claims, business losses, automotive damage, or workers' compensation.

Claimants can opt not to rely on the services of their insurance company's adjuster and may instead choose to hire a public adjuster. These workers assist clients in preparing and presenting claims to insurance companies and in trying to negotiate a fair settlement. They perform the same services as adjusters who work directly for companies, but they work in the best interests of the client rather than the insurance company. Independent adjusters are also self-employed and are typically hired by an insurance carrier on a freelance or contractual basis. Insurance companies may choose to hire independent adjusters in lieu of hiring them as regular employees.

Claims examiners within property and casualty insurance firms may have duties similar to those of an adjuster, but often their primary job is to review the claims submitted in order to ensure that proper guidelines have been followed. They may assist adjusters with complex and complicated claims or when a disaster suddenly greatly increases the volume of claims.

Most claims examiners work for life or health insurance companies. In health insurance companies, examiners review health-related claims to see whether costs are reasonable given the diagnosis. Examiners use guides with information on the average period of disability, the expected treatments, and the average hospital stay for the various ailments. Examiners check claim applications for completeness and accuracy, interview medical specialists, and consult policy files to verify the information reported in a claim. Examiners will then either authorize the appropriate payment or refer the claim to an investigator for a more thorough review. Claims examiners usually specialize in group or individual insurance plans and in hospital, dental, or prescription drug claims.

In life insurance, claims examiners review the causes of death, particularly in the case of an accident, because most life insurance policies pay additional benefits if a death is accidental. Claims examiners also may review new applications for life insurance to make sure that the applicants have no serious illnesses that would make them a high risk to insure and thus disqualify them from obtaining insurance.

Another occupation that plays an important role in the accurate settlement of claims is that of the *appraiser*, whose role is to estimate the cost or value of an insured item. The majority of appraisers employed by insurance companies and independent adjusting firms are *auto damage appraisers*. These appraisers inspect damaged vehicles after an accident and estimate the cost of repairs. This information is then relayed to the adjuster, who incorporates the appraisal into the settlement. Auto damage appraisers are valued by insurance companies because they can provide an unbiased judgment of repair costs. Otherwise, the companies would have to rely on auto mechanics' estimates, which might be unreasonably high.

Many claims adjusters and auto damage appraisers are equipped with laptop computers from which they can download the necessary forms and files from insurance company databases. They also may use digital cameras, which allow photographs of the damage to be sent to the company via the Internet. Many also input information about the damage directly into their computers, where software programs produce estimates of damage on standard forms. These new technologies allow for faster and more efficient processing of claims.

When adjusters or examiners suspect fraud, they refer the claim to an investigator. *Insurance investigators* in an insurance company's special investigative unit handle claims in which the company suspects fraudulent or criminal activity, such as arson, falsified workers' disability claims, staged accidents, or unnecessary medical treatments. The severity of insurance fraud cases can vary greatly, from claimants simply overstating the damage to a vehicle to complicated fraud rings responsible for many claimants and supported by dishonest doctors, lawyers, and even insurance personnel.

Investigators usually start with a database search to obtain background information on claimants and witnesses. Investigators can access certain personal information and identify Social Security numbers, aliases, driver's license numbers, addresses, phone numbers, criminal records, and past claims histories to establish whether a claimant has ever attempted insurance fraud. Then, investigators may visit claimants and witnesses to obtain a recorded statement; take photographs; and inspect facilities, such as doctors' offices, to determine whether the doctors have a proper license. Investigators often consult with legal counsel and can be expert witnesses in court cases.

Often, investigators also perform surveillance work. For example, in a case involving fraudulent workers' compensation claims, an investigator may covertly observe the claimant for several days or even weeks. If the investigator observes the subject performing an activity that is ruled out by injuries stated in a workers' compensation claim, the investigator will take video or still photographs to document the activity and report it to the insurance company.

Work environment. Working environments of claims adjusters, appraisers, examiners, and investigators vary greatly. Many claims adjusters and auto damage appraisers often work outside the office, inspecting damaged buildings and automobiles. Adjusters who inspect damaged buildings must be wary of potential hazards such as collapsed roofs and floors, as well as weakened structures.

Adjusters report to the office every morning to get their assignments, while others simply call in from home and spend their days traveling to claim sites. New technology, such as laptop computers and cellular telephones, is making telecommuting easier for claims adjusters and auto damage appraisers. Many adjusters work inside their office only a few hours a week, while others conduct their business entirely out of their home and automobile. Occasionally, experienced adjusters must be away from home for days—for example, when they travel to the scene of a disaster such as a tornado, hurricane, or flood—to work with local adjusters and government officials.

Most claims examiners employed by life and health insurance companies work a standard five-day, 40-hour week in a typical office environment. In contrast, adjusters often must arrange their work schedules to accommodate evening and weekend appointments with clients. This sometimes results in adjusters working irregular schedules or more than 40 hours a week, especially when they have a lot of claims to investigate. Adjusters often are called to work in the event of emergencies and may have to work 50 or 60 hours a week until all claims are resolved.

© JIST Works

Appraisers spend much of their time offsite at automotive body shops estimating vehicle damage costs. The remaining time may be spent working in the office. Many independent appraisers work from home, which has been made easier through new computer software valuation programs. Auto damage appraisers typically work regular hours and rarely work on the weekends. Self-employed appraisers also have the flexibility to make their own hours, as many appraisals are done by appointment.

Some days, investigators will spend all day in the office searching databases, making telephone calls, and writing reports. Other times, they may be away performing surveillance activities or interviewing witnesses. Some of the work can involve confrontation with claimants and others involved in a case, so the job can be stressful and dangerous. Insurance investigators often work irregular hours because of the need to conduct surveillance and contact people who are not available during normal working hours. Early morning, evening, and weekend work is common.

Training, Other Qualifications, and Advancement

Training and entry requirements vary widely for claims adjusters, appraisers, examiners, and investigators. Although many in these occupations do not have a college degree, most companies prefer to hire college graduates.

Education and training. There are no formal education requirements for any of these occupations, and a high school degree is typically the minimal requirement needed to obtain employment. However, most employers prefer to hire college graduates or people who have some postsecondary training.

No specific college major is recommended, but a variety of degrees can be an asset. For example, a claims adjuster who has a business or an accounting background might be suited to specialize in claims of financial loss due to strikes, breakdowns of equipment, or damage to merchandise. College training in architecture or engineering is helpful in adjusting industrial claims, such as those involving damage from fires or other accidents. A legal background can be beneficial to someone handling workers' compensation and product liability cases. A medical background is useful for those examiners working on medical and life insurance claims.

The following tabulation presents the 2006 percent distribution of all claims adjusters, appraisers, examiners, and investigators by their highest level of educational attainment:

High school graduate or less 22%

Some college, no degree...17

Associate's degree 12

Bachelor's degree 45

Graduate degree 5

For auto damage appraiser jobs, firms typically prefer to hire people who also have experience as an estimator or as a manager of an auto body repair shop. Also, an appraiser must know how to repair vehicles in order to identify and estimate damage. Technical skills are essential. While auto damage appraisers do not require a college education, most companies prefer to hire persons with formal training. Many vocational colleges offer two-year programs in auto body repair and teach students how to estimate the costs to repair damaged vehicles.

For investigator jobs, most insurance companies prefer to hire people trained as law enforcement officers, private investigators, claims adjusters, or examiners because these workers have good interviewing and interrogation skills.

Beginning claims adjusters, appraisers, examiners, and investigators work on small claims under the supervision of experienced workers. As they learn more about claims investigation and settlement, they are assigned larger, more complex claims. Trainees take on more responsibility as they demonstrate competence in handling assignments and progress in their coursework. Auto damage appraisers may also receive some on-the-job training, which may last several months. They may work under close supervision while estimating damage costs until their employer decides they are ready to perform estimates on their own.

Continuing education is very important for claims adjusters, appraisers, examiners, and investigators because federal and state laws and court decisions affect how claims are handled or who is covered by insurance policies. Also, examiners working on life and health claims must be familiar with new medical procedures and prescription drugs. Examiners working on auto claims must be familiar with new car models and repair techniques.

Many companies offer training sessions to inform their employees of industry changes, and a number of schools and associations give courses and seminars on various topics having to with claims. Correspondence courses via the Internet are also making long-distance learning possible.

Licensure. Licensing requirements for claims adjusters, appraisers, examiners, and investigators vary by state. Some states have few requirements, while others require either the completion of prelicensing education, a satisfactory score on a licensing exam, or both. Earning a voluntary professional designation can sometimes substitute for completing an exam. In some states, claims adjusters employed by insurance companies can work under the company license and need not become licensed themselves. Public adjusters may need to meet separate or additional requirements. For example, some states require public adjusters to file a surety bond.

Some states that require licensing also require a certain number of continuing education credits per year in order to renew the license. Workers can fulfill their continuing education requirements by attending classes or workshops, by writing articles for claims publications, or by giving lectures and presentations.

Other qualifications. Claims adjusters, appraisers, and examiners often work closely with claimants, witnesses, and other insurance professionals, so they must be able to communicate effectively with others. Knowledge of computer applications also is very helpful. In addition, a valid driver's license and a good driving record are required for workers who must travel on the job. Some companies require applicants to pass a series of written aptitude tests designed to measure their communication, analytical, and general mathematical skills.

When hiring investigators, employers look for individuals who have ingenuity and who are persistent and assertive. Investigators should not be afraid of confrontation, should communicate well, and should be able to think on their feet. Good interviewing and interrogation skills also are important and usually are acquired in earlier careers in law enforcement.

Certification and advancement. Employees who demonstrate competence in claims work or administrative skills may be promoted to more responsible managerial or administrative jobs. Similarly, claims investigators may rise to become supervisor or manager of the investigations department. Once they achieve expertise, many choose to start their own independent adjusting or auto damage appraising firms.

Numerous examiners and adjusters also earn professional certifications and designations to demonstrate their professional expertise. Although requirements for these designations vary, many entail at least five to 10 years of experience in the claims field and the successful completion of an examination; in addition, a certain number of continuing education credits must be earned each year to retain the designation.

Employment

Adjusters, appraisers, examiners, and investigators held about 319,000 jobs in 2006. Insurance carriers; agencies; brokerages; and related industries, such as private claims adjusting companies, employed more than 7 out of 10 claims adjusters, appraisers, examiners, and investigators. Less than 5 percent of these jobs were held by auto damage insurance appraisers. Relatively few adjusters, appraisers, examiners, and investigators were self-employed.

Job Outlook

Despite average job growth, keen competition for claims adjuster, appraiser, examiner, and investigator jobs is expected, especially in smaller, privately owned companies. For claims adjusters, opportunities will be best for those who have a license and related experience. For appraiser jobs, opportunities will be best for those who have some vocational training and previous auto body repair experience.

Employment change. Employment of claims adjusters, appraisers, examiners, and investigators is expected to grow by 9 percent over the 2006–2016 decade, which is about as fast as the average for all occupations. Many insurance carriers are downsizing their claims staff in an effort to contain costs. Larger companies are relying more on customer service representatives in call centers, for example, to handle the recording of the necessary details of the claim, allowing adjusters to spend more of their time investigating claims. New technology is reducing the amount of time it takes for an adjuster to complete a claim, thereby increasing the number of claims that one adjuster can handle. The demand for these jobs will increase regardless of new technology, however, because they cannot be easily automated. Additionally, a growing need for adjusters, appraisers, examiners, and investigators will stem from more insurance policies being sold to accommodate a growing population. Further, as the elderly population increases, there will be a greater need for health care, resulting in more health insurance claims.

Employment of insurance investigators is not expected to grow significantly despite the expected increase in the number of claims in

litigation and the number and complexity of insurance fraud cases. Technology, such as the Internet, reduces the amount of time it takes investigators to perform background checks, allowing them to handle more cases. However, adjusters are still needed to contact policyholders, inspect damaged property, and consult with experts.

As with claims adjusters, examiners, and investigators, employment of auto damage appraisers should grow by 13 percent, which is also about as fast as the average for all occupations. Insurance companies and agents continue to sell growing numbers of auto insurance policies, leading to more claims being filed that require the attention of an auto damage appraiser. The work of auto damage appraisers is also not easily automated because most appraisals require an on-site inspection, but new technology is making them somewhat more efficient. In addition, some insurance companies are opening their own repair facilities, which may reduce the need for auto damage appraisers.

Job prospects. Numerous job openings also will result from job growth and the need to replace workers who transfer to other occupations or leave the labor force. Overall, college graduates and those with previous related experience will have the best opportunities for jobs as claims adjusters, examiners, and investigators. Auto damage appraisers with related vocational training and auto body shop experience will also have good prospects. People entering these occupations with no previous experience or formal training may find more opportunities working directly for an insurance carrier.

Competition for investigator jobs will remain keen because the occupation attracts many qualified people, including retirees from law enforcement and the military and experienced claims adjusters and examiners who choose to get an investigator license. Heightened media and public awareness of insurance fraud also may attract qualified candidates to this occupation.

Earnings

Earnings of claims adjusters, appraisers, examiners, and investigators vary significantly. Median annual earnings were $50,660 in May 2006 for wage and salary workers. The middle 50 percent earned between $38,520 and $65,210. The lowest 10 percent earned less than $30,890, and the highest 10 percent earned more than $79,170.

Median annual earnings of wage and salary auto damage insurance appraisers were $49,180 in May 2006. The middle 50 percent earned between $40,870 and $57,830. The lowest 10 percent earned less than $34,220, and the highest 10 percent earned more than $68,420.

Many claims adjusters, especially those who work for insurance companies, receive additional bonuses or benefits as part of their job. Adjusters often are furnished a laptop computer, a cellular telephone, and a company car or are reimbursed for the use of their own vehicle for business purposes.

Projections data from the National Employment Matrix

Occupational Title	SOC Code	Employment, 2006	Projected employment, 2016	Change, 2006-16	
				Number	Percent
Claims adjusters, appraisers, examiners, and investigators	13-1030	319,000	347,000	29,000	9
Claims adjusters, examiners, and investigators............................	13-1031	305,000	332,000	27,000	9
Insurance appraisers, auto damage	13-1032	13,000	15,000	1,700	13

NOTE: Data in this table are rounded.

Related Occupations

Property-casualty insurance adjusters and life and health insurance examiners must determine the validity of a claim and negotiate a settlement. They also are responsible for determining how much to reimburse the client. Occupations similar to those of claims adjusters, appraisers, examiners, and investigators include cost estimators; bill and account collectors; medical records and health information technicians; billing and posting clerks; credit authorizers, checkers, and clerks; and bookkeeping, accounting, and auditing clerks.

In determining the validity of a claim, insurance adjusters must inspect the damage in order to assess the magnitude of the loss. Workers who perform similar duties include fire inspectors and investigators and construction and building inspectors.

To ensure that company practices and procedures are followed, property and casualty examiners review insurance claims for which a claims adjuster has already proposed a settlement. Others in occupations that review documents for accuracy and compliance with a given set of rules and regulations are tax examiners, collectors, and revenue agents and accountants and auditors.

Like automotive body and related repairers and automotive service technicians and mechanics, auto damage appraisers must be familiar with the structure and functions of various automobiles and their parts. They must also be familiar with techniques to estimate value, which is a requirement similar to appraisers and assessors of real estate.

Insurance investigators detect and investigate fraudulent claims and criminal activity. Their work is similar to that of private detectives and investigators.

Sources of Additional Information

General information about a career as a claims adjuster, appraiser, examiner, or investigator is available from the home offices of many insurance companies. Information about licensing requirements for claims adjusters may be obtained from the department of insurance in each state.

Information about the property-casualty insurance field can be obtained by contacting

▸ Insurance Information Institute, 110 William St., New York, NY 10038. Internet: http://www.iii.org

Information about the health insurance field can be obtained by contacting

▸ National Association of Health Underwriters, 2000 North 14th Street, Suite 450, Arlington, VA 22201. Internet: http://www.nahu.org

For information about professional designation and training programs, contact any of the following organizations:

▸ American College, 270 South Bryn Mawr Ave., Bryn Mawr, PA 19010-2196. Internet: http://www.theamericancollege.edu

▸ American Institute for Chartered Property Casualty Underwriters and the Insurance Institute of America, 720 Providence Rd., P.O. Box 3016, Malvern, PA 19355-0716. Internet: http://www.aicpcu.org

▸ International Claim Association, 1255 23rd St. NW, Washington, DC 20037. Internet: http://www.claim.org

▸ LOMA, 2300 Windy Ridge Parkway, Suite 600, Atlanta, GA 30339-8443. Internet: http://www.loma.org/

Information on careers in auto damage appraising can be obtained from

▸ Independent Automotive Damage Appraisers Association, P.O. Box 12291, Columbus, GA 31917-2291. Internet: http://www.iada.org

Clinical Laboratory Technologists and Technicians

(O*NET 29-2011.00 and 29-2012.00)

Significant Points

■ Faster than average employment growth and excellent job opportunities are expected.

■ Clinical laboratory technologists usually have a bachelor's degree with a major in medical technology or in one of the life sciences; clinical laboratory technicians generally need either an associate degree or a certificate.

■ Most jobs will continue to be in hospitals, but employment will grow faster in other settings.

Nature of the Work

Clinical laboratory testing plays a crucial role in the detection, diagnosis, and treatment of disease. Clinical laboratory technologists—also referred to as clinical laboratory scientists or medical technologists—and clinical laboratory technicians, also known as medical technicians or medical laboratory technicians, perform most of these tests.

Clinical laboratory personnel examine and analyze body fluids, and cells. They look for bacteria, parasites, and other microorganisms; analyze the chemical content of fluids; match blood for transfusions; and test for drug levels in the blood that show how a patient is responding to treatment. Technologists also prepare specimens for examination, count cells, and look for abnormal cells in blood and body fluids. They use microscopes, cell counters, and other sophisticated laboratory equipment. They also use automated equipment and computerized instruments capable of performing a number of tests simultaneously. After testing and examining a specimen, they analyze the results and relay them to physicians.

With increasing automation and the use of computer technology, the work of technologists and technicians has become less hands-on and more analytical. The complexity of tests performed, the level of judgment needed, and the amount of responsibility workers assume depend largely on the amount of education and experience they have. Clinical laboratory technologists usually do more complex tasks than clinical laboratory technicians do.

Clinical laboratory technologists perform complex chemical, biological, hematological, immunologic, microscopic, and bacteriological tests. Technologists microscopically examine blood and other body fluids. They make cultures of body fluid and tissue samples, to determine the presence of bacteria, fungi, parasites, or other microorganisms. Technologists analyze samples for chemical content or a chemical reaction and determine concentrations of compounds such as blood glucose and cholesterol levels. They also type and cross match blood samples for transfusions.

Clinical laboratory technologists evaluate test results, develop and modify procedures, and establish and monitor programs, to ensure the accuracy of tests. Some technologists supervise clinical laboratory technicians.

Technologists in small laboratories perform many types of tests, whereas those in large laboratories generally specialize. Clinical chemistry technologists, for example, prepare specimens and analyze the chemical and hormonal contents of body fluids. Microbiology technologists examine and identify bacteria and other microorganisms. Blood bank technologists, or immunohematology technologists, collect, type, and prepare blood and its components for transfusions. Immunology technologists examine elements of the human immune system and its response to foreign bodies. Cytotechnologists prepare slides of body cells and examine these cells microscopically for abnormalities that may signal the beginning of a cancerous growth. Molecular biology technologists perform complex protein and nucleic acid testing on cell samples.

Clinical laboratory technicians perform less complex tests and laboratory procedures than technologists do. Technicians may prepare specimens and operate automated analyzers, for example, or they may perform manual tests in accordance with detailed instructions. They usually work under the supervision of medical and clinical laboratory technologists or laboratory managers. Like technologists, clinical laboratory technicians may work in several areas of the clinical laboratory or specialize in just one. Phlebotomists collect blood samples, for example, and histotechnicians cut and stain tissue specimens for microscopic examination by pathologists.

Work environment. Clinical laboratory personnel are trained to work with infectious specimens. When proper methods of infection control and sterilization are followed, few hazards exist. Protective masks, gloves, and goggles often are necessary to ensure the safety of laboratory personnel.

Working conditions vary with the size and type of employment setting. Laboratories usually are well lighted and clean; however, specimens, solutions, and reagents used in the laboratory sometimes produce fumes. Laboratory workers may spend a great deal of time on their feet.

Hours of clinical laboratory technologists and technicians vary with the size and type of employment setting. In large hospitals or in independent laboratories that operate continuously, personnel usually work the day, evening, or night shift and may work weekends and holidays. Laboratory personnel in small facilities may work on rotating shifts, rather than on a regular shift. In some facilities, laboratory personnel are on call several nights a week or on weekends, in case of an emergency.

Training, Other Qualifications, and Advancement

Clinical laboratory technologist generally require a bachelor's degree in medical technology or in one of the life sciences; clinical laboratory technicians usually need an associate degree or a certificate.

Education and training. The usual requirement for an entry-level position as a clinical laboratory technologist is a bachelor's degree with a major in medical technology or one of the life sciences; however, it is possible to qualify for some jobs with a combination of education and on-the-job and specialized training. Universities and hospitals offer medical technology programs.

Bachelor's degree programs in medical technology include courses in chemistry, biological sciences, microbiology, mathematics, and statistics, as well as specialized courses devoted to knowledge and skills used in the clinical laboratory. Many programs also offer or require courses in management, business, and computer applications. The Clinical Laboratory Improvement Act requires technologists who perform highly complex tests to have at least an associate degree.

Medical and clinical laboratory technicians generally have either an associate degree from a community or junior college or a certificate from a hospital, a vocational or technical school, or the Armed Forces. A few technicians learn their skills on the job.

The National Accrediting Agency for Clinical Laboratory Sciences (NAACLS) fully accredits about 470 programs for medical and clinical laboratory technologists, medical and clinical laboratory technicians, histotechnologists and histotechnicians, cytogenetic technologists, and diagnostic molecular scientists. NAACLS also approves about 60 programs in phlebotomy and clinical assisting. Other nationally recognized agencies that accredit specific areas for clinical laboratory workers include the Commission on Accreditation of Allied Health Education Programs and the Accrediting Bureau of Health Education Schools.

Licensure. Some states require laboratory personnel to be licensed or registered. Licensure of technologists often requires a bachelor's degree and the passing of an exam, but requirements vary by state and specialty. Information on licensure is available from state departments of health or boards of occupational licensing.

Certification and other qualifications. Many employers prefer applicants who are certified by a recognized professional association. Associations offering certification include the Board of Registry of the American Society for Clinical Pathology, the American Medical Technologists, the National Credentialing Agency for Laboratory Personnel, and the Board of Registry of the American Association of Bioanalysts. These agencies have different requirements for certification and different organizational sponsors.

In addition to certification, employers seek clinical laboratory personnel with good analytical judgment and the ability to work under pressure. Technologists in particular are expected to be good at problem solving. Close attention to detail is also essential for laboratory personnel because small differences or changes in test substances or numerical readouts can be crucial to a diagnosis. Manual dexterity and normal color vision are highly desirable, and with the widespread use of automated laboratory equipment, computer skills are important.

Advancement. Technicians can advance and become technologists through additional education and experience. Technologists may advance to supervisory positions in laboratory work or may become chief medical or clinical laboratory technologists or laboratory managers in hospitals. Manufacturers of home diagnostic testing kits and laboratory equipment and supplies also seek experienced technologists to work in product development, marketing, and sales.

Professional certification and a graduate degree in medical technology, one of the biological sciences, chemistry, management, or education usually speeds advancement. A doctorate usually is needed to become a laboratory director. Federal regulation requires directors of moderately complex laboratories to have either a master's degree or a bachelor's degree, combined with the appropriate amount of training and experience.

Employment

Clinical laboratory technologists and technicians held about 319,000 jobs in 2006. More than half of jobs were in hospitals. Most of the remaining jobs were in offices of physicians and in medical and diagnostic laboratories. A small proportion was in educational services and in all other ambulatory health care services.

Job Outlook

Rapid job growth and excellent job opportunities are expected. Most jobs will continue to be in hospitals, but employment will grow faster in other settings.

Employment change. Employment of clinical laboratory workers is expected to grow 14 percent between 2006 and 2016, faster than the average for all occupations. The volume of laboratory tests continues to increase with both population growth and the development of new types of tests.

Technological advances will continue to have opposing effects on employment. On the one hand, new, increasingly powerful diagnostic tests will encourage additional testing and spur employment. On the other, research and development efforts targeted at simplifying routine testing procedures may enhance the ability of nonlaboratory personnel—physicians and patients in particular—to perform tests now conducted in laboratories.

Although hospitals are expected to continue to be the major employer of clinical laboratory workers, employment is expected to grow faster in medical and diagnostic laboratories, offices of physicians, and all other ambulatory health care services.

Job prospects. Job opportunities are expected to be excellent because the number of job openings is expected to continue to exceed the number of job seekers. Although significant, job growth will not be the only source of opportunities. As in most occupations, many additional openings will result from the need to replace workers who transfer to other occupations, retire, or stop working for some other reason.

Earnings

Median annual wage-and-salary earnings of medical and clinical laboratory technologists were $49,700 in May 2006. The middle 50 percent earned between $41,680 and $58,560. The lowest 10 percent earned less than $34,660, and the highest 10 percent earned more than $69,260. Median annual earnings in the industries employing the largest numbers of medical and clinical laboratory technologists were

Federal government	$57,360
Medical and diagnostic laboratories	50,740
General medical and surgical hospitals	49,930
Offices of physicians	45,420
Colleges, universities, and professional schools	45,080

Median annual wage-and-salary earnings of medical and clinical laboratory technicians were $32,840 in May 2006. The middle 50 percent earned between $26,430 and $41,020. The lowest 10 percent earned less than $21,830, and the highest 10 percent earned more than $50,250. Median annual earnings in the industries employing the largest numbers of medical and clinical laboratory technicians were

General medical and surgical hospitals	$34,200
Colleges, universities, and professional schools	33,440
Offices of physicians	31,330
Medical and diagnostic laboratories	30,240
Other ambulatory health care services	29,560

According to the American Society for Clinical Pathology, median hourly wages of staff clinical laboratory technologists and technicians in 2005 in various specialties and laboratory types were

	Hospital	Private clinic	Physician office laboratory
Cytotechnoligist	$26.39	$31.64	$25.69
Histotechnologist	21.50	21.63	23.29
Medical technologist	21.77	20.00	20.00
Histotechnician	18.50	20.86	18.27
Medical laboratory technician	17.41	16.94	16.63
Phlebotomist	11.70	12.15	11.25

Related Occupations

Clinical laboratory technologists and technicians analyze body fluids, tissue, and other substances, using a variety of tests. Similar or related procedures are performed by chemists and materials scientists, science technicians, and veterinary technologists and technicians.

Sources of Additional Information

For a list of accredited and approved educational programs for clinical laboratory personnel, contact

▸ National Accrediting Agency for Clinical Laboratory Sciences, 8410 W. Bryn Mawr Ave., Suite 670, Chicago, IL 60631. Internet: http://www.naacls.org

Information on certification is available from

▸ American Association of Bioanalysts, Board of Registry, 906 Olive St., Suite 1200, St. Louis, MO 63101. Internet: http://www.aab.org

▸ American Medical Technologists, 10700 Higgins Rd., Suite 150, Rosemont, IL 60018. Internet: http://www.amt1.com

▸ American Society for Clinical Pathology, 33 West Monroe Street, Suite 1600, Chicago, IL 60603. Internet: http://www.ascp.org

Projections data from the National Employment Matrix

Occupational Title	SOC Code	Employment, 2006	Projected employment, 2016	Change, 2006-2016 Number	Change, 2006-2016 Percent
Clinical laboratory technologists and technicians	29-2010	319,000	362,000	43,000	14
Medical and clinical laboratory technologists	29-2011	167,000	188,000	21,000	12
Medical and clinical laboratory technicians	29-2012	151,000	174,000	23,000	15

NOTE: Data in this table are rounded.

▸ National Credentialing Agency for Laboratory Personnel, P.O. Box 15945, Lenexa, KS 66285. Internet: http://www.nca-info.org

Additional career information is available from

▸ American Association of Blood Banks, 8101 Glenbrook Rd., Bethesda, MD 20814. Internet: http://www.aabb.org

▸ American Society for Clinical Laboratory Science, 6701 Democracy Blvd., Suite 300, Bethesda, MD 20817. Internet: http://www.ascls.org

▸ American Society for Cytopathology, 400 West 9th St., Suite 201, Wilmington, DE 19801. Internet: http://www.cytopathology.org

▸ Clinical Laboratory Management Association, 989 Old Eagle School Rd., Suite 815, Wayne, PA 19087. Internet: http://www.clma.org

Computer Scientists and Database Administrators

(O*NET 15-1011.00, 15-1061.00, 15-1081.00, 15-1099.04, 15-1099.05, and 15-1099.99)

Significant Points

■ Education requirements range from an associate degree to a doctoral degree.

■ Employment is expected to increase much faster than the average as organizations continue to expand their use of technology.

■ Workers must be able to learn new technologies quickly for these constantly evolving occupations.

Nature of the Work

The rapid and widespread use of computers and information technology has generated a need for highly trained workers proficient in various job functions. These computer specialists include computer scientists, database administrators, and network systems and data communication analysts. Job tasks and occupational titles used to describe these workers evolve rapidly and continually, reflecting new areas of specialization or changes in technology, as well as the preferences and practices of employers.

Computer scientists work as theorists, researchers, or inventors. Their jobs are distinguished by the higher level of theoretical expertise and innovation they apply to complex problems and the creation or application of new technology. The areas of computer science research range from complex theory to hardware design to programming-language design. Some researchers work on multidisciplinary projects, such as developing and advancing uses of virtual reality, extending human-computer interaction, or designing robots. They may work on design teams with electrical engineers and other specialists.

Computer science researchers employed by academic institutions have job functions that are similar in many ways to those employed by other organizations. In general, researchers in academic settings have more flexibility to focus on pure theory, while those working in other organizations usually focus on projects that have the possibility of producing patents and profits. However, some researchers in non-academic settings have considerable latitude in determining the direction of their research.

With the Internet and electronic business generating large volumes of data, there is a growing need to be able to store, manage, and extract data effectively. *Database administrators* work with database management systems software and determine ways to organize and store data. They identify user needs and set up new computer databases. In many cases, database administrators must integrate data from outdated systems into a new system. They also test and coordinate modifications to the system when needed, and troubleshoot problems when they occur. An organization's database administrator ensures the performance of the system, understands the platform on which the database runs, and adds new users to the system. Because many databases are connected to the Internet, database administrators also must plan and coordinate security measures with network administrators. With the growing volume of sensitive data and the increasing interconnectedness of computer networks, data integrity, backup systems, and database security have become increasingly important aspects of the job of database administrators.

Network systems and data communications analysts, also referred to as *network architects*, design, test, and evaluate systems such as local area networks (LANs), wide area networks (WANs), the Internet, intranets, and other data communications systems. Systems are configured in many ways and can range from a connection between two offices in the same building to globally distributed networks, voice mail, and e-mail systems of a multinational organization. Network systems and data communications analysts perform network modeling, analysis, and planning, often requiring both hardware and software solutions. For example, a network may involve the installation of several pieces of hardware, such as routers and hubs, wireless adaptors, and cables, while also requiring the installation and configuration of software, such as network drivers. Analysts also may research related products and make necessary hardware and software recommendations.

Telecommunications specialists focus on the interaction between computer and communications equipment. These workers design voice and data communication systems, supervise the installation of the systems, and provide maintenance and other services to clients after the systems are installed.

The growth of the Internet and the expansion of the World Wide Web (the graphical portion of the Internet) have generated a variety of occupations related to the design, development, and maintenance of Web sites and their servers. For example, *webmasters* are responsible for all technical aspects of a Web site, including performance issues such as speed of access, and for approving the content of the site. *Internet developers* or *Web developers*, also called *Web designers*, are responsible for day-to-day site creation and design.

Work environment. Computer scientists and database administrators normally work in offices or laboratories in comfortable surroundings. They typically work about 40 hours a week, the same as many other professional or office workers. However, evening or weekend work may be necessary to meet deadlines or to solve specific problems. Telecommuting is increasingly common for many computer professionals as networks expand, allowing more work to be done from remote locations through modems, laptops, electronic mail, and the Internet. However, some work still must be done in the office for security or other reasons.

Like other workers who spend long periods in front of a computer terminal typing on a keyboard, computer scientists and database administrators are susceptible to eyestrain, back discomfort, and

© JIST Works

hand and wrist problems such as carpal tunnel syndrome or cumulative trauma disorder.

Training, Other Qualifications, and Advancement

Rapidly changing technology requires an increasing level of skill and education on the part of workers in these occupations. Employers look for professionals with an ever-broader background and range of skills, including technical knowledge and also communication and other interpersonal skills.

Education and training. While there is no universally accepted way to prepare for a job as a network systems analyst, computer scientist, or database administrator, most employers place a premium on some formal college education. A bachelor's degree is a prerequisite for many jobs; however, some jobs may require only a two-year degree. Relevant work experience also is very important. For more technically complex jobs, persons with graduate degrees are preferred. Most computer scientist positions require a Ph.D. degree, as their main job function is research. Computer scientists having only a bachelor's or master's degree are generally limited in their ability to advance.

For database administrator and network systems and data communication analyst positions, most employers seek applicants who have bachelor's degrees in computer science, information science, or management information systems (MIS). MIS programs usually are part of the business school or college and differ considerably from computer science programs, emphasizing business and management-oriented coursework and business computing courses. Employers increasingly prefer applicants with a master's degree in business administration (MBA) with a concentration in information systems, as more firms move their business to the Internet. For some network systems and data communication analysts, such as webmasters, an associate degree or certificate is sufficient, although more advanced positions might require a computer-related bachelor's degree.

Most community colleges and many independent technical institutes and proprietary schools offer an associate's degree in computer science or a related information technology field. Many of these programs may be geared more toward meeting the needs of local businesses and are more occupation specific than are four-year degree programs. Some jobs may be better suited to the level of training that such programs offer. Employers usually look for people who have broad knowledge and experience related to computer systems and technologies, strong problem-solving and analytical skills, and good interpersonal skills. Courses in computer science or systems design offer good preparation for a job in these computer occupations. For jobs in a business environment, employers usually want systems analysts to have business management or closely related skills, while a background in the physical sciences, applied mathematics, or engineering is preferred for work in scientifically oriented organizations. Art or graphic design skills may be desirable for webmasters or Web developers.

Despite employers' preference for those with technical degrees, individuals with post-secondary degrees in a variety of other subjects may find employment in these occupations. Given the rapid pace of technological change, a degree generally has more value as a demonstration of an individual's ability to learn, rather than as a certification of a certain skill set. Generally speaking, coursework in computer science and an undergraduate degree are sufficient qualifications, especially if the applicant has a reasonable amount of experience.

Certification and other qualifications. Computer scientists and database administrators must be able to think logically and have good communication skills. Because they often deal with a number of tasks simultaneously, the ability to concentrate and pay close attention to detail also is important. Although computer specialists sometimes work independently, they frequently work in teams on large projects. As a result, they must be able to communicate effectively with computer personnel, such as programmers and managers, as well as with users or other staff who may have no technical computer background.

Jobseekers can enhance their employment opportunities by earning certifications, most of which are offered through private companies, with many related to specific products. Many employers regard these certifications as the industry standard. For example, one method of acquiring enough knowledge to get a job as a database administrator is to become certified in database management with a certain software package. Voluntary certification also is available through various organizations associated with computer specialists. Professional certification may afford a jobseeker a competitive advantage.

Because technology is so closely connected to the functioning of businesses, many workers in these occupations come from elsewhere in the business or industry to become computer specialists. This background can be very useful, in that it helps them to better understand how their networking and database tools are being used within the organization.

Advancement. Computer scientists may advance into managerial or project leadership positions. Many having advanced degrees choose to leave private industry for academic positions. Database administrators may advance into managerial positions, such as chief technology officer, on the basis of their experience managing data and enforcing security. Computer specialists with work experience and considerable expertise in a particular subject or a certain application may find lucrative opportunities as independent consultants or may choose to start their own computer consulting firms.

Technological advances come so rapidly in the computer field that continuous study is necessary to keep one's skills up to date. Employers, hardware and software vendors, colleges and universities, and private training institutions offer continuing education. Additional training may come from professional development seminars offered by professional computing societies.

Employment

Computer scientists and database administrators held about 542,000 jobs in May 2006, including about 58,000 who were self-employed. Employment was distributed among the detailed occupations as follows:

Network systems and data communication
   analysts 262,000
Computer specialists, all other............................136,000
Database administrators 119,000
Computer and information scientists, research 25,000

Although they are increasingly employed in every sector of the economy, the greatest concentration of these workers is in the computer systems design and related services industry. Firms in this industry provide services related to the commercial use of computers on a contract basis, including custom computer programming services; computer systems integration design services; computer facilities management services, including computer systems or data processing facilities support services for clients; and other computer-related services, such as disaster recovery services and software installation. Many computer scientists and database administrators are employed by Internet service providers; Web search portals; and data processing, hosting, and related services firms. Others work for government, manufacturers of computer and electronic products, insurance companies, financial institutions, and universities.

A growing number of computer specialists, such as network and data communications analysts, are employed on a temporary or contract basis; many of these individuals are self-employed, working independently as contractors or consultants. For example, a company installing a new computer system may need the services of several network systems and data communication analysts just to get the system running. Because not all of the analysts would be needed once the system is functioning, the company might contract for such employees with a temporary help agency or consulting firm, or with the network systems analysts themselves. Such jobs may last from several months to 2 years or more. This growing practice enables companies to bring in people with the exact skills they need to complete a particular project, rather than having to spend time or money training or retraining existing workers. Often, experienced consultants then train a company's in-house staff as a project develops.

Job Outlook

Computer scientists and database administrators are projected to be one of the fastest growing occupations over the next decade. Strong employment growth combined with a limited supply of qualified workers will result in excellent employment prospects for this occupation and a high demand for their skills.

Employment change. The computer scientists and database administrators occupation is expected to grow 37 percent from 2006 to 2016, much faster than average for all occupations. Employment of these computer specialists is expected to grow as organizations continue to adopt and integrate increasingly sophisticated technologies. Job increases will be driven by very rapid growth in computer systems design and related services, which is projected to be one of the fastest growing industries in the U.S. economy.

The demand for networking to facilitate the sharing of information, the expansion of client-server environments, and the need for computer specialists to use their knowledge and skills in a problem-solving capacity will be major factors in the rising demand for computer scientists and database administrators. Firms will continue to seek out computer specialists who are able to implement the latest tech-

nologies and are able to apply them to meet the needs of businesses as they struggle to maintain a competitive advantage.

As computers continue to become more central to business functions, more sophisticated and complex technology is being implemented across all organizations, fueling demand for computer scientists and database administrators. There is growing demand for network systems and data communication analysts to help firms maximize their efficiency with available technology. Expansion of electronic commerce—doing business on the Internet—and the continuing need to build and maintain databases that store critical information on customers, inventory, and projects are fueling demand for database administrators familiar with the latest technology. Because of the increasing reliance on the Internet among businesses, information security is an increasing concern.

The development of new technologies leads to demand for various kinds of workers. The expanding integration of Internet technologies into businesses, for example, has resulted in a growing need for specialists who can develop and support Internet and intranet applications. The growth of electronic commerce means that more establishments use the Internet to conduct their business online. It also means more security specialists are needed to protect their systems. The spread of such new technologies translates into a need for information technology professionals who can help organizations use technology to communicate with employees, clients, and consumers. Explosive growth in these areas also is expected to fuel demand for specialists who are knowledgeable about network, data, and communications security.

Job prospects. Computer scientists and database administrators should continue to enjoy excellent job prospects. As technology becomes more sophisticated and complex, however, these positions will demand a higher level of skill and expertise from their employees. Individuals with an advanced degree in computer science or computer engineering or with an MBA with a concentration in information systems should enjoy favorable employment prospects. College graduates with a bachelor's degree in computer science, computer engineering, information science, or MIS also should enjoy favorable prospects, particularly if they have supplemented their formal education with practical experience. Because employers continue to seek computer specialists who can combine strong technical skills with good business skills, individuals with a combination of experience inside and outside the IT arena will have the best job prospects.

In addition to growth, many job openings will arise from the need to replace workers who move into managerial positions or other occupations or who leave the labor force.

Earnings

Median annual earnings of computer and information scientists, research, were $93,950 in May 2006. The middle 50 percent earned

Projections data from the National Employment Matrix

Occupational Title	SOC Code	Employment, 2006	Projected employment, 2016	Change, 2006-2016	
				Number	Percent
Computer scientists and database administrators	—	542,000	742,000	200,000	37
Computer and information scientists, research	15-1011	25,000	31,000	5,400	22
Database administrators	15-1061	119,000	154,000	34,000	29
Network systems and data communications analysts	15-1081	262,000	402,000	140,000	53
Computer specialists, all other	15-1099	136,000	157,000	21,000	15

NOTE: Data in this table are rounded.

between $71,930 and $118,100. The lowest 10 percent earned less than $53,590, and the highest 10 percent earned more than $144,880. Median annual earnings of computer and information scientists employed in computer systems design and related services in May 2006 were $95,340.

Median annual earnings of database administrators were $64,670 in May 2006. The middle 50 percent earned between $48,560 and $84,830. The lowest 10 percent earned less than $37,350, and the highest 10 percent earned more than $103,010. In May 2006, median annual earnings of database administrators employed in computer systems design and related services were $72,510, and for those in management of companies and enterprises, earnings were $67,680.

Median annual earnings of network systems and data communication analysts were $64,600 in May 2006. The middle 50 percent earned between $49,510 and $82,630. The lowest 10 percent earned less than $38,410, and the highest 10 percent earned more than $101,740. Median annual earnings in the industries employing the largest numbers of network systems and data communications analysts in May 2006 are shown below:

Wired telecommunications carriers	$72,480
Management of companies and enterprises	68,490
Management, scientific, and technical consulting services	67,830
Computer systems design and related services	67,080
State government	52,020

Median annual earnings of all other computer specialists were $68,570 in May 2006. Median annual earnings of all other computer specialists employed in computer systems design and related services were $67,370, and, for those in management of companies and enterprises, earnings were $63,610 in May 2006.

Robert Half International, a firm providing specialized staffing services, noted the following salary ranges for computer-related occupations in their 2007 Salary Guide:

Database manager	$84,750	– $116,000
Network architect	78,000	– 112,250
Database developer	73,500	– 103,000
Senior web developer	71,000	– 102,000
Database administrator	70,250	– 102,000
Network manager	68,750	– 93,000
Web developer	54,750	– 81,500
LAN/WAN administrator	51,000	– 71,500
Web administrator	49,750	– 74,750
Web designer	47,000	– 71,500
Telecommunications specialist	47,500	– 69,500

Related Occupations

Others who work with large amounts of data are computer programmers, computer software engineers, computer and information systems managers, engineers, mathematicians, statisticians, and actuaries.

Sources of Additional Information

Further information about computer careers is available from

▸ Association for Computing Machinery (ACM), 1515 Broadway, New York, NY 10036. Internet: http://www.acm.org

▸ Institute of Electrical and Electronics Engineers Computer Society, Headquarters Office, 1730 Massachusetts Ave. NW, Washington, DC 20036-1992. Internet: http://www.computer.org

▸ Software & Information Industry Association, 1090 Vermont Ave. NW, 6th floor, Washington, DC 20005. Internet: http://www.siia.net

Computer Support Specialists and Systems Administrators

(O*NET 15-1041.00, 15-1071.00, and 15-1071.01)

Significant Points

■ Growth in computer support specialist jobs will be about as fast as the average, while growth in network and computer system administrator jobs will be much faster than average.

■ There are many paths of entry to these occupations.

■ Job prospects should be best for college graduates with relevant skills and experience; certifications and practical experience are essential for people without degrees.

Nature of the Work

In the last decade, computers have become an integral part of everyday life at home, work, school, and nearly everywhere else. Of course, almost every computer user encounters a problem occasionally, whether it is the annoyance of a forgotten password or the disaster of a crashing hard drive. The explosive use of computers has created demand for specialists who provide advice to users, as well as for the day-to-day administration, maintenance, and support of computer systems and networks.

Computer support specialists provide technical assistance, support, and advice to customers and other users. This occupational group includes *technical support specialists* and *help-desk technicians*. These troubleshooters interpret problems and provide technical support for hardware, software, and systems. They answer telephone calls, analyze problems by using automated diagnostic programs, and resolve recurring difficulties. Support specialists work either within a company that uses computer systems or directly for a computer hardware or software vendor. Increasingly, these specialists work for help-desk or support services firms, for which they provide computer support to clients on a contract basis.

Technical support specialists respond to inquiries from their organizations' computer users and may run automatic diagnostics programs to resolve problems. They also install, modify, clean, and repair computer hardware and software. In addition, they may write training manuals and train computer users in how to use new computer hardware and software. These workers also oversee the daily performance of their company's computer systems and evaluate how useful software programs are.

Help-desk technicians respond to telephone calls and e-mail messages from customers looking for help with computer problems. In responding to these inquiries, help-desk technicians must listen carefully to the customer, ask questions to diagnose the nature of the problem, and then patiently walk the customer through the problem-solving steps.

Help-desk technicians deal directly with customer issues and companies value them as a source of feedback on their products. They are consulted for information about what gives customers the most trouble, as well as other customer concerns. Most computer support specialists start out at the help desk.

Network and *computer systems administrators* design, install, and support an organization's computer systems. They are responsible for local-area networks (LAN), wide-area networks (WAN), network segments, and Internet and intranet systems. They work in a variety of environments, including professional offices, small businesses, government organizations, and large corporations. They maintain network hardware and software, analyze problems, and monitor networks to ensure their availability to system users. These workers gather data to identify customer needs and then use the information to identify, interpret, and evaluate system and network requirements. Administrators also may plan, coordinate, and implement network security measures.

Systems administrators are responsible for maintaining network efficiency. They ensure that the design of an organization's computer system allows all of the components, including computers, the network, and software, to work properly together. Furthermore, they monitor and adjust the performance of existing networks and continually survey the current computer site to determine future network needs. Administrators also troubleshoot problems reported by users and by automated network monitoring systems and make recommendations for future system upgrades.

In some organizations, *computer security specialists* may plan, coordinate, and implement the organization's information security. These workers educate users about computer security, install security software, monitor networks for security breaches, respond to cyber attacks, and, in some cases, gather data and evidence to be used in prosecuting cyber crime. The responsibilities of computer security specialists have increased in recent years as cyber attacks have become more common. This and other growing specialty occupations reflect an increasing emphasis on client-server applications, the expansion of Internet and intranet applications, and the demand for more end-user support.

Work environment. Computer support specialists and systems administrators normally work in well-lighted, comfortable offices or computer laboratories. They usually work about 40 hours a week, but if their employer requires computer support over extended hours, they may be "on call" for rotating evening or weekend work. Overtime may be necessary when unexpected technical problems arise. Like other workers who type on a keyboard for long periods, computer support specialists and systems administrators are susceptible to eyestrain, back discomfort, and hand and wrist problems such as carpal tunnel syndrome.

Computer support specialists and systems administrators constantly interact with customers and fellow employees as they answer questions and give advice. Those who work as consultants are away from their offices much of the time, sometimes spending months working in a client's office.

As computer networks expand, more computer support specialists and systems administrators may be able to provide technical support from remote locations. This capability would reduce or eliminate travel to the customer's workplace. Systems administrators also can administer and configure networks and servers remotely, although this practice is not as common as it is among computer support specialists.

Training, Other Qualifications, and Advancement

A college degree is required for some computer support specialist positions, but certification and relevant experience may be sufficient for others. A bachelor's degree is required for many network and computer systems administrator positions. For both occupations, strong analytical and communication skills are essential.

Education and training. Due to the wide range of skills required, there are many paths of entry to a job as a computer support specialist or systems administrator. Training requirements for computer support specialist positions vary, but many employers prefer to hire applicants with some formal college education. A bachelor's degree in computer science or information systems is a prerequisite for some jobs; other jobs, however, may require only a computer-related associate degree. And for some jobs, relevant computer experience and certifications may substitute for formal education. For systems administrator jobs, many employers seek applicants with bachelor's degrees, although not necessarily in a computer-related field.

A number of companies are becoming more flexible about requiring a college degree for support positions. In the absence of a degree, however, certification and practical experience are essential. Certification training programs, offered by a variety of vendors and product makers, may help some people to qualify for entry-level positions.

Other qualifications. People interested in becoming a computer support specialist or systems administrator must have strong problem-solving, analytical, and communication skills because troubleshooting and helping others are vital parts of the job. The constant interaction with other computer personnel, customers, and employees requires computer support specialists and systems administrators to communicate effectively on paper, via e-mail, over the phone, or in person. Strong writing skills are useful in preparing manuals for employees and customers.

Advancement. Beginning computer support specialists usually work for organizations that deal directly with customers or in-house users. Support specialists may advance into positions in which they use what they have learned from customers to improve the design and efficiency of future products. Job promotions usually depend more on performance than on formal education. Eventually, some computer support specialists become software engineers, designing products rather than assisting users. Computer support specialists in hardware and software companies often enjoy great upward mobility; advancement sometimes comes within months of becoming employed.

Entry-level network and computer systems administrators are involved in routine maintenance and monitoring of computer systems, typically working behind the scenes in an organization. After gaining experience and expertise, they often are able to advance to more senior-level positions. For example, senior network and computer systems administrators may make presentations to executives and managers on the security of the company computer network. They also may translate the needs of an organization into a set of technical requirements based on the available technology. As with support specialists, administrators may become software engineers involved in system and network design.

As technology continues to improve, computer support specialists and systems administrators must strive to acquire new skills. Many continuing education programs are provided by employers, hardware and software vendors, colleges and universities, and private training institutions. Professional development seminars offered by computing services firms also can enhance skills and advancement opportunities.

Employment

Computer support specialists and systems administrators held about 862,000 jobs in 2006. Of these, approximately 552,000 were computer support specialists and about 309,000 were network and computer systems administrators. Although they worked in a wide range of industries, about 23 percent of all computer support specialists and systems administrators were employed in professional, scientific, and technical services industries, principally computer systems design and related services. Substantial numbers of these workers were also employed in administrative and support services companies, financial institutions, insurance companies, government agencies, educational institutions, software publishers, telecommunications organizations, health care organizations, and management of companies and enterprises.

Employers of computer support specialists and systems administrators range from startup companies to established industry leaders. As computer networks become an integral part of business, industries not typically associated with computers—such as construction—increasingly need computer support workers.

Job Outlook

Employment of computer support specialists and systems administrators is expected to increase faster than the average. Job prospects should be best for those with a college degree and relevant experience.

Employment change. Employment of computer support specialists and systems administrators is expected to increase by 18 percent from 2006 to 2016, which is much faster than the average for all occupations. In addition, this occupation is expected to add 155,000 jobs over the projection decade.

Employment of computer support specialists is expected to increase by 13 percent from 2006 to 2016, which is about as fast as the average for all occupations. Demand for these workers will result as organizations and individuals continue to adopt increasingly sophisticated technology. Job growth will continue to be driven by the ongoing expansion of the computer system design and related services industry, which is projected to remain one of the fastest-growing industries in the U.S. economy. Growth will not be as explosive as during the previous decade, however, because the information

technology industry is maturing and because some of these jobs are expected to be outsourced offshore where prevailing wages are lower. Physical location is not as important for computer support specialists as it is for other occupations because these workers can provide assistance remotely and support services are provided around the clock across time zones.

Job growth among computer support specialists reflects the rapid evolution of technology. As computers and software become more complex, support specialists will be needed to provide technical assistance to customers and other users. The adoption of new mobile technologies, such as the wireless Internet, will continue to create a need for these workers to familiarize and educate computer users. Consulting jobs for computer support specialists also should continue to increase as businesses seek help managing, upgrading, and customizing ever more complex computer systems.

Employment of network and computer systems administrators is expected to increase by 27 percent from 2006 to 2016, which is much faster than the average for all occupations. Computer networks have become an integral part of business, and demand for these workers will increase as firms continue to invest in new technologies. The wide use of electronic commerce and the increasing adoption of mobile technologies mean that more establishments will use the Internet to conduct business online. This growth translates into a need for systems administrators who can help organizations use technology to communicate with employees, clients, and consumers.

Demand for computer security specialists will grow as businesses and government continue to invest heavily in "cyber security," protecting vital computer networks and electronic infrastructures from attack. The information security field is expected to generate many new system administrator jobs over the next decade as firms across all industries place a high priority on safeguarding their data and systems.

Employment of network and computer systems administrators, however, may be tempered somewhat by offshore outsourcing, as firms transfer work to countries with lower-prevailing wages and highly skilled work forces. Systems administrators may increasingly be able to manage computer systems from remote locations as technology advances.

Job prospects. Job prospects should be best for college graduates who possess the latest technological skills, particularly graduates who have supplemented their formal education with relevant work experience. Employers will continue to seek computer specialists who possess strong fundamental computer skills combined with good interpersonal and communication skills. Due to the demand for computer support specialists and systems administrators over the next decade, those who have strong computer skills but do not have a college degree should continue to qualify for some entry-level positions.

Projections data from the National Employment Matrix

Occupational Title	SOC Code	Employment, 2006	Projected employment, 2016	Change, 2006-2016	
				Number	Percent
Computer support specialists and systems administrators...............	—	862,000	1,016,000	155,000	18
Computer support specialists..	15-1041	552,000	624,000	71,000	13
Network and computer systems administrators...........................	15-1071	309,000	393,000	83,000	27

NOTE: Data in this table are rounded.

Earnings

Median annual earnings of wage-and-salary computer support specialists were $41,470 in May 2006. The middle 50 percent earned between $32,110 and $53,640. The lowest 10 percent earned less than $25,290, and the highest 10 percent earned more than $68,540. Median annual earnings in the industries employing the largest numbers of computer support specialists in May 2006 were as follows:

Software publishers $46,270

Management of companies and enterprises 42,770

Computer systems design and related services 42,510

Colleges, universities, and professional schools 40,130

Elementary and secondary schools 37,880

Median annual earnings of wage-and-salary network and computer systems administrators were $62,130 in May 2006. The middle 50 percent earned between $48,520 and $79,160. The lowest 10 percent earned less than $38,610, and the highest 10 percent earned more than $97,080. Median annual earnings in the industries employing the largest numbers of network and computer systems administrators in May 2006 were as follows:

Wired telecommunications carriers $70,790

Computer systems design and related services 66,680

Management of companies and enterprises 66,020

Colleges, universities, and professional schools 54,590

Elementary and secondary schools 53,750

According to Robert Half Technology, starting salaries in 2007 ranged from $27,500 to $37,000 for help-desk workers. Starting salaries for desktop support analysts ranged from $46,500 to $65,250. For systems administrators, starting salaries ranged from $50,000 to $75,750.

Related Occupations

Other computer specialists include computer programmers, computer software engineers, computer systems analysts, and computer scientists and database administrators. Other workers who respond to customer inquiries are customer service representatives.

Sources of Additional Information

For additional information about a career as a computer support specialist, contact

▸ Association of Support Professionals, 122 Barnard Ave., Watertown, MA 02472.

For additional information about a career as a systems administrator, contact

▸ The League of Professional System Administrators, 15000 Commerce Parkway, Suite C, Mount Laurel, NJ 08054. Internet: http://lopsa.org/

▸ National Workforce Center for Emerging Technologies, 3000 Landerholm Circle SE, Bellevue, WA 98007. Internet: http://www.nwcet.org

Construction and Building Inspectors

(O*NET 47-4011.00)

Significant Points

■ About 41 percent of inspectors work for local governments, primarily municipal or county building departments.

■ Many home inspectors are self employed.

■ Opportunities should be best for experienced construction supervisors and craftworkers who have some college education, engineering or architectural training, or certification as construction inspectors or plan examiners.

Nature of the Work

Construction and building inspectors examine buildings, highways and streets, sewer and water systems, dams, bridges, and other structures. They ensure that their construction, alteration, or repair complies with building codes and ordinances, zoning regulations, and contract specifications. Building codes and standards are the primary means by which building construction is regulated in the United States for the health and safety of the general public. National model building and construction codes are published by the International Code Council (ICC), although many localities have additional ordinances and codes that modify or add to the national model codes. To monitor compliance with regulations, inspectors make an initial inspection during the first phase of construction and follow up with further inspections throughout the construction project. However, no inspection is ever exactly the same. In areas where certain types of severe weather or natural disasters—such as earthquakes or hurricanes—are more common, inspectors monitor compliance with additional safety regulations designed to protect structures and occupants during those events.

There are many types of inspectors. *Building inspectors* inspect the structural quality and general safety of buildings. Some specialize in for example, structural steel or reinforced-concrete structures. Before construction begins, *plan examiners* determine whether the plans for the building or other structure comply with building codes and whether they are suited to the engineering and environmental demands of the building site. To inspect the condition of the soil and the positioning and depth of the footings, inspectors visit the worksite before the foundation is poured. Later, they return to the site to inspect the foundation after it has been completed. The size and type of structure, as well as the rate at which it proceeds toward completion, determine the number of other site visits they must make. Upon completion of the project, they make a final, comprehensive inspection.

In addition to structural characteristics, a primary concern of building inspectors is fire safety. They inspect structures' fire sprinklers, alarms, smoke control systems, and fire exits. Inspectors assess the type of construction, contents of the building, adequacy of fire protection equipment, and risks posed by adjoining buildings.

Electrical inspectors examine the installation of electrical systems and equipment to ensure that they function properly and comply with electrical codes and standards. They visit worksites to inspect new and existing sound and security systems, wiring, lighting, motors, and generating equipment. They also inspect the installation of the electrical wiring for heating and air-conditioning systems, appliances, and other components.

Elevator inspectors examine lifting and conveying devices such as elevators, escalators, moving sidewalks, lifts and hoists, inclined railways, ski lifts, and amusement rides.

For information on *Fire inspectors* see this book's job profile of fire fighting occupations.

Home inspectors conduct inspections of newly built or previously owned homes, condominiums, town homes, manufactured homes, apartments, and at times commercial buildings. Home inspection has become a standard practice in the home-purchasing process. Home inspectors are most often hired by prospective home buyers to inspect and report on the condition of a home's systems, components, and structure. Although they look for and report violations of building codes, they do not have the power to enforce compliance with the codes. Typically, they are hired either immediately prior to a purchase offer on a home or as a contingency to a sales contract. In addition to examining structural quality, home inspectors inspect all home systems and features, including roofing as well as the exterior, attached garage or carport, foundation, interior, plumbing, and electrical, heating, and cooling systems. Some home inspections are done for homeowners who want an evaluation of their home's condition, for example, prior to putting the home on the market or as a way to diagnose problems.

Mechanical inspectors inspect the installation of the mechanical components of commercial kitchen appliances, heating and air-conditioning equipment, gasoline and butane tanks, gas and oil piping, and gas-fired and oil-fired appliances. Some specialize in boilers or ventilating equipment as well.

Plumbing inspectors examine plumbing systems, including private disposal systems, water supply and distribution systems, plumbing fixtures and traps, and drain, waste, and vent lines.

Public works inspectors ensure that federal, state, and local government construction of water and sewer systems, highways, streets, bridges, and dams conforms to detailed contract specifications. They inspect excavation and fill operations, the placement of forms for concrete, concrete mixing and pouring, asphalt paving, and grading operations. They record the work and materials used so that contract payments can be calculated. Public works inspectors may specialize in highways, structural steel, reinforced concrete, or ditches. Others specialize in dredging operations required for bridges and dams or for harbors.

The owner of a building or structure under construction employs *specification inspectors* to ensure that work is done according to design specifications. Specification inspectors represent the owner's interests, not those of the general public. Insurance companies and financial institutions also may use their services.

Details concerning construction projects, building and occupancy permits, and other documentation generally are stored on computers so that they can easily be retrieved and updated. For example, inspectors may use laptop computers to record their findings while inspecting a site. Most inspectors use computers to help them monitor the status of construction inspection activities and keep track of permits issued, and some can access all construction and building codes from their computers on the jobsite, decreasing the need for paper binders. However, many inspectors continue to use a paper checklist to detail their findings.

Although inspections are primarily visual, inspectors may use tape measures, survey instruments, metering devices, and equipment such as concrete strength measurers. They keep a log of their work, take photographs, and file reports. Many inspectors also use laptops or other portable electronic devices onsite to facilitate the accuracy of their written reports, as well as e-mail and fax machines to send out the results. If necessary, they act on their findings. For example, government and construction inspectors notify the construction contractor, superintendent, or supervisor when they discover a violation of a code or ordinance or something that does not comply with the contract specifications or approved plans. If the problem is not corrected within a reasonable or otherwise specified period, government inspectors have authority to issue a "stop-work" order.

Many inspectors also investigate construction or alterations being done without proper permits. Inspectors who are employees of municipalities enforce laws pertaining to the proper design, construction, and use of buildings. They direct violators of permit laws to obtain permits and to submit to inspection.

Work environment. Construction and building inspectors usually work alone. However, several may be assigned to large, complex projects, particularly because inspectors tend to specialize in different areas of construction. Although they spend considerable time inspecting construction worksites, inspectors also spend time in a field office reviewing blueprints, answering letters or telephone calls, writing reports, and scheduling inspections.

Many construction sites are dirty and may be cluttered with tools, materials, or debris. Inspectors may have to climb ladders or many flights of stairs or crawl around in tight spaces. Although their work generally is not considered hazardous, inspectors, like other construction workers, wear hardhats and adhere to other safety requirements while at a construction site.

Inspectors normally work regular hours. However, they may work additional hours during periods when a lot of construction is taking place. Also, if an accident occurs at a construction site, inspectors must respond immediately and may work additional hours to complete their report. Non-government inspectors—especially those who are self-employed—may have a varied work schedule, at times working evenings and weekends.

Training, Other Qualifications, and Advancement

Although requirements vary considerably, construction and building inspectors should have a thorough knowledge of construction materials and practices. In some states, construction and building inspectors are required to obtain a special license or certification, so it is important to check with the appropriate state agency.

Education and training. Most employers require at least a high school diploma or the equivalent, even for workers with considerable experience. More often, employers look for persons who have studied engineering or architecture or who have a degree from a community or junior college with courses in building inspection, home inspection, construction technology, drafting, and mathematics. Many community colleges offer certificate or associate degree programs in building inspection technology. Courses in blueprint reading, algebra, geometry, and English also are useful. A growing number of construction and building inspectors are entering the occupation with a college degree, which often can substitute for previous experience. The distribution of all construction and building inspectors by their highest level of educational attainment in 2006 was:

High school graduate or less 31%

Some college, no degree 28%

Associate's degree...12%

Bachelor's degree 26%

Graduate degree...2%

The level of training requirements varies by type of inspector and state. In general, construction and building inspectors receive much of their training on the job, although they must learn building codes and standards on their own. Working with an experienced inspector, they learn about inspection techniques; codes, ordinances, and regulations; contract specifications; and recordkeeping and reporting duties. Supervised onsite inspections also may be a part of the training. Other requirements can include various courses and assigned reading. Some courses and instructional material are available online as well as through formal venues.

Licensure and certification. Many states and local jurisdictions require some type of license or certification for employment as a construction and building inspector. Requirements may vary by state or local municipality. Typical requirements for licensure or certification include previous experience, a minimum educational attainment level, such as a high school diploma, and possibly the passing of a state-approved examination. Some states have individual licensing programs for inspectors, while others may require certification by such associations as the International Code Council, International Association of Plumbing and Mechanical Officials, and National Fire Protection Association.

Similarly, some states require home inspectors to obtain a state issued license or certification. Currently, 33 states have regulations affecting home inspectors. Requirements for a license or certification vary by state, but may include obtaining a minimum level of education, having a set amount of experience with inspections, purchasing liability insurance of a certain amount, and the passing of an examination. Renewal is usually every few years and annual continuing education is almost always required.

Other qualifications. Because inspectors must possess the right mix of technical knowledge, experience, and education, employers prefer applicants who have both formal training and experience. For example, many inspectors previously worked as carpenters, electricians, or plumbers. Home inspectors combine knowledge of multiple specialties, so many of them come into the occupation having a combination of certifications and previous experience in various construction trades.

Construction and building inspectors must be in good physical condition in order to walk and climb about construction and building sites. They also must have a driver's license so that they can get to scheduled appointments.

Advancement. Being a member of a nationally recognized inspection association enhances employment opportunities and may be required by some employers. Even if it is not required, certification can enhance an inspector's opportunities for employment and advancement to more responsible positions. To become certified, inspectors with substantial experience and education must pass examinations on topics including code requirements, construction techniques and materials, standards of practice, and codes of ethics. The International Code Council offers multiple voluntary certifications, as do many other professional associations. Many categories

of certification are awarded for inspectors and plan examiners in a variety of specialties, including the Certified Building Official (CBO) certification, for code compliance, and the Residential Building Inspector (RBI) certification, for home inspectors. In a few cases, there are no education or experience prerequisites, and certification consists of passing an examination in a designated field either at a regional location or online. In addition, federal, state, and many local governments may require inspectors to pass a civil service exam.

Because they advise builders and the general public on building codes, construction practices, and technical developments, construction and building inspectors must keep abreast of changes in these areas. Continuing education is required by many states and certifying organizations. Numerous employers provide formal training to broaden inspectors' knowledge of construction materials, practices, and techniques. Inspectors who work for small agencies or firms that do not conduct their own training programs can expand their knowledge and upgrade their skills by attending state-sponsored training programs, by taking college or correspondence courses, or by attending seminars and conferences sponsored by various related organizations, including professional organizations. An engineering or architectural degree often is required for advancement to supervisory positions.

Employment

Construction and building inspectors held about 110,000 jobs in 2006. Local governments—primarily municipal or county building departments—employed 41 percent. Employment of local government inspectors is concentrated in cities and in suburban areas undergoing rapid growth. Local governments in larger jurisdictions may employ large inspection staffs, including many plan examiners or inspectors who specialize in structural steel, reinforced concrete, and boiler, electrical, and elevator inspection. In smaller jurisdictions, only one or a few inspectors who specialize in multiple areas may be on staff.

Another 26 percent of construction and building inspectors worked for architectural and engineering services firms, conducting inspections for a fee or on a contract basis. Many of these were home inspectors working on behalf of potential real estate purchasers. Most of the remaining inspectors were employed in other service-providing industries or by state governments. About 1 in 10 construction and building inspectors was self-employed. Since many home inspectors are self-employed, it is likely that most self-employed construction and building inspectors were home inspectors.

Job Outlook

Job opportunities in construction and building inspection should be best for highly experienced supervisors and construction craft workers who have some college education, engineering or architectural training, or certification as inspectors or plan examiners. Inspectors should experience faster than average employment growth.

Employment change. Employment of construction and building inspectors is expected to grow by 18 percent over the 2006–2016 decade, which is faster than the average for all occupations. Concern for public safety and a desire for improvement in the quality of construction should continue to stimulate demand for construction and building inspectors in government as well as in firms specializing in architectural, engineering, and related services. As the result of new

Projections data from the National Employment Matrix

Occupational Title	SOC Code	Employment, 2006	Projected employment, 2016	Change, 2006-16	
				Number	Percent
Construction and building inspectors..	47-4011	110,000	130,000	20,000	18

NOTE: Data in this table are rounded.

technology such as building information modeling (BIM), the availability of a richer set of buildings data in a more timely and transparent manner will make it easier to conduct plan reviews. This will lead to more time and resources spent on inspections. In addition, the growing focus on natural and manmade disasters is increasing the level of interest in and need for qualified inspectors. Issues such as green and sustainable design are new areas of focus that will also drive the demand for construction and building inspectors.

The routine practice of obtaining home inspections is a relatively recent development, causing employment of home inspectors to increase rapidly. Although employment of home inspectors is expected to continue to increase, the attention given to this specialty, combined with the desire of some construction workers to move into less strenuous and potentially higher paying work, may result in reduced growth of home inspectors in some areas. In addition, increasing state regulations are starting to limit entry into the specialty only to those who have a given level of previous experience and are certified.

Job prospects. Inspectors are involved in all phases of construction, including maintenance and repair work, and are therefore less likely to lose their jobs when new construction slows during recessions. Those who are self-employed, such as home inspectors, are more likely to be affected by economic downturns or fluctuations in the real estate market. However, those with a thorough knowledge of construction practices and skills in areas such as reading and evaluating blueprints and plans will be better off. Inspectors with previous related experience in construction, a postsecondary degree, and engineering or architectural training will have the best prospects. In addition to openings stemming from the expected employment growth, some job openings will arise from the need to replace inspectors who transfer to other occupations or leave the labor force.

Earnings

Median annual earnings of wage and salary construction and building inspectors were $46,570 in May 2006. The middle 50 percent earned between $36,610 and $58,780. The lowest 10 percent earned less than $29,210, and the highest 10 percent earned more than $72,590. Median annual earnings in the industries employing the largest numbers of construction and building inspectors were

Architectural, engineering, and related services $46,850

Local government 46,040

State government 43,680

Building inspectors, including plan examiners, generally earn the highest salaries. Salaries in large metropolitan areas are substantially higher than those in small jurisdictions.

Benefits vary by place of employment. Those working for the government and private companies typically receive standard benefits, including health and medical insurance, a retirement plan, and paid annual leave. Those who are self-employed may have to provide their own benefits.

More than a quarter of all construction and building inspectors belonged to a union in 2006.

Related Occupations

Because construction and building inspectors are familiar with construction principles, the most closely related occupations are construction occupations, especially carpenters, plumbers, and electricians. Construction and building inspectors also combine knowledge of construction principles and law with an ability to coordinate data, diagnose problems, and communicate with people. Workers in other occupations using a similar combination of skills include architects, except landscape and naval; appraisers and assessors of real estate; construction managers; civil engineers; cost estimators; engineering technicians; and surveyors, cartographers, photogrammetrists, and surveying technicians.

Sources of Additional Information

Information about building codes, certification, and a career as a construction or building inspector is available from

▸ International Code Council, 500 New Jersey Avenue NW, 6th Floor, Washington, DC 20001-2070. Internet: http://www.iccsafe.org

▸ National Fire Protection Association, 1 Batterymarch Park, Quincy, Massachusetts, 02169-7471. Internet: http://www.nfpa.org

For more information about construction inspectors, contact

▸ Association of Construction Inspectors, 1224 North Nokomis NE, Alexandria, MN 56308.

For more information about electrical inspectors, contact

▸ International Association of Electrical Inspectors, 901 Waterfall Way, Suite 602, Richardson, TX 75080-7702. Internet: http://www.iaei.org

For more information about elevator inspectors, contact

▸ National Association of Elevator Safety Authorities International, 6957 Littlerock Rd SW, Ste A, Tumwater, WA 98512. Internet: http://www.naesai.org

For more information about education and training for mechanical and plumbing inspectors, contact

▸ International Association for Plumbing and Mechanical Officials, 5001 E. Philadelphia St., Ontario, CA 91761. Internet: http://www.iapmo.org/iapmo

For information about becoming a home inspector, contact any of the following organizations:

▸ American Society of Home Inspectors, 932 Lee St., Suite 101, Des Plaines, IL 60016. Internet: http://www.ashi.org

▸ National Association of Home Inspectors, 4248 Park Glen Rd., Minneapolis, MN 55416. Internet: http://www.nahi.org

For information about a career as a state or local government construction or building inspector, contact your state or local employment service.

Construction Equipment Operators

(O*NET 47-2071.00, 47-2072.00, and 47-2073.00)

Significant Points

■ Many construction equipment operators acquire their skills on the job, but formal apprenticeship programs provide more comprehensive training.

■ Job opportunities are expected to be very good.

■ Hourly pay is relatively high, but operators of some types of equipment cannot work in inclement weather, so total annual earnings may be reduced.

Nature of the Work

Construction equipment operators use machinery to move construction materials, earth, and other heavy materials at construction sites and mines. They operate equipment that clears and grades land to prepare it for construction of roads, buildings, and bridges. They use machines to dig trenches to lay or repair sewer and other pipelines and hoist heavy construction materials. They may even work off-shore constructing oil rigs. Construction equipment operators also operate machinery that spreads asphalt and concrete on roads and other structures.

These workers also set up and inspect the equipment, make adjustments, and perform some maintenance and minor repairs. Construction equipment operators control equipment by moving levers, foot pedals, operating switches, or joysticks. Construction equipment is more complicated to use than it was in the past. For example, Global Positioning System (GPS) technology is now being used to help with grading and leveling activities.

Included in the construction equipment operator occupation are paving, surfacing, and tamping equipment operators; piledriver operators; and operating engineers. *Paving and surfacing equipment operators* use levers and other controls to operate machines that spread and level asphalt or spread and smooth concrete for roadways or other structures. *Asphalt paving machine operators* turn valves to regulate the temperature and flow of asphalt onto the roadbed. They must take care that the machine distributes the paving material evenly and without voids, and make sure that there is a constant flow of asphalt going into the hopper. *Concrete paving machine operators* control levers and turn handwheels to move attachments that spread, vibrate, and level wet concrete in forms. They must observe the surface of concrete to identify low spots into which workers must add concrete. They use other attachments to smooth the surface of the concrete, spray on a curing compound, and cut expansion joints. *Tamping equipment operators* operate tamping machines that compact earth and other fill materials for roadbeds or other construction sites. They also may operate machines with interchangeable hammers to cut or break up old pavement and drive guardrail posts into the earth.

Piledriver operators use large machines, mounted on skids, barges, or cranes to hammer piles into the ground. Piles are long heavy beams of wood or steel driven into the ground to support retaining walls, bulkheads, bridges, piers, or building foundations. Some piledriver operators work on offshore oil rigs. Piledriver operators move hand and foot levers and turn valves to activate, position, and control the pile-driving equipment.

Operating engineers and other construction equipment operators use one or several types of power construction equipment. They may operate excavation and loading machines equipped with scoops, shovels, or buckets that dig sand, gravel, earth, or similar materials and load it into trucks or onto conveyors. In addition to the familiar bulldozers, they operate trench excavators, road graders, and similar equipment. Sometimes, they may drive and control industrial trucks or tractors equipped with forklifts or booms for lifting materials or with hitches for pulling trailers. They also may operate and maintain air compressors, pumps, and other power equipment at construction sites. Construction equipment operators who are classified as operating engineers are capable of operating several different types of construction equipment.

Work environment. Construction equipment operators work outdoors, in nearly every type of climate and weather condition, although in many areas of the country, some types of construction operations must be suspended in winter. Bulldozers, scrapers, and especially tampers and piledrivers are noisy and shake or jolt the operator. Operating heavy construction equipment can be dangerous. As with most machinery, accidents generally can be avoided by observing proper operating procedures and safety practices. Construction equipment operators are cold in the winter and hot in the summer and often get dirty, greasy, muddy, or dusty. Some operators work in remote locations on large construction projects, such as highways and dams, or in factory or mining operations.

Operators may have irregular hours because work on some construction projects continues around the clock or must be performed late at night or early in the morning.

Training, Other Qualifications, and Advancement

Construction equipment operators usually learn their skills on the job, but formal apprenticeship programs provide more comprehensive training.

Education and training. Employers of construction equipment operators generally prefer to hire high school graduates, although some employers may train non-graduates to operate some types of equipment. High school courses in automobile mechanics are helpful because workers may perform maintenance on their machines. Also useful are courses in science and mechanical drawing.

On the job, workers may start by operating light equipment under the guidance of an experienced operator. Later, they may operate heavier equipment, such as bulldozers and cranes. Technologically advanced construction equipment with computerized controls and improved hydraulics and electronics requires more skill to operate. Operators of such equipment may need more training and some understanding of electronics.

It is generally accepted that formal training provides more comprehensive skills. Some construction equipment operators train in formal operating engineer apprenticeship programs administered by union-management committees of the International Union of Operating Engineers and the Associated General Contractors of America. Because apprentices learn to operate a wider variety of machines than do other beginners, they usually have better job opportunities. Apprenticeship programs consist of at least three years, or 6,000

© JIST Works

hours, of paid on-the-job training together with and 144 hours of related classroom instruction each year.

Private vocational schools offer instruction in the operation of certain types of construction equipment. Completion of such programs may help a person get a job. However, people considering such training should check the school's reputation among employers in the area and find out if the school offers the opportunity to work on actual machines in realistic situations. A large amount of information can be learned in classrooms. But to become a skilled construction equipment operator, a worker needs to actually perform the various tasks. The best training facilities have equipment on-site so that students can do the tasks that they are learning about.

Licensure. Construction equipment operators often obtain a commercial driver's license so that they can haul their equipment to the various job sites. Commercial driver's licenses are issued by states according to each state's rules and regulations. (See the job profile of truck drivers and driver/sales workers elsewhere in this book for more information on commercial driver's licenses.)

Certification and other qualifications. Mechanical aptitude and experience operating related mobile equipment, such as farm tractors or heavy equipment, in the Armed Forces or elsewhere is an asset. Operators need to be in good physical condition and have a good sense of balance, the ability to judge distance, and eye-hand-foot coordination. Some operator positions require the ability to work at heights.

Certification or training in the right school will allow a worker to have opportunities across the country. While attending some vocational schools, operators are able to qualify for or attain various certifications. These certifications prove to potential employers that an operator is able to handle specific types of equipment. Certifications last from three to five years and must be renewed.

Advancement. Construction equipment operators can advance to become supervisors. Some operators choose to teach in training facilities to pass on their knowledge. Other operators start their own contracting businesses although this may be difficult because of high start-up costs.

Employment

Construction equipment operators held about 494,000 jobs in 2006. Jobs were found in every section of the country and were distributed among various types of operators as follows:

Operating engineers and other construction
    equipment operators 424,000

Paving, surfacing, and tamping equipment
    operators 64,000

Pile-driver operators 5,600

About 63 percent of construction equipment operators worked in the construction industry. Many equipment operators worked in heavy construction, building highways, bridges, or railroads. About 17 percent of construction equipment operators worked in state and local government. Others—mostly grader, bulldozer, and scraper operators—worked in mining. Some also worked for manufacturing or utility companies. About 5 percent of construction equipment operators were self-employed.

Job Outlook

Average job growth, reflecting increased demand for their services, and the need to replace workers who leave the occupation should result in very good job opportunities for construction equipment operators.

Employment change. Employment of construction equipment operators is expected to increase 8 percent between 2006 and 2016, about as fast as the average for all occupations. Even though improvements in equipment are expected to continue to raise worker productivity and to moderate the demand for new workers somewhat, employment is expected to increase because population and business growth will create a need for new houses, industrial facilities, schools, hospitals, offices, and other structures.

Specifically, more paving, surfacing, and tamping equipment operators will be needed as a result of expected growth in highway, bridge, and street construction. There has been consistent Congressional support for road projects. Bridge construction is expected to increase most because bridges will need to be repaired or replaced before they become unsafe. In some areas, deteriorating highway conditions also will spur demand for highway maintenance and repair.

More piledriver operators will be needed as construction continues to move into areas that are challenging to build in and require the use of piles as supports. Increases in bridge construction will also create demand for piledriver operators.

Demand for operating engineers and other construction equipment operators will be driven by the demand for new construction. Increases in pipeline construction will also create demand. These operators work in all sectors of construction.

Job prospects. Job opportunities for construction equipment operators are expected to be very good. Some potential workers may choose not to enter training programs because they prefer work that has more comfortable working conditions and is less seasonal in nature. This reluctance makes it easier for willing workers to get operator jobs.

In addition, many job openings will arise from job growth and from the need to replace experienced construction equipment operators who transfer to other occupations, retire, or leave the job for other reasons. Construction equipment operators who can use a large

Projections data from the National Employment Matrix

Occupational Title	SOC Code	Employment, 2006	Projected employment, 2016	Change, 2006-16	
				Number	Percent
Construction equipment operators	47-2070	494,000	536,000	42,000	8
Paving, surfacing, and tamping equipment operators	47-2071	64,000	70,000	5,800	9
Pile-driver operators..	47-2072	5,600	6,000	500	8
Operating engineers and other construction equipment operators	47-2073	424,000	460,000	35,000	8

NOTE: Data in this table are rounded.

variety of equipment will have the best prospects. Operators with pipeline experience will have especially good opportunities.

Employment of construction equipment operators, like that of many other construction workers, is sensitive to the fluctuations in the economy. Workers in these trades may experience periods of unemployment when the overall level of construction falls. On the other hand, shortages of these workers may occur in some areas during peak periods of building activity.

Earnings

Earnings for construction equipment operators vary. In May 2006, median hourly earnings of wage and salary operating engineers and other construction equipment operators were $17.74. The middle 50 percent earned between $13.89 and $23.98. The lowest 10 percent earned less than $11.54, and the highest 10 percent earned more than $30.83. Median hourly earnings in the industries employing the largest numbers of operating engineers were

Highway, street, and bridge construction $19.88

Utility system construction....................................18.62

Other specialty trade contractors...........................18.00

Other heavy and civil engineering construction 17.63

Local government 15.95

Median hourly earnings of wage and salary paving, surfacing, and tamping equipment operators were $15.05 in May 2006. The middle 50 percent earned between $11.98 and $19.71. The lowest 10 percent earned less than $9.97, and the highest 10 percent earned more than $25.30. Median hourly earnings in the industries employing the largest numbers of paving, surfacing, and tamping equipment operators in were as follows:

Other specialty trade contractors $15.26

Highway, street, and bridge construction 15.11

Local government 14.86

In May 2006, median hourly earnings of wage and salary piledriver operators were $22.20. The middle 50 percent earned between $16.31 and $31.65. The lowest 10 percent earned less than $12.83, and the highest 10 percent earned more than $37.28. Median hourly earnings in the industries employing the largest numbers of pile driver operators were as follows:

Other heavy and civil engineering construction $28.60

Highway, street, and bridge construction 22.50

Other specialty trade contractors...........................20.60

Utility system construction....................................18.62

Hourly pay is relatively high, particularly in large metropolitan areas. However, annual earnings of some workers may be lower than hourly rates would indicate because work time may be limited by bad weather. About 28 percent of construction equipment operators belong to a union.

Related Occupations

Other workers who operate mechanical equipment include agricultural equipment operators; truck drivers, heavy and tractor trailer; logging equipment operators; and a variety of material moving occupations.

Sources of Additional Information

For further information about apprenticeships or work opportunities for construction equipment operators, contact a local of the International Union of Operating Engineers, a local apprenticeship committee, or the nearest office of the state apprenticeship agency or employment service. You can also find information on the registered apprenticeship system with links to state apprenticeship programs on the U.S. Department of Labor's Web site: http://www.doleta.gov/atels_bat. Apprenticeship information is also available from the U.S. Department of Labor's toll free helpline: (877) 872-5627.

For general information about the work of construction equipment operators, contact

▸ Associated General Contractors of America, 2300 Wilson Blvd., Suite 400, Arlington, VA 22201. Internet: http://www.agc.org

▸ International Union of Operating Engineers, 1125 17th St. NW, Washington, DC 20036. Internet: http://www.iuoe.org

▸ National Center for Construction Education and Research, P.O. Box 141104, Gainesville, FL 32614-1104. Internet: http://www.nccer.org

▸ Pile Driving Contractors Association, P.O. Box 66208, Orange Park, FL 32065. Internet: http://www.piledrivers.org

For general information on apprenticeships and how to get them, see the *Occupational Outlook Quarterly* article "Apprenticeships: Career training, credentials—and a paycheck in your pocket," online at http://www.bls.gov/opub/ooq/2002/summer/art01.pdf and in print at many libraries and career centers.

Construction Laborers

(O*NET 47-2061.00)

Significant Points

■ Many construction laborer jobs require a variety of basic skills, but others require specialized training and experience.

■ Most construction laborers learn on the job, but formal apprenticeship programs provide the most thorough preparation.

■ Job opportunities vary by locality, but in many areas there will be competition, especially for jobs requiring limited skills.

■ Laborers who have specialized skills or who can relocate near new construction projects should have the best opportunities.

Nature of the Work

Construction laborers can be found on almost all construction sites performing a wide range of tasks from the very easy to the potentially hazardous. They can be found at building, highway, and heavy construction sites; residential and commercial sites; tunnel and shaft excavations; and demolition sites. Many of the jobs they perform require physical strength, training, and experience. Other jobs require little skill and can be learned in a short amount of time. While most construction laborers specialize in a type of construction, such as highway or tunnel construction, some are generalists who perform many different tasks during all stages of construction. Construction laborers, who work in underground construction, such as in tunnels, or in demolition are more likely to specialize in only those areas.

Construction laborers clean and prepare construction sites. They remove trees and debris, tend pumps, compressors and generators, and build forms for pouring concrete. They erect and disassemble scaffolding and other temporary structures. They load, unload, identify, and distribute building materials to the appropriate location according to project plans and specifications. Laborers also tend machines; for example, they may mix concrete using a portable mixer or tend a machine that pumps concrete, grout, cement, sand, plaster, or stucco through a spray gun for application to ceilings and walls. They often help other craftworkers, including carpenters, plasterers, operating engineers, and masons.

Construction laborers are responsible for oversight of the installation and maintenance of traffic control devices and patterns. At highway construction sites, this work may include clearing and preparing highway work zones and rights of way; installing traffic barricades, cones, and markers; and controlling traffic passing near, in, and around work zones. They also dig trenches, install sewer, water, and storm drain pipes, and place concrete and asphalt on roads. Other highly specialized tasks include operating laser guidance equipment to place pipes; operating air, electric, and pneumatic drills; and transporting and setting explosives for tunnel, shaft, and road construction.

Some construction laborers help with the removal of hazardous materials, such as asbestos, lead, or chemicals.

Construction laborers operate a variety of equipment including pavement breakers; jackhammers; earth tampers; concrete, mortar, and plaster mixers; electric and hydraulic boring machines; torches; small mechanical hoists; laser beam equipment; and surveying and measuring equipment. They may use computers and other high-tech input devices to control robotic pipe cutters and cleaners. To perform their jobs effectively, construction laborers must be familiar with the duties of other craftworkers and with the materials, tools, and machinery they use.

Construction laborers often work as part of a team with other skilled craftworkers, jointly carrying out assigned construction tasks. At other times, construction laborers may work alone, reading and interpreting instructions, plans, and specifications with little or no supervision.

Work environment. Most laborers do physically demanding work. They may lift and carry heavy objects, and stoop, kneel, crouch, or crawl in awkward positions. Some work at great heights, or outdoors in all weather conditions. Some jobs expose workers to harmful materials or chemicals, fumes, odors, loud noise, or dangerous machinery. Some laborers may be exposed to lead-based paint, asbestos, or other hazardous substances during their work especially when working in confined spaces. To avoid injury, workers in these jobs wear safety clothing, such as gloves, hardhats, protective chemical suits, and devices to protect their eyes, respiratory system, or hearing. While working in underground construction, construction laborers must be especially alert to safely follow procedures and must deal with a variety of hazards.

Construction laborers generally work 8-hour shifts, although longer shifts are common. Overnight work may be required when working on highways. In some parts of the country, construction laborers may work only during certain seasons. They may also experience weather-related work stoppages at any time of the year.

Training, Other Qualifications, and Advancement

Many construction laborer jobs require a variety of basic skills, but others require specialized training and experience. Most construction laborers learn on the job, but formal apprenticeship programs provide the most thorough preparation.

Education and training. While some construction laborer jobs have no specific educational qualifications or entry-level training, apprenticeships for laborers require a high school diploma or equivalent. High school classes in English, mathematics, physics, mechanical drawing, blueprint reading, welding, and general shop can be helpful.

Most workers start by getting a job with a contractor who provides on-the-job training. Increasingly, construction laborers find work through temporary help agencies that send laborers to construction sites for short-term work. Entry-level workers generally help more experienced workers. They perform routine tasks, such as cleaning and preparing the worksite and unloading materials. When the opportunity arises, they learn from experienced construction trades workers how to do more difficult tasks, such as operating tools and equipment. Construction laborers may also choose or be required to attend a trade or vocational school or community college to receive further trade-related training.

Some laborers receive more formal training. A number of employers, particularly large nonresidential construction contractors with union membership, offer employees formal apprenticeships, which provide the best preparation. These programs include between two and four years of classroom and on-the-job training. In the first 200 hours, workers learn basic construction skills such as blueprint reading, the correct use of tools and equipment, and safety and health procedures. The remainder of the curriculum consists of specialized skills training in three of the largest segments of the construction industry: building construction, heavy and highway construction, and environmental remediation, such as lead or asbestos abatement, and mold or hazardous waste remediation.

Workers who use dangerous equipment or handle toxic chemicals usually receive specialized safety training. Laborers who remove hazardous materials are required to take union or employer-sponsored Occupational Safety and Health Administration safety training.

Apprenticeship applicants usually must be at least 18 years old and meet local requirements. Because the number of apprenticeship programs is limited, however, only a small proportion of laborers learn their trade in this way.

Other qualifications. Laborers need manual dexterity, eye-hand coordination, good physical fitness, a good sense of balance, and an ability to work as a member of a team. The ability to solve arithmetic problems quickly and accurately may be required. In addition, military service or a good work history is viewed favorably by contractors.

Certification and advancement. Laborers may earn certifications in welding, scaffold erecting, and concrete finishing. These certifications help workers prove that they have the knowledge to perform more complex tasks.

Through training and experience, laborers can move into other construction occupations. Laborers may also advance to become construction supervisors or general contractors. For those who would

Projections data from the National Employment Matrix

Occupational Title	SOC Code	Employment, 2006	Projected employment, 2016	Change, 2006-16	
				Number	Percent
Construction laborers	47-2061	1,232,000	1,366,000	134,000	11

NOTE: Data in this table are rounded.

like to advance, it is increasingly important to be able to communicate in both English and Spanish in order to relay instructions and safety precautions to workers with limited understanding of English; Spanish-speaking workers make up a large part of the construction workforce in many areas. Supervisors and contractors need good communication skills to deal with clients and subcontractors.

In addition, supervisors and contractors should be able to identify and estimate the quantity of materials needed to complete a job, and accurately estimate how long a job will take to complete and what it will cost. Computer skills also are important for advancement as construction becomes increasingly mechanized and computerized.

Employment

Construction laborers held about 1.2 million jobs in 2006. They worked throughout the country but, like the general population, were concentrated in metropolitan areas. About 67 percent of construction laborers work in the construction industry, including 30 percent who work for specialty trade contractors. About 17 percent were self-employed in 2006.

Job Outlook

Employment is expected to grow about as fast as the average. In many areas, there will be competition for jobs, especially for those requiring limited skills. Laborers who have specialized skills or who can relocate near new construction projects should have the best opportunities.

Employment change. Employment of construction laborers is expected to grow by 11 percent between 2006 and 2016, about as fast as the average for all occupations. The construction industry in general is expected to grow more slowly than it has in recent years. Due to the large variety of tasks that laborers perform, demand for laborers will mirror the level of overall construction activity.

Construction laborer jobs will be adversely affected by automation as some jobs are replaced by new machinery and equipment that improves productivity and quality. Also, laborers will be increasingly employed by staffing agencies that will contract out laborers to employers on a temporary basis, and in many areas employers will continue to rely on day laborers instead of full-time laborers on staff.

Job prospects. In many geographic areas there will be competition, especially for jobs requiring limited skills, due to a plentiful supply of workers who are willing to work as day laborers. In other areas, however, opportunities will be better. Overall opportunities will be best for those with experience and specialized skills and for those who can relocate to areas with new construction projects. Opportunities will also be better for laborers specializing in road construction.

Employment of construction laborers, like that of many other construction workers, is sensitive to the fluctuations of the economy. Workers in these trades may experience periods of unemployment when the overall level of construction falls. On the other hand, shortages of these workers may occur in some areas during peak periods of building activity.

Earnings

Median hourly earnings of wage and salary construction laborers in May 2006 were $12.66. The middle 50 percent earned between $9.95 and $17.31. The lowest 10 percent earned less than $8.16, and the highest 10 percent earned more than $24.19. Median hourly earnings in the industries employing the largest number of construction laborers were as follows:

Nonresidential building construction	$13.62
Other specialty trade contractors	12.93
Residential building construction	12.82
Foundation, structure, and building exterior contractors	12.41
Employment services	9.90

Earnings for construction laborers can be reduced by poor weather or by downturns in construction activity, which sometimes result in layoffs. Apprentices or helpers usually start out earning about 60 percent of the wage rate paid to experienced workers. Pay increases as apprentices gain experience and learn new skills. Some laborers belong to the Laborers' International Union of North America.

Related Occupations

The work of construction laborers is closely related to other construction occupations. Other workers who perform similar physical work include persons in material moving occupations; forest, conservation, and logging workers; and grounds maintenance workers.

Sources of Additional Information

For information about jobs as a construction laborer, contact local building or construction contractors, local joint labor-management apprenticeship committees, apprenticeship agencies, or the local office of your State Employment Service. You can also find information on the registered apprenticeships together with links to state apprenticeship programs on the U.S. Department of Labor's Web site: http://www.doleta.gov/atels_bat. Apprenticeship information is also available from the U.S. Department of Labor's toll-free helpline: (877) 872-5627. For general information on apprenticeships and how to get them, see the *Occupational Outlook Quarterly* article "Apprenticeships: Career training, credentials—and a paycheck in your pocket," online at http://www.bls.gov/opub/ooq/2002/summer/art01.pdf and in print at many libraries and career centers.

For information on education programs for laborers, contact

▸ Laborers-AGC Education and Training Fund, 37 Deerfield Rd., P.O. Box 37, Pomfret Center, CT 06259. Internet: http://www.laborerslearn.org

▶ National Center for Construction Education and Research, P.O. Box 141104, Gainesville, FL 32614-1104. Internet: http://www.nccer.org

Correctional Officers

(O*NET 33-1011.00, 33-3011.00, and 33-3012.00)

Significant Points

■ The work can be stressful and hazardous.

■ Most correctional officers are employed in state and local government prisons and jails.

■ Job opportunities are expected to be excellent.

Nature of the Work

Correctional officers, also known as *detention officers*, are responsible for overseeing individuals who have been arrested and are awaiting trial or who have been convicted of a crime and sentenced to serve time in a jail, reformatory, or penitentiary.

The jail population changes constantly as some are released, some are convicted and transferred to prison, and new offenders are arrested and enter the system. Correctional officers in local jails admit and process about 12 million people a year, with about 700,000 offenders in jail at any given time. Correctional officers in state and federal prisons watch over the approximately 1.5 million offenders who are incarcerated there at any given time.

Correctional officers maintain security and inmate accountability to prevent disturbances, assaults, and escapes. Officers have no law enforcement responsibilities outside the institution where they work. (For more information on a related occupation, see the profile of police and detectives elsewhere in this book.)

Regardless of the setting, correctional officers maintain order within the institution and enforce rules and regulations. To help ensure that inmates are orderly and obey rules, correctional officers monitor the activities and supervise the work assignments of inmates. Sometimes, officers must search inmates and their living quarters for contraband like weapons or drugs, settle disputes between inmates, and enforce discipline. Correctional officers periodically inspect the facilities, checking cells and other areas of the institution for unsanitary conditions, contraband, fire hazards, and any evidence of infractions of rules. In addition, they routinely inspect locks, window bars, grilles, doors, and gates for signs of tampering. Finally, officers inspect mail and visitors for prohibited items.

Correctional officers report orally and in writing on inmate conduct and on the quality and quantity of work done by inmates. Officers also report security breaches, disturbances, violations of rules, and any unusual occurrences. They usually keep a daily log or record of their activities. Correctional officers cannot show favoritism and must report any inmate who violates the rules. If a crime is committed within their institution or an inmate escapes, they help the responsible law enforcement authorities investigate or search for the escapee. In jail and prison facilities with direct supervision of cellblocks, officers work unarmed. They are equipped with communications devices so that they can summon help if necessary. These officers often work in a cellblock alone, or with another officer, among the 50 to 100 inmates who reside there. The officers enforce regulations primarily through their interpersonal communication

skills and through the use of progressive sanctions, such as the removal of some privileges.

In the highest security facilities, where the most dangerous inmates are housed, correctional officers often monitor the activities of prisoners from a centralized control center with closed-circuit television cameras and a computer tracking system. In such an environment, the inmates may not see anyone but officers for days or weeks at a time and may leave their cells only for showers, solitary exercise time, or visitors. Depending on the offenders' security classification within the institution, correctional officers may have to restrain inmates in handcuffs and leg irons to safely escort them to and from cells and other areas and to see authorized visitors. Officers also escort prisoners between the institution and courtrooms, medical facilities, and other destinations outside the institution.

Bailiffs, also known as *marshals* or *court officers*, are law enforcement officers who maintain safety and order in courtrooms. Their duties, which vary by location, include enforcing courtroom rules, assisting judges, guarding juries from outside contact, delivering court documents, and providing general security for courthouses.

Work environment. Working in a correctional institution can be stressful and hazardous. Every year, correctional officers are injured in confrontations with inmates. Correctional officers may work indoors or outdoors. Some correctional institutions are well lighted, temperature controlled, and ventilated, but others are old, overcrowded, hot, and noisy. Although both jails and prisons can be dangerous places to work, prison populations are more stable than jail populations, and correctional officers in prisons know the security and custodial requirements of the prisoners with whom they are dealing.

Correctional officers usually work an 8-hour day, 5 days a week, on rotating shifts. Because prison and jail security must be provided around the clock, officers work all hours of the day and night, weekends, and holidays. In addition, officers may be required to work paid overtime.

Training, Other Qualifications, and Advancement

Correctional officers learn most of what they need to know for their work through on-the-job training. Qualifications vary by agency, but all agencies require a high school diploma or equivalent, and some also require some college education or full-time work experience.

Education and training. A high school diploma or graduation equivalency degree is required by all employers. The Federal Bureau of Prisons requires entry-level correctional officers to have at least a bachelor's degree; three years of full-time experience in a field providing counseling, assistance, or supervision to individuals; or a combination of the two. Some state and local corrections agencies require some college credits, but law enforcement or military experience may be substituted to fulfill this requirement.

Federal, state, and some local departments of corrections provide training for correctional officers based on guidelines established by the American Correctional Association and the American Jail Association. Some states have regional training academies that are available to local agencies. At the conclusion of formal instruction, all state and local correctional agencies provide on-the-job training, including training on legal restrictions and interpersonal relations. Many systems require firearms proficiency and self-defense skills. Officer trainees typically receive several weeks or months of training in an actual job setting under the supervision of an experienced officer. However, on-the-job training varies widely from agency to agency.

Academy trainees generally receive instruction in a number of subjects, including institutional policies, regulations, and operations, as well as custody and security procedures. New federal correctional officers must undergo 200 hours of formal training within the first year of employment. They also must complete 120 hours of specialized training at the U.S. Federal Bureau of Prisons residential training center at Glynco, GA, within 60 days of their appointment. Experienced officers receive annual in-service training to keep abreast of new developments and procedures.

Some correctional officers are members of prison tactical response teams, which are trained to respond to disturbances, riots, hostage situations, forced cell moves, and other potentially dangerous confrontations. Team members practice disarming prisoners wielding weapons, protecting themselves and inmates against the effects of chemical agents, and other tactics.

Other qualifications. All institutions require correctional officers to be at least 18 to 21 years of age, be a U.S. citizen or permanent resident, and have no felony convictions. Some require previous experience in law enforcement or the military, but college credits can be substituted to fulfill this requirement. Others require demonstration of job stability, usually by accumulating two years of work experience, which need not be related to corrections or law enforcement.

Correctional officers must be in good health. Candidates for employment generally are required to meet formal standards of physical fitness, eyesight, and hearing. In addition, many jurisdictions use standard tests to determine applicant suitability to work in a correctional environment. Good judgment and the ability to think and act quickly are indispensable. Applicants are typically screened for drug abuse, subject to background checks, and required to pass a written examination.

Advancement. Qualified officers may advance to the position of correctional sergeant. Correctional sergeants supervise correctional officers and usually are responsible for maintaining security and directing the activities of other officers during an assigned shift or in an assigned area. Ambitious and qualified correctional officers can be promoted to supervisory or administrative positions all the way up to warden. Promotion prospects may be enhanced by attending college. Officers sometimes transfer to related jobs, such as probation officer, parole officer, and correctional treatment specialist.

Employment

Correctional officers held about 500,000 jobs in 2006. About 3 of every 5 jobs were in state correctional institutions such as prisons, prison camps, and youth correctional facilities. About 18,000 jobs

for correctional officers were in federal correctional institutions, and about 16,000 jobs were in privately owned and managed prisons.

Most of the remaining jobs were in city and county jails or in other institutions run by local governments. Some 300 of these jails, all of them in urban areas, are large, housing over 1,000 inmates. Most correctional officers employed in jails, however, work in institutions located in rural areas with smaller inmate populations.

Other correctional officers oversee individuals being held by the U.S. Immigration and Naturalization Service pending release or deportation or work for correctional institutions that are run by private, for-profit organizations.

Job Outlook

Employment growth is expected to be faster than the average for all occupations, and job opportunities are expected to be excellent.

Employment change. Employment of correctional officers is expected to grow 16 percent between 2006 and 2016, faster than the average for all occupations. Increasing demand for correctional officers will stem from population growth and rising rates of incarceration. Mandatory sentencing guidelines calling for longer sentences and reduced parole for inmates are a primary reason for historically increasing incarceration rates. Some states are reconsidering mandatory sentencing guidelines because of budgetary constraints, court decisions, and doubts about their effectiveness. Additionally, the Supreme Court recently ruled to make federal sentencing guidelines voluntary, rather than mandatory, for judges. It is unclear how many states will change their sentencing policies and how long it will be before any changes affect the prison population. Nevertheless, these developments could moderate future increases in the prison population and cause employment of correctional officers to grow more slowly than they have in the past.

Some employment opportunities also will arise in the private sector, as public authorities contract with private companies to provide and staff corrections facilities. Both state and federal corrections agencies are increasingly using private prisons.

Job prospects. Job opportunities for correctional officers are expected to be excellent. The need to replace correctional officers who transfer to other occupations, retire, or leave the labor force, coupled with rising employment demand, will generate thousands of job openings each year. In the past, some local and state corrections agencies have experienced difficulty in attracting and keeping qualified applicants, largely because of low salaries, shift work, and the concentration of jobs in rural locations. This situation is expected to continue.

Layoffs of correctional officers are rare because of increasing offender populations.

Projections data from the National Employment Matrix

Occupational Title	SOC Code	Employment, 2006	Projected employment, 2016	Change, 2006-16	
				Number	Percent
Correctional officers...:	—	500,000	582,000	82,000	16
First-line supervisors/managers of correctional officers	33-1011	40,000	45,000	5,000	13
Bailiffs, correctional officers, and jailers	33-3010	460,000	537,000	77,000	17
Bailiffs	33-3011	19,000	21,000	2,100	11
Correctional officers and jailers	33-3012	442,000	516,000	75,000	17

NOTE: Data in this table are rounded.

Earnings

Median annual earnings of correctional officers and jailers were $35,760 in May 2006. The middle 50 percent earned between $28,320 and $46,500. The lowest 10 percent earned less than $23,600, and the highest 10 percent earned more than $58,580. Median annual earnings in the public sector were $47,750 in the federal government, $36,140 in state government, and $34,820 in local government. In the facilities support services industry, where the relatively small number of officers employed by privately operated prisons is classified, median annual earnings were $25,050.

Median annual earnings of first-line supervisors/managers of correctional officers were $52,580 in May 2006. The middle 50 percent earned between $38,920 and $67,820. The lowest 10 percent earned less than $33,270, and the highest 10 percent earned more than $81,230. Median annual earnings were $51,500 in state government and $52,940 in local government.

Median annual earnings of bailiffs were $34,210 in May 2006. The middle 50 percent earned between $25,130 and $48,010. The lowest 10 percent earned less than $18,390, and the highest 10 percent earned more than $58,270. Median annual earnings were $30,510 in local government.

According to the Federal Bureau of Prisons, the starting salary for federal correctional officers was $28,862 a year in 2007. Starting federal salaries were slightly higher in areas where prevailing local pay levels were higher.

In addition to typical benefits, correctional officers employed in the public sector usually are provided with uniforms or a clothing allowance to purchase their own uniforms. Civil service systems or merit boards cover officers employed by the federal government and most state governments. Their retirement coverage entitles correctional officers to retire at age 50 after 20 years of service or at any age with 25 years of service.

Related Occupations

A number of options are available to those interested in careers in protective services and security. Security guards and gaming surveillance officers protect people and property against theft, vandalism, illegal entry, and fire. Police and detectives maintain law and order, prevent crime, and arrest offenders. Probation officers and correctional treatment specialists monitor and counsel offenders and evaluate their progress in becoming productive members of society.

Sources of Additional Information

Further information about correctional officers is available from

▸ American Correctional Association, 206 N. Washington St., Suite 200, Alexandria, VA 22314. Internet: http://www.aca.org

▸ American Jail Association, 1135 Professional Ct., Hagerstown, MD 21740. Internet: http://www.corrections.com/aja

▸ Information on entrance requirements, training, and career opportunities for correctional officers at the federal level may be obtained from the Federal Bureau of Prisons. Internet: http://www.bop.gov

Information on obtaining a position as a correctional officer with the federal government is available from the Office of Personnel Management through USAJOBS, the federal government's official employment information system. This resource for locating and applying for job opportunities can be accessed through the Internet at http://www.usajobs.opm.gov or through an interactive voice response telephone system at (703) 724-1850 or TDD (978) 461-8404. These numbers are not toll free, and charges may result.

Counter and Rental Clerks

(O*NET 41-2021.00)

Significant Points

■ Jobs usually require little or no experience or formal education.

■ Employment is projected to grow much faster than average as businesses strive to improve customer service.

■ Many full-time and part-time job opportunities should be available, primarily because of the need to replace workers who leave this occupation.

Nature of the Work

Counter and rental clerks take orders for rentals and services. Many rent cars or home improvement equipment, for example. Regardless of where they work, counter and rental clerks must be knowledgeable about the company's goods and services, policies, and procedures. Depending on the type of establishment, counter and rental clerks use their knowledge to give advice on a wide variety of products and services, ranging from hydraulic tools to shoe repair. For example, in the car rental industry, these workers tell customers about the features of different types of automobiles and about daily and weekly rental costs. They also ensure that customers meet age and other requirements for renting cars, and they indicate when and in what condition the cars must be returned. Those in the equipment rental industry have similar duties but also must know how to operate and care for the machinery rented. In drycleaning establishments, counter clerks inform customers when items will be ready and about the effects, if any, of the chemicals used on certain garments. In video rental stores, counter clerks advise customers about the use of video and game players and the length of the rental period. They scan returned movies and games, restock shelves, handle money, and log daily reports.

When taking orders, counter and rental clerks use various types of equipment. In some establishments, they write out tickets and order forms, although most use computers or barcode scanners. Most of these computer systems are user friendly, require very little data entry, and are customized for each firm. Scanners read the product code and display a description of the item on a computer screen. However, clerks must ensure that the information on the screen matches the product.

Work environment. Firms employing counter and rental clerks usually operate nights and weekends for the convenience of their customers. As a result, many employers offer flexible schedules. Some counter and rental clerks work 40-hour weeks, but many are on part-time schedules—usually during rush periods, such as weekends, evenings, and holidays.

Working conditions usually are pleasant; most stores and service establishments are clean, well lighted, and temperature controlled. However, clerks are on their feet much of the time and may be confined behind a small counter area. Some may need to move, lift, or carry heavy machinery or other equipment. The job requires con-

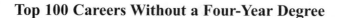

Projections data from the National Employment Matrix

Occupational Title	SOC Code	Employment, 2006	Projected employment, 2016	Change, 2006-16	
				Number	Percent
Counter and rental clerks	41-2021	477,000	586,000	109,000	23

NOTE: Data in this table are rounded.

stant interaction with the public and can be stressful, especially during busy periods.

Training, Other Qualifications, and Advancement

Most counter and rental clerk jobs are entry-level positions that require little or no experience and minimal formal education.

Education and training. Many employers prefer workers with at least a high school diploma. In most companies, counter and rental clerks are trained on the job, sometimes through the use of videos, brochures, and pamphlets.

Clerks usually learn the firm's policies and procedures and how to operate a firm's equipment from more experienced workers. However, some employers have formal classroom training programs lasting between a few hours and a few weeks. Topics covered in this training include the nature of the industry, the company and its policies and procedures, operation of equipment, sales techniques, and customer service. Counter and rental clerks also must become familiar with the different products and services rented or provided by their company to give customers the best possible service.

Other qualifications. Counter and rental clerks should enjoy working with people and should be tactful and polite, even with difficult customers. They also should be able to handle several tasks at once, while continuing to provide friendly service. In addition, good oral and written communication skills are essential.

Advancement. Advancement opportunities depend on the size and type of company. Many establishments that employ counter or rental clerks tend to be small businesses, making advancement difficult. In larger establishments, however, jobs such as counter and rental clerks offer good opportunities for workers to learn about their company's products and business practices. That can lead to more responsible positions. Some counter and rental clerks are promoted to event planner, assistant manager, or salesperson. Some pursue related positions. A clerk that fixes rented equipment might become a mechanic, for example.

In certain industries, such as equipment repair, counter and rental jobs may be an additional or alternative source of income for workers with multiple jobs or for those who are semiretired. For example, retired mechanics could prove invaluable at tool rental centers because of their knowledge of, and familiarity with, tools.

Employment

Counter and rental clerks held about 477,000 jobs in 2006. About 22 percent of clerks worked in consumer goods rental, which includes video rental stores. Other large employers included drycleaning and laundry services; automotive equipment rental and leasing services; automobile dealers; amusement, gambling, and recreation industries; and grocery stores.

Counter and rental clerks are employed throughout the country but are concentrated in metropolitan areas, where personal services and renting and leasing services are in greater demand.

Job Outlook

Much faster than average employment growth coupled with the need to replace workers who leave this occupation should result in many full-time and part-time job opportunities.

Employment change. Employment of counter and rental clerks is expected to increase by 23 percent during the 2006–2016 decade, much faster than the average for all occupations. Because all types of businesses strive to improve customer service by hiring more clerks, fast employment growth is expected in most industries; growth in amusement and recreation industries is expected to be especially fast.

Job prospects. Many full-time and part-time job opportunities should be available, primarily because of the need to replace experienced workers who transfer to other occupations or leave the labor force.

Earnings

Counter and rental clerks typically start at the minimum wage, which, in establishments covered by federal law, was $5.85 an hour in 2007. In some states, the law sets the minimum wage higher, and establishments must pay at least that amount. Wages also tend to be higher in areas where there is intense competition for workers. In addition to wages, some counter and rental clerks receive commissions based on the number of contracts they complete or services they sell.

Median hourly earnings of counter and rental clerks in May 2006 were $9.41. The middle 50 percent earned between $7.58 and $13.05 an hour. The lowest 10 percent earned less than $6.56 an hour, and the highest 10 percent earned more than $18.17 an hour. Median hourly earnings in the industries employing the largest number of counter and rental clerks in May 2006 were

Automobile dealers	$19.15
Automotive equipment rental and leasing	10.79
Lessors of real estate	10.31
Consumer goods rental	8.07
Drycleaning and laundry services	7.95

Full-time workers typically receive health and life insurance, paid vacation, and sick leave. Benefits for counter and rental clerks who work part time or work for independent stores tend to be significantly less than for those who work full time. Many companies offer discounts to full-time and part-time employees on the goods or services they provide.

Related Occupations

Counter and rental clerks take orders and receive payment for services rendered. Other workers with similar duties include tellers, cashiers, food and beverage serving and related workers, gaming cage workers, Postal Service workers, and retail salespersons.

Sources of Additional Information

For general information on employment in the equipment rental industry, contact

▸ American Rental Association, 1900 19th St., Moline, IL 61265. Internet: http://www.ararental.org

For more information about the work of counter clerks in drycleaning and laundry establishments, contact

▸ International Fabricare Institute, 14700 Sweitzer Ln., Laurel, MD 20707. Internet: http://www.ifi.org

Court Reporters

(O*NET 23-2091.00)

Significant Points

■ Job prospects are expected to be excellent, especially for those with certification.

■ Demand for real-time broadcast captioning and translating will spur employment growth.

■ The amount of training required to become a court reporter varies by specialization; licensure requirements vary by state.

Nature of the Work

Court reporters usually create verbatim transcripts of speeches, conversations, legal proceedings, meetings, and other events. Sometimes written accounts of spoken words are necessary for correspondence, records, or legal proof, and court reporters provide those accounts. They play a critical role not only in judicial proceedings, but also at every meeting where the spoken word must be preserved as a written transcript. They are responsible for ensuring a complete, accurate, and secure legal record. In addition to preparing and protecting the legal record, many court reporters assist judges and trial attorneys in a variety of ways, such as organizing and searching for information in the official record or making suggestions to judges and attorneys regarding courtroom administration and procedure. Increasingly, court reporters provide closed-captioning and real-time translating services to the deaf and hard-of-hearing community.

There are several methods of court reporting. The most common method is called stenographic. Using a stenotype machine, stenotypists document all statements made in official proceedings. The machine allows them to press multiple keys at once to record combinations of letters representing sounds, words, or phrases. These symbols are electronically recorded and then translated and displayed as text in a process called computer-aided transcription (CAT). In real-time court reporting, the stenotype machine is linked to computers for real-time captioning, often of television programs. As the reporter keys in the symbols, the spoken word instantly appear as text on the screen.

Another method of court reporting is electronic reporting. This method uses audio equipment to record court proceedings. The court reporter monitors the process, takes notes to identify speakers, and listens to the recording to ensure clarity and quality. The equipment used may include analog tape recorders or digital equipment. Electronic reporters and transcribers often are responsible for producing a written transcript of the recorded proceeding.

Yet another method of court reporting is voice writing. Using the voice-writing method, a court reporter speaks directly into a voice silencer—a hand-held mask containing a microphone. As the reporter repeats the testimony into the recorder, the mask prevents the reporter from being heard during testimony. Voice writers record everything that is said by judges, witnesses, attorneys, and other parties to a proceeding, including gestures and emotional reactions, and prepare transcripts afterwards.

Court reporters are responsible for a number of duties both before and after transcribing events. Stenographic or voice writing reporters must create and maintain the computer dictionary that they use to translate their keystroke codes or voice files into written text. They may customize the dictionary with parts of words, entire words, or terminology specific to the proceeding, program, or event—such as a religious service—they plan to transcribe. After documenting proceedings, stenographic reporters must edit the computer-generated translation for correct grammar. All reporters are responsible for accurate identification of proper names and places. Electronic reporters ensure that the record or testimony is discernible. Reporters usually prepare written transcripts, make copies, and provide information from the transcript to courts, counsels, parties, and the public on request. Court reporters also develop procedures for easy storage and retrieval of all stenographic notes, voice files, commonly referred to as "stenograms", or audio recordings in paper or digital format.

Although many court reporters record official proceedings in the courtroom, others work outside the courts. For example, court reporters—called webcasters—capture sales meetings, press conferences, product introductions, and technical training seminars and instantly transmit them to all parties involved via computers. As participants speak into telephones or microphones, the words appear on all of the participants' computer monitors simultaneously. Still others capture the proceedings taking place in government agencies at all levels, from the U.S. Congress to state and local governing bodies. Court reporters who specialize in captioning live television programming for people with hearing loss are commonly known as broadcast captioners. They work for television networks or cable stations, captioning news, emergency broadcasts, sporting events, and other programming.

A version of the captioning process that allows reporters to provide more personalized services for deaf and hard-of-hearing people is Communication Access Real-time Translation (CART). CART reporters often work with hard-of-hearing students and people who are learning English as a second language, captioning high school and college classes and providing transcripts at the end of the sessions. CART reporters also accompany deaf clients to events, including conventions, doctor appointments, or wherever communication access is needed. CART providers increasingly furnish this service remotely, as an Internet or phone connection allows for immediate communication access regardless of location. With CART and broadcast captioning, the level of understanding gained by a person with hearing loss depends entirely on the skill of the court reporter. In an emergency, such as a tornado or a hurricane, people's safety may depend on the accuracy of information provided in the form of captioning.

Some voice writers produce a transcript in real time, using computer speech recognition technology. Other voice writers prefer to translate their voice files after the proceeding is over, or they transcribe the files manually, without using speech recognition at all. In any event, speech recognition-enabled voice writers pursue not only court reporting careers, but also careers as closed captioners, CART reporters for hearing-impaired individuals, and Internet streaming text providers or caption providers.

Work environment. The majority of court reporters work in comfortable settings, such as offices of attorneys, courtrooms, legislatures, and conventions. An increasing number of court reporters work from home-based offices as independent contractors, or freelancers.

Work in this occupation presents few hazards, although sitting in the same position for long periods can be tiring, and workers can suffer wrist, back, neck, or eye strain. Workers also risk repetitive stress injuries such as carpal tunnel syndrome. In addition, the pressure to be accurate and fast can be stressful.

Many official court reporters work a standard 40-hour week, and they often work additional hours at home preparing transcripts. Self-employed court reporters, or freelancers, usually work flexible hours, including part time, evenings, and weekends, or they may be on call.

Training, Other Qualifications, and Advancement

The amount of training required to become a court reporter varies by specialization. Licensure requirements vary by state.

Education and training. The amount of training required to become a court reporter varies with the type of reporting chosen. It usually takes less than a year to become a novice voice writer, although it takes at least two years to become proficient at realtime voice writing. Electronic reporters and transcribers learn their skills on the job. The average length of time it takes to become a realtime stenotypist is 33 months. Training is offered by about 130 postsecondary vocational and technical schools and colleges. The National Court Reporters Association (NCRA) has certified about 70 programs, all of which offer courses in stenotype computer-aided transcription and real-time reporting. NCRA-certified programs require students to capture a minimum of 225 words per minute, a requirement for federal government employment as well.

Electronic court reporters use audio-capture technology and, therefore, usually learn their skills on the job. Students read manuals, review them with their trainers, and observe skilled electronic transcribers perform procedures. Court electronic transcribers generally obtain initial technical training from a vendor when it is placed in service, with further court-specific training provided on the job. If working for a private company or organization, hands-on training occurs under direct supervision of an established practitioner or firm.

Licensure. Some states require voice writers to pass a test and to earn state licensure. As a substitute for state licensure, the National Verbatim Reporters Association offers three national certifications to voice writers: Certified Verbatim Reporter (CVR), Certificate of Merit (CM), and Real-Time Verbatim Reporter (RVR). Earning these certifications is sufficient to be licensed in states where the

voice method of court reporting is permitted. Candidates for the first certification—the CVR—must pass a written test of spelling, punctuation, vocabulary, legal and medical terminology and three five-minute dictation and transcription examinations that test for speed, accuracy, and silence. The second certification, the CM, requires additional levels of speed, knowledge, and accuracy. The RVR certification measures the candidate's skill at real-time transcription, judicial reporting, CART provision, and captioning, including Webcasting. To retain these certifications, the voice writer must obtain continuing education credits. Credits are given for voice writer education courses, continuing legal education courses, and college courses.

Some states require court reporters to be notary publics. Others require the Certified Court Reporter (CCR) designation, for which a reporter must pass a state test administered by a board of examiners.

Other qualifications. In addition to possessing speed and accuracy, court reporters must have excellent listening skills and hearing, good English grammar and vocabulary, and punctuation skills. They must be aware of business practices and current events as well as the correct spelling of names of people, places, and events that may be mentioned in a broadcast or in court proceedings. For those who work in courtrooms, an expert knowledge of legal terminology and criminal and appellate procedure is essential. Because capturing proceedings requires the use of computerized stenography or speech recognition equipment, court reporters must be knowledgeable about computer hardware and software applications. Voice writers must learn to listen and speak simultaneously and very quickly and quietly, while also identifying speakers and describing peripheral activities in the courtroom or deposition room.

Certification and advancement. Certifications can help court reporters get jobs and advance in their careers. Several associations offer certifications for different types of reporters.

The National Court Reporters Association confers the entry-level designation Registered Professional Reporter (RPR) upon those who pass a four-part examination and participate in mandatory continuing education programs. Although voluntary, the designation is recognized as a mark of distinction in the field.

A court reporter may obtain additional certifications that demonstrate higher levels of experience and competency, such as Registered Merit Reporter (RMR) or Registered Diplomate Reporter (RDR). The NCRA also offers the designations Certified Realtime Reporter (CRR), Certified Broadcast Captioner (CBC), and Certified CART Provider (CCP), designed primarily for those who caption media programs or assist people who are deaf.

With experience and education, court reporters can also receive certification in administrative and management, consulting, or teaching positions.

The United States Court Reporters Association offers another voluntary certification designation, the Federal Certified Realtime Reporter (FCRR), for court reporters working in federal courts. The exam is designed to test the basic real-time skills of federal court reporters and is recognized by the Administrative Office for the United States District Courts for purposes of real-time certification.

The American Association of Electronic Reporters and Transcribers (AAERT) certifies electronic court reporters. Certification is voluntary and includes a written and a practical examination. To be eligible to take the exams, candidates must have at least two years of court reporting or transcribing experience, must be eligible for notary public commissions in their states, and must have completed

Projections data from the National Employment Matrix

Occupational Title	SOC Code	Employment, 2006	Projected employment, 2016	Change, 2006-2016	
				Number	Percent
Court reporters	23-2091	19,000	24,000	4,700	25

NOTE: Data in this table are rounded.

high school. AAERT offers three types of certificates—Certified Electronic Court Reporter (CER), Certified Electronic Court Transcriber (CET), and Certified Electronic Court Reporter and Transcriber (CERT). Some employers may require electronic court reporters and transcribers to obtain certificates once they are eligible.

Employment

Court reporters held about 19,000 jobs in 2006. More than half worked for state and local governments, a reflection of the large number of court reporters working in courts, legislatures, and various agencies. Most of the remaining wage and salary workers were employed by court reporting agencies. Around 8 percent of court reporters were self-employed.

Job Outlook

Employment is projected to grow much faster than the average, reflecting the demand for real-time broadcast captioning and translating. Job opportunities should be excellent, especially for those with certification.

Employment change. Employment of court reporters is projected to grow 25 percent, much faster than the average for all occupations between 2006 and 2016. Demand for court reporter services will be spurred by the continuing need for accurate transcription of proceedings in courts and in pretrial depositions, by the growing need to create captions for live television, and by the need to provide other real-time broadcast captioning and translating services for the deaf and hard-of-hearing.

Increasing numbers of civil and criminal cases are expected to create new jobs for court reporters, but budget constraints are expected to limit the ability of federal, state, and local courts to expand, and thereby also limit the demand for traditional court reporting services in courtrooms and other legal venues. Further, because of the difficulty in attracting court reporters and in efforts to control costs, many courtrooms have installed tape recorders that are maintained by electronic court reporters and transcribers to record court proceedings. However, because courts use electronic reporters and transcribers only in a limited capacity traditional stenographic court reporters will continue to be used in felony trials and other proceedings. Despite the use of audiotape and videotape technology, court reporters can quickly turn spoken words into readable, searchable, permanent text, and they will continue to be needed to produce written legal transcripts and proceedings for publication.

Voice writers have become more widely accepted as the accuracy of speech recognition technology improves. Still, many courts allow only stenotypists to perform court reporting duties.

In addition, more court reporters will be needed to caption outside of legal proceedings. Not only is there federal legislation mandating that all new television programming be captioned for the deaf and hard-of-hearing, all new Spanish-language programming likewise must be captioned by 2010. In addition, the Americans with Disabilities Act gives deaf and hard-of-hearing students in colleges and universities the right to request access to real-time translation in their classes. These factors are expected to continue to increase the demand for court reporters who provide CART services. Although these services forgo transcripts and differ from traditional court reporting, they require the same skills that court reporters learn in their training.

Job prospects. Job opportunities for court reporters are expected to be excellent as job openings continue to outnumber jobseekers in some areas. Court reporters with certification and those who choose to specialize in providing CART, broadcast captioning, and or webcasting services should have the best job opportunities. The favorable job market reflects the fact that fewer people are entering this profession, particularly as stenographic typists.

Earnings

Wage and salary court reporters had median annual earnings of $45,610 in May 2006. The middle 50 percent earned between $33,160 and $61,530. The lowest-paid 10 percent earned less than $23,430, and the highest-paid 10 percent earned more than $77,770. Median annual earnings in May 2006 were $45,080 for court reporters working in local government and $41,720 for those working in business support services.

Compensation and compensation methods for court reporters vary with the type of reporting job, the experience of the individual reporter, the level of certification achieved, and the region of the country. Official court reporters earn a salary and a per-page fee for transcripts. Many salaried court reporters supplement their income by doing freelance work. Freelance court reporters are paid per job and receive a per-page fee for transcripts. CART providers are paid by the hour. Captioners receive a salary and benefits if they work as employees of a captioning company; Captioners working as independent contractors are paid by the hour.

Related Occupations

Workers in several other occupations also type, record information, and process paperwork. Among these are secretaries and administrative assistants; medical transcriptionists; data entry and information processing workers; receptionists and information clerks; and human resources assistants, except payroll and timekeeping. Other workers who provide legal support include paralegals and legal assistants.

Sources of Additional Information

State employment service offices can provide information about job openings for court reporters. For information about careers, training, and certification in court reporting contact

▶ American Association of Electronic Reporters and Transcribers, 23812 Rock Circle, Bothell, WA 98021. Internet: http://www.aaert.org

▸ National Court Reporters Association, 8224 Old Courthouse Rd., Vienna, VA 22182. Internet: http://www.ncraonline.org

▸ National Verbatim Reporters Association, 207 Third Ave., Hattiesburg, MS 39401. Internet: http://www.nvra.org

▸ United States Court Reporters Association, 4731 N. Western Ave., Chicago, IL 60625-2012. Internet: http://www.uscra.org

Customer Service Representatives

(O*NET 43-4051.00, 43-4051.01, and 43-4051.02)

Significant Points

■ Job prospects are expected to be excellent.

■ Most jobs require only a high school diploma but educational requirements are rising.

■ Strong verbal communication and listening skills are important.

Nature of the Work

Customer service representatives are employed by many different types of companies to serve as a direct point of contact for customers. They are responsible for ensuring that their company's customers receive an adequate level of service or help with their questions and concerns. These customers may be individual consumers or other companies, and their service needs can vary considerably.

All customer service representatives interact with customers to provide information in response to inquiries about products or services and to handle and resolve complaints. They communicate with customers through a variety of means—by telephone; by e-mail, fax, regular mail; or in person. Some customer service representatives handle general questions and complaints, whereas others specialize in a particular area.

Many customer inquiries involve routine questions and requests. For example, customer service representatives may be asked to provide a customer with their credit card balance, or to check on the status of an order. However, other questions are more involved, and may require additional research or further explanation on the part of the customer service representative. In handling customers' complaints, they must attempt to resolve the problem according to guidelines established by the company. These procedures may involve asking questions to determine the validity of a complaint; offering possible solutions; or providing customers with refunds, exchanges, or other offers, like discounts or coupons. In some cases, customer service representatives are required to follow up with an individual customer until a question is answered or an issue is resolved.

Some customer service representatives help people decide what types of products or services would best suit their needs. They may even aid customers in completing purchases or transactions. Although the primary function of customer service representatives is not sales, some may spend time encouraging customers to purchase additional products or services. (For information on workers whose primary function is sales, see the job profile of sales representatives, wholesale and manufacturing, elsewhere in this book.) Customer service representatives also may make changes or updates to a customer's profile or account information. They may keep records of transactions and update and maintain databases of information.

Most customer service representatives use computers and telephones extensively in their work. Customer service representatives frequently enter information into a computer as they are speaking to customers. Often, companies have large amounts of data, such as account information, that is pulled up on a computer screen while the representative is talking to a customer so he or she can answer specific questions. Customer service representatives also usually have answers to the most common customer questions, or guidelines for dealing with complaints. In the event that they encounter a question or situation to which they do not know how to respond, workers consult with a supervisor to determine the best course of action. They generally use multiline telephone systems, which may route calls directly to the most appropriate representative. However, at times, they must transfer calls to someone who may be better able to respond to the customer's needs.

In some organizations, customer service representatives spend their entire day on the telephone. In others, they may spend part of their day answering e-mails and the remainder of the day taking calls. For some, most of their contact with the customer is face to face. Customer service representatives need to remain aware of the amount of time spent with each customer so that they can fairly distribute their time among the people who require their assistance. This is particularly important for those whose primary activities are answering telephone calls and whose conversations are required to be kept within a set time limit. For those working in call centers, there is usually very little time between telephone calls. When working in call centers, customer service representatives are likely to be under close supervision. Telephone calls may be taped and reviewed by supervisors to ensure that company policies and procedures are being followed.

Job responsibilities also can differ, depending on the industry in which a customer service representative is employed. For example, those working in the branch office of a bank may assume the responsibilities of other workers, such as teller or new account clerk, as needed. In insurance agencies, a customer service representative interacts with agents, insurance companies, and policyholders. These workers handle much of the paperwork related to insurance policies, such as policy applications and changes and renewals to existing policies. They answer questions regarding policy coverage, help with reporting claims, and do anything else that may need to be done. Although they must have similar credentials and knowledge of insurance products as insurance agents, the duties of a customer service representative differ from those of an agent as they are not responsible for seeking potential customers. Customer service representatives employed by utilities and communications companies assist individuals interested in opening accounts for various utilities such as electricity and gas, or for communication services such as cable television and telephone. They explain various options and receive orders for services to be installed, turned on, turned off, or changed. They also may look into and resolve complaints about billing and other service.

Work environment. Although customer service representatives work in a variety of settings, most work in areas that are clean and well lit. Many work in call or customer contact centers where workers generally have their own workstation or cubicle space equipped with a telephone, headset, and computer. Because many call centers are open extended hours, beyond the traditional work day, or are staffed around the clock, these positions may require workers to take on early morning, evening, or late night shifts. Weekend or holiday work also may be necessary. As a result, the occupation is well suited to flexible work schedules. About 17 percent of customer service representatives work part time. The occupation also offers the opportunity for seasonal work in certain industries, often through temporary help agencies.

Call centers may be crowded and noisy, and work may be repetitive and stressful, with little time between calls. Workers usually must attempt to minimize the length of each call, while still providing excellent service. To ensure that these procedures are followed, conversations may be monitored by supervisors, which be stressful. Also, long periods spent sitting, typing, or looking at a computer screen may cause eye and muscle strain, backaches, headaches, and repetitive motion injuries.

Customer service representatives working outside of a call center environment may interact with customers through several different means. For example, workers employed by an insurance agency or in a grocery store may have customers approach them in person or contact them by telephone, computer, mail, or fax. Many of these customer service representatives work a standard 40-hour week; however, their hours generally depend on their employer's hours of operation. Work environments outside of a call center also vary accordingly. Most customer service representatives work either in an office or at a service or help desk.

Customer service representatives may have to deal with difficult or irate customers, which can be challenging. However, the ability to resolve customers' problems has the potential to be very rewarding.

Training, Other Qualifications, and Advancement

Most jobs require at least a high school diploma. However, employers are increasingly seeking candidates with some college education. Most employers provide training to workers before they begin serving customers.

Education and training. Most customer service representative jobs require only a high school diploma. However, because employers are demanding a higher skilled workforce, many customer service jobs now require an associate or bachelor's degree. High school and college level courses in computers, English, or business are helpful in preparing for a job in customer service.

Training requirements vary by industry. Almost all customer service representatives are provided with some training prior to beginning work. This training generally includes customer service and phone skills; information on products and services; information about common customer problems; the use of the telephone and computer systems; and company policies and regulations. Length of training varies, but usually lasts at least several weeks. Because of a constant need to update skills and knowledge, most customer service representatives continue to receive training throughout their career. This is particularly true of workers in industries such as banking, in which regulations and products are continually changing.

Other qualifications. Because customer service representatives constantly interact with the public, good communication and problem-solving skills are a must. Verbal communication and listening skills are especially important. For workers who communicate through e-mail, good typing, spelling, and writing skills are necessary. Basic to intermediate computer knowledge and good interpersonal skills also

are important qualities for people who wish to be successful in the field.

Customer service representatives play a critical role in providing an interface between customers and companies. As a result, employers seek out people who are friendly and possess a professional manner. The ability to deal patiently with problems and complaints and to remain courteous when faced with difficult or angry people is very important. Also, a customer service representative needs to be able to work independently within specified time constraints. Workers should have a clear and pleasant speaking voice and be fluent in English. However, the ability to speak a foreign language is becoming increasingly necessary.

Although some positions may require previous industry, office, or customer service experience, many customer service jobs are entry level. However, within insurance agencies and brokerages, these jobs usually are not entry-level positions. Workers must have previous experience in insurance and often are required by state regulations to be licensed like insurance sales agents. A variety of designations are available to demonstrate that a candidate has sufficient knowledge and skill, and continuing education courses and training often are offered through the employer.

Advancement. Customer service jobs are often good introductory positions into a company or an industry. In some cases, experienced workers can move up within the company into supervisory or managerial positions or they may move into areas such as product development, in which they can use their knowledge to improve products and services. As they gain more knowledge of industry products and services, customer service representatives in insurance may advance to other, higher level positions, such as insurance sales agent.

Employment

Customer service representatives held about 2.2 million jobs in 2006. Although they were found in a variety of industries, about 23 percent of customer service representatives worked in finance and insurance. The largest numbers were employed by insurance carriers, insurance agencies and brokerages, and banks and credit unions.

About 14 percent of customer service representatives were employed in administrative and support services. These workers were concentrated in the business support services industry (which includes telephone call centers) and employment services (which includes temporary help services and employment placement agencies). Another 11 percent of customer service representatives were employed in retail trade establishments such as general merchandise stores and food and beverage stores. Other industries that employ significant numbers of customer service representatives include information, particularly the telecommunications industry; manufacturing, such as printing and related support activities; and wholesale trade.

Job Outlook

Customer service representatives are expected to experience growth that is much faster than the average for all occupations through the projection period. Furthermore, job prospects should excellent as workers who leave the occupation will need to be replaced.

Employment Change. Employment of customer service representatives is expected to increase 25 percent from 2006 to 2016, which is much faster than the average for all occupations. This occupation will have one of the largest numbers of new jobs arise, about

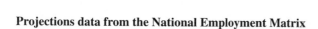

Projections data from the National Employment Matrix

Occupational Title	SOC Code	Employment, 2006	Projected employment, 2016	Change, 2006-16	
				Number	Percent
Customer service representatives..	43-4051	2,202,000	2,747,000	545,000	25

NOTE: Data in this table are rounded.

545,000 over the 2006–2016 projection period. Beyond growth stemming from expansion of the industries in which customer service representatives are employed, a need for additional customer service representatives is likely to result from heightened reliance on these workers. Customer service is very important to the success of any organization that deals with customers, and strong customer service can build sales, visibility, and loyalty as companies try to distinguish themselves from competitors. In many industries, gaining a competitive edge and retaining customers will be increasingly important over the next decade. This is particularly true in industries such as financial services, communications, and utilities, which already employ numerous customer service representatives. As the trend towards consolidation in industries continues, centralized call centers will provide an effective method for delivering a high level of customer service. As a result, employment of customer service representatives may grow at a faster rate in call centers than in other areas. However, this growth may be tempered by a variety of factors such as technological improvements that make it increasingly feasible and cost-effective for call centers to be built or relocated outside of the United States.

Technology is affecting the occupation in many ways. The Internet and automated teller machines have provided customers with means of obtaining information and conducting transactions that do not entail interacting with another person. Technology also allows for greater streamlining of processes, while at the same time increasing the productivity of workers. The use of computer software to filter e-mails, generating automatic responses or directing messages to the appropriate representative, and the use of similar systems to answer or route telephone inquiries are likely to become more prevalent in the future. Also, with rapidly improving telecommunications, some organizations have begun to position their call centers overseas.

Despite such developments, the need for customer service representatives is expected to remain strong. In many ways, technology has heightened consumers' expectations for information and services, and the availability of information online seems to have generated more need for customer service representatives, particularly to respond to e-mail. Also, technology cannot replace human skills. As more sophisticated technologies are able to resolve many customers' questions and concerns, the nature of the inquiries handled by customer service representatives is likely to become increasingly complex.

Furthermore, the job responsibilities of customer service representatives are expanding. As companies downsize or take other measures to increase profitability, workers are being trained to perform additional duties such as opening bank accounts or cross-selling products. As a result, employers increasingly may prefer customer service representatives who have education beyond high school, such as some college or even a college degree.

While jobs in some industries—such as retail trade—may be affected by economic downturns, the customer service occupation generally is resistant to major fluctuations in employment.

Job prospects. Prospects for obtaining a job in this field are expected to be excellent, with more job openings than jobseekers. Bilingual jobseekers, in particular, may enjoy favorable job prospects. In addition, numerous job openings will result from the need to replace experienced customer service representatives who transfer to other occupations or leave the labor force. Replacement needs are expected to be significant in this large occupation because many young people work as customer service representatives before switching to other jobs.

This occupation is well suited to flexible work schedules, and many opportunities for part-time work will continue to be available, particularly as organizations attempt to cut labor costs by hiring more temporary workers.

Earnings

In May 2006, median hourly earnings for wage and salary customer service representatives were $13.62. The middle 50 percent earned between $10.73 and $17.40. The lowest 10 percent earned less than $8.71 and the highest 10 percent earned more than $22.11.

Earnings for customer service representatives vary according to level of skill required, experience, training, location, and size of firm. Median hourly earnings in the industries employing the largest numbers of these workers in May 2006 were

Insurance carriers	$15.00
Agencies, brokerages, and other insurance related activities	14.51
Depository Credit Intermediation	13.68
Employment services	11.74
Telephone call centers	10.29

In addition to receiving an hourly wage, full-time customer service representatives who work evenings, nights, weekends, or holidays may receive shift differential pay. Also, because call centers are often open during extended hours, or even 24 hours a day, some customer service representatives have the benefit of being able to work a schedule that does not conform to the traditional work week. Other benefits can include life and health insurance, pensions, bonuses, employer-provided training, and discounts on the products and services the company offers.

Related Occupations

Customer service representatives interact with customers to provide information in response to inquiries about products and services and to handle and resolve complaints. Other occupations in which workers have similar dealings with customers and the public are information and record clerks; financial clerks such as tellers and new account clerks; insurance sales agents; securities, commodities, and financial services sales agents; retail salespersons; computer support specialists; and gaming services workers.

© JIST Works

Sources of Additional Information

State employment service offices can provide information about employment opportunities for customer service representatives.

Dental Assistants

(O*NET 31-9091.00)

Significant Points

- Job prospects should be excellent.

- Dentists are expected to hire more assistants to perform routine tasks so that they may devote their own time to more complex procedures.

- Many assistants learn their skills on the job, although an increasing number are trained in dental-assisting programs; most programs take 1 year or less to complete.

Nature of the Work

Dental assistants work closely with, and under the supervision of, dentists. Assistants perform a variety of patient care, office, and laboratory duties.

Dental assistants should not be confused with dental hygienists, who are licensed to perform different clinical tasks. (See the job profile of dental hygienists elsewhere in this book.)

Dental assistants sterilize and disinfect instruments and equipment, prepare and lay out the instruments and materials required to treat each patient, and obtain patients' dental records. Assistants make patients as comfortable as possible in the dental chair and prepare them for treatment. During dental procedures, assistants work alongside the dentist to provide assistance. They hand instruments and materials to dentists and keep patients' mouths dry and clear by using suction or other devices. They also instruct patients on postoperative and general oral health care.

Dental assistants may prepare materials for impressions and restorations, take dental x rays, and process x-ray film as directed by a dentist. They also may remove sutures, apply topical anesthetics to gums or cavity-preventive agents to teeth, remove excess cement used in the filling process, and place rubber dams on the teeth to isolate them for individual treatment. Some states are expanding dental assistants' duties to include tasks such as coronal polishing and restorative dentistry functions for those assistants that meet specific training and experience requirements.

Dental assistants with laboratory duties make casts of the teeth and mouth from impressions, clean and polish removable appliances, and make temporary crowns. Those with office duties schedule and confirm appointments, receive patients, keep treatment records, send bills, receive payments, and order dental supplies and materials.

Work environment. Dental assistants work in a well-lighted, clean environment. Their work area usually is near the dental chair so that they can arrange instruments, materials, and medication and hand them to the dentist when needed. Dental assistants must wear gloves, masks, eyewear, and protective clothing to protect themselves and their patients from infectious diseases. Assistants also follow safety procedures to minimize the risks associated with the use of x-ray machines.

About half of dental assistants have a 35- to 40-hour work week. Most of the rest work part-time or have variable schedules. Depending on the hours of the dental office where they work, assistants may have to work on Saturdays or evenings. Some dental assistants hold multiple jobs by working at dental offices that are open on different days or scheduling their work at a second office around the hours they work at their primary office.

Training, Other Qualifications, and Advancement

Many assistants learn their skills on the job, although an increasing number are trained in dental-assisting programs offered by community and junior colleges, trade schools, technical institutes, or the Armed Forces.

Education and training. High school students interested in a career as a dental assistant should take courses in biology, chemistry, health, and office practices. For those wishing to pursue further education, the Commission on Dental Accreditation within the American Dental Association (ADA) approved 269 dental-assisting training programs in 2006. Programs include classroom, laboratory, and preclinical instruction in dental-assisting skills and related theory. In addition, students gain practical experience in dental schools, clinics, or dental offices. Most programs take one year or less to complete and lead to a certificate or diploma. Two-year programs offered in community and junior colleges lead to an associate degree. All programs require a high school diploma or its equivalent, and some require science or computer-related courses for admission. A number of private vocational schools offer four- to six-month courses in dental assisting, but the Commission on Dental Accreditation does not accredit these programs.

A large number of dental assistants learn through on-the-job training. In these situations, the employing dentist or other dental assistants in the dental office teach the new assistant dental terminology, the names of the instruments, how to perform daily duties, how to interact with patients, and other things necessary to help keep the dental office running smoothly. While some things can be picked up easily, it may be a few months before new dental assistants are completely knowledgeable about their duties and comfortable doing all of their tasks without assistance.

A period of on-the-job training is often required even for those that have completed a dental-assisting program or have some previous experience. Different dentists may have their own styles of doing things that need to be learned before an assistant can be comfortable working with them. Office-specific information, such as where files are kept, will need to be learned at each new job. Also, as dental technology changes, dental assistants need to stay familiar with the tools and procedures that they will be using or helping dentists to use. On-the-job training is often sufficient to keep assistants up-to-date on these matters.

Licensure. Most states regulate the duties that dental assistants are allowed to perform. Some states require licensure or registration, which may include passing a written or practical examination. There are a variety of schools offering courses—approximately 10 to 12 months in length—that meet their state's requirements. Other states require dental assistants to complete state-approved education courses of four to 12 hours in length. Some states offer registration of other dental assisting credentials with little or no education required. Some states require continuing education to maintain

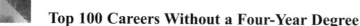
Projections data from the National Employment Matrix

Occupational Title	SOC Code	Employment, 2006	Projected employment, 2016	Change, 2006-16	
				Number	Percent
Dental assistants..	31-9091	280,000	362,000	82,000	29

NOTE: Data in this table are rounded.

licensure or registration. A few states allow dental assistants to perform any function delegated to them by the dentist.

Individual states have adopted different standards for dental assistants who perform certain advanced duties. In some states, for example, dental assistants who perform radiological procedures must complete additional training. Completion of the Radiation Health and Safety examination offered by Dental Assisting National Board (DANB) meets the standards in more than 30 states. Some states require completion of a state-approved course in radiology as well.

Certification and other qualifications. Certification is available through the Dental Assisting National Board (DANB) and is recognized or required in more than 30 states. Certification is an acknowledgment of an assistant's qualifications and professional competence and may be an asset when one is seeking employment. Candidates may qualify to take the DANB certification examination by graduating from an ADA-accredited dental assisting education program or by having two years of full-time, or four years of part-time, experience as a dental assistant. In addition, applicants must have current certification in cardiopulmonary resuscitation. For annual recertification, individuals must earn continuing education credits. Other organizations offer registration, most often at the state level.

Dental assistants must be a second pair of hands for a dentist; therefore, dentists look for people who are reliable, work well with others, and have good manual dexterity.

Advancement. Without further education, advancement opportunities are limited. Some dental assistants become office managers, dental-assisting instructors, dental product sales representatives, or insurance claims processors for dental insurance companies. Others go back to school to become dental hygienists. For many, this entry-level occupation provides basic training and experience and serves as a steppingstone to more highly skilled and higher paying jobs.

Employment

Dental assistants held about 280,000 jobs in 2006. Almost all jobs for dental assistants were in offices of dentists. A small number of jobs were in the federal, state, and local governments or in offices of physicians. About 35 percent of dental assistants worked part time, sometimes in more than one dental office.

Job Outlook

Employment is expected to increase much faster than average; job prospects are expected to be excellent.

Employment change. Employment is expected to grow 29 percent from 2006 to 2016, which is much faster than the average for all occupations. In fact, dental assistants are expected to be among the fastest growing occupations over the 2006–2016 projection period.

Population growth, greater retention of natural teeth by middle-aged and older people, and an increased focus on preventative dental care

for younger generations will fuel demand for dental services. Older dentists, who have been less likely to employ assistants or have employed fewer, are leaving the occupation and will be replaced by recent graduates, who are more likely to use one or more assistants. In addition, as dentists' workloads increase, they are expected to hire more assistants to perform routine tasks, so that they may devote their own time to more complex procedures.

Job prospects. Job prospects for dental assistants should be excellent. In addition to job openings due to employment growth, numerous job openings will arise out of the need to replace assistants who transfer to other occupations, retire, or leave for other reasons. Many opportunities for entry-level positions offer on-the-job training, but some dentists prefer to hire experienced assistants or those who have completed a dental-assisting program.

Earnings

Median hourly earnings of dental assistants were $14.53 in May 2006. The middle 50 percent earned between $11.94 and $17.44 an hour. The lowest 10 percent earned less than $9.87, and the highest 10 percent earned more than $20.69 an hour.

Benefits vary substantially by practice setting and may be contingent upon full-time employment. According to the American Dental Association, 87 percent of dentists offer reimbursement for continuing education courses taken by their assistants.

Related Occupations

Other workers supporting health practitioners include dental hygienists, medical assistants, surgical technologists, pharmacy aides, pharmacy technicians, occupational therapist assistants and aides, and physical therapist assistants and aides.

Sources of Additional Information

Information about career opportunities and accredited dental assistant programs is available from

▸ Commission on Dental Accreditation, American Dental Association, 211 East Chicago Ave., Suite 1814, Chicago, IL 60611. Internet: http://www.ada.org

For information on becoming a Certified Dental Assistant and a list of state boards of dentistry, contact

▸ Dental Assisting National Board, Inc., 676 North Saint Clair St., Suite 1880, Chicago, IL 60611. Internet: http://www.danb.org

For more information on a career as a dental assistant and general information about continuing education, contact

▸ American Dental Assistants Association, 35 East Wacker Dr., Suite 1730, Chicago, IL 60601. Internet: http://www.dentalassistant.org

For more information about continuing education courses, contact

▸ National Association of Dental Assistants, 900 South Washington St., Suite G-13, Falls Church, VA 22046.

Dental Hygienists

(O*NET 29-2021.00)

Significant Points

- A degree from an accredited dental hygiene school and a state license are required for this job.
- Dental hygienists rank among the fastest growing occupations.
- Job prospects are expected to remain excellent.
- More than half work part time, and flexible scheduling is a distinctive feature of this job.

Nature of the Work

Dental hygienists remove soft and hard deposits from teeth, teach patients how to practice good oral hygiene, and provide other preventive dental care. They examine patients' teeth and gums, recording the presence of diseases or abnormalities.

Dental hygienists use an assortment of different tools to complete their tasks. Hand and rotary instruments and ultrasonic devices are used to clean and polish teeth, including removing calculus, stains, and plaque. Hygienists use x-ray machines to take dental pictures, and sometimes develop the film. They may use models of teeth to explain oral hygiene, perform root planning as a periodontal therapy, or apply cavity-preventative agents such as fluorides and pit and fissure sealants. In some states, hygienists are allowed to administer anesthetics, while in others they administer local anesthetics using syringes. Some states also allow hygienists to place and carve filling materials, temporary fillings, and periodontal dressings; remove sutures; and smooth and polish metal restorations.

Dental hygienists also help patients develop and maintain good oral health. For example, they may explain the relationship between diet and oral health or inform patients how to select toothbrushes and show them how to brush and floss their teeth.

Hygienists sometimes make a diagnosis and other times may prepare clinical and laboratory diagnostic tests for the dentist to interpret. Hygienists sometimes work chair side with the dentist during treatment.

Work environment. Dental hygienists work in clean, well-lighted offices. Important health safeguards include strict adherence to proper radiological procedures and the use of appropriate protective devices when administering anesthetic gas. Dental hygienists also wear safety glasses, surgical masks, and gloves to protect themselves and patients from infectious diseases.

Flexible scheduling is a distinctive feature of this job. Full-time, part-time, evening, and weekend schedules are widely available. Dentists frequently hire hygienists to work only 2 or 3 days a week, so hygienists may hold jobs in more than one dental office. More than half of all dental hygienists worked part time—less than 35 hours a week.

Training, Other Qualifications, and Advancement

Prospective dental hygienists must become licensed in the state in which they wish to practice. A degree from an accredited dental hygiene school is usually required along with licensure examinations.

Education and training. A high school diploma and college entrance test scores are usually required for admission to a dental hygiene program. High school students interested in becoming a dental hygienist should take courses in biology, chemistry, and mathematics. Also, some dental hygiene programs require applicants to have completed at least one year of college. Specific entrance requirements vary from one school to another.

In 2006, there were 286 dental hygiene programs accredited by the Commission on Dental Accreditation. Most dental hygiene programs grant an associate degree, although some also offer a certificate, a bachelor's degree, or a master's degree. A minimum of an associate degree or certificate in dental hygiene is generally required for practice in a private dental office. A bachelor's or master's degree usually is required for research, teaching, or clinical practice in public or school health programs.

Schools offer laboratory, clinical, and classroom instruction in subjects such as anatomy, physiology, chemistry, microbiology, pharmacology, nutrition, radiography, histology (the study of tissue structure), periodontology (the study of gum diseases), pathology, dental materials, clinical dental hygiene, and social and behavioral sciences.

Licensure. Dental hygienists must be licensed by the state in which they practice. Nearly all states require candidates to graduate from an accredited dental hygiene school and pass both a written and clinical examination. The American Dental Association's Joint Commission on National Dental Examinations administers the written examination, which is accepted by all states and the District of Columbia. State or regional testing agencies administer the clinical examination. In addition, most states require an examination on the legal aspects of dental hygiene practice. Alabama is the only state that allows candidates to take its examinations if they have been trained through a state-regulated on-the-job program in a dentist's office.

Other qualifications. Dental hygienists should work well with others because they work closely with dentists and dental assistants as well as dealing directly with patients. Hygienists also need good manual dexterity, because they use dental instruments within a patient's mouth, with little room for error.

Employment

Dental hygienists held about 167,000 jobs in 2006. Because multiple job holding is common in this field, the number of jobs exceeds the number of hygienists. Almost all jobs for dental hygienists were in offices of dentists. A very small number worked for employment services, offices of physicians, or other industries.

Job Outlook

Dental hygienists rank among the fastest growing occupations, and job prospects are expected to remain excellent.

Employment change. Employment of dental hygienists is expected to grow 30 percent through 2016, much faster than the average for all occupations. This projected growth ranks dental hygienists among the fastest growing occupations, in response to increasing demand for dental care and the greater use of hygienists.

Projections data from the National Employment Matrix

Occupational Title	SOC Code	Employment, 2006	Projected employment, 2016	Change, 2006-2016	
				Number	Percent
Dental hygienists...	29-2021	167,000	217,000	50,000	30

NOTE: Data in this table are rounded.

The demand for dental services will grow because of population growth, older people increasingly retaining more teeth, and a growing focus on preventative dental care. To meet this demand, facilities that provide dental care, particularly dentists' offices, will increasingly employ dental hygienists, and more hygienists per office, to perform services that have been performed by dentists in the past.

Job prospects. Job prospects are expected to remain excellent. Older dentists, who have been less likely to employ dental hygienists, are leaving the occupation and will be replaced by recent graduates, who are more likely to employ one or more hygienists. In addition, as dentists' workloads increase, they are expected to hire more hygienists to perform preventive dental care, such as cleaning, so that they may devote their own time to more complex procedures.

Earnings

Median hourly earnings of dental hygienists were $30.19 in May 2006. The middle 50 percent earned between $24.63 and $35.67 an hour. The lowest 10 percent earned less than $19.45, and the highest 10 percent earned more than $41.60 an hour.

Earnings vary by geographic location, employment setting, and years of experience. Dental hygienists may be paid on an hourly, daily, salary, or commission basis.

Benefits vary substantially by practice setting and may be contingent upon full-time employment. According to the American Dental Association, 86 percent of hygienists receive hospital and medical benefits.

Related Occupations

Other workers supporting health practitioners in an office setting include dental assistants, medical assistants, occupational therapist assistants and aides, physical therapist assistants and aides, physician assistants, and registered nurses. Dental hygienists sometimes work with radiation technology, as do radiation therapists.

Sources of Additional Information

For information on a career in dental hygiene, including educational requirements, contact

▸ Division of Education, American Dental Hygienists Association, 444 N. Michigan Ave., Suite 3400, Chicago, IL 60611. Internet: http://www.adha.org

For information about accredited programs and educational requirements, contact

▸ Commission on Dental Accreditation, American Dental Association, 211 E. Chicago Ave., Suite 1814, Chicago, IL 60611. Internet: http://www.ada.org

The State Board of Dental Examiners in each state can supply information on licensing requirements.

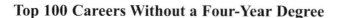

Diagnostic Medical Sonographers

(O*NET 29-2032.00)

Significant Points

■ Job opportunities should be favorable.

■ Employment growth is expected to be faster than average as sonography becomes an increasingly attractive alternative to radiologic procedures.

■ More than half of all sonographers were employed by hospitals, and most of the rest were employed by offices of physicians, medical and diagnostic laboratories, and mobile imaging services.

■ Sonographers may train in hospitals, vocational-technical institutions, colleges and universities, and the Armed Forces; employers prefer those who trained in accredited programs and who are registered.

Nature of the Work

Diagnostic imaging embraces several procedures that aid in diagnosing ailments. The most familiar procedures are the x ray and the magnetic resonance imaging; however, not all imaging technologies use ionizing radiation or radio waves. Sonography, or ultrasonography, is the use of sound waves to generate an image for the assessment and diagnosis of various medical conditions. Sonography commonly is associated with obstetrics and the use of ultrasound imaging during pregnancy, but this technology has many other applications in the diagnosis and treatment of medical conditions throughout the body.

Diagnostic medical sonographers use special equipment to direct nonionizing, high frequency sound waves into areas of the patient's body. Sonographers operate the equipment, which collects reflected echoes and forms an image that may be videotaped, transmitted, or photographed for interpretation and diagnosis by a physician.

Sonographers begin by explaining the procedure to the patient and recording any medical history that may be relevant to the condition being viewed. They then select appropriate equipment settings and direct the patient to move into positions that will provide the best view. To perform the exam, sonographers use a transducer, which transmits sound waves in a cone- or rectangle-shaped beam. Although techniques vary with the area being examined, sonographers usually spread a special gel on the skin to aid the transmission of sound waves.

Viewing the screen during the scan, sonographers look for subtle visual cues that contrast healthy areas with unhealthy ones. They decide whether the images are satisfactory for diagnostic purposes and select which ones to store and show to the physician.

Sonographers take measurements, calculate values, and analyze the results in preliminary findings for the physicians.

In addition to working directly with patients, diagnostic medical sonographers keep patient records and adjust and maintain equipment. They also may prepare work schedules, evaluate equipment purchases, or manage a sonography or diagnostic imaging department.

Diagnostic medical sonographers may specialize in obstetric and gynecologic sonography (the female reproductive system), abdominal sonography (the liver, kidneys, gallbladder, spleen, and pancreas), neurosonography (the brain), or breast sonography. In addition, sonographers may specialize in vascular sonography or cardiac sonography. (Vascular sonographers and cardiac sonographers are covered in this book's job profile of cardiovascular technologists and technicians.)

Obstetric and gynecologic sonographers specialize in the imaging of the female reproductive system. Included in the discipline is one of the more well-known uses of sonography: examining the fetus of a pregnant woman to track the baby's growth and health.

Abdominal sonographers inspect a patient's abdominal cavity to help diagnose and treat conditions primarily involving the gallbladder, bile ducts, kidneys, liver, pancreas, spleen, and male reproductive system. Abdominal sonographers also are able to scan parts of the chest, although studies of the heart using sonography usually are done by echocardiographers.

Neurosonographers focus on the nervous system, including the brain. In neonatal care, neurosonographers study and diagnose neurological and nervous system disorders in premature infants. They also may scan blood vessels to check for abnormalities indicating a stroke in infants diagnosed with sickle-cell anemia. Like other sonographers, neurosonographers operate transducers to perform the sonogram, but use frequencies and beam shapes different from those used by obstetric and abdominal sonographers.

Breast sonographers use sonography to study diseases of the breasts. Sonography aids mammography in the detection of breast cancer. Breast sonography can also track tumors, blood supply conditions, and assist in the accurate biopsy of breast tissue. Breast sonographers use high-frequency transducers, made exclusively to study breast tissue.

Work environment. Sonographers typically work in health care facilities that are clean. They usually work at diagnostic imaging machines in darkened rooms, but also may perform procedures at patients' bedsides. Sonographers may be on their feet for long periods of time and may have to lift or turn disabled patients. In addition, the nature of their work can put sonographers at an increased risk for musculoskeletal disorders such as carpel tunnel syndrome, neck and back strain, and eye strain: however, greater use of ergonomic equipment and an increasing awareness will continue to minimize such risks

Some sonographers work as contract employees and may travel to several health care facilities in an area. Similarly, some sonographers work with mobile imaging service providers and travel to patients and use mobile diagnostic imaging equipment to provide service in areas that otherwise do not have the access to such services.

Most full-time sonographers work about 40 hours a week. Hospital-based sonographers may have evening and weekend hours and times when they are on call and must be ready to report to work on short notice.

Training, Other Qualifications, and Advancement

Diagnostic medical sonography is an occupation where there is no preferred level of education and several avenues of education are widely accepted by employers. Although no level of education is preferred, employers do prefer sonographers who trained in accredited programs and who are registered.

Education and training. There are several avenues for entry into the field of diagnostic medical sonography. Sonographers may train in hospitals, vocational-technical institutions, colleges and universities, and the Armed Forces. Some training programs prefer applicants with a background in science or experience in other health care professions. Some also may consider high school graduates with courses in mathematics and science, as well as applicants with liberal arts backgrounds, but this practice is infrequent.

Colleges and universities offer formal training in both two- and four-year programs, culminating in an associate or a bachelor's degree. Two-year programs are most prevalent. Course work includes classes in anatomy, physiology, instrumentation, basic physics, patient care, and medical ethics.

A few one-year programs that may result in a certificate also are accepted as proper education by employers. These programs typically are satisfactory education for workers already in health care who seek to increase their marketability by training in sonography. These programs are not accredited.

The Commission on Accreditation for Allied Health Education Programs (CAAHEP) accredited 147 training programs in 2006. These programs typically are the formal training programs offered by colleges and universities. Some hospital programs are accredited as well.

Certification and other qualifications. Although no state requires licensure in diagnostic medical sonography, organizations such as the American Registry for Diagnostic Medical Sonography (ARDMS) certify the skills and knowledge of sonographers through credentialing, including registration. Because registration provides an independent, objective measure of an individual's professional standing, many employers prefer to hire registered sonographers. Sonographers registered by the ARDMS are Registered Diagnostic Medical Sonographers (RDMS). Registration with ARDMS requires passing a general physical principles and instrumentation examination, in addition to passing an exam in a specialty such as obstetric and gynecologic sonography, abdominal sonography, or neurosonography. Sonographers must complete a required number of continuing education hours to maintain registration with the ARDMS and to stay abreast of technological advancements related to the occupation.

Sonographers need good communication and interpersonal skills because they must be able to explain technical procedures and results to their patients, some of whom may be nervous about the exam or the problems it may reveal. Good hand-eye coordination is particularly important to obtaining quality images. It is also important that sonographers enjoy learning because continuing education is the key to sonographers staying abreast of the ever-changing field of diagnostic medicine. A background in mathematics and science is helpful for sonographers as well.

Advancement. Sonographers specializing in one particular discipline often seek competency in others. For example, obstetric sonographers

Projections data from the National Employment Matrix

Occupational Title	SOC Code	Employment, 2006	Projected employment, 2016	Change, 2006-2016	
				Number	Percent
Diagnostic medical sonographers	29-2032	46,000	54,000	8,700	19

NOTE: Data in this table are rounded.

might seek training in abdominal sonography to broaden their opportunities and increase their marketability.

Sonographers may also have advancement opportunities in education, administration, research, sales, or technical advising.

Employment

Diagnostic medical sonographers held about 46,000 jobs in 2006. More than half of all sonographer jobs were in public and private hospitals. The rest were typically in offices of physicians, medical and diagnostic laboratories, and mobile imaging services.

Job Outlook

Faster-than-average employment growth is expected. Job opportunities should be favorable.

Employment change. Employment of diagnostic medical sonographers is expected to increase by about 19 percent through 2016—faster than the average for all occupations—as the population ages, increasing the demand for diagnostic imaging and therapeutic technology.

Additional job growth is expected as sonography becomes an increasingly attractive alternative to radiologic procedures, as patients seek safer treatment methods. Unlike most diagnostic imaging methods, sonography does not involve radiation, so harmful side effects and complications from repeated use are less likely for both the patient and the sonographer. Sonographic technology is expected to evolve rapidly and to spawn many new sonography procedures, such as 3D- and 4D-sonography for use in obstetric and ophthalmologic diagnosis. However, high costs and approval by the federal government may limit the rate at which some promising new technologies are adopted.

Hospitals will remain the principal employer of diagnostic medical sonographers. However, employment is expected to grow more rapidly in offices of physicians and in medical and diagnostic laboratories, including diagnostic imaging centers. Healthcare facilities such as these are expected to grow very rapidly through 2016 because of the strong shift toward outpatient care, encouraged by third-party payers and made possible by technological advances that permit more procedures to be performed outside the hospital.

Job prospects. Job opportunities should be favorable. In addition to job openings from growth, some openings will arise from the need to replace sonographers who retire or leave the occupation permanently for some other reason. Pain caused by musculoskeletal disorders has made it difficult for sonographers to perform well. Some are forced to leave the occupation early because of this disorder.

Earnings

Median annual earnings of diagnostic medical sonographers were $57,160 in May 2006. The middle 50 percent earned between $48,890 and $67,670 a year. The lowest 10 percent earned less than $40,960, and the highest 10 percent earned more than $77,520.

Median annual earnings of diagnostic medical sonographers in May 2006 were $56,970 in offices of physicians and $56,850 in general medical and surgical hospitals.

Related Occupations

Diagnostic medical sonographers operate sophisticated equipment to help physicians and other health practitioners diagnose and treat patients. Workers in related occupations include cardiovascular technologists and technicians, clinical laboratory technologists and technicians, nuclear medicine technologists, radiologic technologists and technicians, and respiratory therapists.

Sources of Additional Information

For information on a career as a diagnostic medical sonographer, contact

▸ Society of Diagnostic Medical Sonography, 2745 Dallas Pkwy., Suite 350, Plano, TX 75093-8730. Internet: http://www.sdms.org

For information on becoming a registered diagnostic medical sonographer, contact

▸ American Registry for Diagnostic Medical Sonography, 51 Monroe St., Plaza East 1, Rockville, MD 20850-2400. Internet: http://www.ardms.org

For more information on ultrasound in medicine, contact

▸ American Institute of Ultrasound in Medicine, 14750 Sweitzer Lane, Suite 100, Laurel, MD 20707-5906. Internet: http://www.aium.org

For a current list of accredited education programs in diagnostic medical sonography, contact

▸ Joint Review Committee on Education in Diagnostic Medical Sonography, 2025 Woodlane Dr., St. Paul, MN 55125-2998. Internet: http://www.jrcdms.org

▸ Commission on Accreditation for Allied Health Education Programs, 35 East Wacker Dr., Suite 1970, Chicago, IL 60601. Internet: http://www.caahep.org

Diesel Service Technicians and Mechanics

(O*NET 49-3031.00)

Significant Points

■ A career in diesel engine repair can offer relatively high wages and the challenge of skilled repair work.

■ Opportunities are expected to be very good for people who complete formal training programs.

■ National certification is the recognized standard of achievement for diesel service technicians and mechanics.

Nature of the Work

Diesel-powered engines are more efficient and durable than their gasoline-burning counterparts. These powerful engines are standard in our nation's trucks, locomotives, and buses and are becoming more prevalent in light vehicles, including passenger vehicles, pickups, and other work trucks.

Diesel service technicians and mechanics, including *bus and truck mechanics and diesel engine specialists*, repair and maintain the diesel engines that power transportation equipment. Some diesel technicians and mechanics also work on other heavy vehicles and mobile equipment, including bulldozers, cranes, road graders, farm tractors, and combines. Other technicians repair diesel-powered passenger automobiles, light trucks, or boats. (For information on technicians and mechanics working primarily on gasoline-powered automobiles, see this book's sections on automotive service technicians.)

Increasingly, diesel technicians must be versatile to adapt to customers' needs and new technologies. It is common for technicians to handle all kinds of repairs, working on a vehicle's electrical system one day and doing major engine repairs the next. Diesel maintenance is becoming increasingly complex, as more electronic components are used to control the operation of an engine. For example, microprocessors now regulate and manage fuel timing, increasing the engine's efficiency. Also, new emissions standards require mechanics to retrofit engines with emissions control systems, such as emission filters and catalysts, to comply with pollution regulations. In modern shops, diesel service technicians use hand-held or laptop computers to diagnose problems and adjust engine functions.

Technicians who work for organizations that maintain their own vehicles spend most of their time doing preventive maintenance. During a routine maintenance check, technicians follow a checklist that includes inspecting brake systems, steering mechanisms, wheel bearings, and other important parts. Following inspection, technicians repair or adjust parts that do not work properly or remove and replace parts that cannot be fixed.

Diesel service technicians use a variety of tools in their work, including power tools, such as pneumatic wrenches that remove bolts quickly; machine tools, such as lathes and grinding machines to rebuild brakes; welding and flame-cutting equipment to remove and repair exhaust systems; and jacks and hoists to lift and move large parts. Common handtools—screwdrivers, pliers, and wrenches—are used to work on small parts and get at hard-to-reach places. Diesel service technicians and mechanics also use a variety of computerized testing equipment to pinpoint and analyze malfunctions in electrical systems and engines. Employers typically furnish expensive power tools, computerized engine analyzers, and other diagnostic equipment, but workers usually accumulate their own hand tools over time.

Work environment. Technicians normally work in well-lighted and ventilated areas. However, some shops are drafty and noisy. Many employers provide lockers and shower facilities. Diesel technicians usually work indoors, although they occasionally repair vehicles on the road. Diesel technicians may lift heavy parts and tools, handle greasy and dirty parts, and stand or lie in awkward positions while making repairs. Minor cuts, burns, and bruises are common, although serious accidents can usually be avoided when safety procedures are followed. Technicians may work as a team or be assisted by an apprentice or helper when doing heavy work, such as removing engines and transmissions.

Most service technicians work a standard 40-hour week, although some work longer hours, particularly if they are self-employed. A growing number of shops have expanded their hours to speed repairs and offer more convenience to customers. Technicians employed by truck and bus firms providing service around the clock may work evenings, nights, and weekends.

Training, Other Qualifications, and Advancement

Employers prefer to hire graduates of formal training programs because those workers are able to advance quickly to the journey level of diesel service. Other workers who learn diesel engine repair through on-the-job training need three to four years of experience before becoming journey-level technicians.

Education and training. High school courses in automotive repair, electronics, English, mathematics, and physics provide a strong educational background for a career as a diesel service technician or mechanic. Many mechanics also have additional training after high school.

A large number of community colleges and trade and vocational schools offer programs in diesel engine repair. These programs usually last from six months to two years and may lead to a certificate of completion or an associate degree. Some offer about 30 hours per week of hands-on training with equipment; others offer more lab or classroom instruction. Formal training provides a foundation in the latest diesel technology and instruction in the service and repair of the equipment that technicians will encounter on the job. Training programs also teach technicians to interpret technical manuals and to communicate well with coworkers and customers. Increasingly, employers work closely with representatives of educational programs, providing instructors with the latest equipment, techniques, and tools and offering jobs to graduates.

Although formal training programs lead to the best prospects, some technicians and mechanics learn through on-the-job training. Unskilled beginners generally are assigned tasks such as cleaning parts, fueling and lubricating vehicles, and driving vehicles into and out of the shop. Beginners are usually promoted to trainee positions as they gain experience and as vacancies become available.

After a few months' experience, most trainees can perform routine service tasks and make minor repairs. These workers advance to increasingly difficult jobs as they prove their ability and competence. After technicians master the repair and service of diesel engines, they learn to work on related components, such as brakes, transmissions, and electrical systems. Generally, technicians with at least three to four years of on-the-job experience will qualify as journey-level diesel technicians.

Employers often send experienced technicians and mechanics to special training classes conducted by manufacturers and vendors, in which workers learn about the latest technology and repair techniques.

Other qualifications. Employers usually look for applicants who have mechanical aptitude and strong problem-solving skills and who are at least 18 years old and in good physical condition. Technicians need a state commercial driver's license to test-drive trucks or buses on public roads. Many companies also require applicants to pass a drug test. Practical experience in automobile repair at an automotive service station, in the Armed Forces, or as a hobby is valuable as well.

Certification and advancement. Experienced diesel service technicians and mechanics with leadership ability may advance to shop supervisor or service manager, and some open their own repair shops. Technicians and mechanics with sales ability sometimes become sales representatives.

Although national certification is not required for employment, many diesel engine technicians and mechanics find that it increases their ability to advance. Certification by the National Institute for Automotive Service Excellence (ASE) is the recognized industry credential for diesel and other automotive service technicians and mechanics. Diesel service technicians may be certified as master medium/heavy truck technicians, master school bus technicians, or master truck equipment technicians. They may also be certified in specific areas of truck repair, such as drivetrains, brakes, suspension and steering, electrical and electronic systems, or preventive maintenance and inspection. For certification in each area, a technician must pass one or more of the ASE-administered exams and present proof of two years of relevant work experience. To remain certified, technicians must be retested every five years.

Employment

Diesel service technicians and mechanics held about 275,000 jobs in 2006. These workers were employed in almost every industry, particularly those that use trucks, buses, and equipment to haul, deliver, and transport materials, goods, and people. The largest employer, the truck transportation industry, employed 1 out of 6 diesel service technicians and mechanics. Less than 1 out of 10 were employed by local governments, mainly to repair school buses, waste removal trucks, and road equipment. A similar number were employed by automotive repair and maintenance facilities. The rest were employed throughout the economy, including construction, manufacturing, retail and wholesale trade, and automotive leasing. About 16,000, a relatively small number, were self-employed. Nearly every area of the country employs diesel service technicians and mechanics, although most work is found in towns and cities where trucking companies, bus lines, and other fleet owners have large operations.

Job Outlook

The number of jobs for diesel service technicians and mechanics is projected to grow about as fast as average. Opportunities should be very good for people who complete formal training in diesel mechanics.

Employment change. Employment of diesel service technicians and mechanics is expected to grow 11 percent from 2006 to 2016, about as fast as the average for all occupations. Additional trucks—and truck repairers—will be needed to keep pace with the increasing volume of freight shipped nationwide. Moreover, the greater durability and economy of the diesel engine relative to the gasoline engine is expected to increase the number of buses, trucks, and other vehicles powered by diesel engines.

And because diesel engines are now cleaner burning and more efficient—to comply with emissions and environmental standards—they are expected to be used in more passenger vehicles, which will create jobs for diesel service technicians and mechanics over the long run. In fact, auto industry executives are projecting more sales of diesel passenger vehicles as gasoline prices increase. In the short-run, many older diesel engines in trucks must be retrofitted to comply with the new emissions regulations, creating more jobs for diesel engine mechanics.

Job prospects. People who enter diesel engine repair will find favorable opportunities, especially as the need to replace workers who retire increases over the next decade. Opportunities should be very good for people who complete formal training in diesel mechanics at community colleges or vocational and technical schools. Applicants without formal training will face stiffer competition for jobs.

Most people entering this occupation can expect relatively steady work because changes in economic conditions have less of an effect on the diesel repair business than on other sectors of the economy. During a downturn in the economy, however, employers may be reluctant to hire new workers.

Earnings

Median hourly earnings of bus and truck mechanics and diesel engine specialists, including incentive pay, were $18.11 in May 2006, more than the $17.65 median hourly earnings for all installation, maintenance, and repair occupations. The middle 50 percent earned between $14.48 and $22.07 an hour. The lowest 10 percent earned less than $11.71, and the highest 10 percent earned more than $26.50 an hour. Median hourly earnings in the industries employing the largest numbers of bus and truck mechanics and diesel engine specialists in May 2006 were as follows:

Local government	$21.22
Motor vehicle and motor vehicle parts and supplies merchant wholesalers	18.27
Automotive repair and maintenance	17.53
General freight trucking	17.14
Specialized freight trucking	16.15

Because many experienced technicians employed by truck fleet dealers and independent repair shops receive a commission related to the labor cost charged to the customer, weekly earnings depend on the amount of work completed. Beginners usually earn from 50 to 75 percent of the rate of skilled workers and receive increases as they become more skilled.

About 23 percent of diesel service technicians and mechanics are members of labor unions, including the International Association of Machinists and Aerospace Workers; the Amalgamated Transit Union; the International Union, United Automobile, Aerospace and Agricultural Implement Workers of America; the Transport Workers Union of America; the Sheet Metal Workers' International Associa-

Projections data from the National Employment Matrix

Occupational Title	SOC Code	Employment, 2006	Projected employment, 2016	Change, 2006-16 Number	Percent
Bus and truck mechanics and diesel engine specialists	49-3031	275,000	306,000	32,000	11

NOTE: Data in this table are rounded.

tion; and the International Brotherhood of Teamsters. Labor unions may provide additional benefits for their members.

Related Occupations

Diesel service technicians and mechanics repair trucks, buses, and other diesel-powered equipment. Related technician and mechanic occupations include aircraft and avionics equipment mechanics and service technicians, automotive service technicians and mechanics, heavy vehicle and mobile equipment service technicians and mechanics, and small engine mechanics.

Sources of Additional Information

More details about work opportunities for diesel service technicians and mechanics may be obtained from local employers such as trucking companies, truck dealers, or buslines; locals of the unions previously mentioned; and local offices of your state employment service. Local state employment service offices also may have information about training programs. State boards of postsecondary career schools have information on licensed schools with training programs for diesel service technicians and mechanics.

For general information about a career as a diesel service technician or mechanic, write

▸ Association of Diesel Specialists, 10 Laboratory Dr., PO Box 13966, Research Triangle Park, NC 27709. Internet: http://www.diesel.org

Information on how to become a certified diesel technician of medium to heavy-duty vehicles or a certified bus technician is available from

▸ National Institute for Automotive Service Excellence (ASE), 101 Blue Seal Dr. SE, Suite 101, Leesburg, VA 20175. Internet: http://www.asecert.org

For a directory of accredited private trade and technical schools with training programs for diesel service technicians and mechanics, contact

▸ Accrediting Commission of Career Schools and Colleges of Technology, 2101 Wilson Blvd., Suite 302, Arlington, VA 22201. Internet: http://www.accsct.org

▸ National Automotive Technicians Education Foundation, 101 Blue Seal Dr. SE, Suite 101, Leesburg, VA 20175. Internet: http://www.natef.org

Drafters

(O*NET 17-3011.00, 17-3011.01, 17-3011.02, 17-3012.00, 17-3012.01, 17-3012.02, 17-3013.00, and 17-3019.99)

Significant Points

■ The type and quality of training programs vary considerably so prospective students should be careful in selecting a program.

■ Opportunities should be best for individuals with at least 2 years of postsecondary training in drafting and considerable skill and experience using computer-aided design and drafting systems.

■ Employment is projected to grow more slowly than average.

■ Demand for drafters varies by specialty and depends on the needs of local industry.

Nature of the Work

Drafters prepare technical drawings and plans, which are used to build everything from manufactured products such as toys, toasters, industrial machinery, and spacecraft to structures such as houses, office buildings, and oil and gas pipelines.

In the past, drafters sat at drawing boards and used pencils, pens, compasses, protractors, triangles, and other drafting devices to prepare a drawing by hand. Now, most drafters use Computer Aided Design and Drafting (CADD) systems to prepare drawings. Consequently, some drafters may be referred to as *CADD operators*.

With CADD systems, drafters can create and store drawings electronically so that they can be viewed, printed, or programmed directly into automated manufacturing systems. CADD systems also permit drafters to quickly prepare variations of a design. Although drafters use CADD extensively, it is only a tool. Drafters still need knowledge of traditional drafting techniques, in addition to CADD skills. Despite the nearly universal use of CADD systems, manual drafting and sketching are used in certain applications.

Drafters' drawings provide visual guidelines and show how to construct a product or structure. Drawings include technical details and specify dimensions, materials, and procedures. Drafters fill in technical details using drawings, rough sketches, specifications, and calculations made by engineers, surveyors, architects, or scientists. For example, drafters use their knowledge of standardized building techniques to draw in the details of a structure. Some use their understanding of engineering and manufacturing theory and standards to draw the parts of a machine; they determine design elements, such as the numbers and kinds of fasteners needed to assemble the machine. Drafters use technical handbooks, tables, calculators, and computers to complete their work.

Drafting work has many specialties:

Aeronautical drafters prepare engineering drawings detailing plans and specifications used in the manufacture of aircraft, missiles, and related parts.

Architectural drafters draw architectural and structural features of buildings and other structures. These workers may specialize in a type of structure, such as residential or commercial, or in a kind of material used, such as reinforced concrete, masonry, steel, or timber.

Civil drafters prepare drawings and topographical and relief maps used in major construction or civil engineering projects, such as highways, bridges, pipelines, flood control projects, and water and sewage systems.

Electrical drafters prepare wiring and layout diagrams used by workers who erect, install, and repair electrical equipment and wiring in communication centers, power plants, electrical distribution systems, and buildings.

Electronics drafters draw wiring diagrams, circuit board assembly diagrams, schematics, and layout drawings used in the manufacture, installation, and repair of electronic devices and components.

Mechanical drafters prepare drawings showing the detail and assembly of a wide variety of machinery and mechanical devices, indicating dimensions, fastening methods, and other requirements.

Process piping or pipeline drafters prepare drawings used in the layout, construction, and operation of oil and gas fields, refineries, chemical plants, and process piping systems.

Work environment. Drafters usually work in comfortable offices. They may sit at adjustable drawing boards or drafting tables when doing manual drawings, although most drafters work at computer terminals much of the time. Because they spend long periods in front of computers doing detailed work, drafters may be susceptible to eyestrain, back discomfort, and hand and wrist problems. Most drafters work a standard 40-hour week; only a small number work part time.

Training, Other Qualifications, and Advancement

Employers prefer applicants who have completed postsecondary school training in drafting, which is offered by technical institutes, community colleges, and some four-year colleges and universities. Employers are most interested in applicants with well-developed drafting and mechanical drawing skills; knowledge of drafting standards, mathematics, science, and engineering technology; and a solid background in CADD techniques.

Education and training. High school courses in mathematics, science, computer technology, design, computer graphics, and, where available, drafting are useful for people considering a drafting career. Employers prefer applicants who have also completed training after high school at a technical institute, community college, or four-year college or university.

The kind and quality of drafting training programs vary considerably so prospective students should be careful in selecting a program. They should contact prospective employers to ask which schools they prefer and contact schools to ask for information about the kinds of jobs their graduates have, the type and condition of instructional facilities and equipment, and teacher qualifications.

Technical institutes offer intensive technical training, but they provide a less general education than do community colleges. Either certificates or diplomas may be awarded. Many technical institutes offer two-year associate degree programs, which are similar to, or part of, the programs offered by community colleges or state university systems. Their programs vary considerably in length and in the type of courses offered. Some public vocational-technical schools serve local students and emphasize the type of training preferred by local employers. Most require a high school diploma or its equivalent for admission. Other technical institutes are run by private, often for-profit, organizations sometimes called proprietary schools.

Community colleges offer courses similar to those in technical institutes but include more classes in theory and liberal arts. Often, there is little or no difference between technical institute and community college programs. However, courses taken at community colleges are more likely to be accepted for credit at four-year colleges. After completing a two-year associate degree program, graduates may obtain jobs as drafters or continue their education in a related field at a four-year college. Most four-year colleges do not offer training in drafting, but they do offer classes in engineering, architecture, and mathematics that are useful for obtaining a job as a drafter.

Technical training obtained in the Armed Forces also can be applied in civilian drafting jobs. Some additional training may be necessary, depending on the technical area or military specialty.

Training differs somewhat within the drafting specialties, although the basics, such as mathematics, are similar. In an electronics drafting program, for example, students learn how to depict electronic components and circuits in drawings. In architectural drafting, they learn the technical specifications of buildings.

Certification and other qualifications. Mechanical ability and visual aptitude are important for drafters. Prospective drafters should be able to draw well and perform detailed work accurately and neatly. Artistic ability is helpful in some specialized fields, as is knowledge of manufacturing and construction methods. In addition, prospective drafters should have good interpersonal skills because they work closely with engineers, surveyors, architects, and other professionals and, sometimes, with customers.

The American Design Drafting Association (ADDA) has established a certification program for drafters. Although employers usually do not require drafters to be certified, certification demonstrates knowledge and an understanding of nationally recognized practices. Individuals who wish to become certified must pass the Drafter Certification Test, administered periodically at ADDA-authorized sites. Applicants are tested on basic drafting concepts, such as geometric construction, working drawings, and architectural terms and standards.

Advancement. Entry-level or junior drafters usually do routine work under close supervision. After gaining experience, they may become intermediate drafters and progress to more difficult work with less supervision. At the intermediate level, they may need to exercise more judgment and perform calculations when preparing and modifying drawings. Drafters may eventually advance to senior drafter, designer, or supervisor. Many employers pay for continuing education, and, with appropriate college degrees, drafters may go on to become engineering technicians, engineers, or architects.

Employment

Drafters held about 253,000 jobs in 2006. Architectural and civil drafters held 46 percent of all jobs for drafters, mechanical drafters held about 31 percent, and electrical and electronics drafters held about 14 percent.

About 49 percent of all jobs for drafters were in architectural, engineering, and related services firms that design construction projects or do other engineering work on a contract basis for other industries. Another 25 percent of jobs were in manufacturing industries such as machinery manufacturing, including metalworking and other general machinery; fabricated metal products manufacturing, including architectural and structural metals; computer and electronic products manufacturing, including navigational, measuring, electromedical, and control instruments; and transportation equipment manufacturing, including aerospace products and parts manufacturing, as well as ship and boat building. Most of the rest were employed in construction, government, wholesale trade, utilities, and employment services. Approximately 5 percent were self-employed in 2006.

Job Outlook

Drafters can expect slower than average employment growth through 2016, with the best opportunities expected for those with 2 years of professional training.

Employment change. Employment of drafters is expected to grow by 6 percent between 2006 and 2016, which is slower than the average for all occupations. Industrial growth and increasingly complex design problems associated with new products and manufacturing processes will increase the demand for drafting services. Further-

Projections data from the National Employment Matrix

Occupational Title	SOC Code	Employment, 2006	Projected employment, 2016	Change, 2006-2016	
				Number	Percent
Drafters	17-3010	253,000	268,000	15,000	6
Architectural and civil drafters	17-3011	116,000	123,000	7,000	6
Electrical and electronics drafters	17-3012	35,000	36,000	1,400	4
Mechanical drafters	17-3013	78,000	82,000	4,100	5
Drafters, all other	17-3019	25,000	27,000	2,700	11

NOTE: Data in this table are rounded.

more, drafters are beginning to break out of the traditional drafting role and do work traditionally performed by engineers and architects, also increasing demand. However, drafters tend to be concentrated in slow-growing or declining manufacturing industries. In addition, CADD systems that are more powerful and easier to use are also expected to limit demand for lesser skilled drafters because simple tasks will be made easier or able to be done by other technical professionals. Employment growth also should be slowed by the offshore outsourcing to other countries of some drafting work because some drafting can be done by sending CADD files over the Internet.

Although growth is expected to be greatest for mechanical, architectural, and civil drafters, demand for particular drafting specialties varies throughout the country because employment usually is contingent on the needs of local industry.

Job prospects. Most job openings are expected to arise from the need to replace drafters who transfer to other occupations, leave the labor force, or retire.

Opportunities should be best for individuals with at least 2 years of postsecondary training in a drafting program that provides strong technical skills and considerable experience with CADD systems. CADD has increased the complexity of drafting applications while enhancing the productivity of drafters. It also has enhanced the nature of drafting by creating more possibilities for design and drafting. As technology continues to advance, employers will look for drafters with a strong background in fundamental drafting principles, a high level of technical sophistication, and the ability to apply their knowledge to a broader range of responsibilities.

Employment of drafters remains highly concentrated in industries that are sensitive to cyclical changes in the economy, primarily manufacturing industries. During recessions, drafters may be laid off. However, a growing number of drafters should continue to find employment on a temporary or contract basis as more companies turn to the employment services industry to meet their changing needs.

Earnings

Drafters' earnings vary by specialty, location, and level of responsibility. Median annual earnings of architectural and civil drafters were $41,960 in May 2006. The middle 50 percent earned between $33,550 and $52,220. The lowest 10 percent earned less than $27,010, and the highest 10 percent earned more than $63,310.

Median annual earnings of mechanical drafters were $43,700 in May 2006. The middle 50 percent earned between $34,680 and $55,130. The lowest 10 percent earned less than $28,230, and the highest 10 percent earned more than $67,860. Median annual earnings for mechanical drafters in architectural, engineering, and related services were $44,120.

Median annual earnings of electrical and electronics drafters were $46,830 in May 2006. The middle 50 percent earned between $36,660 and $60,160. The lowest 10 percent earned less than $29,290, and the highest 10 percent earned more than $74,490. In architectural, engineering, and related services, median annual earnings for electrical and electronics drafters were $44,140.

Related Occupations

Other workers who prepare or analyze detailed drawings and make precise calculations and measurements include architects, except landscape and naval; landscape architects; commercial and industrial designers; engineers; engineering technicians; science technicians; and surveyors, cartographers, photogrammetrists, and surveying technicians.

Sources of Additional Information

Information on schools offering programs in drafting and related fields is available from

▸ Accrediting Commission of Career Schools and Colleges of Technology, 2101 Wilson Blvd., Suite 302, Arlington, VA 22201. Internet: http://www.accsct.org

Information about certification is available from

▸ American Design Drafting Association, 105 E. Main St., Newbern, TN 38059. Internet: http://www.adda.org

Drywall Installers, Ceiling Tile Installers, and Tapers

(O*NET 47-2081.00 and 47-2082.00)

Significant Points

■ Most workers learn this trade on the job by starting as helpers to more experienced workers; additional classroom instruction may also be needed.

■ Job prospects are expected to be good.

■ Inclement weather seldom interrupts work, but workers may be idled when downturns in the economy slow construction activity.

Nature of the Work

Drywall consists of a thin layer of gypsum between two layers of heavy paper. It is used to make walls and ceilings in most buildings today because it is faster and cheaper to install than plaster.

There are two kinds of drywall workers—installers and tapers—although many workers do both types of work. Installers, also called *framers* or *hangers*, fasten drywall panels to the inside framework of houses and other buildings. *Tapers* or *finishers*, prepare these panels for painting by taping and finishing joints and imperfections. In addition to drywall workers, ceiling tile installers and lathers also help to build walls and ceilings.

Because drywall panels are manufactured in standard sizes—usually 4 feet by 8 or 12 feet—drywall installers must measure, cut, fit, and fasten them to the inside framework of buildings. Workers cut smaller pieces to go around doors and windows. Installers saw, drill, or cut holes in panels for electrical outlets, air-conditioning units, and plumbing. After making these alterations, installers may glue, nail, or screw the wallboard panels to the wood or metal framework, called studs. Because drywall is heavy and cumbersome, another worker usually helps the installer to position and secure the panel. Installers often use a lift when placing ceiling panels.

After the drywall is installed, tapers fill joints between panels with a joint compound, also called spackle or "mud." Using the wide, flat tip of a special trowel, they spread the compound into and along each side of the joint with brush-like strokes. They immediately use the trowel to press a paper tape—used to reinforce the drywall and to hide imperfections—into the wet compound and to smooth away excess material. Nail and screw depressions also are covered with this compound, as are imperfections caused by the installation of air-conditioning vents and other fixtures. On large projects, finishers may use automatic taping tools that apply the joint compound and tape in one step. Using increasingly wider trowels, tapers apply second and third coats of the compound, sanding the treated areas after each coat to make them as smooth as the rest of the wall surface. This results in a seamless and almost perfect surface. For hard to reach heights and ceilings, sanding poles are commonly used. Some tapers apply textured surfaces to walls and ceilings with trowels, brushes, or spray guns.

Ceiling tile installers, or *acoustical carpenters,* apply or mount acoustical tiles or blocks, strips, or sheets of shock-absorbing materials to ceilings and walls of buildings to reduce reflection of sound or to decorate rooms. First, they measure and mark the surface according to blueprints and drawings. Then, they nail or screw moldings to the wall to support and seal the joint between the ceiling tile and the wall. Finally, they mount the tile, either by applying a cement adhesive to the back of the tile and then pressing the tile into place, or by nailing, screwing, stapling, or wire-tying the lath directly to the structural framework.

Making walls out of plaster requires the work of lathers. Lathers apply the support base for plaster coatings, fireproofing, or acoustical materials. This support base, called lath, is put on walls, ceilings, ornamental frameworks, and partitions of buildings before plaster and other coatings are added. Lathers use handtools and portable power tools, to nail, screw, staple, or wire-tie the lath directly to the structural framework of a building. At one time, lath was made of wooden strips, but now, it is usually made of wire, metal mesh, or gypsum, also known as rockboard. Metal lath is used when the plaster on top of it will be exposed to weather or water or when a surface is curved or irregular and not suitable for drywall.

Work environment. As in many other construction trades, this work is sometimes physically strenuous. Drywall installers, ceiling tile installers, lathers, and tapers spend most of the day on their feet, either standing, bending, stretching, or kneeling. Some tapers use stilts to tape and finish ceiling and angle joints. Installers have to lift and maneuver heavy, cumbersome drywall panels. Hazards include falls from ladders and scaffolds and injuries from power tools and from working with sharp tools, such as utility knives. Because sanding a joint compound to a smooth finish creates a great deal of dust, most finishers wear masks and goggles for protection.

A 40-hour week is standard, but the work weeks often fluctuate depending on the workload. Workers who are paid hourly rates receive premium pay for overtime.

Training, Other Qualifications, and Advancement

Drywall installers, ceiling tile installers, and tapers learn their trade through formal and informal training programs. It can take three to four years of both classroom and paid on-the-job training to become a fully skilled worker, but many skills can be learned within the first year. In general, the more formal the training process, the more skilled the individual becomes, and the more in demand by employers.

Education and training. Training for this profession can begin in a high school, where classes in English, math, mechanical drawing, blueprint reading, and general shop are recommended. The most common way to get a first job is to find an employer who will provide on-the-job training. Entry-level workers generally start as helpers, assisting more experienced workers. Employers may also send new employees to a trade or vocational school or community college to receive classroom training.

Some employers, particularly large nonresidential construction contractors with union membership, offer employees formal apprenticeships. These programs combine on-the-job training with related classroom instruction—at least 144 hours of instruction each year. The length of the apprenticeship program, usually three to four years, varies with the apprentice's skill. Because the number of apprenticeship programs is limited, however, only a small proportion of drywall installers, ceiling tile installers, and tapers learn their trade this way.

Helpers and apprentices start by carrying materials, lifting and holding panels, and cleaning up debris. They also learn to use the tools, machines, equipment, and materials of the trade. Within a few weeks, they learn to measure, cut, and install materials. Eventually, they become fully experienced workers. Tapers learn their job by taping joints and touching up nail holes, scrapes, and other imperfections. They soon learn to install corner guards and to conceal openings around pipes. At the end of their training, drywall installers, ceiling tile installers, and tapers learn to estimate the cost of installing and finishing drywall.

Other jobseekers may choose to obtain their classroom training before seeking a job. There are a number of vocational-technical schools and training academies affiliated with the unions and contractors that offer training in these occupations. Employers often look favorably upon graduates of these training programs and usually start them at a higher level than those without the training.

Other qualifications. Some skills needed to become a drywall installer, ceiling tile installer, and taper include manual dexterity, eye-hand coordination, good physical fitness, and a good sense of balance. The ability to solve basic arithmetic problems quickly and accurately also is required. In addition, a good work history or military service is viewed favorably by contractors.

Projections data from the National Employment Matrix

Occupational Title	SOC Code	Employment, 2006	Projected employment, 2016	Change, 2006-16	
				Number	Percent
Drywall installers, ceiling tile installers, and tapers	47-2080	240,000	258,000	17,000	7
Drywall and ceiling tile installers	47-2081	186,000	199,000	14,000	7
Tapers	47-2082	54,000	58,000	3,900	7

NOTE: Data in this table are rounded.

Supervisors and contractors need good English skills in order to deal with clients and subcontractors. They also should be able to identify and estimate the quantity of materials needed to complete a job, and accurately estimate how long a job will take to complete and at what cost.

Apprentices usually must be at least 18 years old and have a high school diploma or GED. Those who complete apprenticeships registered with the federal or state government receive a journey worker certificate, recognized nationwide.

Advancement. Drywall installers, ceiling tile installers, and tapers may advance to carpentry supervisor or general construction supervisor positions. Others may become independent contractors. For those who would like to advance, it is increasingly important to be able to communicate in both English and Spanish in order to relay instructions and safety precautions to workers with limited understanding of English because Spanish-speaking workers make up a large part of the construction workforce in many areas. Knowing English well also makes it easier to advance.

Employment

Drywall installers, ceiling tile installers, and tapers held about 240,000 jobs in 2006. Most worked for contractors specializing in drywall and ceiling tile installation; others worked for contractors doing many kinds of construction. About 56,000 were self-employed independent contractors.

Most installers and tapers are employed in populous areas. In other areas, where there may not be enough work to keep a drywall or ceiling tile installer employed full time, carpenters and painters usually do the work.

Job Outlook

Employment is expected to increase about as fast as the average for all occupations, largely reflecting overall growth of the construction industry. Good job prospects are expected overall.

Employment change. Employment is expected to grow by 7 percent between 2006 and 2016, about as fast as the average for all occupations. Growth reflects the number of new construction and remodeling projects. New residential construction projects are expected to provide the majority of new jobs during the projection decade, but home improvement and renovation projects are also expected to create jobs because existing residential and nonresidential buildings are getting old and need repair.

Job prospects. Job opportunities for drywall installers, ceiling tile installers, and tapers are expected to be good. Many potential workers are not attracted to this occupation because they prefer work that is less strenuous and has more comfortable working conditions. Experienced workers will have especially favorable opportunities.

Besides those resulting from job growth, many jobs will open up each year because of the need to replace workers who transfer to other occupations or leave the labor force.

Despite the growing use of exterior panels, most drywall installation and finishing is done indoors. Therefore, drywall workers lose less work time because of inclement weather than do some other construction workers. Nevertheless, like many other construction workers, employment is sensitive to the fluctuations of the economy. Workers in these trades may experience periods of unemployment when the overall level of construction falls. On the other hand, shortages of these workers may occur in some areas during peak periods of building activity.

Earnings

In May 2006, the median hourly earnings of wage and salary drywall and ceiling tile installers were $17.38. The middle 50 percent earned between $13.60 and $22.58. The lowest 10 percent earned less than $10.90, and the highest 10 percent earned more than $28.85. The median hourly earnings in the industries employing the largest numbers of drywall and ceiling tile installers were as follows:

Foundation, structure, and building exterior contractors $18.10	
Drywall and insulation contractors 17.42	
Nonresidential building construction 17.26	
Residential building construction.............................17.26	

In May 2006, the median hourly earnings of wage and salary tapers were $19.85. The middle 50 percent earned between $14.65 and $25.70. The lowest 10 percent earned less than $11.59, and the highest 10 percent earned more than $31.23.

Some contractors pay these workers according to the number of panels they install or finish per day; others pay an hourly rate.

Trainees usually start at about half the rate paid to experienced workers and receive wage increases as they became more skilled.

Related Occupations

Drywall installers, ceiling tile installers, and tapers combine strength and dexterity with precision and accuracy to make materials fit according to a plan. Other occupations that require similar abilities include carpenters; carpet, floor, and tile installers and finishers; insulation workers; and plasterers and stucco masons.

Sources of Additional Information

For information about work opportunities in drywall application and finishing and ceiling tile installation, contact local drywall installation and ceiling tile installation contractors, a local joint union-management apprenticeship committee, a state or local chapter of the

Associated Builders and Contractors, or the nearest office of the state employment service or apprenticeship agency. You can also find information on the registered apprenticeship system with links to state apprenticeship programs on the U.S. Department of Labor's Web site: http://www.doleta.gov/atels_bat. Apprenticeship information is also available from the U.S. Department of Labor's toll free helpline: (877) 282-5627.

For details about job qualifications and training programs in drywall application and finishing and ceiling tile installation, contact

▸ Associated Builders and Contractors, 4250 North Fairfax Dr., 9th Floor, Arlington, VA 22203. Internet: http://www.trytools.org

▸ Finishing Trades Institute, International Union of Painters and Allied Trades, 1750 New York Ave. NW, Washington, DC 20006. Internet: http://www.finishingtradesinstitute.org

▸ National Association of Home Builders, Home Builders Institute, 1201 15th St. NW, Washington, DC 20005. Internet: http://www.hbi.org

▸ National Center for Construction Education and Research, P.O. Box 141104, Gainesville, FL 32614-1104. Internet: http://www.nccer.org

▸ United Brotherhood of Carpenters and Joiners of America, Carpenters Training Fund, 6801 Placid St., Las Vegas, NV 89119. Internet: http://www.carpenters.org

For general information on apprenticeships and how to get them, see the *Occupational Outlook Quarterly* article "Apprenticeships: Career training, credentials—and a paycheck in your pocket," online at http://www.bls.gov/opub/ooq/2002/summer/art01.pdf and in print at many libraries and career centers.

Electricians

(O*NET 47-2111.00)

Significant Points

■ Job opportunities should be very good, especially for those with the broadest range of skills.

■ Most electricians acquire their skills by completing an apprenticeship program lasting 4 to 5 years.

■ About 4 out of 5 electricians work in the construction industry or are self employed, but there also will be opportunities for electricians in other industries.

Nature of the Work

Electricians bring electricity into homes, businesses, and factories. They install and maintain the wiring, fuses, and other components through which electricity flows. Many electricians also install and maintain electrical machines in factories.

Electricians usually start their work by reading blueprints. Blueprints are technical diagrams that show the locations of circuits, outlets, load centers, panel boards, and other equipment. To ensure public safety, electricians follow the National Electrical Code, and state and local building codes.

Electricians connect all types of wires to circuit breakers, transformers, outlets, or other components. They join the wires in boxes with various specially designed connectors. When installing wiring, electricians use hand tools such as conduit benders, screwdrivers, pliers, knives, hacksaws, and wire strippers, as well as power tools such as drills and saws. Later, they use ammeters, ohmmeters, voltmeters, oscilloscopes, and other equipment to test connections and ensure the compatibility and safety of components.

Electricians generally focus on either construction or maintenance, although many do both. Electricians specializing in construction primarily install wiring systems into factories, businesses, and new homes. Electricians specializing in maintenance work fix and upgrade existing electrical systems and repair electrical equipment.

When electricians install wiring systems in factories and commercial settings, they first place conduit (pipe or tubing) inside partitions, walls, or other concealed areas as designated by the blueprints. They also fasten small metal or plastic boxes to the walls that will house electrical switches and outlets. They pull insulated wires or cables through the conduit to complete circuits between these boxes. The diameter and number of wires installed depends on how much power will need to run through it. The greater the diameter of the wire, the more electricity it can handle. In residential construction, electricians usually install insulated wire encased in plastic, which does not need to run through conduit.

Some electricians also install low-voltage wiring systems in addition to electrical systems, although line installers and repairers specialize in this work. Low-voltage wiring accommodates voice, data, and video equipment, such as telephones, computers, intercoms, and fire alarm and security systems. Electricians also may install coaxial or fiber optic cable for telecommunications equipment and electronic controls for industrial uses.

Maintenance electricians repair or replace electric and electronic equipment when it breaks. They make needed repairs as quickly as possible in order to minimize inconvenience. They may replace items such as circuit breakers, fuses, switches, electrical and electronic components, or wire. Electricians also periodically inspect all equipment to ensure it is operating properly and to correct problems before breakdowns occur.

Maintenance work varies greatly, depending on where an electrician works. Electricians who focus on residential work perform a wide variety of electrical work for homeowners. They may rewire a home and replace an old fuse box with a new circuit breaker box to accommodate additional appliances, or they may install new lighting and other electric household items, such as ceiling fans. These electricians might also do some construction and installation work.

Electricians in large factories usually do maintenance work that is more complex. They may repair motors, transformers, generators, and electronic controllers on machine tools and industrial robots. Electricians also advise management whether continued operation of equipment could be hazardous. When working with complex electronic devices, they may consult with engineers, engineering technicians, line installers and repairers, or industrial machinery mechanics and maintenance workers. (Profiles of some of these occupations appear elsewhere in this book.)

Work environment. Electricians work indoors and out, at construction sites, in homes, and in businesses or factories. Work may be strenuous at times and may include bending conduit, lifting heavy objects, and standing, stooping, and kneeling for long periods. Electricians risk injury from electrical shock, falls, and cuts. They must follow strict safety procedures to avoid injuries. When working outdoors, they may be subject to inclement weather conditions. Some electricians may have to travel long distances to jobsites.

Most electricians work a standard 40-hour week, although overtime may be required. Those who do maintenance work may work nights or weekends and be on call to go to the worksite when needed. Electricians in industrial settings may have periodic extended overtime during scheduled maintenance or retooling periods. Companies that operate 24 hours a day may employ three shifts of electricians.

Training, Other Qualifications, and Advancement

Most electricians learn their trade through apprenticeship programs. These programs combine on-the-job training with related classroom instruction.

Education and training. Most electricians learn their trade through apprenticeship programs. These programs combine paid on-the-job training with related classroom instruction. Joint training committees made up of local unions of the International Brotherhood of Electrical Workers and local chapters of the National Electrical Contractors Association; individual electrical contracting companies; or local chapters of the Associated Builders and Contractors and the Independent Electrical Contractors Association usually sponsor apprenticeship programs.

Because of the comprehensive training received, those who complete apprenticeship programs qualify to do both maintenance and construction work. Apprenticeship programs usually last four years. Each year includes at least 144 hours of classroom instruction and 2,000 hours of on-the-job training. In the classroom, apprentices learn electrical theory, blueprint reading, mathematics, electrical code requirements, and safety and first aid practices. They also may receive specialized training in soldering, communications, fire alarm systems, and cranes and elevators.

On the job, apprentices work under the supervision of experienced electricians. At first, they drill holes, set anchors, and attach conduit. Later, they measure, fabricate, and install conduit and install, connect, and test wiring, outlets, and switches. They also learn to set up and draw diagrams for entire electrical systems. Eventually, they practice and master all of an electrician's main tasks.

Some people start their classroom training before seeking an apprenticeship. A number of public and private vocational-technical schools and training academies offer training to become an electrician. Employers often hire students who complete these programs and usually start them at a more advanced level than those without this training. A few people become electricians by first working as helpers—assisting electricians by setting up job sites, gathering materials, and doing other nonelectrical work—before entering an apprenticeship program. All apprentices need a high school diploma or a General Equivalency Diploma (G.E.D.). Electricians may also need classes in mathematics because they solve mathematical problems on the job.

Education can continue throughout an electrician's career. Electricians often complete regular safety programs, manufacturer-specific training, and management training courses. Classes on installing low-voltage voice, data, and video systems have recently become common as these systems become more prevalent. Other courses teach electricians how to become contractors.

Licensure. Most states and localities require electricians to be licensed. Although licensing requirements vary from state to state, electricians usually must pass an examination that tests their knowledge of electrical theory, the National Electrical Code, and local electric and building codes. Experienced electricians periodically take courses offered by their employer or union to learn about changes in the National Electrical Code.

Electrical contractors who do electrical work for the public, as opposed to electricians who work for electrical contractors, often need a special license. In some states, electrical contractors need certification as master electricians. Most states require master electricians to have at least seven years of experience as an electrician. Some states require a bachelor's degree in electrical engineering or a related field.

Other qualifications. Applicants for apprenticeships usually must be at least 18 years old and have a high school diploma or a G.E.D. They also may have to pass a test and meet other requirements.

Other skills needed to become an electrician include manual dexterity, eye-hand coordination, physical fitness, and a good sense of balance. They also need good color vision because workers frequently must identify electrical wires by color. In addition, apprenticeship committees and employers view a good work history or military service favorably.

Advancement. Experienced electricians can advance to jobs as supervisors. In construction, they also may become project managers or construction superintendents. Those with sufficient capital and management skills can start their own contracting business, although this often requires a special electrical contractor's license. Supervisors and contractors should be able to identify and estimate costs and prices and the time and materials needed to complete a job. Many electricians also become electrical inspectors.

For those who seek to advance, it is increasingly important to be able to communicate in both English and Spanish in order to relay instructions and safety precautions to workers with limited understanding of English; Spanish-speaking workers make up a large part of the construction workforce in many areas. Spanish-speaking workers who want to advance in this occupation need very good English skills to understand electrician classes and installation instructions, which are usually written in English. and are highly technical.

Employment

Electricians held about 705,000 jobs in 2006. About 68 percent of wage-and-salary workers were employed in the construction industry and the remainder worked as maintenance electricians in other industries. In addition, about 11 percent of electricians were self-employed.

Job Outlook

Average employment growth is expected. Job prospects should be very good, particularly for workers with the widest range of skills, including voice, data, and video wiring.

Employment change. Employment of electricians should increase 7 percent between 2006 and 2016, about as fast as the average for all occupations. As the population and economy grow, more electricians will be needed to install and maintain electrical devices and wiring in homes, factories, offices, and other structures. An increase in power plant construction over the next ten years will require many additional electricians. New technologies also are expected to continue to spur demand for these workers. For example, buildings increasingly need wiring to accommodate computers and telecommunications equipment. Robots and other automated manufacturing

Projections data from the National Employment Matrix

Occupational Title	SOC Code	Employment, 2006	Projected employment, 2016	Change, 2006-16	
				Number	Percent
Electricians...	47-2111	705,000	757,000	52,000	7

NOTE: Data in this table are rounded.

systems in factories also will require the installation and maintenance of more complex wiring systems. As the economy rehabilitates and retrofits older structures, which usually require electrical improvements to meet modern codes, it will create additional jobs.

Job prospects. In addition to jobs created by the increased demand for electrical work, many openings are expected over the next decade as a large number of electricians retire. This will create very good job opportunities, especially for those with the widest range of skills, including voice, data, and video wiring. Job openings for electricians will vary by location and specialty, however, and will be best in the fastest growing regions of the country, especially those areas where power plants are being constructed.

Employment of electricians, like that of many other construction workers, is sensitive to the fluctuations of the economy. Workers in these trades may experience periods of unemployment when the overall level of construction falls. On the other hand, shortages of these workers may occur in some areas during peak periods of building activity.

Although employment of maintenance electricians is steadier than that of construction electricians, those working in the automotive and other manufacturing industries that are sensitive to cyclical swings in the economy may experience lay offs during recessions. In addition, opportunities for maintenance electricians may be limited in many industries by the increased contracting out for electrical services in an effort to reduce operating costs. However, increased job opportunities for electricians in electrical contracting firms should partially offset job losses in other industries.

Earnings

In May 2006, median hourly earnings of wage and salary electricians were $20.97. The middle 50 percent earned between $16.07 and $27.71. The lowest 10 percent earned less than $12.76, and the highest 10 percent earned more than $34.95. Median hourly earnings in the industries employing the largest numbers of electricians were

Motor vehicle parts manufacturing	$31.90
Electric power generation, transmission, and distribution	26.32
Local government	23.80
Nonresidential building construction	20.58
Electrical contractors	20.47
Plumbing, heating, and air-conditioning contractors	19.56
Employment services	17.15

Apprentices usually start at between 40 and 50 percent of the rate paid to fully trained electricians, depending on experience. As apprentices become more skilled, they receive periodic pay increases throughout their training.

Some electricians are members of the International Brotherhood of Electrical Workers. Among unions representing maintenance electricians are the International Brotherhood of Electrical Workers; the International Union of Electronic, Electrical, Salaried, Machine, and Furniture Workers; the International Association of Machinists and Aerospace Workers; the International Union, United Automobile, Aircraft and Agricultural Implement Workers of America; and the United Steelworkers of America.

Related Occupations

To install and maintain electrical systems, electricians combine manual skill and knowledge of electrical materials and concepts. Workers in other occupations involving similar skills include heating, air-conditioning, and refrigeration mechanics and installers; line installers and repairers; electrical and electronics installers and repairers; electronic home entertainment equipment installers and repairers; and elevator installers and repairers.

Sources of Additional Information

For details about apprenticeships or other work opportunities in this trade, contact the offices of the state employment service, the state apprenticeship agency, local electrical contractors or firms that employ maintenance electricians, or local union-management electrician apprenticeship committees. Apprenticeship information is also available from the U.S. Department of Labor's toll free helpline:1 (877) 872-5627.

Information also may be available from local chapters of the Independent Electrical Contractors, Inc.; the National Electrical Contractors Association; the Home Builders Institute; the Associated Builders and Contractors; and the International Brotherhood of Electrical Workers.

For information about union apprenticeship and training programs, contact

▸ National Joint Apprenticeship Training Committee, 301 Prince George's Blvd., Upper Marlboro, MD 20774. Internet: http://www.njatc.org

▸ National Electrical Contractors Association, 3 Metro Center, Suite 1100, Bethesda, MD 20814. Internet: http://www.necanet.org

▸ International Brotherhood of Electrical Workers, 1125 15th St. NW, Washington, DC 20005.

For information about independent apprenticeship programs, contact

▸ Associated Builders and Contractors, Workforce Development Department, 4250 North Fairfax Dr., 9th Floor, Arlington, VA 22203. Internet: http://www.trytools.org

▸ Independent Electrical Contractors, Inc., 4401 Ford Ave., Suite 1100, Alexandria, VA 22302. Internet: http://www.ieci.org

▸ National Association of Home Builders, Home Builders Institute, 1201 15th St. NW, Washington, DC 20005. Internet: http://www.hbi.org

▸ National Center for Construction Education and Research, 3600 NW 43rd St., Bldg. G, Gainesville, FL 32606. Internet: http://www.nccer.org

For general information on apprenticeships and how to get them, see the *Occupational Outlook Quarterly* article "Apprenticeships: Career training, credentials—and a paycheck in your pocket," online at http://www.bls.gov/opub/ooq/2002/summer/art01.pdf and in print at many libraries and career centers.

Emergency Medical Technicians and Paramedics

(O*NET 29-2041.00)

Significant Points

■ Employment is projected to grow faster than the average as paid positions replace unpaid volunteers.

■ Emergency medical technicians and paramedics need formal training and certification, but requirements vary by state.

■ Emergency services function 24 hours a day so emergency medical technicians and paramedics have irregular working hours.

■ Opportunities will be best for those who have earned advanced certifications.

Nature of the Work

People's lives often depend on the quick reaction and competent care of emergency medical technicians (EMTs) and paramedics. Incidents as varied as automobile accidents, heart attacks, slips and falls, childbirth, and gunshot wounds all require immediate medical attention. EMTs and paramedics provide this vital service as they care for and transport the sick or injured to a medical facility.

In an emergency, EMTs and paramedics are typically dispatched by a 911 operator to the scene, where they often work with police and fire fighters. (Police and detectives and fire fighting occupations are discussed elsewhere in this book.) Once they arrive, EMTs and paramedics assess the nature of the patient's condition while trying to determine whether the patient has any pre-existing medical conditions. Following medical protocols and guidelines, they provide appropriate emergency care and, when necessary, transport the patient. Some paramedics are trained to treat patients with minor injuries on the scene of an accident or they may treat them at their home without transporting them to a medical facility. Emergency treatment is carried out under the medical direction of physicians.

EMTs and paramedics may use special equipment, such as back-boards, to immobilize patients before placing them on stretchers and securing them in the ambulance for transport to a medical facility. These workers generally work in teams. During the transport of a patient, one EMT or paramedic drives while the other monitors the patient's vital signs and gives additional care as needed. Some paramedics work as part of a helicopter's flight crew to transport critically ill or injured patients to hospital trauma centers.

At the medical facility, EMTs and paramedics help transfer patients to the emergency department, report their observations and actions to emergency department staff, and may provide additional emergency treatment. After each run, EMTs and paramedics replace used supplies and check equipment. If a transported patient had a contagious disease, EMTs and paramedics decontaminate the interior of the ambulance and report cases to the proper authorities.

EMTs and paramedics also provide transportation for patients from one medical facility to another, particularly if they work for private ambulance services. Patients often need to be transferred to a hospital that specializes in their injury or illness or to a nursing home.

Beyond these general duties, the specific responsibilities of EMTs and paramedics depend on their level of qualification and training. The National Registry of Emergency Medical Technicians (NREMT) certifies emergency medical service providers at five levels: First Responder; EMT-Basic; EMT-Intermediate, which has two levels called 1985 and 1999; and Paramedic. Some states, however, have their own certification programs and use distinct names and titles.

The EMT-Basic represents the first component of the emergency medical technician system. An EMT trained at this level is prepared to care for patients at the scene of an accident and while transporting patients by ambulance to the hospital under medical direction. The EMT-Basic has the emergency skills to assess a patient's condition and manage respiratory, cardiac, and trauma emergencies.

The EMT-Intermediate has more advanced training. However, the specific tasks that those certified at this level are allowed to perform varies greatly from state to state.

EMT-Paramedics provide the most extensive pre-hospital care. In addition to carrying out the procedures of the other levels, paramedics may administer drugs orally and intravenously, interpret electrocardiograms (EKGs), perform endotracheal intubations, and use monitors and other complex equipment. However, like EMT-Intermediate, what paramedics are permitted to do varies by state.

Work environment. EMTs and paramedics work both indoors and out, in all types of weather. They are required to do considerable kneeling, bending, and heavy lifting. These workers risk noise-induced hearing loss from sirens and back injuries from lifting patients. In addition, EMTs and paramedics may be exposed to diseases such as hepatitis-B and AIDS, as well as violence from mentally unstable patients. The work is not only physically strenuous but can be stressful, sometimes involving life-or-death situations and suffering patients. Nonetheless, many people find the work exciting and challenging and enjoy the opportunity to help others.

EMTs and paramedics employed by fire departments work about 50 hours a week. Those employed by hospitals frequently work between 45 and 60 hours a week, and those in private ambulance services, between 45 and 50 hours. Some of these workers, especially those in police and fire departments, are on call for extended periods. Because emergency services function 24 hours a day, EMTs and paramedics have irregular working hours.

Training, Other Qualifications, and Advancement

Generally, a high school diploma is required to enter a training program to become an EMT or paramedic. Workers must complete a formal training and certification process.

Education and training. A high school diploma is usually required to enter a formal emergency medical technician training program. Training is offered at progressive levels: EMT-Basic, EMT-Intermediate, and EMT-Paramedic.

At the EMT-Basic level, coursework emphasizes emergency skills, such as managing respiratory, trauma, and cardiac emergencies, and patient assessment. Formal courses are often combined with time in

Projections data from the National Employment Matrix

Occupational Title	SOC Code	Employment, 2006	Projected employment, 2016	Change, 2006-2016	
				Number	Percent
Emergency medical technicians and paramedics.............................	29-2041	201,000	240,000	39,000	19

NOTE: Data in this table are rounded.

an emergency room or ambulance. The program provides instruction and practice in dealing with bleeding, fractures, airway obstruction, cardiac arrest, and emergency childbirth. Students learn how to use and maintain common emergency equipment, such as backboards, suction devices, splints, oxygen delivery systems, and stretchers. Graduates of approved EMT-Basic training programs must pass a written and practical examination administered by the state certifying agency or the NREMT.

At the EMT-Intermediate level, training requirements vary by state. The nationally defined levels (EMT-Intermediate 1985 and EMT-Intermediate 1999) typically require 30 to 350 hours of training based on scope of practice. Students learn advanced skills such the use of advanced airway devices, intravenous fluids, and some medications.

The most advanced level of training for this occupation is EMT-Paramedic. At this level, the caregiver receives training in anatomy and physiology as well as advanced medical skills. Most commonly, the training is conducted in community colleges and technical schools over one to two years and may result in an associate's degree. Such education prepares the graduate to take the NREMT examination and become certified as a Paramedic. Extensive related coursework and clinical and field experience is required. Refresher courses and continuing education are available for EMTs and paramedics at all levels.

Licensure. All 50 states require certification for each of the EMT levels. In most states and the District of Columbia registration with the NREMT is required at some or all levels of certification. Other states administer their own certification examination or provide the option of taking either the NREMT or state examination. To maintain certification, EMTs and paramedics must recertify, usually every two years. Generally, they must be working as an EMT or paramedic and meet a continuing education requirement.

Other qualifications. EMTs and paramedics should be emotionally stable, have good dexterity, agility, and physical coordination, and be able to lift and carry heavy loads. They also need good eyesight (corrective lenses may be used) with accurate color vision.

Advancement. Paramedics can become supervisors, operations managers, administrative directors, or executive directors of emergency services. Some EMTs and paramedics become instructors, dispatchers, or physician assistants; others move into sales or marketing of emergency medical equipment. A number of people become EMTs and paramedics to test their interest in health care before training as registered nurses, physicians, or other health workers.

Employment

EMTs and paramedics held about 201,000 jobs in 2006. Most career EMTs and paramedics work in metropolitan areas. Volunteer EMTs and paramedics are more common in small cities, towns, and rural areas. These individuals volunteer for fire departments, emergency medical services, or hospitals and may respond to only a few calls

per month. About 30 percent of EMTs or paramedics belong to a union.

Paid EMTs and paramedics were employed in a number of industries. About 4 out of 10 worked as employees of private ambulance services. About 3 out of 10 worked in local government for fire departments, public ambulance services, and emergency medical services. Another 2 out of 10 worked full time in hospitals within the medical facility or responded to calls in ambulances or helicopters to transport critically ill or injured patients. The remainder worked in various industries providing emergency services.

Job Outlook

Employment for EMTs and paramedics is expected to grow faster than the average for all occupations through 2016. Job prospects should be good, particularly in cities and private ambulance services.

Employment change. Employment of emergency medical technicians and paramedics is expected to grow by 19 percent between 2006 and 2016, which is faster than the average for all occupations. Full-time paid EMTs and paramedics will be needed to replace unpaid volunteers. It is becoming increasing difficult for emergency medical services to recruit and retain unpaid volunteers because of the amount of training and the large time commitment these positions require. As a result, more paid EMTs and paramedics are needed. Furthermore, as a large segment of the population—aging members of the baby boom generation—becomes more likely to have medical emergencies, demand will increase for EMTs and paramedics. There also will still be demand for part-time, volunteer EMTs and paramedics in rural areas and smaller metropolitan areas.

Job prospects. Job prospects should be favorable. Many job openings will arise from growth and from the need to replace workers who leave the occupation because of the limited potential for advancement, as well as the modest pay and benefits in private-sector jobs.

Job opportunities should be best in private ambulance services. Competition will be greater for jobs in local government, including fire, police, and independent third-service rescue squad departments which tend to have better salaries and benefits. EMTs and paramedics who have advanced education and certifications, such as Paramedic level certification, should enjoy the most favorable job prospects as clients and patients demand higher levels of care before arriving at the hospital.

Earnings

Earnings of EMTs and paramedics depend on the employment setting and geographic location of their jobs, as well as their training and experience. Median annual earnings of EMTs and paramedics were $27,070 in May 2006. The middle 50 percent earned between $21,290 and $35,210. The lowest 10 percent earned less than $17,300, and the highest 10 percent earned more than $45,280. Median annual earnings in the industries employing the largest

© JIST Works

numbers of EMTs and paramedics in May 2006 were $23,250 in general medical and surgical hospitals and $20,350 in ambulance services.

Those in emergency medical services who are part of fire or police departments typically receive the same benefits as firefighters or police officers. For example, many are covered by pension plans that provide retirement at half pay after 20 or 25 years of service or if the worker is disabled in the line of duty.

Related Occupations

Other workers in occupations that require quick and level-headed reactions to life-or-death situations are air traffic controllers, fire-fighting occupations, physician assistants, police and detectives, and registered nurses.

Sources of Additional Information

General information about emergency medical technicians and paramedics is available from

- National Association of Emergency Medical Technicians, P.O. Box 1400, Clinton, MS 39060-1400. Internet: http://www.naemt.org
- National Highway Traffic Safety Administration, EMS Division, 400 7th St. SW, NTS-14, Washington, DC 20590. Internet: http://www.nhtsa.dot.gov/portal/site/nhtsa/menuitem.2a0771e91315babbbf30811060008a0c/
- National Registry of Emergency Medical Technicians, Rocco V. Morando Bldg., 6610 Busch Blvd., P.O. Box 29233, Columbus, OH 43229. Internet: http://www.nremt.org

Engineering Technicians

(O*NET 17-3021.00, 17-3022.00, 17-3023.00, 17-3023.01, 17-3023.02, 17-3023.03, 17-3024.00, 17-3025.00, 17-3026.00, 17-3027.00, and 17-3029.99)

Significant Points

- Because the type and quality of training programs vary considerably, prospective students should carefully investigate training programs before enrolling.

- Electrical and electronic engineering technicians make up 33 percent of all engineering technicians.

- Employment of engineering technicians often is influenced by the same economic conditions that affect engineers; as a result, job outlook varies by specialty.

- Opportunities will be best for individuals with an associate degree or extensive job training in engineering technology.

Nature of the Work

Engineering technicians use the principles and theories of science, engineering, and mathematics to solve technical problems in research and development, manufacturing, sales, construction, inspection, and maintenance. Their work is more narrowly focused and application-oriented than that of scientists and engineers. Many engineering technicians assist engineers and scientists, especially in research and development. Others work in quality control, inspecting products and processes, conducting tests, or collecting data. In manufacturing, they may assist in product design, development, or production.

Engineering technicians who work in research and development build or set up equipment; prepare and conduct experiments; collect data; calculate or record results; and help engineers or scientists in other ways, such as making prototype versions of newly designed equipment. They also assist in design work, often using computer-aided design and drafting (CADD) equipment.

Most engineering technicians specialize, learning skills and working in the same disciplines as engineers. Occupational titles, therefore, tend to reflect this similarity. This book does not cover in detail some branches of engineering technology, such as chemical engineering technology (the development of new chemical products and processes) and bioengineering technology (the development and implementation of biomedical equipment), for which there are accredited programs of study.

Aerospace engineering and operations technicians construct, test, and maintain aircraft and space vehicles. They may calibrate test equipment and determine causes of equipment malfunctions. Using computer and communications systems, aerospace engineering and operations technicians often record and interpret test data.

Civil engineering technicians help civil engineers plan and oversee the building of highways, buildings, bridges, dams, wastewater treatment systems, and other structures and do related research. Some estimate construction costs and specify materials to be used, and some may even prepare drawings or perform land-surveying duties. Others may set up and monitor instruments used to study traffic conditions. (Construction and building inspectors; drafters; and surveyors, cartographers, photogrammetrists, and surveying technicians are covered elsewhere in this book.)

Electrical and electronics engineering technicians help design, develop, test, and manufacture electrical and electronic equipment such as communication equipment; radar, industrial, and medical monitoring or control devices; navigational equipment; and computers. They may work in product evaluation and testing, using measuring and diagnostic devices to adjust, test, and repair equipment.

Electromechanical engineering technicians combine knowledge of mechanical engineering technology with knowledge of electrical and electronic circuits to design, develop, test, and manufacture electronic and computer-controlled mechanical systems. Their work often overlaps that of both electrical and electronics engineering technicians and mechanical engineering technicians.

Environmental engineering technicians work closely with environmental engineers and scientists in developing methods and devices used in the prevention, control, or correction of environmental hazards. They inspect and maintain equipment related to air pollution and recycling. Some inspect water and wastewater treatment systems to ensure that pollution control requirements are met.

Industrial engineering technicians study the efficient use of personnel, materials, and machines in factories, stores, repair shops, and offices. They prepare layouts of machinery and equipment, plan the flow of work, conduct statistical studies of production time or quality, and analyze production costs.

Mechanical engineering technicians help engineers design, develop, test, and manufacture industrial machinery, consumer products, and other equipment. They may assist in product tests by, for example, setting up instrumentation for auto crash tests. They may make sketches and rough layouts, record and analyze data, make calculations and estimates, and report on their findings. When planning production, mechanical engineering technicians prepare layouts and drawings of the assembly process and of parts to be manufactured. They estimate labor costs, equipment life, and plant space. Some test and inspect machines and equipment or work with engineers to eliminate production problems.

Work environment. Most engineering technicians work 40 hours a week in laboratories, offices, manufacturing or industrial plants, or on construction sites. Some may be exposed to hazards from equipment, chemicals, or toxic materials.

Training, Other Qualifications, and Advancement

Most engineering technicians enter the occupation with an associate degree in engineering technology. Training is available at technical institutes, community colleges, extension divisions of colleges and universities, public and private vocational-technical schools, and in the Armed Forces. Because the type and quality of training programs vary considerably, prospective students should carefully investigate training programs before enrolling.

Education and training. Although it may be possible to qualify for certain engineering technician jobs without formal training, most employers prefer to hire someone with at least a two-year associate degree in engineering technology. People with college courses in science, engineering, and mathematics may qualify for some positions but may need additional specialized training and experience. Prospective engineering technicians should take as many high school science and math courses as possible to prepare for programs in engineering technology after high school.

Most two-year associate degree programs accredited by the Technology Accreditation Commission of the Accreditation Board for Engineering and Technology (ABET) include at least college algebra and trigonometry and one or two basic science courses. Depending on the specialty, more math or science may be required. About 710 ABET-accredited programs are offered in engineering technology specialties.

The type of technical courses required depends on the specialty. For example, prospective mechanical engineering technicians may take courses in fluid mechanics, thermodynamics, and mechanical design; electrical engineering technicians may need classes in electrical circuits, microprocessors, and digital electronics; and those preparing to work in environmental engineering technology need courses in environmental regulations and safe handling of hazardous materials.

Many publicly and privately operated schools provide technical training, but the type and quality of training vary considerably. Therefore, prospective students should carefully select a program in line with their goals. They should ascertain prospective employers' preferences and ask schools to provide information about the kinds of jobs obtained by program graduates, about instructional facilities and equipment, and about faculty qualifications. Graduates of ABET-accredited programs usually are recognized as having achieved an acceptable level of competence in the mathematics, science, and technical courses required for this occupation.

Technical institutes offer intensive technical training through application and practice, but they provide less theory and general educa-

tion than do community colleges. Many technical institutes offer two-year associate degree programs and are similar to or part of a community college or state university system. Other technical institutes are run by private organizations, with programs that vary considerably in length and types of courses offered.

Community colleges offer curriculums that are similar to those in technical institutes but include more theory and liberal arts. There may be little or no difference between programs at technical institutes and community colleges, as both offer associate degrees. After completing the two-year program, some graduates get jobs as engineering technicians, whereas others continue their education at four-year colleges. However, an associate degree in pre-engineering is different from one in engineering technology. Students who enroll in a two-year pre-engineering program may find it very difficult to find work as an engineering technician if they decide not to enter a four-year engineering program because pre-engineering programs usually focus less on hands-on applications and more on academic preparatory work. Conversely, graduates of two-year engineering technology programs may not receive credit for some of the courses they have taken if they choose to transfer to a four-year engineering program. Colleges having four-year programs usually do not offer engineering technician training, but college courses in science, engineering, and mathematics are useful for obtaining a job as an engineering technician. Many four-year colleges offer bachelor's degrees in engineering technology, but graduates of these programs often are hired to work as technologists or applied engineers, not technicians.

Area vocational-technical schools, another source of technical training, include postsecondary public institutions that serve local students and emphasize training needed by local employers. Most require a high school diploma or its equivalent for admission.

Other training in technical areas may be obtained in the Armed Forces. Many military technical training programs are highly regarded by employers. However, skills acquired in military programs are often narrowly focused and may be of limited applicability in civilian industry, which often requires broader training. Therefore, some additional training may be needed, depending on the acquired skills and the kind of job.

Other qualifications. Because many engineering technicians assist in design work, creativity is desirable. Good communication skills and the ability to work well with others also are important as engineering technicians are typically part of a team of engineers and other technicians.

Certification and advancement. Although employers usually do not require engineering technicians to be certified, such certification may provide jobseekers a competitive advantage. The National Institute for Certification in Engineering Technologies has established voluntary certification programs for several engineering technology specialties. Certification is available at various levels, each level combining a written examination in a specialty with a certain amount of job-related experience, a supervisory evaluation, and a recommendation.

Engineering technicians usually begin by performing routine duties under the close supervision of an experienced technician, technologist, engineer, or scientist. As they gain experience, they are given more difficult assignments with only general supervision. Some engineering technicians eventually become supervisors.

Employment

Engineering technicians held 511,000 jobs in 2006. Approximately 33 percent were electrical and electronics engineering technicians, as indicated by the following tabulation.

Electrical and electronic engineering technicians	170,000
Civil engineering technicians	91,000
Industrial engineering technicians	75,000
Mechanical engineering technicians	48,000
Environmental engineering technicians	21,000
Electro-mechanical technicians	16,000
Aerospace engineering and operations technicians	8,500
Engineering technicians, except drafters, all other	82,000

About 35 percent of all engineering technicians worked in manufacturing, mainly in the computer and electronic equipment, transportation equipment, and machinery manufacturing industries. Another 25 percent worked in professional, scientific, and technical service industries, mostly in engineering or business services companies that do engineering work on contract for government, manufacturing firms, or other organizations.

In 2006, the federal government employed 37,000 engineering technicians. State governments employed 29,000, and local governments employed 25,000.

Job Outlook

Overall employment of engineering technicians is expected to grow about as fast as the average for all occupations, but projected growth and job prospects vary by specialty. Opportunities will be best for individuals with an associate degree or extensive job training in engineering technology.

Employment change. Overall employment of engineering technicians is expected to grow 7 percent between 2006 and 2016, about as fast as the average for all occupations. Competitive pressures will force companies to improve and update manufacturing facilities and product designs, resulting in more jobs for engineering technicians.

Growth of engineering technician employment in some design functions may be dampened by increasing globalization of the development process. To reduce costs and speed project completion, some companies may relocate part of their development operations to facilities overseas, impacting both engineers and engineering technicians—particularly in electronics and computer-related specialties. However, much of the work of engineering technicians requires on-site presence, so demand for engineering technicians within the U.S. should continue to grow—particularly in the environmental, civil, and industrial specialties.

Because engineering technicians work closely with engineers, employment of engineering technicians is often influenced by the same local and national economic conditions that affect engineers. As a result, the employment outlook varies with industry and specialization.

Aerospace engineering and operations technicians are expected to have 10 percent employment growth between 2006 and 2016, about as fast as the average for all occupations. Increases in the number

and scope of military aerospace projects likely will generate new jobs. New technologies to be used on commercial aircraft produced during the next decade should also spur demand for these workers.

Civil engineering technicians are expected to have 10 percent employment growth between 2006 and 2016, about as fast as the average for all occupations. Spurred by population growth and the related need to improve the nation's infrastructure, more civil engineering technicians will be needed to expand transportation, water supply, and pollution control systems, as well as large buildings and building complexes. They also will be needed to repair or replace existing roads, bridges, and other public structures.

Electrical and electronic engineering technicians are expected to have 4 percent employment growth between 2006 and 2016, more slowly than the average for all occupations. Although rising demand for electronic goods—including communications equipment, defense-related equipment, medical electronics, and consumer products—should continue to drive demand, foreign competition in design and manufacturing will limit employment growth.

Electro-mechanical technicians are expected to have 3 percent employment growth between 2006 and 2016, more slowly than the average for all occupations. As with the closely-related electrical and electronic engineering technicians and mechanical engineering technicians, job growth should be driven by increasing demand for electro-mechanical products such as unmanned aircraft and robotic equipment. However, growth will be tempered by advances in productivity and strong foreign competition.

Environmental engineering technicians are expected to have 25 percent employment growth between 2006 and 2016, much faster than the average for all occupations. More environmental engineering technicians will be needed to comply with environmental regulations and to develop methods of cleaning up existing hazards. A shift in emphasis toward preventing problems rather than controlling those that already exist, as well as increasing public health concerns resulting from population growth, also will spur demand.

Industrial engineering technicians are expected to have 10 percent employment growth between 2006 and 2016, about as fast as the average for all occupations. As firms continue to seek new means of reducing costs and increasing productivity, demand for industrial engineering technicians to analyze and improve production processes should increase. This should lead to some job growth even in manufacturing industries with slowly growing or declining employment.

Mechanical engineering technicians are expected to have 6 percent employment growth between 2006 and 2016, more slowly than the average for all occupations. As mechanical products and components become increasingly complex, demand for improvements in these products should drive employment growth of mechanical engineering technicians. However, growth is expected to be limited by foreign competition in both design services and manufacturing.

Job prospects. Job prospects will vary by specialty and location, depending on the health and composition of local industry. In general, opportunities will be best for individuals with an associate degree or extensive job training in engineering technology. As technology becomes more sophisticated, employers will continue to look for technicians who are skilled in new technology and require little additional training. An increase in the number of jobs related to public health and safety should create job opportunities for engineering technicians with the appropriate training and certification. In addition to openings from job growth, many job openings will

Projections data from the National Employment Matrix

Occupational Title	SOC Code	Employment, 2006	Projected employment, 2016	Change, 2006-2016	
				Number	Percent
Engineering technicians, except drafters	17-3020	511,000	545,000	34,000	7
Aerospace engineering and operations technicians	17-3021	8,500	9,400	900	10
Civil engineering technicians...	17-3022	91,000	100,000	9,200	10
Electrical and electronic engineering technicians........................	17-3023	170,000	177,000	6,100	4
Electro-mechanical technicians	17-3024	16,000	16,000	400	3
Environmental engineering technicians	17-3025	21,000	26,000	5,200	25
Industrial engineering technicians	17-3026	75,000	82,000	7,500	10
Mechanical engineering technicians..	17-3027	48,000	51,000	3,100	6
Engineering technicians, except drafters, all other	17-3029	82,000	83,000	1,600	2

NOTE: Data in this table are rounded.

stem from the need to replace technicians who retire or leave the labor force.

Earnings

Median annual earnings in May 2006 of engineering technicians by specialty are shown in the following tabulation.

Aerospace engineering and operations
technicians...$53,300

Electrical and electronic engineering
technicians 50,660

Industrial engineering technicians 46,810

Mechanical engineering technicians 45,850

Electro-mechanical technicians 44,720

Civil engineering technicians...............................40,560

Environmental engineering technicians 40,560

Median annual earnings of wage-and-salary electrical and electronics engineering technicians were $50,660 in May 2006. The middle 50 percent earned between $39,270 and $60,470. The lowest 10 percent earned less than $30,120, and the highest 10 percent earned more than $73,200. Median annual earnings in the industries employing the largest numbers of electrical and electronics engineering technicians are:

Wired telecommunications carriers $54,780

Engineering services 48,330

Semiconductor and other electronic component
manufacturing 45,720

Navigational, measuring, electromedical, and
control instruments manufacturing.....................45,140

Employment services 38,910

Median annual earnings of wage-and-salary civil engineering technicians were $40,560 in May 2006. The middle 50 percent earned between $31,310 and $51,230. The lowest 10 percent earned less than $25,250, and the highest 10 percent earned more than $62,920. Median annual earnings in the industries employing the largest numbers of civil engineering technicians are:

Local government $45,800

Architectural services.......................................42,310

Engineering services 41,180

State government 35,870

Testing laboratories 31,800

In May 2006, the median annual salary for aerospace engineering and operations technicians in the aerospace products and parts manufacturing industry was $52,060, and the median annual salary for environmental engineering technicians in the architectural, engineering, and related services industry was $38,060. The median annual salary for industrial engineering technicians in the aerospace product and parts manufacturing industry was $57,330. In the architectural, engineering, and related services industry, the median annual salary for mechanical engineering technicians was $43,920. Electro-mechanical technicians earned a median salary of $41,550 in the navigational, measuring, electromedical, and control instruments manufacturing industry.

Related Occupations

Engineering technicians apply scientific and engineering skills usually gained in postsecondary programs below the bachelor's degree level. Similar occupations include science technicians; drafters; surveyors, cartographers, photogrammetrists, and surveying technicians; and broadcast and sound engineering technicians and radio operators.

Sources of Additional Information

For information about careers in engineering technology, contact

▸ JETS (Junior Engineering Technical Society) Guidance, 1420 King St., Suite 405, Alexandria, VA 22314. Internet: http://www.jets.org

Information on engineering technology programs accredited by the Accreditation Board for Engineering and Technology is available from

▸ ABET, Inc., 111 Market Place, Suite 1050, Baltimore, MD 21202. Internet: http://www.abet.org

Information on certification, as well as job and career information, is available from

▸ National Institute for Certification in Engineering Technologies, 1420 King St., Alexandria, VA 22314. Internet: http://www.nicet.org

© JIST Works

Farmers, Ranchers, and Agricultural Managers

(O*NET 11-9011.00, 11-9011.01, 11-9011.02, 11-9011.03, and 11-9012.00)

Significant Points

■ Modern farming requires knowledge of new developments in agriculture, as well as work experience often gained through growing up on a farm or through postsecondary education.

■ Overall employment is projected to decline because of increasing productivity and consolidation of farms.

■ Horticulture and organic farming will provide better employment opportunities.

■ Small-scale farming is a major growth area and offers the best opportunity for entering the occupation.

Nature of the Work

American farmers, ranchers, and agricultural managers direct the activities of one of the world's largest and most productive agricultural sectors. They produce enough food and fiber to meet the needs of the United States and for export. *Farmers and ranchers* own and operate mainly family-owned farms. They also may lease land from a landowner and operate it as a working farm. *Agricultural managers* manage the day-to-day activities of one or more farms, ranches, nurseries, timber tracts, greenhouses, or other agricultural establishments for farmers, absentee landowners, or corporations. Their duties and responsibilities vary widely but focus on the business aspects of running a farm. On small farms, they may oversee the entire operation; on larger farms, they may oversee a single activity, such as marketing.

Farmers, ranchers, and agricultural managers make many managerial decisions. Farm output and income are strongly influenced by the weather, disease, fluctuations in prices of domestic and foreign farm products, and federal farm programs. In crop-production operations, farmers and managers usually determine the best time to plant seed, apply fertilizer and chemicals, and harvest and market the crops. Many carefully plan the combination of crops they grow so that if the price of one crop drops, they will have sufficient income from another crop to make up the loss. Farmers, ranchers, and managers monitor the constantly changing prices for their products. They use different strategies to protect themselves from unpredictable changes in the markets for agricultural products. If they plan ahead, they may be able to store their crops or keep their livestock to take advantage of higher prices later in the year. Those who participate in the risky futures market buy contracts on future production of agricultural goods. These contracts can minimize the risk of sudden price changes by guaranteeing a certain price for farmers' and ranchers' agricultural goods when they are ready to sell.

While most farm output is sold directly to food-processing companies, some farmers—particularly operators of smaller farms—may choose to sell their goods directly to consumers through farmers' markets. Some use cooperatives to reduce their financial risk and to gain a larger share of the prices consumers pay. For example, in community-supported agriculture, cooperatives sell shares of a harvest to consumers prior to the planting season, thus freeing the farmer from having to bear all the financial risks and ensuring the farmer a market for the produce of the coming season. Farmers, ranchers, and agricultural managers also negotiate with banks and other credit lenders to get the best financing deals for their equipment, livestock, and seed.

Like other businesses, farming operations have become more complex in recent years, so many farmers use computers to keep financial and inventory records. They also use computer databases and spreadsheets to manage breeding, dairy, and other farm operations.

The type of farm farmers, ranchers, and agricultural managers operate determines their specific tasks. On crop farms—farms growing grain, cotton, other fibers, fruit, and vegetables—farmers are responsible for preparing, tilling, planting, fertilizing, cultivating, spraying, and harvesting. After the harvest, they make sure that the crops are properly packaged, stored, and marketed. Livestock, dairy, and poultry farmers and ranchers feed and care for animals and keep barns, pens, coops, and other farm buildings clean and in good condition. They also plan and oversee breeding and marketing activities. Both farmers and ranchers operate machinery and maintain equipment and facilities, and both track technological improvements in animal breeding and seeds and choose new or existing products.

The size of the farm or ranch often determines which of these tasks farmers and ranchers handle themselves. Operators of small farms usually perform all tasks, physical and administrative. They keep records for management and tax purposes, service machinery, maintain buildings, and grow vegetables and raise animals. Operators of large farms, by contrast, have employees who help with the physical work that small-farm operators do themselves. Although employment on most farms is limited to the farmer and one or two family workers or hired employees, some large farms have 100 or more full-time and seasonal workers. Some of these employees are in nonfarm occupations, working as truck drivers, sales representatives, bookkeepers, and computer specialists.

Agricultural managers usually do not plant, harvest, or perform other production activities; instead, they hire and supervise farm and livestock workers, who perform most daily production tasks. Managers may establish output goals; determine financial constraints; monitor production and marketing; hire, assign, and supervise workers; determine crop transportation and storage requirements; and oversee maintenance of the property and equipment.

Two types of farmers that are growing in importance are horticultural specialty farmers and aquaculture farmers. *Horticultural specialty farmers* oversee the production of fruits, vegetables, flowers, and ornamental plants used in landscaping, including turf. They also grow nuts, berries, and grapes for wine. *Aquaculture farmers* raise fish and shellfish in marine, brackish, or fresh water, usually in ponds, floating net pens, raceways, or recirculating systems. They stock, feed, protect, and otherwise manage aquatic life sold for consumption or used for recreational fishing.

Work environment. The work of full-time farmers, ranchers, and agricultural managers is often strenuous; work hours are frequently long; and these workers rarely have days off during the planting, growing, and harvesting seasons. Nevertheless, for those who enter farming or ranching, the hard work is counterbalanced by their enjoyment of living in a rural area, working outdoors, being self-employed, and making a living off the land.

Farmers and farm managers on crop farms usually work from sunrise to sunset during the planting and harvesting seasons. The rest of

© JIST Works

the year, they plan next season's crops, market their output, and repair machinery.

On livestock-producing farms and ranches, work goes on throughout the year. Animals, unless they are grazing, must be fed and watered every day, and dairy cows must be milked two or three times a day. Many livestock and dairy farmers monitor and attend to the health of their herds, which may include assisting in the birthing of animals. Such farmers and farm managers rarely get the chance to get away unless they hire an assistant or arrange for a temporary substitute.

Farmers and farm managers who grow produce and perishables have different demands on their time depending on the crop grown and the season. They may work very long hours during planting and harvesting season, but shorter hours at other times. Some farmers maintain cover crops during the cold months, which keep them busy beyond the typical growing season.

On very large farms, farmers and farm managers spend substantial time meeting farm supervisors in charge of various activities. Professional farm managers overseeing several farms may divide their time between traveling to meet farmers or landowners and planning the farm operations in their offices. As farming practices and agricultural technology become more sophisticated, farmers and farm managers are spending more time in offices and at computers, where they electronically manage many aspects of their businesses. Some farmers also attend conferences to exchange information, particularly during the winter months.

Farm work can be hazardous. Tractors and other farm machinery can cause serious injury, and workers must be constantly alert on the job. The proper operation of equipment and handling of chemicals are necessary to avoid accidents, safeguard health, and protect the environment.

Training, Other Qualifications, and Advancement

Experience gained from growing up on or working on a family farm is the most common way farmers learn their trade. However, modern farming requires increasingly complex scientific, business, and financial decisions, so postsecondary education in agriculture is important even for people who were raised on farms.

Education and training. Most farmers receive their training on the job, often by being raised on a farm. However, the completion of a two-year associate degree or a four-year bachelor's degree at a college of agriculture is becoming increasingly important for farm managers and for farmers and ranchers who expect to make a living at farming. A degree in farm management or in business with a concentration in agriculture is important.

Students should select the college most appropriate to their interests and location. All state university systems have at least one land-grant college or university with a school of agriculture. Common programs of study include agronomy, dairy science, agricultural economics and business, horticulture, crop and fruit science, and animal science. For students interested in aquaculture, formal programs are available and include coursework in fisheries biology, fish culture, hatchery management and maintenance, and hydrology.

Agricultural colleges teach technical knowledge of crops, growing conditions, and plant diseases. They also teach prospective ranchers and dairy farmers the basics of veterinary science and animal husbandry. Students also study how the environment is affected by farm operations—for example, how various pesticides affect local animals.

New farmers, ranchers, and agricultural managers often spend time working under an experienced farmer to learn how to apply the skills learned through academic training. Those without academic training often take many years to learn how weather, fertilizers, seed, feeding, or breeding affect the growth of crops or the raising of animals in addition to other aspects of farming. A small number of farms offer formal apprenticeships to help young people learn the practical skills of farming and ranching.

Other qualifications. Farmers, ranchers, and agricultural managers need managerial skills to organize and operate a business. A basic knowledge of accounting and bookkeeping is essential in keeping financial records, and knowledge of credit sources is vital for buying seed, fertilizer, and other needed inputs. Workers must also be familiar with complex safety regulations and requirements of governmental agricultural support programs. Computer skills are becoming increasingly important, especially on large farms, where computers are widely used for recordkeeping and business analysis. In addition, skills in personnel management, communication, and conflict resolution are important in the operation of a farm or ranch business.

Mechanical aptitude and the ability to work with tools of all kinds also are valuable skills for a small-farm operator, who often maintains and repairs machinery or farm structures.

Certification and advancement. Because of rapid changes in the industry, farmers, ranchers, and agricultural managers need to stay informed about continuing advances in agricultural methods, both in the United States and abroad. They need to monitor changes in governmental regulations that may affect production methods or markets for particular crops. Besides print journals that inform the agricultural community, farmers and managers use the Internet for quick access to the latest developments in areas such as agricultural marketing; legal arrangements; and growing crops, vegetables, and livestock.

Agricultural managers can enhance their professional status through voluntary certification as an Accredited Farm Manager (AFM) by the American Society of Farm Managers and Rural Appraisers. Accreditation requires several years of farm management experience, the appropriate academic background—a bachelor's degree or, preferably, a master's degree in a field of agricultural science—and the passing of courses and examinations related to the business, financial, and legal aspects of farm and ranch management.

Employment

Farmers, ranchers, and agricultural managers held nearly 1.3 million jobs in 2006. About 80 percent are self-employed farmers and ranchers, and the remainder is agricultural managers. Most farmers, ranchers, and agricultural managers oversee crop-production activities, while others manage livestock and dairy production. Most farmers and ranchers operate small farms on a part-time basis.

The soil, topography of the land, and climate often determine the type of farming and ranching done in a particular area. California, Texas, Iowa, Nebraska, and Kansas are the leading agricultural states in terms of agricultural output measured in dollars. Texas, Missouri, Iowa, Kentucky, and Tennessee are the leading agricultural states in terms of numbers of farms.

Job Outlook

The long-term trend toward the consolidation of farms into fewer and larger ones is expected to continue over the 2006–16 decade and to result in a continued moderate decline in employment of self-employed farmers and ranchers and little or no change in employment of salaried agricultural managers. Nevertheless, a number of jobs will be available because of the need to replace the large number of farmers expected to retire or leave the profession over the next decade.

Employment change. Employment of self-employed farmers is expected to decline moderately by 8 percent over the 2006–2016 decade. The continuing ability of the agriculture sector to produce more with fewer workers will cause some farmers to go out of business as market pressures leave little room for the marginally successful farmer. As land, machinery, seed, and chemicals become more expensive, only well-capitalized farmers and corporations will be able to buy many of the farms that become available. These larger, more productive farms are better able to withstand the adverse effects of climate and price fluctuations on farm output and income. Larger farms also have advantages in obtaining government subsidies and payments because these payments are usually based on acreage owned and per-unit production.

In contrast, agricultural managers are projected to gain jobs, growing by 1 percent—effectively little or no change in the occupation. Owners of large tracts of land, who often do not live on the property they own, increasingly will seek the expertise of agricultural managers to run their farms and ranches in a business-like manner.

Despite the expected continued consolidation of farmland and the projected decline in overall employment of this occupation, an increasing number of small-scale farmers have developed successful market niches that involve personalized direct contact with their customers. Many are finding opportunities in organic food production, which is the fastest-growing segment in agriculture. Others use farmers' markets that cater directly to urban and suburban consumers, allowing the farmers to capture a greater share of consumers' food dollars. Some small-scale farmers belong to collectively owned marketing cooperatives that process and sell their product. Other farmers participate in community-supported agriculture cooperatives that allow consumers to directly buy a share of the farmer's harvest.

Aquaculture may continue to provide some new employment opportunities over the 2006–16 decade. Concerns about overfishing and the depletion of the stock of some wild fish species will likely lead to more restrictions on deep-sea fishing, even as public demand for the consumption of seafood continues to grow. This has spurred the growth of aquaculture farms that raise selected aquatic species—such as shrimp, salmon, trout, and catfish—in pens or ponds. Aquaculture has increased even in landlocked states as farmers attempt to diversify.

Job prospects. Job prospects are expected to be favorable for those who want to go into farming. With fewer people wanting to become farmers and a large number of farmers expected to retire or give up their farms in the next decade, there will be some opportunities to own or lease a farm. The market for agricultural products is projected to be good for most products over the next decade, and thus many farmers who retire will need to be replaced. Farmers who produce corn used to produce ethanol will be in particular demand as ethanol plays a greater role in energy production as fuel for automobiles. Farmers who grow crops used in landscaping, such as trees, shrubs, turf, and other ornamentals, also will have better job prospects as people put more money into landscaping their homes and businesses.

Earnings

Incomes of farmers and ranchers vary greatly from year to year because prices of farm products fluctuate with weather conditions and the other factors that influence the quantity and quality of farm output and the demand for those products. A farm that shows a large profit one year may show a loss the following year. According to the U.S. Department of Agriculture, the average net cash farm business income for farm operator households in 2005 was $15,603. This figure, however, does not reflect the fact that farmers often receive government subsidies or other payments that supplement their incomes and reduce some of the risk of farming. Additionally, most farmers—primarily operators of small farms—have income from off-farm business activities or careers, which is often greater than that of their farm income.

Full-time, salaried farm managers had median weekly earnings of $1,001 in May 2006. The middle half earned between $766 and $1,382. The highest-paid 10 percent earned more than $1,924, and the lowest-paid 10 percent earned less than $572.

Self-employed farmers must procure their own health and life insurance. As members of farm organizations, they may receive group discounts on health and life insurance premiums.

Related Occupations

Farmers, ranchers, and agricultural managers strive to improve the quality of agricultural products and the efficiency of farms. Others whose work relates to agriculture include agricultural engineers, agricultural and food scientists, agricultural workers, and purchasing agents and buyers of farm products.

Sources of Additional Information

For general information about farming and agricultural occupations, contact either of the following organizations:

▸ Center for Rural Affairs, P.O. Box 406, Walthill, NE 68067. Internet: http://www.cfra.org

Projections data from the National Employment Matrix

Occupational Title	SOC Code	Employment, 2006	Projected employment, 2016	Change, 2006-16	
				Number	Percent
Agricultural managers..	11-9010	1,317,000	1,230,000	-87,000	-7
Farm, ranch, and other agricultural managers............................	11-9011	258,000	261,000	2,900	1
Farmers and ranchers	11-9012	1,058,000	969,000	-90,000	-8

NOTE: Data in this table are rounded.

▸ National FFA Organization, The National FFA Center, Attention Career Information Requests, P.O. Box 68690, Indianapolis, IN 46268. Internet: http://www.ffa.org

For information about certification as an accredited farm manager, contact

▸ American Society of Farm Managers and Rural Appraisers, 950 Cherry St., Suite 508, Denver, CO 80222. Internet: http://www.asfmra.org

For information on the USDA's program to help small farmers get started, contact

▸ Small Farm Program, U.S. Department of Agriculture, Cooperative State, Research, Education, and Extension Service, Stop 2220, Washington, DC 20250. Internet: http://www.csrees.usda.gov/smallfarms.cfm

For information about organic farming, horticulture, and internships, contact

▸ Alternative Farming System Information Center, NAL, 10301 Baltimore Ave., Room 132, Beltsville, MD 20705. Internet: http://www.nal.usda.gov

▸ ATTRA, National Sustainable Agriculture Information Service, P.O. Box 3657, Fayetteville, AR 72702. Internet: http://www.attra.ncat.org

To learn more about how technological and other changes are affecting agricultural careers, see the *Occupational Outlook Quarterly* article "Farming in the 21st century: A modern business in the modern world," online at http://www.bls.gov/opub/ooq/2005/spring/art02.pdf and in print at many libraries and career centers.

Fire Fighting Occupations

(O*NET 33-1021.00, 33-1021.01, 33-1021.02, 33-2011.00, 33-2011.01, 33-2011.02, 33-2021.00, 33-2021.01, 33-2021.02, and 33-2022.00)

Significant Points

■ Fire fighting involves hazardous conditions and long, irregular hours.

■ About 9 out of 10 fire fighting workers are employed by local governments.

■ Applicants for city fire fighting jobs generally must pass written, physical, and medical examinations.

■ Although employment is expected to grow faster than the average, keen competition for jobs is expected because this occupation attracts many qualified candidates.

Nature of the Work

Every year, fires and other emergencies take thousands of lives and destroy property worth billions of dollars. Fire fighters help protect the public against these dangers by responding to fires and a variety of other emergencies. In addition to putting out fires, they are frequently the first emergency personnel at the scene of a traffic accident or medical emergency and may be called upon to treat injuries or perform other vital functions.

During duty hours, fire fighters must be prepared to respond immediately to a fire or others emergency. Fighting fires is dangerous and complex, therefore requires organization and teamwork. At every emergency scene, fire fighters perform specific duties assigned by a superior officer. At fires, they connect hose lines to hydrants and operate a pump to send water to high-pressure hoses. Some carry hoses, climb ladders, and enter burning buildings—using systematic and careful procedures—to put out fires. At times, they may need to use tools, like an ax, to make their way through doors, walls, and debris, sometimes with the aid of information about a building's floor plan. Some find and rescue occupants who are unable to safely leave the building without assistance. They also provide emergency medical attention, ventilate smoke-filled areas, and attempt to salvage the contents of buildings. Fire fighters' duties may change several times while the company is in action. Sometimes they remain at the site of a disaster for days at a time, rescuing trapped survivors, and assisting with medical treatment.

Fire fighters work in a variety of settings, including metropolitan areas, rural areas with grasslands and forests, airports, chemical plants and other industrial sites. They have also assumed a range of responsibilities, including emergency medical services. In fact, most calls to which fire fighters respond involve medical emergencies. In addition, some fire fighters work in hazardous materials units that are specially trained for the control, prevention, and cleanup of hazardous materials, such as oil spills or accidents involving the transport of chemicals.

Workers specializing forest fires utilize different methods and equipment than other fire fighters. In national forests and parks, *forest fire inspectors and prevention specialists* spot fires from watchtowers and report the fires to headquarters by telephone or radio. Forest rangers also patrol to ensure that travelers and campers comply with fire regulations. When fires break out, crews of fire fighters are brought in to suppress the blaze with heavy equipment and water hoses. Fighting forest fires, like fighting urban fires, is rigorous work. One of the most effective means of fighting a forest fire is creating fire lines—cutting down trees and digging out grass and all other combustible vegetation in the path of the fire—to deprive it of fuel. Elite fire fighters called smoke jumpers parachute from airplanes to reach otherwise inaccessible areas. This tactic, however, can be extremely hazardous.

When they aren't responding to fires and other emergencies, fire fighters clean and maintain equipment, study fire science and fire fighting techniques, conduct practice drills and fire inspections, and participate in physical fitness activities. They also prepare written reports on fire incidents and review fire science literature to stay informed about technological developments and changing administrative practices and policies.

Most fire departments have a fire prevention division, usually headed by a fire marshal and staffed by *fire inspectors*. Workers in this division conduct inspections of structures to prevent fires by ensuring compliance with fire codes. These inspectors also work with developers and planners to check and approve plans for new buildings and inspect buildings under construction.

Some fire fighters become *fire investigators*, who determine the causes of fires. They collect evidence, interview witnesses, and prepare reports on fires in cases where the cause may be arson or criminal negligence. They often are asked to testify in court. In some cities, these investigators work in police departments, and some are employed by insurance companies.

Work environment. Fire fighters spend much of their time at fire stations, which are usually similar to dormitories. When an alarm sounds, fire fighters respond, regardless of the weather or hour. Fire fighting involves the risk of death or injury from floors caving in, walls toppling, traffic accidents, and exposure to flames and smoke. Fire fighters also may come into contact with poisonous, flammable, or explosive gases and chemicals and radioactive materials, which may have immediate or long-term effects on their health. For these reasons, they must wear protective gear that can be very heavy and hot.

Work hours of fire fighters are longer and more varied than the hours of most other workers. Many fire fighters work more than 50 hours a week, and sometimes they may work longer. In some agencies, fire fighters are on duty for 24 hours, then off for 48 hours, and receive an extra day off at intervals. In others, they work a day shift of 10 hours for 3 or 4 days, a night shift of 14 hours for 3 or 4 nights, have 3 or 4 days off, and then repeat the cycle. In addition, fire fighters often work extra hours at fires and other emergencies and are regularly assigned to work on holidays. Fire lieutenants and fire captains often work the same hours as the fire fighters they supervise.

Training, Other Qualifications, and Advancement

Applicants for fire fighting jobs are usually required to have at least a high school diploma, but candidates with some education after high school are increasingly preferred. Most municipal jobs require passing written and physical tests. All fire fighters receive extensive training after being hired.

Education and training. Most fire fighters have a high school diploma, however, the completion of community college courses, or in some cases, an associate degree, in fire science may improve an applicant's chances for a job. A number of colleges and universities offer courses leading to two- or four-year degrees in fire engineering or fire science. In recent years, an increasing proportion of new fire fighters have had some education after high school.

As a rule, entry-level workers in large fire departments are trained for several weeks at the department's training center or academy. Through classroom instruction and practical training, the recruits study fire fighting techniques, fire prevention, hazardous materials control, local building codes, and emergency medical procedures, including first aid and cardiopulmonary resuscitation (CPR). They also learn how to use axes, chain saws, fire extinguishers, ladders, and other fire fighting and rescue equipment. After successfully completing this training, the recruits are assigned to a fire company, where they undergo a period of probation.

Many fire departments have accredited apprenticeship programs lasting up to four years. These programs combine formal instruction with on-the-job training under the supervision of experienced fire fighters.

Almost all departments require fire fighters to be certified as emergency medical technicians. (For more information, see the section of this book on emergency medical technicians and paramedics.) Although most fire departments require the lowest level of certification, Emergency Medical Technician-Basic (EMT-Basic), larger departments in major metropolitan areas increasingly require paramedic certification. Some departments include this training in the fire academy, whereas others prefer that recruits earn EMT certification on their own but will give them up to one year to do it.

In addition to participating in training programs conducted by local fire departments, some fire fighters attend training sessions sponsored by the U.S. National Fire Academy. These training sessions cover topics such as executive development, anti-arson techniques, disaster preparedness, hazardous materials control, and public fire safety and education. Some states also have either voluntary or mandatory fire fighter training and certification programs. Many fire departments offer fire fighters incentives such as tuition reimbursement or higher pay for completing advanced training.

Other qualifications. Applicants for municipal fire fighting jobs usually must pass a written exam; tests of strength, physical stamina, coordination, and agility; and a medical examination that includes a drug screening. Workers may be monitored on a random basis for drug use after accepting employment. Examinations are generally open to people who are at least 18 years of age and have a high school education or its equivalent. Those who receive the highest scores in all phases of testing have the best chances of being hired.

Among the personal qualities fire fighters need are mental alertness, self-discipline, courage, mechanical aptitude, endurance, strength, and a sense of public service. Initiative and good judgment also are extremely important because fire fighters make quick decisions in emergencies. Members of a crew live and work closely together under conditions of stress and danger for extended periods, so they must be dependable and able to get along well with others. Leadership qualities are necessary for officers, who must establish and maintain discipline and efficiency, as well as direct the activities of the fire fighters in their companies.

Advancement. Most experienced fire fighters continue studying to improve their job performance and prepare for promotion examinations. To progress to higher level positions, they acquire expertise in advanced fire fighting equipment and techniques, building construction, emergency medical technology, writing, public speaking, management and budgeting procedures, and public relations.

Opportunities for promotion depend upon the results of written examinations, as well as job performance, interviews, and seniority. Hands-on tests that simulate real-world job situations are also used by some fire departments.

Usually, fire fighters are first promoted to engineer, then lieutenant, captain, battalion chief, assistant chief, deputy chief, and, finally, chief. For promotion to positions higher than battalion chief, many fire departments now require a bachelor's degree, preferably in fire science, public administration, or a related field. An associate degree is required for executive fire officer certification from the National Fire Academy.

Employment

In 2006, total paid employment in firefighting occupations was about 361,000. Fire fighters held about 293,000 jobs, first-line supervisors/managers of fire fighting and prevention workers held about 52,000, and fire inspectors and investigators held about 14,000 jobs. These employment figures include only paid career fire fighters—they do not cover volunteer fire fighters, who perform the same duties and may constitute the majority of fire fighters in a residential area. According to the U.S. Fire Administration, about 71 percent of fire companies were staffed entirely by volunteer fire fighters in 2005.

About 9 out of 10 fire fighting workers were employed by local government. Some large cities have thousands of career fire fighters, while many small towns have only a few. Most of the remainder worked in fire departments on federal and state installations,

Projections data from the National Employment Matrix

Occupational Title	SOC Code	Employment, 2006	Projected employment, 2016	Change, 2006-16	
				Number	Percent
Fire fighting occupations..	—	361,000	404,000	43,000	12
First-line supervisors/managers of fire fighting and prevention workers..........	33-1021	52,000	58,000	6,000	11
Fire fighting and prevention workers	33-2000	308,000	345,000	37,000	12
Fire fighters	33-2011	293,000	328,000	35,000	12
Fire inspectors...	33-2020	16,000	17,000	1,600	10
Fire inspectors and investigators..	33-2021	14,000	15,000	1,500	11
Forest fire inspectors and prevention specialists..................	33-2022	1,800	1,900	0	2

NOTE: Data in this table are rounded.

including airports. Private fire fighting companies employ a small number of fire fighters.

In response to the expanding role of fire fighters, some municipalities have combined fire prevention, public fire education, safety, and emergency medical services into a single organization commonly referred to as a public safety organization. Some local and regional fire departments are being consolidated into countywide establishments to reduce administrative staffs, cut costs, and establish consistent training standards and work procedures.

Job Outlook

Although employment is expected to grow as fast as the average for all jobs, candidates for these positions are expected to face keen competition as these positions are highly attractive and sought after.

Employment change. Employment of workers in fire fighting occupations is expected to grow by 12 percent over the 2006–2016 decade, which is as fast as the average for all occupations. Most job growth will stem from volunteer fire fighting positions being converted to paid positions. In recent years, it has become more difficult for volunteer fire departments to recruit and retain volunteers. This may be the result of the considerable amount of training and time commitment required. Furthermore, a trend towards more people living in and around cities has increased the demand for fire fighters. When areas develop and become more densely populated, emergencies and fires affect more buildings and more people and therefore require more fire fighters.

Job prospects. Prospective fire fighters are expected to face keen competition for available job openings. Many people are attracted to fire fighting because, it is challenging and provides the opportunity to perform an essential public service; a high school education is usually sufficient for entry; and a pension is usually guaranteed after 25 years work. Consequently, the number of qualified applicants in most areas far exceeds the number of job openings, even though the written examination and physical requirements eliminate many applicants. This situation is expected to persist in coming years. Applicants with the best chances are those who are physically fit and score the highest on physical conditioning and mechanical aptitude exams. Those who have completed some fire fighter education at a community college and have EMT or paramedic certification will have an additional advantage.

Earnings

Median annual earnings of fire fighters were $41,190 in May 2006. The middle 50 percent earned between $29,550 and $54,120. The lowest 10 percent earned less than $20,660, and the highest 10

percent earned more than $66,140. Median annual earnings were $41,600 in local government, $41,070 in the federal government, and $37,000 in state governments.

Median annual earnings of first-line supervisors/managers of fire fighting and prevention workers were $62,900 in May 2006. The middle 50 percent earned between $50,180 and $79,060. The lowest 10 percent earned less than $36,820, and the highest 10 percent earned more than $97,820. First-line supervisors/managers of fire fighting and prevention workers employed in local government earned a median of about $64,070 a year.

Median annual earnings of fire inspectors and investigators were $48,050 in May 2006. The middle 50 percent earned between $36,960 and $61,160 a year. The lowest 10 percent earned less than $29,840, and the highest 10 percent earned more than $74,930. Fire inspectors and investigators employed in local government earned a median of about $49,690 a year.

According to the International City-County Management Association, average salaries in 2006 for sworn full-time positions were as follows:

	Minimum annual base salary	Maximum annual base salary
Fire chief	$73,435	$95,271
Deputy chief..............................	66,420	84,284
Assistant fire chief	61,887	78,914
Battalion chief	62,199	78,611
Fire captain	51,808	62,785
Fire lieutenant	47,469	56,511
Fire prevention/code inspector	45,951	58,349
Engineer	43,232	56,045

Fire fighters who average more than a certain number of work hours per week are required to be paid overtime. The hours threshold is determined by the department. Fire fighters often earn overtime for working extra shifts to maintain minimum staffing levels or during special emergencies.

Fire fighters receive benefits that usually include medical and liability insurance, vacation and sick leave, and some paid holidays. Almost all fire departments provide protective clothing (helmets, boots, and coats) and breathing apparatus, and many also provide dress uniforms. Fire fighters generally are covered by pension plans, often providing retirement at half pay after 25 years of service or if the individual is disabled in the line of duty.

Related Occupations

Like fire fighters, emergency medical technicians and paramedics and police and detectives respond to emergencies and save lives.

Sources of Additional Information

Information about a career as a fire fighter may be obtained from local fire departments and from either of the following organizations:

▸ International Association of Fire Fighters, 1750 New York Ave. NW, Washington, DC 20006. Internet: http://www.iaff.org

▸ U.S. Fire Administration, 16825 South Seton Ave., Emmitsburg, MD 21727. Internet: http://www.usfa.dhs.gov

Information about professional qualifications and a list of colleges and universities offering two- or four-year degree programs in fire science or fire prevention may be obtained from

▸ National Fire Academy, 16825 South Seton Ave., Emmitsburg, MD 21727. Internet: http://www.usfa.dhs.gov/nfa/index.htm

Fitness Workers

(O*NET 39-9031.00)

Significant Points

■ Many fitness and personal training jobs are part time, but many workers increase their hours by working at several different facilities or at clients' homes.

■ Night and weekend hours are common.

■ Most fitness workers need to be certified.

■ Job prospects are expected to be good.

Nature of the Work

Fitness workers lead, instruct, and motivate individuals or groups in exercise activities, including cardiovascular exercise, strength training, and stretching. They work in health clubs, country clubs, hospitals, universities, yoga and Pilates studios, resorts, and clients' homes. Increasingly, fitness workers also are found in workplaces, where they organize and direct health and fitness programs for employees of all ages. Although gyms and health clubs offer a variety of exercise activities such as weightlifting, yoga, cardiovascular training, and karate, fitness workers typically specialize in only a few areas.

Personal trainers work one-on-one with clients either in a gym or in the client's home. They help clients assess their level of physical fitness and set and reach fitness goals. Trainers also demonstrate various exercises and help clients improve their exercise techniques. They may keep records of their clients' exercise sessions to monitor clients' progress toward physical fitness. They may also advise their clients on how to modify their lifestyle outside of the gym to improve their fitness.

Group exercise instructors conduct group exercise sessions that usually include aerobic exercise, stretching, and muscle conditioning. Cardiovascular conditioning classes are often set to music. Instructors choose and mix the music and choreograph a corresponding exercise sequence. Two increasingly popular conditioning methods taught in exercise classes are Pilates and yoga. In these classes, instructors demonstrate the different moves and positions of the particular method; they also observe students and correct those who are doing the exercises improperly. Group exercise instructors are responsible for ensuring that their classes are motivating, safe, and challenging, yet not too difficult for the participants.

Fitness directors oversee the fitness-related aspects of a health club or fitness center. They create and oversee programs that meet the needs of the club's members, including new member orientations, fitness assessments, and workout incentive programs. They also select fitness equipment; coordinate personal training and group exercise programs; hire, train, and supervise fitness staff; and carry out administrative duties.

Fitness workers in smaller facilities with few employees may perform a variety of functions in addition to their fitness duties, such as tending the front desk, signing up new members, giving tours of the fitness center, writing newsletter articles, creating posters and flyers, and supervising the weight training and cardiovascular equipment areas. In larger commercial facilities, personal trainers are often required to sell their services to members and to make a specified number of sales. Some fitness workers may combine the duties of group exercise instructors and personal trainers, and in smaller facilities, the fitness director may teach classes and do personal training.

Work environment. Most fitness workers spend their time indoors at fitness centers and health clubs. Fitness directors and supervisors, however, typically spend most of their time in an office. Those in smaller fitness centers may split their time among office work, personal training, and teaching classes. Directors and supervisors generally engage in less physical activity than do lower-level fitness workers. Nevertheless, workers at all levels risk suffering injuries during physical activities.

Since most fitness centers are open long hours, fitness workers often work nights and weekends and even occasional holidays. Some may travel from place to place throughout the day, to different gyms or to clients' homes, to maintain a full work schedule.

Fitness workers generally enjoy a lot of autonomy. Group exercise instructors choreograph or plan their own classes, and personal trainers have the freedom to design and implement their clients' workout routines.

Training, Other Qualifications, and Advancement

For most fitness workers, certification is critical. Personal trainers usually must have certification to begin working with clients or with members of a fitness facility. Group fitness instructors may begin without a certification, but they are often encouraged or required by their employers to become certified.

Education and training. Fitness workers usually do not receive much on-the-job training; they are expected to know how to do their jobs when they are hired. Workers may receive some organizational training to learn about the operations of their new employer. They occasionally receive specialized training if they are expected to teach or lead a specific method of exercise or focus on a particular age or ability group. Because the requirements vary from employer to employer, it may be helpful to contact your local fitness centers or other potential employers to find out what background they prefer before pursuing training.

The education and training required depends on the specific type of fitness work: personal training, group fitness, or a specialization such as Pilates or yoga each need different preparation. Personal trainers often start out by taking classes to become certified. They then may begin by working alongside an experienced trainer before being allowed to train clients alone. Group fitness instructors often get started by participating in exercise classes until they are ready to successfully audition as instructors and begin teaching class. They also may improve their skills by taking training courses or attending fitness conventions. Most employers require instructors to work toward becoming certified.

Training for Pilates and yoga instructors is changing. Because interest in these forms of exercise has exploded in recent years, the demand for teachers has grown faster than the ability to train them properly. However, because inexperienced teachers have contributed to student injuries, there has been a push toward more standardized, rigorous requirements for teacher training.

Pilates and yoga teachers need specialized training in their particular method of exercise. For Pilates, training options range from weekend-long workshops to year-long programs, but the trend is toward requiring more training. The Pilates Method Alliance has established training standards that recommend at least 200 hours of training; the group also has standards for training schools and maintains a list of training schools that meet the requirements. However, some Pilates teachers are certified group exercise instructors who attend short Pilates workshops; currently, many fitness centers hire people with minimal Pilates training if the applicants have a fitness certification and group fitness experience.

Training requirements for yoga teachers are similar to those for Pilates teachers. Training programs range from a few days to more than two years. Many people get their start by taking yoga; eventually, their teachers may consider them ready to assist or to substitute teach. Some students may begin teaching their own classes when their yoga teachers think they are ready; the teachers may even provide letters of recommendation. Those who wish to pursue teaching more seriously usually pursue formal teacher training.

Currently, there are many training programs through the yoga community as well as programs through the fitness industry. The Yoga Alliance has established training standards requiring at least 200 training hours, with a specified number of hours in areas including techniques, teaching methodology, anatomy, physiology, and philosophy. The Yoga Alliance also registers schools that train students to its standards. Because some schools may meet the standards but not be registered, prospective students should check the requirements and decide if particular schools meet them.

An increasing number of employers require fitness workers to have a bachelor's degree in a field related to health or fitness, such as exercise science or physical education. Some employers allow workers to substitute a college degree for certification, but most employers who require a bachelor's degree also require certification.

Certification and other qualifications. Most personal trainers must obtain certification in the fitness field to gain employment. Group fitness instructors do not necessarily need certification to begin working. The most important characteristic that an employer looks for in a new fitness instructor is the ability to plan and lead a class that is motivating and safe. However, most organizations encourage their group instructors to become certified over time, and many require it.

In the fitness field, there are many organizations—some of which are listed in the last section of this statement—that offer certification.

Becoming certified by one of the top certification organizations is increasingly important, especially for personal trainers. One way to ensure that a certifying organization is reputable is to see that it is accredited by the National Commission for Certifying Agencies.

Most certifying organizations require candidates to have a high school diploma, be certified in cardiopulmonary resuscitation (CPR), and pass an exam. All certification exams have a written component, and some also have a practical component. The exams measure knowledge of human physiology, proper exercise techniques, assessment of client fitness levels, and development of appropriate exercise programs. There is no particular training program required for certifications; candidates may prepare however they prefer. Certifying organizations do offer study materials, including books, CD-ROMs, other audio and visual materials, and exam preparation workshops and seminars, but exam candidates are not required to purchase materials to take exams.

Certification generally is good for two years, after which workers must become recertified by attending continuing education classes or conferences, writing articles, or giving presentations. Some organizations offer more advanced certification, requiring an associate or bachelor's degree in an exercise-related subject for individuals interested in training athletes, working with people who are injured or ill, or advising clients on general health.

Pilates and yoga instructors usually do not need group exercise certifications to maintain employment. It is more important that they have specialized training in their particular method of exercise. However, the Pilates Method Alliance does offer certification.

People planning fitness careers should be outgoing, excellent communicators, good at motivating people, and sensitive to the needs of others. Excellent health and physical fitness are important due to the physical nature of the job. Those who wish to be personal trainers in a large commercial fitness center should have strong sales skills. All personal trainers should have the personality and motivation to attract and retain clients.

Advancement. A bachelor's degree in exercise science, physical education, kinesiology (the study of muscles, especially the mechanics of human motion), or a related area, along with experience, usually is required to advance to management positions in a health club or fitness center. Some organizations require a master's degree. As in other occupations, managerial skills are also needed to advance to supervisory or managerial positions. College courses in management, business administration, accounting, and personnel management may be helpful, but many fitness companies have corporate universities in which they train employees for management positions.

Personal trainers may advance to head trainer, with responsibility for hiring and overseeing the personal training staff and for bringing in new personal training clients. Group fitness instructors may be promoted to group exercise director, responsible for hiring instructors and coordinating exercise classes. Later, a worker might become the fitness director, who manages the fitness budget and staff. Workers might also become the general manager, whose main focus is the financial aspects of an organization, particularly setting and achieving sales goals; in a small fitness center, however, the general manager is usually involved with all aspects of running the facility. Some workers go into business for themselves and open their own fitness centers.

© JIST Works

Projections data from the National Employment Matrix

Occupational Title	SOC Code	Employment, 2006	Projected employment, 2016	Change, 2006-16	
				Number	Percent
Fitness trainers and aerobics instructors	39-9031	235,000	298,000	63,000	27

NOTE: Data in this table are rounded.

Employment

Fitness workers held about 235,000 jobs in 2006. Almost all personal trainers and group exercise instructors worked in physical fitness facilities, health clubs, and fitness centers, mainly in the amusement and recreation industry or in civic and social organizations. About 8 percent of fitness workers were self-employed; many of these were personal trainers, while others were group fitness instructors working on a contract basis with fitness centers. Many fitness jobs are part time, and many workers hold multiple jobs, teaching or doing personal training at several different fitness centers and at clients' homes.

Job Outlook

Jobs for fitness workers are expected to increase much faster than the average for all occupations. Fitness workers should have good opportunities due to rapid job growth in health clubs, fitness facilities, and other settings where fitness workers are concentrated.

Employment change. Employment of fitness workers is expected to increase 27 percent over the 2006–2016 decade, much faster than the average for all occupations. These workers are expected to gain jobs because an increasing number of people are spending time and money on fitness, and more businesses are recognizing the benefits of health and fitness programs for their employees.

Aging baby boomers are concerned with staying healthy, physically fit, and independent. Moreover, the reduction of physical education programs in schools, combined with parents' growing concern about childhood obesity, has resulted in rapid increases in children's health club membership. Increasingly, parents are also hiring personal trainers for their children, and the number of weight-training gyms for children is expected to continue to grow. Health club membership among young adults also has grown steadily, driven by concern with physical fitness and by rising incomes.

As health clubs strive to provide more personalized service to keep their members motivated, they will continue to offer personal training and a wide variety of group exercise classes. Participation in yoga and Pilates is expected to continue to increase, driven partly by the aging population that demands low-impact forms of exercise and seeks relief from arthritis and other ailments.

Job prospects. Opportunities are expected to be good for fitness workers because of rapid job growth in health clubs, fitness facilities, and other settings where fitness workers are concentrated. In addition, many job openings will stem from the need to replace the large numbers of workers who leave these occupations each year. Part-time jobs will be easier to find than full-time jobs.

Earnings

Median annual earnings of fitness trainers and aerobics instructors in May 2006 were $25,910. The middle 50 percent earned between $18,010 and $41,040. The bottom 10 percent earned less than $14,880, while the top 10 percent earned $56,750 or more. These figures do not include the earnings of the self-employed. Earnings of successful self-employed personal trainers can be much higher. Median annual earnings in the industries employing the largest numbers of fitness workers in 2006 were as follows:

General medical and surgical hospitals $29,640

Local government 27,720

Fitness and recreational sports centers 27,200

Other schools and instruction 22,770

Civic and social organizations 22,630

Because many fitness workers work part time, they often do not receive benefits such as health insurance or retirement plans from their employers. They are able to use fitness facilities at no cost, however.

Related Occupations

Other occupations that focus on physical fitness include athletes, coaches, umpires, and related workers. Physical therapists also do related work when they create exercise plans to improve their patients' flexibility, strength, and endurance. Dietitians and nutritionists advise individuals on improving and maintaining their health, like fitness workers do. Also like fitness workers, many recreation workers lead groups in physical activities.

Sources of Additional Information

For more information about fitness careers and universities and other institutions offering programs in health and fitness, contact

▸ IDEA Health and Fitness Association, 10455 Pacific Center Ct., San Diego, CA 92121-4339.

▸ National Strength and Conditioning Association, 1885 Bob Johnson Drive, Colorado Springs, CO 80906. Internet: http://www.nsca-lift.org

For information about personal trainer and group fitness instructor certifications, contact

▸ American College of Sports Medicine, P.O. Box 1440, Indianapolis, IN 46206-1440. Internet: http://www.acsm.org

▸ American Council on Exercise, 4851 Paramount Dr., San Diego, CA 92123. Internet: http://www.acefitness.org

▸ National Academy of Sports Medicine, 26632 Agoura Rd., Calabasas, CA 91302. Internet: http://www.nasm.org

▸ NSCA Certification Commission, 3333 Landmark Circle, Lincoln, NE 68504. Internet: http://www.nsca-cc.org

For information about Pilates certification and training programs, contact

▸ Pilates Method Alliance, P.O. Box 370906, Miami, FL 33137-0906. Internet: http://www.pilatesmethodalliance.org

For information on yoga teacher training programs, contact

▸ Yoga Alliance, 7801 Old Branch Ave., Suite 400, Clinton, MD 20735. Internet: http://www.yogaalliance.org

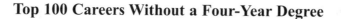

To find accredited fitness certification programs, contact

▸ National Commission for Certifying Agencies, 2025 M St. NW, Suite 800, Washington, DC 20036. Internet: http://www.noca.org/ncca/accredorg.htm

For information about health clubs and sports clubs, contact

▸ International Health, Racquet, and Sportsclub Association, 263 Summer St., Boston, MA 02210. Internet: http://www.ihrsa.org

Flight Attendants

(O*NET 39-6031.00)

Significant Points

■ Competition for positions is expected to remain keen because the opportunity for travel attracts more applicants than there are jobs.

■ Job duties are learned through formal on-the-job training at a flight training center.

■ A high school diploma is the minimum educational requirement; however, applicants with a college degree and with experience in dealing with the public are likely to have the best job opportunities.

Nature of the Work

Major airlines are required by law to provide flight attendants for the safety and security of the traveling public. Although the primary job of the flight attendants is to ensure that security and safety regulations are followed, attendants also try to make flights comfortable and enjoyable for passengers.

At least 1 hour before each flight, attendants are briefed by the captain—the pilot in command—on such things as emergency evacuation procedures, coordination of the crew, the length of the flight, expected weather conditions, and special issues having to do with passengers. Flight attendants make sure that first-aid kits and other emergency equipment are aboard and in working order and that the passenger cabin is in order, with adequate supplies of food, beverages, and any other provided amenities. As passengers board the plane, flight attendants greet them, check their tickets, and tell them where to store carry-on items.

Before the plane takes off, flight attendants instruct all passengers in the use of emergency equipment and check to see that seatbelts are fastened, seat backs are in upright positions, and all carry-on items are properly stowed. In the air, helping passengers in the event of an emergency is the most important responsibility of a flight attendant. Safety-related actions may range from reassuring passengers during rough weather to directing passengers who must evacuate a plane following an emergency landing. Flight attendants also answer questions about the flight; distribute reading material, pillows, and blankets; and help small children, elderly or disabled persons, and any others needing assistance. They may administer first aid to passengers who become ill. Flight attendants generally serve beverages and other refreshments and, on many flights, especially international, heat and distribute precooked meals or snacks. Prior to landing, flight attendants take inventory of headsets, alcoholic beverages, and moneys collected. They also report any medical problems passengers may have had, the condition of cabin equipment, and lost and found articles.

Lead, or first, flight attendants, sometimes known as pursers, oversee the work of the other attendants aboard the aircraft, while performing most of the same duties.

Work environment. Because airlines operate around the clock and year round, flight attendants may work nights, holidays, and weekends. In most cases, agreements between the airline and the employees' union determine the total daily and monthly working time. Scheduled on-duty time usually is limited to 12 hours per day although some contracts provide daily actual maximums of 14 hours, with somewhat greater maximums for international flying.

Attendants usually fly 65 to 90 hours a month and generally spend another 50 hours a month on the ground preparing planes for flights, writing reports following completed flights, and waiting for planes to arrive. Most airlines guarantee a minimum of 65 to 85 flight hours per month, with the option to work additional hours. Flight attendants receive extra compensation for increased hours.

Flight attendants may be away from their home base at least one-third of the time. During this period, the airlines provide hotel accommodations and an allowance for meal expenses.

Flight attendants must be flexible and willing to relocate. However, many flight attendants elect to live in one place and commute to their assigned home base. Home bases and routes worked are bid for on a seniority basis. The longer the flight attendant has been employed, the more likely he or she is to work on chosen flights. Almost all flight attendants start out working on reserve status or on call. On small corporate airlines, flight attendants often work on an as-needed basis and must adapt to varying environments and passengers.

The combination of free time and discount airfares provides flight attendants the opportunity to travel and see new places. However, the work can be strenuous and trying. Flight attendants stand during much of the flight and must remain pleasant and efficient, regardless of how tired they are or how demanding passengers may be. Occasionally, flight attendants must deal with disruptive passengers. Also, turbulent flights can add to possible difficulties regarding service, including potential injuries to passengers.

Working in a moving aircraft leaves flight attendants susceptible to injuries. For example, back injuries and mishaps can occur when opening overhead compartments or while pushing heavy service carts. In addition, medical problems can arise from irregular sleeping and eating patterns, dealing with stressful passengers, working in a pressurized environment, and breathing recycled air.

Training, Other Qualifications, and Advancement

Flight attendants must be certified by the Federal Aviation Administration (FAA). A high school diploma is the minimum educational requirement, but airlines increasingly prefer applicants who have a college degree. Experience in dealing with the public is important because flight attendants must be able to interact comfortably with strangers and remain calm under duress.

Education and training. A high school diploma is the minimum educational requirement. However, airlines increasingly prefer applicants with a college degree and with experience in dealing with the public. Applicants who attend schools and colleges that offer flight attendant training may have an advantage over other applicants. Highly desirable areas of concentration include people-oriented disciplines such as psychology, communications, sociology, nursing, anthropology, police or fire science, travel and tourism, hospitality and education. Flight attendants for international airlines generally must speak a foreign language fluently. For their international flights, some of the major airlines prefer candidates who can speak two major foreign languages.

Once hired, all candidates must undergo a period of formal training. The length of training, ranging from three to eight weeks, depends on the size and type of carrier and takes place at the airline's flight training center. Airlines that do not operate training centers generally send new employees to the center of another airline. Some airlines may provide transportation to the training centers and an allowance for room, board, and school supplies, while other airlines charge individuals for training. New trainees are not considered employees of the airline until they successfully complete the training program. Trainees learn emergency procedures such as evacuating an airplane, operating emergency systems and equipment, administering first aid, and surviving in the water. In addition, trainees are taught how to deal with disruptive passengers and with hijacking and terrorist situations. New hires learn flight regulations and duties, gain knowledge of company operations and policies, and receive instruction on personal grooming and weight control. Trainees for the international routes get additional instruction in passport and customs regulations. Trainees must perform many drills and duties unaided, in front of the training staff. Throughout training, they also take tests designed to eliminate unsuccessful trainees. Toward the end of their training, students go on practice flights. Upon successful completion of training, flight attendants receive the FAA's Certificate of Demonstrated Proficiency. Flight attendants also are required to go through periodic retraining and pass an FAA safety examination to continue flying.

Licensure and certification. All flight attendants must be certified by the FAA. In order to be certified, flight attendants are required to successfully complete training requirements, such as evacuation, fire fighting, medical emergency, and security procedures established by the FAA and the Transportation Security Administration. They also must perform the assigned duties of a cabin crew member and complete an approved proficiency check. Flight attendants are certified for specific types of aircraft, regardless of the carrier. Therefore, only one-day or two-day recurrent training, with the new carrier, is needed for those flight attendants who change airlines, as long as the type of aircraft remains the same.

Other qualifications. Airlines prefer to hire poised, tactful, and resourceful people who can interact comfortably with strangers and remain calm under duress. Flight attendants must be in excellent health, and have the ability to speak clearly. Airlines usually have age, physical, and appearance requirements. Applicants usually must be at least 18 to 21 years old, although some carriers may have higher minimum-age requirements. Applicants must meet height requirements for reaching overhead bins, which often contain emergency equipment, and most airlines want candidates with weight proportionate to height. Vision is required to be correctable to 20/30 or better with glasses or contact lenses (uncorrected no worse than 20/200). Men must have their hair cut above the collar and be clean shaven. Airlines prefer applicants with no visible tattoos, body piercing, or unusual hairstyles or makeup.

In addition to education and training, airlines conduct a thorough background check as required by the FAA, which goes back as many as 10 years. Everything about an applicant is investigated, including date of birth, employment history, criminal record, school records,

and gaps in employment. Employment is contingent on a successful background check. An applicant will not be offered a job or will be immediately dismissed if his or her background check shows any discrepancies. All U.S. airlines require that applicants be citizens of the United States or registered aliens with legal rights to obtain employment in the United States.

Advancement. After completing initial training, flight attendants are assigned to one of their airline's bases. New flight attendants are placed on reserve status and are called either to staff extra flights or to fill in for crewmembers who are sick, on vacation, or rerouted. When they are not on duty, reserve flight attendants must be available to report for flights on short notice. They usually remain on reserve for at least one year but, in some cities, it may take five to 10 years or longer to advance from reserve status. Flight attendants who no longer are on reserve bid monthly for regular assignments. Because assignments are based on seniority, usually only the most experienced attendants get their choice of assignments. Advancement takes longer today than in the past because experienced flight attendants are remaining in this career longer than in the past.

Some flight attendants become supervisors, moving from senior or lead flight attendant, to check flight attendant, to flight attendant supervisor, then on to base manager, and finally to manager or vice president of in-flight operations. They may take on additional duties such as recruiting, instructing, or developing in-flight products. Their experience also may qualify them for numerous airline-related jobs involving contact with the public, such as reservation ticket agent or public relations specialist. Flight attendants who do not want to travel often for various reasons may move to a position as an administrative assistant. With additional education, some flight attendants may decide to transfer to other areas of the airline for which they work, such as risk management or human resources.

Employment

Flight attendants held about 97,000 jobs in 2006. Commercial airlines employed the vast majority of flight attendants, most of whom lived in their employer's home-base city. A small number of flight attendants worked for large companies that operated aircraft for business purposes.

Job Outlook

Competition for jobs is expected to remain keen because the opportunity for travel attracts more applicants than there are jobs.

Employment change. Employment of flight attendants is expected to grow 11 percent, about as fast as the average for all occupations over the 2006–2016 projection period. Population growth and an improving economy are expected to boost the number of airline passengers. As airlines expand their capacity to meet rising demand by increasing the number and size of planes in operation, more flight attendants will be needed.

Job prospects. Despite growing demand for flight attendants, competition is expected to be keen because this job usually attracts more applicants than there are jobs, with only the most qualified eventually being hired. College graduates who have experience dealing with the public should have the best chance of being hired. Job opportunities may be better with the faster growing regional and commuter, low-cost, and charter airlines. There also are job opportunities for professionally trained flight attendants to work for companies operating private aircraft for their executives.

Projections data from the National Employment Matrix

Occupational Title	SOC Code	Employment, 2006	Projected employment, 2016	Change, 2006-16	
				Number	Percent
Flight attendants..	39-6031	97,000	107,000	10,000	11

NOTE: Data in this table are rounded.

The majority of job opportunities through the year 2016 will arise from the need to replace flight attendants who leave the labor force or transfer to other occupations, often for higher earnings or a more stable lifestyle. With the job now viewed increasingly as a profession, however, fewer flight attendants leave their jobs, and job turnover is not as high as in the past. The average job tenure of attendants is currently more than 14 years and is increasing.

In the long run, opportunities for persons seeking flight attendant jobs should improve as the airline industry expands. Over the next decade, however, demand for flight attendants will fluctuate with the demand for air travel, which is highly sensitive to swings in the economy. During downturns, as air traffic declines, the hiring of flight attendants declines, and some experienced attendants may be laid off until traffic recovers.

Earnings

Median annual earnings of flight attendants were $53,780 in May 2006. The middle 50 percent earned between $33,320 and $77,410. The lowest 10 percent earned less than $24,250, and the highest 10 percent earned more than $99,300.

According to data from the Association of Flight Attendants, beginning attendants had median earnings of $15,849 a year in 2006. Beginning pay scales for flight attendants vary by carrier, however. New hires usually begin at the same pay scale regardless of experience, and all flight attendants receive the same future pay increases based on an established pay scale.

Some airlines offer incentive pay for working holidays, night and international flights, or taking positions that require additional responsibility or paperwork.

Flight attendants and their immediate families are entitled to free or discounted fares on their own airline and reduced fares on most other airlines. Some airlines require that the flight attendant be with an airline for 3 to 6 months before taking advantage of this benefit. Other benefits may include medical, dental, and life insurance; 401K or other retirement plan; sick leave; paid holidays; stock options; paid vacations; and tuition reimbursement. Flight attendants also receive a "per diem" allowance for meal expenses while on duty away from home. Flight attendants are required to purchase uniforms and wear them while on duty. The airlines usually pay for uniform replacement items, and may provide a small allowance to cover cleaning and upkeep of the uniforms.

The majority of flight attendants hold union membership, primarily with the Association of Flight Attendants. Other unions that represent flight attendants include the Transport Workers Union of America and the International Brotherhood of Teamsters.

Related Occupations

Other jobs that involve helping people as a safety professional, while requiring the ability to be calm even under trying circumstances, include emergency medical technicians and paramedics as well as firefighting occupations.

Sources of Additional Information

Information about job opportunities and qualifications required for work at a particular airline may be obtained by writing to the airline's human resources office.

For further information on flight attendants, contact

▸ Association of Flight Attendants, 501 Third St. NW, Washington, DC 20001. Internet: http://www.afanet.org

Food and Beverage Serving and Related Workers

(O*NET 35-3011.00, 35-3021.00, 35-3022.00, 35-3031.00, 35-3041.00, 35-9011.00, 35-9021.00, 35-9031.00, and 35-9099.99)

Significant Points

■ Most jobs are part time and have few educational requirements, attracting many young people to the occupation—more than one-fifth of these workers are 16 to 19 years old, about five times the proportion for all workers.

■ Job openings are expected to be abundant through 2016, which will create excellent opportunities for jobseekers.

■ Tips comprise a major portion of earnings, so keen competition is expected for jobs in fine dining and more popular restaurants where potential tips are greatest.

Nature of the Work

Food and beverage serving and related workers are the front line of customer service in restaurants, coffee shops, and other food service establishments. These workers greet customers, escort them to seats and hand them menus, take food and drink orders, and serve food and beverages. They also answer questions, explain menu items and specials, and keep tables and dining areas clean and set for new diners. Most work as part of a team, helping coworkers to improve workflow and customer service.

Waiters and waitresses, the largest group of these workers, take customers' orders, serve food and beverages, prepare itemized checks, and sometimes accept payment. Their specific duties vary considerably, depending on the establishment. In coffee shops serving routine, straightforward fare, such as salads, soups, and sandwiches, servers are expected to provide fast, efficient, and courteous service. In fine dining restaurants, where more complicated meals are prepared and often served over several courses, waiters and waitresses provide more formal service emphasizing personal, attentive treatment and a more leisurely pace. They may recommend certain dishes and identify ingredients or explain how various items on the menu are prepared. Some prepare salads, desserts, or other menu items tableside. Additionally, servers may meet with managers and chefs, before each shift to discuss the menu and any new items or specials, review ingredients for any potential food allergies, or talk about any food safety concerns, coordination between the kitchen and the dining room, and any customer service issues from the previous day or shift. Servers usually also check the identification of patrons to ensure they meet the minimum age requirement for the purchase of alcohol and tobacco products wherever those items are sold.

Waiters and waitresses sometimes perform the duties of other food and beverage service workers. These tasks may include escorting guests to tables, serving customers seated at counters, clearing and setting up tables, or operating a cash register. However, full-service restaurants frequently hire other staff, such as hosts and hostesses, cashiers, or dining room attendants, to perform these duties.

Bartenders fill drink orders either taken directly from patrons at the bar or through waiters and waitresses who place drink orders for dining room customers. Bartenders check the identification of customers seated at the bar to ensure they meet the minimum age requirement for the purchase of alcohol and tobacco products. They prepare mixed drinks, serve bottled or draught beer, and pour wine or other beverages. Bartenders must know a wide range of drink recipes and be able to mix drinks accurately, quickly, and without waste. Besides mixing and serving drinks, bartenders stock and prepare garnishes for drinks; maintain an adequate supply of ice, glasses, and other bar supplies; and keep the bar area clean for customers. They also may collect payment, operate the cash register, wash glassware and utensils, and serve food to customers who dine at the bar. Bartenders usually are responsible for ordering and maintaining an inventory of liquor, mixes, and other bar supplies.

Most bartenders directly serve and interact with patrons. Bartenders should be friendly and at ease talking with customers. Bartenders at service bars, on the other hand, have less contact with customers. They work in small bars often located off the kitchen in restaurants, hotels, and clubs where only waiters and waitresses place drink orders. Some establishments, especially larger, higher volume ones, use equipment that automatically measures, pours, and mixes drinks at the push of a button. Bartenders who use this equipment, however, still must work quickly to handle a large volume of drink orders and be familiar with the ingredients for special drink requests. Much of a bartender's work still must be done by hand.

Hosts and hostesses welcome guests and maintain reservation or waiting lists. They may direct patrons to coatrooms, restrooms, or to a place to wait until their table is ready. Hosts and hostesses assign guests to tables suitable for the size of their group, escort patrons to their seats, and provide menus. They also schedule dining reservations, arrange parties, and organize any special services that are required. In some restaurants, they act as cashiers.

Dining room and cafeteria attendants and bartender helpers assist waiters, waitresses, and bartenders by cleaning tables, removing dirty dishes, and keeping serving areas stocked with supplies. Sometimes called backwaiters or runners, they bring meals out of the kitchen and assist waiters and waitresses by distributing dishes to individual diners. They also replenish the supply of clean linens, dishes, silverware, and glasses in the dining room and keep the bar stocked with glasses, liquor, ice, and drink garnishes. Dining room attendants set tables with clean tablecloths, napkins, silverware, glasses, and dishes and serve ice water, rolls, and butter. At the conclusion of meals, they remove dirty dishes and soiled linens from tables. *Cafeteria attendants* stock serving tables with food, trays, dishes, and silverware and may carry trays to dining tables for patrons. Bartender helpers keep bar equipment clean and glasses

washed. *Dishwashers* clean dishes, cutlery, and kitchen utensils and equipment.

Counter attendants take orders and serve food in cafeterias, coffee shops, and carryout eateries. In cafeterias, they serve food displayed on steam tables, carve meat, dish out vegetables, ladle sauces and soups, and fill beverage glasses. In lunchrooms and coffee shops, counter attendants take orders from customers seated at the counter, transmit orders to the kitchen, and pick up and serve food. They also fill cups with coffee, soda, and other beverages and prepare fountain specialties, such as milkshakes and ice cream sundaes. Counter attendants also take carryout orders from diners and wrap or place items in containers. They clean counters, write itemized bills, and sometimes accept payment. Some counter attendants may prepare short-order items, such as sandwiches and salads.

Some food and beverage serving workers take orders from customers at counters or drive-through windows at fast-food restaurants. They assemble orders, hand them to customers, and accept payment. Many of these are *combined food preparation and serving workers* who also cook and package food, make coffee, and fill beverage cups using drink-dispensing machines.

Other workers serve food to patrons outside of a restaurant environment. They might deliver room service meals in hotels or meals to hospital rooms or act as carhops, bringing orders to parked cars.

Work environment. Food and beverage service workers are on their feet most of the time and often carry heavy trays of food, dishes, and glassware. During busy dining periods, they are under pressure to serve customers quickly and efficiently. The work is relatively safe, but care must be taken to avoid slips, falls, and burns.

Part-time work is more common among food and beverage serving and related workers than among workers in almost any other occupation. In 2006, those on part-time schedules included half of all waiters and waitresses and 39 percent of all bartenders.

Food service and drinking establishments typically maintain long dining hours and offer flexible and varied work opportunities. Many food and beverage serving and related workers work evenings, weekends, and holidays. Many students and teenagers seek part time or seasonal work as food and beverage serving and related workers as a first job to gain work experience or to earn spending money. More than one-fifth of all food and beverage serving and related workers were 16 to 19 years old—about five times the proportion for all workers.

Training, Other Qualifications, and Advancement

Most food and beverage service jobs require little or no previous experience and provide training on the job.

Education and training. There are no specific educational requirements for most food and beverage service jobs. Many employers prefer to hire high school graduates for waiter and waitress, bartender, and host and hostess positions, but completion of high school usually is not required for fast-food workers, counter attendants, dishwashers, and dining room attendants and bartender helpers. For many people, a job as a food and beverage service worker serves as a source of immediate income, rather than a career. Many entrants to these jobs are in their late teens or early twenties and have a high school education or less. Usually, they have little or no work experience. Many are full-time students or homemakers. Food and beverage service jobs are a major source of part-time employment for high school and college students.

All new employees receive some training from their employer. They learn safe food handling procedures and sanitation practices, for example. Some employers, particularly those in fast-food restaurants, teach new workers using self-study programs, on-line programs, audiovisual presentations, and instructional booklets that explain food preparation and service skills. But most food and beverage serving and related workers pick up their skills by observing and working with more experienced workers. Some full-service restaurants also provide new dining room employees with some form of classroom training that alternates with periods of on-the-job work experience. These training programs communicate the operating philosophy of the restaurant, help establish a personal rapport with other staff, teach formal serving techniques, and instill a desire to work as a team. They also provide an opportunity to discuss customer service situations and the proper ways of handling unpleasant circumstances or unruly patrons.

Some food serving workers can acquire more skills by attending relevant classes offered by public or private vocational schools, restaurant associations, or large restaurant chains. Some bartenders also acquire their skills by attending a bartending or vocational and technical school. These programs often include instruction on state and local laws and regulations, cocktail recipes, proper attire and conduct, and stocking a bar. Some of these schools help their graduates find jobs. Although few employers require any minimum level of educational attainment, some specialized training is usually needed in food handling and legal issues surrounding serving alcoholic beverages. Employers are more likely to hire and promote based on people skills and personal qualities rather than education.

Other qualifications. Restaurants rely on good food and quality customer service to retain loyal customers and succeed in a competitive industry. Food and beverage serving and related workers who exhibit excellent personal qualities—such as a neat clean appearance, a well-spoken manner, an ability to work as a part of a team, and a pleasant way with patrons—will be highly sought after. All workers who serve alcoholic beverages must be at least 21 years of age in most jurisdictions and should be familiar with state and local laws concerning the sale of alcoholic beverages. For bartender jobs, many employers prefer to hire people who are 25 or older.

Waiters and waitresses need a good memory to avoid confusing customers' orders and to recall faces, names, and preferences of frequent patrons. These workers also should be comfortable using computers to place orders and generate customers' bills. Some may need to be quick at arithmetic so they can total bills manually. Knowledge of a foreign language is helpful to communicate with a diverse clientele and staff. Prior experience waiting on tables is preferred by restaurants and hotels that have rigid table service standards. Jobs at these establishments often offer higher wages and have greater income potential from tips, but they may also have stiffer employment requirements, such as prior table service experience or higher education than other establishments.

Advancement. Due to the relatively small size of most food-serving establishments, opportunities for promotion are limited. After gaining experience, some dining room and cafeteria attendants and bartender helpers advance to waiter, waitress, or bartender jobs. For waiters, waitresses, and bartenders, advancement usually is limited to finding a job in a busier or more expensive restaurant or bar where prospects for tip earnings are better. Some bartenders, hosts

and hostesses, and waiters and waitresses advance to supervisory jobs, such as dining room supervisor, *maitre d'hotel*, assistant manager, or restaurant general manager. A few bartenders open their own businesses. In larger restaurant chains, food and beverage service workers who excel often are invited to enter the company's formal management training program. (For more information, see the section on food service managers elsewhere in this book.)

Employment

Food and beverage serving and related workers held 7.4 million jobs in 2006. The distribution of jobs among the various food and beverage serving occupations was as follows:

Combined food preparation and serving workers, including fast food	2,503,000
Waiters and waitresses	2,361,000
Counter attendants, cafeteria, food concession, and coffee shop	533,000
Dishwashers	517,000
Bartenders	495,000
Dining room and cafeteria attendants and bartender helpers	416,000
Hosts and hostesses, restaurant, lounge, and coffee shop	351,000
Food servers, non restaurant	189,000
All other food preparation and serving related workers	56,000

The overwhelming majority of jobs for food and beverage serving and related workers were found in food services and drinking places, such as restaurants, sandwich shops, and catering or contract food service operators. Other jobs were in hotels, motels, and other traveler accommodation establishments; amusement, gambling, and recreation establishments; educational services; grocery stores; nursing care facilities; civic and social organizations; and hospitals.

Jobs are located throughout the country but are typically plentiful in large cities and tourist areas. Vacation resorts offer seasonal employment, and some workers alternate between summer and winter resorts.

Job Outlook

Average employment growth is expected, and job opportunities should be excellent for food and beverage serving and related workers, but job competition is often keen at upscale restaurants.

Employment change. Overall employment of these workers is expected to increase by 13 percent over the 2006–2016 decade, which is about as fast as the average for all occupations. Food and beverage serving and related workers are projected to have one of the largest numbers of new jobs arise, about 993,000, over this period. The popularity of eating out is expected to increase as the population expands and as customers seek the convenience of restaurants and other dining options. Projected employment growth varies somewhat by job type. Employment of combined food preparation and serving workers, which includes fast-food workers, is expected to increase faster than the average in response to the continuing fast-paced lifestyle of many Americans and the addition of healthier foods at many fast-food restaurants. Average employment growth is expected for waiters and waitresses, hosts and hostesses,

Projections data from the National Employment Matrix

Occupational Title	SOC Code	Employment, 2006	Projected employment, 2016	Change, 2006-16	
				Number	Percent
Food and beverage serving and related workers	—	7,422,000	8,415,000	993,000	13
Food and beverage serving workers...	35-3000	6,081,000	6,927,000	846,000	14
Bartenders	35-3011	495,000	551,000	56,000	11
Fast food and counter workers	35-3020	3,036,000	3,542,000	506,000	17
Combined food preparation and serving workers, including fast food	35-3021	2,503,000	2,955,000	452,000	18
Counter attendants, cafeteria, food concession, and coffee shop..	35-3022	533,000	587,000	54,000	10
Waiters and waitresses	35-3031	2,361,000	2,615,000	255,000	11
Food servers, nonrestaurant	35-3041	189,000	219,000	30,000	16
Other food preparation and serving related workers....................	35-9000	1,341,000	1,488,000	147,000	11
Dining room and cafeteria attendants and bartender helpers	35-9011	416,000	466,000	49,000	12
Dishwashers	35-9021	517,000	571,000	54,000	10
Hosts and hostesses, restaurant, lounge, and coffee shop	35-9031	351,000	388,000	37,000	10
Food preparation and serving related workers, all other...........	35-9099	56,000	64,000	7,300	13

NOTE: Data in this table are rounded.

and bartenders. Restaurants that offer table service, more varied menus, and an active bar scene are growing in number in response to consumer demands for convenience and to increases in disposable income, especially among families who frequent casual family-oriented restaurants; affluent young professionals, who patronize trendier, more upscale establishments; and retirees and others who dine out as a way to socialize. Employment of dishwashers, dining room and cafeteria attendants, and bartender helpers also will grow about as fast as average.

Job prospects. Job opportunities at most eating and drinking places will be excellent because many people in service sector occupations change jobs frequently and the number of food service outlets needing food service workers will continue to grow. Many of these workers, such as teens, those seeking part-time employment, or multiple jobholders, do so to satisfy short-term income needs before moving on to jobs in other occupations or leaving the workforce. Keen competition is expected, however, for jobs in popular restaurants and fine dining establishments, where potential earnings from tips are greatest.

Earnings

Food and beverage serving and related workers derive their earnings from a combination of hourly wages and customer tips. Earnings vary greatly, depending on the type of job and establishment. For example, fast-food workers and hosts and hostesses usually do not receive tips, so their wage rates may be higher than those of waiters and waitresses and bartenders in full-service restaurants but their overall earnings might be lower. In many full-service restaurants, tips are higher than wages. In some restaurants, workers contribute all or a portion of their tips to a tip pool, which is distributed among qualifying workers. Tip pools allow workers who don't usually receive tips directly from customers, such as dining room attendants, to feel a part of a team and to share in the rewards of good service.

In May 2006, median hourly wage-and-salary earnings (including tips) of waiters and waitresses were $7.14. The middle 50 percent earned between $6.42 and $9.14. The lowest 10 percent earned less than $5.78, and the highest 10 percent earned more than $12.46 an hour. For most waiters and waitresses, higher earnings are primarily the result of receiving more in tips rather than higher hourly wages.

Tips usually average between 10 and 20 percent of guests' checks; waiters and waitresses working in busy, expensive restaurants earn the most.

Bartenders had median hourly wage-and-salary earnings (including tips) of $7.86. The middle 50 percent earned between $6.77 and $10.10. The lowest 10 percent earned less than $6.00, and the highest 10 percent earned more than $13.56 an hour. Like waiters and waitresses, bartenders employed in public bars may receive more than half of their earnings as tips. Service bartenders often are paid higher hourly wages to offset their lower tip earnings.

Median hourly wage-and-salary earnings (including tips) of dining room and cafeteria attendants and bartender helpers were $7.36. The middle 50 percent earned between $6.62 and $8.59. The lowest 10 percent earned less than $5.91, and the highest 10 percent earned more than $10.60 an hour. Most received over half of their earnings as wages; the rest of their income was a share of the proceeds from tip pools.

Median hourly wage-and-salary earnings of hosts and hostesses were $7.78. The middle 50 percent earned between $6.79 and $8.97. The lowest 10 percent earned less than $5.99, and the highest 10 percent earned more than $10.80 an hour. Wages comprised the majority of their earnings. In some cases, wages were supplemented by proceeds from tip pools.

Median hourly wage-and-salary earnings of combined food preparation and serving workers, including fast food, were $7.24. The middle 50 percent earned between $6.47 and $8.46. The lowest 10 percent earned less than $5.79, and the highest 10 percent earned more than $10.16 an hour. Although some combined food preparation and serving workers receive a part of their earnings as tips, fast-food workers usually do not.

Median hourly wage-and-salary earnings of counter attendants in cafeterias, food concessions, and coffee shops (including tips) were $7.76. The middle 50 percent earned between $6.85 and $9.00 an hour. The lowest 10 percent earned less than $6.11, and the highest 10 percent earned more than $10.86 an hour.

Median hourly wage-and-salary earnings of dishwashers were $7.57. The middle 50 percent earned between $6.78 and $8.62. The lowest 10 percent earned less than $6.01, and the highest 10 percent earned more than $10.00 an hour.

Median hourly wage-and-salary earnings of food servers outside of restaurants were $8.70. The middle 50 percent earned between $7.27 and $10.87. The lowest 10 percent earned less than $6.36, and the highest 10 percent earned more than $13.81 an hour.

Many beginning or inexperienced workers earn the federal minimum wage of $5.85 an hour. However, a few states set minimum wages higher than the federal minimum. Under federal law, this wage will increase to $6.55 in the summer of 2008 and to $7.25 in the summer of 2009. Also, various minimum wage exceptions apply under specific circumstances to disabled workers, full-time students, youth under age 20 in their first 90 days of employment, tipped employees, and student-learners. Tipped employees are those who customarily and regularly receive more than $30 a month in tips. The employer may consider tips as part of wages, but the employer must pay at least $2.13 an hour in direct wages.

Many employers provide free meals and furnish uniforms, but some may deduct from wages the cost, or fair value, of any meals or lodging provided. Food and beverage service workers who work full time often receive typical benefits, but part-time workers usually do not. In some large restaurants and hotels, food and beverage serving and related workers belong to unions—principally the Unite HERE and the Service Employees International Union.

Related Occupations

Other workers who prepare food for diners include chefs, cooks, and food preparation workers. Those whose job involves serving customers and handling money include cashiers, flight attendants, gaming services workers, and retail salespersons.

Sources of Additional Information

Information about job opportunities may be obtained from local employers and local offices of state employment services agencies.

A guide to careers in restaurants plus a list of two- and four-year colleges offering food service programs and related scholarship information is available from

▸ National Restaurant Association, 1200 17th St. NW, Washington, DC 20036. Internet: http://www.restaurant.org

For general information on hospitality careers, contact

▸ International Council on Hotel, Restaurant, and Institutional Education, 2810 North Parham Rd., Suite 230, Richmond, VA 23294. Internet: http://www.chrie.org

Food Service Managers

(O*NET 11-9051.00)

Significant Points

■ Experience in food and beverage preparation and serving jobs is necessary for most food service manager positions.

■ Food service managers coordinate a wide range of activities, but their most difficult task may be dealing with irate customers and uncooperative employees.

■ Job opportunities for food service managers should be good as the number of outlets of restaurant chains increases to meet customer demand for convenience and value.

Nature of the Work

Food service managers are responsible for the daily operations of restaurants and other establishments that prepare and serve meals and beverages to customers. Besides coordinating activities among various departments, such as kitchen, dining room, and banquet operations, food service managers ensure that customers are satisfied with their dining experience. In addition, they oversee the inventory and ordering of food, equipment, and supplies and arrange for the routine maintenance and upkeep of the restaurant's equipment and facilities. Managers generally are responsible for all of the administrative and human-resource functions of running the business, including recruiting new employees and monitoring employee performance and training.

Managers interview, hire, train, and, when necessary, fire employees. Retaining good employees is a major challenge facing food service managers. Managers recruit employees at career fairs, contact schools that offer academic programs in hospitality or culinary arts, and arrange for newspaper advertising to attract additional applicants. Managers oversee the training of new employees and explain the establishment's policies and practices. They schedule work hours, making sure that enough workers are present to cover each shift. If employees are unable to work, managers may have to call in alternates to cover for them or fill in themselves when needed. Some managers may help with cooking, clearing tables, or other tasks when the restaurant becomes extremely busy.

Food service managers ensure that diners are served properly and in a timely manner. They investigate and resolve customers' complaints about food quality or service. They monitor orders in the kitchen to determine where backups may occur, and they work with the chef to remedy any delays in service. Managers direct the cleaning of the dining areas and the washing of tableware, kitchen utensils, and equipment to comply with company and government sanitation standards. Managers also monitor the actions of their employees and patrons on a continual basis to ensure the personal safety of everyone. They make sure that health and safety standards and local liquor regulations are obeyed.

In addition to their regular duties, food service managers perform a variety of administrative assignments, such as keeping employee work records; preparing the payroll; and completing paperwork to comply with licensing laws and tax, wage and hour, unemployment compensation, and Social Security laws. Some of this work may be delegated to an assistant manager or bookkeeper, or it may be contracted out, but most general managers retain responsibility for the accuracy of business records. Managers also maintain records of supply and equipment purchases and ensure that accounts with suppliers are paid.

Managers tally the cash and charge receipts received and balance them against the record of sales. They are responsible for depositing the day's receipts at the bank or securing them in a safe place. Finally, managers are responsible for locking up the establishment; checking that ovens; grills, and lights are off, and switching on alarm systems.

Technology influences the jobs of food service managers in many ways, enhancing efficiency and productivity. Many restaurants use computers to track orders, inventory, and the seating of patrons. Point-of-service (POS) systems allow servers to key in a customer's order—either at the table, using a hand-held device, or from a computer terminal in the dining room—and send the order to the kitchen instantaneously so preparation can begin. The same system totals and prints checks, functions like a cash register, connects to credit card authorizers, and tracks sales. To minimize food costs and spoilage, many managers use inventory-tracking software to compare sales records with a record of the current inventory. Some establishments enter an inventory of standard ingredients and suppliers into their POS system. When supplies of particular ingredients run low, they can be ordered directly from the supplier, using preprogrammed information. Computers also allow restaurant and food service managers to keep track of employee schedules and paychecks more efficiently.

Food service managers use the Internet to track industry news, find recipes, conduct market research, purchase supplies or equipment, recruit employees, and train staff. Internet access also makes service to customers more efficient. Many restaurants maintain Web sites that include menus and online promotions, provide information about the restaurant's location, and offer patrons the option of making a reservation.

In most full-service restaurants and institutional food service facilities, the management team consists of a *general manager*, one or more *assistant managers*, and an *executive chef*. The executive chef is responsible for all food preparation activities, including running kitchen operations, planning menus, and maintaining quality standards for food service. In limited-service eating places, such as sandwich shops, coffee bars, or fast-food establishments, managers, not executive chefs, are responsible for supervising routine food preparation operations. Assistant managers in full-service facilities generally oversee service in the dining rooms and banquet areas. In larger restaurants and fast-food or other food service facilities that serve meals daily and maintain longer business hours, individual assistant managers may supervise different shifts of workers. In smaller restaurants, formal titles may be less important, and one person may undertake the work of one or more food service positions. For example, the executive chef also may be the general manager or even sometimes an owner. (For additional information on these other workers, see the job profile of chefs, cooks, and food preparation workers elsewhere in this book.)

In restaurants where there are both food service managers and executive chefs, the managers often help the chefs select successful menu items. This task varies by establishment, depending on the seasonality of menu items; the frequency with which restaurants change their menus; and the introduction of daily, weekly, or seasonal specials. Many restaurants rarely change their menus while others make frequent alterations. Managers or executive chefs select menu items, taking into account the likely number of customers and the past popularity of dishes. Other issues considered when planning a menu include whether there was any food left over from prior meals that should not be wasted, the need for variety, and the seasonal availability of foods. Managers or executive chefs analyze the recipes of the dishes to determine food, labor, and overhead costs; work out the portion size and nutritional content of each plate; and assign prices to various menu items. Menus must be developed far enough in advance that supplies can be ordered and received in time.

Managers or executive chefs estimate food needs, place orders with distributors, and schedule the delivery of fresh food and supplies. They plan for routine services or deliveries, such as linen services or the heavy cleaning of dining rooms or kitchen equipment, to occur during slow times or when the dining room is closed. Managers also arrange for equipment maintenance and repairs and coordinate a variety of services such as waste removal and pest control. Managers or executive chefs receive deliveries and check the contents against order records. They inspect the quality of fresh meats, poultry, fish, fruits, vegetables, and baked goods to ensure that expectations are met. They meet with representatives from restaurant supply companies and place orders to replenish stocks of tableware, linens, paper products, cleaning supplies, cooking utensils, and furniture and fixtures.

Work environment. Food service managers are among the first to arrive in the morning and the last to leave at night. Long hours—12 to 15 per day, 50 or more per week, and sometimes 7 days a week—are common. Managers of institutional food service facilities, such as school, factory, or office cafeterias, work more regular hours because the operating hours of these establishments usually conform to the operating hours of the business or facility they serve. However, hours for many managers are unpredictable.

Managers should be calm; flexible; and able to work through emergencies, such as a fire or flood, to ensure everyone's safety. They also should be able to fill in for absent workers on short notice. Managers often experience the pressures of simultaneously coordinating a wide range of activities. When problems occur, it is the manager's responsibility to resolve them with minimal disruption to customers. The job can be hectic, and dealing with irate customers or uncooperative employees can be stressful.

Managers also may experience the typical minor injuries of other restaurant workers, such as muscle aches, cuts, or burns. They might endure physical discomfort from moving tables or chairs to accommodate large parties, receiving and storing daily supplies from vendors, or making minor repairs to furniture or equipment.

Training, Other Qualifications, and Advancement

Experience in the food services industry, whether as a cook, waiter or waitress, or counter attendant, is the most common training for food service managers. Many restaurant and food service manager positions, particularly self-service and fast-food, are filled by promoting experienced food and beverage preparation and service workers.

Education and training. Experience as a waiter or waitress, cook, or counter help is the most common way to enter the occupation. Executive chefs, in particular, need extensive experience working as chefs. Many food service management companies and national or regional restaurant chains recruit management trainees from two- and four-year college hospitality management programs, which require internships and real-life experience to graduate. Some restaurant chains prefer to hire people with degrees in restaurant and institutional food service management, but they often hire graduates with degrees in other fields who have demonstrated experience, interest, and aptitude.

Postsecondary education is preferred for many food service manager positions, but it is not a significant qualification for many others: More than 40 percent of food service managers have a high school diploma or less; less than one-quarter have a bachelor's or graduate degree. However, a postsecondary degree is preferred by higher-end full-service restaurants and for many corporate positions, such as managing a regional or national restaurant chain or franchise or overseeing contract food service operations at sports and entertainment complexes, school campuses, and institutional facilities. A college degree also is beneficial for those who want to own or manage their own restaurant.

Almost 1,000 colleges and universities offer four-year programs in restaurant and hospitality management or institutional food service management; a growing number of university programs offer graduate degrees in hospitality management or similar fields. For those not interested in pursuing a four-year degree, community and junior colleges, technical institutes, and other institutions offer programs in the field leading to an associate degree or other formal certification.

Both two- and four-year programs provide instruction in subjects such as nutrition, sanitation, and food planning and preparation, as well as accounting, business law and management, and computer science. Some programs combine classroom and laboratory study with internships providing on-the-job experience. In addition, many educational institutions offer culinary programs in food preparation. Such training can lead to careers as cooks or chefs and provide a foundation for advancement to executive chef positions.

Many larger food service operations will provide, or offer to pay for, technical training, such as computer or business courses, so that employees can acquire the business skills necessary to read spreadsheets or understand the concepts and practices of running a business. Generally, this requires a long-term commitment on the employee's part to both the employer and to the profession.

Most restaurant chains and food service management companies have rigorous training programs for management positions. Through a combination of classroom and on-the-job training, trainees receive instruction and gain work experience in all aspects of the operation of a restaurant or institutional food service facility. Areas include food preparation, nutrition, sanitation, security, company policies and procedures, personnel management, recordkeeping, and preparation of reports. Training on use of the restaurant's computer system is increasingly important as well. Usually, after six months or a year, trainees receive their first permanent assignment as an assistant manager.

Other qualifications. Most employers emphasize personal qualities when hiring managers. Workers who are reliable, show initiative, and have leadership qualities are highly sought after for promotion. Other qualities that managers look for are good problem-solving skills and the ability to concentrate on details. A neat and clean appearance is important because food service managers must convey self-confidence and show respect in dealing with the public. Because food service management can be physically demanding, good health and stamina are important.

Managers must be good communicators, as they deal with customers, employees, and suppliers for most of the day. They must be able to motivate employees to work as a team to ensure that food and service meet appropriate standards. Additionally, the ability to speak multiple languages is helpful to communicate with staff and patrons.

Certification and advancement. The certified Foodservice Management Professional (FMP) designation is a measure of professional achievement for food service managers, and although not a requirement for employment or necessary for advancement, voluntary certification can provide recognition of professional competence, particularly for managers who acquired their skills largely on the job. The National Restaurant Association Educational Foundation awards the FMP designation to managers who achieve a qualifying score on a written examination, complete a series of courses that cover a range of food service management topics, and meet standards of work experience in the field.

Willingness to relocate often is essential for advancement to positions with greater responsibility. Managers typically advance to larger or more prominent establishments or regional management positions within restaurant chains. Some may open their own food service establishments or franchise operation.

Employment

Food service managers held about 350,000 jobs in 2006. The majority of managers are salaried, but 45 percent are self-employed as owners of independent restaurants or other small food service establishments. Thirty-eight percent of all salaried jobs for food service managers are in full-service restaurants or limited-service eating places, such as fast-food restaurants and cafeterias. Other salaried jobs are in special food services—an industry that includes food service contractors who supply food services at institutional, governmental, commercial, or industrial locations, and educational services, primarily in elementary and secondary schools. A smaller number of salaried jobs are in hotels; amusement, gambling, and recreation industries; nursing care facilities; and hospitals. Jobs are located throughout the country, with large cities and resort areas providing more opportunities for full-service dining positions.

Job Outlook

Food service manager jobs are expected to grow 5 percent, or more slowly than the average for all occupations through 2016. However, job opportunities should be good because, in addition to job growth, many more openings will arise from the need to replace managers who leave the occupation.

Employment change. Employment of food service managers is expected to grow 5 percent, or more slowly than the average for all occupations, during the 2006–2016 decade. New eating and drinking places will open to meet the growing demand for convenience and value from a growing population, generating new employment opportunities for food service managers. Employment growth is projected to vary by industry. Most new jobs will be in full-service restaurants, but they are expected to decline among limited-service restaurants. Manager jobs will also increase in special food services, an industry that includes food service contractors that provide food for schools, health care facilities, and other commercial businesses and in nursing and residential care for the elderly. Self-employment of these workers will generate nearly 30 percent of new jobs.

Job prospects. In addition to job openings from employment growth, the need to replace managers who transfer to other occupations or stop working will create good job opportunities. Although practical experience is an integral part of finding a food service

Projections data from the National Employment Matrix

Occupational Title	SOC Code	Employment, 2006	Projected employment, 2016	Change, 2006-16	
				Number	Percent
Food service managers...	11-9051	350,000	368,000	18,000	5

NOTE: Data in this table are rounded.

management position, applicants with a degree in restaurant, hospitality or institutional food service management will have an edge when competing for jobs at upscale restaurants and for advancement in a restaurant chain or into corporate management.

Earnings

Median annual earnings of salaried food service managers were $43,020 in May 2006. The middle 50 percent earned between $34,210 and $55,100. The lowest 10 percent earned less than $27,400, and the highest 10 percent earned more than $70,810. Median annual earnings in the industries employing the largest numbers of food service managers were as follows:

Traveler accommodation	$48,890
Special food services	48,710
Full-service restaurants	45,650
Elementary and secondary schools	39,650
Limited-service eating places	39,070

In addition to receiving typical benefits, most salaried food service managers are provided free meals and the opportunity for additional training, depending on their length of service. Some food service managers, especially those in full-service restaurants, may earn bonuses depending on sales volume or revenue.

Related Occupations

Food service managers direct the activities of a hospitality-industry business and provide a service to customers. Other managers and supervisors in hospitality-oriented businesses include gaming managers, lodging managers, sales worker supervisors, and first-line supervisors or managers of food preparation and serving workers.

Sources of Additional Information

Information about a career as a food service manager, two- and four-year college programs in restaurant and food service management, and certification as a Foodservice Management Professional is available from

▶ National Restaurant Association Educational Foundation, 175 West Jackson Blvd., Suite 1500, Chicago, IL 60604-2702. Internet: http://www.nraef.org

Career information about food service managers, as well as a directory of two- and four-year colleges that offer courses or programs that prepare persons for food service careers is available from

▶ National Restaurant Association, 1200 17th St. NW, Washington, DC 20036-3097. Internet: http://www.restaurant.org

General information on hospitality careers may be obtained from

▶ The International Council on Hotel, Restaurant, and Institutional Education, 2810 North Parham Rd., Suite 230, Richmond, VA 23294. Internet: http://www.chrie.org

Additional information about job opportunities in food service management may be obtained from local employers and from local offices of state employment services agencies.

Funeral Directors

(O*NET 11-9061.00)

Significant Points

■ Job opportunities should be good, particularly for those who also embalm.

■ Some mortuary science graduates relocate to get a job.

■ Funeral directors are licensed by the state in which they practice.

■ Funeral directors need the ability to communicate easily and compassionately and to comfort people in a time of sorrow.

Nature of the Work

Funeral practices and rites vary greatly among cultures and religions. However, funeral practices usually share some common elements—removing the deceased to a mortuary, preparing the remains, performing a ceremony that honors the deceased and addresses the spiritual needs of the family, and carrying out final disposition of the deceased. Funeral directors arrange and direct these tasks for grieving families.

Funeral directors also are called morticians or undertakers. This career may not appeal to everyone, but those who work as funeral directors take great pride in their ability to provide comforting and appropriate services.

Funeral directors arrange the details and handle the logistics of funerals. They interview the family to learn their wishes about the funeral, the clergy or other people who will officiate, and the final disposition of the remains. Sometimes, the deceased leaves detailed instructions for his or her own funeral. Together with the family, funeral directors establish the location, dates, and times of wakes, memorial services, and burials. They arrange for a hearse to carry the body to the funeral home or mortuary. They also comfort the family and friends of the deceased.

Funeral directors prepare obituary notices and have them placed in newspapers; arrange for pallbearers and clergy; schedule the opening and closing of a grave with a representative of the cemetery; decorate and prepare the sites of all services; and provide transportation for the deceased, mourners, and flowers between sites. They also direct preparation and shipment of the body for out-of-state burial.

Most funeral directors also are trained, licensed, and practicing embalmers. Embalming is a sanitary, cosmetic, and preservative process through which the body is prepared for interment. If more than 24 hours elapse between death and interment, state laws usually require that the remains be refrigerated or embalmed.

When embalming a body, funeral directors wash the body with germicidal soap and replace the blood with embalming fluid to preserve the tissues. They may reshape and reconstruct bodies, using materials such as clay, cotton, plaster of Paris, and wax. They also may apply cosmetics to provide a natural appearance, dress the body, and place it in a casket. Funeral directors maintain records such as embalming reports and itemized lists of clothing or valuables delivered with the body. In large funeral homes, an embalming staff of two or more plus several apprentices may be employed.

Funeral services may take place in a home, at a house of worship, at a funeral home, or at the gravesite or crematory. Some services are not religious, but many are, reflecting the religion of the family. Funeral directors must be familiar with the funeral and burial customs of many faiths, ethnic groups, and fraternal organizations. For example, members of some religions seldom have the deceased embalmed or cremated.

Burial in a casket is the most common method of disposing of remains in this country, although entombment also occurs. Cremation, which is the burning of the body in a special furnace, is increasingly selected because it can be less expensive and is becoming more appealing, in part because memorial services can be held anywhere, and at any time, sometimes months later when all relatives and friends can come together. A funeral service followed by cremation need not be any different from a funeral service followed by a burial. Usually, cremated remains are placed in some type of permanent receptacle, or urn, before being committed to a final resting place. The urn may be buried, placed in an indoor or outdoor mausoleum or columbarium, or interred in a special urn garden that many cemeteries provide for cremated remains.

Funeral directors handle the paperwork involved with the person's death, including submitting papers to state authorities so that a formal death certificate may be issued and copies distributed to the heirs. They may help family members apply for veterans' burial benefits, and they notify the Social Security Administration of the death. Also, funeral directors may apply for the transfer of any pensions, insurance policies, or annuities on behalf of survivors.

Funeral directors also work with those who want to plan their own funerals in advance. This provides peace of mind by ensuring that the client's wishes will be taken care of in a way that is satisfying to the client and to the client's survivors.

Most funeral homes are small, family-run businesses, and many funeral directors are owner-operators or employees with managerial responsibilities. Funeral directors, therefore, are responsible for the success and the profitability of their businesses. Directors keep records of expenses, purchases, and services rendered; prepare and send invoices for services; prepare and submit reports for unemployment insurance; prepare federal, state, and local tax forms; and prepare itemized bills for customers. Funeral directors increasingly use computers for billing, bookkeeping, and marketing. Some are beginning to use the Internet to communicate with clients who are planning their funerals in advance or to assist them by developing electronic obituaries and guest books. Directors strive to foster a cooperative spirit and friendly attitude among employees and a compassionate demeanor toward the families. Increasingly, funeral directors also are helping individuals adapt to changes in their lives following a death through aftercare services and support groups.

Most funeral homes have a chapel, one or more viewing rooms, a casket-selection room, and a preparation room. Many also have a crematory on the premises. Equipment may include a hearse, a flower car, limousines, and sometimes an ambulance. Funeral homes usually stock a selection of caskets and urns for families to purchase or rent.

Work environment. Funeral directors occasionally come into contact with bodies that had contagious diseases, but the possibility of infection is remote if health regulations are followed.

Funeral directors often work long, irregular hours, and the occupation can be highly stressful. Many are on call at all hours because they may be needed to remove remains in the middle of the night.

Shift work sometimes is necessary because funeral home hours include evenings and weekends. In smaller funeral homes, working hours vary, but in larger establishments, employees usually work 8 hours a day, 5 or 6 days a week.

Training, Other Qualifications, and Advancement

Funeral directors are licensed in all states. State licensing laws vary, but most require applicants to be 21 years old, have two years of formal education, serve a one-year apprenticeship, and pass an examination.

Education and training. College programs in mortuary science usually last from two to four years. The American Board of Funeral Service Education accredits about 50 mortuary science programs. A few community and junior colleges offer two-year programs, and a few colleges and universities offer both two-year and four-year programs. Mortuary science programs include courses in anatomy, physiology, pathology, embalming techniques, restorative art, business management, accounting and use of computers in funeral home management, and client services. They also include courses in the social sciences and in legal, ethical, and regulatory subjects such as psychology, grief counseling, oral and written communication, funeral service law, business law, and ethics.

Many state and national associations offer continuing education programs designed for licensed funeral directors. These programs address issues in communications, counseling, and management. More than 30 states have requirements that funeral directors receive continuing education credits to maintain their licenses.

Apprenticeships must be completed under the direction of an experienced and licensed funeral director. Some states require apprenticeships. Depending on state regulations, apprenticeships last from one to three years and may be served before, during, or after mortuary school. Apprenticeships provide practical experience in all facets of the funeral service, from embalming to transporting remains.

High school students can start preparing for a career as a funeral director by taking courses in biology and chemistry and participating in public speaking or debate clubs. Part-time or summer jobs in funeral homes also provide good experience. These jobs consist mostly of maintenance and cleanup tasks, such as washing and polishing limousines and hearses, but they can help students become familiar with the operation of funeral homes.

Licensure. All states require funeral directors to be licensed. Licensing laws vary by state, but most require applicants to be 21 years old, have two years of formal education that includes studies in mortuary science, serve a one-year apprenticeship, and pass a qualifying examination. After becoming licensed, new funeral directors may join the staff of a funeral home.

Some states require all funeral directors to be licensed in embalming. Others have separate licenses for directors and embalmers, but in those states funeral directors who embalm need to be licensed in embalming, and most workers obtain both licenses.

State board licensing examinations vary, but they usually consist of written and oral parts and include a demonstration of practical skills. People who want to work in another state may have to pass the examination for that state; however, some states have reciprocity arrangements and will grant licenses to funeral directors from

Projections data from the National Employment Matrix

Occupational Title	SOC Code	Employment, 2006	Projected employment, 2016	Change, 2006-16	
				Number	Percent
Funeral directors	11-9061	29,000	32,000	3,600	12

NOTE: Data in this table are rounded.

another state without further examination. People interested in a career as a funeral director should contact their state licensing board for specific requirements.

Other qualifications. Funeral directors need composure, tact, and the ability to communicate easily and compassionately with the public. Funeral directors also should have the desire and ability to comfort people in a time of sorrow.

To show proper respect and consideration for the families and the dead, funeral directors must dress appropriately. The professions usually require short, neat haircuts and trim beards, if any, for men. Suits and ties for men and dresses for women are customary.

Advancement. Advancement opportunities generally are best in larger funeral homes. Funeral directors may earn promotions to higher-paying positions such as branch manager or general manager. Some directors eventually acquire enough money and experience to establish their own funeral home businesses.

Employment

Funeral directors held about 29,000 jobs in 2006. About 20 percent were self-employed. Nearly all worked in the death care services industry.

Job Outlook

Job opportunities are expected to be good, particularly for those who also embalm. Some mortuary science graduates relocate to get a job.

Employment change. Employment of funeral directors is expected to increase by 12 percent during the 2006–2016 decade, about as fast as the average for all occupations. Projected job growth reflects growth in the death care services industry, where funeral directors are employed.

Job prospects. In addition to employment growth, the need to replace funeral directors who retire or leave the occupation for other reasons will provide a number of job opportunities. Funeral directors are older, on average, than workers in most other occupations and are expected to retire in greater numbers over the coming decade. In addition, some funeral directors leave the profession because of the long and irregular hours. Some mortuary science graduates relocate to get a job.

Earnings

Median annual earnings for wage and salary funeral directors were $49,620 in May 2006. The middle 50 percent earned between $37,200 and $65,260. The lowest 10 percent earned less than $28,410 and the top 10 percent earned more than $91,800.

Salaries of funeral directors depend on the number of years of experience in funeral service, the number of services performed, the number of facilities operated, the area of the country, and the director's level of formal education. Funeral directors in large cities usually earn more than their counterparts in small towns and rural areas.

Related Occupations

The job of a funeral director requires tact, discretion, and compassion when dealing with grieving people. Others who need these qualities include social workers, psychologists, physicians and surgeons, and other health practitioners involved in diagnosis and treatment.

Sources of Additional Information

For a list of accredited mortuary science programs and information on the funeral service profession, write to

▸ The National Funeral Directors Association, 13625 Bishop's Dr., Brookfield, WI 53005. Internet: http://www.nfda.org

For information about college programs in mortuary science, scholarships, and funeral service as a career, contact

▸ The American Board of Funeral Service Education, 3432 Ashland Ave., Suite U, St. Joseph, MO 64506. Internet: http://www.abfse.org

▸ For information on specific state licensing requirements, contact the state's licensing board.

For more information about funeral directors and their work, see the *Occupational Outlook Quarterly* article "Jobs in weddings and funerals: Working with the betrothed and the bereaved," available in many libraries and career centers and online at http://www.bls.gov/opub/ooq/2006/winter/art03.pdf.

Grounds Maintenance Workers

(O*NET 37-1012.00, 37-3011.00, 37-3012.00, 37-3013.00, and 37-3019.99)

Significant Points

■ Opportunities should be very good, especially for workers willing to work seasonal or variable schedules, because of significant job turnover and increased demand for landscaping.

■ Many beginning jobs have low earnings and are physically demanding.

■ Most workers learn through short-term on-the-job training.

Nature of the Work

Attractively designed, healthy, and well-maintained lawns, gardens, and grounds create a positive impression, establish a peaceful mood, and increase property values. Grounds maintenance workers perform the variety of tasks necessary to achieve a pleasant and functional outdoor environment. They also care for indoor gardens and plantings in commercial and public facilities, such as malls, hotels, and botanical gardens.

These workers use handtools such as shovels, rakes, pruning and handsaws, hedge and brush trimmers, and axes, as well as power lawnmowers, chain saws, snowblowers, and electric clippers. Some use equipment such as tractors and twin-axle vehicles. Landscaping and groundskeeping workers at parks, schools, cemeteries, and golf courses may lay sod after preparing the ground. Workers at sod farms use sod cutters to harvest sod that will be replanted elsewhere.

Grounds maintenance workers can be divided into landscaping workers and groundskeeping workers, depending on whether they mainly install new landscape elements or maintain existing ones, but their duties often overlap. Other grounds maintenance workers are pesticide handlers and tree trimmers.

Landscaping workers install plants and other elements into landscaped areas and often maintain them. They might mow, edge, trim, fertilize, dethatch, water, and mulch lawns and grounds many times during the growing season. They grade property by creating or smoothing hills and inclines, install lighting or sprinkler systems, and build walkways, terraces, patios, decks, and fountains. They also transport and plant new vegetation, and transplant, mulch, fertilize, and water existing plants, trees, and shrubs. A growing number of residential and commercial clients, such as managers of office buildings, shopping malls, multiunit residential buildings, and hotels and motels, favor full-service landscape maintenance.

Groundskeeping workers, also called *groundskeepers*, usually focus on maintaining existing grounds. They might work on athletic fields, golf courses, cemeteries, university campuses, and parks. In addition to caring for sod, plants, and trees, they rake and mulch leaves, clear snow from walkways and parking lots, and use irrigation methods to adjust the amount of water consumption and prevent waste. They see to the proper upkeep and repair of sidewalks, parking lots, groundskeeping equipment, pools, fountains, fences, planters, and benches.

Groundskeeping workers who care for athletic fields keep natural and artificial turf in top condition, mark out boundaries, and paint turf with team logos and names before events. They must make sure that the underlying soil on fields with natural turf has the required composition to allow proper drainage and to support the grasses used on the field. Groundskeeping workers mow, water, fertilize, and aerate the fields regularly. In sports venues, they vacuum and disinfect synthetic turf after its use to prevent the growth of harmful bacteria, and they remove the turf and replace the cushioning pad periodically.

Groundskeepers in parks and recreation facilities care for lawns, trees, and shrubs; maintain playgrounds; clean buildings; and keep parking lots, picnic areas, and other public spaces free of litter. They also may erect and dismantle snow fences, and maintain swimming pools. These workers inspect buildings and equipment, make needed repairs, and keep everything freshly painted.

Workers who maintain golf courses are called *greenskeepers*. Greenskeepers do many of the same things as other groundskeepers, but they also periodically relocate the holes on putting greens to prevent uneven wear of the turf and to add interest and challenge to the game. Greenskeepers also keep canopies, benches, ball washers, and tee markers repaired and freshly painted.

Some groundskeepers specialize in caring for cemeteries and memorial gardens. They dig graves to specified depths, generally using a backhoe. They mow grass regularly, apply fertilizers and other chemicals, prune shrubs and trees, plant flowers, and remove debris from graves.

Pesticide handlers, sprayers, and applicators, vegetation mix herbicides, fungicides, or insecticides and apply them through sprays, dusts, or vapors into the soil or onto plants. Those working for chemical lawn service firms are more specialized, inspecting lawns for problems and applying fertilizers, pesticides, and other chemicals to stimulate growth and prevent or control weeds, diseases, or insect infestation. Many practice integrated pest-management techniques.

Tree trimmers and pruners cut away dead or excess branches from trees or shrubs to clear roads, sidewalks, or utilities' equipment or to improve the appearance, health, and value of trees. Some of these workers also specialize in pruning, trimming and shaping ornamental trees and shrubs for private residences, golf courses, or other institutional grounds. Tree trimmers and pruners use handsaws, pole saws, shears, and clippers. When trimming near power lines, they usually work on truck-mounted lifts and use power pruners.

Supervisors of landscaping and groundskeeping workers oversee grounds maintenance work. They prepare cost estimates, schedule work for crews on the basis of weather conditions or the availability of equipment, perform spot checks to ensure the quality of the service, and suggest changes in work procedures. In addition, supervisors train workers in their tasks; keep employees' time records and record work performed; and even assist workers when deadlines are near. Supervisors who own their own business are also known as *landscape contractors*. They also often call themselves *landscape designers* if they create landscape design plans. Landscape designers also design exterior floral displays by planting annual or perennial flowers. Some work with landscape architects. Supervisors of workers on golf courses are known as *superintendents*.

Supervisors of tree trimmers and pruners are called *arborists*. Arborists specialize in the care of individual trees, diagnosing and treating tree diseases and recommending preventative health measures. Some arborists plant trees. Most can recommend types of trees that are appropriate for a specific location, as the wrong tree in the wrong location could lead to future problems with crowding, insects, diseases, or poor growth.

Arborists are employed by cities to improve urban green space, utilities to maintain power distribution networks, companies to care for residential and commercial properties, as well as many other settings.

Work environment. Many grounds maintenance jobs are seasonal, available mainly in the spring, summer, and fall, when most planting, mowing, trimming, and cleanup are necessary. Most of the work is performed outdoors in all kinds of weather. It can be physically demanding and repetitive, involving much bending, lifting, and shoveling. Workers in landscaping and groundskeeping may be under pressure to get the job completed, especially when they are preparing for scheduled events such as athletic competitions.

Those who work with pesticides, fertilizers, and other chemicals, as well as dangerous equipment and tools such as power lawnmowers, chain saws, and power clippers, must exercise safety precautions. Workers who use motorized equipment must take care to protect their hearing.

Training, Other Qualifications, and Advancement

Most grounds maintenance workers learn on-the-job. However, some occupations may require formal training in areas such as landscape design, horticulture, or business management.

Education and training. There usually are no minimum educational requirements for entry-level positions in grounds maintenance. In 2006, most workers had a high school education or less. Short-term on-the-job training generally is sufficient to teach new hires how to operate and repair equipment such as mowers, trimmers, leaf blowers, and small tractors and to follow correct safety procedures. They must also learn proper planting and maintenance procedures for their localities. Large institutional employers such as golf courses or municipalities may supplement on-the-job training with coursework in subjects like horticulture or small engine repair for those employees showing ability and willingness to learn.

Landscaping supervisors or contractors who own their own business, arborists, and landscape designers usually need formal training in landscape design, horticulture, arboriculture, or business. A bachelor's degree may be needed for those who want to become specialists or own their own business.

Licensure. Most states require licensure or certification for workers who apply pesticides. Requirements vary but usually include passing a test on the proper use and disposal of insecticides, herbicides, and fungicides. Some states require that landscape contractors be licensed.

Other qualifications. Employers look for responsible, self-motivated individuals because grounds maintenance workers often work with little supervision. Employers want people who can learn quickly and follow instructions accurately so that time is not wasted and plants are not damaged. Workers who deal directly with customers must get along well with people.

Driving a vehicle is often needed for these jobs. If driving is required, preference is given to applicants with a driver's license, a good driving record, and experience driving a truck.

Certification and advancement. The Professional Grounds Management Society offers voluntary certification to grounds managers who have a bachelor's degree in a relevant major with at least four years of experience, including two years as a supervisor; an associate degree in a relevant major with six years of experience, including three years as a supervisor; or eight years of experience including four years as a supervisor, and no degree. Additionally, candidates for certification must pass an examination covering subjects such as equipment management, personnel management, environmental issues, turf care, ornamentals, and circulatory systems. Certification as a grounds technician is also offered by this organization.

The Professional Landcare Network offers six certifications to those who seek to demonstrate specific knowledge in an area of landscaping and grounds maintenance. Obtaining certification may be an asset for career advancement. The Tree Care Industry Association offers four levels of credentials. Currently available credentials include Tree Care Apprentice, Ground Operations Specialist, Tree Climber Specialist, and Tree Care Specialist, as well as a certification program in safety.

Laborers who demonstrate a willingness to work hard and quickly, have good communication skills, and take an interest in the business may advance to crew leader or other supervisory positions. Becoming a grounds manager or landscape contractor usually requires some formal education beyond high school and several years of progressively more responsible experience. Some workers with groundskeeping backgrounds may start their own businesses after several years of experience.

Employment

Grounds maintenance workers held about 1.5 million jobs in 2006. Employment was distributed as follows:

Landscaping and groundskeeping workers 1,220,000

First-line supervisors/managers of landscaping, lawn service, and groundskeeping workers..........202,000

Tree trimmers and pruners 41,000

Pesticide handlers, sprayers, and applicators, vegetation 31,000

Grounds maintenance workers, all other 28,000

More than one-third of the workers in grounds maintenance were employed in companies providing landscaping services to buildings and dwellings. Others worked for amusement and recreation facilities, such as golf courses and racetracks; educational institutions, both public, and private; and property management and real-estate development firms. Some were employed by local governments, installing and maintaining landscaping for parks, hospitals, and other public facilities. Almost 24 percent of grounds maintenance workers were self-employed, providing landscape maintenance directly to customers on a contract basis.

About 14 percent of grounds maintenance workers worked part time; about 9 percent were younger than age twenty.

Job Outlook

Those interested in grounds maintenance occupations should find very good job opportunities in the future. Employment of grounds maintenance workers is expected to grow faster than average for all occupations through the year 2016.

Employment change. Employment of grounds maintenance workers is expected to grow about 18 percent during the 2006–2016 decade. Grounds maintenance workers will have among the largest numbers of new jobs arise, around 270,000 over the 2006–2016 period.

More workers will be needed to keep up with increasing demand by lawn care and landscaping companies. Increased construction of office buildings, shopping malls, and residential housing and of highways and parks is expected to increase demand for grounds maintenance workers. In addition, the upkeep and renovation of existing landscaping and grounds are continuing sources of demand for grounds maintenance workers. Major institutions, such as universities and corporate headquarters, recognize the importance of good landscape design in attracting personnel and clients and are expected to use grounds maintenance services more extensively to maintain and upgrade their properties. Grounds maintenance workers working for state and local governments, however, may face budget cuts, which may affect hiring.

Homeowners are a growing source of demand for grounds maintenance workers. Many two-income households lack the time to take care of their lawns so they increasingly hire people to maintain them. Also, as the population ages, more elderly homeowners will require lawn care services to help maintain their yards. In addition, there is a growing interest by homeowners in their backyards and a desire to make yards more attractive for outdoor entertaining. With many newer homes having more and bigger windows overlooking the property, it is becoming more important to maintain and beautify the grounds.

Projections data from the National Employment Matrix

Occupational Title	SOC Code	Employment, 2006	Projected employment, 2016	Change, 2006-16	
				Number	Percent
Grounds maintenance workers and related first-line supervisors/ managers	—	1,521,000	1,791,000	270,000	18
First-line supervisors/managers of landscaping, lawn service, and groundskeeping workers	37-1012	202,000	237,000	36,000	18
Grounds maintenance workers..	37-3000	1,319,000	1,554,000	235,000	18
Landscaping and groundskeeping workers	37-3011	1,220,000	1,441,000	221,000	18
Pesticide handlers, sprayers, and applicators, vegetation	37-3012	31,000	35,000	4,300	14
Tree trimmers and pruners	37-3013	41,000	45,000	4,500	11
Grounds maintenance workers, all other.................................	37-3019	28,000	33,000	4,600	17

NOTE: Data in this table are rounded.

Job opportunities for tree trimmers and pruners should also increase as utility companies step up pruning of trees around electric lines to prevent power outages. Additionally, tree trimmers and pruners will be needed to help combat infestations caused by new species of insects from other countries. For example, ash trees from Chicago to Washington, D.C. are under threat by a pest from China, and preventative eradication may be employed to control the pest.

Job prospects. Jobs for grounds maintenance workers are increasing, and because wages for beginners are low and the work is physically demanding, many employers have difficulty attracting enough workers to fill all openings, creating very good job opportunities.

Job opportunities for nonseasonal work are more numerous in regions with temperate climates, where landscaping and lawn services are required all year. Opportunities may vary with local economic conditions.

Earnings

Median hourly earnings in May 2006 of grounds maintenance workers were as follows:

First-line supervisors/managers of landscaping,
lawn service, and groundskeeping workers $17.93

Tree trimmers and pruners 13.58

Pesticide handlers, sprayers, and applicators,
vegetation 12.84

Landscaping and groundskeeping workers 10.22

Grounds maintenance workers, all others 9.82

Median hourly earnings in the industries employing the largest numbers of landscaping and groundskeeping workers were as follows:

Local government $11.64

Services to buildings and dwellings 10.17

Landscaping services 10.17

Other amusement and recreation industries................9.47

Employment services 9.09

Related Occupations

Grounds maintenance workers perform most of their work outdoors and have some knowledge of plants and soils. Others whose jobs may require that they work outdoors are agricultural workers; farmers, ranchers, and agricultural managers; forest, conservation, and logging workers; landscape architects; and biological scientists.

Sources of Additional Information

For career and certification information on tree trimmers and pruners, contact

▸ Tree Care Industry Association, 3 Perimeter Rd., Unit I, Manchester, NH 03103-3341. Internet: http://www.treecareindustry.org

▸ International Society of Arboriculture, P.O. Box 3129, Champaign, IL 61826-3129. Internet: http://www.isa-arbor.com/ careersInArboriculture/careers.aspx

For information on work as a landscaping and groundskeeping worker, contact the following organizations:

▸ Professional Grounds Management Society, 720 Light St., Baltimore, MD 21230-3816. Internet: http://www.pgms.org

▸ Professional Landcare Network, 950 Herndon Parkway, Suite 450, Herndon, VA 20170-5528. Internet: http://www.landcarenetwork.org/

For information on becoming a licensed pesticide applicator, contact your state's Department of Agriculture or Department of Environmental Protection or Conservation.

Heating, Air-Conditioning, and Refrigeration Mechanics and Installers

(O*NET 49-9021.00, 49-9021.01, and 49-9021.02)

Significant Points

■ Employment is projected to grow as fast as the average.

■ Job prospects are expected to be excellent.

■ Employers prefer to hire those who have completed technical school training or a formal apprenticeship.

Nature of the Work

Heating and air-conditioning systems control the temperature, humidity, and the total air quality in residential, commercial, industrial, and other buildings. Refrigeration systems make it possible to store and transport food, medicine, and other perishable items. Heating, air-conditioning, and refrigeration mechanics and installers—also called technicians—install, maintain, and repair such systems. Because heating, ventilation, air-conditioning, and refrigeration systems often are referred to as HVACR systems, these workers also may be called HVACR technicians.

Heating, air-conditioning, and refrigeration systems consist of many mechanical, electrical, and electronic components, such as motors, compressors, pumps, fans, ducts, pipes, thermostats, and switches. In central forced air heating systems, for example, a furnace heats air, which is then distributed via a system of metal or fiberglass ducts. Technicians must be able to maintain, diagnose, and correct problems throughout the entire system. To do this, they adjust system controls to recommended settings and test the performance of the system using special tools and test equipment.

Technicians often specialize in either installation or maintenance and repair, although they are trained to do both. They also may specialize in doing heating work or air-conditioning or refrigeration work. Some specialize in one type of equipment—for example, hydronics (water-based heating systems), solar panels, or commercial refrigeration. Some technicians also sell service contracts to their clients. Service contracts provide for regular maintenance of the heating and cooling systems and they help to reduce the seasonal fluctuations of this type of work.

Technicians follow blueprints or other specifications to install oil, gas, electric, solid-fuel, and multiple-fuel heating systems and air-conditioning systems. After putting the equipment in place, they install fuel and water supply lines, air ducts and vents, pumps, and other components. They may connect electrical wiring and controls and check the unit for proper operation. To ensure the proper functioning of the system, furnace installers often use combustion test equipment, such as carbon dioxide testers, carbon monoxide testers, combustion analyzers, and oxygen testers. These tests ensure that the system will operate safely and at peak efficiency.

After a furnace or air-conditioning unit has been installed, technicians often perform routine maintenance and repair work to keep the systems operating efficiently. They may adjust burners and blowers and check for leaks. If the system is not operating properly, they check the thermostat, burner nozzles, controls or other parts to diagnose and correct the problem.

Technicians also install and maintain heat pumps, which are similar to air conditioners but can be reversed so that they both heat and cool a home. Because of the added complexity and the fact that they run both in summer and winter, these systems often require more maintenance and need to be replaced more frequently than traditional furnaces and air conditioners.

During the summer, when heating systems are not being used, heating equipment technicians do maintenance work, such as replacing filters, ducts, and other parts of the system that may accumulate dust and impurities during the operating season. During the winter, air-conditioning mechanics inspect the systems and do required maintenance, such as overhauling compressors.

Refrigeration mechanics install, service, and repair industrial and commercial refrigerating systems and a variety of refrigeration equipment. They follow blueprints, design specifications, and manufacturers' instructions to install motors, compressors, condensing units, evaporators, piping, and other components. They connect this equipment to the ductwork, refrigerant lines, and electrical power source. After making the connections, they charge the system with refrigerant, check it for proper operation and leaks, and program control systems.

When air-conditioning and refrigeration technicians service equipment, they must use care to conserve, recover, and recycle the refrigerants used in air-conditioning and refrigeration systems. The release of these refrigerants can be harmful to the environment. Technicians conserve the refrigerant by making sure that there are no leaks in the system; they recover it by venting the refrigerant into proper cylinders; they recycle it for reuse with special filter-dryers; or they ensure that the refrigerant is properly disposed of.

Heating, air-conditioning, and refrigeration mechanics and installers are adept at using a variety of tools, including hammers, wrenches, metal snips, electric drills, pipe cutters and benders, measurement gauges, and acetylene torches, to work with refrigerant lines and air ducts. They use voltmeters, thermometers, pressure gauges, manometers, and other testing devices to check airflow, refrigerant pressure, electrical circuits, burners, and other components.

Other craft workers sometimes install or repair cooling and heating systems. For example, on a large air-conditioning installation job, especially where workers are covered by union contracts, ductwork might be done by sheet metal workers and duct installers; electrical work by electricians; and installation of piping, condensers, and other components by pipelayers, plumbers, pipefitters, and steamfitters. Home appliance repairers usually service room air-conditioners and household refrigerators. (Additional information about many of these occupations appears elsewhere in this book.)

Work environment. Heating, air-conditioning, and refrigeration mechanics and installers work in homes, retail establishments, hospitals, office buildings, and factories—anywhere there is climate-control equipment that needs to be installed, repaired, or serviced. They may be assigned to specific job sites at the beginning of each day or may be dispatched to a variety of locations if they are making service calls.

Technicians may work outside in cold or hot weather or in buildings that are uncomfortable because the air-conditioning or heating equipment is broken. In addition, technicians might work in awkward or cramped positions and sometimes are required to work in high places. Hazards include electrical shock, burns, muscle strains, and other injuries from handling heavy equipment. Appropriate safety equipment is necessary when handling refrigerants because contact can cause skin damage, frostbite, or blindness. Inhalation of refrigerants when working in confined spaces also is a possible hazard.

The majority of mechanics and installers work at least a 40-hour week. During peak seasons, they often work overtime or irregular hours. Maintenance workers, including those who provide maintenance services under contract, often work evening or weekend shifts and are on call. Most employers try to provide a full work week year-round by scheduling both installation and maintenance work, and many manufacturers and contractors now provide or even require year-round service contracts. In most shops that service both heating and air-conditioning equipment, employment is stable throughout the year.

Training, Other Qualifications, and Advancement

Because of the increasing sophistication of heating, air-conditioning, and refrigeration systems, employers prefer to hire those who have completed technical school training or a formal apprenticeship. Some mechanics and installers, however, still learn the trade informally on the job.

Education and training. Many secondary and postsecondary technical and trade schools, junior and community colleges, and the U.S. Armed Forces offer six-month to two-year programs in heating, air-conditioning, and refrigeration. Students study theory of temperature control, equipment design and construction, and electronics. They also learn the basics of installation, maintenance, and repair. Three accrediting agencies have set academic standards for HVACR programs. These accrediting bodies are HVAC Excellence, the National Center for Construction Education and Research, and the Partnership for Air-Conditioning, Heating, and Refrigeration Accreditation. After completing these programs, new technicians generally need between an additional six months and two years of field experience before they are considered proficient.

Many technicians train through apprenticeships. Apprenticeship programs frequently are run by joint committees representing local chapters of the Air-Conditioning Contractors of America, the Mechanical Contractors Association of America, Plumbing-Heating-Cooling Contractors—National Association, and locals of the sheet metal workers' International Association or the United Association of Journeymen and Apprentices of the Plumbing and Pipefitting Industry of the United States and Canada. Local chapters of the Associated Builders and Contractors and the National Association of Home Builders sponsor other apprenticeship programs. Formal apprenticeship programs normally last three to five years and combine paid on-the-job training with classroom instruction. Classes include subjects such as the use and care of tools, safety practices, blueprint reading, and the theory and design of heating, ventilation, air-conditioning, and refrigeration systems. In addition to understanding how systems work, technicians must learn about refrigerant products and the legislation and regulations that govern their use.

Applicants for apprenticeships must have a high school diploma or equivalent. Math and reading skills are essential. After completing an apprenticeship program, technicians are considered skilled trades workers and capable of working alone. These programs are also a pathway to certification and, in some cases, college credits.

Those who acquire their skills on the job usually begin by assisting experienced technicians. They may begin by performing simple tasks such as carrying materials, insulating refrigerant lines, or cleaning furnaces. In time, they move on to more difficult tasks, such as cutting and soldering pipes and sheet metal and checking electrical and electronic circuits.

Several organizations have begun to offer basic self-study, classroom, and Internet courses for individuals with limited experience.

Licensure. Heating, air-conditioning, and refrigeration mechanics and installers are required to be licensed by some states and localities. Requirements for licensure vary greatly, but all states or localities that require a license have a test that must be passed. The contents of these tests vary by state or locality, with some requiring extensive knowledge of electrical codes and others focusing more on HVACR-specific knowledge. Completion of an apprenticeship program or two to five years of experience are also common requirements.

In addition, all technicians who purchase or work with refrigerants must be certified in their proper handling. To become certified to purchase and handle refrigerants, technicians must pass a written examination specific to the type of work in which they specialize. The three possible areas of certification are: Type I—servicing small appliances; Type II—high-pressure refrigerants; and Type III—low-pressure refrigerants. Exams are administered by organizations approved by the U.S. Environmental Protection Agency, such as trade schools, unions, contractor associations, or building groups.

Other qualifications. High school courses in shop math, mechanical drawing, applied physics and chemistry, electronics, blueprint reading, and computer applications provide a good background for those interested in entering this occupation. Some knowledge of plumbing or electrical work also is helpful. A basic understanding of electronics is becoming more important because of the increasing use of electronics in equipment controls. Because technicians frequently deal directly with the public, they should be courteous and tactful, especially when dealing with an aggravated customer. They also should be in good physical condition because they sometimes have to lift and move heavy equipment.

Certification and advancement. Throughout the learning process, technicians may have to take a number of tests that measure their skills. For those with relevant coursework and less than one year of experience, the industry has developed a series of exams to test basic competency in residential heating and cooling, light commercial heating and cooling, and commercial refrigeration. These are referred to as "Entry-level" certification exams and are commonly conducted at both secondary and postsecondary technical and trade schools. HVACR technicians who have at least one year of experience performing installations and two years of experience performing maintenance and repair can take a number of different tests to certify their competency in working with specific types of equipment, such as oil-burning furnaces. These tests are offered through the Refrigeration Service Engineers Society, HVAC Excellence, Carbon Monoxide Safety Association, Air-Conditioning and Refrigeration Safety Coalition, and North American Technician Excellence, Inc., among others. Employers increasingly recommend taking and passing these tests and obtaining certification; doing so may increase advancement opportunities.

Advancement usually takes the form of higher wages. Some technicians, however, may advance to positions as supervisor or service manager. Others may move into sales and marketing. Still others may become building superintendents, cost estimators, system test and balance specialists, or, with the necessary certification, teachers. Those with sufficient money and managerial skill can open their own contracting business.

Employment

Heating, air-conditioning, and refrigeration mechanics and installers held about 292,000 jobs in 2006; about 55 percent worked for plumbing, heating, and air-conditioning contractors. The rest were employed in a variety of industries throughout the country, reflecting a widespread dependence on climate-control systems. Some worked for fuel oil dealers, refrigeration and air-conditioning service and repair shops, schools, and stores that sell heating and air-conditioning systems. Local governments, the federal government, hospitals, office buildings, and other organizations that operate large air-conditioning, refrigeration, or heating systems also employed these workers. About 13 percent of these workers were self-employed.

Job Outlook

With average job growth and numerous expected retirements, heating, air-conditioning, and refrigeration mechanics and installers should have excellent employment opportunities.

Projections data from the National Employment Matrix

Occupational Title	SOC Code	Employment, 2006	Projected employment, 2016	Change, 2006-16	
				Number	Percent
Heating, air conditioning, and refrigeration mechanics and installers	49-9021	292,000	317,000	25,000	9

NOTE: Data in this table are rounded.

Employment change. Employment of heating, air-conditioning, and refrigeration mechanics and installers is projected to increase 9 percent during the 2006–2016 decade, as fast as the average for all occupations. As the population and stock of buildings grows, so does the demand for residential, commercial, and industrial climate-control systems. Residential HVACR systems generally need replacement after 10 to 15 years; the large number of homes built in recent years will enter this replacement timeframe by 2016. The increased complexity of HVACR systems, which increases the possibility that equipment may malfunction, also will create opportunities for service technicians. A growing focus on improving indoor air quality and the increasing use of refrigerated equipment by a growing number of stores and gasoline stations that sell food should also create more jobs for heating, air-conditioning, and refrigeration technicians.

Concern for the environment has prompted the development of new energy-saving heating and air-conditioning systems. An emphasis on better energy management should lead to the replacement of older systems and the installation of newer, more efficient systems in existing homes and buildings. Also, demand for maintenance and service work should increase as businesses and homeowners strive to keep increasingly complex systems operating at peak efficiency. Regulations prohibiting the discharge and production of older types of refrigerants that pollute the atmosphere should continue to result in the need to replace many existing air conditioning systems or to modify them to use new environmentally safe refrigerants. The pace of replacement in the commercial and industrial sectors will quicken if Congress or individual states change tax rules designed to encourage companies to buy new HVACR equipment.

Job prospects. Job prospects for heating, air-conditioning, and refrigeration mechanics and installers are expected to be excellent, particularly for those who have completed training from an accredited technical school or a formal apprenticeship. Job opportunities should be best in the fastest growing areas of the country. A growing number of retirements of highly skilled technicians are expected to generate many job openings. Many contractors have reported problems finding enough workers to meet the demand for service and installation of HVACR systems.

Technicians who specialize in installation work may experience periods of unemployment when the level of new construction activity declines, but maintenance and repair work usually remains relatively stable. People and businesses depend on their climate-control or refrigeration systems and must keep them in good working order, regardless of economic conditions.

Earnings

Median hourly wage-and-salary earnings of heating, air-conditioning, and refrigeration mechanics and installers were $18.11 in May 2006. The middle 50 percent earned between $14.12 and $23.32 an hour. The lowest 10 percent earned less than $11.38, and the top 10 percent earned more than $28.57. Median hourly earnings in the industries employing the largest numbers of heating, air-conditioning, and refrigeration mechanics and installers were

Hardware, and plumbing and heating equipment
and supplies merchant wholesalers $20.53

Commercial and industrial machinery and
equipment (except automotive and electronic)
repair and maintenance 19.95

Direct selling establishments 19.12

Plumbing, heating, and air-conditioning
contractors 17.46

Electrical contractors 16.74

Apprentices usually begin at about 50 percent of the wage rate paid to experienced workers. As they gain experience and improve their skills, they receive periodic increases until they reach the wage rate of experienced workers.

Heating, air-conditioning, and refrigeration mechanics and installers enjoy a variety of employer-sponsored benefits. In addition to typical benefits such as health insurance and pension plans, some employers pay for work-related training and provide uniforms, company vans, and tools.

About 14 percent of heating, air-conditioning, and refrigeration mechanics and installers are members of a union. The unions to which the greatest numbers of mechanics and installers belong are the sheet metal workers International Association and the United Association of Journeymen and Apprentices of the Plumbing and Pipefitting Industry of the United States and Canada.

Related Occupations

Heating, air-conditioning, and refrigeration mechanics and installers work with sheet metal and piping, and repair machinery, such as electrical motors, compressors, and burners. Other workers who have similar skills include boilermakers; home appliance repairers; electricians; sheet metal workers; and pipelayers, plumbers, pipefitters, and steamfitters.

Sources of Additional Information

For more information about opportunities for training, certification, and employment in this trade, contact local vocational and technical schools; local heating, air-conditioning, and refrigeration contractors; a local of the unions or organizations previously mentioned; a local joint union-management apprenticeship committee; or the nearest office of the state employment service or apprenticeship agency. You can also find information on the registered apprenticeship system with links to state apprenticeship programs on the U.S. Department of Labor's Web site: http://www.doleta.gov/atles_bat. Apprenticeship information is also available from the U.S. Department of Labor's toll free helpline: (877) 872-5627.

For information on career opportunities, training, and technician certification, contact

▸ Air-Conditioning Contractors of America, 2800 Shirlington Rd., Suite 300, Arlington, VA 22206. Internet: http://www.acca.org

▸ Air-Conditioning and Refrigeration Institute, 4100 North Fairfax Dr., Suite 200, Arlington, VA 22203. Internet: http://www.coolcareers.org and http://www.ari.org

▸ Associated Builders and Contractors, Workforce Development Department, 4250 North Fairfax Dr., 9th Floor, Arlington, VA 22203. Internet: http://www.trytools.org

▸ Carbon Monoxide Safety Association, P.O. Box 669, Eastlake, CO 80614. Internet: http://www.cosafety.org

▸ Home Builders Institute, National Association of Home Builders, 1201 15th St. NW, 6th Floor, Washington, DC 20005. Internet: http://www.hbi.org

▸ HVAC Excellence, P.O. Box 491, Mt. Prospect, IL 60056. Internet: http://www.hvacexcellence.org

▸ Mechanical Contractors Association of America, Mechanical Service Contractors of America, 1385 Piccard Dr., Rockville, MD 20850. Internet: http://www.mcaa.org and http://www.mcaa.org/msca

▸ National Center for Construction Education and Research, P.O. Box 141104, Gainesville, FL 32601. Internet: http://www.nccer.org

▸ National Occupational Competency Testing Institute. Internet: http://www.nocti.org

▸ North American Technician Excellence, 4100 North Fairfax Dr., Suite 210, Arlington, VA 22203. Internet: http://www.natex.org

▸ Plumbing-Heating-Cooling Contractors, 180 S. Washington, St., P.O. Box 6808, Falls Church, VA 22046. Internet: http://www.phccweb.org org

▸ Refrigeration Service Engineers Society, 1666 Rand Rd., Des Plaines, IL 60016. Internet: http://www.rses.org

▸ Sheet Metal and Air-Conditioning Contractors National Association, 4201 Lafayette Center Dr., Chantilly, VA 20151. Internet: http://www.smacna.org

▸ United Association of Journeymen and Apprentices of the Plumbing and Pipefitting Industry, 901 Massachusetts Ave. NW, Washington, DC 20001. Internet: http://www.ua.org

Industrial Machinery Mechanics and Maintenance Workers

(O*NET 49-9041.00 and 49-9043.00)

Significant Points

■ Most of these workers are employed in manufacturing, but a growing number work for industrial equipment dealers and repair shops.

■ Machinery maintenance workers learn on the job, while industrial machinery mechanics usually need some education after high school plus experience working on specific machines.

■ Applicants with broad skills in machine repair and maintenance should have favorable job prospects.

Nature of the Work

Imagine an automobile assembly line: a large conveyor system moves unfinished automobiles down the line, giant robotic welding arms bond the different body panels together, hydraulic lifts move the motor into the body of the car, and giant presses stamp body parts from flat sheets of steel. All of these machines—the hydraulic lifts, the robotic welders, the conveyor system, and the giant presses—sometimes break down. When the assembly line stops because a machine breaks down, it costs the company money. Industrial machinery mechanics and machinery maintenance workers maintain and repair these very different, and often very expensive, machines.

The most basic tasks are performed by *machinery maintenance workers*. These employees are responsible for cleaning and lubricating machinery, performing basic diagnostic tests, checking performance, and testing damaged machine parts to determine whether major repairs are necessary. In carrying out these tasks, maintenance workers must follow machine specifications and adhere to maintenance schedules. Maintenance workers may perform minor repairs, but major repairs are generally left to machinery mechanics.

Industrial machinery mechanics, also called industrial machinery repairers or maintenance machinists, are highly skilled workers who maintain and repair machinery in a plant or factory. To do this effectively, they must be able to detect minor problems and correct them before they become major. Machinery mechanics use technical manuals, their understanding of the equipment, and careful observation to discover the cause of the problem. For example, after hearing a vibration from a machine, the mechanic must decide whether it is due to worn belts, weak motor bearings, or some other problem. Mechanics need years of training and experience to diagnose problems, but computerized diagnostic systems and vibration analysis techniques provide aid in determining the nature of the problem.

After diagnosing the problem, the industrial machinery mechanic disassembles the equipment to repair or replace the necessary parts. When repairing electronically controlled machinery, mechanics may work closely with electronic repairers or electricians who maintain the machine's electronic parts. (Information about electricians appears elsewhere in this book.) Increasingly, mechanics are expected to have the electrical, electronics, and computer programming skills to repair sophisticated equipment on their own. Once a repair is made, mechanics perform tests to ensure that the machine is running smoothly.

Primary responsibilities of industrial machinery mechanics also often include preventive maintenance and the installation of new machinery. For example, they adjust and calibrate automated manufacturing equipment, such as industrial robots. Part of setting up equipment is programming the programmable logic control (PLC), a frequently used type of computer used as the control system for automated industrial machines. Situating and installing machinery has traditionally been the job of millwrights, but as plants retool and invest in new equipment, companies increasingly rely on mechanics to do this task for some machinery.

Industrial machinery mechanics and machinery maintenance workers use a variety of tools to perform repairs and preventive maintenance. They may use handtools to adjust a motor or a chain hoist to lift a heavy printing press off the ground. When replacements for broken or defective parts are not readily available, or when a machine must be quickly returned to production, mechanics may

© **JIST Works**

create a new part using lathes, grinders, or drill presses. Mechanics use catalogs to order replacement parts and often follow blueprints, technical manuals, and engineering specifications to maintain and fix equipment. By keeping complete and up-to-date records, mechanics try to anticipate trouble and service equipment before factory production is interrupted.

Work environment. In production facilities, these workers are subject to common shop injuries such as cuts, bruises, and strains. They also may work in awkward positions, including on top of ladders or in cramped conditions under large machinery, which exposes them to additional hazards. They often use protective equipment such as hardhats, safety glasses, steel-tipped shoes, hearing protectors, and belts.

Because factories and other facilities cannot afford to have industrial machinery out of service for long periods, mechanics may be on call or assigned to work nights or on weekends. Overtime is common among full-time industrial machinery mechanics; about 30 percent work over 40 hours a week.

Training, Other Qualifications, and Advancement

Machinery maintenance workers can usually get a job with little more than a high school diploma or its equivalent—most learn on the job. Industrial machinery mechanics, on the other hand, usually need some education after high school plus experience working on specific machines before they can be considered a mechanic.

Education and training. Employers prefer to hire those who have taken courses in mechanical drawing, mathematics, blueprint reading, computer programming, or electronics. Entry-level machinery maintenance worker positions generally require a high school diploma, GED, or its equivalent. However, employers increasingly prefer to hire machinery maintenance workers with some training in industrial technology or an area of it, such as fluid power. Machinery maintenance workers typically receive on-the-job training lasting a few months to a year to perform routine tasks, such as setting up, cleaning, lubricating, and starting machinery. This training may be offered by experienced workers, professional trainers, or representatives of equipment manufacturers.

Industrial machinery mechanics usually need a year or more of formal education and training after high school to learn the growing range of mechanical and technical skills that they need. While mechanics used to specialize in one area, such as hydraulics or electronics, many factories now require every mechanic to have knowledge of electricity, electronics, hydraulics, and computer programming.

Workers can get this training in a number of different ways. Experience in the military repairing equipment, particularly ships, is highly valued by employers. Also, two-year associate degree programs in industrial maintenance are good preparation. Some employers offer four-year apprenticeship programs that combine classroom instruction with paid on-the-job-training. Apprenticeship programs usually are sponsored by a local trade union. Other mechanics may start as helpers or in other factory jobs and learn the skills of the trade informally and by taking courses offered through their employer. Classroom instruction focuses on subjects such as shop mathematics, blueprint reading, welding, electronics, and computer training. In addition to classroom training, it is important that mechanics train on the specific machines they will repair. They can get this training

on the job, through dealer or manufacturer's representatives or in a classroom.

Other qualifications. Mechanical aptitude and manual dexterity are important for workers in this occupation. Good reading comprehension is also necessary to understand the technical manuals of a wide range of machines. And, good physical conditioning and agility are necessary because repairers sometimes have to lift heavy objects or climb to reach equipment.

Advancement. Opportunities for advancement vary by specialty. Machinery maintenance workers, if they take classes and gain additional skills, may advance to industrial machinery mechanic or supervisor. Industrial machinery mechanics also advance by working with more complicated equipment and gaining additional repair skills. The most highly skilled repairers can be promoted to supervisor, master mechanic, or millwright.

Employment

Industrial machinery mechanics and maintenance workers held about 345,000 jobs in 2006. Of these, 261,000 were held by the more highly skilled industrial machinery mechanics, while machinery maintenance workers accounted for 84,000 jobs. The majority of both types of workers were employed in the manufacturing sector in industries such as food processing and chemical, fabricated metal product, machinery, and motor vehicle and parts manufacturing. Additionally, about 9 percent work in wholesale trade, mostly for dealers of industrial equipment. Manufacturers often rely on these dealers to make complex repairs to specific machines. About 7 percent of mechanics work for the commercial and industrial machinery and equipment repair and maintenance industry, often making site visits to companies to repair equipment. Local governments employ a number of machinery maintenance workers, but few mechanics.

Job Outlook

Employment of industrial machinery mechanics and maintenance workers is projected to grow about as fast as average, and job prospects should be favorable for those with a variety of repair skills.

Employment change. Employment of industrial machinery mechanics and maintenance workers is expected to grow 7 percent from 2006 to 2016, about as fast as the average for all occupations. As factories become increasingly automated, these workers will be needed to maintain and repair the automated equipment. However, many new machines are more reliable and capable of self-diagnosis, making repairs easier and quicker and somewhat slowing the growth of repairer jobs.

Industrial machinery mechanics and maintenance workers are not as affected by changes in production levels as other manufacturing workers. During slack periods, when some plant workers are laid off, mechanics often are retained to do major overhaul jobs and to keep expensive machinery in working order. In addition, replacing highly skilled and experienced industrial maintenance workers is quite difficult, which discourages lay-offs.

Job prospects. Applicants with broad skills in machine repair and maintenance should have favorable job prospects. Many mechanics are expected to retire in coming years, and employers have reported difficulty in recruiting young workers with the necessary skills to be industrial machinery mechanics. In addition to openings from

Projections data from the National Employment Matrix

Occupational Title	SOC Code	Employment, 2006	Projected employment, 2016	Change, 2006-16	
				Number	Percent
Industrial machinery mechanics and maintenance workers..............	—	345,000	368,000	23,000	7
Industrial machinery mechanics	49-9041	261,000	284,000	24,000	9
Maintenance workers, machinery	49-9043	84,000	83,000	-900	-1

NOTE: Data in this table are rounded.

growth, most job openings will stem from the need to replace workers who transfer to other occupations or who retire or leave the labor force for other reasons.

Earnings

Median hourly wage-and-salary earnings of industrial machinery mechanics were $19.74 in May 2006. The middle 50 percent earned between $15.87 and $24.46. The lowest 10 percent earned less than $12.84, and the highest 10 percent earned more than $29.85.

Machinery maintenance workers earned somewhat less than the higher skilled industrial machinery mechanics. Median hourly wage-and-salary earnings of machinery maintenance workers were $16.61 in May 2006. The middle 50 percent earned between $12.91 and $21.53. The lowest 10 percent earned less than $10.29, and the highest 10 percent earned more than $26.46.

Earnings vary by industry and geographic region. Median hourly wage-and-salary earnings in the industries employing the largest numbers of industrial machinery mechanics are:

Electric power generation, transmission, and
distribution $26.02
Motor vehicle parts manufacturing...........................24.97
Machinery, equipment, and supplies merchant
wholesalers 18.94
Plastics product manufacturing 18.79
Commercial and industrial machinery and equipment
(except automotive and electronic) repair and
maintenance 17.78

About 18 percent of industrial machinery mechanics and maintenance workers are union members. Labor unions that represent these workers include the United Steelworkers of America; the United Auto Workers; the International Association of Machinists and Aerospace Workers; the United Brotherhood of Carpenters and Joiners of America; and the International Union of Electronic, Electrical, Salaried, Machine, and Furniture Workers-Communications Workers of America.

Related Occupations

Other occupations that involve repairing and maintaining industrial machinery include machinists; maintenance and repair workers, general; millwrights; electrical and electronics installers and repairers; electricians; and pipelayers, plumbers, pipefitters, and steamfitters.

Sources of Additional Information

Information about employment and apprenticeship opportunities may be obtained from local employers and from local offices of the state employment service. For further information on apprenticeship

programs, write to the Apprenticeship Council of your state's labor department or local firms that employ machinery mechanics and repairers. You can also find information on registered apprenticeships, together with links to state apprenticeship programs, on the U.S. Department of Labor's Web site: http://www.doleta.gov/atels_bat. Apprenticeship information is also available from the U.S. Department of Labor's toll free helpline: (877) 872-5627.

Interior Designers

(O*NET 27-1025.00)

Significant Points

■ Keen competition is expected for jobs because many talented individuals are attracted to this occupation.

■ About 26 percent are self employed.

■ Postsecondary education—especially a bachelor's degree—is recommended for entry-level positions; some states license interior designers.

Nature of the Work

Interior designers draw upon many disciplines to enhance the function, safety, and aesthetics of interior spaces. Their main concerns are with how different colors, textures, furniture, lighting, and space work together to meet the needs of a building's occupants. Designers plan interior spaces of almost every type of building, including offices, airport terminals, theaters, shopping malls, restaurants, hotels, schools, hospitals, and private residences. Good design can boost office productivity, increase sales, attract a more affluent clientele, provide a more relaxing hospital stay, or increase a building's market value.

Traditionally, most interior designers focused on decorating—choosing a style and color palette and then selecting appropriate furniture, floor and window coverings, artwork, and lighting. However, an increasing number of designers are becoming involved in architectural detailing, such as crown molding and built-in bookshelves, and in planning layouts of buildings undergoing renovation, including helping to determine the location of windows, stairways, escalators, and walkways.

Interior designers must be able to read blueprints, understand building and fire codes, and know how to make space accessible to people who are disabled. Designers frequently collaborate with architects, electricians, and building contractors to ensure that designs are safe and meet construction requirements.

Whatever space they are working on, almost all designers follow the same process. The first step, known as programming, is to determine the client's needs and wishes. The designer usually meets face-to-face with the client to find out how the space will be used and to get an idea of the client's preferences and budget. For example, the designer might inquire about a family's cooking habits if the family is remodeling a kitchen or ask about a store or restaurant's target customer in order to pick an appropriate motif. The designer also will visit the space to take inventory of existing furniture and equipment and identify positive attributes of the space and potential problems.

Then, the designer formulates a design plan and estimates costs. Today, designs often are created with the use of computer-aided design (CAD), which provides more detail and easier corrections than sketches made by hand. Once the designer completes the proposed design, he or she will present it to the client and make revisions based on the client's input.

When the design concept is decided upon, the designer will begin specifying the materials, finishes, and furnishings required, such as furniture, lighting, flooring, wall covering, and artwork. Depending on the complexity of the project, the designer also might submit drawings for approval by a construction inspector to ensure that the design meets building codes. If a project requires structural work, the designer works with an architect or engineer for that part of the project. Most designs also require the hiring of contractors to do technical work, such as lighting, plumbing, or electrical wiring. Often designers choose contractors and write work contracts.

Finally, the designer develops a timeline for the project, coordinates contractor work schedules, and makes sure work is completed on time. The designer oversees the installation of the design elements, and after the project is complete, the designer, together with the client, pay follow-up visits to the building site to ensure that the client is satisfied. If the client is not satisfied, the designer makes corrections.

Designers who work for furniture or home and garden stores sell merchandise in addition to offering design services. In-store designers provide services, such as selecting a style and color scheme that fits the client's needs or finding suitable accessories and lighting, similar to those offered by other interior designers. However, in-store designers rarely visit clients' spaces and use only a particular store's products or catalogs.

Interior designers sometimes supervise assistants who carry out their plans and perform administrative tasks, such as reviewing catalogues and ordering samples. Designers who run their own businesses also may devote considerable time to developing new business contacts, examining equipment and space needs, and attending to business matters.

Although most interior designers do many kinds of projects, some specialize in one area of interior design. Some specialize in the type of building space—usually residential or commercial—while others specialize in a certain design element or type of client, such as health care facilities. The most common specialties of this kind are lighting, kitchen and bath, and closet designs. However, designers can specialize in almost any area of design, including acoustics and noise abatement, security, electronics and home theaters, home spas, and indoor gardens.

Three areas of design that are becoming increasingly popular are ergonomic design, elder design, and environmental—or green—design. Ergonomic design involves designing work spaces and furniture that emphasize good posture and minimize muscle strain on the body. Elder design involves planning interior space to aid in the movement of people who are elderly and disabled. Green design involves selecting furniture and carpets that are free of chemicals

and hypoallergenic and selecting construction materials that are energy efficient or are made from renewable resources

Work environment. Working conditions and places of employment vary. Interior designers employed by large corporations or design firms generally work regular hours in well-lighted and comfortable settings. Designers in smaller design consulting firms or those who freelance generally work on a contract, or job, basis. They frequently adjust their workday to suit their clients' schedules and deadlines, meeting with clients during evening or weekend hours when necessary. Consultants and self-employed designers tend to work longer hours and in smaller, more congested environments.

Interior designers may work under stress to meet deadlines, stay on budget, and please clients. Self-employed designers also are under pressure to find new clients to maintain a steady income.

Designers may work in their own offices or studios or in clients' homes or offices. They also may travel to other locations, such as showrooms, design centers, clients' exhibit sites, and manufacturing facilities. With the increased speed and sophistication of computers and advanced communications networks, designers may form international design teams, serve a more geographically dispersed clientele, research design alternatives by using information on the Internet, and purchase supplies electronically.

Training, Other Qualifications, and Advancement

Postsecondary education, especially a bachelor's degree, is recommended for entry-level positions in interior design. Two-year and three-year programs also are available. Some states license interior designers.

Education and training. Postsecondary education, especially a bachelor's degree, is recommended for entry-level positions in interior design. Training programs are available from professional design schools or from colleges and universities and usually take two to four years to complete. Graduates of two-year or three-year programs are awarded certificates or associate degrees in interior design and normally qualify as assistants to interior designers upon graduation. Graduates with a bachelor's degree usually qualify for a formal design apprenticeship program.

The National Association of Schools of Art and Design accredits approximately 250 postsecondary institutions with programs in art and design. Most of these schools award a degree in interior design. Applicants may be required to submit sketches and other examples of their artistic ability. Basic coursework includes computer-aided design (CAD), drawing, perspective, spatial planning, color and fabrics, furniture design, architecture, ergonomics, ethics, and psychology.

The National Council for Interior Design Accreditation also accredits interior design programs that lead to a bachelor's degree. In 2007, there were 145 accredited bachelor's degree programs in interior design in the United States; most are part of schools or departments of art, architecture, and home economics.

After the completion of formal training, interior designers will enter a one-year to three-year apprenticeship to gain experience before taking a licensing exam. Most apprentices work in design or architecture firms under the supervision of an experienced designer. Apprentices also may choose to gain experience working as an in-store designer in furniture stores. The National Council of Interior

Design offers the Interior Design Experience Program, which helps entry-level interior designers gain valuable work experience by supervising work experience and offering mentoring services and workshops to new designers.

Licensure. Twenty-three states, the District of Columbia, and Puerto Rico register or license interior designers. The National Council administers the licensing exam for Interior Design Qualification. To be eligible to take the exam, applicants must have at least six years of combined education and experience in interior design, of which at least two years must be postsecondary education in design.

Once candidates have passed the qualifying exam, they are granted the title of Certified, Registered, or Licensed Interior Designer, depending on the state. Continuing education is required to maintain licensure.

Other qualifications. Membership in a professional association is one indication of an interior designer's qualifications and professional standing. The American Society of Interior Designers is the largest professional association for interior designers in the United States. Interior designers can qualify for membership with at least a two-year degree and work experience.

Employers increasingly prefer interior designers who are familiar with computer-aided design software and the basics of architecture and engineering to ensure that their designs meet building safety codes.

In addition to possessing technical knowledge, interior designers must be creative, imaginative, and persistent and must be able to communicate their ideas visually, verbally, and in writing. Because tastes in style can change quickly, designers need to be well read, open to new ideas and influences, and quick to react to changing trends. Problem-solving skills and the ability to work independently and under pressure are additional important traits. People in this field need self-discipline to start projects on their own, to budget their time, and to meet deadlines and production schedules. Good business sense and sales ability also are important, especially for those who freelance or run their own business.

Certification and advancement. Optional certifications in kitchen and bath design are available from the National Kitchen and Bath Association. The association offers three different levels of certification for kitchen and bath designers, each achieved through training seminars and certification exams.

Beginning interior designers receive on-the-job training and normally need one to three years of training before they can advance to higher level positions. Experienced designers in large firms may advance to chief designer, design department head, or some other supervisory position. Some experienced designers open their own firms or decide to specialize in one aspect of interior design. Other designers leave the occupation to become teachers in schools of design or in colleges and universities. Many faculty members continue to consult privately or operate small design studios to complement their classroom activities.

Employment

Interior designers held about 72,000 jobs in 2006. Approximately 26 percent were self-employed. About 26 percent of interior designers worked in specialized design services. The rest of the interior designers provided design services in architectural and landscape architectural services, furniture and home-furnishing stores, building material and supplies dealers, and residential building construction

companies. Many interior designers also performed freelance work in addition to holding a salaried job in interior design or another occupation.

Job Outlook

Employment of interior designers is expected to be faster than average; however, keen competition for jobs is expected.

Employment change. Employment of interior designers is expected to grow 19 percent from 2006 to 2016, faster than average for all occupations. Economic expansion, growing homeowner wealth, and an increasing interest in interior design will increase demand for designers.

Recent increases in homeowner wealth and the growing popularity of home improvement television programs have increased demand for residential design services. Homeowners have been using the equity in their homes to finance new additions, remodel aging kitchens and bathrooms, and update the general décor of the home. Many homeowners also have requested design help in creating year-round outdoor living spaces.

However, this same growth in home improvement television programs and discount furniture stores has spurred a trend in do-it-yourself design, which could hamper employment growth of designers. Nevertheless, some clients will still hire designers for initial consultations.

Demand from businesses in the hospitality industry—hotels, resorts, and restaurants—is expected to be high because of an expected increase in tourism. Demand for interior design services from the health care industry also is expected to be high because of an anticipated increase in demand for facilities that will accommodate the aging population. Designers will be needed to make these facilities as comfortable and homelike as possible for patients.

Some interior designers choose to specialize in one design element to create a niche for themselves in an increasingly competitive market. The demand for kitchen and bath design is growing in response to the growing demand for home remodeling. Designs using the latest technology in, for example, home theaters, state-of-the-art conference facilities, and security systems are expected to be especially popular. In addition, demand for home spas, indoor gardens, and outdoor living space should continue to increase.

Extensive knowledge of ergonomics and green design are expected to be in demand. Ergonomic design has gained in popularity with the growth in the elderly population and workplace safety requirements. The public's growing awareness of environmental quality and the growing number of individuals with allergies and asthma are expected to increase the demand for green design.

Job prospects. Interior designers are expected to face keen competition for available positions because many talented individuals are attracted to this profession. Individuals with little or no formal training in interior design, as well as those lacking creativity and perseverance, will find it very difficult to establish and maintain a career in this occupation.

As the economy grows, more private businesses and consumers will request the services of interior designers. However, design services are considered a luxury expense and may be subject to fluctuations in the economy. For example, decreases in consumer and business income and spending caused by a slow economy can have a detrimental effect on employment of interior designers.

Projections data from the National Employment Matrix

Occupational Title	SOC Code	Employment, 2006	Projected employment, 2016	Change, 2006-2016	
				Number	Percent
Interior designers	27-1025	72,000	86,000	14,000	19

NOTE: Data in this table are rounded.

Earnings

Median annual earnings for wage and salary interior designers were $42,260 in May 2006. The middle 50 percent earned between $31,830 and $57,230. The lowest 10 percent earned less than $24,270, and the highest 10 percent earned more than $78,760. Median annual earnings in the industries employing the largest numbers of interior designers in May 2006 were

Architectural, engineering, and related services	....$46,750
Architectural services	46,750
Specialized design services	43,250
Furniture stores	38,980
Building material and supplies dealers	36,650

Interior design salaries vary widely with the specialty, type of employer, number of years of experience, and reputation of the individuals. Among salaried interior designers, those in large specialized design and architectural firms tend to earn higher and more stable salaries. Interior designers working in retail stores usually earn a commission, which can be irregular.

For residential design projects, self-employed interior designers and those working in smaller firms usually earn a per-hour consulting fee, plus a percentage of the total cost of furniture, lighting, artwork, and other design elements. For commercial projects, they might charge a per-hour consulting fee, charge by the square footage, or charge a flat fee for the whole project. Also, designers who use specialty contractors usually earn a percentage of the contractor's earnings on the project in return for hiring the contractor. Self-employed designers must provide their own benefits.

Related Occupations

Workers in other occupations who design or arrange objects to enhance their appearance and function include architects, except landscape and naval; artists and related workers; commercial and industrial designers; fashion designers; floral designers; graphic designers; and landscape architects.

Sources of Additional Information

For information on degrees, continuing education, and licensure programs in interior design and interior design research, contact

▸ American Society of Interior Designers, 608 Massachusetts Ave. NE, Washington, DC 20002. Internet: http://www.asid.org

For a list of schools with accredited bachelor's degree programs in interior design, contact

▸ Council for Interior Design Accreditation, 146 Monroe Center NW, Suite 1318, Grand Rapids, MI 49503. Internet: http://www.accredit-id.org

For general information about art and design and a list of accredited college-level programs, contact

▸ National Association of Schools of Art and Design, 11250 Roger Bacon Dr., Suite 21, Reston, VA 20190. Internet: http://nasad.arts-accredit.org

For information on state licensing requirements and exams, and the Interior Design Experience Program, contact

▸ National Council for Interior Design Qualification, 1200 18th St. NW, Suite 1001, Washington, DC 20036-2506. Internet: http://www.ncidq.org

For information on careers, continuing education, and certification programs in the interior design specialty of residential kitchen and bath design, contact

▸ National Kitchen and Bath Association, 687 Willow Grove St., Hackettstown, NJ 07840. Internet: http://www.nkba.org/student

Interpreters and Translators

(O*NET 27-3091.00)

Significant Points

■ About 22 percent of interpreters and translators are self employed.

■ Work is often sporadic, and many of these workers are part time.

■ In addition to needing fluency in at least two languages, many interpreters and translators need a bachelor's degree. Many also complete job-specific training programs.

■ Job outlook varies by specialty.

Nature of the Work

Interpreters and translators enable the cross-cultural communication necessary in today's society by converting one language into another. However, these language specialists do more than simply translate words—they relay concepts and ideas between languages. They must thoroughly understand the subject matter in which they work in order to accurately convert information from one language, known as the source language, into another, the target language. In addition, they must be sensitive to the cultures associated with their languages of expertise.

Interpreters and translators are often discussed together because they share some common traits. For example, both must be fluent in at least two languages—a native, or active, language and a secondary, or passive, language; a small number of interpreters and translators are fluent in two or more passive languages. Their active language is the one that they know best and into which they interpret or translate, and their passive language is one for which they have nearly perfect knowledge.

Although some people do both, interpretation and translation are different professions. Interpreters deal with spoken words, translators with written words. Each task requires a distinct set of skills and aptitudes, and most people are better suited for one or the other. While interpreters often work into and from both languages, translators generally work only into their active language.

Interpreters convert one spoken language into another—or, in the case of sign-language interpreters, between spoken communication and sign language. This requires interpreters to pay attention carefully, understand what is communicated in both languages, and express thoughts and ideas clearly. Strong research and analytical skills, mental dexterity, and an exceptional memory also are important.

The first part of an interpreter's work begins before arriving at the jobsite. The interpreter must become familiar with the subject matter that the speakers will discuss, a task that may involve research to create a list of common words and phrases associated with the topic. Next, the interpreter usually travels to the location where his or her services are needed. Physical presence may not be required for some work, such as telephone interpretation. But it is usually important that the interpreter see the communicators in order to hear and observe the person speaking and to relay the message to the other party.

There are two types of interpretation: simultaneous and consecutive. Simultaneous interpretation requires interpreters to listen and speak (or sign) at the same time. In simultaneous interpretation, the interpreter begins to convey a sentence being spoken while the speaker is still talking. Ideally, simultaneous interpreters should be so familiar with a subject that they are able to anticipate the end of the speaker's sentence. Because they need a high degree of concentration, simultaneous interpreters work in pairs, with each interpreting for 20- to 30-minute periods. This type of interpretation is required at international conferences and is sometimes used in the courts.

In contrast to simultaneous interpretation's immediacy, consecutive interpretation begins only after the speaker has verbalized a group of words or sentences. Consecutive interpreters often take notes while listening to the speakers, so they must develop some type of note-taking or shorthand system. This form of interpretation is used most often for person-to-person communication, during which the interpreter is positioned near both parties.

Translators convert written materials from one language into another. They must have excellent writing and analytical ability. And because the documents that they translate must be as flawless as possible, they also need good editing skills.

Assignments may vary in length, writing style, and subject matter. When translators first receive text to convert into another language, they usually read it in its entirety to get an idea of the subject. Next, they identify and look up any unfamiliar words. Multiple additional readings are usually needed before translators begin to actually write and finalize the translation. Translators also might do additional research on the subject matter if they are unclear about anything in the text. They consult with the text's originator or issuing agency to clarify unclear or unfamiliar ideas, words, or acronyms.

Translating involves more than replacing a word with its equivalent in another language; sentences and ideas must be manipulated to flow with the same coherence as those in the source document so that the translation reads as though it originated in the target language. Translators also must bear in mind any cultural references that may need to be explained to the intended audience, such as colloquialisms, slang, and other expressions that do not translate literally. Some subjects may be more difficult than others to translate because words or passages may have multiple meanings that make

several translations possible. Not surprisingly, translated work often goes through multiple revisions before final text is submitted.

The way in which translators do their jobs has changed with advances in technology. Today, nearly all translation work is done on a computer, and most assignments are received and submitted electronically. This enables translators to work from almost anywhere, and a large percentage of them work from home. The Internet provides advanced research capabilities and valuable language resources, such as specialized dictionaries and glossaries. In some cases, use of machine-assisted translation—including memory tools that provide comparisons of previous translations with current work—helps save time and reduce repetition.

The services of interpreters and translators are needed in a number of subject areas. While these workers may not completely specialize in a particular field or industry, many do focus on one area of expertise. Some of the most common areas are described below; however, interpreters and translators also may work in a variety of other areas, including business, social services, or entertainment.

Conference interpreters work at conferences that have non-English-speaking attendees. This work includes international business and diplomacy, although conference interpreters interpret for any organization that works with foreign language speakers. Employers prefer high-level interpreters who have the ability to translate from at least two passive languages into one active (native) language—for example, the ability to interpret from Spanish and French into English. For some positions, such as those with the United Nations, this qualification is mandatory.

Much of the interpreting performed at conferences is simultaneous; however, at some meetings with a small number of attendees, consecutive interpreting also may be used. Usually, interpreters sit in soundproof booths, listening to the speakers through headphones and interpreting into a microphone what is said. The interpreted speech is then relayed to the listener through headsets. When interpreting is needed for only one or two people, the interpreter generally sits behind or next to the attendee and whispers a translation of the proceedings.

Guide or escort interpreters accompany either U.S. visitors abroad or foreign visitors in the United States to ensure that they are able to communicate during their stay. These specialists interpret on a variety of subjects, both on an informal basis and on a professional level. Most of their interpretation is consecutive, and work is generally shared by two interpreters when the assignment requires more than an 8-hour day. Frequent travel, often for days or weeks at a time, is common, an aspect of the job that some find particularly appealing.

Judiciary interpreters and translators help people appearing in court who are unable or unwilling to communicate in English. These workers must remain detached from the content of their work and not alter or modify the meaning or tone of what is said. Legal translators must be thoroughly familiar with the language and functions of the U.S. judicial system, as well as other countries' legal systems. Court interpreters work in a variety of legal settings, such as attorney-client meetings, preliminary hearings, depositions, trials, and arraignments. Success as a court interpreter requires an understanding of both legal terminology and colloquial language. In addition to interpreting what is said, court interpreters also may be required to translate written documents and read them aloud, also known as sight translation.

© **JIST Works**

Literary translators adapt written literature from one language into another. They may translate any number of documents, including journal articles, books, poetry, and short stories. Literary translation is related to creative writing; literary translators must create a new text in the target language that reproduces the content and style of the original. Whenever possible, literary translators work closely with authors to best capture their intended meanings and literary characteristics.

This type of work often is done as a sideline by university professors; however, opportunities exist for well-established literary translators. As with writers, finding a publisher and maintaining a network of contacts in the publishing industry is a critical part of the job. Most aspiring literary translators begin by submitting a short sample of their work, in the hope that it will be printed and give them recognition. For example, after receiving permission from the author, they might submit to a publishing house a previously unpublished short work, such as a poem or essay.

Localization translators constitute a relatively recent and rapidly expanding specialty. Localization involves the complete adaptation of a product for use in a different language and culture. At its earlier stages, this work dealt primarily with software localization, but the specialty has expanded to include the adaptation of Internet sites and products in manufacturing and other business sectors. The goal of these specialists is to make the product to appear as if it were originally manufactured in the country where it will be sold and supported.

Medical interpreters and translators provide language services to health care patients with limited English proficiency. Medical interpreters help patients to communicate with doctors, nurses, and other medical staff. Translators working in this specialty primarily convert patient materials and informational brochures issued by hospitals and medical facilities into the desired language. Medical interpreters need a strong grasp of medical and colloquial terminology in both languages, along with cultural sensitivity regarding how the patient receives the information. They must remain detached but aware of the patient's feelings and pain.

Sign language interpreters facilitate communication between people who are deaf or hard of hearing and people who can hear. Sign language interpreters must be fluent in English and in American Sign Language (ASL), which combines signing, finger spelling, and specific body language. ASL has its own grammatical rules, sentence structure, idioms, historical contexts, and cultural nuances. Sign language interpreting, like foreign language interpreting, involves more than simply replacing a word of spoken English with a sign representing that word.

Most sign language interpreters either interpret, aiding communication between English and ASL, or transliterate, facilitating communication between English and contact signing—a form of signing that uses a more English language-based word order. Some interpreters specialize in oral interpreting for deaf or hard of hearing people who lip-read instead of sign. Other specialties include tactile signing, which is interpreting for people who are blind as well as deaf by making manual signs into a person's hands; cued speech; and signing exact English.

Self-employed and freelance interpreters and translators need general business skills to successfully manage their finances and careers. They must set prices for their work, bill customers, keep financial records, and market their services to attract new business and build their client base.

Work environment. Interpreters work in a variety of settings, such as hospitals, courtrooms, and conference centers. They are required to travel to the site—whether it is in a neighboring town or on the other side of the world—where their services are needed. Interpreters who work over the telephone generally work in call centers in urban areas, and keep to a standard five-day, 40-hour work week. Interpreters for deaf students in schools usually work in a school setting for 9 months out of the year. Translators usually work alone, and they must frequently perform under pressure of deadlines and tight schedules. Many translators choose to work at home; however, technology allows translators to work from almost anywhere.

Because many interpreters and translators freelance, their schedules are often erratic, with extensive periods of no work interspersed with periods requiring long, irregular hours. For those who freelance, a significant amount of time must be dedicated to looking for jobs. In addition, freelancers must manage their own finances, and payment for their services may not always be prompt. Freelancing, however, offers variety and flexibility, and allows many workers to choose which jobs to accept or decline.

The work can be stressful and exhausting, and translation can be lonesome. However, interpreters and translators may use their irregular schedules to pursue other interests, such as traveling, dabbling in a hobby, or working a second job. Many interpreters and translators enjoy what they do and value the ability to control their schedules and workloads.

Training, Other Qualifications, and Advancement

Interpreters and translators must be fluent in at least two languages. Their educational backgrounds may vary widely, but most have a bachelor's degree. Many also complete job-specific training programs.

Education and training. The educational backgrounds of interpreters and translators vary. Knowing at least two languages is essential. Although it is not necessary to have been raised bilingual to succeed, many interpreters and translators grew up speaking two languages.

In high school, students can prepare for these careers by taking a broad range of courses that include English writing and comprehension, foreign languages, and basic computer proficiency. Other helpful pursuits include spending time abroad, engaging in direct contact with foreign cultures, and reading extensively on a variety of subjects in English and at least one other language.

Beyond high school, there are many educational options. Although a bachelor's degree is often required, interpreters and translators note that it is acceptable to major in something other than a language. An educational background in a particular field of study provides a natural area of subject matter expertise. However, specialized training in how to do the work is generally required. Formal programs in interpreting and translation are available at colleges nationwide and through nonuniversity training programs, conferences, and courses. Many people who work as conference interpreters or in more technical areas—such as localization, engineering, or finance—have master's degrees, while those working in the community as court or medical interpreters or translators are more likely to complete job-specific training programs.

Other qualifications. Experience is an essential part of a successful career in either interpreting or translation. In fact, many agencies or companies use only the services of people who have worked in the field for three to five years or who have a degree in translation studies or both.

A good way for translators to learn firsthand about the profession is to start out working in-house for a translation company; however, such jobs are not very numerous. People seeking to enter interpreter or translator jobs should begin by getting experience whatever way they can—even if it means doing informal or unpaid work.

Volunteer opportunities are available through community organizations, hospitals, and sporting events, such as marathons, that involve international competitors. The American Translators Association works with the Red Cross to provide volunteer interpreters in crisis situations. All translation can be used as examples for potential clients, even translation done as practice.

Paid or unpaid internships and apprenticeships are other ways for interpreters and translators to get started. Escort interpreting may offer an opportunity for inexperienced candidates to work alongside a more seasoned interpreter. Interpreters might also find it easier to break into areas with particularly high demand for language services, such as court or medical interpretation.

Whatever path of entry they pursue, new interpreters and translators should establish mentoring relationships to build their skills, confidence, and a professional network. Mentoring may be formal, such as through a professional association, or informal with a coworker or an acquaintance who has experience as an interpreter or translator. Both the American Translators Association and the Registry of Interpreters for the Deaf offer formal mentoring programs.

Translators working in localization need a solid grasp of the languages to be translated, a thorough understanding of technical concepts and vocabulary, and a high degree of knowledge about the intended target audience or users of the product. Because software often is involved, it is not uncommon for people who work in this area of translation to have a strong background in computer science or to have computer-related work experience.

Certification and advancement. There is currently no universal form of certification required of interpreters and translators in the United States, but there are a variety of different tests that workers can take to demonstrate proficiency. The American Translators Association provides certification in more than 24 language combinations for its members; other options include a certification program offered by The Translators and Interpreters Guild. Many interpreters are not certified.

Federal courts have certification for Spanish, Navajo, and Haitian Creole interpreters, and many state and municipal courts offer their own forms of certification. The National Association of Judiciary Interpreters and Translators also offers certification for court interpreting.

The U.S. Department of State has a three-test series for interpreters, including simple consecutive interpreting (for escort work), simultaneous interpreting (for court or seminar work), and conference-level interpreting (for international conferences). These tests are not referred to directly as certification, but successful completion often indicates that a person has an adequate level of skill to work in the field.

The National Association of the Deaf and the Registry of Interpreters for the Deaf (RID) jointly offer certification for general sign interpreters. In addition, the registry offers specialty tests in legal interpreting, speech reading, and deaf-to-deaf interpreting—which includes interpreting between deaf speakers with different native languages and from ASL to tactile signing.

Once interpreters and translators have gained sufficient experience, they may then move up to more difficult or prestigious assignments, may seek certification, may be given editorial responsibility, or may eventually manage or start a translation agency.

Many self-employed interpreters and translators start businesses by submitting resumes and samples to many different employment agencies and then wait to be contacted when an agency matches their skills with a job. After establishing a few regular clients, interpreters and translators may receive enough work from a few clients to stay busy, and they often hear of subsequent jobs by word of mouth or through referrals from existing clients.

Employment

Interpreters and translators held about 41,000 jobs in 2006. However, the actual number of interpreters and translators is probably significantly higher because many work in the occupation only sporadically. Interpreters and translators are employed in a variety of industries, reflecting the diversity of employment options in the field. About 33 worked in public and private educational institutions, such as schools, colleges, and universities. About 12 worked in health care and social assistance, many of whom worked for hospitals. Another 10 worked in other areas of government, such as federal, state and local courts. Other employers of interpreters and translators include publishing companies, telephone companies, airlines, and interpreting and translating agencies.

About 22 percent of interpreters and translators are self-employed. Many who freelance in the occupation work only part time, relying on other sources of income to supplement earnings from interpreting or translation.

Job Outlook

Interpreters and translators can expect much faster than average employment growth over the next decade. Job prospects vary by specialty.

Employment change. Employment of interpreters and translators is projected to increase 24 percent over the 2006–2016 decade, much faster than the average for all occupations. This growth will be driven partly by strong demand in health care settings and work related to homeland security. Additionally, higher demand for interpreters and translators results directly from the broadening of international ties and the increase in the number of foreign language speakers in the United States. Both of these trends are expected to continue, contributing to relatively rapid growth in the number of jobs for interpreters and translators.

Current events and changing political environments, often difficult to foresee, will increase the need for people who can work with other languages. For example, homeland security needs are expected to drive increasing demand for interpreters and translators of Middle Eastern and North African languages, primarily in federal government agencies.

Demand will remain strong for translators of the languages referred to as "PFIGS"—Portuguese, French, Italian, German, and Spanish; Arabic and other Middle Eastern languages; and the principal Asian languages—Chinese, Japanese, and Korean. Demand for American Sign Language interpreters will grow rapidly, driven by the increasing use of video relay services, which allow individuals to conduct

Projections data from the National Employment Matrix

Occupational Title	SOC Code	Employment, 2006	Projected employment, 2016	Change, 2006-2016	
				Number	Percent
Interpreters and translators...	27-3091	41,000	51,000	9,700	24

NOTE: Data in this table are rounded.

video calls using a sign language interpreter over an Internet connection.

Technology has made the work of interpreters and translators easier. However, technology is not likely to have a negative impact on employment of interpreters and translators because such innovations are incapable of producing work comparable with work produced by these professionals.

Job prospects. Urban areas, especially Washington D.C., New York, and cities in California, provide the largest numbers of employment possibilities, especially for interpreters; however, as the immigrant population spreads into more rural areas, jobs in smaller communities will become more widely available.

Job prospects for interpreters and translators vary by specialty. There should be demand for specialists in localization, driven by imports and exports and the expansion of the Internet; however, demand may be dampened somewhat by outsourcing of localization work to other countries. Demand is expected to be strong in other technical areas, such as medicine and law. Given the shortage of interpreters and translators meeting the desired skill level of employers, interpreters for the deaf will continue to have favorable employment prospects. On the other hand, job opportunities are expected to be limited for both conference interpreters and literary translators.

Earnings

Salaried interpreters and translators had median hourly earnings of $17.10 in May 2006. The middle 50 percent earned between $12.94 and $22.60. The lowest 10 percent earned less than $9.88, and the highest 10 percent earned more than $30.91.

Earnings depend on language, subject matter, skill, experience, education, certification, and type of employer, and salaries of interpreters and translators can vary widely. Interpreters and translators who know languages for which there is a greater demand, or which relatively few people can translate, often have higher earnings as do those with specialized expertise, such as those working in software localization. Individuals classified as language specialists for the federal government earned an average of $76,287 annually in 2007. Limited information suggests that some highly skilled interpreters and translators—for example, high-level conference interpreters—working full time can earn more than $100,000 annually.

For those who are not salaried, earnings may fluctuate, depending on the availability of work. Freelance interpreters usually earn an hourly rate, whereas translators who freelance typically earn a rate per word or per hour.

Related Occupations

Interpreters and translators use their multilingual skills, as do teachers of languages. These include preschool, kindergarten, elementary, middle, and secondary school teachers; postsecondary school teachers; special education teachers; adult literacy and remedial education teachers; and self-enrichment education teachers. The work of

interpreters, particularly guide or escort interpreters, is similar to that of tour guides and escorts, in that they accompany individuals or groups on tours or to places of interest.

The work of translators is similar to that of writers and editors, in that they communicate information and ideas in writing and prepare texts for publication or dissemination. Furthermore, interpreters or translators working in a legal or health care environment are required to have a knowledge of terms and concepts that is similar to that of professionals working in these fields, such as court reporters or medical transcriptionists.

Sources of Additional Information

Organizations dedicated to these professions can provide valuable advice and guidance to people interested in learning more about interpretation and translation. The language services division of local hospitals or courthouses also may have information about available opportunities.

For general career information, contact the organizations listed below:

▸ American Translators Association, 225 Reinekers Ln., Suite 590, Alexandria, VA 22314. Internet: http://www.atanet.org

For more detailed information by specialty, contact the association affiliated with that subject area:

▸ American Literary Translators Association, The University of Texas at Dallas, Box 830688 Mail Station J051, Richardson, TX 75083-0688. Internet: http://www.literarytranslators.org

▸ Localization Industry Standards Association, Domaine en Prael, CH-1323 Romainmtier, Switzerland. Internet: http://www.lisa.org

▸ National Association of Judiciary Interpreters and Translators, 603 Stewart St., Suite 610, Seattle, WA 98101. Internet: http://www.najit.org

▸ National Council on Interpreting in Health Care, 270 West Lawrence St., Albany, NY 12208. Internet: http://www.ncihc.org

▸ Registry of Interpreters for the Deaf, 333 Commerce St., Alexandria, VA 22314. Internet: http://www.rid.org

For information about testing to become a contract interpreter or translator with the U.S. State Department, contact

▸ U.S. Department of State, Office of Language Services, 2401 E St. NW, SA-1, Room H1400, Washington, DC 20520-2204.

Information on obtaining positions as interpreters and translators with the federal government is available from the Office of Personnel Management through USAJOBS, the federal government's official employment information system. This resource for locating and applying for job opportunities can be accessed through the Internet at http://www.usajobs.opm.gov or through an interactive voice response telephone system at (703) 724-1850 or TDD (978) 461-8404. These numbers are not toll free, and charges may result. For advice on how to find and apply for federal jobs, see the *Occupational Outlook Quarterly* article "How to get a job in the Federal Government," online at http://www.bls.gov/opub/ooq/2004/summer/art01.pdf.

(O*NET 29-2061.00)

Licensed Practical and Licensed Vocational Nurses

Significant Points

- Most training programs, lasting about 1 year, are offered by vocational or technical schools or community or junior colleges.

- Overall job prospects are expected to be very good, but job outlook varies by industry.

- Replacement needs will be a major source of job openings, as many workers leave the occupation permanently.

Nature of the Work

Licensed practical nurses (LPNs), or licensed vocational nurses (LVNs), care for people who are sick, injured, convalescent, or disabled under the direction of physicians and registered nurses. (The work of registered nurses is described elsewhere in this book.) The nature of the direction and supervision required varies by state and job setting.

LPNs care for patients in many ways. Often, they provide basic bedside care. Many LPNs measure and record patients' vital signs such as height, weight, temperature, blood pressure, pulse, and respiration. They also prepare and give injections and enemas, monitor catheters, dress wounds, and give alcohol rubs and massages. To help keep patients comfortable, they assist with bathing, dressing, and personal hygiene, moving in bed, standing, and walking. They might also feed patients who need help eating. Experienced LPNs may supervise nursing assistants and aides.

As part of their work, LPNs collect samples for testing, perform routine laboratory tests, and record food and fluid intake and output. They clean and monitor medical equipment. Sometimes, they help physicians and registered nurses perform tests and procedures. Some LPNs help to deliver, care for, and feed infants.

LPNs also monitor their patients and report adverse reactions to medications or treatments. LPNs gather information from patients, including their health history and how they are currently feeling. They may use this information to complete insurance forms, preauthorizations, and referrals, and they share information with registered nurses and doctors to help determine the best course of care for a patient.

LPNs often teach family members how to care for a relative or teach patients about good health habits.

Most LPNs are generalists and work in all areas of health care. However, some work in a specialized setting, such as a nursing home, a doctor's office, or in home health care. LPNs in nursing care facilities help to evaluate residents' needs, develop care plans, and supervise the care provided by nursing aides. In doctors' offices and clinics, they may be responsible for making appointments, keeping records, and performing other clerical duties. LPNs who work in home health care may prepare meals and teach family members simple nursing tasks.

In some states, LPNs are permitted to administer prescribed medicines, start intravenous fluids, and provide care to ventilator-dependent patients.

Work environment. Most licensed practical nurses in hospitals and nursing care facilities work a 40-hour week, but because patients need round-the-clock care, some work nights, weekends, and holidays. They often stand for long periods and help patients move in bed, stand, or walk.

LPNs may face hazards from caustic chemicals, radiation, and infectious diseases. They are subject to back injuries when moving patients. They often must deal with the stress of heavy workloads. In addition, the patients they care for may be confused, agitated, or uncooperative.

Training, Other Qualifications, and Advancement

Most training programs, lasting about one year, are offered by vocational or technical schools or community or junior colleges. LPNs must be licensed to practice. Successful completion of a practical nurse program and passing an examination are required to become licensed.

Education and training. All states and the District of Columbia require LPNs to pass a licensing examination, known as the NCLEX-PN, after completing a state-approved practical nursing program. A high school diploma or its equivalent usually is required for entry, although some programs accept candidates without a diploma, and some programs are part of a high school curriculum.

In 2006, there were more than 1,500 state-approved training programs in practical nursing. Most training programs are available from technical and vocational schools or community and junior colleges. Other programs are available through high schools, hospitals, and colleges and universities.

Most year-long practical nursing programs include both classroom study and supervised clinical practice (patient care). Classroom study covers basic nursing concepts and subjects related to patient care, including anatomy, physiology, medical-surgical nursing, pediatrics, obstetrics, psychiatric nursing, the administration of drugs, nutrition, and first aid. Clinical practice usually is in a hospital but sometimes includes other settings.

Licensure. The NCLEX-PN licensing exam is required in order to obtain licensure as an LPN. The exam is developed and administered by the National Council of State Boards of Nursing. The NCLEX-PN is a computer-based exam and varies in length. The exam covers four major categories: safe and effective care environment, health promotion and maintenance, psychosocial integrity, and physiological integrity.

Other qualifications. LPNs should have a caring, sympathetic nature. They should be emotionally stable because working with the sick and injured can be stressful. They also need to be observant, and to have good decision-making and communication skills. As part of a health-care team, they must be able to follow orders and work under close supervision.

Advancement. In some employment settings, such as nursing homes, LPNs can advance to become charge nurses who oversee the work of other LPNs and of nursing aides. Some LPNs also choose to become registered nurses through numerous LPN-to-RN training programs.

Projections data from the National Employment Matrix

Occupational Title	SOC Code	Employment, 2006	Projected employment, 2016	Change, 2006-2016	
				Number	Percent
Licensed practical and licensed vocational nurses............................	29-2061	749,000	854,000	105,000	14

NOTE: Data in this table are rounded.

Employment

Licensed practical nurses held about 749,000 jobs in 2006. About 26 percent of LPNs worked in hospitals, 26 percent in nursing care facilities, and another 12 percent in offices of physicians. Others worked for home health care services; employment services; residential care facilities; community care facilities for the elderly; outpatient care centers; and federal, state, and local government agencies. About 19 percent worked part time.

Job Outlook

Employment of LPNs is projected to grow faster than average. Overall job prospects are expected to be very good, but job outlook varies by industry. The best job opportunities will occur in nursing care facilities and home health care services, while applicants for jobs in hospitals may face competition.

Employment change. Employment of LPNs is expected to grow 14 percent between 2006 and 2016, faster than the average for all occupations, in response to the long-term care needs of an increasing elderly population and the general increase in demand for health care services.

Many procedures once performed only in hospitals are being performed in physicians' offices and in outpatient care centers such as ambulatory surgical and emergency medical centers, largely because of advances in technology. LPNs care for patients who undergo these and other procedures, so employment of LPNs is projected to decline in traditional hospitals, but is projected to grow faster than average in most settings outside of hospitals. However, some hospitals are assigning a larger share of nursing duties to LPNs, which will temper the employment decline in the industry.

Employment of LPNs is expected to grow much faster than average in home health care services. Home health care agencies will offer a large number of new jobs for LPNs because of an increasing number of older people with functional disabilities, consumer preference for care in the home, and technological advances that make it possible to bring increasingly complex treatments into the home.

Employment of LPNs in nursing care facilities is expected to grow faster than average, and provide the most new jobs for LPNs, because of the growing number of people who are aged and disabled and in need of long-term care. In addition, LPNs in nursing care facilities will be needed to care for the increasing number of patients who have been discharged from the hospital but who have not recovered enough to return home.

Job prospects. Replacement needs will be a major source of job openings, as many workers leave the occupation permanently. Very good job opportunities are expected. Rapid employment growth is projected in most health care industries, with the best job opportunities occurring in nursing care facilities and in home health care services. However, applicants for jobs in hospitals may face competition as the number of hospital jobs for LPNs declines.

Earnings

Median annual earnings of licensed practical nurses were $36,550 in May 2006. The middle 50 percent earned between $31,080 and $43,640. The lowest 10 percent earned less than $26,380, and the highest 10 percent earned more than $50,480. Median annual earnings in the industries employing the largest numbers of licensed practical nurses in May 2006 were

Employment services $42,110
Nursing care facilities 38,320
Home health care services 37,880
General medical and surgical hospitals 35,000
Offices of physicians 32,710

Related Occupations

LPNs work closely with people while helping them. So do emergency medical technicians and paramedics; medical assistants; nursing, psychiatric, and home health aides; registered nurses; athletic trainers; social and human service assistants; pharmacy technicians; pharmacy aides; and surgical technologists.

Sources of Additional Information

For information about practical nursing, contact the following organizations:

▸ National Association for Practical Nurse Education and Service, Inc., P.O. Box 25647, Alexandria, VA 22313. Internet: http://www.napnes.org

▸ National Federation of Licensed Practical Nurses, Inc., 605 Poole Dr., Garner, NC 27529. Internet: http://www.nflpn.org

▸ National League for Nursing, 61 Broadway, New York, NY 10006. Internet: http://www.nln.org

Information on the NCLEX-PN licensing exam is available from

▸ National Council of State Boards of Nursing, 111 East Wacker Dr., Suite 2900, Chicago, IL 60611. Internet: http://www.ncsbn.org

A list of state-approved LPN programs is available from individual state boards of nursing.

Line Installers and Repairers

(O*NET 49-9051.00 and 49-9052.00)

Significant Points

■ Earnings are higher than in most other occupations that do not require postsecondary education.

■ A growing number of retirements should create very good job opportunities, especially for electrical power-line installers and repairers.

- Line installers and repairers often work outdoors, and conditions can be hazardous.

- Most line installers and repairers require several years of long-term on-the-job training.

Nature of the Work

Line installers and repairers work on the vast networks of wires and cables that provide customers with electrical power and voice, video and data communications services. *Electrical power-line installers and repairers,* also called *line erectors,* install and maintain the networks of powerlines that go from generating plants to the customer. *Telecommunications line installers and repairers* install and repair the lines and cable that provide such services as cable television, telephone service, and the Internet to residential and commercial customers.

All line installers construct new lines by erecting utility poles and towers, or digging underground trenches, to carry the wires and cables. They may use a variety of construction equipment, including digger derricks, trenchers, cable plows, and borers. Digger derricks are trucks equipped with augers and cranes. Workers use augers to dig holes in the ground and use cranes to set utility poles in place. Trenchers and cable plows are used to cut openings in the earth for the laying of underground cables. Borers, which tunnel under the earth, are used to install tubes for the wire without opening a trench in the soil.

When construction is complete, line installers string cable along poles and towers or through tunnels and trenches. While working on poles and towers, installers use truck-mounted buckets to elevate themselves to the top of the structure, but sometimes they have to physically climb the pole or tower. Next, they pull up cable from large reels mounted on trucks, set the line in place, and pull up the slack so that it has the correct amount of tension. Finally, line installers attach the cable securely to the structure using hand and hydraulic tools. When working with electrical powerlines, installers bolt or clamp insulators onto the poles before attaching the cable. Underground cable is laid directly in a trench, pulled through a tunnel, or strung through a conduit running through a trench.

Other installation duties include setting up service for customers and installing network equipment. To set up service, line installers string cable between the customers' premises and the nearest lines running on poles or towers or in trenches. They connect wiring to houses and check the connection for proper voltage readings. Line installers also may install a variety of network equipment. When setting up telephone and cable television lines, they install amplifiers and repeaters that maintain the strength of communications transmissions. When running electrical powerlines, they install and replace transformers, circuitbreakers, switches, fuses, and other equipment to control and direct the electrical current.

In addition to installation, line installers and repairers are responsible for maintenance of electrical, telecommunications, and cable television lines. Workers periodically travel in trucks, helicopters, and airplanes to visually inspect the wires and cables. Sensitive monitoring equipment can automatically detect malfunctions on the network, such as loss of current flow. When line repairers identify a problem, they travel to the location of the malfunction and repair or replace defective cables or equipment.

Bad weather or natural disasters can cause extensive damage to networks of lines. Line installers and repairers must respond quickly to these emergencies to restore critical utility and communications services. This can often involve working outdoors in adverse weather conditions.

Installation and repair work may require splicing, or joining together, separate pieces of cable. Each cable contains numerous individual wires; splicing the cables together requires that each wire in one piece of cable be joined to another wire in the matching piece. Line installers join these wires and the surrounding cables using small hand tools, epoxy (an especially strong glue), or mechanical equipment. At each splice, they place insulation over the conductor and seal the splice with moistureproof covering. At some companies, specialized *cable splicing technicians* perform splices on larger lines.

Telecommunications networks are in the process of replacing older conventional wire or metal cables with new fiber optic cables. Fiber optic cables are made of hair-thin strands of glass, which convey pulses of light. These cables carry much more information at higher speeds than conventional cables. Splicing fiber optic cable requires specialized equipment that carefully slices, matches, and aligns individual glass fibers. The fibers are joined by either electrical fusion (welding) or a mechanical fixture and gel (glue).

The work performed by electrical power-line installers and telecommunications line installers and is quite similar, but there are some differences. Working with powerlines requires specialized knowledge of transformers, electrical power distribution systems, and substations. In contrast, working with telecommunications lines requires specialized knowledge of fiber optics and telecommunications switches and routers.

Work environment. Line installers and repairers must climb and maintain their balance while working on poles and towers. They lift equipment and work in a variety of positions, such as stooping or kneeling. Their work often requires that they drive utility vehicles, travel long distances, and work outdoors under a variety of weather conditions.

Line installers and repairers encounter serious hazards on their jobs and must follow safety procedures to minimize potential danger. They wear safety equipment when entering utility holes and test for the presence of gas before going underground. Electric powerline workers have the more hazardous jobs. High-voltage powerlines can instantly electrocute a worker who comes in contact with a live cable, so line installers and repairers must use electrically insulated protective devices and tools when working with such cables. Powerlines are typically higher than telephone and cable television lines, increasing the risk of severe injury due to falls. To prevent these injuries, line installers and repairers must use fall-protection equipment when working on poles or towers.

Since line installers and repairers fix damage from storms, they may be asked to work long and irregular hours. They can expect frequently to be on-call and work overtime. When performing normal maintenance and constructing new lines, line installers work more normal hours.

Training, Other Qualifications, and Advancement

Most line installers and repairers require several years of long-term on-the-job training and some classroom work to become proficient. Formal apprenticeships are common.

Education and training. Line installers and repairers usually need at least a high school diploma. Employers look for people with basic knowledge of algebra and trigonometry and good reading and writing skills. Some also prefer to hire people with technical knowledge of electricity or electronics obtained through vocational programs, community colleges, or the Armed Forces.

Programs in telecommunications, electronics, or electricity, many of which are operated with assistance from local employers and unions, are offered by many community or technical colleges. Some programs work with local companies to offer one-year certificates that emphasize hands-on field work. More advanced two-year associate degree programs provide students with a broader knowledge of the technology used in telecommunications and electrical utilities. They offer courses in electricity, electronics, fiber optics, and microwave transmission. Employers often prefer to hire graduates of these programs for line installer and repairer jobs.

Line installers and repairers receive most of their training on the job. Electrical line installers and repairers often must complete formal apprenticeships or other employer training programs. These programs, which can last up to five years, combine on-the-job training with formal classroom courses and are sometimes administered jointly by the employer and the union representing the workers. Unions include the International Brotherhood of Electrical Workers, the Communications Workers of America, and the Utility Workers Union of America. Government safety regulations strictly define the training and education requirements for apprentice electrical line installers.

Line installers and repairers working for telephone and cable television companies receive several years of on-the-job training. They also may attend training or take online courses provided by equipment manufacturers, schools, unions, or industry training organizations.

Other qualifications. Line installers and repairers must be able to read instructions, write reports, and solve problems. If they deal directly with customers, they also must have good customer service skills. They should also be mechanically inclined and like working with computers and new technology.

Physical fitness is important because they must be able to climb, lift heavy objects (many employers require applicants to be able to lift at least 50 pounds), and do other physical activity that requires stamina, strength, and coordination. Line installers and repairers often must work at a considerable height above the ground so they cannot be afraid of heights. Normal ability to distinguish colors is necessary because wires and cables may be color-coded. In addition, they often need a commercial driver's licenses to operate company-owned vehicles, so a good driving record is important.

Certification and advancement. Entry-level line installers may be hired as ground workers, helpers, or tree trimmers, who clear branches from telephone and powerlines. These workers may advance to positions stringing cable and performing service installations. With experience, they may advance to more sophisticated maintenance and repair positions responsible for increasingly larger portions of the network. Promotion to supervisory or training positions also is possible, but more advanced supervisory positions often require a college degree.

Advancement for telecommunications line installers is also made easier by earning certifications—formal recognition by a respected organization of one's knowledge of current technology. The Society of Cable Television Engineers (SCTE), for example, offers certification programs for line installers and repairers employed in the cable television industry. Candidates for certification can attend training sessions at local SCTE chapters.

Employment

Line installers and repairers held about 275,000 jobs in 2006. Approximately 162,000 were telecommunications line installers and repairers; the remainder were electrical power-line installers and repairers. Nearly all line installers and repairers worked for telecommunications companies, including both cable television distribution and telecommunications companies; construction contractors; or electric power generation, transmission, and distribution companies.

Approximately 6,100 line installers and repairers were self-employed. Many of these were contractors employed by the telecommunications companies to handle customer service problems and installations.

Job Outlook

Employment of line installers and repairers is projected to grow more slowly than average, but retirements are expected to create very good job opportunities for new workers, particularly for electrical power-line installers.

Employment change. Overall employment of line installers and repairers will grow 6 percent between 2006 and 2016, slower than the average for all occupations. Growth will reflect an increasing demand for electricity and telecommunications services as the population grows. However, productivity gains—particularly in maintaining these networks—will keep employment growth slow.

Employment of telecommunications line installers and repairers will grow more slowly than the average for all occupations. As the population expands, installers will be needed to lay the wiring for new developments and provide new telecommunications and cable television services. Additionally, old copper wiring will need to be replaced with fiber optic cable, also requiring more installers. The fiber optic lines will allow companies to give customers high-speed access to data, video, and graphics. Fiber optic lines allow for greater amounts of data to be transmitted through the cables at a faster rate. Fiber optic lines are expected to be more reliable in the long run, however, so they will require fewer workers.

Growth of wireless communications will also slow job increases for line installers and repairers in the long run. More households are switching to wireless delivery of their communications, video, and data services. Although wireless networks use lines to connect cellular towers to central offices, they do not require as many line installers to maintain and expand their systems. Satellite television providers—another major portion of the wireless communications industry—will also reduce demand for wire-based phone, Internet, and cable TV.

Employment of electrical power-line installers and repairers is expected to grow about as fast as the average for all occupations. Despite consistently rising demand for electricity, power companies will cut costs by shifting more work to outside contractors and hire fewer installers and repairers. Most new jobs for electrical power-line installers and repairers are expected to arise among contracting firms in the construction industry.

Job prospects. Very good job opportunities are expected, especially for electrical power-line installers and repairers. A growing number of retirements will create many job openings.

Projections data from the National Employment Matrix

Occupational Title	SOC Code	Employment, 2006	Projected employment, 2016	Change, 2006-16	
				Number	Percent
Line installers and repairers	49-9050	275,000	290,000	16,000	6
Electrical power-line installers and repairers	49-9051	112,000	120,000	8,100	7
Telecommunications line installers and repairers	49-9052	162,000	170,000	7,500	5

NOTE: Data in this table are rounded.

Earnings

Earnings for line installers and repairers are higher than those in most other occupations that do not require postsecondary education. Median hourly earnings for electrical power-line installers and repairers were $24.41 in May 2006. The middle 50 percent earned between $18.73 and $28.90. The lowest 10 percent earned less than $13.96, and the highest 10 percent earned more than $34.20. Median hourly earnings in the industries employing the largest numbers of electrical power-line installers and repairers in May 2006 are shown below:

Electric power generation, transmission, and
   distribution $25.90

Wired telecommunications carriers...........................24.82

Local government 23.06

Building equipment contractors..............................22.04

Utility system construction....................................19.29

Median hourly earnings for telecommunications line installers and repairers were $22.25 in May 2006. The middle 50 percent earned between $15.56 and $28.40. The lowest 10 percent earned less than $11.88, and the highest 10 percent earned more than $32.80. Median hourly earnings in the industries employing the largest numbers of telecommunications line installers and repairers in May 2006 are shown below:

Wired telecommunications carriers $27.61

Building equipment contractors..............................17.89

Cable and other subscription programming 17.72

Cable and other program distribution......................17.45

Utility system construction....................................15.41

Many line installers and repairers belong to unions, principally the Communications Workers of America, the International Brotherhood of Electrical Workers, and the Utility Workers Union of America. For these workers, union contracts set wage rates, wage increases, and the time needed to advance from one job level to the next.

Good health, education, and vacation benefits are common in the occupation.

Related Occupations

Other workers who install and repair electrical and electronic equipment include electricians; power plant operators, distributors, and dispatchers; and radio and telecommunications equipment installers and repairers.

Sources of Additional Information

For more details about employment opportunities, contact the telephone, cable television, or electrical power companies in your community. For general information and educational resources on line installer and repairer jobs, contact

▸ Communications Workers of America, 501 3rd St. NW, Washington, DC 20001. Internet: http://www.cwa-union.org/jobs

▸ National Joint Apprenticeship and Training Center (NJATC), 301 Prince Georges Blvd., Suite D, Upper Marlboro MD 20774. Internet: http://www.njatc.org

For information on training and professional certifications for those already employed by cable telecommunications firms, contact

▸ Society of Cable Telecommunications Engineers, Certification Department, 140 Phillips Rd., Exton, PA 19341-1318. Internet: http://www.scte.org

Maintenance and Repair Workers, General

(O*NET 49-9042.00)

Significant Points

■ General maintenance and repair workers are employed in almost every industry.

■ Many workers learn their skills informally on the job.

■ Job growth and turnover in this large occupation should result in excellent job opportunities, especially for people with experience in maintenance and related fields.

Nature of the Work

Most craft workers specialize in one kind of work, such as plumbing or carpentry. General maintenance and repair workers, however, have skills in many different crafts. They repair and maintain machines, mechanical equipment, and buildings and work on plumbing, electrical, and air-conditioning and heating systems. They build partitions, make plaster or drywall repairs, and fix or paint roofs, windows, doors, floors, woodwork, and other parts of building structures. They also maintain and repair specialized equipment and machinery found in cafeterias, laundries, hospitals, stores, offices, and factories.

Typical duties include troubleshooting and fixing faulty electrical switches, repairing air-conditioning motors, and unclogging drains. New buildings sometimes have computer-controlled systems that allow maintenance workers to make adjustments in building settings and monitor for problems from a central location. For example, they can remotely control light sensors that turn off lights automatically after a set amount of time or identify a broken ventilation fan that needs to be replaced.

General maintenance and repair workers inspect and diagnose problems and determine the best way to correct them, frequently checking blueprints, repair manuals, and parts catalogs. They obtain supplies and repair parts from distributors or storerooms. Using common hand and power tools such as screwdrivers, saws, drills, wrenches, and hammers, as well as specialized equipment and electronic testing devices, these workers replace or fix worn or broken parts, where necessary, or make adjustments to correct malfunctioning equipment and machines.

General maintenance and repair workers also perform routine preventive maintenance and ensure that machines continue to run smoothly, building systems operate efficiently, and the physical condition of buildings does not deteriorate. Following a checklist, they may inspect drives, motors, and belts, check fluid levels, replace filters, and perform other maintenance actions. Maintenance and repair workers keep records of their work.

Employees in small establishments, where they are often the only maintenance worker, make all repairs, except for very large or difficult jobs. In larger establishments, duties may be limited to the maintenance of everything in a workshop or a particular area.

Work environment. General maintenance and repair workers often carry out several different tasks in a single day, at any number of locations. They may work inside a single building or in several different buildings. They may have to stand for long periods, lift heavy objects, and work in uncomfortably hot or cold environments, in awkward and cramped positions, or on ladders. Those employed in small establishments often work with only limited supervision. Those in larger establishments frequently work under the direct supervision of an experienced worker. Some tasks put workers at risk of electrical shock, burns, falls, cuts, and bruises.

Most general maintenance workers work a 40-hour week. Some work evening, night, or weekend shifts or are on call for emergency repairs.

Training, Other Qualifications, and Advancement

Many general maintenance and repair workers learn their skills informally on the job as helpers to other repairers or to carpenters, electricians, and other construction workers.

Education and training. General maintenance and repair workers often learn their skills informally on the job. They start as helpers, watching and learning from skilled maintenance workers. Helpers begin by doing simple jobs, such as fixing leaky faucets and replacing light bulbs, and progress to more difficult tasks, such as overhauling machinery or building walls. Some learn their skills by working as helpers to other types of repair or construction workers, including machinery repairers, carpenters, or electricians.

Several months of on-the-job training are required to become fully qualified, depending on the skill level required. Some jobs require a year or more to become fully qualified. Because a growing number of new buildings rely on computers to control their systems, general maintenance and repair workers may need basic computer skills, such as how to log onto a central computer system and navigate through a series of menus. Companies that install computer-controlled equipment usually provide on-site training for general maintenance and repair workers.

Many employers prefer to hire high school graduates. High school courses in mechanical drawing, electricity, woodworking, blueprint reading, science, mathematics, and computers are useful. Because of the wide variety of tasks performed by maintenance and repair workers, technical education is an important part of their training. Maintenance and repair workers often need to do work that involves electrical, plumbing, and heating and air-conditioning systems, or painting and roofing tasks. Although these basic tasks may not require a license to do the work, a good working knowledge of many repair and maintenance tasks is required. Many maintenance and repair workers learn some of these skills in high school shop classes and postsecondary trade or vocational schools or community colleges.

Licensure. Licensing requirements vary by state and locality. In some cases, workers may need to be licensed in a particular specialty such as electrical or plumbing work.

Other qualifications. Mechanical aptitude, the ability to use shop mathematics, and manual dexterity are important. Good health is necessary because the job involves much walking, standing, reaching, and heavy lifting. Difficult jobs require problem-solving ability, and many positions require the ability to work without direct supervision.

Advancement. Many general maintenance and repair workers in large organizations advance to maintenance supervisor or become craftworkers such as electricians, heating and air-conditioning mechanics, or plumbers. Within small organizations, promotion opportunities may be limited.

Employment

General maintenance and repair workers held 1.4 million jobs in 2006. They were employed in almost every industry. Around 19 percent worked in manufacturing industries, almost evenly distributed through all sectors, while about 10 percent worked for federal, state, and local governments. Others worked for wholesale and retail firms and for real estate firms that operate office and apartment buildings.

Job Outlook

Average employment growth is expected. Job growth and the need to replace those who leave this large occupation should result in excellent job opportunities, especially for those with experience in maintenance and related fields.

Employment change. Employment of general maintenance and repair workers is expected to grow 10 percent during the 2006–2016 decade, about as fast as the average for all occupations. Employment is related to the number of buildings—for example, office and apartment buildings, stores, schools, hospitals, hotels, and factories—and the amount of equipment needing maintenance and repair. One

Projections data from the National Employment Matrix

Occupational Title	SOC Code	Employment, 2006	Projected employment, 2016	Change, 2006-16	
				Number	Percent
Maintenance and repair workers, general	49-9042	1,391,000	1,531,000	140,000	10

NOTE: Data in this table are rounded.

factor limiting job growth is that computers allow buildings to be monitored more efficiently, partially reducing the need for workers.

Job prospects. Job opportunities should be excellent, especially for those with experience in maintenance or related fields. General maintenance and repair is a large occupation, generating many job openings due to growth and the need to replace those who leave the occupation. Many job openings are expected to result from the retirement of experienced maintenance workers over the next decade.

Earnings

Median hourly earnings of general maintenance and repair workers were $15.34 in May 2006. The middle 50 percent earned between $11.66 and $19.90. The lowest 10 percent earned less than $9.20, and the highest 10 percent earned more than $24.44. Median hourly earnings in the industries employing the largest numbers of general maintenance and repair workers in May 2006 are shown in the following tabulation:

Local government	$15.85
Elementary and secondary schools	15.76
Activities related to real estate	13.44
Lessors of real estate	13.06
Traveler accommodation	11.76

Some general maintenance and repair workers are members of unions including the American Federation of State, County, and Municipal Employees and the United Auto Workers.

Related Occupations

Some duties of general maintenance and repair workers are similar to those of carpenters; pipelayers, plumbers, pipefitters, and steamfitters; electricians; and heating, air-conditioning, and refrigeration mechanics. Other duties are similar to those of coin, vending, and amusement machine servicers and repairers; electrical and electronics installers and repairers; electronic home entertainment equipment installers and repairers; and radio and telecommunications equipment installers and repairers.

Sources of Additional Information

Information about job opportunities may be obtained from local employers and local offices of the state.

For information related to maintenance managers contact

▸ International Maintenance Institute, P.O. Box 751896, Houston, TX 77275-1896. Internet: http://www.imionline.org

Massage Therapists

(O*NET 31-9011.00)

Significant Points

■ Employment is expected to grow faster than average over the 2006–2016 period as more people learn about the benefits of massage therapy.

■ Many states require formal training and national certification in order to practice massage therapy.

■ This occupation includes a large percentage of part-time and self-employed workers.

Nature of the Work

The medical benefits of "friction" were first documented in Western culture by the Greek physician Hippocrates around 400 BC. Today, massage therapy is being used as a means of treating painful ailments, decompressing tired and overworked muscles, reducing stress, rehabilitating sports injuries, and promoting general health. This is done by manipulating the soft tissue muscles of the body in order to improve circulation and remove waste products from the muscles.

Clients may seek massage for medical benefit or for relaxation purposes, and there is a wide range of massage treatment available to meet these distinct needs. Massage therapy that aims to improve physical health typically differs in duration and technique from massage that is intended to simply relax or rejuvenate clients. The training background of those who perform the two types of massage therapy differs as well.

Massage therapists can specialize in over 80 different types of massage, called modalities. Swedish massage, deep tissue massage, reflexology, acupressure, sports massage, and neuromuscular massage are just a few of the many approaches to massage therapy. Most massage therapists specialize in several modalities, which require different techniques. Some use exaggerated strokes ranging the length of a body part, while others use quick, percussion-like strokes with a cupped or closed hand. A massage can be as long as 2 hours or as short as 5 or 10 minutes. Usually, the type of massage given depends on the client's needs and the client's physical condition. For example, therapists may use special techniques for elderly clients that they would not use for athletes, and they would use approaches for clients with injuries that would not be appropriate for clients seeking relaxation. There are also some forms of massage that are given solely to one type of client, for example prenatal massage and infant massage.

Massage therapists work by appointment. Before beginning a massage therapy session, therapists conduct an informal interview with the client to find out about the person's medical history and desired results from the massage. This gives therapists a chance to discuss which techniques could be beneficial to the client and which could be harmful. Because massage therapists tend to specialize in only a few areas of massage, customers will often be referred to or seek a therapist with a certain type of massage in mind. Based on the person's goals, ailments, medical history, and stress- or pain-related problem areas, a massage therapist will conclude whether a massage would be harmful, and if not, move forward with the session. While giving the massage, therapists alter their approach or concentrate on any areas of particular discomfort as necessary.

Many modalities of massage therapy use massage oils, lotions, or creams to massage and rub the client's muscles. Most massage therapists, particularly those who are self-employed, supply their own table or chair, sheets, pillows, and body lotions or oils. Most modalities of massage require clients to be covered in a sheet or blanket, and require clients to be undressed or to wear loose-fitting clothing. The therapist only exposes the body part being massaged. Some types of massage are done without oils or lotions and are performed with the client fully-clothed.

Massage therapists must develop a rapport with their clients if repeat customers are to be secured. Because those who seek a therapist tend to make regular visits, developing a loyal clientele is an important part of becoming successful.

Work environment. Massage therapists work in an array of settings both private and public: private offices, studios, hospitals, nursing homes, fitness centers, sports medicine facilities, airports, and shopping malls, for example. Some massage therapists also travel to clients' homes or offices to provide a massage. It is not uncommon for full-time massage therapists to divide their time among several different settings, depending on the clients and locations scheduled.

Most massage therapists give massages in dimly lit settings. Using candles and/or incense is not uncommon. Ambient or other calm, soothing music is often played. The dim lighting, smells, and background noise are meant to put clients at ease. On the other hand, when visiting a client's office, a massage therapist may not have those amenities. The working conditions depend heavily on a therapist's location and what the client wants.

Because massage is physically demanding, massage therapists can succumb to injury if the proper technique is not used. Repetitive motion problems and fatigue from standing for extended periods of time are most common. This risk can be limited by use of good technique, proper spacing between sessions, exercise, and in many cases by the therapists themselves receiving a massage on a regular basis.

Because of the physical nature of the work and time needed in between sessions, massage therapists typically give massages less than 40 hours per week. Most therapists who work 15 to 30 hours per week consider themselves to be full-time workers, because when time for travel, equipment set-up, and business functions, such as billing, are added, a massage therapist's hours per week may very well be more than 40 hours. About 42 percent of all massage therapists worked part time and 20 percent had variable schedules in 2006.

Training, Other Qualifications, and Advancement

In 2007, 38 states and the District of Columbia had laws regulating massage therapy in some way. Most of the boards governing massage therapy in these states require practicing massage therapists to complete a formal education program and pass a national certification examination or a state exam. It is best to check information on licensing, certification, and accreditation on a state-by-state basis.

Education and training. Training standards and requirements for massage therapists vary greatly by state and locality. There are roughly 1,500 massage therapy postsecondary schools, college programs, and training programs throughout the country. Massage therapy programs generally cover subjects such as anatomy; physiology, the study of organs and tissues; kinesiology, the study of motion and body mechanics; business; ethics; as well as hands-on practice of massage techniques. Training programs may concentrate on certain modalities of massage. Several programs also provide alumni services such as post-graduate job placement and continuing educational services. Both full- and part-time programs are available.

These programs vary in accreditation. Massage therapy training programs are generally approved by a state board, and may also be accredited by an independent accrediting agency. In states that regulate massage therapy, graduation from an approved school or training program is usually required in order to practice. Some state regulations require that therapists keep up on their knowledge and technique through continuing education.

Licensure. After completion of a training program, many massage therapists opt to take the National Certification Examination for Therapeutic Massage and Bodywork (NCETMB). Many states require that therapists pass this test in order to practice massage therapy. The exam is administered by the National Certification Board for Therapeutic Massage and Bodywork (NCBTMB), which has several eligibility requirements. In states that require massage therapy program approval, a candidate must graduate from a state-approved training institute or submit a portfolio of training experience for NCBTMB review to qualify for the test. In locations that do not require accredited training programs, this is unnecessary.

When a therapist passes the NCETMB, he or she can use the recognized national credential: Nationally Certified in Therapeutic Massage and Bodywork (NCTMB). The credential must be renewed every four years. In order to remain certified, a therapist must perform at least 200 hours of therapeutic massage and complete continuing education requirements during this time. In 2005, the NCBTMB introduced a new national certification test and corresponding professional credential. The new test covers the same topics as the traditional national certification exam, but covers fewer modalities of massage therapy. Recognition of this new national certification varies by state.

Recently, a second multi-state examination program has begun to take shape. The Federation of State Massage Therapy Boards offers a licensure program that is also accepted by many states.

Massage therapy licensure boards decide which certifications and tests to accept on a state-by-state basis. Therefore, those wishing to practice massage therapy should look into legal requirements for the state and locality in which they intend to practice.

Other qualifications. Both strong communication skills and a friendly, empathetic personality are extremely helpful qualities for fostering a trusting relationship with clients and in turn, expanding one's client base. Massage can be a delicate issue for some clients and because of this, making clients feel comfortable is one of the most important abilities for massage therapists.

Advancement. Membership in a professional massage therapy association may help therapists network and in turn, find new clients. Some of these associations require that members graduate from a nationally credentialed training program, have a state license, or be nationally certified by the NCBTMB.

Because of the nature of massage therapy, opportunities for advancement are limited. However, with increased experience and an expanding client base, there are opportunities for therapists to increase client fees and, therefore, income. In addition, those who are well organized and have an entrepreneurial spirit may go into business for themselves. Self-employed massage therapists with a large client base have the highest earnings.

Employment

Massage therapists held about 118,000 jobs in 2006. About 64 percent were self-employed. There are many more people who practice massage therapy as a secondary source of income. As a result, some industry sources estimate that more than 200,000 people practice massage therapy in some capacity.

Of those self-employed, most owned their own business, and the rest worked as independent contractors. Others found employment in

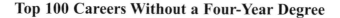

Projections data from the National Employment Matrix

Occupational Title	SOC Code	Employment, 2006	Projected employment, 2016	Change, 2006-16	
				Number	Percent
Massage therapists	31-9011	118,000	142,000	24,000	20

NOTE: Data in this table are rounded.

salons and spas; the offices of physicians and chiropractors; fitness and recreational sports centers; and hotels. While massage therapists can find jobs throughout the country, employment is concentrated in metropolitan areas, as well as resort and destination locales.

Job Outlook

Employment growth for massage therapists is expected to be faster than average for all occupations with very good job prospects, particularly for those seeking part-time work.

Employment change. Employment for massage therapists is expected to increase 20 percent from 2006 to 2016, faster than average for all occupations. Employment will grow as more people learn about the benefits of massage therapy.

Increased interest in alternative medicine and holistic healing will translate into new openings for those skilled in massage therapy. Healthcare providers and medical insurance companies are beginning to recognize massage therapy as a legitimate treatment and preventative measure for several types of injuries and illnesses. The health care industry is using massage therapy more often as a supplement to conventional medical techniques for ailments such as muscle problems, some sicknesses and diseases, and stress-related health problems. Massage therapy's growing acceptance as a medical tool, particularly by the medical provider and insurance industries, will have the greatest impact on new job growth for massage therapists.

Massage is an increasingly popular technique for relaxation and reduction of stress. As workplaces try to distinguish themselves as employee-friendly, providing professional in-office, seated massages for employees is becoming a popular on-the-job benefit.

Older citizens in nursing homes or assisted living facilities are also finding benefits from massage, such as increased energy levels and reduced health problems. Demand for massage therapy should grow among older age groups because they increasingly enjoy longer, more active lives and persons age 55 and older are projected to be the most rapidly growing segment of the U.S. population over the next decade. However, demand for massage therapy is presently greatest among young adults, and they are likely to continue to enjoy the benefits of massage therapy as they age.

Job prospects. In states that regulate massage therapy, those who complete formal training programs and pass the national certification exam are likely to have very good opportunities. However, new massage therapists should expect to work only part-time in spas, hotels, hospitals, physical therapy centers, and other businesses until they can build a client base of their own. Because referrals are a very important source of work for massage therapists, networking will increase the number of job opportunities. Joining a state or local chapter of a professional association can also help build strong contacts and further increase the likelihood of steady work.

Female massage therapists will continue to enjoy slightly better job prospects, as some clients—both male and female—are uncomfortable with male physical contact. In 2006, 84 percent of all massage therapists were female.

Earnings

Median wage and salary hourly earnings of massage therapists, including gratuities, were $16.06 in May 2006. The middle 50 percent earned between $10.98 and $24.22. The lowest 10 percent earned less than $7.48, and the highest 10 percent earned more than $33.83. Generally, massage therapists earn 15 to 20 percent of their income as gratuities. For those who work in a hospital or other clinical setting, however, tipping is not common.

As is typical for most workers who are self-employed and work part-time, few benefits are provided.

Related Occupations

Other workers associated with the healthcare industry who provide therapy to clients include athletic trainers, physical therapists, physical therapist assistants and aides, chiropractors, and workers in other occupations that use touch to aid healing or relieve stress.

Sources of Additional Information

General information on becoming a massage therapist is available from state regulatory boards.

For more information on becoming a massage therapist, contact

▸ Associated Bodywork & Massage Professionals, 1271 Sugarbush Dr., Evergreen, CO 80439. Internet: http://www.massagetherapy.com/careers/index.php

▸ American Massage Therapy Association, 500 Davis St., Suite 900, Evanston, IL 60201. Internet: http://www.amtamassage.org

For a directory of schools providing accredited massage therapy training programs, contact

▸ Commission on Massage Therapy Accreditation, 1007 Church St., Suite 302, Evanston, IL 60201. Internet: http://www.comta.org

▸ Accrediting Commission of Career Schools and Colleges of Technology, 2101 Wilson Blvd., Suite 302, Arlington, VA 22201. Internet: http://www.accsct.org

Information on national testing and national certification is available from

▸ National Certification Board for Therapeutic Massage and Bodywork, 1901 S. Meyers Rd., Suite 240, Oakbrook Terrace, IL 60181. Internet: http://www.ncbtmb.com

▸ Federation of State Massage Therapy Boards, 7111 W 151st Street, Suite 356, Overland Park, Kansas 66223. Internet: http://www.fsmtb.org

Medical Assistants

(O*NET 31-9092.00)

Significant Points

■ About 62 percent of medical assistants work in offices of physicians.

- Some medical assistants are trained on the job, but many complete 1-year or 2-year programs.

- Employment is projected to grow much faster than average, ranking medical assistants among the fastest growing occupations over the 2006–2016 decade.

- Job prospects should be excellent.

Nature of the Work

Medical assistants perform administrative and clinical tasks to keep the offices of physicians, podiatrists, chiropractors, and other health practitioners running smoothly. They should not be confused with Physician assistants, who examine, diagnose, and treat patients under the direct supervision of a physician.

The duties of medical assistants vary from office to office, depending on the location and size of the practice and the practitioner's specialty. In small practices, medical assistants usually do many different kinds of tasks, handling both administrative and clinical duties and reporting directly to an office manager, physician, or other health practitioner. Those in large practices tend to specialize in a particular area, under the supervision of department administrators.

Medical assistants who perform administrative tasks have many duties. They update and file patients' medical records, fill out insurance forms, and arrange for hospital admissions and laboratory services. They also perform tasks less specific to medical settings, such as answering telephones, greeting patients, handling correspondence, scheduling appointments, and handling billing and bookkeeping.

For clinical medical assistants, duties vary according to what is allowed by state law. Some common tasks include taking medical histories and recording vital signs, explaining treatment procedures to patients, preparing patients for examinations, and assisting physicians during examinations. Medical assistants collect and prepare laboratory specimens and sometimes perform basic laboratory tests on the premises, dispose of contaminated supplies, and sterilize medical instruments. They might instruct patients about medications and special diets, prepare and administer medications as directed by a physician, authorize drug refills as directed, telephone prescriptions to a pharmacy, draw blood, prepare patients for x-rays, take electrocardiograms, remove sutures, and change dressings.

Medical assistants also may arrange examining room instruments and equipment, purchase and maintain supplies and equipment, and keep waiting and examining rooms neat and clean.

Ophthalmic medical assistants, *optometric assistants*, and *podiatric medical assistants* are examples of specialized assistants who have additional duties. Ophthalmic medical assistants help ophthalmologists provide eye care. They conduct diagnostic tests, measure and record vision, and test eye muscle function. They also show patients how to insert, remove, and care for contact lenses, and they apply eye dressings. Under the direction of the physician, ophthalmic medical assistants may administer eye medications. They also maintain optical and surgical instruments and may assist the ophthalmologist in surgery. Optometric assistants also help provide eye care, working with optometrists. They provide chair-side assistance, instruct patients about contact lens use and care, conduct preliminary tests on patients, and otherwise provide assistance while working directly with an optometrist. Podiatric medical assistants make castings of feet, expose and develop x rays, and assist podiatrists in surgery.

Work environment. Medical assistants work in well-lighted, clean environments. They constantly interact with other people and may have to handle several responsibilities at once. Most full-time medical assistants work a regular 40-hour week. However, many medical assistants work part time, evenings, or weekends.

Training, Other Qualifications, and Advancement

Some medical assistants are trained on the job, but many complete one-year or two-year programs.

Education and training. Postsecondary medical assisting programs are offered in vocational-technical high schools, postsecondary vocational schools, and community and junior colleges. Programs usually last either one year and result in a certificate or diploma, or two years and result in an associate degree. Courses cover anatomy, physiology, and medical terminology, as well as typing, transcription, recordkeeping, accounting, and insurance processing. Students learn laboratory techniques, clinical and diagnostic procedures, pharmaceutical principles, the administration of medications, and first aid. They study office practices, patient relations, medical law, and ethics. There are various organizations that accredit medical assisting programs. Accredited programs often include an internship that provides practical experience in physicians' offices, hospitals, or other health care facilities.

Formal training in medical assisting, while generally preferred, is not always required. Some medical assistants are trained on the job, although this practice is less common than in the past. Applicants usually need a high school diploma or the equivalent. Recommended high school courses include mathematics, health, biology, typing, bookkeeping, computers, and office skills. Volunteer experience in the health care field also is helpful. Medical assistants who are trained on the job usually spend their first few months attending training sessions and working closely with more experienced workers.

Some states allow medical assistants to perform more advanced procedures, such as giving injections, after passing a test or taking a course.

Certification and other qualifications. Employers prefer to hire experienced workers or those who are certified. Although not required, certification indicates that a medical assistant meets certain standards of competence. There are various associations—some listed in the sources of information below—that award certification credentials to medical assistants, and the certification process varies. It also is possible to become certified in a specialty, such as podiatry, optometry, or ophthalmology.

Medical assistants deal with the public; therefore, they must be neat and well groomed and have a courteous, pleasant manner and they must be able to put patients at ease and explain physicians' instructions. They must respect the confidential nature of medical information. Clinical duties require a reasonable level of manual dexterity and visual acuity.

Advancement. Medical assistants may advance to other occupations through experience or additional training. For example, some may go on to teach medical assisting, and others pursue additional education to become nurses or other health care workers. Administrative medical assistants may advance to office manager, or qualify for a variety of administrative support occupations.

Projections data from the National Employment Matrix

Occupational Title	SOC Code	Employment, 2006	Projected employment, 2016	Change, 2006-16	
				Number	Percent
Medical assistants	31-9092	417,000	565,000	148,000	35

NOTE: Data in this table are rounded.

Employment

Medical assistants held about 417,000 jobs in 2006. About 62 percent worked in offices of physicians; 12 percent worked in public and private hospitals, including inpatient and outpatient facilities; and 11 percent worked in offices of other health practitioners, such as chiropractors, optometrists, and podiatrists. Most of the remainder worked in other health care industries such as outpatient care centers and nursing and residential care facilities.

Job Outlook

Employment is projected to grow much faster than average, ranking medical assistants among the fastest growing occupations over the 2006–2016 decade. Job opportunities should be excellent, particularly for those with formal training or experience, and certification.

Employment change. Employment of medical assistants is expected to grow 35 percent from 2006 to 2016, much faster than the average for all occupations. As the health care industry expands because of technological advances in medicine and the growth and aging of the population, there will be an increased need for all health care workers. Increasing use of medical assistants in the rapidly growing health care industry will further stimulate job growth.

Helping to drive job growth is the increasing number of group practices, clinics, and other health care facilities that need a high proportion of support personnel, particularly medical assistants who can handle both administrative and clinical duties. In addition, medical assistants work primarily in outpatient settings, a rapidly growing sector of the health care industry.

Job prospects. Job seekers who want to work as a medical assistant should find excellent job prospects. Medical assistants are projected to account for a very large number of new jobs, and many other opportunities will come from the need to replace workers leaving the occupation. Those with formal training or experience—particularly those with certification—should have the best job opportunities.

Earnings

The earnings of medical assistants vary, depending on their experience, skill level, and location. Median annual earnings of wage-and-salary medical assistants were $26,290 in May 2006. The middle 50 percent earned between $21,970 and $31,210. The lowest 10 percent earned less than $18,860, and the highest 10 percent earned more than $36,840. Median annual earnings in the industries employing the largest numbers of medical assistants in May 2006 were

General medical and surgical hospitals	$27,340
Outpatient care centers	26,840
Offices of physicians	26,620
Offices of chiropractors	22,940
Offices of optometrists	22,850

Related Occupations

Medical assistants perform work similar to the tasks completed by other workers in medical support occupations. Administrative medical assistants do work similar to that of medical secretaries, medical transcriptionists, and medical records and health information technicians. Clinical medical assistants perform duties similar to those of dental assistants; dental hygienists; occupational therapist assistants and aides; pharmacy aides; licensed practical and licensed vocational nurses; surgical technologists; physical therapist assistants and aides; and nursing, psychiatric, and home health aides.

Sources of Additional Information

Information about career opportunities and certification for medical assistants is available from

▸ American Association of Medical Assistants, 20 North Wacker Dr., Suite 1575, Chicago, IL 60606. Internet: http://www.aama-ntl.org

▸ American Medical Technologists, 10700 West Higgins Rd., Suite 150, Rosemont, IL 60018. Internet: http://www.amt1.com

▸ National Healthcareer Association, 7 Ridgedale Ave., Suite 203, Cedar Knolls, NJ 07927.

Information about career opportunities, training programs, and certification for ophthalmic medical personnel is available from

▸ Joint Commission on Allied Health Personnel in Ophthalmology, 2025 Woodlane Dr., St. Paul, MN 55125. Internet: http://www.jcahpo.org/newsite/index.htm

Information about career opportunities, training programs and certification for optometric assistants is available from

▸ American Optometric Association, 243 N. Lindbergh Blvd., St. Louis, MO 63141. Internet: http://www.aoa.org

Information about certification for podiatric assistants is available from

▸ American Society of Podiatric Medical Assistants, 2124 South Austin Blvd., Cicero, IL 60804. Internet: http://www.aspma.org

For lists of accredited educational programs in medical assisting, contact

▸ Accrediting Bureau of Health Education Schools, 7777 Leesburg Pike, Suite 314 N, Falls Church, VA 22043. Internet: http://www.abhes.org

▸ Commission on Accreditation of Allied Health Education Programs, 1361 Park St., Clearwater, FL 33756. Internet: http://www.caahep.org

Medical Records and Health Information Technicians

(O*NET 29-2071.00)

Significant Points

■ Employment is expected to grow faster than average.

■ Job prospects should be very good; technicians with a strong background in medical coding will be in particularly high demand.

■ Entrants usually have an associate degree.

■ This is one of the few health occupations in which there is little or no direct contact with patients.

Nature of the Work

Every time a patient receives health care, a record is maintained of the observations, medical or surgical interventions, and treatment outcomes. This record includes information that the patient provides concerning his or her symptoms and medical history, the results of examinations, reports of X rays and laboratory tests, diagnoses, and treatment plans. Medical records and health information technicians organize and evaluate these records for completeness and accuracy.

Technicians assemble patients' health information, making sure that patients' initial medical charts are complete, that all forms are completed and properly identified and authenticated, and that all necessary information is in the computer. They regularly communicate with physicians and other health care professionals to clarify diagnoses or to obtain additional information. Technicians regularly use computer programs to tabulate and analyze data to improve patient care, better control cost, provide documentation for use in legal actions, or use in research studies.

Medical records and health information technicians' duties vary with the size of the facility where they work. In large to medium-size facilities, technicians might specialize in one aspect of health information or might supervise health information clerks and transcriptionists while a medical records and health information administrator manages the department. In small facilities, a credentialed medical records and health information technician may have the opportunity to manage the department.

Some medical records and health information technicians specialize in coding patients' medical information for insurance purposes. Technicians who specialize in coding are called *health information coders, medical record coders, coder/abstractors,* or *coding specialists.* These technicians assign a code to each diagnosis and procedure, relying on their knowledge of disease processes. Technicians then use classification systems software to assign the patient to one of several hundred "diagnosis-related groups," or DRGs. The DRG determines the amount for which the hospital will be reimbursed if the patient is covered by Medicare or other insurance programs using the DRG system. In addition to the DRG system, coders use other coding systems, such as those required for ambulatory settings, physician offices, or long-term care.

Medical records and health information technicians also may specialize in cancer registry. *Cancer* (or tumor) *registrars* maintain facility, regional, and national databases of cancer patients. Registrars review patient records and pathology reports, and assign codes for the diagnosis and treatment of different cancers and selected benign tumors. Registrars conduct annual followups on all patients in the registry to track their treatment, survival, and recovery. Physicians and public health organizations then use this information to calculate survivor rates and success rates of various types of treatment, locate geographic areas with high incidences of certain cancers, and identify potential participants for clinical drug trials. Public health officials also use cancer registry data to target areas for the allocation of resources to provide intervention and screening.

Work environment. Medical records and health information technicians work in pleasant and comfortable offices. This is one of the few health-related occupations in which there is little or no direct contact with patients. Because accuracy is essential in their jobs, technicians must pay close attention to detail. Technicians who work at computer monitors for prolonged periods must guard against eyestrain and muscle pain.

Medical records and health information technicians usually work a 40-hour week. Some overtime may be required. In hospitals—where health information departments often are open 24 hours a day, 7 days a week—technicians may work day, evening, and night shifts.

Training, Other Qualifications, and Advancement

Medical records and health information technicians entering the field usually have an associate degree from a community or junior college. Many employers favor technicians who have become Registered Health Information Technicians (RHIT). Advancement opportunities for medical record and health information technicians are typically achieved by specialization or promotion to a management position.

Education and training. Medical records and health information technicians generally obtain an associate degree from a community or junior college. Typically, community and junior colleges offer flexible course scheduling or online distance learning courses. In addition to general education, coursework includes medical terminology, anatomy and physiology, legal aspects of health information, health data standards, coding and abstraction of data, statistics, database management, quality improvement methods, and computer science. Applicants can improve their chances of admission into a program by taking biology, math, chemistry, health, and computer science courses in high school.

Certification and other qualifications. Most employers prefer to hire Registered Health Information Technicians (RHIT), who must pass a written examination offered by the American Health Information Management Association (AHIMA). To take the examination, a person must graduate from a two-year associate degree program accredited by the Commission on Accreditation for Health Informatics and Information Management Education (CAHIIM). Technicians trained in non-CAHIIM-accredited programs or trained on the job are not eligible to take the examination. In 2007, there were about 245 CAHIIM accredited programs in Health Informantics and Information Management Education.

Some employers prefer candidates with experience in a health care setting. Experience is valuable in demonstrating certain skills or desirable qualities. It is beneficial for health information technicians to possess good communication skills, as they often serve as a liaison between health care facilities, insurance companies, and other establishments. Accuracy is also essential to technicians because they must pay close attention to detail. A candidate who exhibits proficiency with computers will become more valuable as health care facilities continue to adopt electronic medical records.

Certification and advancement. Experienced medical records and health information technicians usually advance in one of two ways—by specializing or by moving into a management position. Many senior technicians specialize in coding, in cancer registry, or in privacy and security. Most coding and registry skills are learned on the job. A number of schools offer certificate programs in coding or include

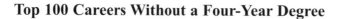

Projections data from the National Employment Matrix

Occupational Title	SOC Code	Employment, 2006	Projected employment, 2016	Change, 2006-2016	
				Number	Percent
Medical records and health information technicians	29-2071	170,000	200,000	30,000	18

NOTE: Data in this table are rounded.

coding as part of the associate degree program for health information technicians, although there are no formal degree programs in coding. For cancer registry, there are a few formal two-year certificate programs approved by the National Cancer Registrars Association (NCRA). Some schools and employers offer intensive one- to two-week training programs in either coding or cancer registry.

Certification in coding is available from several organizations. Coding certification within specific medical specialty areas is available from the Board of Medical Specialty Coding and the Professional Association of Healthcare Coding Specialist (PAHCS). The American Academy of Professional Coders (AAPC) offers three distinct certification programs in coding. The AHIMA also offers certification for Certified Healthcare Privacy and Security because of growing concerns for the security of electronic medical records. Certification in cancer registry is available from the NCRA. Continuing education units are typically required to renew credentials.

In large medical records and health information departments, experienced technicians may advance to section supervisor, overseeing the work of the coding, correspondence, or discharge sections, for example. Senior technicians with RHIT credentials may become director or assistant director of a medical records and health information department in a small facility. However, in larger institutions, the director usually is an administrator with a bachelor's degree in medical records and health information administration.

Hospitals sometimes advance promising health information clerks to jobs as medical records and health information technicians, although this practice may be less common in the future. Advancement usually requires two to four years of job experience and completion of a hospital's in-house training program.

Employment

Medical records and health information technicians held about 170,000 jobs in 2006. About 2 out of 5 jobs were in hospitals. The rest were mostly in offices of physicians, nursing care facilities, outpatient care centers, and home health care services. Insurance firms that deal in health matters employ a small number of health information technicians to tabulate and analyze health information. Public health departments also employ technicians to supervise data collection from health care institutions and to assist in research.

Job Outlook

Employment is expected to grow faster than average. Job prospects should be very good; technicians with a strong background in medical coding will be in particularly high demand.

Employment change. Employment of medical records and health information technicians is expected to increase by 18 percent through 2016—faster than the average for all occupations—because of rapid growth in the number of medical tests, treatments, and procedures that will be increasingly scrutinized by health insurance companies, regulators, courts, and consumers. Also, technicians will be needed to enter patient information into computer databases to comply with federal legislation mandating the use of electronic medical records.

New jobs are expected in offices of physicians as a result of increasing demand for detailed records, especially in large group practices. New jobs also are expected in home health care services, outpatient care centers, and nursing and residential care facilities. Although employment growth in hospitals will not keep pace with growth in other health care industries, many new jobs will, nevertheless, be created.

Cancer registrars should experience job growth. As the population continues to age, the incidence of cancer may increase.

Job prospects. Job prospects should be very good. In addition to job growth, openings will result from the need to replace technicians who retire or leave the occupation permanently.

Technicians with a strong background in medical coding will be in particularly high demand. Changing government regulations and the growth of managed care have increased the amount of paperwork involved in filing insurance claims. Additionally, health care facilities are having some difficulty attracting qualified workers, primarily because employers prefer trained and experienced technicians prepared to work in an increasingly electronic environment with the integration of electronic health records. Job opportunities may be especially good for coders employed through temporary help agencies or by professional services firms.

Earnings

Median annual earnings of medical records and health information technicians were $28,030 in May 2006. The middle 50 percent earned between $22,420 and $35,990. The lowest 10 percent earned less than $19,060, and the highest 10 percent earned more than $45,260. Median annual earnings in the industries employing the largest numbers of medical records and health information technicians in May 2006 were

General medical and surgical hospitals $29,400
Nursing care facilities 28,410
Outpatient care centers 26,680
Offices of physicians 24,170

Related Occupations

Medical records and health information technicians need a strong clinical background to analyze the contents of medical records. Medical secretaries and medical transcriptionists also must be knowledgeable about medical terminology, anatomy, and physiology even though they have little or no direct contact with patients.

Sources of Additional Information

Information on careers in medical records and health information technology, and a list of accredited training programs is available from

▸ American Health Information Management Association, 233 N. Michigan Ave., Suite 2150, Chicago, IL 60601-5800. Internet: http://www.ahima.org

Information on training and certification for medical coders is available from

▸ American Academy of Professional Coders, 2480 South 3850 West, Suite B, Salt Lake City, UT 84120. Internet: http://www.aapc.com

Information on cancer registrars is available from

▸ National Cancer Registrars Association, 1340 Braddock Place Suite 203, Alexandria, VA 22314. Internet: http://www.ncra-usa.org

Musicians, Singers, and Related Workers

(O*NET 27-2041.00, 27-2041.01, 27-2041.04, 27-2042.00, 27-2042.01, and 27-2042.02)

Significant Points

■ Part-time schedules—typically at night and on weekends—intermittent unemployment, and rejection when auditioning for work are common; many musicians and singers supplement their income with earnings from other sources.

■ Aspiring musicians and singers begin studying an instrument or training their voices at an early age.

■ Competition for jobs is keen; talented individuals who can play several instruments and perform a wide range of musical styles should enjoy the best job prospects.

Nature of the Work

Musicians, singers, and related workers play musical instruments, sing, compose or arrange music, or conduct groups in instrumental or vocal performances. They may perform solo or as part of a group. Musicians, singers, and related workers entertain live audiences in nightclubs, concert halls, and theaters; others perform in recording or production studios. Regardless of the setting, musicians, singers, and related workers spend considerable time practicing, alone and with their bands, orchestras, or other musical ensembles.

Musicians play one or more musical instruments. Many musicians learn to play several related instruments and can perform equally well in several musical styles. Instrumental musicians, for example, may play in a symphony orchestra, rock group, or jazz combo one night, appear in another ensemble the next, and work in a studio band the following day. Some play a variety of string, brass, woodwind, or percussion instruments or electronic synthesizers.

Singers interpret music and text, using their knowledge of voice production, melody, and harmony. They sing character parts or perform in their own individual style. Singers are often classified according to their voice range—soprano, contralto, tenor, baritone, or bass, for example—or by the type of music they sing, such as rock, pop, folk, opera, rap, or country.

Music directors and *conductors* conduct, direct, plan, and lead instrumental or vocal performances by musical groups, such as orchestras, choirs, and glee clubs. These leaders audition and select musicians, choose the music most appropriate for their talents and abilities, and direct rehearsals and performances. *Choral directors* lead choirs and glee clubs, sometimes working with a band or an orchestra conductor. Directors audition and select singers and lead them at rehearsals and performances to achieve harmony, rhythm, tempo, shading, and other desired musical effects.

Composers create original music such as symphonies, operas, sonatas, radio and television jingles, film scores, and popular songs. They transcribe ideas into musical notation, using harmony, rhythm, melody, and tonal structure. Although most composers and songwriters practice their craft on instruments and transcribe the notes with pen and paper, some use computer software to compose and edit their music.

Arrangers transcribe and adapt musical compositions to a particular style for orchestras, bands, choral groups, or individuals. Components of music—including tempo, volume, and the mix of instruments needed—are arranged to express the composer's message. While some arrangers write directly into a musical composition, others use computer software to make changes.

Work environment. Musicians typically perform at night and on weekends. They spend much additional time practicing or in rehearsal. Full-time musicians with long-term employment contracts, such as those with symphony orchestras or television and film production companies, enjoy steady work and less travel. Nightclub, solo, or recital musicians frequently travel to perform in a variety of local settings and may tour nationally or internationally. Because many musicians find only part-time or intermittent work, experiencing unemployment between engagements, they often supplement their income with other types of jobs. The stress of constantly looking for work leads many musicians to accept permanent, full-time jobs in other occupations, while working part time as musicians.

Most instrumental musicians work closely with a variety of other people, including their colleagues, agents, employers, sponsors, and audiences. Although they usually work indoors, some perform outdoors for parades, concerts, and festivals. In some nightclubs and restaurants, smoke and odors may be present and lighting and ventilation may be poor.

Training, Other Qualifications, and Advancement

Long-term on-the-job training is the most common way people learn to become musicians or singers. Aspiring musicians begin studying an instrument at an early age. They may gain valuable experience playing in a school or community band or an orchestra or with a group of friends. Singers usually start training when their voices mature. Participation in school musicals or choirs often provides good early training and experience. Composers and music directors usually require a bachelor's degree in a related field.

Education and training. Musicians need extensive and prolonged training and practice to acquire the necessary skills and knowledge to interpret music at a professional level. Like other artists, musicians and singers continually strive to improve their abilities. Formal training may be obtained through private study with an accomplished musician, in a college or university music program, or in a music conservatory. An audition generally is necessary to qualify for university or conservatory study. The National Association of Schools of Music accredits more than 600 college-level programs in music. Courses typically include music theory, music interpretation, composition, conducting, and performance in a particular instru-

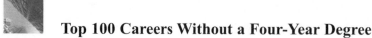
Projections data from the National Employment Matrix

Occupational Title	SOC Code	Employment, 2006	Projected employment, 2016	Change, 2006-2016	
				Number	Percent
Musicians, singers, and related workers	27-2040	264,000	293,000	29,000	11
Music directors and composers..	27-2041	68,000	77,000	8,800	13
Musicians and singers	27-2042	196,000	216,000	20,000	10

NOTE: Data in this table are rounded.

ment or in voice. Music directors, composers, conductors, and arrangers need considerable related work experience or advanced training in these subjects.

A master's or doctoral degree usually is required to teach advanced music courses in colleges and universities; a bachelor's degree may be sufficient to teach basic courses. A degree in music education qualifies graduates for a state certificate to teach music in public elementary or secondary schools. Musicians who do not meet public school music education requirements may teach in private schools and recreation associations or instruct individual students in private sessions.

Other qualifications. Musicians must be knowledgeable about a broad range of musical styles as well as the type of music that interests them most. Having a broader range of interest, knowledge, and training can help expand employment opportunities and musical abilities. Voice training and private instrumental lessons, especially when taken at a young age, also help develop technique and enhance one's performance.

Young persons considering careers in music should have musical talent, versatility, creativity, poise, and a good stage presence. Self-discipline is vital because producing a quality performance on a consistent basis requires constant study and practice. Musicians who play in concerts or in nightclubs and those who tour must have physical stamina to endure frequent travel and an irregular performance schedule. Musicians and singers also must be prepared to face the anxiety of intermittent employment and of rejection when auditioning for work.

Advancement. Advancement for musicians usually means becoming better known, finding work more easily, and performing for higher earnings. Successful musicians often rely on agents or managers to find them performing engagements, negotiate contracts, and develop their careers.

Employment

Musicians, singers, and related workers held about 264,000 jobs in 2006. Around 35 percent worked part time; 48 percent were self-employed. Many found jobs in cities in which entertainment and recording activities are concentrated, such as New York, Los Angeles, Las Vegas, Chicago, and Nashville.

Musicians, singers, and related workers are employed in a variety of settings. Of those who earn a wage or salary, 35 percent were employed by religious organizations and 11 percent by performing arts companies such as professional orchestras, small chamber music groups, opera companies, musical theater companies, and ballet troupes. Musicians and singers also perform in nightclubs and restaurants and for weddings and other events. Well-known musicians and groups may perform in concerts, appear on radio and television broadcasts, and make recordings and music videos. The U.S.

Armed Forces also offer careers in their bands and smaller musical groups.

Job Outlook

Employment is expected to grow about as fast as the average for all occupations. Keen competition for jobs, especially full-time jobs, is expected to continue. Talented individuals who are skilled in multiple instruments or musical styles will have the best job prospects.

Employment change. Overall employment of musicians, singers, and related workers is expected to grow 11 percent during the 2006–2016 decade, about as fast as the average for all occupations. Most new wage-and-salary jobs for musicians will arise in religious organizations. Five percent growth is expected for self-employed musicians, who generally perform in nightclubs, concert tours, and other venues. The Internet and other new forms of media may provide independent musicians and singers alternative methods to distribute music.

Job prospects. Growth in demand for musicians will generate a number of job opportunities, and many openings also will arise from the need to replace those who leave the field each year because they are unable to make a living solely as musicians or singers, or for other reasons.

Competition for jobs as musicians, singers, and related workers is expected to be keen, especially for full-time jobs. The vast number of people with the desire to perform will continue to greatly exceed the number of openings. New musicians or singers will have their best chance of landing a job with smaller, community-based performing arts groups or as freelance artists. Talented individuals who are skilled in multiple instruments or musical styles will have the best job prospects. However, talent alone is no guarantee of success: many people start out to become musicians or singers but leave the profession because they find the work difficult, the discipline demanding, and the long periods of intermittent unemployment a hardship.

Earnings

Median hourly earnings of wage-and-salary musicians and singers were $19.73 in May 2006. The middle 50 percent earned between $10.81 and $36.55. The lowest 10 percent earned less than $7.08, and the highest 10 percent earned more than $57.37. Median hourly earnings were $23.37 in performing arts companies and $13.57 in religious organizations. Annual earnings data for musicians and singers were not available because of the wide variation in the number of hours worked by musicians and singers and the short-term nature of many jobs. It is rare for musicians and singers to have guaranteed employment that exceeds 3 to 6 months.

Median annual earnings of salaried music directors and composers were $39,750 in May 2006. The middle 50 percent earned between

$23,660 and $60,350. The lowest 10 percent earned less than $15,210, and the highest 10 percent earned more than $110,850.

For self-employed musicians and singers, earnings typically reflect the number of jobs a freelance musician or singer played or the number of hours and weeks of contract work, in addition to a performer's professional reputation and setting. Performers who can fill large concert halls, arenas, or outdoor stadiums generally command higher pay than those who perform in local clubs. Soloists or headliners usually receive higher earnings than band members or opening acts. The most successful musicians earn performance or recording fees that far exceed the median earnings.

The American Federation of Musicians negotiates minimum contracts for major orchestras during the performing season. Each orchestra works out a separate contract with its local union, but individual musicians may negotiate higher salaries. In regional orchestras, minimum salaries are often less because fewer performances are scheduled. Regional orchestra musicians often are paid for their services, without any guarantee of future employment. Community orchestras often have more limited funding and offer salaries that are much lower for seasons of shorter duration.

Although musicians employed by some symphony orchestras work under master wage agreements, which guarantee a season's work up to 52 weeks, many other musicians face relatively long periods of unemployment between jobs. Even when employed, many musicians and singers work part time in unrelated occupations. Thus, their earnings for music usually are lower than earnings in many other occupations. Moreover, because they may not work steadily for one employer, some performers cannot qualify for unemployment compensation, and few have typical benefits such as sick leave or paid vacations. For these reasons, many musicians give private lessons or take jobs unrelated to music to supplement their earnings as performers.

Many musicians belong to a local of the American Federation of Musicians. Professional singers who perform live often belong to a branch of the American Guild of Musical Artists; those who record for the broadcast industries may belong to the American Federation of Television and Radio Artists.

Related Occupations

Musical instrument repairers and tuners (part of the precision instrument and equipment repairers occupation) require technical knowledge of musical instruments. Others whose work involves the performing arts include actors, producers, and directors; announcers; and dancers and choreographers. School teachers and self-enrichment education teachers who teach music often use some of the same knowledge and skills as musicians and singers.

Sources of Additional Information

For general information about music and music teacher education and a list of accredited college-level programs, contact

▶ National Association of Schools of Music, 11250 Roger Bacon Dr., Suite 21, Reston, VA 20190. Internet: http://nasm.arts-accredit. org

Nuclear Medicine Technologists

(O*NET 29-2033.00)

Significant Points

- Two-thirds of nuclear medicine technologists work in hospitals.
- Nuclear medicine technology programs range in length from 1 to 4 years and lead to a certificate, an associate degree, or a bachelor's degree.
- Faster-than-average job growth will arise from an increase in the number of middle-aged and elderly persons, who are the primary users of diagnostic and treatment procedures.
- The number of job openings each year will be relatively low because the occupation is small; technologists who also are trained in other diagnostic methods, such as radiologic technology or diagnostic medical sonography, will have the best prospects.

Nature of the Work

Diagnostic imaging embraces several procedures that aid in diagnosing ailments, the most familiar being the x ray. In nuclear medicine, radionuclides—unstable atoms that emit radiation spontaneously—are used to diagnose and treat disease. Radionuclides are purified and compounded to form radiopharmaceuticals. Nuclear medicine technologists administer radiopharmaceuticals to patients and then monitor the characteristics and functions of tissues or organs in which the drugs localize. Abnormal areas show higher-than-expected or lower-than-expected concentrations of radioactivity. Nuclear medicine differs from other diagnostic imaging technologies because it determines the presence of disease on the basis of metabolic changes rather than changes in organ structure.

Nuclear medicine technologists operate cameras that detect and map the radioactive drug in a patient's body to create diagnostic images. After explaining test procedures to patients, technologists prepare a dosage of the radiopharmaceutical and administer it by mouth, injection, inhalation, or other means. They position patients and start a gamma scintillation camera, or "scanner," which creates images of the distribution of a radiopharmaceutical as it localizes in, and emits signals from, the patient's body. The images are produced on a computer screen or on film for a physician to interpret.

When preparing radiopharmaceuticals, technologists adhere to safety standards that keep the radiation exposure as low as possible to workers and patients. Technologists keep patient records and document the amount and type of radionuclides that they receive, use, and discard.

Work environment. Physical stamina is important because nuclear medicine technologists are on their feet much of the day and may have to lift or turn disabled patients. In addition, technologists must operate complicated equipment that requires mechanical ability and manual dexterity.

Although the potential for radiation exposure exists in this field, it is minimized by the use of shielded syringes, gloves, and other protective devices and by adherence to strict radiation safety guidelines.

The amount of radiation in a nuclear medicine procedure is comparable to that received during a diagnostic x-ray procedure. Technologists also wear badges that measure radiation levels. Because of safety programs, badge measurements rarely exceed established safety levels.

Nuclear medicine technologists generally work a 40-hour week, perhaps including evening or weekend hours, in departments that operate on an extended schedule. Opportunities for part-time and shift work also are available. In addition, technologists in hospitals may have on-call duty on a rotational basis, and those employed by mobile imaging services may be required to travel to several locations.

Training, Other Qualifications, and Advancement

Nuclear medicine technology programs range in length from one to four years and lead to a certificate, an associate degree, or a bachelor's degree. Many employers and an increasing number of states require certification or licensure. Aspiring nuclear medicine technologists should check the requirements of the state in which they plan to work.

Education and training. Completion of a nuclear medicine technology program takes one to four years and leads to a certificate, an associate degree, or a bachelor's degree. Generally, certificate programs are offered in hospitals, associate degree programs in community colleges, and bachelor's degree programs in four-year colleges and universities. Courses cover the physical sciences, biological effects of radiation exposure, radiation protection and procedures, the use of radiopharmaceuticals, imaging techniques, and computer applications.

One-year certificate programs are for health professionals who already possess an associate degree—especially radiologic technologists and diagnostic medical sonographers—but who wish to specialize in nuclear medicine. The programs also attract medical technologists, registered nurses, and others who wish to change fields or specialize.

The Joint Review Committee on Education Programs in Nuclear Medicine Technology accredits most formal training programs in nuclear medicine technology. In 2006, there were about 100 accredited programs in the continental United States and Puerto Rico.

Licensure and certification. Educational requirements for nuclear medicine technologists vary from state to state, so it is important that aspiring technologists check the requirements of the state in which they plan to work. More than half of all states require certification or licensing of nuclear medicine technicians. Certification is available from the American Registry of Radiologic Technologists (ARRT) and from the Nuclear Medicine Technology Certification Board (NMTCB). Although not required, some workers receive certification from both agencies. Nuclear medicine technologists must meet the minimum federal standards on the administration of radioactive drugs and the operation of radiation detection equipment.

The most common way to become eligible for certification by ARRT or NMTCB is to complete a training program recognized by those organizations. Other ways to become eligible are completing a bachelor's or associate degree in biological science or related health field, such as registered nursing, or acquiring, under supervision, a certain number of hours of experience in nuclear medicine technology. ARRT and NMTCB have different requirements, but in all cases, one must pass a comprehensive exam to become certified.

In addition to the general certification requirements, certified technicians also must complete a certain number of continuing education hours. Continuing education is required primarily because of the frequent technological and innovative changes in the field of nuclear medicine. Typically, technologists must register annually with both the ARRT and the NMTCB.

Other qualifications. Nuclear medicine technologists should have excellent communication skills, be detail-oriented, and have a desire to continue learning. Technologists must effectively interact with patients and their families and should be sensitive to patients' physical and psychological needs. Nuclear medicine technologists must be able to work independently as they usually have little direct supervision. Technologists also must be detailed-oriented and meticulous when performing procedures to assure that all regulations are being followed.

Advancement. Technologists may advance to supervisor, then to chief technologist, and to department administrator or director. Some technologists specialize in a clinical area such as nuclear cardiology or computer analysis or leave patient care to take positions in research laboratories. Some become instructors in, or directors of, nuclear medicine technology programs, a step that usually requires a bachelor's or master's degree in the subject. Others leave the occupation to work as sales or training representatives for medical equipment and radiopharmaceutical manufacturing firms or as radiation safety officers in regulatory agencies or hospitals.

Employment

Nuclear medicine technologists held about 20,000 jobs in 2006. About 67 percent of all nuclear medicine technologists jobs were in hospitals—private and government. Most of the rest were in offices of physicians or in medical and diagnostic laboratories, including diagnostic imaging centers.

Job Outlook

Faster-than-average job growth will arise from an increase in the number of middle-aged and elderly persons, who are the primary users of diagnostic and treatment procedures. However, the number of job openings each year will be relatively low because the occupation is small.

Employment change. Employment of nuclear medicine technologists is expected to increase by 15 percent from 2006 to 2016, faster

Projections data from the National Employment Matrix

Occupational Title	SOC Code	Employment, 2006	Projected employment, 2016	Change, 2006-2016	
				Number	Percent
Nuclear medicine technologists	29-2033	20,000	23,000	2,900	15

NOTE: Data in this table are rounded.

than the average for all occupations. Growth will arise from technological advancement, the development of new nuclear medicine treatments, and an increase in the number of middle-aged and older persons, who are the primary users of diagnostic procedures, including nuclear medicine tests.

Technological innovations may increase the diagnostic uses of nuclear medicine. New nuclear medical imaging technologies, including positron emission tomography (PET) and single photon emission computed tomography (SPECT), are expected to be used increasingly and to contribute further to employment growth. The wider use of nuclear medical imaging to observe metabolic and biochemical changes during neurology, cardiology, and oncology procedures also will spur demand for nuclear medicine technologists.

Nonetheless, cost considerations will affect the speed with which new applications of nuclear medicine grow. Some promising nuclear medicine procedures, such as positron emission tomography, are extremely costly, and hospitals contemplating these procedures will have to consider equipment costs, reimbursement policies, and the number of potential users.

Job prospects. In spite of fast growth in nuclear medicine, the number of openings into the occupation each year will be relatively low because of the small size of the occupation. Technologists who have additional training in other diagnostic methods, such as radiologic technology or diagnostic medical sonography, will have the best prospects.

Earnings

Median annual earnings of nuclear medicine technologists were $62,300 in May 2006. The middle 50 percent earned between $53,530 and $72,410. The lowest 10 percent earned less than $46,490, and the highest 10 percent earned more than $82,310. Median annual earnings of nuclear medicine technologists in 2006 were $61,230 in general medical and surgical hospitals.

Related Occupations

Nuclear medical technologists operate sophisticated equipment to help physicians and other health practitioners diagnose and treat patients. Cardiovascular technologists and technicians, clinical laboratory technologists and technicians, diagnostic medical sonographers, radiation therapists, radiologic technologists and technicians, and respiratory therapists perform similar functions.

Sources of Additional Information

Additional information on a career as a nuclear medicine technologist is available from

▸ American Society of Radiologic Technologists, 15000 Central Ave. SE, Albuquerque, NM 87123-3917. Internet: http://www.asrt.org

▸ American Registry of Radiologic Technologists, 1255 Northland Dr., St. Paul, MN 55120-1155. Internet: http://www.arrt.org

▸ Society of Nuclear Medicine Technologists, 1850 Samuel Morse Dr., Reston, VA 20190-5316. Internet: http://www.snm.org

For a list of accredited programs in nuclear medicine technology, contact

▸ Joint Review Committee on Educational Programs in Nuclear Medicine Technology, 716 Black Point Rd., Polson, MT 59860. Internet: http://www.jrcnmt.org

Information on certification is available from

▸ Nuclear Medicine Technology Certification Board, 2970 Clairmont Rd., Suite 935, Atlanta, GA 30329-4421. Internet: http://www.nmtcb.org

Nursing, Psychiatric, and Home Health Aides

(O*NET 31-1011.00, 31-1012.00, and 31-1013.00)

Significant Points

■ Numerous job openings and excellent job opportunities are expected.

■ Most jobs are in nursing and residential care facilities, hospitals, and home health care services.

■ This occupation is characterized by modest entry requirements, low pay, high physical and emotional demands, and limited advancement opportunities.

Nature of the Work

Nursing and psychiatric aides help care for physically or mentally ill, injured, disabled, or infirm individuals in hospitals, nursing care facilities, and mental health settings. Home health aides have duties that are similar, but they work in patients' homes or residential care facilities. Nursing aides and home health aides are among the occupations commonly referred to as direct care workers, due to their role in working with patients who need long-term care. The specific care they give depends on their specialty.

Nursing aides also known as nurse aides, nursing assistants, certified nursing assistants, geriatric aides, unlicensed assistive personnel, orderlies, or hospital attendants provide hands-on care and perform routine tasks under the supervision of nursing and medical staff. Specific tasks vary, with aides handling many aspects of a patient's care. They often help patients to eat, dress, and bathe. They also answer calls for help, deliver messages, serve meals, make beds, and tidy up rooms. Aides sometimes are responsible for taking a patient's temperature, pulse rate, respiration rate, or blood pressure. They also may help provide care to patients by helping them get into and out of bed and walk, escorting them to operating and examining rooms, or providing skin care. Some aides help other medical staff by setting up equipment, storing and moving supplies, and assisting with some procedures. Aides also observe patients' physical, mental, and emotional conditions and report any change to the nursing or medical staff.

Nurse aides employed in nursing care facilities often are the principal caregivers, having far more contact with residents than do other members of the staff. Because some residents may stay in a nursing care facility for months or even years, aides develop ongoing relationships with them and interact with them in a positive, caring way.

Home health aides help elderly, convalescent, or disabled persons live in their own homes instead of health care facilities. Under the direction of nursing or medical staff, they provide health-related services, such as administering oral medications. (Personal and home care aides, who provide mainly housekeeping and routine personal care services, are discussed elsewhere in this book.) Like nursing aides, home health aides may check patients' pulse rate, temperature, and respiration rate; help with simple prescribed exercises; and help patients to get in and out of bed, bathe, dress, and groom. Occasionally, they change nonsterile dressings, give massages and provide skin care, or assist with braces and artificial limbs. Experienced home health aides, with training, also may assist with medical equipment such as ventilators, which help patients breathe.

Most home health aides work with elderly or disabled persons who need more extensive care than family or friends can provide. Some help discharged hospital patients who have relatively short-term needs.

In home health agencies, a registered nurse, physical therapist, or social worker usually assigns specific duties to and supervises home health aides, who keep records of the services they perform and record each patient's condition and progress. The aides report changes in a patient's condition to the supervisor or case manager.

Psychiatric aides, also known as mental health assistants or psychiatric nursing assistants, care for mentally impaired or emotionally disturbed individuals. They work under a team that may include psychiatrists, psychologists, psychiatric nurses, social workers, and therapists. In addition to helping patients to dress, bathe, groom themselves, and eat, psychiatric aides socialize with them and lead them in educational and recreational activities. Psychiatric aides may play card games or other games with patients, watch television with them, or participate in group activities, such as playing sports or going on field trips. They observe patients and report any physical or behavioral signs that might be important for the professional staff to know. They accompany patients to and from therapy and treatment. Because they have such close contact with patients, psychiatric aides can have a great deal of influence on their outlook and treatment.

Work environment. Work as an aide can be physically demanding. Aides spend many hours standing and walking, and they often face heavy workloads. Aides must guard against back injury because they may have to move patients into and out of bed or help them to stand or walk. It is important for aides to be trained in and to follow the proper procedures for lifting and moving patients. Aides also may face hazards from minor infections and major diseases, such as hepatitis, but can avoid infections by following proper procedures.

Aides also perform tasks that some may consider unpleasant, such as emptying bedpans and changing soiled bed linens. The patients they care for may be disoriented, irritable, or uncooperative. Psychiatric aides must be prepared to care for patients whose illness may cause violent behavior. Although their work can be emotionally demanding, many aides gain satisfaction from assisting those in need.

Home health aides may go to the same patient's home for months or even years. However, most aides work with a number of different patients, each job lasting a few hours, days, or weeks. Home health aides often visit multiple patients on the same day.

Home health aides generally work alone, with periodic visits from their supervisor. They receive detailed instructions explaining when to visit patients and what services to perform. Aides are individually responsible for getting to patients' homes, and they may spend a good portion of the working day traveling from one patient to another. Because mechanical lifting devices available in institutional settings are not as frequently available in patients' homes, home

health aides must take extra care to avoid injuries resulting from overexertion when they assist patients.

Most full-time aides work about 40 hours per week, but because patients need care 24 hours a day, some aides work evenings, nights, weekends, and holidays. In 2006, 23 percent of aides worked part time compared with 15 percent of all workers.

Training, Other Qualifications, and Advancement

In many cases, a high school diploma or equivalent is necessary for a job as a nursing or psychiatric aide. However, a high school diploma generally is not required for jobs as home health aides. Specific qualifications vary by occupation, state laws, and work setting. Advancement opportunities are limited.

Education and training. Nursing and psychiatric aide training is offered in high schools, vocational-technical centers, some nursing care facilities, and some community colleges. Courses cover body mechanics, nutrition, anatomy and physiology, infection control, communication skills, and resident rights. Personal care skills, such as how to help patients to bathe, eat, and groom themselves, also are taught. Hospitals may require previous experience as a nursing aide or home health aide. Some states also require psychiatric aides to complete a formal training program. However, most psychiatric aides learn their skills on the job from experienced workers.

Home health aides are generally not required to have a high school diploma. They usually are trained on the job by registered nurses, licensed practical nurses, or experienced aides. Also, clients may prefer that tasks are done a certain way, and make those suggestions to the home health aide. A competency evaluation may be required to ensure the aide can perform the required tasks.

Some employers provide classroom instruction for newly hired aides, while others rely exclusively on informal on-the-job instruction by a licensed nurse or an experienced aide. Such training may last from several days to a few months. Aides also may attend lectures, workshops, and in-service training.

Licensure and certification. The federal government has guidelines for home health aides whose employers receive reimbursement from Medicare. Federal law requires home health aides to pass a competency test covering a wide range of areas. A home health aide may receive training before taking the competency test. In addition, the National Association for Home Care and Hospice offers voluntary certification for home health aides. Some states also require aides to be licensed.

Similar federal requirements exist for nurse aides who work in nursing care facilities. These aides must complete a minimum of 75 hours of state-approved training and pass a competency evaluation. Aides who complete the program are known as certified nurse assistants (CNAs) and are placed on the state registry of nurse aides.

Other qualifications. Aides must be in good health. A physical examination, including state-regulated tests such as those for tuberculosis, may be required. A criminal background check also is usually required for employment.

Applicants should be tactful, patient, understanding, emotionally stable, and dependable and should have a desire to help people. They also should be able to work as part of a team, have good communication skills, and be willing to perform repetitive, routine tasks. Home health aides should be honest and discreet because they work

Projections data from the National Employment Matrix

Occupational Title	SOC Code	Employment, 2006	Projected employment, 2016	Change, 2006-16	
				Number	Percent
Nursing, psychiatric, and home health aides	31-1000	2,296,000	2,944,000	647,000	28
Home health aides...	31-1011	787,000	1,171,000	384,000	49
Nursing aides, orderlies, and attendants	31-1012	1,447,000	1,711,000	264,000	18
Psychiatric aides...	31-1013	62,000	62,000	0	0

NOTE: Data in this table are rounded.

in private homes. They also will need access to a car or public transportation to reach patients' homes.

Advancement. Opportunities for advancement within these occupations are limited. Aides generally need additional formal training or education to enter other health occupations. The most common health care occupations for former aides are licensed practical nurse, registered nurse, and medical assistant.

For some individuals, these occupations serve as entry-level jobs. For example, some high school and college students gain experience working in these occupations while attending school. In addition, experience as an aide can help individuals decide whether to pursue a career in health care.

Employment

Nursing, psychiatric, and home health aides held about 2.3 million jobs in 2006. Nursing aides held the most jobs—approximately 1.4 million. Home health aides held roughly 787,000 jobs, and psychiatric aides held about 62,000 jobs. About 52 percent of nursing aides worked in nursing and residential care facilities and another 29 percent worked in hospitals. Home health aides were mainly employed by home health care services, nursing and residential care facilities and social assistance agencies. About 47 percent of all psychiatric aides worked in hospitals, primarily in psychiatric and substance abuse hospitals, although some also worked in the psychiatric units of general medical and surgical hospitals. Others were employed in state government agencies; residential mental retardation, mental health, and substance abuse facilities; and nursing and residential care facilities.

Job Outlook

Excellent job opportunities for nursing, psychiatric, and home health aides will arise from a combination of rapid employment growth and the need to replace the many workers who leave the occupation each year.

Employment change. Overall employment of nursing, psychiatric, and home health aides is projected to grow 28 percent between 2006 and 2016, much faster than the average for all occupations. However, growth will vary for the individual occupations. Home health aides are expected to gain jobs faster than other aides as a result of growing demand for home services from an aging population and efforts to contain costs by moving patients out of hospitals and nursing care facilities as quickly as possible. Consumer preference for care in the home and improvements in medical technologies for in-home treatment also will contribute to much-faster-than-average employment growth for home health aides.

Nursing aide employment will not grow as fast as home health aide employment, largely because nursing aides are concentrated in relatively slower-growing industries. Employment of nursing aides is

expected to grow faster than the average for all occupations through 2016, in response to the long-term care needs of an increasing elderly population. Financial pressures on hospitals to discharge patients as soon as possible should boost admissions to nursing care facilities. As a result, job openings will be more numerous in nursing and residential care facilities than in hospitals. Modern medical technology also will drive demand for nursing aides because as the technology saves and extends more lives, it increases the need for long-term care provided by aides.

Little or no change is expected in employment of psychiatric aides—the smallest of the three occupations. Most psychiatric aides currently work in hospitals, but the industries most likely to see growth will be residential facilities for people with developmental disabilities, mental illness, and substance abuse problems. There is a long-term trend toward treating psychiatric patients outside of hospitals because it is more cost effective and allows patients to live more independent lives. Demand for psychiatric aides in residential facilities will rise in response to the increase in the number of older persons, many of whom will require mental health services. Growing demand for these workers also rests on an increasing number of mentally disabled adults who were formerly cared for by their elderly parents and who will continue to need care. Job growth also could be affected by changes in government funding of programs for the mentally ill.

Job prospects. High replacement needs for nursing, psychiatric, and home health aides reflect modest entry requirements, low pay, high physical and emotional demands, and limited opportunities for advancement within the occupation. For these same reasons, the number of people looking to enter the occupation will be limited. Many aides leave the occupation to attend training programs for other health care occupations. Therefore, people who are interested in, and suited for, this work should have excellent job opportunities.

Earnings

Median hourly earnings of nursing aides, orderlies, and attendants were $10.67 in May 2006. The middle 50 percent earned between $9.09 and $12.80 an hour. The lowest 10 percent earned less than $7.78, and the highest 10 percent earned more than $14.99 an hour. Median hourly earnings in the industries employing the largest numbers of nursing aides, orderlies, and attendants in May 2006 were

Local government $12.15
Employment services 11.47
General medical and surgical hospitals 11.06
Nursing care facilities 10.37
Community care facilities for the elderly..................10.07

Nursing and psychiatric aides in hospitals generally receive at least 1 week of paid vacation after 1 year of service. Paid holidays and sick leave, hospital and medical benefits, extra pay for late-shift work, and pension plans also are available to many hospital employees and to some nursing care facility employees.

Median hourly earnings of home health aides were $9.34 in May 2006. The middle 50 percent earned between $7.99 and $10.90 an hour. The lowest 10 percent earned less than $7.06, and the highest 10 percent earned more than $13.00 an hour. Median hourly earnings in the industries employing the largest numbers of home health aides in May 2006 were

Nursing care facilities $9.76

Residential mental retardation facilities 9.34

Services for the elderly and persons with
disabilities 9.26

Home health care services 9.14

Community care facilities for the elderly 8.87

Home health aides receive slight pay increases with experience and added responsibility. Usually, they are paid only for the time worked in the home, not for travel time between jobs, and must pay for their travel costs from their earnings. Most employers hire only on-call hourly workers and provide no benefits.

Median hourly earnings of psychiatric aides were $11.49 in May 2006. The middle 50 percent earned between $9.20 and $14.46 an hour. The lowest 10 percent earned less than $7.75, and the highest 10 percent earned more than $17.32 an hour. Median hourly earnings in the industries employing the largest numbers of psychiatric aides in May 2006 were

State government $13.27

General medical and surgical hospitals 12.31

Psychiatric and substance abuse hospitals 11.76

Residential mental health and substance abuse
facilities 9.65

Residential mental retardation facilities 8.80

Related Occupations

Nursing, psychiatric, and home health aides help people who need routine care or treatment. So do child care workers, licensed practical and licensed vocational nurses, medical assistants, occupational therapist assistants and aides, personal and home care aides, physical therapist assistants and aides, radiation therapists, and registered nurses. Social and human service assistants, who sometimes work with mental health patients, do work similar to that of psychiatric aides.

Sources of Additional Information

Information about employment opportunities may be obtained from local hospitals, nursing care facilities, home health care agencies, psychiatric facilities, state boards of nursing, and local offices of the state employment service.

Information on licensing requirements for nursing and home health aides, and lists of state-approved nursing aide programs are available from state departments of public health, departments of occupational licensing, boards of nursing, and home care associations.

For more information on training and requirements for home health aides, contact

▶ National Association for Home Care and Hospice, 228 7th St. SE, Washington, DC 20003. Internet: http://www.nahc.org

For more information on the home health care industry, contact

▶ Visiting Nurse Associations of America, 8403 Colesville Rd., Suite 1550, Silver Spring, MD 20910-6374. Internet: http://www.vnaa.org

For more information on the health care workforce, contact

▶ The Center for the Health Professions, 3333 California St., San Francisco, CA 94118. Internet: http://www.futurehealth.ucsf.edu

Occupational Therapist Assistants and Aides

(O*NET 31-2011.00 and 31-2012.00)

Significant Points

◾ Occupational therapist assistants generally must complete an associate degree or a certificate program; in contrast, occupational therapist aides usually receive most of their training on the job.

◾ Employment is projected to grow much faster than the average as demand for occupational therapy services rises and as occupational therapists increasingly use assistants and aides.

◾ Job prospects should be very good for occupational therapist assistants; job seekers holding only a high school diploma might face keen competition for occupational therapist aide jobs.

Nature of the Work

Occupational therapist assistants and aides work under the direction of occupational therapists to provide rehabilitative services to persons with mental, physical, emotional, or developmental impairments. The ultimate goal is to improve clients' quality of life and ability to perform daily activities. For example, occupational therapist assistants help injured workers re-enter the labor force by teaching them how to compensate for lost motor skills or help individuals with learning disabilities increase their independence.

Occupational therapist assistants, commonly known as *occupational therapy assistants*, help clients with rehabilitative activities and exercises outlined in a treatment plan developed in collaboration with an occupational therapist. Activities range from teaching the proper method of moving from a bed into a wheelchair to the best way to stretch and limber the muscles of the hand. Assistants monitor an individual's activities to make sure that they are performed correctly and to provide encouragement. They also record their client's progress for the occupational therapist. If the treatment is not having the intended effect, or the client is not improving as expected, the therapist may alter the treatment program in hopes of obtaining better results. In addition, occupational therapist assistants document the billing of the client's health insurance provider.

Occupational therapist aides typically prepare materials and assemble equipment used during treatment. They are responsible for a range of clerical tasks, including scheduling appointments, answering the telephone, restocking or ordering depleted supplies, and filling out insurance forms or other paperwork. Aides are not licensed, so the law does not allow them to perform as wide a range of tasks as occupational therapist assistants.

Work environment. Occupational therapist assistants and aides need to have a moderate degree of strength because of the physical exertion required to assist patients. For example, assistants and aides may need to lift patients. Constant kneeling, stooping, and standing for long periods also are part of the job.

The hours and days that occupational therapist assistants and aides work vary by facility and with whether they are full- or part time. For example, many outpatient therapy offices and clinics have evening and weekend hours to coincide with patients' schedules.

Training, Other Qualifications, and Advancement

An associate degree or a certificate from an accredited community college or technical school is generally required to qualify for occupational therapist assistant jobs. In contrast, occupational therapist aides usually receive most of their training on the job.

Education and training. There were 126 accredited occupational therapist assistant programs in 2007. The first year of study typically involves an introduction to health care, basic medical terminology, anatomy, and physiology. In the second year, courses are more rigorous and usually include occupational therapist courses in areas such as mental health, adult physical disabilities, gerontology, and pediatrics. Students also must complete 16 weeks of supervised fieldwork in a clinic or community setting.

Applicants to occupational therapist assistant programs can improve their chances of admission by taking high school courses in biology and health and by performing volunteer work in nursing care facilities, occupational or physical therapists' offices, or other health care settings.

Occupational therapist aides usually receive most of their training on the job. Qualified applicants must have a high school diploma, strong interpersonal skills, and a desire to help people in need. Applicants may increase their chances of getting a job by volunteering their services, thus displaying initiative and aptitude to the employer.

Licensure. In most states, occupational therapist assistants are regulated and must pass a national certification examination after they graduate. Those who pass the test are awarded the title "Certified Occupational Therapy Assistant."

Other qualifications. Assistants and aides must be responsible, patient, and willing to take directions and work as part of a team. Furthermore, they should be caring and want to help people who are not able to help themselves.

Advancement. Occupational therapist assistants may advance into administration positions. They might organize all the assistants in a large occupational therapy department or act as the director for a

specific department such as sports medicine. Some assistants go on to teach classes in accredited occupational therapist assistant academic programs or lead health risk reduction classes for the elderly.

Employment

Occupational therapist assistants and aides held about 33,000 jobs in 2006. Occupational therapist assistants held about 25,000 jobs, and occupational therapist aides held approximately 8,000. About 29 percent of jobs for assistants and aides were in hospitals, 23 percent were in offices of occupational therapists, and 21 percent were in nursing and residential care facilities. The rest were primarily in community care facilities for the elderly, home health care services, individual and family services, and state government agencies.

Job Outlook

Employment is expected to grow much faster than average as demand for occupational therapy services rises and as occupational therapists increasingly use assistants and aides. Job prospects should be very good for occupational therapist assistants. Job seekers holding only a high school diploma might face keen competition for occupational therapist aide jobs.

Employment change. Employment of occupational therapist assistants and aides is expected to grow 25 percent from 2006 to 2016, much faster than the average for all occupations. In the short run, the impact of proposed federal legislation imposing limits on reimbursement for therapy services may adversely affect the job market for occupational therapist assistants and aides. Over the long run, however, demand for occupational therapist assistants and aides will continue to rise because of the increasing number of individuals with disabilities or limited function.

The growing elderly population is particularly vulnerable to chronic and debilitating conditions that require therapeutic services. These patients often need additional assistance in their treatment, making the roles of assistants and aides vital. Also, the large baby-boom generation is entering the prime age for heart attacks and strokes, further increasing the demand for cardiac and physical rehabilitation. In addition, future medical developments should permit an increased percentage of trauma victims to survive, creating added demand for therapy services. An increase of sensory disorders in children will also spur demand for occupational therapy services.

Occupational therapists are expected to increasingly utilize assistants and aides to reduce the cost of occupational therapy services. Once a patient is evaluated and a treatment plan is designed by the therapist, the occupational therapist assistant can provide many aspects of treatment, as prescribed by the therapist.

Job prospects. Opportunities for individuals interested in becoming occupational therapist assistants are expected to be very good. In addition to employment growth, job openings will result from the need to replace occupational therapist assistants and aides who leave

Projections data from the National Employment Matrix

Occupational Title	SOC Code	Employment, 2006	Projected employment, 2016	Change, 2006-16	
				Number	Percent
Occupational therapist assistants and aides	31-2010	33,000	41,000	8,200	25
Occupational therapist assistants	31-2011	25,000	31,000	6,400	25
Occupational therapist aides	31-2012	8,200	10,000	1,800	22

NOTE: Data in this table are rounded.

the occupation permanently over the 2006–2016 period. Occupational therapist assistants and aides with prior experience working in an occupational therapy office or other health care setting will have the best job opportunities. However, individuals with only a high school diploma may face keen competition for occupational therapist aide jobs.

Earnings

Median annual earnings of occupational therapist assistants were $42,060 in May 2006. The middle 50 percent earned between $34,130 and $50,230. The lowest 10 percent earned less than $26,050, and the highest 10 percent earned more than $58,270. Median annual earnings in the industries employing the largest numbers of occupational therapist assistants in May 2006 were

Offices of physical, occupational and speech
  therapists, and audiologists $45,130

Nursing care facilities 43,280

General medical and surgical hospitals 40,060

Median annual earnings of occupational therapist aides were $25,020 in May 2006. The middle 50 percent earned between $20,460 and $32,160. The lowest 10 percent earned less than $17,060, and the highest 10 percent earned more than $44,130. Median annual earnings in the industries employing the largest numbers of occupational therapist aides in May 2006 were

Offices of physical, occupational and speech
  therapists, and audiologists $26,960

General medical and surgical hospitals 26,360

Nursing care facilities 25,520

Related Occupations

Occupational therapist assistants and aides work under the supervision and direction of occupational therapists. Other workers in the health care field who work under similar supervision include dental assistants; medical assistants; nursing, psychiatric, and home health aides; personal and home care aides; pharmacy aides; pharmacy technicians; and physical therapist assistants and aides.

Sources of Additional Information

For information on a career as an occupational therapist assistant or aide, and a list of accredited programs, contact

▸ American Occupational Therapy Association, 4720 Montgomery Lane, Bethesda, MD 20824-1220. Internet: http://www.aota.org

Office and Administrative Support Worker Supervisors and Managers

(O*NET 43-1011.00, 43-1011.01, and 43-1011.02)

Significant Points

■ Most jobs are filled by promoting office or administrative support workers from within the organization.

■ Office automation will cause employment in some office and administrative support occupations to grow slowly or even decline, resulting in slower-than-average growth among supervisors and managers.

■ Applicants are likely to encounter keen competition because their numbers should greatly exceed the number of job openings.

Nature of the Work

All organizations need timely and effective office and administrative support to operate efficiently. Office and administrative support supervisors and managers coordinate this support. These workers are employed in virtually every sector of the economy, working in positions as varied as teller supervisor, customer services manager, or shipping and receiving supervisor.

Although specific functions of office and administrative support supervisors and managers vary significantly, they share many common duties. For example, supervisors perform administrative tasks to ensure that their staffs can work efficiently. Equipment and machinery used in their departments must be in good working order. If the computer system goes down or a fax machine malfunctions, the supervisors must try to correct the problem or alert repair personnel. They also request new equipment or supplies for their department when necessary.

Planning work and supervising staff are key functions of this job. To do these effectively, the supervisor must know the strengths and weaknesses of each member of the staff, as well as the results required and time allotted to each job. Supervisors must make allowances for unexpected staff absences and other disruptions by adjusting assignments or performing the work themselves if the situation requires it.

After allocating work assignments and issuing deadlines, office and administrative support supervisors and managers oversee the work to ensure that it is proceeding on schedule and meeting established quality standards. This may involve reviewing each person's work on a computer—as in the case of accounting clerks—or listening to how a worker deals with customers—as in the case of customer services representatives. When supervising long-term projects, the supervisor may meet regularly with staff members to discuss their progress.

Office and administrative support supervisors and managers also evaluate each worker's performance. If a worker has done a good job, the supervisor indicates that in the employee's personnel file and may recommend a promotion or other award. Alternatively, if a worker is performing inadequately, the supervisor discusses the problem with the employee to determine the cause and helps the worker to improve his or her performance. This might require sending the employee to a training course or arranging personal counseling. If the situation does not improve, the supervisor may recommend a transfer, demotion, or dismissal.

Office and administrative support supervisors and managers usually interview and evaluate prospective employees. When new workers arrive on the job, supervisors greet them and provide orientation to acquaint them with their organization and its operating routines. Some supervisors may be actively involved in recruiting new workers—for example, by making presentations at high schools and business colleges. They also may serve as the primary liaisons between their offices and the general public through direct contact and by preparing promotional information.

Supervisors help train new employees in organization and office procedures. They may teach new employees how to use the telephone system and operate office equipment. Because most administrative support work is computerized, they also must teach new employees to use the organization's computer system. When new office equipment or updated computer software is introduced, supervisors train experienced employees to use it efficiently or, if this is not possible, arrange for their employees to receive special outside training.

Office and administrative support supervisors and managers often act as liaisons between the administrative support staff and the professional, technical, and managerial staff. This may involve implementing new company policies or restructuring the workflow in their departments. They also must keep their superiors informed of their progress and any potential problems. Often, this communication takes the form of research projects and progress reports. Because supervisors and managers have access to information such as their department's performance records, they may compile and present these data for use in planning or designing new policies.

Office and administrative support supervisors and managers also may have to resolve interpersonal conflicts among the staff. In organizations covered by union contracts, supervisors must know the provisions of labor-management agreements and run their departments accordingly. They also may meet with union representatives to discuss work problems or grievances.

Work environment. Office and administrative support supervisors and managers are employed in a wide variety of work settings, but most work in clean and well-lit offices that usually are comfortable.

Most office and administrative support supervisors and managers work a standard 40-hour week. However, some organizations operate around the clock, so some supervisors may have to work nights, weekends, and holidays. Sometimes, supervisors rotate among the three 8-hour shifts in a workday; in other cases, shifts are assigned on the basis of seniority.

Training, Other Qualifications, and Advancement

Most firms fill office and administrative support supervisory and managerial positions by promoting office or administrative support workers from within their organizations. To become eligible for promotion to a supervisory position, administrative support workers must prove they are capable of handling additional responsibilities.

Education and training. Many employers require office and administrative support supervisors and managers to have postsecondary training—and in some cases, an associate or even a bachelor's degree. Good working knowledge of the organization's computer system is also an advantage. In addition, supervisors must pay close attention to detail in order to identify and correct errors made by the staff they oversee.

Most office and administrative support worker supervisors and managers are promoted from within the company. Several years of on-the-job experience are usually the best preparation to become a supervisor or manager. After acquiring some experience, the employee should have a thorough knowledge of other personnel and company operations.

Administrative support workers with potential supervisory abilities may be given occasional supervisory assignments. To prepare for full-time supervisory duties, workers may attend in-house training or take courses in time management, project management, or interpersonal relations.

Other qualifications. When evaluating candidates, supervisors look for strong teamwork, problem-solving, leadership, and communication skills, as well as determination, loyalty, poise, and confidence. They also look for more specific supervisory attributes, such as the ability to organize and coordinate work efficiently, to set priorities, and to motivate others. Increasingly, supervisors need a broad base of office skills coupled with personal flexibility to adapt to changes in organizational structure and move among departments when necessary.

Advancement. For office and administrative supervisors and managers promoted from within, advancement opportunities may be limited without a postsecondary degree, depending on the company. The knowledge required to move into more business and financial related occupations may not necessarily be learned through working in an office or administrative occupation.

In some managerial positions, office and administrative support supervisor positions are filled with people from outside the organization. These positions may serve as entry-level training for potential higher level managers. New college graduates may rotate through departments of an organization at this level to learn the work of the organization before moving on to a higher level position.

Employment

Office and administrative support supervisors and managers held 1.4 million jobs in 2006. Although jobs for office and administrative support supervisors and managers are found in practically every industry, the largest number are found in organizations with a large administrative support workforce, such as banks, wholesalers, government agencies, retail establishments, business service firms, health care facilities, schools, and insurance companies. Because of most organizations' need for continuity of supervision, few office and administrative support supervisors and managers work on a temporary or part-time basis.

Job Outlook

Employment of office and administrative support supervisors and managers is expected to grow more slowly than the average for all occupations through the year 2016. Keen competition is expected for prospective job applicants.

Employment change. Employment is expected to grow by 6 percent during the 2006–2016 period, which is more slowly than the average for all occupations. Employment of office and administrative support supervisors and managers is determined largely by the demand for administrative support workers. New technology should increase office and administrative support workers' productivity and allow a wider variety of tasks to be performed by people in professional positions. These trends will cause employment in some administrative support occupations to grow slowly or even decline. As a result, supervisors will direct smaller permanent staffs—supplemented by increased use of temporary administrative support staff—and perform more professional tasks. Office and administrative support managers will coordinate the increasing amount of

Projections data from the National Employment Matrix

Occupational Title	SOC Code	Employment, 2006	Projected employment, 2016	Change, 2006-16	
				Number	Percent
First-line supervisors/managers of office and administrative support workers...	43-1011	1,418,000	1,500,000	82,000	6

NOTE: Data in this table are rounded.

administrative work and make sure that the technology is applied and running properly. However, organizational restructuring should continue to reduce employment in some managerial positions, distributing more responsibility to office and administrative support supervisors.

Job prospects. Like those seeking other supervisory and managerial occupations, applicants for jobs as office and administrative support worker supervisors and managers are likely to encounter keen competition because the number of applicants should greatly exceed the number of job openings. Besides the job openings arising from growth, a large number of openings will stem from the need to replace workers who transfer to other occupations or leave this large occupation for other reasons.

Earnings

Median annual earnings of office and administrative support supervisors and managers were $43,510 in May 2006; the middle 50 percent earned between $33,730 and $56,130. The lowest-paid 10 percent earned less than $26,530, while the highest-paid 10 percent earned more than $71,340. In May 2006, median annual earnings in the industries employing the largest numbers of office and administrative support supervisors and managers were

Management of companies and enterprises	$49,160
Local government	45,520
General medical and surgical hospitals	44,250
Offices of physicians	42,110
Depository credit intermediation	40,900

In addition to typical benefits, some office and administrative support supervisors and managers, particularly in the private sector, may receive additional compensation in the form of bonuses and stock options.

Related Occupations

Office and administrative support supervisors and managers must understand and sometimes perform the work of those whom they oversee, including bookkeeping, accounting, and auditing clerks; secretaries and administrative assistants; communications equipment operators; customer service representatives; data entry and information processing workers; general office clerks; receptionists and information clerks; stock clerks and order fillers; and order clerks. Their supervisory and administrative duties are similar to those of other supervisors and managers, such as education administrators and administrative services managers.

Sources of Additional Information

For information related to a wide variety of management occupations, including educational programs and certified designations, contact

▶ International Association of Administrative Professionals, 10502 NW Ambassador Dr., P.O. Box 20404, Kansas City, MO 64195-0404. Internet: http://www.iaap-hq.org

▶ American Management Association, 1601 Broadway, New York, NY 10019. Internet: http://www.amanet.org

▶ Association of Professional Office Managers, 1 Research Court, Suite 450, Rockville, MD 20850. Internet: http://www.apomonline.org

Office Clerks, General

(O*NET 43-9061.00)

Significant Points

■ Employment growth and high replacement needs in this large occupation will result in numerous job openings.

■ Prospects should be best for those with knowledge of basic computer applications and office machinery as well as good communication skills.

■ Part-time and temporary positions are common.

Nature of the Work

Rather than performing a single specialized task, general office clerks have responsibilities that often change daily with the needs of the specific job and the employer. Some clerks spend their days filing or keyboarding. Others enter data at a computer terminal. They also operate photocopiers, fax machines, and other office equipment; prepare mailings; proofread documents; and answer telephones and deliver messages.

The specific duties assigned to a clerk vary significantly, depending on the type of office in which he or she works. An office clerk in a doctor's office, for example, would not perform the same tasks that a clerk in a large financial institution or in the office of an auto parts wholesaler would. Although all clerks may sort checks, keep payroll records, take inventory, and access information, they also perform duties unique to their employer, such as organizing medications in a doctor's office, preparing materials for presentations in a corporate office, or filling orders received by fax machine for a wholesaler.

Clerks' duties also vary by level of experience. Whereas inexperienced employees make photocopies, stuff envelopes, or record inquiries, experienced clerks usually are given additional responsibilities. For example, they may maintain financial or other records, set up spreadsheets, verify statistical reports for accuracy and completeness, handle and adjust customer complaints, work with vendors, make travel arrangements, take inventory of equipment and supplies, answer questions on departmental services and functions, or help prepare invoices or budgetary requests. Senior office clerks may be expected to monitor and direct the work of lower level clerks.

Work environment. For the most part, general office clerks work in comfortable office settings. Those on full-time schedules usually work a standard 40-hour week; however, some work shifts or overtime during busy periods. About 26 percent of clerks work part time in 2006. Many clerks also work in temporary positions.

Training, Other Qualifications, and Advancement

Office clerks often need to know how to use word processing and other business software and office equipment. Experience working in an office is helpful, but office clerks also learn skills on the job.

Education and training. Although most office clerk jobs are entry-level positions, employers may prefer or require previous office or business experience. Employers usually require a high school diploma or equivalent, and some require basic computer skills, including familiarity with word processing software, as well as other general office skills.

Training for this occupation is available through business education programs offered in high schools, community and junior colleges, and postsecondary vocational schools. Courses in office practices, word processing, and other computer applications are particularly helpful.

Other qualifications. Because general office clerks usually work with other office staff, they should be cooperative and able to work as part of a team. Employers prefer individuals who can perform a variety of tasks and satisfy the needs of the many departments within a company. In addition, applicants should have good communication skills, be detail oriented, and adaptable.

Advancement. General office clerks who exhibit strong communication, interpersonal, and analytical skills may be promoted to supervisory positions. Others may move into different, more senior administrative jobs, such as receptionist, secretary, or administrative assistant. After gaining some work experience or specialized skills, many workers transfer to jobs with higher pay or greater advancement potential. Advancement to professional occupations within an organization normally requires additional formal education, such as a college degree.

Employment

General office clerks held about 3.2 million jobs in 2006. Most are employed in relatively small businesses. Although they work in every sector of the economy, about 43 percent worked in local government, health care and social assistance, administrative and support services, finance and insurance, or professional, scientific, and technical services industries.

Job Outlook

Employment growth and high replacement needs in this large occupation is expected to result in numerous job openings for general office clerks.

Employment change. Employment of general office clerks is expected to grow 13 percent between 2006 and 2016, which is about as fast as the average for all occupations. The employment outlook for these workers will continue to be affected by the increasing use of technology, expanding office automation, and the consolidation of administrative support tasks. These factors have led to a consolidation of administrative support staffs and a diversification of job responsibilities. However, this consolidation will increase the demand for general office clerks because they perform a variety of administrative support tasks, as opposed to clerks with very specific functions. It will become increasingly common within businesses, especially those smaller in size, to find only general office clerks in charge of all administrative support work.

Job prospects. Many job openings for general office clerks are expected to be for full-time jobs; there will also be a demand for part-time and temporary positions. Prospects should be best for those who have good writing and communication skills and knowledge of basic computer applications and office machinery—such as fax machines, telephone systems, and scanners. As general administrative support duties continue to be consolidated, employers will increasingly seek well-rounded individuals with highly developed communication skills and the ability to perform multiple tasks.

Job opportunities may vary from year to year because the strength of the economy affects demand for general office clerks. Companies tend to employ more workers when the economy is strong. Industries least likely to be affected by economic fluctuations tend to be the most stable places for employment.

Earnings

Median annual earnings of general office clerks were $23,710 in May 2006; the middle 50 percent earned between $18,640 and $30,240 annually. The lowest 10 percent earned less than $14,850, and the highest 10 percent earned more than $37,600. Median annual salaries in the industries employing the largest numbers of general office clerks in May 2006 were

Local government	$26,590
General medical and surgical hospitals	26,050
Elementary and secondary schools	24,230
Colleges, universities, and professional schools	23,980
Employment services	21,890

Related Occupations

The duties of general office clerks can include a combination of bookkeeping, keyboarding, office machine operation, and filing. Other office and administrative support workers who perform similar duties include bookkeeping, accounting, and auditing clerks; communications equipment operators; customer service representatives; data entry and information processing workers; order clerks; receptionists and information clerks; secretaries and administrative assistants; stock clerks and order fillers; and tellers. Nonclerical

Projections data from the National Employment Matrix

Occupational Title	SOC Code	Employment, 2006	Projected employment, 2016	Change, 2006-16	
				Number	Percent
Office clerks, general	43-9061	3,200,000	3,604,000	404,000	13

NOTE: Data in this table are rounded.

entry-level workers include cashiers; counter and rental clerks; and food and beverage serving and related workers.

Sources of Additional Information

State employment service offices and agencies can provide information about job openings for general office clerks.

For information related to administrative occupations, including educational programs and certified designations, contact

▸ International Association of Administrative Professionals, 10502 NW Ambassador Dr., P.O. Box 20404, Kansas City, MO 64195-0404. Internet: http://www.iaap-hq.org

▸ American Management Association, 1601 Broadway, New York, NY 10019. Internet: http://www.amanet.org

Painters and Paperhangers

(O*NET 47-2141.00 and 47-2142.00)

Significant Points

■ Employment prospects for painters should be excellent due to the large numbers of workers who leave the occupation for other jobs; paperhangers will face very limited opportunities.

■ Most workers learn informally on the job as helpers, but some experts recommend completion of an apprenticeship program.

■ About 42 percent of painters and paperhangers are self employed.

Nature of the Work

Paint and wall coverings make surfaces clean, attractive, and bright. In addition, paints and other sealers protect exterior surfaces from wear caused by exposure to the weather.

Painters apply paint, stain, varnish, and other finishes to buildings and other structures. They choose the right paint or finish for the surface to be covered, taking into account durability, ease of handling, method of application, and customers' wishes. Painters first prepare the surfaces to be covered, so that the paint will adhere properly. This may require removing the old coat of paint by stripping, sanding, wire brushing, burning, or water and abrasive blasting. Painters also wash walls and trim to remove dirt and grease, fill nail holes and cracks, sandpaper rough spots, and brush off dust. On new surfaces, they apply a primer or sealer to prepare the surface for the finish coat. Painters also mix paints and match colors, relying on knowledge of paint composition and color harmony. In large paint shops or hardware stores, mixing and matching are automated.

There are several ways to apply paint and similar coverings. Painters must be able to choose the right paint applicator for each job, depending on the surface to be covered, the characteristics of the finish, and other factors. Some jobs need only a good bristle brush with a soft, tapered edge; others require a dip or fountain pressure roller; still others are best done using a paint sprayer. Many jobs need several types of applicators. In fact, painters may use an assortment of brushes, edgers, and rollers for a single job. The right tools speed the painter's work and also produce the most attractive surface.

Some painting artisans specialize in creating unique finishes by using one of many decorative techniques. These techniques often involve "broken color," a process created by applying one or more colors in broken layers over a different base coat to produce a mottled or textured effect. Often these techniques employ glazes or washes applied over a solid colored background. Glazes are made of oil-based paints and give a sleek glow to walls. Washes are made of latex-based paints that have been thinned with water and can add a greater sense of depth and texture. Other decorative painting techniques include sponging, rag-rolling, stippling, sheen striping, dragging, distressing, color blocking, marbling, and faux finishes.

Some painters specialize in painting industrial structures to prevent deterioration. One example is applying a protective coating to steel bridges to fight corrosion. The coating most commonly used is a waterborne acrylic solvent that is easy to apply and environmentally friendly, but other specialized and sometimes difficult-to-apply coatings may be used. Painters may also coat interior and exterior manufacturing facilities and equipment such as storage tanks, plant buildings, lockers, piping, structural steel, and ships.

When painting any industrial structure, workers must take necessary safety precautions depending on their project. Those who specialize in interior applications such as painting the inside of storage tanks, for example, must wear a full-body protective suit. When working on bridges, painters are often suspended by cables and may work at extreme heights. When working on tall buildings, painters erect scaffolding, including "swing stages," scaffolds suspended by ropes, or cables attached to roof hooks. When painting steeples and other conical structures, they use a bosun's chair, a swing-like device.

Paperhangers cover walls and ceilings with decorative wall coverings made of paper, vinyl, or fabric. They first prepare the surface to be covered by applying "sizing," which seals the surface and makes the covering adhere better. When redecorating, they may first remove the old covering by soaking, steaming, or applying solvents. When necessary, they patch holes and take care of other imperfections before hanging the new wall covering.

After the surface has been prepared, paperhangers must prepare the paste or other adhesive, unless they are using pretreated paper. They then measure the area to be covered, check the covering for flaws, cut the covering into strips of the proper size, and closely examine the pattern in order to match it when the strips are hung. Much of this process can now be handled by specialized equipment.

The next step is to brush or roll the adhesive onto the back of the covering, if needed, and to then place the strips on the wall or ceiling, making sure the pattern is matched, the strips are straight, and the edges are butted together to make tight, closed seams. Finally, paperhangers smooth the strips to remove bubbles and wrinkles, trim the top and bottom with a razor knife, and wipe off any excess adhesive.

Work environment. Most painters and paperhangers work 40 hours a week or less; about 24 percent have variable schedules or work part time. Painters and paperhangers must stand for long periods, often working from scaffolding and ladders. Their jobs also require a considerable amount of climbing, bending, and stretching. These workers must have stamina because much of the work is done with their arms raised overhead. Painters, especially industrial painters, often work outdoors, almost always in dry, warm weather. Those who paint bridges or building infrastructure may be exposed to extreme heights and uncomfortable positions; some painters work suspended with ropes or cables.

Some painting jobs can leave a worker covered with paint. Drywall dust created by electric sanders prior to painting requires workers to wear protective safety glasses and a dust mask. Painters and

© JIST Works

paperhangers sometimes work with materials that are hazardous or toxic, such as when they are required to remove lead-based paints. In the most dangerous situations, painters work in a sealed self-contained suit to prevent inhalation of or contact with hazardous materials. Although workers are subject to falls from ladders, the occupation is not as hazardous as some other construction occupations.

Training, Other Qualifications, and Advancement

Painting and paperhanging is learned mostly on the job, but some experts recommend completion of an apprenticeship program.

Education and training. Most painters and paperhangers learn through on-the-job training and by working as a helper to an experienced painter. However, there are a number of formal and informal training programs that provide more thorough instruction and a better career foundation. In general, the more formal the training received, the more likely the individual will enter the profession at a higher level. There are limited informal training opportunities for paperhangers because there are fewer paperhangers and helpers are usually not required.

If available, apprenticeships generally provide a mixture of classroom instruction and paid on-the-job training. Apprenticeships for painters and paperhangers consist of two to four years of on-the-job training, supplemented by a minimum of 144 hours of related classroom instruction each year. A high school education or its equivalent, with courses in mathematics, usually is required to enter an apprenticeship program. Apprentices receive instruction in color harmony, use and care of tools and equipment, surface preparation, application techniques, paint mixing and matching, characteristics of different finishes, blueprint reading, wood finishing, and safety.

Besides apprenticeships, some workers gain skills by attending technical schools that offer training prior to employment. These schools can take about a year to complete. Others receive training through local vocational high schools.

Whether a painter learns the trade through a formal apprenticeship or informally as a helper, on-the-job instruction covers similar skill areas. Under the direction of experienced workers, trainees carry supplies, erect scaffolds, and do simple painting and surface preparation tasks while they learn about paint and painting equipment. As they gain experience, trainees learn to prepare surfaces for painting and paperhanging, to mix paints, and to apply paint and wall coverings efficiently and neatly. Near the end of their training, they may learn decorating concepts, color coordination, and cost-estimating techniques. In addition to learning craft skills, painters must become familiar with safety and health regulations so that their work complies with the law.

Other qualifications. Painters and paperhangers should have good manual dexterity, vision, and color sense. They also need physical stamina and balance to work on ladders and platforms. Apprentices or helpers generally must be at least 18 years old and in good physical condition, in addition to the high school diploma or equivalent that most apprentices need.

Certification and advancement. Some organizations offer training and certification to enhance the skills of their members. People interested in industrial painting, for example, can earn several designations from the National Association of Corrosion Engineers in several areas of specialization, including one for coating applicators,

called Protective Coating Specialist. Courses range from one day to several weeks depending on the certification program and specialty.

Painters and paperhangers may advance to supervisory or estimating jobs with painting and decorating contractors. Many establish their own painting and decorating businesses. For those who would like to advance, it is increasingly important to be able to communicate in both English and Spanish in order to relay instructions and safety precautions to workers with limited English skills; Spanish-speaking workers make up a large part of the construction workforce in many areas. Painting contractors need good English skills to deal with clients and subcontractors.

Employment

Painters and paperhangers held about 473,000 jobs in 2006; about 98 percent were painters. Around 38 percent of painters and paperhangers work for painting and wall covering contractors engaged in new construction, repair, restoration, or remodeling work. In addition, organizations that own or manage large buildings—such as apartment complexes—may employ painters, as do some schools, hospitals, factories, and government agencies.

Self-employed independent painting contractors accounted for 42 percent of all painters and paperhangers, significantly greater than the 20 percent of all construction trades workers combined.

Job Outlook

Employment of painters and paperhangers is expected to grow about as fast as the average for all occupations, reflecting increases in the stock of buildings and other structures that require maintenance and renovation. Excellent employment opportunities are expected for painters due to the need to replace the large number of workers who leave the occupation; paperhangers will have very limited opportunities.

Employment change. Overall employment is expected to grow by 11 percent between 2006 and 2016, about as fast as the average for all occupations. Driving employment growth will be retiring baby boomers who either purchase second homes or otherwise leave their existing homes that then require interior painting. Investors who sell properties or rent them out will also require the services of painters prior to completing a transaction. The relatively short life of exterior paints in residential homes as well as changing color and application trends will continue to support demand for painters. Painting is labor-intensive and not susceptible to technological changes that might make workers more productive and slow employment growth.

Growth of industrial painting will be driven by the need to prevent corrosion and deterioration of the many industrial structures by painting or coating them. Applying a protective coating to steel bridges, for example, is cost effective and can add years to the life expectancy of a bridge.

Employment of paperhangers should decline rapidly as many homeowners take advantage of easy application materials and resort to cheaper alternatives, such as painting.

Job prospects. Job prospects for painters should be excellent because of the need to replace workers who leave the occupation for other jobs. There are no strict training requirements for entry into these jobs, so many people with limited skills work as painters or helpers for a relatively short time and then move on to other types of work with higher pay or better working conditions.

Projections data from the National Employment Matrix

Occupational Title	SOC Code	Employment, 2006	Projected employment, 2016	Change, 2006-16	
				Number	Percent
Painters and paperhangers..	47-2140	473,000	526,000	53,000	11
Painters, construction and maintenance	47-2141	463,000	517,000	54,000	12
Paperhangers	47-2142	9,900	8,700	-1,200	-12

NOTE: Data in this table are rounded.

Opportunities for industrial painters should be excellent as the positions available should be greater than the pool of qualified individuals to fill them. While industrial structures that require painting are located throughout the nation, the best employment opportunities should be in the petrochemical industry in the Gulf Coast region, where strong demand and the largest concentration of workers exists.

Very few openings will arise for paperhangers because the number of these jobs is comparatively small and cheaper, more modern decorative finishes such as faux effects and sponging have gained in popularity at the expense of paper, vinyl, or fabric wall coverings.

Jobseekers considering these occupations should expect some periods of unemployment, especially until they gain experience. Many construction projects are of short duration, and construction activity is cyclical in nature. Remodeling, restoration, and maintenance projects, however, should continue as homeowners undertake renovation projects and hire painters even in economic downturns. Nonetheless, workers in these trades may experience periods of unemployment when the overall level of construction falls. On the other hand, shortages of these workers may occur in some areas during peak periods of building activity.

Earnings

In May 2006, median hourly earnings of wage and salary painters, construction and maintenance, were $15.00, not including the earnings of the self-employed. The middle 50 percent earned between $12.19 and $19.51. The lowest 10 percent earned less than $9.97, and the highest 10 percent earned more than $25.62. Median hourly earnings in the industries employing the largest numbers of painters were as follows:

Local government	$20.11
Drywall and insulation contractors	16.18
Nonresidential building construction	15.68
Residential building construction	15.04
Painting and wall covering contractors	14.62

In May 2006, median earnings for wage and salary paperhangers were $16.21. The middle 50 percent earned between $13.12 and $20.62. The lowest 10 percent earned less than $10.34, and the highest 10 percent earned more than $26.77.

Earnings for painters may be reduced on occasion because of bad weather and the short-term nature of many construction jobs. Hourly wage rates for apprentices usually start at 40 to 50 percent of the rate for experienced workers and increase periodically.

Some painters and paperhangers are members of the International Brotherhood of Painters and Allied Trades. Some painters are members of other unions.

Related Occupations

Painters and paperhangers apply various coverings to decorate and protect wood, drywall, metal, and other surfaces. Other construction occupations in which workers do finishing work include carpenters; carpet, floor, and tile installers and finishers; drywall installers, ceiling tile installers, and tapers; painting and coating workers, except construction and maintenance; and plasterers and stucco masons.

Sources of Additional Information

For details about painting and paperhanging apprenticeships or work opportunities, contact local painting and decorating contractors, local trade organizations, a local of the International Union of Painters and Allied Trades, a local joint union-management apprenticeship committee, or an office of the state apprenticeship agency or employment service.

For information about the work of painters and paperhangers and training opportunities, contact

▸ Associated Builders and Contractors, Workforce Development Department, 4250 North Fairfax Dr., 9th Floor, Arlington, VA 22203. Internet: http://www.trytools.org

▸ International Union of Painters and Allied Trades, 1750 New York Ave. NW, Washington, DC 20006. Internet: http://www.iupat.org

▸ National Center for Construction Education and Research, P.O. Box 141104, Gainesville, FL 32614. Internet: http://www.nccer.org

▸ Painting and Decorating Contractors of America, 1801 Park 270 Dr., Suite 220, St. Louis, MO 63146. Internet: http://www.pdca.org

For general information about the work of industrial painters and opportunities for training and certification as a protective coating specialist, contact

▸ National Association of Corrosion Engineers, 1440 South Creek Dr., Houston, TX 77084. Internet: http://www.nace.org

Paralegals and Legal Assistants

(O*NET 23-2011.00)

Significant Points

■ Most entrants have an associate degree in paralegal studies, or a bachelor's degree coupled with a certificate in paralegal studies.

■ About 7 out of 10 work for law firms; others work for corporate legal departments and government agencies.

■ Employment is projected to grow much faster than average, as employers try to reduce costs by hiring paralegals to perform tasks once done by lawyers.

■ Competition for jobs should continue; experienced, formally trained paralegals should have the best employment opportunities.

Nature of the Work

While lawyers assume ultimate responsibility for legal work, they often delegate many of their tasks to paralegals. In fact, paralegals—also called legal assistants—are continuing to assume a growing range of tasks in legal offices and perform many of the same tasks as lawyers. Nevertheless, they are explicitly prohibited from carrying out duties considered to be the practice of law, such as setting legal fees, giving legal advice, and presenting cases in court.

One of a paralegal's most important tasks is helping lawyers prepare for closings, hearings, trials, and corporate meetings. Paralegals might investigate the facts of cases and ensure that all relevant information is considered. They also identify appropriate laws, judicial decisions, legal articles, and other materials that are relevant to assigned cases. After they analyze and organize the information, paralegals may prepare written reports that attorneys use in determining how cases should be handled. If attorneys decide to file lawsuits on behalf of clients, paralegals may help prepare the legal arguments, draft pleadings and motions to be filed with the court, obtain affidavits, and assist attorneys during trials. Paralegals also organize and track files of all important case documents and make them available and easily accessible to attorneys.

In addition to this preparatory work, paralegals perform a number of other functions. For example, they help draft contracts, mortgages, and separation agreements. They also may assist in preparing tax returns, establishing trust funds, and planning estates. Some paralegals coordinate the activities of other law office employees and maintain financial office records.

Computer software packages and the Internet are used to search legal literature stored in computer databases and on CD-ROM. In litigation involving many supporting documents, paralegals usually use computer databases to retrieve, organize, and index various materials. Imaging software allows paralegals to scan documents directly into a database, while billing programs help them to track hours billed to clients. Computer software packages also are used to perform tax computations and explore the consequences of various tax strategies for clients.

Paralegals are found in all types of organizations, but most are employed by law firms, corporate legal departments, and various government offices. In these organizations, they can work in many different areas of the law, including litigation, personal injury, corporate law, criminal law, employee benefits, intellectual property, labor law, bankruptcy, immigration, family law, and real estate. As the law becomes more complex, paralegals become more specialized. Within specialties, functions are often broken down further. For example, paralegals specializing in labor law may concentrate exclusively on employee benefits. In small and medium-size law firms, duties are often more general.

The tasks of paralegals differ widely according to the type of organization for which they work. A corporate paralegal often assists attorneys with employee contracts, shareholder agreements, stock-option plans, and employee benefit plans. They also may help prepare and file annual financial reports, maintain corporate minutes' record resolutions, and prepare forms to secure loans for the corporation. Corporate paralegals often monitor and review government regulations to ensure that the corporation is aware of new requirements and is operating within the law. Increasingly, experienced corporate paralegals or paralegal managers are assuming additional supervisory responsibilities such as overseeing team projects.

The duties of paralegals who work in the public sector usually vary by agency. In general, litigation paralegals analyze legal material for internal use, maintain reference files, conduct research for attorneys, and collect and analyze evidence for agency hearings. They may prepare informative or explanatory material on laws, agency regulations, and agency policy for general use by the agency and the public. Paralegals employed in community legal-service projects help the poor, the aged, and others who are in need of legal assistance. They file forms, conduct research, prepare documents, and, when authorized by law, may represent clients at administrative hearings.

Work environment. Paralegals handle many routine assignments, particularly when they are inexperienced. As they gain experience, paralegals usually assume more varied tasks with additional responsibility. Paralegals do most of their work in offices and law libraries. Occasionally, they travel to gather information and perform other duties.

Paralegals employed by corporations and government usually work a standard 40-hour week. Although most paralegals work year round, some are temporarily employed during busy times of the year and then released. Paralegals who work for law firms sometimes work very long hours when under pressure to meet deadlines.

Training, Other Qualifications, and Advancement

Most entrants have an associate degree in paralegal studies, or a bachelor's degree coupled with a certificate in paralegal studies. Some employers train paralegals on the job.

Education and training. There are several ways to become a paralegal. The most common is through a community college paralegal program that leads to an associate degree. Another common method of entry, mainly for those who already have a college degree, is earning a certificate in paralegal studies. A small number of schools offer a bachelor's and master's degree in paralegal studies. Finally, some employers train paralegals on the job.

Associate and bachelor's degree programs usually combine paralegal training with courses in other academic subjects. Certificate programs vary significantly, with some only taking a few months to complete. Most certificate programs provide intensive paralegal training for individuals who already hold college degrees.

About 1,000 colleges and universities, law schools, and proprietary schools offer formal paralegal training programs. Approximately 260 paralegal programs are approved by the American Bar Association (ABA). Although many employers do not require such approval, graduation from an ABA-approved program can enhance employment opportunities. Admission requirements vary. Some require certain college courses or a bachelor's degree, while others accept high school graduates or those with legal experience. A few schools require standardized tests and personal interviews.

The quality of paralegal training programs varies; some programs may include job placement services. If possible, prospective students should examine the experiences of recent graduates before enrolling in a paralegal program. Any training program usually includes courses in legal research and the legal applications of computers. Many paralegal training programs also offer an internship in which students gain practical experience by working for several months in a private law firm, the office of a public defender or attorney general, a corporate legal department, a legal aid organization, a bank, or a government agency. Internship experience is an asset when one is seeking a job after graduation.

Some employers train paralegals on the job, hiring college graduates with no legal experience or promoting experienced legal secretaries. Other entrants have experience in a technical field that is useful to law firms, such as a background in tax preparation or criminal justice. Nursing or health administration experience is valuable in personal injury law practices.

Certification and other qualifications. Although most employers do not require certification, earning a voluntary certification from a professional society may offer advantages in the labor market. The National Association of Legal Assistants (NALA), for example, has established standards for certification requiring various combinations of education and experience. Paralegals who meet these standards are eligible to take a two-day examination. Those who pass the exam may use the Certified Legal Assistant (CLA) or Certified Paralegal (CP) credential. The NALA also offers the Advanced Paralegal Certification for experienced paralegals who want to specialize. The Advanced Paralegal Certification program is a curriculum based program offered on the Internet.

The American Alliance of Paralegals, Inc. offers the American Alliance Certified Paralegal (AACP) credential, a voluntary certification program. Paralegals seeking the AACP certification must possess at least five years of paralegal experience and meet one of the three educational criteria. Certification must be renewed every two years, including the completion 18 hours of continuing education.

In addition, the National Federation of Paralegal Association offers the Registered Paralegal (RP) designation to paralegals with a bachelor's degree and at least two years of experience who pass an exam. To maintain the credential, workers must complete 12 hours of continuing education every two years. The National Association for Legal Professionals offers the Professional Paralegal (PP) certification to those who pass a four-part exam. Recertification requires 75 hours of continuing education.

Paralegals must be able to document and present their findings and opinions to their supervising attorney. They need to understand legal terminology and have good research and investigative skills. Familiarity with the operation and applications of computers in legal research and litigation support also is important. Paralegals should stay informed of new developments in the laws that affect their area of practice. Participation in continuing legal education seminars allows paralegals to maintain and expand their knowledge of the law. In fact, all paralegals in California must complete four hours of mandatory continuing education in either general law or in a specialized area of law.

Because paralegals frequently deal with the public, they should be courteous and uphold the ethical standards of the legal profession. The National Association of Legal Assistants, the National Federation of Paralegal Associations, and a few states have established ethical guidelines for paralegals to follow.

Advancement. Paralegals usually are given more responsibilities and require less supervision as they gain work experience. Experienced paralegals who work in large law firms, corporate legal departments, or government agencies may supervise and delegate assignments to other paralegals and clerical staff. Advancement opportunities also include promotion to managerial and other law-related positions within the firm or corporate legal department. However, some paralegals find it easier to move to another law firm when seeking increased responsibility or advancement.

Employment

Paralegals and legal assistants held about 238,000 jobs in 2006. Private law firms employed 7 out of 10 paralegals and legal assistants; most of the remainder worked for corporate legal departments and various levels of government. Within the federal government, the U.S. Department of Justice is the largest employer, followed by the Social Security Administration and the U.S. Department of the Treasury. A small number of paralegals own their own businesses and work as freelance legal assistants, contracting their services to attorneys or corporate legal departments.

Job Outlook

Despite projected rapid employment growth, competition for jobs is expected to continue as many people seek to go into this profession; experienced, formally trained paralegals should have the best employment opportunities.

Employment change. Employment of paralegals and legal assistants is projected to grow 22 percent between 2006 and 2016, much faster than the average for all occupations. Employers are trying to reduce costs and increase the availability and efficiency of legal services by hiring paralegals to perform tasks once done by lawyers. Paralegals are performing a wider variety of duties, making them more useful to businesses.

Demand for paralegals also is expected to grow as an expanding population increasingly requires legal services, especially in areas such as intellectual property, health care, international law, elder issues, criminal law, and environmental law. The growth of prepaid legal plans also should contribute to the demand for legal services.

Private law firms will continue to be the largest employers of paralegals, but a growing array of other organizations, such as corporate legal departments, insurance companies, real estate and title insurance firms, and banks also hire paralegals. Corporations in particular are expected to increase their in-house legal departments to cut costs. In part because of the range of tasks they can perform, paralegals are also increasingly employed in small and medium-size establishments of all types.

Job prospects. In addition to new jobs created by employment growth, more job openings will arise as people leave the occupation. There will be demand for paralegals who specialize in areas such as real estate, bankruptcy, medical malpractice, and product liability. Community legal service programs, which provide assistance to the poor, elderly, minorities, and middle-income families, will employ additional paralegals to minimize expenses and serve the most people. Job opportunities also are expected in federal, state, and local government agencies, consumer organizations, and the courts. However, this occupation attracts many applicants, creating competition for jobs. Experienced, formally trained paralegals should have the best job prospects.

To a limited extent, paralegal jobs are affected by the business cycle. During recessions, demand declines for some discretionary legal services, such as planning estates, drafting wills, and handling real estate transactions. Corporations are less inclined to initiate certain types of litigation when falling sales and profits lead to fiscal belt

Projections data from the National Employment Matrix

Occupational Title	SOC Code	Employment, 2006	Projected employment, 2016	Change, 2006-2016	
				Number	Percent
Paralegals and legal assistants..	23-2011	238,000	291,000	53,000	22

NOTE: Data in this table are rounded.

tightening. As a result, full-time paralegals employed in offices adversely affected by a recession may be laid off or have their work hours reduced. However, during recessions, corporations and individuals are more likely to face problems that require legal assistance, such as bankruptcies, foreclosures, and divorces. Paralegals, who provide many of the same legal services as lawyers at a lower cost, tend to fare relatively better in difficult economic conditions.

Earnings

Earnings of paralegals and legal assistants vary greatly. Salaries depend on education, training, experience, the type and size of employer, and the geographic location of the job. In general, paralegals who work for large law firms or in large metropolitan areas earn more than those who work for smaller firms or in less populated regions. In May 2006, full-time wage-and-salary paralegals and legal assistants had median annual earnings, including bonuses, of $43,040. The middle 50 percent earned between $33,920 and $54,690. The top 10 percent earned more than $67,540, and the bottom 10 percent earned less than $27,450. Median annual earnings in the industries employing the largest numbers of paralegals were

Federal government	$56,080
Management of companies and enterprises	52,220
Local government	42,170
Legal services	41,460
State government	38,020

In addition to earning a salary, many paralegals receive bonuses, in part, to compensate them for sometimes having to work long hours. Paralegals also receive vacation, paid sick leave, a 401 savings plan, life insurance, personal paid time off, dental insurance, and reimbursement for continuing legal education.

Related Occupations

Among the other occupations that call for a specialized understanding of the law but do not require the extensive training of a lawyer, are law clerks; title examiners, abstractors, and searchers; claims adjusters, appraisers, examiners, and investigators; and occupational health and safety specialists and technicians.

Sources of Additional Information

General information on a career as a paralegal can be obtained from

▸ Standing Committee on Paralegals, American Bar Association, 321 North Clark St., Chicago, IL 60610. Internet: http://www.abanet.org/legalservices/paralegals

For information on the Certified Legal Assistant exam, schools that offer training programs in a specific state, and standards and guidelines for paralegals, contact

▸ National Association of Legal Assistants, Inc., 1516 South Boston St., Suite 200, Tulsa, OK 74119. Internet: http://www.nala.org

Information on the Paralegal Advanced Competency Exam, paralegal careers, paralegal training programs, job postings, and local associations is available from

▸ National Federation of Paralegal Associations, PO Box 2016, Edmonds, WA 98020. Internet: http://www.paralegals.org

Information on paralegal training programs, including the pamphlet *How to Choose a Paralegal Education Program,* may be obtained from

▸ American Association for Paralegal Education, 19 Mantua Rd., Mt. Royal, NJ 08061. Internet: http://www.aafpe.org

Information on paralegal careers, certification, and job postings is available from

▸ American Alliance of Paralegals, Inc., 16815 East Shea Boulevard, Suite 110, No. 101, Fountain Hills, Arizona, 85268. Internet: http://www.aapipara.org

For information on the Professional Paralegal exam, schools that offer training programs in a specific state, and standards and guidelines for paralegals, contact

▸ NALS, 314 E. 3rd St., Suite 210, Tulsa, OK 74120. Internet: http://www.nals.org

Information on obtaining positions as a paralegal or legal assistant with the federal government is available from the Office of Personnel Management through USAJOBS, the federal government's official employment information system. This resource for locating and applying for job opportunities can be accessed through the Internet at http://www.usajobs.opm.gov or through an interactive voice response telephone system at (703) 724-1850 or TDD (978) 461-8404. These numbers are not toll free, and charges may result. For advice on how to find and apply for federal jobs, see the *Occupational Outlook Quarterly* article "How to get a job in the Federal Government," online at http://www.bls.gov/opub/ooq/2004/summer/art01.pdf.

Personal and Home Care Aides

(O*NET 39-9021.00)

Significant Points

■ Job opportunities are expected to be excellent because of rapid growth in home health care and high replacement needs.

■ Skill requirements are low, as is the pay.

■ About 1 out of 3 personal and home care aides work part time; most aides work with a number of different clients, each job lasting a few hours, days, or weeks.

Nature of the Work

Personal and home care aides help people who are elderly, disabled, ill, and/or mentally disabled to live in their own homes or in residential care facilities instead of in health facilities or institutions. Most personal and home care aides work with elderly or physically or mentally disabled clients who need more extensive personal and home care than family or friends can provide. Some aides work with families in which a parent is incapacitated and small children need care. Others help discharged hospital patients who have relatively short-term needs. (*Home health aides*—who provide health-related services are discussed in the job profile of nursing, psychiatric, and home health aides, elsewhere in this book.)

Personal and home care aides—also called *homemakers, caregivers, companions*, and *personal attendants*—provide housekeeping and routine personal care services. They clean clients' houses, do laundry, and change bed linens. Aides may plan meals (including special diets), shop for food, and cook. Aides also may help clients get out of bed, bathe, dress, and groom. Some accompany clients to doctors' appointments or on other errands.

Personal and home care aides provide instruction and psychological support to their patients. They may advise families and patients on nutrition, cleanliness, and household tasks. Aides also may assist in toilet training a severely mentally handicapped child, or they may just listen to clients talk.

In home health care agencies, a registered nurse, physical therapist, or social worker assigns specific duties and supervises personal and home care aides. Aides keep records of services performed and of clients' condition and progress. They report changes in the client's condition to the supervisor or case manager. In carrying out their work, aides cooperate with health care professionals, including registered nurses, therapists, and other medical staff.

The personal and home care aide's daily routine may vary. Aides may go to the same home every day for months or even years. Aides often visit four or five clients on the same day. However, some aides may work solely with one client who is in need of more care and attention. In some situations, this may involve working with other aides in shifts so the client has an aide throughout the day and night.

Personal and home care aides generally work on their own, with periodic visits by their supervisor. They receive detailed instructions explaining when to visit clients and what services to perform for them.

Aides are individually responsible for getting to the client's home. They may spend a good portion of the work day traveling from one client to another. Aides must be careful to avoid over-exertion or injury when they assist clients.

Work environment. Surroundings differ from case to case. Some homes are neat and pleasant, whereas others are untidy and depressing. Some clients are pleasant and cooperative; others are angry, abusive, depressed, or otherwise difficult. Aides may spend a large portion of each day traveling between clients' homes.

About 33 percent of aides work part time, and some work weekends or evenings to suit the needs of their clients.

Training, Other Qualifications, and Advancement

In some states, the only requirement for employment is on-the-job training, which generally is provided by employers. Other states may require formal training, which is available from community colleges, vocational schools, elder care programs, and home health care agencies.

Education and training. Most personal and home care aides receive short term on-the-job training in a range of job functions. Aides are instructed on how to properly cook for a client, which includes information on nutrition and special diets. Furthermore, they may be trained on basic housekeeping tasks, such as making a bed and keeping the home sanitary and safe for the client. Generally, they are taught how to respond to an emergency situation, learning basic safety techniques. Employers may also train aides to conduct themselves in a professional and courteous manner while in a clients' home.

Other qualifications. Personal and home care aides should have a desire to help people and not mind hard work. They should be responsible, compassionate, patient, emotionally stable, and cheerful. In addition, aides should be tactful, honest, and discreet because they work in private homes. Aides also must be in good health. A physical examination, including state-mandated tests for tuberculosis and other diseases, may be required. A criminal background check, credit check, and good driving record may also be required for employment. Additionally, personal and home care aides are responsible for their own transportation to reach patients' homes.

Certification and advancement. The National Association for Home Care and Hospice (NAHC) offers national certification for personal and home care aides. Certification is a voluntary demonstration that the individual has met industry standards. Certification requires the completion of a 75-hour course, observation and documentation of 17 skills for competency assessed by a registered nurse and passing a written exam developed by NAHC.

Advancement for personal and home care aides is limited. In some agencies, workers start out performing homemaker duties, such as cleaning. With experience and training, they may take on more personal care duties. Some aides choose to receive additional training to become nursing and home health aides, licensed practical nurses, or registered nurses. Some experienced personal and home care aides may start their own home care agency or work as a self-employed aide. Self-employed aides have no agency affiliation or supervision and accept clients, set fees, and arrange work schedules on their own.

Employment

Personal and home care aides held about 767,000 jobs in 2006. The majority of jobs were in home health care services; individual and family services; residential care facilities; and private households. In 2006, about 8 percent of personal and home care aides were self-employed.

Job Outlook

Excellent job opportunities are expected for this occupation because rapid employment growth and high replacement needs are projected to produce a large number of job openings.

Employment change. Employment of personal and home care aides is projected to grow by 51 percent between 2006 and 2016, which is much faster than the average for all occupations. This occupation will be amongst the occupations adding the most new jobs, growing by about 389,000 jobs. The expected growth is due, in large part, to the projected rise in the number of elderly people, an age group that often has mounting health problems and that needs some assistance with daily activities. The elderly and other patients, such as the mentally disabled, increasingly rely on home care.

Projections data from the National Employment Matrix

Occupational Title	SOC Code	Employment, 2006	Projected employment, 2016	Change, 2006-16	
				Number	Percent
Personal and home care aides	39-9021	767,000	1,156,000	389,000	51

NOTE: Data in this table are rounded.

This trend reflects several developments. Inpatient care in hospitals and nursing homes can be extremely expensive, so more patients return to their homes from these facilities as quickly as possible to contain costs. Patients who need assistance with everyday tasks and household chores rather than medical care can reduce medical expenses by returning to their homes. Furthermore, most patients—particularly the elderly—increasingly prefer care in their homes rather than in nursing homes or other in-patient facilities. This trend is aided by the realization that treatment can be more effective in familiar surroundings. Finally, home care has become easier and more feasible with the development of better medical technologies for in-home treatment.

Job prospects. In addition to job openings created by the increased demand for these workers, replacement needs are expected to lead to many openings. The relatively low skill requirements, low pay, and high emotional demands of the work result in high replacement needs. For these same reasons, many people are reluctant to seek jobs in the occupation. Therefore, persons who are interested in and suited for this work—particularly those with experience or training as personal care, home health, or nursing aides—should have excellent job prospects.

Earnings

Median hourly earnings of wage-and-salary personal and home care aides were $8.54 in May 2006. The middle 50 percent earned between $7.09 and $10.19 an hour. The lowest 10 percent earned less than $6.05, and the highest 10 percent earned more than $11.60 an hour. Median hourly earnings in the industries employing the largest numbers of personal and home care aides were as follows:

Residential mental retardation facilities $9.54

Services for the elderly and persons with
    disabilities 9.18

Home health care services 7.19

Most employers give slight pay increases with experience and added responsibility. Aides usually are paid only for the time they work in the home, not for travel time between jobs. Employers often hire on-call hourly workers and provide no benefits.

Related Occupations

Personal and home care aides combine the duties of caregivers and social service workers. Workers in related occupations that involve personal contact to help others include childcare workers; nursing, psychiatric, and home health aides; occupational therapist assistants and aides; physical therapist assistants and aides; and social and human service assistants.

Sources of Additional Information

Information about employment opportunities may be obtained from local hospitals, nursing care facilities, home health care agencies,

psychiatric facilities, residential mental health facilities, social assistance agencies, and local offices of the state employment service.

For information about voluntary credentials for personal and home care aides, contact

▸ National Association for Homecare and Hospice, 228 Seventh St. SE, Washington, DC 20003. Internet: http://www.nahc.org

Pharmacy Technicians

(O*NET 29-2052.00)

Significant Points

■ Job opportunities are expected to be good, especially for those with certification or previous work experience.

■ Many technicians work evenings, weekends, and holidays.

■ About 71 percent of jobs are in retail pharmacies, grocery stores, department stores, or mass retailers.

Nature of the Work

Pharmacy technicians help licensed pharmacists provide medication and other health care products to patients. Technicians usually perform routine tasks to help prepare prescribed medication, such as counting tablets and labeling bottles. They also perform administrative duties, such as answering phones, stocking shelves, and operating cash registers. Technicians refer any questions regarding prescriptions, drug information, or health matters to a *pharmacist*.

Pharmacy technicians who work in retail or mail-order pharmacies have varying responsibilities, depending on state rules and regulations. Technicians receive written prescriptions or requests for prescription refills from patients. They also may receive prescriptions sent electronically from the doctor's office. They must verify that information on the prescription is complete and accurate. To prepare the prescription, technicians must retrieve, count, pour, weigh, measure, and sometimes mix the medication. Then, they prepare the prescription labels, select the type of prescription container, and affix the prescription and auxiliary labels to the container. Once the prescription is filled, technicians price and file the prescription, which must be checked by a pharmacist before it is given to the patient. Technicians may establish and maintain patient profiles, prepare insurance claim forms, and stock and take inventory of prescription and over-the-counter medications.

In hospitals, nursing homes, and assisted-living facilities, technicians have added responsibilities, including reading patients' charts and preparing the appropriate medication. After the pharmacist checks the prescription for accuracy, the pharmacy technician may deliver it to the patient. The technician then copies the information about the prescribed medication onto the patient's profile. Technicians also may assemble a 24-hour supply of medicine for every patient. They package and label each dose separately. The packages are then placed in the medicine cabinets of patients until the supervising pharmacist checks them for accuracy, and only then is the medication given to the patients.

Pharmacy aides work closely with pharmacy technicians. They often are clerks or cashiers who primarily answer telephones, handle money, stock shelves, and perform other clerical duties. Pharmacy technicians usually perform more complex tasks than pharmacy aides, although in some states their duties and job titles may overlap.

Work environment. Pharmacy technicians work in clean, organized, well-lighted, and well-ventilated areas. Most of their workday is spent on their feet. They may be required to lift heavy boxes or to use stepladders to retrieve supplies from high shelves.

Technicians work the same hours that pharmacists work. These may include evenings, nights, weekends, and holidays, particularly in facilities that are open 24 hours a day such as hospitals and some retail pharmacies. As their seniority increases, technicians often acquire increased control over the hours they work. There are many opportunities for part-time work in both retail and hospital settings.

Training, Other Qualifications, and Advancement

Most pharmacy technicians are trained on-the-job, but employers favor applicants who have formal training, certification, or previous experience. Strong customer service skills also are important. Pharmacy technicians may become supervisors, may move into specialty positions or into sales, or may become pharmacists.

Education and training. Although most pharmacy technicians receive informal on-the-job training, employers favor those who have completed formal training and certification. However, there are currently few state and no federal requirements for formal training or certification of pharmacy technicians. Employers who have insufficient resources to give on-the-job training often seek formally educated pharmacy technicians. Formal education programs and certification emphasize the technician's interest in and dedication to the work. In addition to the military, some hospitals, proprietary schools, vocational or technical colleges, and community colleges offer formal education programs.

Formal pharmacy technician education programs require classroom and laboratory work in a variety of areas, including medical and pharmaceutical terminology, pharmaceutical calculations, pharmacy recordkeeping, pharmaceutical techniques, and pharmacy law and ethics. Technicians also are required to learn medication names, actions, uses, and doses. Many training programs include internships, in which students gain hands-on experience in actual pharmacies. After completion, students receive a diploma, a certificate, or an associate's degree, depending on the program.

Prospective pharmacy technicians with experience working as an aide in a community pharmacy or volunteering in a hospital may have an advantage. Employers also prefer applicants with experience managing inventories, counting tablets, measuring dosages, and using computers. In addition, a background in chemistry, English, and health education may be beneficial.

Certification and other qualifications. Two organizations, the Pharmacy Technician Certification Board and the Institute for the Certification of Pharmacy Technicians, administer national certification examinations. Certification is voluntary in most states, but is required by some states and employers. Some technicians are hired

without formal training, but under the condition that they obtain certification within a specified period of time. To be eligible for either exam, candidates must have a high school diploma or GED, no felony convictions of any kind within five years of applying, and no drug or pharmacy related felony convictions at any point. Employers, often pharmacists, know that individuals who pass the exam have a standardized body of knowledge and skills. Many employers also will reimburse the costs of the exam.

Under both programs, technicians must be recertified every two years. Recertification requires 20 hours of continuing education within the two-year certification period. At least one hour must be in pharmacy law. Continuing education hours can be earned from several different sources, including colleges, pharmacy associations, and pharmacy technician training programs. Up to 10 hours of continuing education can be earned on the job under the direct supervision and instruction of a pharmacist.

Strong customer service and teamwork skills are needed because pharmacy technicians interact with patients, coworkers, and health care professionals. Mathematics, spelling, and reading skills also are important. Successful pharmacy technicians are alert, observant, organized, dedicated, and responsible. They should be willing and able to take directions, but be able to work independently without constant instruction. They must be precise; details are sometimes a matter of life and death. Candidates interested in becoming pharmacy technicians cannot have prior records of drug or substance abuse.

Advancement. In large pharmacies and health-systems, pharmacy technicians with significant training, experience and certification can be promoted to supervisory positions, mentoring and training pharmacy technicians with less experience. Some may advance into specialty positions such as chemo therapy technician and nuclear pharmacy technician. Others move into sales. With a substantial amount of formal training, some pharmacy technicians go on to become pharmacists.

Employment

Pharmacy technicians held about 285,000 jobs in 2006. About 71 percent of jobs were in retail pharmacies, either independently owned or part of a drugstore chain, grocery store, department store, or mass retailer. About 18 percent of jobs were in hospitals and a small proportion was in mail-order and Internet pharmacies, offices of physicians, pharmaceutical wholesalers, and the federal government.

Job Outlook

Employment is expected to increase much faster than the average through 2016, and job opportunities are expected to be good.

Employment change. Employment of pharmacy technicians is expected to increase by 32 percent from 2006 to 2016, which is much faster than the average for all occupations. The increased number of middle-aged and elderly people—who use more prescription drugs than younger people—will spur demand for technicians throughout the projection period. In addition, as scientific advances bring treatments for an increasing number of conditions, more pharmacy technicians will be needed to fill a growing number of prescriptions.

As cost-conscious insurers begin to use pharmacies as patient-care centers, pharmacy technicians will assume responsibility for some

Projections data from the National Employment Matrix

Occupational Title	SOC Code	Employment, 2006	Projected employment, 2016	Change, 2006-2016	
				Number	Percent
Pharmacy technicians..	29-2052	285,000	376,000	91,000	32

NOTE: Data in this table are rounded.

of the more routine tasks previously performed by pharmacists. In addition, they will adopt some of the administrative duties that were previously performed by pharmacy aides, such as answering phones and stocking shelves.

Reducing the need for pharmacy technicians to some degree, however, will be the growing use of drug dispensing machines. These machines increase productivity by completing some of the pharmacy technician's duties, namely counting pills and placing them into prescription containers. These machines are only used for the most common medications, however, and their effect on employment should be minimal.

Almost all states have legislated the maximum number of technicians who can safely work under a pharmacist at one time. Changes in these laws could directly affect employment.

Job prospects. Good job opportunities are expected for full-time and part-time work, especially for technicians with formal training or previous experience. Job openings for pharmacy technicians will result from employment growth, and from the need to replace workers who transfer to other occupations or leave the labor force.

Earnings

Median hourly earnings of wage-and-salary pharmacy technicians in May 2006 were $12.32. The middle 50 percent earned between $10.10 and $14.92. The lowest 10 percent earned less than $8.56, and the highest 10 percent earned more than $17.65. Median hourly earnings in the industries employing the largest numbers of pharmacy technicians in May 2006 were

General medical and surgical hospitals $13.86

Grocery stores...12.78

Pharmacies and drug stores 11.50

Certified technicians may earn more. Shift differentials for working evenings or weekends also can increase earnings. Some technicians belong to unions representing hospital or grocery store workers.

Related Occupations

This occupation is most closely related to pharmacists and pharmacy aides. Workers in other medical support occupations include dental assistants, medical transcriptionists, medical records and health information technicians, occupational therapist assistants and aides, and physical therapist assistants and aides.

Sources of Additional Information

For information on pharmacy technician certification programs, contact

▸ Pharmacy Technician Certification Board, 2215 Constitution Ave. NW, Washington DC 20037-2985. Internet: http://www.ptcb.org

▸ Institute for the Certification of Pharmacy Technicians, 2536 S. Old Hwy 94, Suite 214, St. Charles, MO 63303. Internet: http://www.nationaltechexam.org

For a list of accredited pharmacy technician training programs, contact

▸ American Society of Health-System Pharmacists, 7272 Wisconsin Ave., Bethesda, MD 20814. Internet: http://www.ashp.org

For pharmacy technician career information, contact

▸ National Pharmacy Technician Association, P.O. Box 683148, Houston, TX 77268. Internet: http://www.pharmacytechnician.org

Physical Therapist Assistants and Aides

(O*NET 31-2021.00 and 31-2022.00)

Significant Points

■ Employment is projected to increase much faster than average.

■ Assistants should have very good job prospects; on the other hand, aides may face keen competition from the large pool of qualified applicants.

■ Aides usually learn skills on the job, while assistants generally have an associate degree; some states require licensing for assistants.

■ About 71 percent of jobs are in offices of physical therapists or in hospitals.

Nature of the Work

Physical therapist assistants and aides help physical therapists to provide treatment that improves patient mobility, relieves pain, and prevents or lessens physical disabilities of patients. A physical therapist might ask an assistant to help patients exercise or learn to use crutches, for example, or an aide to gather and prepare therapy equipment. Patients include accident victims and individuals with disabling conditions such as lower-back pain, arthritis, heart disease, fractures, head injuries, and cerebral palsy.

Physical therapist assistants perform a variety of tasks. Under the direction and supervision of physical therapists, they provide part of a patient's treatment. This might involve exercises, massages, electrical stimulation, paraffin baths, hot and cold packs, traction, and ultrasound. Physical therapist assistants record the patient's responses to treatment and report the outcome of each treatment to the physical therapist.

Physical therapist aides help make therapy sessions productive, under the direct supervision of a physical therapist or physical therapist assistant. They usually are responsible for keeping the treatment area clean and organized and for preparing for each patient's therapy. When patients need assistance moving to or from a treatment area, aides push them in a wheelchair or provide them with a shoulder to lean on. Because they are not licensed, aides do not perform the clinical tasks of a physical therapist assistant in states where licensure is required.

The duties of aides include some clerical tasks, such as ordering depleted supplies, answering the phone, and filling out insurance forms and other paperwork. The extent to which an aide or an assistant performs clerical tasks depends on the size and location of the facility.

Work environment. Physical therapist assistants and aides need a moderate degree of strength because of the physical exertion required in assisting patients with their treatment. In some cases, assistants and aides need to lift patients. Frequent kneeling, stooping, and standing for long periods also are part of the job.

The hours and days that physical therapist assistants and aides work vary with the facility. About 23 percent of all physical therapist assistants and aides work part time. Many outpatient physical therapy offices and clinics have evening and weekend hours, to coincide with patients' personal schedules.

Training, Other Qualifications, and Advancement

Most physical therapist aides are trained on the job, but most physical therapist assistants earn an associate degree from an accredited physical therapist assistant program. Some states require licensing for physical therapist assistants.

Education and training. Employers typically require physical therapist aides to have a high school diploma. They are trained on the job, and most employers provide clinical on-the-job training.

In many states, physical therapist assistants are required by law to hold at least an associate degree. According to the American Physical Therapy Association, there were 233 accredited physical therapist assistant programs in the United States as of 2006. Accredited programs usually last two years, or four semesters, and culminate in an associate degree.

Programs are divided into academic study and hands-on clinical experience. Academic course work includes algebra, anatomy and physiology, biology, chemistry, and psychology. Clinical work includes certifications in CPR and other first aid and field experience in treatment centers. Both educators and prospective employers view clinical experience as essential to ensuring that students understand the responsibilities of a physical therapist assistant.

Licensure. Licensing is not required to practice as a physical therapist aide. However, some states require licensure or registration in order to work as a physical therapist assistant. states that require licensure stipulate specific educational and examination criteria. Additional requirements may include certification in cardiopulmonary resuscitation (CPR) and other first aid and a minimum number of hours of clinical experience. Complete information on regulations can be obtained from state licensing boards.

Other qualifications. Physical therapist assistants and aides should be well-organized, detail oriented, and caring. They usually have strong interpersonal skills and a desire to help people in need.

Advancement. Some physical therapist aides advance to become therapist assistants after gaining experience and, often, additional education. Sometimes, this education is required by law.

Some physical therapist assistants advance by specializing in a clinical area. They gain expertise in treating a certain type of patient, such as geriatric or pediatric, or a type of ailment, such as sports injuries. Many physical therapist assistants advance to administration positions. These positions might include organizing all the assistants in a large physical therapy organization or acting as the director for a specific department such as sports medicine. Other assistants go on to teach in an accredited physical therapist assistant academic program, lead health risk reduction classes for the elderly, or organize community activities related to fitness and risk reduction.

Employment

Physical therapist assistants and aides held about 107,000 jobs in 2006. Physical therapist assistants held about 60,000 jobs; physical therapist aides, approximately 46,000. Both work with physical therapists in a variety of settings. About 71 percent of jobs were in offices of physical therapists or in hospitals. Others worked primarily in nursing care facilities, offices of physicians, home health care services, and outpatient care centers.

Job Outlook

Employment is expected to grow much faster than average because of increasing consumer demand for physical therapy services. Job prospects for physical therapist assistants are expected to be very good. Aides should experience keen competition for jobs.

Employment change. Employment of physical therapist assistants and aides is expected to grow by 29 percent over the 2006–2016 decade, much faster than the average for all occupations. The impact of federal limits on Medicare and Medicaid reimbursement for therapy services may adversely affect the short-term job outlook for physical therapist assistants and aides. However, long-term demand for physical therapist assistants and aides will continue to rise, as the number of individuals with disabilities or limited function grows.

The increasing number of people who need therapy reflects, in part, the increasing elderly population. The elderly population is particularly vulnerable to chronic and debilitating conditions that require therapeutic services. These patients often need additional assistance in their treatment, making the roles of assistants and aides vital. In addition, the large baby-boom generation is entering the prime age for heart attacks and strokes, further increasing the demand for cardiac and physical rehabilitation. Moreover, future medical developments should permit an increased percentage of trauma victims to survive, creating added demand for therapy services.

Physical therapists are expected to increasingly use assistants to reduce the cost of physical therapy services. Once a patient is eval-

Projections data from the National Employment Matrix

Occupational Title	SOC Code	Employment, 2006	Projected employment, 2016	Change, 2006-16	
				Number	Percent
Physical therapist assistants and aides	31-2020	107,000	137,000	31,000	29
Physical therapist assistants	31-2021	60,000	80,000	20,000	32
Physical therapist aides	31-2022	46,000	58,000	11,000	24

NOTE: Data in this table are rounded.

uated and a treatment plan is designed by the physical therapist, the physical therapist assistant can provide many parts of the treatment, as approved by the therapist.

Job prospects. Opportunities for individuals interested in becoming physical therapist assistants are expected to be very good. Physical therapist aides may face keen competition from the large pool of qualified individuals. In addition to employment growth, job openings will result from the need to replace workers who leave the occupation permanently. Physical therapist assistants and aides with prior experience working in a physical therapy office or other health care setting will have the best job opportunities.

Earnings

Median annual earnings of physical therapist assistants were $41,360 in May 2006. The middle 50 percent earned between $33,840 and $49,010. The lowest 10 percent earned less than $26,190, and the highest 10 percent earned more than $57,220. Median annual earnings in the industries employing the largest numbers of physical therapist assistants in May 2006 were

Home health care services	$46,390
Nursing care facilities	44,460
Offices of physical, occupational and speech therapists, and audiologists	40,780
General medical and surgical hospitals	40,670
Offices of physicians	39,290

Median annual earnings of physical therapist aides were $22,060 in May 2006. The middle 50 percent earned between $18,550 and $26,860. The lowest 10 percent earned less than $15,850, and the highest 10 percent earned more than $32,600. Median annual earnings in the industries employing the largest numbers of physical therapist aides in May 2006 were

Nursing care facilities	$24,170
Offices of physicians	22,680
General medical and surgical hospitals	22,680
Offices of physical, occupational and speech therapists, and audiologists	21,230

Related Occupations

Physical therapist assistants and aides work under the supervision of physical therapists. Other workers in the health care field who work under similar supervision include dental assistants; medical assistants; occupational therapist assistants and aides; pharmacy aides; pharmacy technicians; nursing, psychiatric, and home health aides; personal and home care aides; and social and human service assistants.

Sources of Additional Information

Career information on physical therapist assistants and a list of schools offering accredited programs can be obtained from

▸ The American Physical Therapy Association, 1111 North Fairfax St., Alexandria, VA 22314-1488. Internet: http://www.apta.org

Pipelayers, Plumbers, Pipefitters, and Steamfitters

(O*NET 47-2151.00, 47-2152.00, 47-2152.01, and 47-2152.02)

Significant Points

■ Job opportunities should be very good, especially for workers with welding experience.

■ Pipelayers, plumbers, pipefitters, and steamfitters comprise one of the largest and highest paid construction occupations.

■ Most states and localities require plumbers to be licensed.

■ Apprenticeship programs generally provide the most comprehensive training, but many workers train in career or technical schools or community colleges.

Nature of the Work

Most people are familiar with plumbers who come to their home to unclog a drain or install an appliance. In addition to these activities, however, pipelayers, plumbers, pipefitters, and steamfitters install, maintain, and repair many different types of pipe systems. For example, some systems move water to a municipal water treatment plant and then to residential, commercial, and public buildings. Other systems dispose of waste, provide gas to stoves and furnaces, or provide for heating and cooling needs. Pipe systems in powerplants carry the steam that powers huge turbines. Pipes also are used in manufacturing plants to move material through the production process. Specialized piping systems are very important in both pharmaceutical and computer-chip manufacturing.

Although pipelaying, plumbing, pipefitting, and steamfitting sometimes are considered a single trade, workers generally specialize in one of five areas. *Pipelayers* lay clay, concrete, plastic, or cast-iron pipe for drains, sewers, water mains, and oil or gas lines. Before laying the pipe, pipelayers prepare and grade the trenches either manually or with machines. After laying the pipe, they weld, glue, cement, or otherwise join the pieces together. *Plumbers* install and repair the water, waste disposal, drainage, and gas systems in homes and commercial and industrial buildings. Plumbers also install plumbing fixtures—bathtubs, showers, sinks, and toilets—and appliances such as dishwashers and water heaters. *Pipefitters* install and repair both high-pressure and low-pressure pipe systems used in manufacturing, in the generation of electricity, and in the heating and cooling of buildings. They also install automatic controls that are increasingly being used to regulate these systems. Some pipefitters specialize in only one type of system. *Steamfitters* install pipe systems that move liquids or gases under high pressure. *Sprinklerfitters* install automatic fire sprinkler systems in buildings.

Pipelayers, plumbers, pipefitters, and steamfitters use many different materials and construction techniques, depending on the type of project. Residential water systems, for example, incorporate copper, steel, and plastic pipe that can be handled and installed by one or two plumbers. Municipal sewerage systems, on the other hand, are made of large cast-iron pipes; installation normally requires crews of pipefitters. Despite these differences, all pipelayers, plumbers, pipefitters, and steamfitters must be able to follow building plans or blueprints and instructions from supervisors, lay out the job, and work efficiently with the materials and tools of their trade.

Computers and specialized software are used to create blueprints and plan layouts.

When construction plumbers install piping in a new house, for example, they work from blueprints or drawings that show the planned location of pipes, plumbing fixtures, and appliances. Recently, plumbers have become more involved in the design process. Their knowledge of codes and the operation of plumbing systems can cut costs. They first lay out the job to fit the piping into the structure of the house with the least waste of material. Then they measure and mark areas in which pipes will be installed and connected. Construction plumbers also check for obstructions such as electrical wiring and, if necessary, plan the pipe installation around the problem.

Sometimes, plumbers have to cut holes in walls, ceilings, and floors of a house. For some systems, they may hang steel supports from ceiling joists to hold the pipe in place. To assemble a system, plumbers—using saws, pipe cutters, and pipe-bending machines— cut and bend lengths of pipe. They connect lengths of pipe with fittings, using methods that depend on the type of pipe used. For plastic pipe, plumbers connect the sections and fittings with adhesives. For copper pipe, they slide a fitting over the end of the pipe and solder it in place with a torch.

After the piping is in place in the house, plumbers install the fixtures and appliances and connect the system to the outside water or sewer lines. Finally, using pressure gauges, they check the system to ensure that the plumbing works properly.

Work environment. Pipefitters and steamfitters most often work in industrial and power plants. Plumbers work in commercial and residential settings where water and septic systems need to be installed and maintained. Pipelayers work outdoors, sometime in remote areas, as they build the pipelines that connect sources of oil, gas, and chemicals with the users of these materials. Sprinklerfitters work in all buildings that require the use of fire sprinkler systems.

Because pipelayers, plumbers, pipefitters, and steamfitters frequently must lift heavy pipes, stand for long periods, and sometimes work in uncomfortable or cramped positions, they need physical strength and stamina. They also may have to work outdoors in inclement weather. In addition, they are subject to possible falls from ladders, cuts from sharp tools, and burns from hot pipes or soldering equipment.

Pipelayers, plumbers, pipefitters, and steamfitters engaged in construction generally work a standard 40-hour week; those involved in maintaining pipe systems, including those who provide maintenance services under contract, may have to work evening or weekend shifts and work on call. These maintenance workers may spend a lot of time traveling to and from worksites.

Training, Other Qualifications, and Advancement

Most pipelayers, plumbers, pipefitters, and steamfitters train in career or technical schools or community colleges, and on the job through apprenticeships.

Education and training. Pipelayers, plumbers, pipefitters, and steamfitters enter into the occupation in a variety of ways. Most residential and industrial plumbers get their training in career and technical schools and community colleges and from on-the-job training. Pipelayers, plumbers, pipefitters, and steamfitters who work for nonresidential enterprises are usually trained through formal apprenticeship programs.

Apprenticeship programs generally provide the most comprehensive training available for these jobs. They are administered either by union locals and their affiliated companies or by nonunion contractor organizations. Organizations that sponsor apprenticeships include: the United Association of Journeymen and Apprentices of the Plumbing and Pipefitting Industry of the United States and Canada; local employers of either the Mechanical Contractors Association of America or the National Association of Plumbing-Heating-Cooling Contractors; a union associated with a member of the National Fire Sprinkler Association; the Associated Builders and Contractors; the National Association of Plumbing-Heating-Cooling Contractors; the American Fire Sprinkler Association, or the Home Builders Institute of the National Association of Home Builders.

Apprenticeships—both union and nonunion—consist of four or five years of paid on-the-job training and at least 144 hours of related classroom instruction per year. Classroom subjects include drafting and blueprint reading, mathematics, applied physics and chemistry, safety, and local plumbing codes and regulations. On the job, apprentices first learn basic skills, such as identifying grades and types of pipe, using the tools of the trade, and safely unloading materials. As apprentices gain experience, they learn how to work with various types of pipe and how to install different piping systems and plumbing fixtures. Apprenticeship gives trainees a thorough knowledge of all aspects of the trade. Although most pipelayers, plumbers, pipefitters, and steamfitters are trained through apprenticeship, some still learn their skills informally on the job.

Licensure. Although there are no uniform national licensing requirements, most states and communities require plumbers to be licensed. Licensing requirements vary, but most localities require workers to have two to five years of experience and to pass an examination that tests their knowledge of the trade and of local plumbing codes before working independently. Several states require a special license to work on gas lines. A few states require pipe fitters to be licensed. These licenses usually require a test, experience, or both.

Other qualifications. Applicants for union or nonunion apprentice jobs must be at least 18 years old and in good physical condition. A drug test may be required. Apprenticeship committees may require applicants to have a high school diploma or its equivalent. Armed Forces training in pipelaying, plumbing, and pipefitting is considered very good preparation. In fact, people with this background may be given credit for previous experience when entering a civilian apprenticeship program. High school or postsecondary courses in shop, plumbing, general mathematics, drafting, blueprint reading, computers, and physics also are good preparation.

Advancement. With additional training, some pipelayers, plumbers, pipefitters, and steamfitters become supervisors for mechanical and plumbing contractors. Others, especially plumbers, go into business for themselves, often starting as a self-employed plumber working from home. Some eventually become owners of businesses employing many workers and may spend most of their time as managers rather than as plumbers. Others move into closely related areas such as construction management or building inspection.

For those who would like to advance, it is increasingly important to be able to communicate in both English and Spanish in order to relay instructions and safety precautions to workers with limited understanding of English; Spanish-speaking workers make up a

© JIST Works

large part of the construction workforce in many areas. Supervisors and contractors need good communication skills to deal with clients and subcontractors.

Employment

Pipelayers, plumbers, pipefitters, and steamfitters constitute one of the largest construction occupations, holding about 569,000 jobs in 2006. About 55 percent worked for plumbing, heating, and air-conditioning contractors engaged in new construction, repair, modernization, or maintenance work. Others did maintenance work for a variety of industrial, commercial, and government employers. For example, pipefitters were employed as maintenance personnel in the petroleum and chemical industries, both of which move liquids and gases through pipes. About 12 percent of pipelayers, plumbers, pipefitters, and steamfitters were self-employed.

Job Outlook

Average employment growth is projected. Job opportunities are expected to be very good, especially for workers with welding experience.

Employment change. Employment of pipelayers, plumbers, pipefitters, and steamfitters is expected to grow 10 percent between 2006 and 2016, about as fast as the average for all occupations. Demand for plumbers will stem from new construction and building renovation. Bath remodeling, in particular, is expected to continue to grow and create more jobs for plumbers. In addition, repair and maintenance of existing residential systems will keep plumbers employed. Demand for pipefitters and steamfitters will be driven by maintenance and construction of places such as powerplants, water and wastewater treatment plants, office buildings, and factories, with extensive pipe systems. Growth of pipelayer jobs will stem from the building of new water and sewer lines and pipelines to new oil and gas fields. Demand for sprinklerfitters will increase because of changes to state and local rules for fire protection in homes and businesses.

Job prospects. Job opportunities are expected to be very good, as demand for skilled pipelayers, plumbers, pipefitters, and steamfitters is expected to outpace the supply of workers well trained in this craft in some areas. Some employers report difficulty finding workers with the right qualifications. In addition, many people currently working in these trades are expected to retire over the next 10 years, which will create additional job openings. Workers with welding experience should have especially good opportunities.

Traditionally, many organizations with extensive pipe systems have employed their own plumbers or pipefitters to maintain equipment and keep systems running smoothly. But, to reduce labor costs, many of these firms no longer employ full-time, in-house plumbers or pipefitters. Instead, when they need a plumber, they rely on workers provided under service contracts by plumbing and pipefitting contractors.

Construction projects generally provide only temporary employment. When a project ends, some pipelayers, plumbers, pipefitters, and steamfitters may be unemployed until they can begin work on a new project, although most companies are trying to limit these periods of unemployment to retain workers. In addition, the jobs of pipelayers, plumbers, pipefitters, and steamfitters are generally less sensitive to changes in economic conditions than jobs in other construction trades. Even when construction activity declines, maintenance, rehabilitation, and replacement of existing piping systems, as well as the increasing installation of fire sprinkler systems, provide many jobs for pipelayers, plumbers, pipefitters, and steamfitters.

Earnings

Pipelayers, plumbers, pipefitters, and steamfitters are among the highest paid construction occupations. Median hourly earnings of wage and salary plumbers, pipefitters, and steamfitters were $20.56. The middle 50 percent earned between $15.62 and $27.54. The lowest 10 percent earned less than $12.30, and the highest 10 percent earned more than $34.79. Median hourly earnings in the industries employing the largest numbers of plumbers, pipefitters, and steamfitters were

Natural gas distribution	$24.91
Nonresidential building construction	21.30
Plumbing, heating, and air-conditioning contractors	20.44
Utility system construction	19.18
Local government	17.86

In May 2006, median hourly earnings of wage and salary pipelayers were $14.58. The middle 50 percent earned between $11.75 and $19.76. The lowest 10 percent earned less than $9.73, and the highest 10 percent earned more than $25.73.

Apprentices usually begin at about 50 percent of the wage rate paid to experienced workers. Wages increase periodically as skills improve. After an initial waiting period, apprentices receive the same benefits as experienced pipelayers, plumbers, pipefitters, and steamfitters.

About 30 percent of pipelayers, plumbers, pipefitters, and steamfitters belonged to a union. Many of these workers are members of the United Association of Journeymen and Apprentices of the Plumbing and Pipefitting Industry of the United States and Canada.

Related Occupations

Other workers who install and repair mechanical systems in buildings include boilermakers; electricians; elevator installers and repairers; heating, air-conditioning, and refrigeration mechanics and installers; industrial machinery mechanics and maintenance workers; millwrights; sheet metal workers; and stationary engineers and

Projections data from the National Employment Matrix

Occupational Title	SOC Code	Employment, 2006	Projected employment, 2016	Change, 2006-16 Number	Change, 2006-16 Percent
Pipelayers, plumbers, pipefitters, and steamfitters	47-2150	569,000	628,000	59,000	10
Pipelayers	47-2151	67,000	72,000	5,800	9
Plumbers, pipefitters, and steamfitters	47-2152	502,000	555,000	53,000	11

NOTE: Data in this table are rounded.

boiler operators. Other related occupations include construction managers and construction and building inspectors.

Sources of Additional Information

For information about apprenticeships or work opportunities in pipelaying, plumbing, pipefitting, and steamfitting, contact local plumbing, heating, and air-conditioning contractors; a local or state chapter of the National Association of Plumbing, Heating, and Cooling Contractors; a local chapter of the Mechanical Contractors Association; a local chapter of the United Association of Journeymen and Apprentices of the Plumbing and Pipefitting Industry of the United States and Canada; or the nearest office of your state employment service or apprenticeship agency. Apprenticeship information is also available from the U.S. Department of Labor's toll free helpline: 1 (877) 872-5627.

For information about apprenticeship opportunities for pipelayers, plumbers, pipefitters, and steamfitters, contact

▸ United Association of Journeymen and Apprentices of the Plumbing and Pipefitting Industry, 901 Massachusetts Ave. NW, Washington, DC 20001. Internet: http://www.ua.org

For more information about training programs for pipelayers, plumbers, pipefitters, and steamfitters, contact

▸ Associated Builders and Contractors, Workforce Development Department, 4250 North Fairfax Dr., 9th Floor, Arlington, VA 22203. Internet: http://www.trytools.org

▸ Home Builders Institute, National Association of Home Builders, 1201 15th St. NW, Washington, DC 20005. Internet: http://www.hbi.org

For general information about the work of pipelayers, plumbers, and pipefitters, contact

▸ Mechanical Contractors Association of America, 1385 Piccard Dr., Rockville, MD 20850. Internet: http://www.mcaa.org

▸ National Center for Construction Education and Research, 3600 NW 43rd St., Bldg. G, Gainesville, FL 32606. Internet: http://www.nccer.org

▸ Plumbing-Heating-Cooling Contractors—National Association, 180 S. Washington St., Falls Church, VA 22040. Internet: http://www.phccweb.org

For general information about the work of sprinklerfitters, contact

▸ American Fire Sprinkler Association, Inc., 12750 Merit Dr., Suite 350, Dallas, TX 75251. Internet: http://www.firesprinkler.org

▸ National Fire Sprinkler Association, 40 Jon Barrett Rd., Patterson, NY 12563. Internet: http://www.nfsa.org

For general information on apprenticeships and how to get them, see the *Occupational Outlook Quarterly* article "Apprenticeships: Career training, credentials—and a paycheck in your pocket," online at http://www.bls.gov/opub/ooq/2002/summer/art01.pdf and in print at many libraries and career centers.

Police and Detectives

(O*NET 33-1012.00, 33-3021.00, 33-3021.01, 33-3021.02, 33-3021.03, 33-3021.04, 33-3021.05, 33-3031.00, 33-3051.00, 33-3051.01, 33-3051.02, 33-3051.03, and 33-3052.00)

Significant Points

■ Police work can be dangerous and stressful.

■ Education requirements range from a high school diploma to a college degree or higher.

■ Job opportunities in most local police departments will be excellent for qualified individuals, while competition is expected for jobs in state and federal agencies.

■ Applicants with college training in police science or military police experience will have the best opportunities.

Nature of the Work

People depend on police officers and detectives to protect their lives and property. Law enforcement officers, some of whom are state or federal special agents or inspectors, perform these duties in a variety of ways depending on the size and type of their organization. In most jurisdictions, they are expected to exercise authority when necessary, whether on or off duty.

Police and detectives pursue and apprehend individuals who break the law and then issue citations or give warnings. A large proportion of their time is spent writing reports and maintaining records of incidents they encounter. Most police officers patrol their jurisdictions and investigate any suspicious activity they notice. Detectives, who are often called agents or special agents, perform investigative duties such as gathering facts and collecting evidence.

The daily activities of police and detectives differ depending on their occupational specialty—such as police officer, game warden, or detective—and whether they are working for a local, state, or federal agency. Duties also differ substantially among various federal agencies, which enforce different aspects of the law. Regardless of job duties or location, police officers and detectives at all levels must write reports and maintain meticulous records that will be needed if they testify in court.

Uniformed police officers have general law enforcement duties, including maintaining regular patrols and responding to calls for service. Much of their time is spent responding to calls and doing paperwork. They may direct traffic at the scene of an accident, investigate a burglary, or give first aid to an accident victim. In large police departments, officers usually are assigned to a specific type of duty. Many urban police agencies are involved in community policing—a practice in which an officer builds relationships with the citizens of local neighborhoods and mobilizes the public to help fight crime.

Police agencies are usually organized into geographic districts, with uniformed officers assigned to patrol a specific area such as part of the business district or outlying residential neighborhoods. Officers may work alone, but in large agencies, they often patrol with a partner. While on patrol, officers attempt to become thoroughly familiar with their patrol area and remain alert for anything unusual. Suspicious circumstances and hazards to public safety are investigated or noted, and officers are dispatched to individual calls for assistance within their district. During their shift, they may identify, pursue, and arrest suspected criminals; resolve problems within the community; and enforce traffic laws.

Some agencies have special geographic jurisdictions and enforcement responsibilities. Public college and university police forces, public school district police, and agencies serving transportation systems and facilities are examples. Most law enforcement workers in special agencies are uniformed officers; a smaller number are investigators.

© JIST Works

Some police officers specialize in a particular field, such as chemical and microscopic analysis, training and firearms instruction, or handwriting and fingerprint identification. Others work with special units, such as horseback, bicycle, motorcycle, or harbor patrol; canine corps; special weapons and tactics (SWAT); or emergency response teams. A few local and special law enforcement officers primarily perform jail-related duties or work in courts. (For information on other officers who work in jails and prisons, see correctional officers elsewhere in this book.)

Sheriffs and deputy sheriffs enforce the law on the county level. Sheriffs are usually elected to their posts and perform duties similar to those of a local or county police chief. Sheriffs' departments tend to be relatively small, most having fewer than 50 sworn officers. Deputy sheriffs have law enforcement duties similar to those of officers in urban police departments. Police and sheriffs' deputies who provide security in city and county courts are sometimes called bailiffs

State police officers, sometimes called *state troopers* or *highway patrol officers*, arrest criminals statewide and patrol highways to enforce motor vehicle laws and regulations. State police officers often issue traffic citations to motorists. At the scene of accidents, they may direct traffic, give first aid, and call for emergency equipment. They also write reports used to determine the cause of the accident. State police officers are frequently called upon to render assistance to other law enforcement agencies, especially those in rural areas or small towns.

State law enforcement agencies operate in every state except Hawaii. Most full-time sworn personnel are uniformed officers who regularly patrol and respond to calls for service. Others work as investigators, perform court-related duties, or carry out administrative or other assignments.

Detectives are plainclothes investigators who gather facts and collect evidence for criminal cases. Some are assigned to interagency task forces to combat specific types of crime. They conduct interviews, examine records, observe the activities of suspects, and participate in raids or arrests. Detectives and state and federal agents and inspectors usually specialize in investigating one type of violation, such as homicide or fraud. They are assigned cases on a rotating basis and work on them until an arrest and conviction is made or until the case is dropped.

Fish and game wardens enforce fishing, hunting, and boating laws. They patrol hunting and fishing areas, conduct search and rescue operations, investigate complaints and accidents, and aid in prosecuting court cases.

The federal government works in many areas of law enforcement. *Federal Bureau of Investigation (FBI) agents* are the Government's principal investigators, responsible for investigating violations of more than 200 categories of federal law and conducting sensitive national security investigations. Agents may conduct surveillance, monitor court-authorized wiretaps, examine business records, investigate white-collar crime, or participate in sensitive undercover assignments. The FBI investigates a wide range of criminal activity, including organized crime, public corruption, financial crime, bank robbery, kidnapping, terrorism, espionage, drug trafficking, and cyber crime.

There are many other federal agencies that enforce particular types of laws. *U.S. Drug Enforcement Administration (DEA) agents* enforce laws and regulations relating to illegal drugs. *U.S. marshals and deputy marshals* protect the federal courts and ensure the effective operation of the judicial system. *Bureau of Alcohol, Tobacco, Firearms, and Explosives agents* enforce and investigate violations of federal firearms and explosives laws, as well as federal alcohol and tobacco tax regulations. The U.S. Department of State *Bureau of Diplomatic Security special agents* are engaged in the battle against terrorism.

The *Department of Homeland Security* also employs numerous law enforcement officers within several different agencies, including Customs and Border Protection, Immigration and Customs Enforcement, and the U.S. Secret Service. *U.S. Border Patrol agents* protect more than 8,000 miles of international land and water boundaries. *Immigration inspectors* interview and examine people seeking entrance to the United States and its territories. *Customs inspectors* enforce laws governing imports and exports by inspecting cargo, baggage, and articles worn or carried by people, vessels, vehicles, trains, and aircraft entering or leaving the United States. *Federal Air Marshals* provide air security by guarding against attacks targeting U.S. aircraft, passengers, and crews. *U.S. Secret Service special agents* and U.S. *Secret Service uniformed officers* protect the President, Vice President, their immediate families, and other public officials. Secret Service special agents also investigate counterfeiting, forgery of Government checks or bonds, and fraudulent use of credit cards.

Other federal agencies employ police and special agents with sworn arrest powers and the authority to carry firearms. These agencies include the Postal Service, the Bureau of Indian Affairs Office of Law Enforcement, the Forest Service, and the National Park Service.

Work environment. Police and detective work can be very dangerous and stressful. In addition to the obvious dangers of confrontations with criminals, police officers and detectives need to be constantly alert and ready to deal appropriately with a number of other threatening situations. Many law enforcement officers witness death and suffering resulting from accidents and criminal behavior. A career in law enforcement may take a toll on their private lives.

The jobs of some federal agents such as U.S. Secret Service and DEA special agents require extensive travel, often on very short notice. They may relocate a number of times over the course of their careers. Some special agents in agencies such as the U.S. Border Patrol work outdoors in rugged terrain for long periods and in all kinds of weather.

Uniformed officers, detectives, agents, and inspectors are usually scheduled to work 40-hour weeks, but paid overtime is common. Shift work is necessary because protection must be provided around the clock. Junior officers frequently work weekends, holidays, and nights. Police officers and detectives are required to work whenever they are needed and may work long hours during investigations. Officers in most jurisdictions, whether on or off duty, are expected to be armed and to exercise their authority when necessary.

Training, Other Qualifications, and Advancement

Most police and detectives learn much of what they need to know on the job, often in their agency's police academy. Civil service regulations govern the appointment of police and detectives in most states, large municipalities, and special police agencies, as well as in many smaller jurisdictions. Candidates must be U.S. citizens, usually at least 20 years old, and must meet rigorous physical and personal qualifications.

Education and training. Applicants usually must have at least a high school education, and some departments require one or two years of college coursework or, in some cases, a college degree.

Law enforcement agencies encourage applicants to take courses or training related to law enforcement subjects after high school. Many entry-level applicants for police jobs have completed some formal postsecondary education, and a significant number are college graduates. Many junior colleges, colleges, and universities offer programs in law enforcement or administration of justice.

Physical education classes and participating in sports are also helpful in developing the competitiveness, stamina, and agility needed for many law enforcement positions. Knowledge of a foreign language is an asset in many federal agencies and urban departments.

Many agencies pay all or part of the tuition for officers to work toward degrees in criminal justice, police science, administration of justice, or public administration and pay higher salaries to those who earn such a degree.

Before their first assignments, officers usually go through a period of training. In state and large local police departments, recruits get training in their agency's police academy, often for 12 to 14 weeks. In small agencies, recruits often attend a regional or state academy. Training includes classroom instruction in constitutional law and civil rights, state laws and local ordinances, and accident investigation. Recruits also receive training and supervised experience in patrol, traffic control, the use of firearms, self-defense, first aid, and emergency response. Police departments in some large cities hire high school graduates who are still in their teens as police cadets or trainees. They do clerical work and attend classes, usually for one to two years, until they reach the minimum age requirement and can be appointed to the regular force.

To be considered for appointment as an FBI agent, an applicant must be a college graduate and have at least three years of professional work experience, or have an advanced degree plus two years of professional work experience. An applicant who meets these criteria must also have one of the following: a college major in accounting, electrical engineering, information technology, or computer science; fluency in a foreign language; a degree from an accredited law school; or three years of related full-time work experience. All new FBI agents undergo 18 weeks of training at the FBI Academy on the U.S. Marine Corps base in Quantico, Virginia.

Most other federal law enforcement agencies require either a bachelor's degree or related work experience or a combination of the two. Federal law enforcement agents undergo extensive training, usually at the U.S. Marine Corps base in Quantico, Virginia, or the Federal Law Enforcement Training Center in Glynco, Georgia. The educational requirements, qualifications, and training information for a particular federal agency can be found on the agency's Web site, most of which are listed in the last section of this statement.

Fish and game wardens also must meet specific requirements. Most states require at least two years of college study. Once hired, fish and game wardens attend a training academy lasting from three to 12 months, sometimes followed by further training in the field.

Other qualifications. Civil service regulations govern the appointment of police and detectives in most states, large municipalities, and special police agencies, as well as in many smaller jurisdictions. Candidates must be U.S. citizens, usually at least 20 years old, and

must meet rigorous physical and personal qualifications. Physical examinations for entrance into law enforcement often include tests of vision, hearing, strength, and agility. Eligibility for appointment usually depends on performance in competitive written examinations and previous education and experience.

Candidates should enjoy working with people and meeting the public. Because personal characteristics such as honesty, sound judgment, integrity, and a sense of responsibility are especially important in law enforcement, candidates are interviewed by senior officers, and their character traits and backgrounds are investigated. In some agencies, candidates are interviewed by a psychiatrist or a psychologist or given a personality test. Most applicants are subjected to lie detector examinations or drug testing. Some agencies subject sworn personnel to random drug testing as a condition of continuing employment.

Advancement. Police officers usually become eligible for promotion after a probationary period ranging from six months to three years. In large departments, promotion may enable an officer to become a detective or to specialize in one type of police work, such as working with juveniles. Promotions to corporal, sergeant, lieutenant, and captain usually are made according to a candidate's position on a promotion list, as determined by scores on a written examination and on-the-job performance.

Continuing training helps police officers, detectives, and special agents improve their job performance. Through police department academies, regional centers for public safety employees established by the states, and federal agency training centers, instructors provide annual training in self-defense tactics, firearms, use-of-force policies, sensitivity and communications skills, crowd-control techniques, relevant legal developments, and advances in law enforcement equipment.

Employment

Police and detectives held about 861,000 jobs in 2006. Seventy-nine percent were employed by local governments. State police agencies employed about 11 percent, and various federal agencies employed about 7 percent. A small proportion worked for educational services, rail transportation, and contract investigation and security services.

According to the U.S. Bureau of Justice Statistics, police and detectives employed by local governments primarily worked in cities with more than 25,000 inhabitants. Some cities have very large police forces, while thousands of small communities employ fewer than 25 officers each.

Job Outlook

Job opportunities in most local police departments will be excellent for qualified individuals, while competition is expected for jobs in state and federal agencies. Average employment growth is expected.

Employment change. Employment of police and detectives is expected to grow 11 percent over the 2006–2016 decade, about as fast as the average for all occupations. A more security-conscious society and population growth will contribute to the increasing demand for police services.

Job prospects. Overall opportunities in local police departments will be excellent for individuals who meet the psychological, personal, and physical qualifications. In addition to openings from employment growth, many openings will be created by the need to replace workers who retire and those who leave local agencies for federal

Projections data from the National Employment Matrix

Occupational Title	SOC Code	Employment, 2006	Projected employment, 2016	Change, 2006-16	
				Number	Percent
Police and detectives	—	861,000	959,000	97,000	11
First-line supervisors/managers of police and detectives	33-1012	93,000	102,000	8,500	9
Detectives and criminal investigators..	33-3021	106,000	125,000	18,000	17
Fish and game wardens	33-3031	8,000	8,000	0	0
Police officers..	33-3050	654,000	724,000	70,000	11
Police and sheriff's patrol officers	33-3051	648,000	719,000	70,000	11
Transit and railroad police	33-3052	5,600	5,900	400	6

NOTE: Data in this table are rounded.

jobs and private sector security jobs. There will be more competition for jobs in federal and state law enforcement agencies than for jobs in local agencies. Less competition for jobs will occur in departments that offer relatively low salaries or those in urban communities where the crime rate is relatively high. Applicants with military experience or college training in police science will have the best opportunities in local and state departments. Applicants with a bachelor's degree and several years of law enforcement or military experience, especially investigative experience, will have the best opportunities in federal agencies.

The level of government spending determines the level of employment for police and detectives. The number of job opportunities, therefore, can vary from year to year and from place to place. Layoffs, on the other hand, are rare because retirements enable most staffing cuts to be handled through attrition. Trained law enforcement officers who lose their jobs because of budget cuts usually have little difficulty finding jobs with other agencies.

Earnings

Police and sheriff's patrol officers had median annual earnings of $47,460 in May 2006. The middle 50 percent earned between $35,600 and $59,880. The lowest 10 percent earned less than $27,310, and the highest 10 percent earned more than $72,450. Median annual earnings were $43,510 in federal government, $52,540 in state government, and $47,190 in local government.

In May 2006, median annual earnings of police and detective supervisors were $69,310. The middle 50 percent earned between $53,900 and $83,940. The lowest 10 percent earned less than $41,260, and the highest 10 percent earned more than $104,410. Median annual earnings were $85,170 in federal government, $68,990 in state government, and $68,670 in local government.

In May 2006, median annual earnings of detectives and criminal investigators were $58,260. The middle 50 percent earned between $43,920 and $76,350. The lowest 10 percent earned less than $34,480, and the highest 10 percent earned more than $92,590. Median annual earnings were $69,510 in federal government, $49,370 in state government, and $52,520 in local government.

Federal law provides special salary rates to federal employees who serve in law enforcement. Additionally, federal special agents and inspectors receive law enforcement availability pay (LEAP)—equal to 25 percent of the agent's grade and step—awarded because of the large amount of overtime that these agents are expected to work. For example, in 2007, FBI agents entered federal service as GS-10 employees on the pay scale at a base salary of $48,159, yet they earned about $60,199 a year with availability pay. They could advance to the GS-13 grade level in field nonsupervisory assign-

ments at a base salary of $75,414, which was worth $94,268 with availability pay. FBI supervisory, management, and executive positions in grades GS-14 and GS-15 paid a base salary of about $89,115 and $104,826 a year, respectively, which amounted to $111,394 or $131,033 per year including availability pay. Salaries were slightly higher in selected areas where the prevailing local pay level was higher. Because federal agents may be eligible for a special law enforcement benefits package, applicants should ask their recruiter for more information.

Total earnings for local, state, and special police and detectives frequently exceed the stated salary because of payments for overtime, which can be significant.

According to the International City-County Management Association's annual Police and Fire Personnel, Salaries, and Expenditures Survey, average salaries for sworn full-time positions in 2006 were

	Minimum annual base salary	Maximum annual base salary
Police chief...............................	$78,547	$99,698
Deputy chief	68,797	87,564
Police captain	65,408	81,466
Police lieutenant	59,940	72,454
Police sergeant	53,734	63,564
Police corporal	44,160	55,183

In addition to the common benefits—paid vacation, sick leave, and medical and life insurance—most police and sheriffs' departments provide officers with special allowances for uniforms. Because police officers usually are covered by liberal pension plans, many retire at half-pay after 25 or 30 years of service.

Related Occupations

Police and detectives maintain law and order, collect evidence and information, and conduct investigations and surveillance. Workers in related occupations include correctional officers, private detectives and investigators, probation officers and correctional treatment specialists, and security guards and gaming surveillance officers. Like police and detectives, firefighters and emergency medical technicians and paramedics provide public safety services and respond to emergencies.

Sources of Additional Information

Information about entrance requirements may be obtained from federal, state, and local law enforcement agencies.

For general information about sheriffs and to learn more about the National Sheriffs' Association scholarship, contact

> ▶ National Sheriffs' Association, 1450 Duke St., Alexandria, VA 22314. Internet: http://www.sheriffs.org

> ▶ Information about qualifications for employment as a FBI Special Agent is available from the nearest state FBI office. The address and phone number are listed in the local telephone directory. Internet: http://www.fbi.gov

> ▶ Information on career opportunities, qualifications, and training for U.S. Secret Service Special Agents and Uniformed Officers is available from the Secret Service Personnel Division at (202) 406-5800, (888) 813-877, or (888) 813-USSS. Internet: http://www.secretservice.gov/join

> ▶ Information about qualifications for employment as a DEA Special Agent is available from the nearest DEA office, or call (800) DEA-4288. Internet: http://www.usdoj.gov/dea

Information about career opportunities, qualifications, and training to become a deputy marshal is available from

> ▶ U.S. Marshals Service, Human Resources Division—Law Enforcement Recruiting, Washington, DC 20530-1000. Internet: http://www.usmarshals.gov

For information on operations and career opportunities in the U.S. Bureau of Alcohol, Tobacco, Firearms, and Explosives, contact

> ▶ U.S. Bureau of Alcohol, Tobacco, Firearms, and Explosives, Office of Governmental and Public Affairs, 650 Massachusetts Ave. NW, Room 8290, Washington D.C., 20226. Internet: http://www.atf.gov

Information about careers in U.S. Customs and Border Protection is available from

> ▶ U.S. Customs and Border Protection, 1300 Pennsylvania Ave. NW, Washington, DC 20229. Internet: http://www.cbp.gov

Information about law enforcement agencies within the Department of Homeland Security is available from

> ▶ U.S. Department of Homeland Security, Washington, DC 20528. Internet: http://www.dhs.gov

To find federal, state, and local law enforcement job fairs and other recruiting events across the country, contact

> ▶ National Law Enforcement Recruiters Association, 2045 15th St. North, Suite 210, Arlington, VA 22201. Internet: http://www.nlera.org

Production, Planning, and Expediting Clerks

(O*NET 43-5061.00)

Significant Points

- Production, planning, and expediting clerks work closely with supervisors who must approve production and work schedules.

- Many production, planning, and expediting jobs are at the entry level and do not require more than a high school diploma.

- Manufacturing firms and wholesale and retail trade establishments are the primary employers.

- Slower-than-average employment growth is projected.

Nature of the Work

Production, planning, and expediting clerks coordinate and facilitate the flow of information, work, and materials within or among offices. Most of their work is done according to production, work, or shipment schedules that are developed by supervisors who determine work progress and completion dates. Clerks compile reports on the progress of work and on production problems, and also may set worker schedules, estimate costs, schedule the shipment of parts, keep an inventory of materials, inspect and assemble materials, and write special orders for services and merchandise. In addition, they may route and deliver parts to ensure that production quotas are met and that merchandise is delivered on the date promised.

Production and planning clerks compile records and reports on various aspects of production, such as materials and parts used, products produced, machine and instrument readings, and frequency of defects. These workers prepare work tickets or other production guides and distribute them to other workers. Production and planning clerks coordinate, schedule, monitor, and chart production and its progress, either manually or electronically. They also gather information from customers' orders or other specifications and use the information to prepare a detailed production sheet that serves as a guide in assembling or manufacturing the product.

Expediting clerks contact vendors and shippers to ensure that merchandise, supplies, and equipment are forwarded on the specified shipping dates. They communicate with transportation companies to prevent delays in transit, and they may arrange for the distribution of materials upon their arrival. They may even visit work areas of vendors and shippers to check the status of orders. Expediting clerks locate materials and distribute them to specified production areas. They may inspect products for quality and quantity to ensure their adherence to specifications. They also keep a chronological list of due dates and may move work that does not meet the production schedule to the top of the list.

Work environment. Although their offices or desks may be near a production plant or warehouse, production, planning, and expediting clerks generally work in clean and environmentally-controlled conditions. They spend most of their day either on the phone or on the computer while working closely with supervisors who must approve production and work schedules. The typical work week is Monday through Friday.

Training, Other Qualifications, and Advancement

Training requirements for production, planning, and expediting clerks are limited. Usually a high school diploma is sufficient, although computer skills also are essential.

Education and training. Many production, planning, and expediting jobs are at the entry level and do not require more than a high school diploma. However, applicants who have taken business courses or have specific job-related experience may be preferred. Production, planning, and expediting clerks usually learn the job by doing routine tasks under close supervision. They learn how to count and mark stock, and then they start keeping records and taking inventory. Production, planning, and expediting clerks must learn both how their company operates and the company's priorities before they can begin to write production and work schedules efficiently.

Projections data from the National Employment Matrix

Occupational Title	SOC Code	Employment, 2006	Projected employment, 2016	Change, 2006-16	
				Number	Percent
Production, planning, and expediting clerks	43-5061	293,000	305,000	12,000	4

NOTE: Data in this table are rounded.

Other qualifications. Employers prefer to hire those familiar with computers and other electronic office and business equipment. Because communication with other people is an integral part of some jobs in the occupation, good oral and written communication skills are essential. Typing, filing, recordkeeping, and other clerical skills also are important. Strength, stamina, good eyesight, and an ability to work at repetitive tasks, sometimes under pressure, are other important characteristics that employers look for in prospective workers.

Advancement. Advancement opportunities for production, planning, and expediting clerks vary with the place of employment, but often require additional education.

Employment

Clerks engaged in production, planning, and expediting activities work in almost every sector of the economy, overseeing inventory control and assuring that schedules and deadlines are met. In 2006, production, planning, and expediting clerks held 293,000 jobs. Jobs in manufacturing made up 41 percent. Another 15 percent were in wholesale and retail trade establishments. Others worked in advertising firms and for telecommunications companies, among other places.

Job Outlook

Employment of production, planning, and expediting clerks is expected to increase more slowly than average.

Employment change. The number of production, planning, and expediting clerks is expected to grow by 4 percent from 2016 to 2016, slower than the average for all occupations. As a greater emphasis is placed on the timely delivery of goods and services throughout the economy, there will be increasing need for production, planning, and expediting clerks at all levels of the supply chain. However, the expected employment decline in manufacturing will limit the overall growth of this occupation. The work of production, planning, and expediting clerks is less likely to be automated than the work of many other administrative support occupations.

Job prospects. In addition to openings due to employment growth, job openings will arise from the need to replace production, planning, and expediting clerks who leave the labor force or transfer to other occupations. Opportunities will be better in fields that are experiencing faster growth, such as wholesale trade and warehousing.

Earnings

Median annual earnings of production, planning, and expediting clerks in May 2006 were $38,620. The middle 50 percent earned between $29,560 and $48,900. The lowest 10 percent earned less than $23,470, and the highest 10 percent earned more than $59,080.

These workers usually receive the same benefits as most other workers.

Related Occupations

Other workers who coordinate the flow of information to assist the production process include cargo and freight agents; shipping, receiving, and traffic clerks; stock clerks and order fillers; and weighers, measurers, checkers, and samplers, recordkeeping.

Sources of Additional Information

Information about job opportunities may be obtained from local employers and from local offices of the state employment service.

Purchasing Managers, Buyers, and Purchasing Agents

(O*NET 11-3061.00, 13-1021.00, 13-1022.00, and 13-1023.00)

Significant Points

- About 43 percent are employed in wholesale trade or manufacturing establishments.
- Some firms prefer to promote existing employees to these positions, while others recruit and train college graduates.
- Employment is projected to have little or no job growth.
- Opportunities should be best for those with a college degree.

Nature of the Work

Purchasing managers, buyers, and purchasing agents shop for a living. They buy the goods and services the company or institution needs, either to resell to customers or for the establishment's own use. *Wholesale and retail buyers* purchase goods, such as clothing or electronics, for resale. *Purchasing agents* buy goods and services for use by their own company or organization; they might buy raw materials for manufacturing or office supplies, for example. *Purchasing agents and buyers of farm products* purchase goods such as grain, Christmas trees, and tobacco for further processing or resale.

Purchasing professionals consider price, quality, availability, reliability, and technical support when choosing suppliers and merchandise. They try to get the best deal for their company by obtaining the highest-quality goods and services at the lowest possible cost to their companies. In order to accomplish this successfully, purchasing managers, buyers, and purchasing agents study sales records and inventory levels of current stock, identify foreign and domestic suppliers, and keep abreast of changes affecting both the supply of and demand for needed products and materials. To be effective, purchasing specialists must have a working technical knowledge of the goods or services to be purchased.

In large industrial organizations, a distinction often is drawn between the work of a buyer or purchasing agent and that of a *purchasing manager.* Purchasing agents commonly focus on routine purchasing tasks, often specializing in a commodity or group of related commodities, such as steel, lumber, cotton, grains, fabricated metal products, or petroleum products. Purchasing agents usually track market conditions, price trends, and futures markets. Purchasing managers usually handle the more complex or critical purchases and may supervise a group of purchasing agents handling other goods and services. Whether a person is titled purchasing manager, buyer, or purchasing agent depends somewhat on specific industry and employer practices. But purchasing managers often have a much larger range of duties than purchasing agents. They may actively seek new technologies and suppliers. They may create and oversee systems that allow individuals within their organizations to buy their own supplies, lowering the cost of each transaction.

Purchasing specialists employed by government agencies or manufacturing firms usually are called purchasing directors, managers, or agents or contract specialists. These workers acquire materials, parts, machines, supplies, services, and other inputs to the production of a final product. Purchasing agents and managers obtain items ranging from raw materials, fabricated parts, machinery, and office supplies to construction services and airline tickets. Some purchasing managers specialize in negotiating and supervising supply contracts and are called contract or supply managers.

Often, purchasing specialists in government place solicitations for services and accept bids and offers through the Internet. Government purchasing agents and managers must follow strict laws and regulations in their work in order to avoid any appearance of impropriety.

Purchasing specialists who buy finished goods for resale are employed by wholesale and retail establishments, where they commonly are known as buyers or merchandise managers. Wholesale and retail buyers are an integral part of a complex system of distribution and merchandising that caters to the vast array of consumer needs and desires. Wholesale buyers purchase goods directly from manufacturers or from other wholesale firms for resale to retail firms, commercial establishments, institutions, and other organizations. In retail firms, buyers purchase goods from wholesale firms or directly from manufacturers for resale to the public.

Buyers largely determine which products their establishment will sell. Therefore, it is essential that they have the ability to predict what will appeal to consumers. They must constantly stay informed of the latest trends, because failure to do so could jeopardize profits and the reputation of their company. They keep track of inventories and sales levels through computer software that is linked to the store's cash registers. Buyers also follow ads in newspapers and other media to check competitors' sales activities, and they watch general economic conditions to anticipate consumer buying patterns. Buyers working for large and medium-sized firms usually specialize in acquiring one or two lines of merchandise, whereas buyers working for small stores may purchase the establishment's complete inventory.

The use of private-label merchandise and the consolidation of buying departments have increased the responsibilities of retail buyers. Private-label merchandise, produced for a particular retailer, requires buyers to work closely with vendors to develop and obtain the desired product. The downsizing and consolidation of buying departments increases the demands placed on buyers because, although the amount of work remains unchanged, there are fewer people to accomplish it. The result is an increase in the workloads and levels of responsibility for all.

Many merchandise managers assist in the planning and implementation of sales promotion programs. Working with merchandise executives, they determine the nature of the sale and purchase items accordingly. Merchandise managers may work with advertising personnel to create an ad campaign. For example, they may determine in which media the advertisement will be placed—newspapers, direct mail, television, or some combination of all three. In addition, merchandise managers often visit the selling floor to ensure that goods are properly displayed. Buyers stay in constant contact with store and department managers to find out what products are selling well and which items the customers are demanding to be added to the product line. Often, assistant buyers are responsible for placing orders and checking shipments.

Evaluating suppliers is one of the most critical functions of a purchasing manager, buyer, or purchasing agent. Many firms now run on a lean manufacturing schedule and use just-in-time inventories, so any delays in the supply chain can shut down production and cost the firm its customers and reputation. Purchasing professionals use many resources to find out all they can about potential suppliers. The Internet has become an effective tool in searching catalogs, trade journals, and industry and company publications and directories. Purchasing professionals will attend meetings, trade shows, and conferences to learn of new industry trends and make contacts with suppliers. Purchasing managers, agents, and buyers will usually interview prospective suppliers and visit their plants and distribution centers to asses their capabilities. It is important to make certain that the supplier is capable of delivering the desired goods or services on time and in the correct quantities without sacrificing quality. Once all of the necessary information on suppliers is gathered, orders are placed and contracts are awarded to those suppliers who meet the purchaser's needs. Most of the transaction process is now automated using electronic purchasing systems that link the supplier and firms together through the Internet.

Purchasing professionals can gain instant access to specifications for thousands of commodities, inventory records, and their customers' purchase records to avoid overpaying for goods and to avoid shortages of popular goods or surpluses of goods that do not sell as well. These systems permit faster selection, customization, and ordering of products, and they allow buyers to concentrate on the qualitative and analytical aspects of the job. Long-term contracts are an important strategy of purchasing professionals because they allow purchasers to consolidate their supply bases around fewer suppliers. In today's global economy, purchasing managers, buyers, and purchasing agents should expect to deal with foreign suppliers. which may require travel to other countries, and should be familiar with other cultures and languages.

Changing business practices have altered the traditional roles of purchasing or supply management specialists in many industries. For example, manufacturing companies increasingly involve workers in this occupation at most stages of product development because of their ability to forecast a part's or material's cost, availability, and suitability for its intended purpose. Furthermore, potential problems with the supply of materials may be avoided by consulting the purchasing department in the early stages of product design.

Purchasing specialists often work closely with other employees in their own organization when deciding on purchases, an arrangement sometimes called "team buying." For example, before submitting an order, they may discuss the design of custom-made products with company design engineers, talk about problems involving the quality of purchased goods with quality assurance engineers and

© JIST Works

production supervisors, or mention shipment problems to managers in the receiving department.

Work environment. Most purchasing managers, buyers, and purchasing agents work in comfortable offices. They frequently work more than the standard 40-hour week because of special sales, conferences, or production deadlines. Evening and weekend work also is common before holiday and back-to-school seasons for those working in retail trade. Consequently, many retail firms discourage the use of vacation time during peak periods.

Buyers and merchandise managers often work under great pressure. Because wholesale and retail stores are so competitive, buyers need physical stamina to keep up with the fast-paced nature of their work.

Many purchasing managers, buyers, and purchasing agents travel at least several days a month. Purchasers for worldwide manufacturing companies and large retailers, as well as buyers of high fashion, may travel outside the United States.

Training, Other Qualifications, and Advancement

Qualified people may begin as trainees, purchasing clerks, expediters, junior buyers, or assistant buyers. They often need continuing education, certification, or a bachelor's degree to advance. Retail and wholesale firms prefer to hire applicants who have a college degree and who are familiar with the merchandise they sell and with wholesaling and retailing practices. Some retail firms promote qualified employees to assistant buyer positions; others recruit and train college graduates as assistant buyers. Most employers use a combination of methods.

Education and training. Educational requirements tend to vary with the size of the organization. Large stores and distributors prefer applicants who have completed a bachelor's degree program with a business emphasis. Many manufacturing firms put an even greater emphasis on formal training, preferring applicants with a bachelor's or master's degree in engineering, business, economics, or one of the applied sciences. A master's degree is essential for advancement to many top-level purchasing manager jobs.

Regardless of academic preparation, new employees must learn the specifics of their employer's business. Training periods vary in length, with most lasting one to five years. In wholesale and retail establishments, most trainees begin by selling merchandise, supervising sales workers, checking invoices on material received, and keeping track of stock. As they progress, trainees are given increased buying-related responsibilities.

In manufacturing, new purchasing employees often are enrolled in company training programs and spend a considerable amount of time learning about their firm's operations and purchasing practices. They work with experienced purchasers to learn about commodities, prices, suppliers, and markets. In addition, they may be assigned to the production planning department to learn about the material requirements system and the inventory system the company uses to keep production and replenishment functions working smoothly.

Other qualifications. Purchasing managers, buyers, and purchasing agents must know how to use word-processing and spreadsheet software and the Internet. Other important qualities include the ability to analyze technical data in suppliers' proposals; good communication, negotiation, and mathematical skills; knowledge of supply-chain management; and the ability to perform financial analyses.

People who wish to become wholesale or retail buyers should be good at planning and decision making and have an interest in merchandising. Anticipating consumer preferences and ensuring that goods are in stock when they are needed require resourcefulness, good judgment, and self-confidence. Buyers must be able to make decisions quickly and to take risks. Marketing skills and the ability to identify products that will sell also are very important. Employers often look for leadership ability, too, because buyers spend a large portion of their time supervising assistant buyers and dealing with manufacturers' representatives and store executives.

Experienced buyers may advance by moving to a department that manages a larger volume or by becoming a merchandise manager. Others may go to work in sales for a manufacturer or wholesaler.

Certification and advancement. An experienced purchasing agent or buyer may become an assistant purchasing manager in charge of a group of purchasing professionals before advancing to purchasing manager, supply manager, or director of materials management. At the top levels, duties may overlap with other management functions, such as production, planning, logistics, and marketing.

Regardless of industry, continuing education is essential for advancement. Many purchasing managers, buyers, and purchasing agents participate in seminars offered by professional societies and take college courses in supply management. Professional certification is becoming increasingly important, especially for those just entering the occupation.

There are several recognized credentials for purchasing agents and purchasing managers. The Certified Purchasing Manager (CPM) designation is conferred by the Institute for Supply Management. In 2008, this certification will be replaced by the Certified Professional in Supply Management (CPSM) credential, covering the wider scope of duties now performed by purchasing professionals. The Certified Purchasing Professional (CPP) and Certified Professional Purchasing Manager (CPPM) designations are conferred by the American Purchasing Society. The Certified Supply Chain Professional credential is conferred by APICS, the Association for Operations Management. For workers in federal, state, and local government, the National Institute of Governmental Purchasing offers the designations of Certified Professional Public Buyer (CPPB) and Certified Public Purchasing Officer (CPPO). Most of these certifications are awarded only after work-related experience and education requirements are met and written or oral exams are successfully completed.

Employment

Purchasing managers, buyers, and purchasing agents held about 529,000 jobs in 2006. About 43 percent worked in the wholesale trade and manufacturing industries and another 11 percent worked in retail trade. The remainder worked mostly in service establishments, such as management of companies and enterprises, or in different levels of government. A small number were self-employed.

The following tabulation shows the distribution of employment by occupational specialty:

Purchasing agents, except wholesale, retail, and farm products	287,000
Wholesale and retail buyers, except farm products	157,000
Purchasing managers	70,000
Purchasing agents and buyers, farm products	16,000

Projections data from the National Employment Matrix

Occupational Title	SOC Code	Employment, 2006	Projected employment, 2016	Change, 2006-16	
				Number	Percent
Purchasing managers, buyers, and purchasing agents	—	529,000	531,000	1,200	0
Purchasing managers	11-3061	70,000	72,000	2,400	3
Purchasing agents and buyers, farm products.............................	13-1021	16,000	15,000	-1,400	-9
Wholesale and retail buyers, except farm products	13-1022	157,000	156,000	-200	0
Purchasing agents, except wholesale, retail, and farm products ...	13-1023	287,000	288,000	400	0

NOTE: Data in this table are rounded.

Job Outlook

Employment of purchasing managers, buyers, and purchasing agents is expected to have little or no job growth through the year 2016. Generally, opportunities will be best for individuals with a bachelor's degree. In government and in large companies, opportunities will be best for those with a master's degree.

Employment change. No change in overall employment of purchasing managers, buyers, and purchasing agents is expected during the 2006–2016 decade.

Demand for purchasing workers will be limited by improving software, which has eliminated much of the paperwork involved in ordering and procuring supplies, and also by the growing number of purchases being made electronically through the Internet and electronic data interchange (EDI). Demand will also be limited by off-shoring of routine purchasing actions to other countries and by consolidation of purchasing departments, which makes purchasing agents more efficient.

Demand for purchasing workers in the manufacturing sector will be less than demand in the services sector, as the overall service sector grows more rapidly than the manufacturing sector. Also, many purchasing agents are now charged with procuring services that traditionally had been done in-house, such as computer and IT (information technology) support, in addition to traditionally contracted services such as advertising.

Employment of purchasing managers is expected to grow more slowly than average. The use of the Internet to conduct electronic commerce has made information easier to obtain, thus increasing the productivity of purchasing managers. The Internet also allows both large and small companies to bid on contracts. Exclusive supply contracts and long-term contracting have allowed companies to negotiate with fewer suppliers less frequently.

Employment of wholesale and retail buyers, except farm products, is expected to have little or no change in employment. In the retail industry, mergers and acquisitions have caused buying departments to consolidate. In addition, larger retail stores are eliminating local buying departments and centralizing them at their headquarters.

Employment of purchasing agents, except wholesale, retail, and farm products, is expected to have little or no change in employment, primarily because of the increased globalization of the U.S. economy. As more materials and supplies come from abroad, firms have begun to outsource more of their purchasing duties to foreign purchasing agents who are located closer to the foreign suppliers of goods and materials they will need. This trend is expected to continue, but it will likely be limited to routine transactions, with complex and critical purchases still being handled in-house.

Finally, employment of purchasing agents and buyers, farm products, is projected to decline 9 percent as overall growth in agricultural industries and retailers in the grocery-related industries consolidate.

Job prospects. Persons who have a bachelor's degree in business should have the best chance of obtaining a buyer position in wholesale or retail trade or within government. A bachelor's degree, combined with industry experience and knowledge of a technical field, will be an advantage for those interested in working for a manufacturing or industrial company. Government agencies and larger companies usually require a master's degree in business or public administration for top-level purchasing positions.

Earnings

Median annual earnings of purchasing managers were $81,570 in May 2006. The middle 50 percent earned between $60,890 and $105,780 a year. The lowest 10 percent earned less than $46,540, and the highest 10 percent earned more than $132,040 a year.

Median annual earnings for purchasing agents and buyers of farm products were $46,770 in May 2006. The middle 50 percent earned between $34,770 and $64,100 a year. The lowest 10 percent earned less than $26,520, and the highest 10 percent earned more than $88,650 a year.

Median annual earnings for wholesale and retail buyers, except farm products, were $44,640 in May 2006. The middle 50 percent earned between $33,640 and $60,590 a year. The lowest 10 percent earned less than $26,270, and the highest 10 percent earned more than $83,080 a year. Median annual earnings in the industries employing the largest numbers of wholesale and retail buyers, except farm products, were

Management of companies and enterprises $54,390
Grocery and related product wholesalers 46,080
Wholesale electronic markets and agents and brokers 45,020
Building material and supplies dealers 40,380
Grocery stores..34,210

Median annual earnings for purchasing agents, except wholesale, retail, and farm products, were $50,730 in May 2006. The middle 50 percent earned between $39,000 and $66,730 a year. The lowest 10 percent earned less than $31,350, and the highest 10 percent earned more than $83,900 a year. Median annual earnings in the industries employing the largest numbers of purchasing agents, except wholesale, retail, and farm products, were

Federal executive branch....................................$68,500
Aerospace product and parts manufacturing 59,390
Navigational, measuring, electromedical, and control instruments manufacturing......................55,620

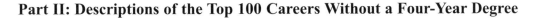

Management of companies and enterprises 54,820

Local government 48,170

Purchasing managers, buyers, and purchasing agents receive the same benefits package as other workers, including vacations, sick leave, life and health insurance, and pension plans. In addition to receiving standard benefits, retail buyers often earn cash bonuses based on their performance and may receive discounts on merchandise bought from their employer.

Related Occupations

Like purchasing managers, buyers, and purchasing agents, procurement clerks work to obtain materials and goods for businesses. Workers in other occupations who need a knowledge of marketing and the ability to assess consumer demand include those in advertising, marketing, promotions, public relations, and sales managers; food service managers; insurance sales agents; lodging managers; sales engineers; and sales representatives, wholesale and manufacturing.

Sources of Additional Information

Further information about education, training, employment, and certification for purchasing careers is available from

▸ American Purchasing Society, North Island Center, Suite 203, 8 East Galena Blvd., Aurora, IL 60506.

▸ Association for Operations Management, APICS, 5301 Shawnee Rd., Alexandria, VA 22312-2317. Internet: http://www.apics.org

▸ Institute for Supply Management, P.O. Box 22160, Tempe, AZ 85285-2160. Internet: http://www.ism.ws

▸ National Institute of Governmental Purchasing, Inc., 151 Spring St., Suite 300, Herndon, VA 20170-5223. Internet: http://www.nigp.org

Radiation Therapists

(O*NET 29-1124.00)

Significant Points

■ A bachelor's degree, associate degree, or certificate in radiation therapy is generally required.

■ Good job opportunities are expected.

■ Employment is projected to grow much faster than the average for all occupations.

Nature of the Work

Treating cancer in the human body is the principal use of radiation therapy. As part of a medical radiation oncology team, radiation therapists use machines—called linear accelerators—to administer radiation treatment to patients. Linear accelerators, used in a procedure called external beam therapy, project high-energy x rays at targeted cancer cells. As the x rays collide with human tissue, they produce highly energized ions that can shrink and eliminate cancerous tumors. Radiation therapy is sometimes used as the sole treatment for cancer, but is usually used in conjunction with chemotherapy or surgery.

The first step in the radiation therapy process is simulation. During simulation, the radiation therapist uses an x-ray imaging machine or computer tomography (CT) scan to pinpoint the location of the tumor. The therapist then positions the patient and adjusts the linear accelerator so that, when treatment begins, radiation exposure is concentrated on the tumor cells. The radiation therapist then develops a treatment plan in conjunction with a radiation oncologist (a physician who specializes in therapeutic radiology), and a dosimetrist (a technician who calculates the dose of radiation that will be used for treatment). The therapist later explains the treatment plan to the patient and answers any questions that the patient may have.

The next step in the process is treatment. To begin, the radiation therapist positions the patient and adjusts the linear accelerator according to the guidelines established in simulation. Then, from a separate room that is protected from the x-ray radiation, the therapist operates the linear accelerator and monitors the patient's condition through a TV monitor and an intercom system. Treatment can take anywhere from 10 to 30 minutes and is usually administered once a day, 5 days a week, for 2 to 9 weeks.

During the treatment phase, the radiation therapist monitors the patient's physical condition to determine if any adverse side effects are taking place. The therapist must also be aware of the patient's emotional wellbeing. Because many patients are under stress and are emotionally fragile, it is important for the therapist to maintain a positive attitude and provide emotional support.

Radiation therapists keep detailed records of their patients' treatments. These records include information such as the dose of radiation used for each treatment, the total amount of radiation used to date, the area treated, and the patient's reactions. Radiation oncologists and dosimetrists review these records to ensure that the treatment plan is working, to monitor the amount of radiation exposure that the patient has received, and to keep side effects to a minimum.

Radiation therapists also assist medical radiation physicists, workers who monitor and adjust the linear accelerator. Because radiation therapists often work alone during the treatment phase, they need to be able to check the linear accelerator for problems and make any adjustments that are needed. Therapists also may assist dosimetrists with routine aspects of dosimetry, the process used to calculate radiation dosages.

Work environment. Radiation therapists work in hospitals or in cancer treatment centers. These places are clean, well lighted, and well ventilated. Therapists do a considerable amount of lifting and must be able to help disabled patients get on and off treatment tables. They spend most of their time on their feet

Radiation therapists generally work 40 hours a week, and unlike those in other health care occupations, they normally work only during the day. However, because radiation therapy emergencies do occur, some therapists are required to be on call and may have to work outside of their normal hours.

Working with cancer patients can be stressful, but many radiation therapists also find it rewarding. Because they work around radioactive materials, radiation therapists take great care to ensure that they are not exposed to dangerous levels of radiation. Following standard safety procedures can prevent overexposure.

Training, Other Qualifications, and Advancement

A bachelor's degree, associate degree, or certificate in radiation therapy generally is required. Many states also require radiation therapists to be licensed. With experience, therapists can advance to managerial positions.

Education and training. Employers usually require applicants to complete an associate or a bachelor's degree program in radiation therapy. Individuals also may become qualified by completing an associate or a bachelor's degree program in radiography, which is the study of radiological imaging, and then completing a 12-month certificate program in radiation therapy. Radiation therapy programs include core courses on radiation therapy procedures and the scientific theories behind them. In addition, such programs often include courses on human anatomy and physiology, physics, algebra, precalculus, writing, public speaking, computer science, and research methodology. In 2007 there were 123 radiation therapy programs accredited by the American Registry of Radiologic Technologists (ARRT).

Licensure. In 2007, 32 states required radiation therapists to be licensed by a state accrediting board. Licensing requirements vary by state, but many states require applicants to pass the ARRT certification examination. Further information is available from individual state licensing offices.

Certification and other qualifications. Some states, as well as many employers, require that radiation therapists be certified by ARRT. To become ARRT-certified, an applicant must complete an accredited radiation therapy program, adhere to ARRT ethical standards, and pass the ARRT certification examination. The examination and accredited academic programs cover radiation protection and quality assurance, clinical concepts in radiation oncology, treatment planning, treatment delivery, and patient care and education. Candidates also must demonstrate competency in several clinical practices including patient care activities; simulation procedures; dosimetry calculations; fabrication of beam modification devices; low-volume, high-risk procedures, and the application of radiation.

ARRT certification is valid for one year, after which therapists must renew their certification. Requirements for renewal include abiding by the ARRT ethical standards, paying annual dues, and satisfying continuing education requirements. Continuing education requirements must be met every two years and include either the completion of 24 credits of radiation therapy-related courses or the attainment of ARRT certification in a discipline other than radiation therapy. Certification renewal, however, may not be required by all states or employers that require initial certification.

All radiation therapists need good communication skills because their work involves a great deal of patient interaction. Individuals interested in becoming radiation therapists should be psychologically capable of working with cancer patients. They should be caring and empathetic because they work with patients who are ill and under stress. They should be able to keep accurate, detailed records.

They also should be physically fit because they work on their feet for long periods and lift and move disabled patients.

Advancement. Experienced radiation therapists may advance to manage radiation therapy programs in treatment centers or other health care facilities. Managers generally continue to treat patients while taking on management responsibilities. Other advancement opportunities include teaching, technical sales, and research. With additional training and certification, therapists also can become dosimetrists, who use complex mathematical formulas to calculate proper radiation doses.

Employment

Radiation therapists held about 15,000 jobs in 2006. About 73 percent worked in hospitals, and about 17 percent worked in the offices of physicians. A small proportion worked in outpatient care centers.

Job Outlook

Employment is expected to increase much faster than the average from 2006 to 2016, and job prospects should be good.

Employment change. Employment of radiation therapists is projected to grow by 25 percent between 2006 and 2016, which is much faster than the average for all occupations. As the U.S. population grows and an increasing share of it is in the older age groups, the number of people needing treatment is expected to increase and to spur demand for radiation therapists. In addition, as radiation technology advances and is able to treat more types of cancer, radiation therapy will be prescribed more often.

Job prospects. Job prospects are expected to be good. Job openings will result from employment growth and from the need to replace workers who retire or leave the occupation for other reasons. Applicants who are certified should have the best opportunities.

Earnings

Median annual earnings of wage-and-salary radiation therapists were $66,170 in May 2006. The middle 50 percent earned between $54,170 and $78,550. The lowest 10 percent earned less than $44,840, and the highest 10 percent earned more than $92,110. Median annual earnings in the industries that employed the largest numbers of radiation therapists in May 2006 are as follows:

Outpatient care centers $73,810
Offices of physicians 70,050
General medical and surgical hospitals 63,580

Some employers also reimburse their employees for the cost of continuing education.

Related Occupations

Radiation therapists use advanced machinery to administer medical treatment to patients. Other occupations that perform similar duties include radiologic technologists and technicians, diagnostic medical

Projections data from the National Employment Matrix

Occupational Title	SOC Code	Employment, 2006	Projected employment, 2016	Change, 2006-2016	
				Number	Percent
Radiation therapists...	29-1124	15,000	18,000	3,600	25

NOTE: Data in this table are rounded.

sonographers, nuclear medicine technologists, cardiovascular technologists and technicians, dental hygienists, respiratory therapists, physical therapist assistants and aides, registered nurses, and physicians and surgeons.

Other occupations that build relationships with patients and provide them with emotional support include nursing, psychiatric, and home health aides; counselors; psychologists; social workers; and social and human service assistants.

Sources of Additional Information

Information on certification by the American Registry of Radiologic Technologists and on accredited radiation therapy programs may be obtained from

▶ American Registry of Radiologic Technologists, 1255 Northland Dr., St. Paul, MN 55120. Internet: http://www.arrt.org

Information on careers in radiation therapy may be obtained from

▶ American Society of Radiologic Technologists, 15000 Central Ave. SE, Albuquerque, NM 87123. Internet: http://www.asrt.org

Radiologic Technologists and Technicians

(O*NET 29-2034.00, 29-2034.01, and 29-2034.02)

Significant Points

■ Employment is projected to grow faster than average, and job opportunities are expected to be favorable.

■ Formal training programs in radiography are offered in hospitals, colleges and universities, and less frequently at vocational-technical institutes; range in length from 1 to 4 years; and lead to a certificate, an associate degree, or a bachelor's degree.

■ Although hospitals will remain the primary employer, a number of new jobs will be found in physicians' offices and diagnostic imaging centers.

Nature of the Work

Radiologic technologists take x rays and administer nonradioactive materials into patients' bloodstreams for diagnostic purposes.

Radiologic technologists also referred to as *radiographers,* produce x-ray films (radiographs) of parts of the human body for use in diagnosing medical problems. They prepare patients for radiologic examinations by explaining the procedure, removing jewelry and other articles through which x rays cannot pass, and positioning patients so that the parts of the body can be appropriately radiographed. To prevent unnecessary exposure to radiation, these workers surround the exposed area with radiation protection devices, such as lead shields, or limit the size of the x-ray beam. Radiographers position radiographic equipment at the correct angle and height over the appropriate area of a patient's body. Using instruments similar to a measuring tape, they may measure the thickness of the section to be radiographed and set controls on the x-ray machine to produce radiographs of the appropriate density, detail, and contrast. They place the x-ray film under the part of the patient's body to be examined and make the exposure. They then remove the film and develop it.

Radiologic technologists must follow physicians' orders precisely and conform to regulations concerning the use of radiation to protect themselves, their patients, and their coworkers from unnecessary exposure.

In addition to preparing patients and operating equipment, radiologic technologists keep patient records and adjust and maintain equipment. They also may prepare work schedules, evaluate purchases of equipment, or manage a radiology department.

Experienced radiographers may perform more complex imaging procedures. When performing fluoroscopies, for example, radiographers prepare a solution of contrast medium for the patient to drink, allowing the radiologist (a physician who interprets radiographs) to see soft tissues in the body.

Some radiographers specialize in computed tomography (CT), and are sometimes referred to as *CT technologists.* CT scans produce a substantial amount of cross-sectional x rays of an area of the body. From those cross-sectional x rays, a three-dimensional image is made. The CT uses ionizing radiation; therefore, it requires the same precautionary measures that radiographers use with other x rays.

Radiographers also can specialize in Magnetic Resonance Imaging as an *MR technologist.* MR, like CT, produces multiple cross-sectional images to create a 3-dimensional image. Unlike CT, MR uses non-ionizing radio frequency to generate image contrast.

Another common specialty for radiographers specialize in is mammography. Mammographers use low dose x-ray systems to produce images of the breast.

In addition to radiologic technologists, others who conduct diagnostic imaging procedures include cardiovascular technologists and technicians, diagnostic medical sonographers, and nuclear medicine technologists. (Each is discussed elsewhere in this book.)

Work environment. Physical stamina is important in this occupation because technologists are on their feet for long periods and may lift or turn disabled patients. Technologists work at diagnostic machines but also may perform some procedures at patients' bedsides. Some travel to patients in large vans equipped with sophisticated diagnostic equipment.

Although radiation hazards exist in this occupation, they are minimized by the use of lead aprons, gloves, and other shielding devices, as well as by instruments monitoring exposure to radiation. Technologists wear badges measuring radiation levels in the radiation area, and detailed records are kept on their cumulative lifetime dose.

Most full-time radiologic technologists work about 40 hours a week. They may, however, have evening, weekend, or on-call hours. Opportunities for part-time and shift work also are available.

Training, Other Qualifications, and Advancement

Preparation for this profession is offered in hospitals, colleges and universities, and less frequently at vocational-technical institutes. Hospitals employ most radiologic technologists. Employers prefer to hire technologists with formal training.

Education and training. Formal training programs in radiography range in length from one to four years and lead to a certificate, an associate degree, or a bachelor's degree. Two-year associate degree programs are most prevalent.

Some one-year certificate programs are available for experienced radiographers or individuals from other health occupations, such as medical technologists and registered nurses, who want to change fields. A bachelor's or master's degree in one of the radiologic technologies is desirable for supervisory, administrative, or teaching positions.

The Joint Review Committee on Education in Radiologic Technology accredits most formal training programs for the field. The committee accredited more than 600 radiography programs in 2007. Admission to radiography programs require, at a minimum, a high school diploma or the equivalent. High school courses in mathematics, physics, chemistry, and biology are helpful. The programs provide both classroom and clinical instruction in anatomy and physiology, patient care procedures, radiation physics, radiation protection, principles of imaging, medical terminology, positioning of patients, medical ethics, radiobiology, and pathology.

Licensure. Federal legislation protects the public from the hazards of unnecessary exposure to medical and dental radiation by ensuring that operators of radiologic equipment are properly trained. Under this legislation, the federal government sets voluntary standards that the states may use for accrediting training programs and licensing individuals who engage in medical or dental radiography. In 2007, 40 states required licensure for practicing radiologic technologists and technicians.

Certification and other qualifications. The American Registry of Radiologic Technologists (ARRT) offers voluntary certification for radiologic technologists. In addition, 35 states use ARRT-administered exams for state licensing purposes. To be eligible for certification, technologists generally must graduate from an accredited program and pass an examination. Many employers prefer to hire certified radiographers. To be recertified, radiographers must complete 24 hours of continuing education every two years.

Radiologic technologists should be sensitive to patients' physical and psychological needs. They must pay attention to detail, follow instructions, and work as part of a team. In addition, operating complicated equipment requires mechanical ability and manual dexterity.

Advancement. With experience and additional training, staff technologists may become specialists, performing CT scanning, MR, and angiography, a procedure during which blood vessels are x rayed to find clots. Technologists also may advance, with additional education and certification, to become a radiologist assistant.

Experienced technologists also may be promoted to supervisor, chief radiologic technologist, and, ultimately, department administrator or director. Depending on the institution, courses or a master's degree in business or health administration may be necessary for the director's position.

Some technologists progress by specializing in the occupation to become instructors or directors in radiologic technology programs; others take jobs as sales representatives or instructors with equipment manufacturers.

Employment

Radiologic technologists held about 196,000 jobs in 2006. More than 60 percent of all jobs were in hospitals. Most other jobs were in offices of physicians; medical and diagnostic laboratories, including diagnostic imaging centers; and outpatient care centers.

Job Outlook

Employment is projected to grow faster than average, and job opportunities are expected to be favorable.

Employment change. Employment of radiologic technologists is expected to increase by about 15 percent from 2006 to 2016, faster than the average for all occupations. As the population grows and ages, there will be an increasing demand for diagnostic imaging. Although health care providers are enthusiastic about the clinical benefits of new technologies, the extent to which they are adopted depends largely on cost and reimbursement considerations. As technology advances many imaging modalities are becoming less expensive and their adoption is becoming more widespread. For example, digital imaging technology can improve the quality of the images and the efficiency of the procedure, but it remains slightly more expensive than analog imaging, a procedure during which the image is put directly on film. Despite this, digital imaging is becoming more widespread in many imaging facilities because of the advantages it provides over analog.

Although hospitals will remain the principal employer of radiologic technologists, a number of new jobs will be found in offices of physicians and diagnostic imaging centers. Health facilities such as these are expected to grow through 2016, because of the shift toward outpatient care, encouraged by third-party payers and made possible by technological advances that permit more procedures to be performed outside the hospital.

Job prospects. In addition to job growth, job openings also will arise from the need to replace technologists who leave the occupation. Radiologic technologists are willing to relocate and who also are experienced in more than one diagnostic imaging procedure—such as CT, MR, and mammography—will have the best employment opportunities as employers seek to control costs by using multi-credentialed employees.

CT is becoming a frontline diagnosis tool. Instead of taking x rays to decide whether a CT is needed, as was the practice before, it is often the first choice for imaging because of its accuracy. MR also is increasing in frequency of use. Technologists with credentialing in either of these specialties will be very marketable to employers.

Earnings

Median annual earnings of radiologic technologists were $48,170 in May 2006. The middle 50 percent earned between $39,840 and $57,940. The lowest 10 percent earned less than $32,750, and the highest 10 percent earned more than $68,920. Median annual earnings in the industries employing the largest numbers of radiologic technologists in 2006 were

Projections data from the National Employment Matrix

Occupational Title	SOC Code	Employment, 2006	Projected employment, 2016	Change, 2006-2016	
				Number	Percent
Radiologic technologists and technicians	29-2034	196,000	226,000	30,000	15

NOTE: Data in this table are rounded.

Medical and diagnostic laboratories $51,280

General medical and surgical hospitals 48,830

Offices of physicians 45,500

Related Occupations

Radiologic technologists operate sophisticated equipment to help physicians, dentists, and other health practitioners diagnose and treat patients. Workers in related occupations include cardiovascular technologists and technicians, clinical laboratory technologists and technicians, diagnostic medical sonographers, nuclear medicine technologists, radiation therapists, and respiratory therapists.

Sources of Additional Information

For information on careers in radiologic technology, contact

▸ American Society of Radiologic Technologists, 15000 Central Ave. SE, Albuquerque, NM 87123-3917. Internet: http://www.asrt.org

For the current list of accredited education programs in radiography, write to

▸ Joint Review Committee on Education in Radiologic Technology, 20 N. Wacker Dr., Suite 2850, Chicago, IL 60606-3182. Internet: http://www.jrcert.org

For certification information, contact

▸ American Registry of Radiologic Technologists, 1255 Northland Dr., St. Paul, MN 55120-1155. Internet: http://www.arrt.org

Real Estate Brokers and Sales Agents

(O*NET 41-9021.00 and 41-9022.00)

Significant Points

■ Real estate brokers and sales agents often work evenings and weekends and usually are on call to suit the needs of clients.

■ A license is required in every state and the District of Columbia.

■ Although gaining a job may be relatively easy, beginning workers face competition from well-established, more experienced agents and brokers.

■ Employment is sensitive to swings in the economy, especially interest rates; during periods of declining economic activity and rising interest rates, the volume of sales and the resulting demand for sales workers fall.

Nature of the Work

One of the most complex and significant financial events in peoples' lives is the purchase or sale of a home or investment property. Because of this complexity and significance, people typically seek the help of real estate brokers and sales agents when buying or selling real estate.

Real estate brokers and sales agents have a thorough knowledge of the real estate market in their communities. They know which neighborhoods will best fit clients' needs and budgets. They are familiar with local zoning and tax laws and know where to obtain financing.

Agents and brokers also act as intermediaries in price negotiations between buyers and sellers.

When selling property, brokers and agents arrange for title searches to verify ownership and for meetings between buyers and sellers during which they agree to the details of the transactions and in a final meeting, the new owners take possession of the property. They also may help to arrange favorable financing from a lender for the prospective buyer; often, this makes the difference between success and failure in closing a sale. In some cases, brokers and agents assume primary responsibility for closing sales; in others, lawyers or lenders do.

Agents and brokers spend a significant amount of time looking for properties to sell. They obtain listings—agreements by owners to place properties for sale with the firm. When listing a property for sale, agents and brokers compare the listed property with similar properties that recently sold, in order to determine a competitive market price for the property. Following the sale of the property, both the agent who sold it and the agent who obtained the listing receive a portion of the commission. Thus, agents who sell a property that they themselves have listed can increase their commission.

Before showing residential properties to potential buyers, agents meet with them to get an idea of the type of home the buyers would like. In this prequalifying phase, the agent determines how much the buyers can afford to spend. In addition, the agent and the buyer usually sign a loyalty contract, which states that the agent will be the only one to show houses to the buyer. An agent or broker then generates lists of properties for sale, their location and description, and available sources of financing. In some cases, agents and brokers use computers to give buyers a virtual tour of properties that interest them.

Agents may meet several times with prospective buyers to discuss and visit available properties. Agents identify and emphasize the most pertinent selling points. To a young family looking for a house, for example, they may emphasize the convenient floor plan, the area's low crime rate, and the proximity to schools and shopping. To a potential investor, they may point out the tax advantages of owning a rental property and the ease of finding a renter. If bargaining over price becomes necessary, agents must follow their client's instructions carefully and may have to present counteroffers to get the best possible price.

Once the buyer and seller have signed a contract, the real estate broker or agent must make sure that all special terms of the contract are met before the closing date. The agent must make sure that any legally mandated or agreed-upon inspections, such as termite and radon inspections, take place. In addition, if the seller agrees to any repairs, the broker or agent ensures they are made. Increasingly, brokers and agents are handling environmental problems as well, by making sure that the properties they sell meet environmental regulations. For example, they may be responsible for dealing with lead paint on the walls. Loan officers, attorneys, or other people handle many details, but the agent must ensure that they are carried out.

Most real estate brokers and sales agents sell residential property. A small number—usually employed in large or specialized firms—sell commercial, industrial, agricultural, or other types of real estate. Every specialty requires knowledge of that particular type of property and clientele. Selling or leasing business property requires an understanding of leasing practices, business trends, and the location of the property. Agents who sell or lease industrial properties must know about the region's transportation, utilities, and labor supply.

Whatever the type of property, the agent or broker must know how to meet the client's particular requirements.

Brokers and agents do the same type of work, but brokers are licensed to manage their own real estate businesses. Agents must work with a broker. They usually provide their services to a licensed real estate broker on a contract basis. In return, the broker pays the agent a portion of the commission earned from the agent's sale of the property. Brokers, as independent businesspeople, often sell real estate owned by others; they also may rent or manage properties for a fee.

Work environment. Advances in telecommunications and the ability to retrieve data about properties over the Internet allow many real estate brokers and sales agents to work out of their homes instead of real estate offices. Even with this convenience, workers spend much of their time away from their desks—showing properties to customers, analyzing properties for sale, meeting with prospective clients, or researching the real estate market.

Agents and brokers often work more than a standard 40-hour week. They usually work evenings and weekends and are usually on call to respond to the needs of clients. Although the hours are long and frequently irregular, most agents and brokers have the freedom to determine their own schedule. They can arrange their work so that they have time off when they want it. Business usually is slower during the winter season.

Training, Other Qualifications, and Advancement

In every state and the District of Columbia, real estate brokers and sales agents must be licensed. Prospective agents must be high school graduates, be at least 18 years old, and pass a written test.

Education and training. Agents and brokers must be high school graduates. In fact, as real estate transactions have become more legally complex, many firms have turned to college graduates to fill positions. A large number of agents and brokers have some college training. College courses in real estate, finance, business administration, statistics, economics, law, and English are helpful. For those who intend to start their own company, business courses such as marketing and accounting are as important as courses in real estate or finance.

More than 1,000 universities, colleges, and community colleges offer courses in real estate. Most offer an associate or bachelor's degree in real estate; some offer graduate degrees. Many local real estate associations that are members of the National Association of Realtors sponsor courses covering the fundamentals and legal aspects of the field. Advanced courses in mortgage financing, property development and management, and other subjects also are available.

Many firms offer formal training programs for both beginners and experienced agents. Larger firms usually offer more extensive programs than smaller firms do.

Licensure. In every state and the District of Columbia, real estate brokers and sales agents must be licensed. Prospective brokers and agents must pass a written examination. The examination—more comprehensive for brokers than for agents—includes questions on basic real estate transactions and laws affecting the sale of property. Most states require candidates for the general sales license to complete between 30 and 90 hours of classroom instruction. To get a broker's license an individual needs between 60 and 90 hours of formal training and a specific amount of experience selling real estate, usually one to three years. Some states waive the experience requirements for the broker's license for applicants who have a bachelor's degree in real estate.

State licenses typically must be renewed every one or two years; usually, no examination is needed. However, many states require continuing education for license renewals. Prospective agents and brokers should contact the real estate licensing commission of the state in which they wish to work to verify the exact licensing requirements.

Other qualifications. Personality traits are as important as academic background. Brokers look for agents who have a pleasant personality, honesty, and a neat appearance. Maturity, good judgment, trustworthiness, and enthusiasm for the job are required to attract prospective customers in this highly competitive field. Agents should be well organized, be detail oriented, and have a good memory for names, faces, and business particulars. They must be at least 18 years old.

Those interested in jobs as real estate agents often begin in their own communities. Their knowledge of local neighborhoods is a clear advantage. Under the direction of an experienced agent, beginners learn the practical aspects of the job, including the use of computers to locate or list available properties and identify sources of financing.

Advancement. As agents gain knowledge and expertise, they become more efficient in closing a greater number of transactions and increase their earnings. In many large firms, experienced agents can advance to sales manager or general manager. People who earn their broker's license may open their own offices. Others with experience and training in estimating property value may become real estate appraisers, and people familiar with operating and maintaining rental properties may become property managers. Experienced agents and brokers with a thorough knowledge of business conditions and property values in their localities may enter mortgage financing or real estate investment counseling.

Employment

In 2006, real estate brokers and sales agents held about 564,000 jobs; real estate sales agents held approximately 77 percent of these jobs.

Many real estate brokers and sales agents worked part time, combining their real estate activities with other careers. About 61 percent real estate brokers and sales agents were self-employed. Real estate is sold in all areas, but employment is concentrated in large urban areas and in rapidly growing communities.

Most real estate firms are relatively small; indeed, some are one-person businesses. By contrast, some large real estate firms have several hundred agents operating out of numerous branch offices. Many brokers have franchise agreements with national or regional real estate organizations. Under this type of arrangement, the broker pays a fee in exchange for the privilege of using the more widely known name of the parent organization. Although franchised brokers often receive help in training sales staff and running their offices, they bear the ultimate responsibility for the success or failure of their firms.

Projections data from the National Employment Matrix

Occupational Title	SOC Code	Employment, 2006	Projected employment, 2016	Change, 2006-16	
				Number	Percent
Real estate brokers and sales agents	41-9020	564,000	624,000	60,000	11
Real estate brokers	41-9021	131,000	146,000	15,000	11
Real estate sales agents	41-9022	432,000	478,000	46,000	11

NOTE: Data in this table are rounded.

Job Outlook

Average employment growth is expected because of the increasing housing needs of a growing population, as well as the perception that real estate is a good investment. Beginning agents and brokers face competition from their well-established, more experienced counterparts.

Employment change. Employment of real estate brokers and sales agents is expected to grow 11 percent during the 2006–2016 projection decade—about as fast as the average for all occupations. Relatively low interest rates and the perception that real estate usually is a good investment may continue to stimulate sales of real estate, resulting in the need for more agents and brokers. However, job growth will be somewhat limited by the increasing use of technology, which is improving the productivity of agents and brokers. For example, prospective customers often can perform their own searches for properties that meet their criteria by accessing real estate information on the Internet. The increasing use of technology is likely to be more detrimental to part-time or temporary real estate agents than to full-time agents because part-time agents generally are not able to compete with full-time agents who have invested in new technology. Changing legal requirements, such as disclosure laws, also may dissuade some who are not serious about practicing full time from continuing to work part time.

Job prospects. In addition to job growth, a large number of job openings will arise from the need to replace workers who transfer to other occupations or leave the labor force. Real estate brokers and sales agents are older, on average, than are most other workers. Historically, many homemakers and retired people were attracted to real estate sales by the flexible and part-time work schedules characteristic of the field. These individuals could enter, leave, and later return to the occupation, depending on the strength of the real estate market, their family responsibilities, or other personal circumstances. Recently, however, the attractiveness of part-time real estate work has declined, as increasingly complex legal and technological requirements are raising startup costs associated with becoming an agent.

Employment of real estate brokers and sales agents often is sensitive to swings in the economy, especially interest rates. During periods of declining economic activity and rising interest rates, the volume of sales and the resulting demand for sales workers falls. As a result, the earnings of agents and brokers decline, and many work fewer hours or leave the occupation altogether.

This occupation is relatively easy to enter and is attractive because of its flexible working conditions; the high interest in, and familiarity with, local real estate markets that entrants often have; and the potential for high earnings. Therefore, although gaining a job as a real estate agent or broker may be relatively easy, beginning agents and brokers face competition from their well-established, more experienced counterparts in obtaining listings and in closing an adequate number of sales.

Well-trained, ambitious people who enjoy selling—particularly those with extensive social and business connections in their communities—should have the best chance for success.

Earnings

The median annual earnings, including commissions, of salaried real estate sales agents were $39,760 in May 2006. The middle 50 percent earned between $26,790 and $65,270 a year. The lowest 10 percent earned less than $20,170, and the highest 10 percent earned more than $111,500. Median annual earnings in the industries employing the largest number of real estate sales agents in May 2006 were

Residential building construction $53,390

Land subdivision 49,230

Offices of real estate agents and brokers...............39,930

Activities related to real estate 36,510

Lessors of real estate 32,580

Median annual earnings, including commissions, of salaried real estate brokers were $60,790 in May 2006. The middle 50 percent earned between $37,800 and $102,180 a year. Median annual earnings in the industries employing the largest number of real estate brokers in May 2006 were

Offices of real estate agents and brokers..............$64,350

Lessors of real estate 61,030

Activities related to real estate 48,250

Commissions on sales are the main source of earnings of real estate agents and brokers. The rate of commission varies according to whatever the agent and broker agree on, the type of property, and its value. The percentage paid on the sale of farm and commercial properties or unimproved land is typically higher than the percentage paid for selling a home.

Commissions may be divided among several agents and brokers. The broker or agent who obtains a listing usually shares the commission with the broker or agent who sells the property and with the firms that employ each of them. Although an agent's share varies greatly from one firm to another, often it is about half of the total amount received by the firm. Agents who both list and sell a property maximize their commission.

Income usually increases as an agent gains experience, but individual motivation, economic conditions, and the type and location of the property affect earnings, too. Sales workers who are active in community organizations and in local real estate associations can broaden their contacts and increase their earnings. A beginner's earnings often are irregular because a few weeks or even months may go by without a sale. Although some brokers allow an agent to draw against future earnings from a special account, the practice is not common with new employees. The beginner, therefore, should have enough money to live for about 6 months or until commissions increase.

Related Occupations

Selling expensive items such as homes requires maturity, tact, and a sense of responsibility. Other sales workers who find these character traits important in their work include insurance sales agents; retail salespersons; sales representatives, wholesale and manufacturing; and securities, commodities, and financial services sales agents. Although not involving sales, others who need an understanding of real estate include property, real estate, and community association managers, as well as appraisers and assessors of real estate.

Sources of Additional Information

Information on licensing requirements for real estate brokers and sales agents is available from most local real estate organizations or from the state real estate commission or board.

More information about opportunities in real estate is available on the Internet site of the following organization:

▸ National Association of Realtors. Internet: http://www.realtor.org

Receptionists and Information Clerks

(O*NET 43-4171.00)

Significant Points

■ Good interpersonal skills are critical.

■ A high school diploma or its equivalent is the most common educational requirement.

■ Employment is expected to grow faster than average for all occupations.

Nature of the Work

Receptionists and information clerks are charged with a responsibility that may affect the success of an organization: making a good first impression. Receptionists and information clerks answer telephones, route and screen calls, greet visitors, respond to inquiries from the public, and provide information about the organization. Some are responsible for the coordination of all mail into and out of the office. In addition, they contribute to the security of an organization by helping to monitor the access of visitors—a function that has become increasingly important.

Whereas some tasks are common to most receptionists and information clerks, their specific responsibilities vary with the type of establishment in which they work. For example, receptionists and information clerks in hospitals and in doctors' offices may gather patients' personal and insurance information and direct them to the proper waiting rooms. In corporate headquarters, they may greet visitors and manage the scheduling of the board room or common conference area. In beauty or hair salons, they arrange appointments, direct customers to the hairstylist, and may serve as cashiers. In factories, large corporations, and government offices, receptionists and information clerks may provide identification cards and arrange for escorts to take visitors to the proper office. Those working for bus

and train companies respond to inquiries about departures, arrivals, stops, and other related matters.

Increasingly, receptionists and information clerks use multiline telephone systems, personal computers, and fax machines. Despite the widespread use of automated answering systems or voice mail, many receptionists and clerks still take messages and inform other employees of visitors' arrivals or cancellation of an appointment. When they are not busy with callers, most workers are expected to perform a variety of office duties, including opening and sorting mail, collecting and distributing parcels, and transmitting and delivering facsimiles. Other duties include updating appointment calendars, preparing travel vouchers, and performing basic bookkeeping, word processing, and filing.

Work environment. Receptionists and information clerks who greet customers and visitors usually work in areas that are highly visible and designed and furnished to make a good impression. Most work stations are clean, well lighted, and relatively quiet. The work performed by some receptionists and information clerks may be tiring, repetitious, and stressful as they may spend all day answering continuously ringing telephones and sometimes encounter difficult or irate callers. The work environment, however, may be very friendly and motivating for individuals who enjoy greeting customers face to face and making them feel comfortable.

Training, Other Qualifications, and Advancement

A high school diploma or its equivalent is the most common educational requirement, although hiring requirements for receptionists and information clerks vary by industry. Good interpersonal skills and being technologically proficient also are important to employers.

Education and training. Receptionists and information clerks generally need a high school diploma or equivalent as most of their training is received on the job. However, employers often look for applicants who already possess certain skills, such as prior computer experience or answering telephones. Some employers also may prefer some formal office education or training. On the job, they learn how to operate the telephone system and computers. They also learn the proper procedures for greeting visitors and for distributing mail, fax messages, and parcels. While many of these skills can be learned quickly, those who are charged with relaying information to visitors or customers may need several months to learn details about the organization.

Other qualifications. Good interpersonal and customer service skills—being courteous, professional, and helpful—are critical for this job. Being an active listener often is a key quality needed by receptionists and information clerks that requires the ability to listen patiently to the points being made, to wait to speak until others have finished, and to ask appropriate questions when necessary. In addition, the ability to relay information accurately to others is important.

The ability to operate a wide range of office technology also is helpful, as receptionists and information clerks are often asked to work on other assignments during the day.

Advancement. Advancement for receptionists generally comes about either by transferring to an occupation with more responsibility or by being promoted to a supervisory position. Receptionists

Projections data from the National Employment Matrix

Occupational Title	SOC Code	Employment, 2006	Projected employment, 2016	Change, 2006-16	
				Number	Percent
Receptionists and information clerks...	43-4171	1,173,000	1,375,000	202,000	17

NOTE: Data in this table are rounded.

with especially strong computer skills may advance to a better pay-ing job as a secretary or an administrative assistant.

Employment

Receptionists and information clerks held about 1.2 million jobs in 2006. The health care and social assistance industries—including offices of physicians, hospitals, nursing homes, and outpatient care facilities—employed about 33 percent of all receptionists and infor-mation clerks. Manufacturing, wholesale and retail trade, govern-ment, and real estate industries also employed large numbers of receptionists and information clerks. More than 3 of every 10 recep-tionists and information clerks work part time.

Job Outlook

Employment of receptionists and information clerks is expected to grow faster than average for all occupations. Receptionists and information clerks will have a very large number of new jobs arise, more than 200,000 over the 2006–2016 period. Additional job opportunities will result from the need to replace workers who trans-fer to other occupations or leave the labor force.

Employment change. Receptionists and information clerks are expected to increase by 17 percent from 2006 to 2016, which is faster than the average for all occupations. Employment growth will result from rapid growth in the following industries: offices of physicians, legal services, employment services, and management and technical consulting.

Technology will have conflicting effects on employment growth for receptionists and information clerks. The increasing use of voice mail and other telephone automation reduces the need for reception-ists by allowing one receptionist to perform work that formerly required several. At the same time, however, the increasing use of other technology has caused a consolidation of clerical responsibil-ities and growing demand for workers with diverse clerical and tech-nical skills. Because receptionists and information clerks may perform a wide variety of clerical tasks, they should continue to be in demand. Further, they perform many tasks that are interpersonal in nature and are not easily automated, ensuring continued demand for their services in a variety of establishments.

Job prospects. In addition to job growth, numerous job opportuni-ties will be created as receptionists and information clerks transfer to other occupations or leave the labor force altogether. Opportuni-ties should be best for persons with a wide range of clerical and technical skills, particularly those with related work experience.

Earnings

Median hourly earnings of receptionists and information clerks in May 2006 were $11.01. The middle 50 percent earned between $9.06 and $13.51. The lowest 10 percent earned less than $7.54, and the highest 10 percent earned more than $16.23. Median hourly earnings in the industries employing the largest number of recep-tionists and information clerks in May 2006 were

Offices of dentists $12.89
General medical and surgical hospitals 11.74
Offices of physicians 11.44
Employment services 10.72
Personal care services 8.57

Related Occupations

Receptionists deal with the public and often direct people to others who can assist them. Other workers who perform similar duties include dispatchers, secretaries and administrative assistants, and customer service representatives.

Sources of Additional Information

State employment offices can provide information on job openings for receptionists.

Registered Nurses

(O*NET 29-1111.00)

Significant Points

■ Registered nurses constitute the largest health care occupation, with 2.5 million jobs.

■ About 59 percent of jobs are in hospitals.

■ The three major educational paths to registered nursing are a bachelor's degree, an associate degree, and a diploma from an approved nursing program.

■ Registered nurses are projected to generate about 587,000 new jobs over the 2006–2016 period, one of the largest numbers among all occupations; overall job opportunities are expected to be excellent, but may vary by employment setting.

Nature of the Work

Registered nurses (RNs), regardless of specialty or work setting, treat patients, educate patients and the public about various medical conditions, and provide advice and emotional support to patients' family members. RNs record patients' medical histories and symp-toms, help perform diagnostic tests and analyze results, operate medical machinery, administer treatment and medications, and help with patient follow-up and rehabilitation.

RNs teach patients and their families how to manage their illness or injury, explaining post-treatment home care needs; diet, nutrition, and exercise programs; and self-administration of medication and physical therapy. Some RNs work to promote general health by edu-cating the public on warning signs and symptoms of disease. RNs also might run general health screening or immunization clinics, blood drives, and public seminars on various conditions.

When caring for patients, RNs establish a plan of care or contribute to an existing plan. Plans may include numerous activities, such as administering medication, including careful checking of dosages and avoiding interactions; starting, maintaining, and discontinuing intravenous (IV) lines for fluid, medication, blood, and blood products; administering therapies and treatments; observing the patient and recording those observations; and consulting with physicians and other health care clinicians. Some RNs provide direction to licensed practical nurses and nursing aids regarding patient care. RNs with advanced educational preparation and training may perform diagnostic and therapeutic procedures and may have prescriptive authority.

RNs can specialize in one or more areas of patient care. There generally are four ways to specialize. RNs can choose a particular work setting or type of treatment, such as perioperative nurses, who work in operating rooms and assist surgeons. RNs also may choose to specialize in specific health conditions, as do diabetes management nurses, who assist patients to manage diabetes. Other RNs specialize in working with one or more organs or body system types, such as dermatology nurses, who work with patients who have skin disorders. RNs also can choose to work with a well-defined population, such as geriatric nurses, who work with the elderly. Some RNs may combine specialties. For example, pediatric oncology nurses deal with children and adolescents who have cancer.

There are many options for RNs who specialize in a work setting or type of treatment. *Ambulatory care nurses* provide preventive care and treat patients with a variety of illnesses and injuries in physicians' offices or in clinics. Some ambulatory care nurses are involved in telehealth, providing care and advice through electronic communications media such as videoconferencing, the Internet, or by telephone. *Critical care nurses* provide care to patients with serious, complex, and acute illnesses or injuries that require very close monitoring and extensive medication protocols and therapies. Critical care nurses often work in critical or intensive care hospital units. *Emergency*, or *trauma, nurses* work in hospital or stand-alone emergency departments, providing initial assessments and care for patients with life-threatening conditions. Some emergency nurses may become qualified to serve as *transport nurses*, who provide medical care to patients who are transported by helicopter or airplane to the nearest medical facility. *Holistic nurses* provide care such as acupuncture, massage and aroma therapy, and biofeedback, which are meant to treat patients' mental and spiritual health in addition to their physical health. *Home health care nurses* provide at-home nursing care for patients, often as follow-up care after discharge from a hospital or from a rehabilitation, long-term care, or skilled nursing facility. *Hospice and palliative care nurses* provide care, most often in home or hospice settings, focused on maintaining quality of life for terminally ill patients. *Infusion nurses* administer medications, fluids, and blood to patients through injections into patients' veins. *Long- term care nurses* provide health care services on a recurring basis to patients with chronic physical or mental disorders, often in long-term care or skilled nursing facilities. *Medical-surgical nurses* provide health promotion and basic medical care to patients with various medical and surgical diagnoses. *Occupational health nurses* seek to prevent job-related injuries and illnesses, provide monitoring and emergency care services, and help employers implement health and safety standards. *Perianesthesia nurses* provide preoperative and postoperative care to patients undergoing anesthesia during surgery or other procedure. *Perioperative nurses* assist surgeons by selecting and handling instruments,

controlling bleeding, and suturing incisions. Some of these nurses also can specialize in plastic and reconstructive surgery. *Psychiatric-mental health nurses* treat patients with personality and mood disorders. *Radiology nurses* provide care to patients undergoing diagnostic radiation procedures such as ultrasounds, magnetic resonance imaging, and radiation therapy for oncology diagnoses. *Rehabilitation nurses* care for patients with temporary and permanent disabilities. *Transplant nurses* care for both transplant recipients and living donors and monitor signs of organ rejection.

RNs specializing in a particular disease, ailment, or health care condition are employed in virtually all work settings, including physicians' offices, outpatient treatment facilities, home health care agencies, and hospitals. *Addictions nurses* care for patients seeking help with alcohol, drug, tobacco, and other addictions. *Intellectual and developmental disabilities nurses* provide care for patients with physical, mental, or behavioral disabilities; care may include help with feeding, controlling bodily functions, sitting or standing independently, and speaking or other communication. *Diabetes management nurses* help diabetics to manage their disease by teaching them proper nutrition and showing them how to test blood sugar levels and administer insulin injections. *Genetics nurses* provide early detection screenings, counseling, and treatment of patients with genetic disorders, including cystic fibrosis and Huntington's disease. *HIV/AIDS nurses* care for patients diagnosed with HIV and AIDS. *Oncology nurses* care for patients with various types of cancer and may assist in the administration of radiation and chemotherapies and follow-up monitoring. *Wound, ostomy, and continence nurses* treat patients with wounds caused by traumatic injury, ulcers, or arterial disease; provide postoperative care for patients with openings that allow for alternative methods of bodily waste elimination; and treat patients with urinary and fecal incontinence.

RNs specializing in treatment of a particular organ or body system usually are employed in hospital specialty or critical care units, specialty clinics, and outpatient care facilities. *Cardiovascular nurses* treat patients with coronary heart disease and those who have had heart surgery, providing services such as postoperative rehabilitation. *Dermatology nurses* treat patients with disorders of the skin, such as skin cancer and psoriasis. *Gastroenterology nurses* treat patients with digestive and intestinal disorders, including ulcers, acid reflux disease, and abdominal bleeding. Some nurses in this field also assist in specialized procedures such as endoscopies, which look inside the gastrointestinal tract using a tube equipped with a light and a camera that can capture images of diseased tissue. *Gynecology nurses* provide care to women with disorders of the reproductive system, including endometriosis, cancer, and sexually transmitted diseases. *Nephrology nurses* care for patients with kidney disease caused by diabetes, hypertension, or substance abuse. *Neuroscience nurses* care for patients with dysfunctions of the nervous system, including brain and spinal cord injuries and seizures. *Ophthalmic nurses* provide care to patients with disorders of the eyes, including blindness and glaucoma, and to patients undergoing eye surgery. *Orthopedic nurses* care for patients with muscular and skeletal problems, including arthritis, bone fractures, and muscular dystrophy. *Otorhinolaryngology nurses* care for patients with ear, nose, and throat disorders, such as cleft palates, allergies, and sinus disorders. *Respiratory nurses* provide care to patients with respiratory disorders such as asthma, tuberculosis, and cystic fibrosis. *Urology nurses* care for patients with disorders of the kidneys, urinary tract, and male reproductive organs, including infections, kidney and bladder stones, and cancers.

© JIST Works

RNs who specialize by population provide preventive and acute care in all health care settings to the segment of the population in which they specialize, including newborns (neonatology), children and adolescents (pediatrics), adults, and the elderly (gerontology or geriatrics). RNs also may provide basic health care to patients outside of health care settings in such venues as including correctional facilities, schools, summer camps, and the military. Some RNs travel around the United States and abroad providing care to patients in areas with shortages of health care workers.

Most RNs work as staff nurses as members of a team providing critical health care . However, some RNs choose to become advanced practice nurses, who work independently or in collaboration with physicians, and may focus on the provision of primary care services. *Clinical nurse specialists* provide direct patient care and expert consultations in one of many nursing specialties, such as psychiatric-mental health. *Nurse anesthetists* provide anesthesia and related care before and after surgical, therapeutic, diagnostic and obstetrical procedures. They also provide pain management and emergency services, such as airway management. *Nurse-midwives* provide primary care to women, including gynecological exams, family planning advice, prenatal care, assistance in labor and delivery, and neonatal care. *Nurse practitioners* serve as primary and specialty care providers, providing a blend of nursing and health care services to patients and families. The most common specialty areas for nurse practitioners are family practice, adult practice, women's health, pediatrics, acute care, and geriatrics. However, there are a variety of other specialties that nurse practitioners can choose, including neonatology and mental health. Advanced practice nurses can prescribe medications in all states and in the District of Columbia.

Some nurses have jobs that require little or no direct patient care, but still require an active RN license. *Case managers* ensure that all of the medical needs of patients with severe injuries and severe or chronic illnesses are met. *Forensics nurses* participate in the scientific investigation and treatment of abuse victims, violence, criminal activity, and traumatic accident. *Infection control nurses* identify, track, and control infectious outbreaks in health care facilities and develop programs for outbreak prevention and response to biological terrorism. *Legal nurse consultants* assist lawyers in medical cases by interviewing patients and witnesses, organizing medical records, determining damages and costs, locating evidence, and educating lawyers about medical issues. *Nurse administrators* supervise nursing staff, establish work schedules and budgets, maintain medical supply inventories, and manage resources to ensure high-quality care. *Nurse educators* plan, develop, implement, and evaluate educational programs and curricula for the professional development of student nurses and RNs. *Nurse informaticists* manage and communicate nursing data and information to improve decision making by consumers, patients, nurses, and other health care providers. RNs also may work as health care consultants, public policy advisors, pharmaceutical and medical supply researchers and salespersons, and medical writers and editors.

Work environment. Most RNs work in well-lighted, comfortable health care facilities. Home health and public health nurses travel to patients' homes, schools, community centers, and other sites. RNs may spend considerable time walking, bending, stretching, and standing. Patients in hospitals and nursing care facilities require 24-hour care; consequently, nurses in these institutions may work nights, weekends, and holidays. RNs also may be on call—available to work on short notice. Nurses who work in offices, schools, and other settings that do not provide 24-hour care are more likely to

work regular business hours. About 21 percent of RNs worked part time in 2006, and 7 percent held more than one job.

Nursing has its hazards, especially in hospitals, nursing care facilities, and clinics, where nurses may be in close contact with individuals who have infectious diseases and with toxic, harmful, or potentially hazardous compounds, solutions, and medications. RNs must observe rigid, standardized guidelines to guard against disease and other dangers, such as those posed by radiation, accidental needle sticks, chemicals used to sterilize instruments, and anesthetics. In addition, they are vulnerable to back injury when moving patients, shocks from electrical equipment, and hazards posed by compressed gases. RNs also may suffer emotional strain from caring for patients suffering unrelieved intense pain, close personal contact with patients' families, the need to make critical decisions, and ethical dilemmas and concerns.

Training, Other Qualifications, and Advancement

The three major educational paths to registered nursing are a bachelor's degree, an associate degree, and a diploma from an approved nursing program. Nurses most commonly enter the occupation by completing an associate degree or bachelor's degree program. Individuals then must complete a national licensing examination in order to obtain a nursing license. Further training or education can qualify nurses to work in specialty areas, and may help improve advancement opportunities.

Education and training. There are three major educational paths to registered nursing—a bachelor's of science degree in nursing (BSN), an associate degree in nursing (ADN), and a diploma. BSN programs, offered by colleges and universities, take about four years to complete. In 2006, 709 nursing programs offered degrees at the bachelor's level. ADN programs, offered by community and junior colleges, take about two to three years to complete. About 850 RN programs granted associate degrees. Diploma programs, administered in hospitals, last about three years. Only about 70 programs offered diplomas. Generally, licensed graduates of any of the three types of educational programs qualify for entry-level positions.

Many RNs with an ADN or diploma later enter bachelor's programs to prepare for a broader scope of nursing practice. Often, they can find an entry-level position and then take advantage of tuition reimbursement benefits to work toward a BSN by completing an RN-to-BSN program. In 2006, there were 629 RN-to-BSN programs in the United States. Accelerated master's degree in nursing (MSN) programs also are available by combining one year of an accelerated BSN program with two years of graduate study. In 2006, there were 149 RN-to-MSN programs.

Accelerated BSN programs also are available for individuals who have a bachelor's or higher degree in another field and who are interested in moving into nursing. In 2006, 197 of these programs were available. Accelerated BSN programs last 12 to 18 months and provide the fastest route to a BSN for individuals who already hold a degree. MSN programs also are available for individuals who hold a bachelor's or higher degree in another field.

Individuals considering nursing should carefully weigh the advantages and disadvantages of enrolling in a BSN or MSN program because, if they do, their advancement opportunities usually are broader. In fact, some career paths are open only to nurses with a bachelor's or master's degree. A bachelor's degree often is necessary for administrative positions and is a prerequisite for admission to graduate nursing programs in research, consulting, and teaching, and all four advanced practice nursing specialties—clinical nurse specialists, nurse anesthetists, nurse-midwives, and nurse practitioners. Individuals who complete a bachelor's receive more training in areas such as communication, leadership, and critical thinking, all of which are becoming more important as nursing care becomes more complex. Additionally, bachelor's degree programs offer more clinical experience in nonhospital settings. Education beyond a bachelor's degree can also help students looking to enter certain fields or increase advancement opportunities. In 2006, 448 nursing schools offered master's degrees, 108 offered doctoral degrees, and 58 offered accelerated BSN-to-doctoral programs.

All four advanced practice nursing specialties require at least a master's degree. Most programs include about two years of full-time study and require a BSN degree for entry; some programs require at least one to two years of clinical experience as an RN for admission. In 2006, there were 342 master's and post-master's programs offered for nurse practitioners, 230 master's and post-master's programs for clinical nurse specialists, 106 programs for nurse anesthetists, and 39 programs for nurse-midwives.

All nursing education programs include classroom instruction and supervised clinical experience in hospitals and other health care facilities. Students take courses in anatomy, physiology, microbiology, chemistry, nutrition, psychology and other behavioral sciences, and nursing. Coursework also includes the liberal arts for ADN and BSN students.

Supervised clinical experience is provided in hospital departments such as pediatrics, psychiatry, maternity, and surgery. A growing number of programs include clinical experience in nursing care facilities, public health departments, home health agencies, and ambulatory clinics.

Licensure and certification. In all states, the District of Columbia, and U.S. territories, students must graduate from an approved nursing program and pass a national licensing examination, known as the NCLEX-RN, in order to obtain a nursing license. Nurses may be licensed in more than one state, either by examination or by the endorsement of a license issued by another state. The Nurse Licensure Compact Agreement allows a nurse who is licensed and permanently resides in one of the member states to practice in the other member states without obtaining additional licensure. In 2006, 20 states were members of the Compact, while two more were pending membership. All states require periodic renewal of licenses, which may require continuing education.

Certification is common, and sometimes required, for the four advanced practice nursing specialties—clinical nurse specialists, nurse anesthetists, nurse-midwives, and nurse practitioners. Upon completion of their educational programs, most advanced practice nurses become nationally certified in their area of specialty. Certification also is available in specialty areas for all nurses. In some states, certification in a specialty is required in order to practice that specialty.

Foreign-educated and foreign-born nurses wishing to work in the United States must obtain a work visa. To obtain the visa, nurses must undergo a federal screening program to ensure that their education and licensure are comparable to that of a U.S. educated nurse, that they have proficiency in written and spoken English, and that they have passed either the Commission on Graduates of Foreign Nursing Schools (CGFNS) Qualifying Examination or the

NCLEX-RN. CGFNS administers the VisaScreen Program. (The Commission is an immigration-neutral, nonprofit organization that is recognized internationally as an authority on credentials evaluation in the health care field.) Nurses educated in Australia, Canada (except Quebec), Ireland, New Zealand, and the United Kingdom, or foreign-born nurses who were educated in the United States, are exempt from the language proficiency testing. In addition to these national requirements, foreign-born nurses must obtain state licensure in order to practice in the United States. Each state has its own requirements for licensure.

Other qualifications. Nurses should be caring, sympathetic, responsible, and detail oriented. They must be able to direct or supervise others, correctly assess patients' conditions, and determine when consultation is required. They need emotional stability to cope with human suffering, emergencies, and other stresses.

Advancement. Some RNs start their careers as licensed practical nurses or nursing aides, and then go back to school to receive their RN degree. Most RNs begin as staff nurses in hospitals, and with experience and good performance often move to other settings or are promoted to more responsible positions. In management, nurses can advance from assistant unit manger or head nurse to more senior-level administrative roles of assistant director, director, vice president, or chief nurse. Increasingly, management-level nursing positions require a graduate or an advanced degree in nursing or health services administration. Administrative positions require leadership, communication and negotiation skills, and good judgment.

Some nurses move into the business side of health care. Their nursing expertise and experience on a health care team equip them to manage ambulatory, acute, home-based, and chronic care. Employers—including hospitals, insurance companies, pharmaceutical manufacturers, and managed care organizations, among others—need RNs for health planning and development, marketing, consulting, policy development, and quality assurance. Other nurses work as college and university faculty or conduct research.

Employment

As the largest health care occupation, registered nurses held about 2.5 million jobs in 2006. Hospitals employed the majority of RNs, with 59 percent of jobs. Other industries also employed large shares of workers. About 8 percent of jobs were in offices of physicians, 5 percent in home health care services, 5 percent in nursing care facilities, 4 percent in employment services, and 3 percent in outpatient care centers. The remainder worked mostly in government agencies, social assistance agencies, and educational services. About 21 percent of RNs worked part time.

Job Outlook

Overall job opportunities for registered nurses are expected to be excellent, but may vary by employment and geographic setting. Employment of RNs is expected to grow much faster than the average for all occupations through 2016 and, because the occupation is very large, many new jobs will result. In fact, registered nurses are projected to generate 587,000 new jobs, among the largest number of new jobs for any occupation. Additionally, hundreds of thousands of job openings will result from the need to replace experienced nurses who leave the occupation.

Employment change. Employment of registered nurses is expected to grow 23 percent from 2006 to 2016, much faster than the average for all occupations. Growth will be driven by technological advances in patient care, which permit a greater number of health problems to be treated, and by an increasing emphasis on preventive care. In addition, the number of older people, who are much more likely than younger people to need nursing care, is projected to grow rapidly.

However, employment of RNs will not grow at the same rate in every industry. The projected growth rates for RNs in the industries with the highest employment of these workers are:

Offices of physicians 39%

Home health care services 39

Outpatient care centers, except mental health
and substance abuse 34

Employment services 27

General medical and surgical hospitals, public
and private 22

Nursing care facilities 20

Employment is expected to grow more slowly in hospitals—health care's largest industry—than in most other health care industries. While the intensity of nursing care is likely to increase, requiring more nurses per patient, the number of inpatients (those who remain in the hospital for more than 24 hours) is not likely to grow by much. Patients are being discharged earlier, and more procedures are being done on an outpatient basis, both inside and outside hospitals. Rapid growth is expected in hospital outpatient facilities, such as those providing same-day surgery, rehabilitation, and chemotherapy.

More and more sophisticated procedures, once performed only in hospitals, are being performed in physicians' offices and in outpatient care centers, such as freestanding ambulatory surgical and emergency centers. Accordingly, employment is expected to grow very fast in these places as health care in general expands.

Employment in nursing care facilities is expected to grow because of increases in the number of elderly, many of whom require long-term care. However, this growth will be relatively slower than in other health care industries because of the desire of patients to be treated at home or in residential care facilities, and the increasing availability of that type of care. The financial pressure on hospitals to discharge patients as soon as possible should produce more admissions to nursing and residential care facilities and to home health care. Job growth also is expected in units that provide specialized long-term rehabilitation for stroke and head injury patients, as well as units that treat Alzheimer's victims.

Employment in home health care is expected to increase rapidly in response to the growing number of older persons with functional disabilities, consumer preference for care in the home, and technological advances that make it possible to bring increasingly complex treatments into the home. The type of care demanded will require nurses who are able to perform complex procedures.

Rapid employment growth in employment services industry is expected as hospitals, physician's offices, and other health care establishments utilize temporary workers to fill short-term staffing needs. And as the demand for nurses grows, temporary nurses will be needed more often, further contributing to employment growth in this industry.

Job prospects. Overall job opportunities are expected to be excellent for registered nurses. Employers in some parts of the country and in certain employment settings report difficulty in attracting and retaining an adequate number of RNs, primarily because of an aging RN workforce and a lack of younger workers to fill positions. Enrollments in nursing programs at all levels have increased more rapidly in the past few years as students seek jobs with stable employment. However, many qualified applicants are being turned away because of a shortage of nursing faculty. The need for nursing faculty will only increase as many instructors near retirement. Many employers also are relying on foreign-educated nurses to fill vacant positions.

Even though overall employment opportunities for all nursing specialties are expected to be excellent, they can vary by employment setting. Despite the slower employment growth in hospitals, job opportunities should still be excellent because of the relatively high turnover of hospital nurses. RNs working in hospitals frequently work overtime and night and weekend shifts and also treat seriously ill and injured patients, all of which can contribute to stress and burnout. Hospital departments in which these working conditions occur most frequently—critical care units, emergency departments, and operating rooms—generally will have more job openings than other departments. To attract and retain qualified nurses, hospitals may offer signing bonuses, family-friendly work schedules, or subsidized training. A growing number of hospitals also are experimenting with online bidding to fill open shifts, in which nurses can volunteer to fill open shifts at premium wages. This can decrease the amount of mandatory overtime that nurses are required to work.

Although faster employment growth is projected in physicians' offices and outpatient care centers, RNs may face greater competition for these positions because they generally offer regular working hours and more comfortable working environments. There also may be some competition for jobs in employment services, despite a high rate of employment growth, because a large number of workers are attracted by the industry's relatively high wages and the flexibility of the work in this industry.

Generally, RNs with at least a bachelor's degree will have better job prospects than those without a bachelor's. In addition, all four advanced practice specialties—clinical nurse specialists, nurse practitioners, nurse-midwives, and nurse anesthetists—will be in high demand, particularly in medically underserved areas such as inner cities and rural areas. Relative to physicians, these RNs increasingly serve as lower-cost primary care providers.

Earnings

Median annual earnings of registered nurses were $57,280 in May 2006. The middle 50 percent earned between $47,710 and $69,850.

Projections data from the National Employment Matrix

Occupational Title	SOC Code	Employment, 2006	Projected employment, 2016	Change, 2006-2016	
				Number	Percent
Registered nurses	29-1111	2,505,000	3,092,000	587,000	23

NOTE: Data in this table are rounded.

The lowest 10 percent earned less than $40,250, and the highest 10 percent earned more than $83,440. Median annual earnings in the industries employing the largest numbers of registered nurses in May 2006 were

Employment services	$64,260
General medical and surgical hospitals	58,550
Home health care services	54,190
Offices of physicians	53,800
Nursing care facilities	52,490

Many employers offer flexible work schedules, child care, educational benefits, and bonuses.

Related Occupations

Because of the number of specialties for registered nurses, and the variety of responsibilities and duties, many other health care occupations are similar in some aspect of the job. Other occupations that deal directly with patients when providing care include licensed practical and licensed vocational nurses, physicians and surgeons, athletic trainers, respiratory therapists, massage therapists, dietitians and nutritionists, occupational therapists, physical therapists, and emergency medical technicians and paramedics. Other occupations that use advanced medical equipment to treat patients include cardiovascular technologists and technicians, diagnostic medical sonographers, radiologic technologists and technicians, radiation therapists, and surgical technologists. Workers who also assist other health care professionals in providing care include nursing, psychiatric, and home health aides; physician assistants; and dental hygienists. Some nurses take on a management role, similar to medical and health services managers.

Sources of Additional Information

For information on a career as a registered nurse and nursing education, contact

▸ National League for Nursing, 61 Broadway, New York, NY 10006. Internet: http://www.nln.org

For information on baccalaureate and graduate nursing education, nursing career options, and financial aid, contact

▸ American Association of Colleges of Nursing, 1 Dupont Circle NW, Suite 530, Washington, DC 20036. Internet: http://www.aacn.nche.edu

For additional information on registered nurses, including credentialing, contact

▸ American Nurses Association, 8515 Georgia Ave., Suite 400, Silver Spring, MD 20910. Internet: http://nursingworld.org

For information on the NCLEX-RN exam and a list of individual state boards of nursing, contact

▸ National Council of State Boards of Nursing, 111 E. Wacker Dr., Suite 2900, Chicago, IL 60611. Internet: http://www.ncsbn.org

For information on the nursing population, including workforce shortage facts, contact

▸ Bureau of Health Professions, 5600 Fishers Lane, Room 8-05, Rockville, MD 20857. Internet: http://bhpr.hrsa.gov

For information on obtaining U.S. certification and work visas for foreign-educated nurses, contact

▸ Commission on Graduates of Foreign Nursing Schools, 3600 Market St., Suite 400, Philadelphia, PA 19104. Internet: http://www.cgfns.org

For a list of accredited clinical nurse specialist programs, contact

▸ National Association of Clinical Nurse Specialists, 2090 Linglestown Rd., Suite 107, Harrisburg, PA 17110. Internet: http://www.nacns.org

For information on nurse anesthetists, including a list of accredited programs, contact

▸ American Association of Nurse Anesthetists, 222 Prospect Ave., Park Ridge, IL 60068.

For information on nurse-midwives, including a list of accredited programs, contact

▸ American College of Nurse-Midwives, 8403 Colesville Rd., Suite 1550, Silver Spring, MD 20910. Internet: http://www.midwife.org

For information on nurse practitioners, including a list of accredited programs, contact

▸ American Academy of Nurse Practitioners, P.O. Box 12846, Austin, TX 78711. Internet: http://www.aanp.org

For information on nurse practitioners education, contact

▸ National Organization of Nurse Practitioner Faculties, 1522 K St. NW, Suite 702, Washington, DC 20005. Internet: http://www.nonpf.org

For information on critical care nurses, contact

▸ American Association of Critical-Care Nurses, 101 Columbia, Aliso Viejo, CA 92656. Internet: http://www.aacn.org

For additional information on registered nurses in all fields and specialties, contact

▸ American Society of Registered Nurses, 1001 Bridgeway, Suite 411, Sausalito, CA 94965. Internet: http://www.asrn.org

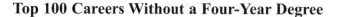

Respiratory Therapists

(O*NET 29-1126.00 and 29-2054.00)

Significant Points

■ Job opportunities should be very good.

■ An associate degree is the minimum educational requirement, but a bachelor's or master's degree may be important for advancement.

■ All states, except Alaska and Hawaii, require respiratory therapists to be licensed.

■ Hospitals will account for the vast majority of job openings, but a growing number of openings will arise in other settings.

Nature of the Work

Respiratory therapists and *respiratory therapy technicians*—also known as respiratory care practitioners—evaluate, treat, and care for patients with breathing or other cardiopulmonary disorders. Practicing under the direction of a physician, respiratory therapists assume primary responsibility for all respiratory care therapeutic treatments and diagnostic procedures, including the supervision of respiratory therapy technicians. Respiratory therapy technicians follow specific, well-defined respiratory care procedures under the direction of respiratory therapists and physicians.

In clinical practice, many of the daily duties of therapists and technicians overlap. However, therapists generally have greater responsibility than technicians. For example, respiratory therapists consult with physicians and other health care staff to help develop and modify patient care plans. Respiratory therapists also are more likely to provide complex therapy requiring considerable independent judgment, such as caring for patients on life support in intensive-care units of hospitals. In this job profile, the term *respiratory therapist* includes both respiratory therapists and respiratory therapy technicians.

Respiratory therapists evaluate and treat all types of patients, ranging from premature infants whose lungs are not fully developed to elderly people whose lungs are diseased. Respiratory therapists provide temporary relief to patients with chronic asthma or emphysema, and they give emergency care to patients who are victims of a heart attack, stroke, drowning, or shock.

To evaluate patients, respiratory therapists interview them, perform limited physical examinations, and conduct diagnostic tests. For example, respiratory therapists test a patient's breathing capacity and determine the concentration of oxygen and other gases in a patient's blood. They also measure a patient's pH, which indicates the acidity or alkalinity of the blood. To evaluate a patient's lung capacity, respiratory therapists have the patient breathe into an instrument that measures the volume and flow of oxygen during inhalation and exhalation. By comparing the reading with the norm for the patient's age, height, weight, and sex, respiratory therapists can provide information that helps determine whether the patient has any lung deficiencies. To analyze oxygen, carbon dioxide, and blood pH levels, therapists draw an arterial blood sample, place it in a blood gas analyzer, and relay the results to a physician, who then makes treatment decisions.

To treat patients, respiratory therapists use oxygen or oxygen mixtures, chest physiotherapy, and aerosol medications—liquid medications suspended in a gas that forms a mist which is inhaled. They teach patients how to inhale the aerosol properly to ensure its effectiveness. When a patient has difficulty getting enough oxygen into his or her blood, therapists increase the patient's concentration of oxygen by placing an oxygen mask or nasal cannula on the patient and setting the oxygen flow at the level prescribed by a physician. Therapists also connect patients who cannot breathe on their own to ventilators that deliver pressurized oxygen into the lungs. The therapists insert a tube into the patient's trachea, or windpipe; connect the tube to the ventilator; and set the rate, volume, and oxygen concentration of the oxygen mixture entering the patient's lungs.

Therapists perform regular assessments of patients and equipment. If a patient appears to be having difficulty breathing or if the oxygen, carbon dioxide, or pH level of the blood is abnormal, therapists change the ventilator setting according to the doctor's orders or check the equipment for mechanical problems.

Respiratory therapists perform chest physiotherapy on patients to remove mucus from their lungs and make it easier for them to breathe. Therapists place patients in positions that help drain mucus, and then vibrate the patients' rib cages, often by tapping on the chest, and tell the patients to cough. Chest physiotherapy may be needed after surgery, for example, because anesthesia depresses respiration. As a result, physiotherapy may be prescribed to help get the patient's lungs back to normal and to prevent congestion. Chest physiotherapy also helps patients suffering from lung diseases, such as cystic fibrosis, that cause mucus to collect in the lungs.

Therapists who work in home care teach patients and their families to use ventilators and other life-support systems. In addition, these therapists visit patients in their homes to inspect and clean equipment, evaluate the home environment, and ensure that patients have sufficient knowledge of their diseases and the proper use of their medications and equipment. Therapists also make emergency visits if equipment problems arise.

In some hospitals, therapists perform tasks that fall outside their traditional role. Therapists are becoming involved in areas such as pulmonary rehabilitation, smoking cessation counseling, disease prevention, case management, and polysomnography—the diagnosis of breathing disorders during sleep, such as apnea. Respiratory therapists also increasingly treat critical care patients, either as part of surface and air transport teams or as part of rapid-response teams in hospitals.

Work environment. Respiratory therapists generally work between 35 and 40 hours a week. Because hospitals operate around the clock, therapists may work evenings, nights, or weekends. They spend long periods standing and walking between patients' rooms. In an emergency, therapists work under the stress of the situation. Respiratory therapists employed in home health care must travel frequently to patients' homes.

Respiratory therapists are trained to work with gases stored under pressure. Adherence to safety precautions and regular maintenance and testing of equipment minimize the risk of injury. As in many other health occupations, respiratory therapists are exposed to infectious diseases, but by carefully following proper procedures they can minimize the risks.

Training, Other Qualifications, and Advancement

An associate degree is the minimum educational requirement, but a bachelor's or master's degree may be important for advancement. All states, except Alaska and Hawaii, require respiratory therapists to be licensed.

Education and training. An associate degree is required to become a respiratory therapist. Training is offered at the postsecondary level by colleges and universities, medical schools, vocational-technical institutes, and the Armed Forces. Most programs award associate or bachelor's degree and prepare graduates for jobs as advanced respiratory therapists. A limited number of associate degree programs lead to jobs as entry-level respiratory therapists. According to the Commission on Accreditation of Allied Health Education Programs (CAAHEP), 45 entry-level and 334 advanced respiratory therapy programs were accredited in the United States in 2006.

Among the areas of study in respiratory therapy programs are human anatomy and physiology, pathophysiology, chemistry, physics, microbiology, pharmacology, and mathematics. Other courses deal with therapeutic and diagnostic procedures and tests, equipment, patient assessment, cardiopulmonary resuscitation, the application of clinical practice guidelines, patient care outside of hospitals, cardiac and pulmonary rehabilitation, respiratory health promotion and disease prevention, and medical recordkeeping and reimbursement.

High school students interested in applying to respiratory therapy programs should take courses in health, biology, mathematics, chemistry, and physics. Respiratory care involves basic mathematical problem solving and an understanding of chemical and physical principles. For example, respiratory care workers must be able to compute dosages of medication and calculate gas concentrations.

Licensure and certification. A license is required to practice as a respiratory therapist, except in Alaska and Hawaii. Also, most employers require respiratory therapists to maintain a cardiopulmonary resuscitation (CPR) certification.

Licensure is usually based, in large part, on meeting the requirements for certification from the National Board for Respiratory Care (NBRC). The board offers the Certified Respiratory Therapist (CRT) credential to those who graduate from entry-level or advanced programs accredited by CAAHEP or the Committee on Accreditation for Respiratory Care (CoARC) and who also pass an exam.

The board also awards the Registered Respiratory Therapist (RRT) to CRTs who have graduated from advanced programs and pass two separate examinations. Supervisory positions and intensive-care specialties usually require the RRT.

Other qualifications. Therapists should be sensitive to a patient's physical and psychological needs. Respiratory care practitioners must pay attention to detail, follow instructions, and work as part of a team. In addition, operating advanced equipment requires proficiency with computers.

Advancement. Respiratory therapists advance in clinical practice by moving from general care to the care of critically ill patients who have significant problems in other organ systems, such as the heart or kidneys. Respiratory therapists, especially those with a bachelor's or master's degree, also may advance to supervisory or managerial positions in a respiratory therapy department. Respiratory therapists in home health care and equipment rental firms may become branch managers. Some respiratory therapists advance by moving into teaching positions. Some others use the knowledge gained as a respiratory therapist to work in another industry, such as developing, marketing, or selling pharmaceuticals and medical devices.

Employment

Respiratory therapists held about 122,000 jobs in 2006. About 79 percent of jobs were in hospitals, mainly in departments of respiratory care, anesthesiology, or pulmonary medicine. Most of the remaining jobs were in offices of physicians or other health practitioners, consumer-goods rental firms that supply respiratory equipment for home use, nursing care facilities, and home health care services. Holding a second job is relatively common for respiratory therapists. About 12 percent held another job, compared with 5 percent of workers in all occupations.

Job Outlook

Faster-than-average employment growth is projected for respiratory therapists. Job opportunities should be very good, especially for respiratory therapists with cardiopulmonary care skills or experience working with infants.

Employment change. Employment of respiratory therapists is expected to grow 19 percent from 2006 to 2016, faster than the average for all occupations. The increasing demand will come from substantial growth in the middle-aged and elderly population—a development that will heighten the incidence of cardiopulmonary disease. Growth in demand also will result from the expanding role of respiratory therapists in case management, disease prevention, emergency care, and the early detection of pulmonary disorders.

Older Americans suffer most from respiratory ailments and cardiopulmonary diseases such as pneumonia, chronic bronchitis, emphysema, and heart disease. As their numbers increase, the need for respiratory therapists is expected to increase as well. In addition, advances in inhalable medications and in the treatment of lung transplant patients, heart attack and accident victims, and premature infants (many of whom are dependent on a ventilator during part of their treatment) will increase the demand for the services of respiratory care practitioners.

Job prospects. Job opportunities are expected to be very good. The vast majority of job openings will continue to be in hospitals. However, a growing number of openings are expected to be outside of hospitals, especially in home health care services, offices of physicians or other health practitioners, consumer-goods rental firms, or in the employment services industry as a temporary worker in various settings.

Earnings

Median annual earnings of wage-and-salary respiratory therapists were $47,420 in May 2006. The middle 50 percent earned between $40,840 and $56,150. The lowest 10 percent earned less than $35,200, and the highest 10 percent earned more than $64,190.

Median annual earnings of wage-and-salary respiratory therapy technicians were $39,120 in May 2006. The middle 50 percent earned between $32,050 and $46,930. The lowest 10 percent earned less than $25,940, and the highest 10 percent earned more than $56,220.

Related Occupations

Under the supervision of a physician, respiratory therapists administer respiratory care and life support to patients with heart and lung difficulties. Other workers who care for, treat, or train people to improve their physical condition include registered nurses, occupational therapists, physical therapists, radiation therapists, and athletic trainers. Respiratory care practitioners work with advanced medical technology, as do other health care technicians including cardiovascular technologists and technicians, nuclear medicine technologists, radiologic technologists and technicians, and diagnostic medical sonographers.

Projections data from the National Employment Matrix

Occupational Title	SOC Code	Employment, 2006	Projected employment, 2016	Change, 2006-2016	
				Number	Percent
Respiratory therapists............................	—	122,000	145,000	23,000	19
Respiratory therapists............................	29-1126	102,000	126,000	23,000	23
Respiratory therapy technicians	29-2054	19,000	19,000	200	1

NOTE: Data in this table are rounded.

Sources of Additional Information

Information concerning a career in respiratory care is available from

▶ American Association for Respiratory Care, 9425 N. MacArthur Blvd., Suite 100, Irving, TX 75063. Internet: http://www.aarc.org

For a list of accredited educational programs for respiratory care practitioners, contact either of the following organizations:

▶ Commission on Accreditation for Allied Health Education Programs, 1361 Park St., Clearwater, FL 33756. Internet: http://www.caahep.org

▶ Committee on Accreditation for Respiratory Care, 1248 Harwood Rd., Bedford, TX 76021.

Information on gaining credentials in respiratory care and a list of state licensing agencies can be obtained from

▶ National Board for Respiratory Care, Inc., 18000 W. 105th St., Olathe, KS 66061. Internet: http://www.nbrc.org

Retail Salespersons

(O*NET 41-2031.00)

Significant Points

■ Good employment opportunities are expected because of the need to replace the large number of workers who leave the occupation each year.

■ Most salespersons work evenings and weekends, particularly during sales and other peak retail periods.

■ Employers look for people who enjoy working with others and who have tact, patience, an interest in sales work, a neat appearance, and the ability to communicate clearly.

Nature of the Work

Consumers spend millions of dollars every day on merchandise and often rely on a store's sales force for help. Whether selling shoes, computer equipment, or automobiles, retail salespersons assist customers in finding what they are looking for and try to interest them in buying the merchandise. Most are able to describe a product's features, demonstrate its use, or show various models and colors.

In addition to selling, most retail salespersons—especially those who work in department and apparel stores—make out sales checks; receive cash, checks, debit, and charge payments; bag or package purchases; and give change and receipts. Depending on the hours they work, retail salespersons may have to open or close cash registers. This work may include counting the money in the register; separating charge slips, coupons, and exchange vouchers; and making deposits at the cash office. Salespersons often are held responsible for the contents of their registers, and repeated shortages are cause for dismissal in many organizations.

Retailers stress the importance of providing courteous and efficient service to remain competitive. For example, when a customer wants an item that is not on the sales floor, the salesperson may check the stockroom, place a special order, or call another store to locate the item.

For some sales jobs, particularly those involving expensive and complex items, retail salespersons need special knowledge or skills. For example, salespersons who sell automobiles must be able to explain the features of various models, the manufacturers' specifications, the types of options and financing available, and the warranty.

Salespersons also may handle returns and exchanges of merchandise, wrap gifts, and keep their work areas neat. In addition, they may help stock shelves or racks, arrange for mailing or delivery of purchases, mark price tags, take inventory, and prepare displays.

Frequently, salespersons must be aware of special sales and promotions. They also must recognize security risks and thefts and know how to handle or prevent such situations.

Work environment. Most salespersons in retail trade work in clean, comfortable, well-lit stores. However, they often stand for long periods and may need supervisory approval to leave the sales floor. They also may work outdoors if they sell items such as cars, plants, or lumber yard materials.

The Monday-through-Friday, 9-to-5 work week is the exception rather than the rule in retail trade. Most salespersons work evenings and weekends, particularly during sales and other peak retail periods. The end-of-year holiday season is the busiest time for most retailers. As a result, many employers limit the use of vacation time between Thanksgiving and the beginning of January.

This occupation offers many opportunities for part-time work and is especially appealing to students, retirees, and others seeking to supplement their income. More than 32 percent of retail salespersons worked part-time in 2006. However, most of those selling big-ticket items work full time and have substantial experience.

Training, Other Qualifications, and Advancement

Retail salespeople typically learn their skills through on-the-job training. Although advancement opportunities are limited, having a college degree or a great deal of experience may help retail salespersons move into management positions.

Education and training. There usually are no formal education requirements for this type of work, although a high school diploma or the equivalent is often preferred. A college degree may be required for management trainee positions, especially in larger retail establishments.

In most small stores, an experienced employee or the store owner instructs newly hired sales personnel in making out sales checks and operating cash registers. In large stores, training programs are more formal and are usually conducted over several days. Topics discussed often include customer service, security, the store's policies and procedures, and how to work a cash register. Depending on the type of product they are selling, employees may be given additional specialized training by sales representatives. For example, those working in cosmetics receive instruction on the types of products the store offers and for whom the cosmetics would be most beneficial. Likewise, salespersons employed by motor vehicle dealers may be instructed on the technical details of standard and optional equipment available on new vehicle models. Since providing the best possible service to customers is a high priority for many employers, employees often are given periodic training to update and refine their skills.

Other qualifications. Employers look for people who enjoy working with others and who have the tact and patience to deal with difficult customers. Among other desirable characteristics are an interest in sales work, a neat appearance, and the ability to communicate clearly and effectively. The ability to speak more than one language may be helpful for employment in communities where people from various cultures live and shop. Before hiring a salesperson, some employers may conduct a background check, especially for a job selling high-priced items.

Advancement. Opportunities for advancement vary. In some small establishments, advancement is limited because one person—often the owner—does most of the managerial work. In others, some salespersons are promoted to assistant manager. Large retail businesses usually prefer to hire college graduates as management trainees, making a college education increasingly important. However, motivated and capable employees without college degrees still may advance to administrative or supervisory positions in large establishments.

As salespersons gain experience and seniority, they usually move to positions of greater responsibility and may be given their choice of departments in which to work. This often means moving to areas with higher potential earnings and commissions. The highest earnings potential usually lies in selling "big-ticket" items—such as cars, jewelry, furniture, and electronic equipment—although doing so often requires extensive knowledge of the product and an extraordinary talent for persuasion.

Retail selling experience may be an asset when applying for sales positions with larger retailers or in nonretail industries, such as financial services, wholesale trade, or manufacturing.

Employment

Retail salespersons held about 4.5 million jobs in 2006. They worked in stores ranging from small specialty shops employing a few workers to giant department stores with hundreds of salespersons. In addition, some were self-employed representatives of direct-sales companies and mail-order houses. The largest employers of retail salespersons are department stores, clothing and clothing accessories stores, building material and garden equipment and supplies dealers, other general merchandise stores, and motor vehicle and parts dealers.

Because retail stores are found in every city and town, employment is distributed geographically in much the same way as the population.

Job Outlook

Due to the high level of turnover in this occupation, opportunities are expected to be good. The average projected employment growth in this occupation reflects the expansion of the economy and consumer spending.

Employment change. Employment is expected to grow by 12 percent over the 2006–2016 decade, which is about as fast as the average for all occupations. In fact, due to the size of this occupation, retail salespersons will have one of the largest numbers of new jobs arise, about 557,000 over the projections decade. This growth reflects rising retail sales stemming from a growing population.

Many retail establishments will continue to expand in size and number, leading to new retail sales positions. Since retail salespeople must be available to assist customers in person, this is not an occupation that will suffer negative effects from advancements in technology. To the contrary, software that integrates purchase transactions, inventory management, and purchasing has greatly changed retailing, but retail salespersons continue to be essential in dealing with customers. There will also be an increased demand for retail salespersons in warehouse clubs and supercenters, which sell a wide assortment of goods at low prices, since they continue to grow as many consumers prefer these stores.

Despite the growing popularity of electronic commerce, the impact of electronic commerce on employment of retail salespersons is expected to be minimal. Internet sales have not decreased the need for retail salespersons. Retail stores commonly use an online presence to complement their in-store sales; there are a limited number of Internet-only apparel and specialty stores. Retail salespersons will remain important in assuring customers, providing specialized service, and increasing customer satisfaction. Most shoppers continue to prefer to make their purchases in stores, and growth of retail sales will continue to generate employment growth in various retail establishments.

Job prospects. As in the past, employment opportunities for retail salespersons are expected to be good because of the need to replace the large number of workers who transfer to other occupations or leave the labor force each year. Warehouse clubs and supercenters are expected to have excellent job prospects as they continue to grow in popularity with consumers. In addition, many new jobs will be created for retail salespersons as businesses seek to expand operations and enhance customer service.

Opportunities for part-time work should be abundant, and demand will be strong for temporary workers during peak selling periods, such as the end-of-year holiday season. The availability of part-time and temporary work attracts many people seeking to supplement their income.

During economic downturns, sales volumes and the resulting demand for sales workers usually decline. Purchases of costly items, such as cars, appliances, and furniture, tend to be postponed during difficult economic times. In areas of high unemployment, sales of many types of goods decline. However, because many retail salespersons constantly transfer to other occupations in search of better pay or career opportunities, employers often can adjust employment levels simply by not replacing all those who leave.

Earnings

Median hourly earnings of retail salespersons, including commissions, were $9.50 in May 2006. The middle 50 percent earned between $7.81 and $12.83 an hour. The lowest 10 percent earned less than $6.79, and the highest 10 percent earned more than $18.48 an hour. Median hourly earnings in the industries employing the largest numbers of retail salespersons in May 2006 were as follows:

Projections data from the National Employment Matrix

Occupational Title	SOC Code	Employment, 2006	Projected employment, 2016	Change, 2006-16	
				Number	Percent
Retail salespersons	41-2031	4,477,000	5,034,000	557,000	12

NOTE: Data in this table are rounded.

© JIST Works

Automobile dealers $18.70

Building material and supplies dealers 11.37

Other general merchandise stores 8.79

Department stores...8.70

Clothing stores...8.53

Many beginning or inexperienced workers earn the federal minimum wage of $5.85 an hour, but many states set minimum wages higher than the federal minimum. Under federal law, this wage will increase to $6.55 in the summer of 2008 and to $7.25 in the summer of 2009. In areas where employers have difficulty attracting and retaining workers, wages tend to be higher than the legislated minimum.

Compensation systems can vary by type of establishment and merchandise sold. Salespersons receive hourly wages, commissions, or a combination thereof. Under a commission system, salespersons receive a percentage of the sales they make. This system offers sales workers the opportunity to increase their earnings considerably, but they may find that their earnings strongly depend on their ability to sell their product and on the ups and downs of the economy.

Benefits may be limited in smaller stores, but benefits in large establishments usually are comparable to those offered by other employers. In addition, nearly all salespersons are able to buy their store's merchandise at a discount, with the savings depending on the type of merchandise. Also, to bolster revenue, employers may use incentive programs such as awards, banquets, bonuses, and profit-sharing plans to promote teamwork among the sales staff.

Related Occupations

Salespersons use sales techniques, coupled with their knowledge of merchandise, to assist customers and encourage purchases. Workers in other occupations who use these same skills include sales representatives, wholesale and manufacturing; securities, commodities, and financial services sales agents; counter and rental clerks; real estate brokers and sales agents; purchasing managers, buyers, and purchasing agents; insurance sales agents; sales engineers; and cashiers.

Sources of Additional Information

Information on careers in retail sales may be obtained from the personnel offices of local stores or from state merchants' associations.

General information about retailing is available from

▸ National Retail Federation, 325 7th St. NW, Suite 1100, Washington, DC 20004.

Information about training for a career in automobile sales is available from

▸ National Automobile Dealers Association, Public Relations Department, 8400 Westpark Dr., McLean, VA 22102-3591. Internet: http://www.nada.org

Roofers

(O*NET 47-2181.00)

Significant Points

■ Most roofers learn their skills informally on the job; some roofers train through 3-year apprenticeships.

■ Most job openings will arise from the need to replace those who leave the occupation because the work is hot, strenuous, and dirty, causing many people to switch to jobs in other construction trades.

■ Demand for roofers is less susceptible to downturns in the economy than demand for other construction trades because most roofing work consists of repair and reroofing.

Nature of the Work

A leaky roof can damage ceilings, walls, and furnishings. Roofers repair and install roofs made of tar or asphalt and gravel; rubber or thermoplastic; metal; or shingles to protect buildings and their contents from water damage. Repair and reroofing—replacing old roofs on existing buildings—makes up the majority of work for roofers.

There are two types of roofs—low-slope and steep-slope. Low-slope roofs rise 4 inches per horizontal foot or less and are installed in layers. Steep-slope roofs rise more than 4 inches per horizontal foot and are usually covered in shingles. Most commercial, industrial, and apartment buildings have low-slope roofs. Most houses have steep-slope roofs. Some roofers work on both types; others specialize.

Most low-slope roofs are covered with several layers of materials. Roofers first put a layer of insulation on the roof deck. Over the insulation, they often spread a coat of molten bitumen, a tarlike substance. Next, they install partially overlapping layers of roofing felt—a fabric saturated in bitumen—over the surface. Roofers use a mop to spread hot bitumen over the felt before adding another layer of felt. This seals the seams and makes the surface watertight. Roofers repeat these steps to build up the desired number of layers, called "plies." The top layer is glazed to make a smooth finish or has gravel embedded in the hot bitumen to create a rough surface.

An increasing number of low-slope roofs are covered with a single-ply membrane of waterproof rubber or thermoplastic compounds. Roofers roll these sheets over the roof's insulation and seal the seams. Adhesive, mechanical fasteners, or stone ballast hold the sheets in place. Roofers must make sure the building is strong enough to hold the stone ballast.

A small but growing number of buildings now have "green" roofs that incorporate plants. A "green" roof begins with a single or multiply waterproof layer. After it is proven to be leak free, roofers put a root barrier over it, and then layers of soil, in which trees and grass are planted. Roofers are usually responsible for making sure the roof is watertight and can withstand the weight and water needs of the plants.

Most residential steep-slope roofs are covered with shingles. To apply shingles, roofers first lay, cut, and tack 3-foot strips of roofing felt over the entire roof. Starting from the bottom edge, the roofer then staples or nails overlapping rows of shingles to the roof. Roofers measure and cut the felt and shingles to fit intersecting roof surfaces and to fit around vent pipes and chimneys. Wherever two roof surfaces intersect, or shingles reach a vent pipe or chimney, roofers cement or nail flashing-strips of metal or shingle over the joints to make them watertight. Finally, roofers cover exposed nail-heads with roofing cement or caulking to prevent water leakage. Roofers who use tile, metal shingles, or shakes (rough wooden shingles) follow a similar process.

Roofers also install equipment that requires cutting through roofs, such as ventilation ducts and attic fans. Some roofers are expert in waterproofing; some waterproof and dampproof masonry and concrete walls, floors, and foundations. To prepare surfaces for waterproofing, they hammer and chisel away rough spots or remove them with a rubbing brick, before applying a coat of liquid waterproofing compound. They also may paint or spray surfaces with a waterproofing material or attach waterproofing membrane to surfaces. Roofers usually spray a bitumen-based coating on interior or exterior surfaces when dampproofing.

Work environment. Roofing work is strenuous. It involves heavy lifting, as well as climbing, bending, and kneeling. Roofers work outdoors in all types of weather, particularly when making repairs. However, they rarely work when it rains or in very cold weather as ice can be dangerous. In northern states, roofing work is generally not performed during winter months. During the summer, roofers may work overtime to complete jobs quickly, especially before forecasted rainfall.

Workers risk slips or falls from scaffolds, ladders, or roofs or burns from hot bitumen, but safety precautions, can prevent most accidents. In addition, roofs can become extremely hot during the summer, causing heat-related illnesses. In 2005, the rate of injuries for roofing contractors in construction was almost twice that of workers overall.

Training, Other Qualifications, and Advancement

Most roofers learn their skills informally by working as helpers for experienced roofers and by taking classes, including safety training, offered by their employers; some complete three-year apprenticeships.

Education and training. A high school education, or its equivalent, is helpful and so are courses in mechanical drawing and basic mathematics. Although most workers learn roofing as helpers for experienced workers, some roofers train through three-year apprenticeship programs administered by local union-management committees representing roofing contractors and locals of the United Union of Roofers, Waterproofers, and Allied Workers. Apprenticeship programs usually include at least 2,000 hours of paid on-the-job training each year, plus a minimum of 144 hours of classroom instruction a year in tools and their use, arithmetic, safety, and other topics. On-the-job training for apprentices is similar to the training given to helpers, but an apprenticeship program is more structured and comprehensive. Apprentices, for example, learn to dampproof and waterproof walls.

Trainees start by carrying equipment and material and erecting scaffolds and hoists. Within two or three months, they are taught to measure, cut, and fit roofing materials and, later, to lay asphalt or fiberglass shingles. Because some roofing materials are used infrequently, it can take several years to get experience working on all types of roofing.

Other qualifications. Good physical condition and good balance are essential for roofers. They cannot be afraid of heights. Experience

with metal-working is helpful for workers who install metal roofing. Usually, apprentices must be at least 18 years old.

Advancement. Roofers may advance to become supervisors or estimators for a roofing contractor or become contractors themselves.

Employment

Roofers held about 156,000 jobs in 2006. Almost all salaried roofers worked for roofing contractors. About 20 percent of roofers were self-employed. Many self-employed roofers specialized in residential work.

Job Outlook

Most job openings will arise from turnover, because the work is hot, strenuous, and dirty, causing many people to switch to jobs in other construction trades. Faster-than-average employment growth is expected.

Employment change. Employment of roofers is expected to grow 14 percent between 2006 and 2016, which is faster than the average for all occupations. Roofs deteriorate faster than most other parts of buildings, and they need to be repaired or replaced more often. So as the number of buildings continues to increase, demand for roofers is expected to grow. In addition to repair work, the need to install roofs on new buildings is also expected to add to the demand for roofers.

Job prospects. Job opportunities for roofers will arise primarily because of the need to replace workers who leave the occupation. The proportion of roofers who leave the occupation each year is higher than in most construction trades—roofing work is hot, strenuous, and dirty, and a significant number of workers treat roofing as a temporary job until they find other work. Some roofers leave the occupation to go into other construction trades. Jobs should be easiest to find during spring and summer.

Employment of roofers who install new roofs, like that of many other construction workers, is sensitive to the fluctuations of the economy. Workers in these trades may experience periods of unemployment when the overall level of construction falls. On the other hand, shortages of these workers may occur in some areas during peak periods of building activity. Nevertheless, roofing is more heavily concentrated on repair and replacement rather than new installation, making demand for roofers less susceptible to the business cycle than it is for some other construction trades.

Earnings

In May 2006, median hourly earnings of wage and salary roofers were $15.51. The middle 50 percent earned between $12.12 and $20.79. The lowest 10 percent earned less than $9.81, and the highest 10 percent earned more than $26.79. The median hourly earnings of roofers in the foundation, structure, and building exterior contractors industry were $15.54. Earnings may be reduced on occasion when poor weather limits the time roofers can work.

Projections data from the National Employment Matrix

Occupational Title	SOC Code	Employment, 2006	Projected employment, 2016	Change, 2006-16	
				Number	Percent
Roofers..	47-2181	156,000	179,000	22,000	14

NOTE: Data in this table are rounded.

Apprentices usually start earning about 40 percent to 50 percent of the rate paid to experienced roofers. They receive periodic raises as they master the skills of the trade.

Some roofers are members of the United Union of Roofers, Waterproofers, and Allied Workers. Hourly wages and fringe benefits are generally higher for union workers.

Related Occupations

Roofers use shingles, bitumen and gravel, single-ply plastic or rubber sheets, or other materials to waterproof building surfaces. Workers in other occupations who cover surfaces with special materials for protection and decoration include carpenters; carpet, floor, and tile installers and finishers; cement masons, concrete finishers, segmental pavers, and terrazzo workers; drywall installers, ceiling tile installers, and tapers; plasterers and stucco masons; and sheet metal workers.

Sources of Additional Information

For information about apprenticeships or job opportunities in roofing, contact local roofing contractors, a local chapter of the roofers union, a local joint union-management apprenticeship committee, or the nearest office of your state employment service or apprenticeship agency. You can also find information on the registered apprenticeship system with links to state apprenticeship programs on the U.S. Department of Labor's Web site: http://www.doleta.gov/atels_bat. Apprenticeship information is also available from the U.S. Department of Labor's toll free helpline: 1 (877) 872-5627.

For information about the work of roofers, contact

▸ National Roofing Contractors Association, 10255 W. Higgins Rd., Suite 600, Rosemont, IL 60018-5607. Internet: http://www.nrca.net

▸ United Union of Roofers, Waterproofers, and Allied Workers, 1660 L St. NW, Suite 800, Washington, DC 20036. Internet: http://www.unionroofers.org

For general information on apprenticeships and how to get them, see the *Occupational Outlook Quarterly* article "Apprenticeships: Career training, credentials—and a paycheck in your pocket," online at http://www.bls.gov/opub/ooq/2002/summer/art01.pdf and in print at many libraries and career centers.

Sales Representatives, Wholesale and Manufacturing

(O*NET 41-4011.00 and 41-4012.00)

Significant Points

■ Competition for jobs is expected, but opportunities will be best for those with a college degree, the appropriate technical expertise, and the personal traits necessary for successful selling.

■ Job prospects for sales representatives will be better for those working with essential goods, since the demand for these products do not fluctuate with the economy.

■ Earnings of sales representatives are relatively high and usually are based on a combination of salary and commission.

Nature of the Work

Sales representatives are an important part of manufacturers' and wholesalers' success. Regardless of the type of product they sell, sales representatives' primary duties are to make wholesale and retail buyers and purchasing agents interested in their merchandise and to address any of their clients' questions and concerns. Sales representatives demonstrate their products and explain how using those products can reduce costs and increase sales.

Sales representatives may represent one or several manufacturers or wholesale distributors by selling one product or a complementary line of products. The clients of sales representatives span almost every industry and include other manufacturers, wholesale and retail establishments, construction contractors, and government agencies.

The process of promoting and selling products can take up to several months. Sales representatives present their products to a customer and negotiate the sale. Whether in person or over the phone, they can make a persuasive sales pitch and often will immediately answer technical and non-technical questions about the products. They may also record any interactions with clients and their respective sales to better match their future needs and sales potential.

There are two major categories of products that sales representatives work with: technical and scientific products and all products except technical and scientific products. Technical and scientific products may include anything from agricultural and mechanical equipment to electrical and pharmaceutical goods. Products included in the later category are more everyday items, including goods such as food, office supplies, and apparel.

Sales representatives stay abreast of new products and the changing needs of their customers in a variety of ways. They attend trade shows at which new products and technologies are showcased. They also attend conferences and conventions to meet other sales representatives and clients and discuss new product developments. In addition, the entire sales force may participate in company-sponsored meetings to review sales performance, product development, sales goals, and profitability.

Frequently, sales representatives who lack the necessary expertise about a given product may team with a technical expert. In this arrangement, the technical expert—sometimes a sales engineer—attends the sales presentation to explain the product and answer questions or concerns. The sales representative makes the preliminary contact with customers, introduces the company's product, and closes the sale. The representative is then able to spend more time maintaining and soliciting accounts and less time acquiring technical knowledge. After the sale, representatives may make follow-up visits to ensure that the equipment is functioning properly and may even help train customers' employees to operate and maintain new equipment. Those selling technical goods may also help set up the installation. Those selling consumer goods often suggest how and where merchandise should be displayed. When working with retailers, they may help arrange promotional programs, store displays, and advertising.

Obtaining new accounts is an important part of the job for all sales representatives. Sales representatives follow leads from other clients, track advertisements in trade journals, participate in trade shows and conferences, and may visit potential clients unannounced. In addition, they may spend time meeting with and entertaining prospective clients during evenings and weekends.

Sales representatives have several duties beyond selling products. They analyze sales statistics; prepare reports; and handle administrative duties, such as filing expense accounts, scheduling appointments, and making travel plans. They also read about new and existing products and monitor the sales, prices, and products of their competitors.

Sales representatives, regardless of where they are employed, may work in either inside sales or outside "field" sales. *Inside sales representatives* may spend a lot of their time on the phone, taking orders and resolving any problems or complaints about the merchandise. These sales representatives typically do not leave the office. *Outside sales representatives* spend much of their time traveling to and visiting with current clients and prospective buyers. During a sales call, they discuss the client's needs and suggest how their merchandise or services can meet those needs. They may show samples or catalogs that describe items their company stocks and inform customers about prices, availability, and ways in which their products can save money and boost productivity. Given that a number of manufacturers and wholesalers sell similar products, sales representatives must emphasize any unique qualities of their products and services. Since many sales representatives sell several complementary products made by different manufacturers, they may take a broad approach to their customers' business. For example, sales representatives may help install new equipment and train employees in its use.

Sales representatives working at an independent sales agency usually sell several products from multiple manufacturers. Additionally, these firms may only cover a certain territory, ranging from local areas to several states. These independent firms are called "manufacturers' representative companies" because their selling is on behalf of the manufacturers.

Depending on where they work, sales representatives may have different job titles. *Manufacturers' agents* or *manufacturers' representatives*, for example, are self-employed sales workers who own independent firms which contract their services to all types of manufacturing companies.

Work environment. Some sales representatives have large territories and travel considerably. Because a sales region may cover several states, representatives may be away from home for several days or weeks at a time. Others work near their home base and travel mostly by car. Sales representatives often are on their feet for long periods and may carry heavy sample products, necessitating some physical stamina.

Sales representatives may work more than 40 hours per week because of the nature of the work and the amount of travel. Since sales calls take place during regular working hours, most of the planning and paperwork involved with sales must be completed during the evening and on the weekends. Although the hours are long and often irregular, many sales representatives working for independent sales companies have the freedom to determine their own schedules.

Dealing with different types of people can be stimulating but demanding. Sales representatives often face competition from representatives of other companies. Companies usually set goals or quotas that representatives are expected to meet. Because their earnings depend on commissions, manufacturers' representatives are also under the added pressure to maintain and expand their clientele.

Training, Other Qualifications, and Advancement

Many employers hire individuals with previous sales experience who lack a college degree, but hiring candidates with a college degree is becoming increasingly common. Regardless of educational background, factors such as personality, the ability to sell, and familiarity with brands are essential to being a successful sales representative.

Education and training. Since there is no formal educational requirement for sales representative, their levels of education varies. Having a bachelor's degree can be highly desirable, especially for sales representatives who work with technical and scientific products. This is because technological advances result in new and more complex products. Additionally, manufacturers' representatives who start their own independent sales company might have an MBA. As shown in the tabulation below, in 2006 many sales representatives had a bachelor's degree, and many others had some college classes. Some, however, had no degree or formal training, but these workers often had sales experience or potential.

High school graduate or less	27%
Some college, no degree	19
Associate's degree	9
Bachelor's degree	38
Graduate degree	6

Many sales representatives attend seminars in sales techniques or take courses in marketing, economics, communication, or even a foreign language to provide the extra edge needed to make sales. Often, companies have formal training programs for beginning sales representatives lasting up to two years. However, most businesses accelerate these programs to reduce costs and expedite the returns from training. In some programs, trainees rotate among jobs in plants and offices to learn all phases of production, installation, and distribution of the product. In others, trainees take formal classroom instruction at the plant, followed by on-the-job training under the supervision of a field sales manager.

Regardless of where they work, new employees may get training by accompanying experienced workers on their sales calls. As they gain familiarity with the firm's products and clients, the new workers are given increasing responsibility until they are eventually assigned their own territory. As businesses experience greater competition, representatives face more pressure to produce sales.

Other qualifications. For sales representative jobs, companies seek the best and brightest individuals who have the personality and desire to sell. Those who want to become sales representatives should be goal oriented, persuasive, and able to work well both independently and as part of a team. A pleasant personality and appearance, the ability to communicate well with people, and problem-solving skills are highly valued. Patience and perseverance are also keys to completing a sale, which can take up to several months. Sales representatives also need to be able to work with computers since computers are increasingly used to place and track orders and to monitor inventory levels.

Manufacturers' representatives who operate a sales agency must also manage their business. This requires organizational and general business skills, as well as knowledge of accounting, marketing, and administration. Usually, however, sales representatives gain

© JIST Works

experience and recognition with a manufacturer or wholesaler before becoming self-employed.

Certification and advancement. Certifications are available that provide formal recognition of the skills of sales representatives, wholesale and manufacturing. Many obtaining certification in this profession have either the Certified Professional Manufacturers' Representative (CPMR) or the Certified Sales Professional (CSP), offered by the Manufacturers' Representatives Education Research Foundation. Certification typically involves completion of formal training and passing an examination.

Frequently, promotion takes the form of an assignment to a larger account or territory where commissions are likely to be greater. Those who have good sales records and leadership ability may advance to higher level positions such as sales supervisor, district manager, or vice president of sales. Others find opportunities in purchasing, advertising, or marketing research.

Advancement opportunities typically depend on whether the sales representatives are working directly for a manufacturer or wholesaler or if they are working with an independent sales agency. Experienced sales representatives working directly for a manufacturer or wholesaler may move into jobs as sales trainers and instruct new employees on selling techniques and company policies and procedures. Some leave the manufacturer or wholesaler and start their own independent sales company. Those working for an independent sales company can also advance by going into business for themselves or by receiving higher pay.

Employment

Manufacturers' and wholesale sales representatives held about 2 million jobs in 2006. About 21 percent worked with technical and scientific products. Almost 60 percent of all representatives worked in wholesale trade. Others were employed in manufacturing, retail trade, information, and construction. Because of the diversity of products and services sold, employment opportunities are available throughout the country in a wide range of industries. In addition to those working directly for a firm, some sales representatives are self-employed manufacturers' agents. They often form small sales firms that may start with just themselves and gradually grow to employ a small staff.

Job Outlook

Job growth of sales representatives, wholesale and manufacturing, is expected to be average, but keen competition is expected for these highly paid sales jobs.

Employment change. Employment of sales representatives, wholesale and manufacturing, is expected to grow by 9 percent between 2006 and 2016, which is about as fast as the average for all occupations. Given the size of this occupation, a large number of new jobs,

about 182,000 will arise over the projections decade. This is primarily because of continued growth in the variety and number of goods sold throughout the economy. Technological progress will also have an impact on job growth. Sales representatives can help ensure that retailers offer the latest technology available to their customers or that businesses acquire the right technical products that will increase their efficiency in operations. Advances in technology will therefore lead to more products being demanded and sold, and thus growth in the sales representative profession.

At the same time, however, computers and other information technology are also making sales representatives more effective and productive, allowing sales representatives to handle more clients, and thus hindering job growth somewhat.

Employment growth will be greatest in independent sales companies as manufacturers and wholesalers continue to outsource sales activities to independent agents rather than using in-house or direct sales workers. Independent agent companies are paid only if they sell, a practice that reduces the overhead cost to their clients. Also, by using agents who usually contract their services to more than one company, companies can share costs of the agents with each other. As the customers of independent agents continue to merge with other companies, independent agent companies and other wholesale trade firms will also merge with each other in response to better serve their clients.

Job prospects. Earnings of sales representatives, wholesale and manufacturing are relatively high, especially for those selling technical and scientific products, so keen competition is likely for jobs. Prospects will be best for those with a solid technical background and the personal traits necessary for successful selling. Opportunities will be better for sales representatives working for an independent sales company as opposed to working directly for a manufacturer because manufacturers are expected to continue contracting out field sales duties.

Opportunities for sales representatives in manufacturing are likely to be best for those selling products for which there is strong demand. Jobs will be most plentiful in small wholesale and manufacturing firms because a growing number of these companies will rely on agents to market their products as a way to control their costs and expand their customer base.

Employment opportunities and earnings may fluctuate from year to year because sales are affected by changing economic conditions, legislative issues, and consumer preferences. Also, many job openings will result from the need to replace workers who transfer to other occupations or leave the labor force.

Earnings

Median annual earnings of wage and salary sales representatives, wholesale and manufacturing, technical and scientific products,

Projections data from the National Employment Matrix

Occupational Title	SOC Code	Employment, 2006	Projected employment, 2016	Change, 2006-16	
				Number	Percent
Sales representatives, wholesale and manufacturing	41-4000	1,973,000	2,155,000	182,000	9
Sales representatives, wholesale and manufacturing, technical and scientific products	41-4011	411,000	462,000	51,000	12
Sales representatives, wholesale and manufacturing, except technical and scientific products	41-4012	1,562,000	1,693,000	131,000	8

NOTE: Data in this table are rounded.

were $64,440, including commissions, in May 2006. The middle 50 percent earned between $45,630 and $91,090 a year. The lowest 10 percent earned less than $33,410, and the highest 10 percent earned more than $121,850 a year. Median annual earnings in the industries employing the largest numbers of sales representatives, technical and scientific products, were as follows:

Computer systems design and related services $75,240

Wholesale electronic markets and agents and
brokers 69,510

Professional and commercial equipment and
supplies merchant wholesalers 67,700

Drugs and druggists' sundries merchant
wholesalers 66,210

Electrical and electronic goods merchant
wholesalers 61,000

Median annual earnings of wage and salary sales representatives, wholesale and manufacturing, except technical and scientific products, were $49,610, including commission, in May 2006. The middle 50 percent earned between $35,460 and $71,650 a year. The lowest 10 percent earned less than $26,030, and the highest 10 percent earned more than $101,030 a year. Median annual earnings in the industries employing the largest numbers of sales representatives, except technical and scientific products, were as follows:

Wholesale electronic markets and agents
and brokers $54,900

Professional and commercial equipment and
supplies merchant wholesalers 49,730

Machinery, equipment, and supplies merchant
wholesalers 48,620

Grocery and related product wholesalers 46,150

Miscellaneous nondurable goods merchant
wholesalers 42,530

Compensation methods for those representatives working for an independent sales company vary significantly by the type of firm and the product sold. Most employers use a combination of salary and commissions or salary plus bonus. Commissions usually are based on the amount of sales, whereas bonuses may depend on individual performance, on the performance of all sales workers in the group or district, or on the company's performance. Unlike those working directly for a manufacturer or wholesaler, sales representatives working for an independent sales company usually are not reimbursed for expenses. Depending on the type of product or products they are selling, their experience in the field, and the number of clients they have, they can earn significantly more or less than those working in direct sales for a manufacturer or wholesaler.

In addition to their earnings, sales representatives working directly for a manufacturer or wholesaler usually are reimbursed for expenses such as transportation costs, meals, hotels, and entertaining customers. They often receive benefits such as health and life insurance, pension plans, vacation and sick leave, personal use of a company car, and frequent flyer mileage. Some companies offer incentives such as free vacation trips or gifts for outstanding sales workers.

Related Occupations

Sales representatives, wholesale and manufacturing, must have sales ability and knowledge of the products they sell. Other occupations

that require similar skills include advertising, marketing, promotions, public relations, and sales managers; insurance sales agents; purchasing managers, buyers, and purchasing agents; real estate brokers and sales agents; retail salespersons; sales engineers; and securities, commodities, and financial services sales agents.

Sources of Additional Information

Information on careers for manufacturers' representatives and sales agents is available from

▶ Manufacturers' Agents National Association, One Spectrum Pointe, Suite 150, Lake Forest, CA 92630. Internet: http://www.manaonline.org

▶ Manufacturers' Representatives Educational Research Foundation, 8329 Cole St., Arvada, CO 80005. Internet: http://www.mrerf.org

Sales Worker Supervisors

(O*NET 41-1011.00 and 41-1012.00)

Significant Points

■ Overall employment is projected to grow more slowly than average.

■ Applicants with retail experience should have the best job opportunities.

■ Long, irregular hours, including evenings and weekends, are common.

Nature of the Work

Sales worker supervisors oversee the work of sales and related workers, such as retail salespersons, cashiers, customer service representatives, stock clerks and order fillers, sales engineers, and wholesale sales representatives. Sales worker supervisors are responsible for interviewing, hiring, and training employees. They also may prepare work schedules and assign workers to specific duties. Many of these supervisors hold job titles such as *sales manager* or *department manager*. Under the occupational classification system used in this book, however, workers who mainly supervise workers and who do not focus on broader managerial issues of planning and strategy are classified as *supervisors*.

In retail establishments, sales worker supervisors ensure that customers receive satisfactory service and quality goods. They also answer customers' inquiries, deal with complaints, and sometimes handle purchasing, budgeting, and accounting.

Responsibilities vary with the size and type of establishment. As the size of retail stores and the types of goods and services increase, supervisors tend to specialize in one department or one aspect of merchandising. Sales worker supervisors in large retail establishments are often referred to as department supervisors or managers. They provide day-to-day oversight of individual departments, such as shoes, cosmetics, or housewares in department stores; produce or meat in grocery stores; and car sales in automotive dealerships. Department supervisors establish and implement policies, goals, and procedures for their specific departments; coordinate activities with other department heads; and strive for smooth operations within their departments. They supervise employees who price and ticket goods and place them on display; clean and organize shelves, displays, and inventories in stockrooms; and inspect merchandise to ensure that nothing is outdated. Sales worker supervisors also review inventory and sales records, develop merchandising techniques, and coordinate sales promotions. In addition, they may greet and assist customers and promote sales and good public relations.

Sales worker supervisors in non-retail establishments oversee and coordinate the activities of sales workers who sell industrial products, insurance policies, or services such as advertising, financial, or Internet services. They may prepare budgets, make personnel decisions, devise sales-incentive programs, and approve sales contracts.

In small or independent companies and retail stores, sales worker supervisors not only directly supervise sales associates, but they also are responsible for the operation of the entire company or store. Some are self-employed business or store owners.

Work environment. Most sales worker supervisors have offices. In retail trade, their offices are within the stores, usually close to the areas they oversee. Although they spend some time in the office completing merchandise orders or arranging work schedules, a large portion of their workday is spent on the sales floor, supervising employees or selling.

Work hours of supervisors vary greatly among establishments because work schedules usually depend on customers' needs. Supervisors generally work at least 40 hours a week. Long, irregular hours are common, particularly during sales, holidays, and busy shopping seasons and at times when inventory is taken. Supervisors are expected to work some evenings and weekends but usually are given a day off during the week. Hours can change weekly, and supervisors sometimes must report to work on short notice, especially when employees are absent. Independent owners often can set their own schedules, but hours must be convenient to customers.

Training, Other Qualifications, and Advancement

Sales worker supervisors usually gain knowledge of management principles and practices through work experience. Many supervisors begin their careers on the sales floor as salespersons, cashiers, or customer service representatives. These workers should be patient, decisive, and sales-oriented.

Education and training. The educational backgrounds of sales worker supervisors vary widely. Supervisors who have postsecondary education often hold associate or bachelor's degrees in liberal arts, social sciences, business, or management. Recommended high school or college courses include those related to business, such as accounting, marketing, management, and sales, and those related to social science, such as psychology, sociology, and communication. Supervisors also must know how to use computers because almost all cash registers, inventory control systems, and sales quotes and contracts are computerized. To gain experience, many college students participate in internship programs that usually are developed jointly by schools and businesses.

Having previous sales experience is usually a requirement for becoming a sales worker supervisor. Most sales worker supervisors have retail sales experience or experience as a customer service representative. In these positions, they learn merchandising, customer service, and the basic policies and procedures of the company.

The type and amount of training available to supervisors varies by company. Many national retail chains and companies have formal training programs for management trainees that include both classroom and on-site training. Training time may be as brief as one week or may last more than one year, giving trainees experience during all sales seasons.

Ordinarily, classroom training includes topics such as interviewing, customer service skills, inventory management, employee relations, and scheduling. Management trainees may work in one specific department while training on the job, or they may rotate through several departments to gain a well-rounded knowledge of the company's operation. Training programs for retail franchises are generally extensive, covering all functions of the company's operation, including budgeting, marketing, management, finance, purchasing, product preparation, human resource management, and compensation. College graduates usually can enter management training programs directly, without much experience.

Other qualifications. Sales worker supervisors must get along with all types of people. They need initiative, self-discipline, good judgment, and decisiveness. Patience and a conciliatory temperament are necessary when dealing with demanding customers. Supervisors also must be able to motivate, organize, and direct the work of subordinates and communicate clearly and persuasively with customers and other supervisors.

Advancement. Supervisors who display leadership and team-building skills, self-confidence, motivation, and decisiveness become candidates for promotion to assistant manager or manager. A postsecondary degree may speed their advancement into management because employers view it as a sign of motivation and maturity—qualities deemed important for promotion to more responsible positions. In many retail establishments, managers are promoted from within the company. In small retail establishments, where the number of positions is limited, advancement to a higher management position may come slowly. Large establishments often have extensive career ladder programs and may offer supervisors the opportunity to transfer to another store in the chain or to the central office. Although promotions may occur more quickly in large establishments, some managers may need to relocate every several years in order to advance.

Supervisors also can become advertising, marketing, promotions, public relations, and sales managers—workers who coordinate marketing plans, monitor sales, and propose advertisements and promotions—or purchasing managers, buyers, or purchasing agents—workers who purchase goods and supplies for their organization or for resale.

Some supervisors who have worked in their industry for a long time open their own stores or sales firms. However, retail trade and sales occupations are highly competitive, and although many independent owners succeed, some fail to cover expenses and eventually go out of business. To prosper, owners usually need good business sense and strong customer service and public relations skills.

Employment

Sales worker supervisors held about 2.2 million jobs in 2006. Approximately 37 percent were self-employed, most of whom were store owners. About 44 percent of sales worker supervisors were wage-and-salary workers employed in the retail sector; some of the largest employers were grocery stores, department stores, motor vehicle and parts dealers, and clothing and clothing accessory stores. The remaining sales worker supervisors worked in non-retail establishments.

Job Outlook

Despite slower than average growth, retail sales worker supervisors with previous experience in sales are expected to have good job prospects because of the large size of the occupation and the need to replace workers who leave their positions.

Employment change. Employment of sales worker supervisors is expected to grow by 4 percent between 2006 and 2016, which is more slowly than the average for all occupations. Growth in the occupation will be limited as retail companies increase the responsibilities of retail salespersons and existing sales worker supervisors.

The Internet and electronic commerce are creating new opportunities to reach and communicate with potential customers. Some firms are hiring Internet sales supervisors, who are in charge of maintaining an Internet site and answering inquiries relating to the product, to prices, and to the terms of delivery. However, Internet sales and electronic commerce may reduce the number of additional sales workers needed in stores, thus reducing the total number of additional supervisors required. Overall, the impact of electronic commerce on employment of sales worker supervisors should be minimal.

Projected employment growth of sales worker supervisors will mirror, in part, the patterns of employment growth in the industries in which they work. For example, faster-than-average employment growth is expected in many of the rapidly growing service-providing industries. In contrast, the number of self-employed sales worker supervisors is expected to grow slowly as independent retailers face increasing competition from national chains.

Unlike mid-level and top-level managers, retail store managers generally will not be affected by the restructuring and consolidation taking place at the corporate headquarters of many retail chains.

Job prospects. Candidates who have retail experience—as a salesperson, cashier, or customer service representative, for example—will have the best opportunities for jobs as supervisors, especially in retail establishments. Stronger competition for supervisory jobs is expected in non-retail establishments, particularly those with the most attractive earnings and work environment.

Some of the job openings over the next decade will occur as experienced supervisors move into higher levels of management, transfer to other occupations, or leave the labor force. However, these job openings will not be great in number since, as with other supervisory and managerial occupations, the separation rate is low. This is the case especially for non-retail sales worker supervisors.

Earnings

Salaries of sales worker supervisors vary substantially, depending on a worker's level of responsibility and length of service and the type, size, and location of the firm.

Salaried supervisors of retail sales workers had median annual earnings of $33,960, including commissions, in May 2006. The middle 50 percent earned between $26,490 and $44,570 a year. The lowest 10 percent earned less than $21,420, and the highest 10 percent earned more than $59,710 a year. Median annual earnings in the industries employing the largest numbers of salaried supervisors of retail sales workers were as follows:

Building material and supplies dealers	$35,820
Grocery stores	33,390
Clothing stores	33,140
Gasoline stations	29,270
Other general merchandise stores	28,870

Salaried supervisors of nonretail sales workers had median annual earnings of, $65,510, including commissions, in May 2006. The middle 50 percent earned between $48,900 and $94,670 a year. The lowest 10 percent earned less than $34,840, and the highest 10 percent earned more than $135,270 a year. Median annual earnings in the industries employing the largest numbers of salaried supervisors of nonretail sales workers were as follows:

Professional and commercial equipment and supplies merchant wholesalers	$80,650
Wholesale electronic markets and agents and brokers	78,260
Machinery, equipment, and supplies merchant wholesalers	65,660
Postal service	58,640
Business support services	45,490

Compensation systems vary by type of establishment and by merchandise sold. Many supervisors receive a commission or a combination of salary and commission. Under a commission system, supervisors receive a percentage of department or store sales. Thus, these supervisors' earnings depend on their ability to sell their product and the condition of the economy. Those who sell large amounts of merchandise or exceed sales goals often receive bonuses or other awards.

Related Occupations

Sales worker supervisors serve customers, supervise workers, and direct and coordinate the operations of an establishment. Workers with similar responsibilities include financial managers, food service managers, lodging managers, office and administrative support worker supervisors and managers, and medical and health services managers.

Sources of Additional Information

Information on employment opportunities for sales worker supervisors may be obtained from the employment offices of various retail establishments or from state employment service offices.

Projections data from the National Employment Matrix

Occupational Title	SOC Code	Employment, 2006	Projected employment, 2016	Change, 2006-16	
				Number	Percent
Supervisors, sales workers	41-1000	2,206,000	2,296,000	91,000	4
First-line supervisors/managers of retail sales workers	41-1011	1,676,000	1,747,000	71,000	4
First-line supervisors/managers of non-retail sales workers	41-1012	530,000	549,000	19,000	4

NOTE: Data in this table are rounded.

General information on management careers in retail establishments is available from

▶ National Retail Federation, 325 7th St. NW, Suite 1100, Washington, DC 20004.

Information about management careers and training programs in the motor vehicle dealers industry is available from

▶ National Automobile Dealers Association, Public Relations Dept., 8400 Westpark Dr., McLean, VA 22102-3591. Internet: http://www.nada.org

Information about management careers in convenience stores is available from

▶ National Association of Convenience Stores, 1600 Duke St., Alexandria, VA 22314-3436.

Science Technicians

(O*NET 19-4011.00, 19-4011.01, 19-4011.02, 19-4021.00, 19-4031.00, 19-4041.00, 19-4041.01, 19-4041.02, 19-4051.00, 19-4051.01, 19-4051.02, 19-4091.00, 19-4092.00, 19-4093.00, and 19-4099.99)

Significant Points

■ Science technicians in production jobs can be employed on day, evening, or night shifts; other technicians work outdoors, sometimes in remote locations.

■ Most science technicians need an associate degree or a certificate in applied science or science-related technology; biological and forensic science technicians usually need a bachelor's degree.

■ Projected job growth varies among occupational specialties; for example, forensic science technicians will grow much faster than average, while chemical technicians will grow more slowly than average.

■ Job opportunities are expected to be best for graduates of applied science technology programs who are well trained on equipment used in laboratories or production facilities.

Nature of the Work

Science technicians use the principles and theories of science and mathematics to solve problems in research and development and to help invent and improve products and processes. However, their jobs are more practically oriented than those of scientists. Technicians set up, operate, and maintain laboratory instruments, monitor experiments, make observations, calculate and record results, and often develop conclusions. They must keep detailed logs of all of their work. Those who perform production work monitor manufacturing processes and may ensure quality by testing products for proper proportions of ingredients, for purity, or for strength and durability.

As laboratory instrumentation and procedures have become more complex, the role of science technicians in research and development has expanded. In addition to performing routine tasks, many technicians, under the direction of scientists, now develop and adapt laboratory procedures to achieve the best results, interpret data, and devise solutions to problems. Technicians must develop expert knowledge of laboratory equipment so that they can adjust settings when necessary and recognize when equipment is malfunctioning.

Most science technicians specialize, learning their skills and working in the same disciplines in which scientists work. Occupational titles, therefore, tend to follow the same structure as those for scientists.

Agricultural and food science technicians work with related scientists to conduct research, development, and testing on food and other agricultural products. Agricultural technicians are involved in food, fiber, and animal research, production, and processing. Some conduct tests and experiments to improve the yield and quality of crops or to increase the resistance of plants and animals to disease, insects, or other hazards. Other agricultural technicians breed animals for the purpose of investigating nutrition. Food science technicians assist food scientists and technologists in research and development, production technology, and quality control. For example, food science technicians may conduct tests on food additives and preservatives to ensure compliance with Food and Drug Administration regulations regarding color, texture, and nutrients. These technicians analyze, record, and compile test results; order supplies to maintain laboratory inventory; and clean and sterilize laboratory equipment.

Biological technicians work with biologists studying living organisms. Many assist scientists who conduct medical research—helping to find a cure for cancer or AIDS, for example. Those who work in pharmaceutical companies help develop and manufacture medicine. Those working in the field of microbiology generally work as laboratory assistants, studying living organisms and infectious agents. Biological technicians also analyze organic substances, such as blood, food, and drugs. Biological technicians working in biotechnology apply knowledge and techniques gained from basic research, including gene splicing and recombinant DNA, and apply them to product development.

Chemical technicians work with chemists and chemical engineers, developing and using chemicals and related products and equipment. Generally, there are two types of chemical technicians: research technicians who work in experimental laboratories and process control technicians who work in manufacturing or other industrial plants. Many chemical technicians working in research and development conduct a variety of laboratory procedures, from routine process control to complex research projects. For example, they may collect and analyze samples of air and water to monitor pollution levels, or they may produce compounds through complex organic synthesis. Most *process technicians* work in manufacturing, testing packaging for design, integrity of materials, and environmental acceptability. Often, process technicians who work in plants focus on quality assurance, monitoring product quality or production processes and developing new production techniques. A few work in shipping to provide technical support and expertise.

Environmental science and protection technicians perform laboratory and field tests to monitor environmental resources and determine the contaminants and sources of pollution in the environment. They may collect samples for testing or be involved in abating and controlling sources of environmental pollution. Some are responsible for waste management operations, control and management of hazardous materials inventory, or general activities involving regulatory compliance. Many environmental science technicians employed at private consulting firms work directly under the supervision of an environmental scientist.

Forensic science technicians investigate crimes by collecting and analyzing physical evidence. Often, they specialize in areas such as DNA analysis or firearm examination, performing tests on weapons

© JIST Works

or on substances such as fiber, glass, hair, tissue, and body fluids to determine their significance to the investigation. Proper collection and storage methods are important to protect the evidence. Forensic science technicians also prepare reports to document their findings and the laboratory techniques used, and they may provide information and expert opinions to investigators. When criminal cases come to trial, forensic science technicians often give testimony as expert witnesses on laboratory findings by identifying and classifying substances, materials, and other evidence collected at the scene of a crime. Some forensic science technicians work closely with other experts or technicians. For example, a forensic science technician may consult either a medical expert about the exact time and cause of a death or another technician who specializes in DNA typing in hopes of matching a DNA type to a suspect.

Forest and conservation technicians compile data on the size, content, and condition of forest land. These workers usually work in a forest under the supervision of a forester, doing specific tasks such as measuring timber, supervising harvesting operations, assisting in road building operations, and locating property lines and features. They also may gather basic information, such as data on populations of trees, disease and insect damage, tree seedling mortality, and conditions that may pose a fire hazard. In addition, forest and conservation technicians train and lead forest and conservation workers in seasonal activities, such as planting tree seedlings, and maintaining recreational facilities. Increasing numbers of forest and conservation technicians work in urban forestry—the study of individual trees in cities—and other nontraditional specialties, rather than in forests or rural areas.

Geological and petroleum technicians measure and record physical and geologic conditions in oil or gas wells, using advanced instruments lowered into the wells or analyzing the mud from the wells. In oil and gas exploration, technicians collect and examine geological data or test geological samples to determine their petroleum content and their mineral and element composition. Some petroleum technicians, called scouts, collect information about oil well and gas well drilling operations, geological and geophysical prospecting, and land or lease contracts.

Nuclear technicians operate nuclear test and research equipment, monitor radiation, and assist nuclear engineers and physicists in research. Some also operate remote controlled equipment to manipulate radioactive materials or materials exposed to radioactivity. Workers who control nuclear reactors are classified as *nuclear power reactor operators*, and are not included in this statement.

Other science technicians perform a wide range of activities. Some collect weather information or assist oceanographers; others work as laser technicians or radiographers.

Work environment. Science technicians work under a wide variety of conditions. Most work indoors, usually in laboratories, and have regular hours. Some occasionally work irregular hours to monitor experiments that cannot be completed during regular working hours. Production technicians often work in 8-hour shifts around the clock. Others, such as agricultural, forest and conservation, geological and petroleum, and environmental science and protection technicians, perform much of their work outdoors, sometimes in remote locations.

Advances in automation and information technology require technicians to operate more sophisticated laboratory equipment. Science technicians make extensive use of computers, electronic measuring equipment, and traditional experimental apparatus.

Some science technicians may be exposed to hazards from equipment, chemicals, or toxic materials. Chemical technicians sometimes work with toxic chemicals or radioactive isotopes; nuclear technicians may be exposed to radiation, and biological technicians sometimes work with disease-causing organisms or radioactive agents. Forensic science technicians often are exposed to human body fluids and firearms. However, these working conditions pose little risk if proper safety procedures are followed. For forensic science technicians, collecting evidence from crime scenes can be distressing and unpleasant.

Training, Other Qualifications, and Advancement

Most science technicians need an associate degree or a certificate in applied science or science-related technology. Biological and forensic science technicians usually need a bachelor's degree. Science technicians with a high school diploma and no college degree typically begin work as trainees under the direct supervision of a more experienced technician, and eventually earn a two-year degree in science technology.

Education and training. There are several ways to qualify for a job as a science technician. Many employers prefer applicants who have at least two years of specialized training or an associate degree in applied science or science-related technology. Because employers' preferences vary, however, some science technicians have a bachelor's degree in chemistry, biology, or forensic science or have completed several science and math courses at a four-year college.

Most biological technician jobs, for example, require a bachelor's degree in biology or a closely related field. Forensic science positions also typically require a bachelor's degree to work in the field. Knowledge and understanding of legal procedures also can be helpful. Chemical technician positions in research and development also often have a bachelor's degree, but most chemical process technicians have a two-year degree instead, usually an associate degree in process technology. In some cases, a high school diploma is sufficient. These workers usually receive additional on-the-job training. Entry-level workers whose college training encompasses extensive hands-on experience with a variety of diagnostic laboratory equipment generally require less on-the-job training.

Whatever their degree, science technicians usually need hands-on training either in school or on the job. Most can get good career preparation through two-year formal training programs that combine the teaching of scientific principles and theory with practical hands-on application in a laboratory setting with up-to-date equipment. Graduates of bachelor's degree programs in science who have considerable experience in laboratory-based courses, have completed internships, or have held summer jobs in laboratories also are well qualified for science technician positions and are preferred by some employers.

Job candidates, who have extensive hands-on experience with a variety of laboratory equipment, including computers and related equipment, usually require a short period of on-the-job training. Those with a high school diploma and no college degree typically begin work as trainees under the direct supervision of a more experienced technician. Many with a high school diploma eventually earn a two-year degree in science technology, often paid for by their employer.

Many technical and community colleges offer associate degrees in a specific technology or more general education in science and mathematics. A number of associate degree programs are designed to provide easy transfer to bachelor's degree programs at colleges or universities. Technical institutes usually offer technician training, but they provide less theory and general education than do community colleges. The length of programs at technical institutes varies, although one-year certificate programs and two-year associate degree programs are common. Prospective forestry and conservation technicians can choose from more than 20 associate degree programs in forest technology accredited by the Society of American Foresters.

Approximately 30 colleges and universities offer a bachelor's degree program in forensic science; about another 25 schools offer a bachelor's degree in a natural science with an emphasis on forensic science or criminology; a few additional schools offer a bachelor's degree with an emphasis in a specialty area, such as criminology, pathology, jurisprudence, investigation, odontology, toxicology, or forensic accounting.

Some schools offer cooperative-education or internship programs, allowing students the opportunity to work at a local company or some other workplace while attending classes during alternate terms. Participation in such programs can significantly enhance a student's employment prospects.

People interested in careers as science technicians should take as many high school science and math courses as possible. Science courses taken beyond high school, in an associate or bachelor's degree program, should be laboratory oriented, with an emphasis on bench skills. A solid background in applied chemistry, physics, and math is vital.

Other qualifications. Communication skills are important because technicians are often required to report their findings both orally and in writing. In addition, technicians should be able to work well with others. Because computers often are used in research and development laboratories, technicians should also have strong computer skills, especially in computer modeling. Organizational ability, an eye for detail, and skill in interpreting scientific results are important as well, as are a high mechanical aptitude, attention to detail, and analytical thinking.

Advancement. Technicians usually begin work as trainees in routine positions under the direct supervision of a scientist or a more experienced technician. As they gain experience, technicians take on more responsibility and carry out assignments under only general supervision, and some eventually become supervisors. However, technicians employed at universities often have job prospects tied to those of particular professors; when those professors retire or leave, these technicians face uncertain employment prospects.

Employment

Science technicians held about 267,000 jobs in 2006. As indicated by the following tabulation, chemical and biological technicians accounted for 52 percent of all jobs:

Biological technicians 79,000

Chemical technicians 61,000

Environmental science and protection technicians, including health 37,000

Forest and conservation technicians.....................34,000

Agricultural and food science technicians 26,000

Forensic science technicians 13,000

Geological and petroleum technicians....................12,000

Nuclear technicians 6,500

About 30 percent of biological technicians worked in professional, scientific, or technical services firms; most other biological technicians worked in educational services, federal, state, and local governments, or pharmaceutical and medicine manufacturing. Chemical technicians held jobs in a wide range of manufacturing and service-providing industries. About 39 percent worked in chemical manufacturing and another 30 percent worked in professional, scientific, or technical services firms. Most environmental science and protection technicians worked for state and local governments and professional, scientific, and technical services firms. About 76 percent of forest and conservation technicians held jobs in the federal government, mostly in the Forest Service; another 17 percent worked for state governments. Around 32 percent of agricultural and food science technicians worked in educational services and 20 percent worked for food processing companies; most of the rest were employed in agriculture. Forensic science technicians worked primarily for state and local governments. Approximately 37 percent of all geological and petroleum technicians worked for oil and gas extraction companies and 49 percent of nuclear technicians worked for utilities.

Job Outlook

Employment of science technicians is projected to grow about as fast as the average, although employment change will vary by specialty. Job opportunities are expected to be best for graduates of applied science technology programs who are well trained on equipment used in laboratories or production facilities.

Employment change. Overall employment of science technicians is expected to grow 12 percent during the 2006–2016 decade, about as fast as the average for all occupations. The continued growth of scientific and medical research—particularly research related to biotechnology—will be the primary driver of employment growth, but the development and production of technical products should also stimulate demand for science technicians in many industries.

Employment of biological technicians should increase faster than the average, as the growing number of agricultural and medicinal products developed with the use of biotechnology techniques boosts demand for these workers. Also, an aging population and stronger competition among pharmaceutical companies are expected to contribute to the need for innovative and improved drugs, further spurring demand. Most growth in employment will be in professional, scientific, and technical services and in educational services.

Job growth for chemical technicians is projected to grow more slowly than the average. The chemical manufacturing industry, except pharmaceutical and medicine manufacturing, is anticipated to experience a decline in overall employment as companies downsize and turn to outside contractors to provide specialized services. Some of these contractors will be in other countries with lower average wages, further limiting employment growth. An increasing focus on quality assurance will require a greater number of process technicians, however, stimulating demand for these workers.

Employment of environmental science and protection technicians is expected to grow much faster than the average; these workers will

Projections data from the National Employment Matrix

Occupational Title	SOC Code	Employment, 2006	Projected employment, 2016	Change, 2006-2016	
				Number	Percent
Science technicians	—	267,000	300,000	33,000	12
Agricultural and food science technicians	19-4011	26,000	28,000	1,700	7
Biological technicians	19-4021	79,000	91,000	13,000	16
Chemical technicians	19-4031	61,000	65,000	3,600	6
Geological and petroleum technicians	19-4041	12,000	13,000	1,000	9
Nuclear technicians	19-4051	6,500	6,900	400	7
Environmental science and protection technicians, including health	19-4091	37,000	47,000	10,000	28
Forensic science technicians	19-4092	13,000	17,000	4,000	31
Forest and conservation technicians	19-4093	34,000	33,000	-700	-2

NOTE: Data in this table are rounded.

be needed to help regulate waste products; to collect air, water, and soil samples for measuring levels of pollutants; to monitor compliance with environmental regulations; and to clean up contaminated sites. Over 80 percent of this growth is expected to be in professional, scientific, and technical services as environmental monitoring, management, and regulatory compliance increase.

An expected decline in employment of forest and conservation technicians within the federal government will lead to little or no change in employment in this specialty, due to budgetary constraints and continued reductions in demand for timber management on federal lands. However, opportunities at state and local governments within specialties such as urban forestry may provide some new jobs. In addition, an increased emphasis on specific conservation issues, such as environmental protection, preservation of water resources, and control of exotic and invasive pests, may provide some employment opportunities.

Employment of agricultural and food science technicians is projected to grow about as fast as the average. Research in biotechnology and other areas of agricultural science will increase as it becomes more important to balance greater agricultural output with protection and preservation of soil, water, and the ecosystem. In particular, research will be needed to combat insects and diseases as they adapt to pesticides and as soil fertility and water quality continue to need improvement.

Jobs for forensic science technicians are expected to increase much faster than the average. Employment growth in state and local government should be driven by the increasing application of forensic science to examine, solve, and prevent crime. Crime scene technicians who work for state and county crime labs should experience favorable employment prospects resulting from strong job growth.

Average employment growth is expected for geological and petroleum technicians. Job growth should be strongest in professional, scientific, and technical services firms because geological and petroleum technicians will be needed to assist environmental scientists and geoscientists as they provide consultation services for companies regarding environmental policy and federal government mandates, such as those requiring lower sulfur emissions.

Nuclear technicians should grow about as fast as the average as more are needed to monitor the nation's aging fleet of nuclear reactors and research future advances in nuclear power. Although no new nuclear powerplants have been built for decades in the United States, energy demand has recently renewed interest in this form of electricity generation and may lead to future construction.

Technicians also will be needed to work in defense-related areas, to develop nuclear medical technology, and to improve and enforce waste management and safety standards.

Job prospects. In addition to job openings created by growth, many openings should arise from the need to replace technicians who retire or leave the labor force for other reasons. Job opportunities are expected to be best for graduates of applied science technology programs who are well trained on equipment used in laboratories or production facilities. As the instrumentation and techniques used in industrial research, development, and production become increasingly more complex, employers will seek individuals with highly developed technical skills. Good communication skills are also increasingly sought by employers.

Job opportunities vary by specialty. The best opportunities for agricultural and food science technicians will be in agricultural biotechnology, specifically in research and development on biofuels. Geological and petroleum technicians should experience little competition for positions because of the relatively small number of new entrants. Forensic science technicians with a bachelor's degree in a forensic science will enjoy much better opportunities than those with an associate degree. During periods of economic recession, science technicians may be laid off.

Earnings

Median hourly earnings of science technicians in May 2006 were as follows:

Nuclear technicians	$31.49
Geological and petroleum technicians	22.19
Forensic science technicians	21.79
Chemical technicians	18.87
Environmental science and protection technicians, including health	18.31
Biological technicians	17.17
Agricultural and food science technicians	15.26
Forest and conservation technicians	14.84

In 2007, the average annual salary in the federal government was $40,629 for biological science technicians; $53,026 for physical science technicians; $40,534 for forestry technicians; $54,081 for geodetic technicians; $50,337 for hydrologic technicians; and $63,396 for meteorological technicians.

Related Occupations

Other technicians who apply scientific principles and who usually have a 2-year associate degree include engineering technicians, broadcast and sound engineering technicians and radio operators, drafters, and health technologists and technicians—especially clinical laboratory technologists and technicians, diagnostic medical sonographers, and radiologic technologists and technicians.

Sources of Additional Information

For information about a career as a chemical technician, contact

▶ American Chemical Society, Education Division, Career Publications, 1155 16th St. NW, Washington, DC 20036. Internet: http://www.acs.org

For career information and a list of undergraduate, graduate, and doctoral programs in forensic sciences, contact

▶ American Academy of Forensic Sciences, P.O. Box 669, Colorado Springs, CO 80901. Internet: http://www.aafs.org

For general information on forestry technicians and a list of schools offering education in forestry, send a self-addressed, stamped business envelope to

▶ Society of American Foresters, 5400 Grosvenor Ln., Bethesda, MD 20814. Internet: http://www.safnet.org

Secretaries and Administrative Assistants

(O*NET 43-6011.00, 43-6012.00, 43-6013.00, and 43-6014.00)

Significant Points

■ This occupation is expected to be among those with the largest number of new jobs.

■ Opportunities should be best for applicants with extensive knowledge of software applications.

■ Secretaries and administrative assistants today perform fewer clerical tasks and are increasingly taking on the roles of information and communication managers.

Nature of the Work

As the reliance on technology continues to expand in offices, the role of the office professional has greatly evolved. Office automation and organizational restructuring have led secretaries and administrative assistants to assume responsibilities once reserved for managerial and professional staff. In spite of these changes, however, the core responsibilities for secretaries and administrative assistants have remained much the same: Performing and coordinating an office's administrative activities and storing, retrieving, and integrating information for dissemination to staff and clients.

Secretaries and administrative assistants perform a variety of administrative and clerical duties necessary to run an organization efficiently. They serve as information and communication managers for an office; plan and schedule meetings and appointments; organize and maintain paper and electronic files; manage projects; conduct research; and disseminate information by using the telephone, mail services, Web sites, and e-mail. They also may handle travel and guest arrangements.

Secretaries and administrative assistants use a variety of office equipment, such as fax machines, photocopiers, scanners, and videoconferencing and telephone systems. In addition, secretaries and administrative assistants often use computers to do tasks previously handled by managers and professionals, such as: create spreadsheets; compose correspondence; manage databases; and create presentations, reports, and documents using desktop publishing software and digital graphics. They also may negotiate with vendors, maintain and examine leased equipment, purchase supplies, manage areas such as stockrooms or corporate libraries, and retrieve data from various sources. At the same time, managers and professionals have assumed many tasks traditionally assigned to secretaries and administrative assistants, such as keyboarding and answering the telephone. Because secretaries and administrative assistants do less dictation and word processing, they now have time to support more members of the executive staff. In a number of organizations, secretaries and administrative assistants work in teams to work flexibly and share their expertise.

Many secretaries and administrative assistants now provide training and orientation for new staff, conduct research on the Internet, and operate and troubleshoot new office technologies.

Specific job duties vary with experience and titles. *Executive secretaries and administrative assistants* provide high-level administrative support for an office and for top executives of an organization. Generally, they perform fewer clerical tasks than do secretaries and more information management. In addition to arranging conference calls and supervising other clerical staff, they may handle more complex responsibilities such as reviewing incoming memos, submissions, and reports in order to determine their significance and to plan for their distribution. They also prepare agendas and make arrangements for meetings of committees and executive boards. They also may conduct research and prepare statistical reports.

Some secretaries and administrative assistants, such as legal and medical secretaries, perform highly specialized work requiring knowledge of technical terminology and procedures. For instance, *legal secretaries* prepare correspondence and legal papers such as summonses, complaints, motions, responses, and subpoenas under the supervision of an attorney or a paralegal. They also may review legal journals and assist with legal research—for example, by verifying quotes and citations in legal briefs. Additionally, legal secretaries often teach newly minted lawyers how to prepare documents for submission to the courts. *Medical secretaries* transcribe dictation, prepare correspondence, and assist physicians or medical scientists with reports, speeches, articles, and conference proceedings. They also record simple medical histories, arrange for patients to be hospitalized, and order supplies. Most medical secretaries need to be familiar with insurance rules, billing practices, and hospital or laboratory procedures. Other technical secretaries who assist engineers or scientists may prepare correspondence, maintain their organization's technical library, and gather and edit materials for scientific papers.

Secretaries employed in elementary schools and high schools perform important administrative functions for the school. They are responsible for handling most of the communications between parents, the community, and teachers and administrators who work at the school. As such, they are required to know details about registering students, immunizations, and bus schedules, for example. They schedule appointments, keep track of students' academic records, and make room assignments for classes. Those who work directly for principals screen inquiries from parents and handle those matters not needing a principal's attention. They also may set a principal's calendar to help set her or his priorities for the day.

Work environment. Secretaries and administrative assistants usually work in schools, hospitals, corporate settings, government agencies, or legal and medical offices. Their jobs often involve sitting for long periods. If they spend a lot of time keyboarding, particularly at a computer monitor, they may encounter problems of eyestrain, stress, and repetitive motion ailments such as carpal tunnel syndrome.

Almost one-fifth of secretaries work part time and many others work in temporary positions. A few participate in job-sharing arrangements, in which two people divide responsibility for a single job. The majority of secretaries and administrative assistants, however, are full-time employees who work a standard 40-hour week.

Training, Other Qualifications, and Advancement

Word processing, writing, and communication skills are essential for all secretaries and administrative assistants. However, employers increasingly require extensive knowledge of software applications, such as desktop publishing, project management, spreadsheets, and database management.

Education and training. High school graduates who have basic office skills may qualify for entry-level secretarial positions. They can acquire these skills in various ways. Training ranges from high school vocational education programs that teach office skills and typing to one- and two-year programs in office administration offered by business and vocational-technical schools, and community colleges. Many temporary placement agencies also provide formal training in computer and office skills. Most medical and legal secretaries must go through specialized training programs that teach them the language of the industry.

Employers of executive secretaries increasingly are seeking candidates with a college degree, as these secretaries work closely with top executives. A degree related to the business or industry in which a person is seeking employment may provide the job seeker with an advantage in the application process.

Most secretaries and administrative assistants, once hired, tend to acquire more advanced skills through on-the-job instruction by other employees or by equipment and software vendors. Others may attend classes or participate in online education to learn how to operate new office technologies, such as information storage systems, scanners, or new updated software packages. As office automation continues to evolve, retraining and continuing education will remain integral parts of secretarial jobs.

Other qualifications. Secretaries and administrative assistants should be proficient in typing and good at spelling, punctuation, grammar, and oral communication. Employers also look for good customer service and interpersonal skills because secretaries and administrative assistants must be tactful in their dealings with people. Discretion, good judgment, organizational or management ability, initiative, and the ability to work independently are especially important for higher-level administrative positions. Changes in the office environment have increased the demand for secretaries and administrative assistants who are adaptable and versatile.

Certification and advancement. Testing and certification for proficiency in office skills are available through organizations such as the International Association of Administrative Professionals; National

Association of Legal Secretaries (NALS), Inc.; and Legal Secretaries International, Inc. As secretaries and administrative assistants gain experience, they can earn several different designations. Prominent designations include the Certified Professional Secretary (CPS) and the Certified Administrative Professional (CAP), which can be earned by meeting certain experience or educational requirements and passing an examination. Similarly, those with one year of experience in the legal field, or who have concluded an approved training course and who want to be certified as a legal support professional, can acquire the Accredited Legal Secretary (ALS) designation through a testing process administered by NALS.

NALS offers two additional designations: Professional Legal Secretary (PLS), considered an advanced certification for legal support professionals, and a designation for proficiency as a paralegal. Legal Secretaries International confers the Certified Legal Secretary Specialist (CLSS) designation in areas such as intellectual property, criminal law, civil litigation, probate, and business law to those who have five years of legal experience and pass an examination. In some instances, certain requirements may be waived.

Secretaries and administrative assistants generally advance by being promoted to other administrative positions with more responsibilities. Qualified administrative assistants who broaden their knowledge of a company's operations and enhance their skills may be promoted to senior or executive secretary or administrative assistant, clerical supervisor, or office manager. Secretaries with word processing or data entry experience can advance to jobs as word processing or data entry trainers, supervisors, or managers within their own firms or in a secretarial, word processing, or data entry service bureau. Secretarial and administrative support experience also can lead to jobs such as instructor or sales representative with manufacturers of software or computer equipment. With additional training, many legal secretaries become paralegals.

Employment

Secretaries and administrative assistants held more than 4.2 million jobs in 2006, ranking it among the largest occupations in the U.S. economy. The following tabulation shows the distribution of employment by secretarial specialty:

Secretaries, except legal, medical, and executive	1,940,000
Executive secretaries and administrative assistants	1,618,000
Medical secretaries	408,000
Legal secretaries	275,000

Secretaries and administrative assistants are employed in organizations of every type. Around 9 out of 10 secretaries and administrative assistants are employed in service providing industries, ranging from education and health care to government and retail trade. Most of the rest work for firms engaged in manufacturing or construction.

Job Outlook

Employment of secretaries and administrative assistants is expected to grow about as fast as average for all occupations. Secretaries and administrative assistants will have among the largest numbers of new jobs arise, about 362,000 over the 2006–2016 period. Additional opportunities will result from the need to replace workers who transfer to other occupations or leave this occupation.

Projections data from the National Employment Matrix

Occupational Title	SOC Code	Employment, 2006	Projected employment, 2016	Change, 2006-16	
				Number	Percent
Secretaries and administrative assistants	43-6000	4,241,000	4,603,000	362,000	9
Executive secretaries and administrative assistants	43-6011	1,618,000	1,857,000	239,000	15
Legal secretaries..	43-6012	275,000	308,000	32,000	12
Medical secretaries..	43-6013	408,000	477,000	68,000	17
Secretaries, except legal, medical, and executive	43-6014	1,940,000	1,962,000	22,000	1

NOTE: Data in this table are rounded.

Employment change. Employment of secretaries and administrative assistants is expected to increase about 9 percent, which is about as fast as average for all occupations, between 2006 and 2016. Projected employment varies by occupational specialty. Above average employment growth in the health care and social assistance industry should lead to faster than average growth for medical secretaries, while moderate growth in legal services is projected to lead to average growth in employment of legal secretaries. Employment of executive secretaries and administrative assistants is projected to grow faster than average for all occupations. Growing industries—such as administrative and support services; health care and social assistance; and professional, scientific, and technical services—will continue to generate the most new jobs. Little or no change in employment is expected for secretaries, except legal, medical, or executive, who account for about 46 percent of all secretaries and administrative assistants.

Increasing office automation and organizational restructuring will continue to make secretaries and administrative assistants more productive in coming years. Computers, e-mail, scanners, and voice message systems will allow secretaries and administrative assistants to accomplish more in the same amount of time. The use of automated equipment also is changing the distribution of work in many offices. In some cases, traditional secretarial duties as typing, filing, photocopying, and bookkeeping are being done by clerks in other departments or by the professionals themselves. For example, professionals and managers increasingly do their own word processing and data entry, and handle much of their own correspondence. Also, in some law and medical offices, paralegals and medical assistants are assuming some tasks formerly done by secretaries.

Developments in office technology are certain to continue. However, many secretarial and administrative duties are of a personal, interactive nature and, therefore, are not easily automated. Responsibilities such as planning conferences, working with clients, and instructing staff require tact and communication skills. Because technology cannot substitute for these personal skills, secretaries and administrative assistants will continue to play a key role in most organizations.

As paralegals and medical assistants assume more of the duties traditionally assigned to secretaries, there is a trend in many offices for professionals and managers to replace the traditional arrangement of one secretary per manager with secretaries and administrative assistants who support the work of systems, departments, or units. This approach often means that secretaries and administrative assistants assume added responsibilities and are seen as valuable members of a team.

Job prospects. In addition to jobs created from growth, numerous job opportunities will arise from the need to replace secretaries and administrative assistants who transfer to other occupations, especially exceptionally skilled executive secretaries and administrative assistants who often move into professional occupations. Job opportunities should be best for applicants with extensive knowledge of software applications and for experienced secretaries and administrative assistants. Opportunities also should be very good for those with advanced communication and computer skills. Applicants with a bachelor's degree will be in great demand to act more as managerial assistants and to perform more complex tasks.

Earnings

Median annual earnings of secretaries, except legal, medical, and executive, were $27,450 in May 2006. The middle 50 percent earned between $21,830 and $34,250. The lowest 10 percent earned less than $17,560, and the highest 10 percent earned more than $41,550. Median annual earnings in the industries employing the largest numbers of secretaries, except legal, medical, and executive in May 2006 were

Local government $30,350

General medical and surgical hospitals 28,810

Colleges, universities, and professional schools 28,700

Elementary and secondary schools 28,120

Employment services 26,810

Median annual earnings of executive secretaries and administrative assistants were $37,240 in May 2006. The middle 50 percent earned between $30,240 and $46,160. The lowest 10 percent earned less than $25,190, and the highest 10 percent earned more than $56,740. Median annual earnings in the industries employing the largest numbers of executive secretaries and administrative assistants in May 2006 were

Management of companies and enterprises $41,570

Local government 38,670

Colleges, universities, and professional schools 36,510

State government 35,830

Employment services 31,600

Median annual earnings of legal secretaries were $38,190 in May 2006. The middle 50 percent earned between $29,650 and $48,520. The lowest 10 percent earned less than $23,870, and the highest 10 percent earned more than $58,770. Medical secretaries earned a median annual salary of $28,090 in May 2006. The middle 50 percent earned between $23,250 and $34,210. The lowest 10 percent earned less than $19,750, and the highest 10 percent earned more than $40,870.

Salaries vary a great deal, however, reflecting differences in skill, experience, and level of responsibility. Certification in this field may be rewarded by a higher salary.

Related Occupations

Workers in a number of other occupations also type, record information, and process paperwork. Among them are bookkeeping, accounting, and auditing clerks; receptionists and information clerks; communications equipment operators; court reporters; human resources assistants, except payroll and timekeeping; computer operators; data entry and information processing workers; paralegals and legal assistants; medical assistants; and medical records and health information technicians. A growing number of secretaries and administrative assistants share in managerial and human resource responsibilities. Occupations requiring these skills include office and administrative support worker supervisors and managers; computer and information systems managers; administrative services managers; and human resources, training, and labor relations managers and specialists.

Sources of Additional Information

State employment offices provide information about job openings for secretaries and administrative assistants.

For information on the latest trends in the profession, career development advice, and the CPS or CAP designations, contact

▶ International Association of Administrative Professionals, 10502 NW Ambassador Dr., P.O. Box 20404, Kansas City, MO 64195-0404. Internet: http://www.iaap-hq.org

▶ Association of Executive and Administrative Professionals, Suite G-13, 900 South Washington Street, Falls Church, VA 22406-4009. Internet: http://www.theaeap.com

Information on the CLSS designation can be obtained from

▶ Legal Secretaries International Inc., 2302 Fannin Street, Suite 500, Houston, TX 77002-9136. Internet: http://www.legalsecretaries.org

Information on the ALS, PLS, and paralegal certifications are available from

▶ National Association of Legal Secretaries, Inc., 314 East Third St., Suite 210, Tulsa, OK 74120. Internet: http://www.nals.org

Security Guards and Gaming Surveillance Officers

(O*NET 33-9031.00 and 33-9032.00)

Significant Points

■ Jobs should be plentiful, but competition is expected for higher paying positions at facilities requiring longer periods of training and a high level of security, such as nuclear power plants and weapons installations.

■ Because of limited formal training requirements and flexible hours, this occupation attracts many individuals seeking a second or part-time job.

■ Some positions, such as those of armored car guards, are hazardous.

Nature of the Work

Security guards, also called *security officers*, patrol and inspect property to protect against fire, theft, vandalism, terrorism, and illegal activity. These workers protect their employer's investment, enforce laws on the property, and deter criminal activity and other problems. They use radio and telephone communications to call for assistance from police, fire, or emergency medical services as the situation dictates. Security guards write comprehensive reports outlining their observations and activities during their assigned shift. They also may interview witnesses or victims, prepare case reports, and testify in court.

Although all security guards perform many of the same duties, their specific tasks depend on whether they work in a "static" security position or on a mobile patrol. Guards assigned to static security positions usually stay at one location for a specified length of time. These guards must become closely acquainted with the property and people associated with their station and must often monitor alarms and closed-circuit TV cameras. In contrast, guards assigned to mobile patrol drive or walk from one location to another and conduct security checks within an assigned geographical zone. They may detain or arrest criminal violators, answer service calls concerning criminal activity or problems, and issue traffic violation warnings.

The security guard's job responsibilities also vary with the size, type, and location of the employer. In department stores, guards protect people, records, merchandise, money, and equipment. They often work with undercover store detectives to prevent theft by customers or employees, and help apprehend shoplifting suspects prior to the arrival of the police. Some shopping centers and theaters have officers who patrol their parking lots to deter car thefts and robberies. In office buildings, banks, and hospitals, guards maintain order and protect the institution's customers, staff and property. At air, sea, and rail terminals and other transportation facilities, guards protect people, freight, property, and equipment. Using metal detectors and high-tech equipment, they may screen passengers and visitors for weapons and explosives, ensure that nothing is stolen while a vehicle is being loaded or unloaded, and watch for fires and criminals.

Guards who work in public buildings such as museums or art galleries protect paintings and exhibits by inspecting people and packages entering and leaving the building. In factories, laboratories, government buildings, data processing centers, and military bases, security officers protect information, products, computer codes, and defense secrets and check the credentials of people and vehicles entering and leaving the premises. Guards working at universities, parks, and sports stadiums perform crowd control, supervise parking and seating, and direct traffic. Security guards stationed at the entrance to bars and nightclubs, prevent access by minors, collect cover charges at the door, maintain order among customers, and protect patrons and property.

Armored car guards protect money and valuables during transit. In addition, they protect individuals responsible for making commercial bank deposits from theft or injury. They pick up money or other valuables from businesses to transport to another location. Carrying money between the truck and the business can be extremely hazardous. As a result, armored car guards usually wear bulletproof vests.

Gaming surveillance officers, also known as *surveillance agents*, and *gaming investigators* act as security agents for casino managers and patrons. Using primarily audio and video equipment in an observation room, they observe casino operations for irregular activities, such as cheating or theft, and monitor compliance to rules, regulations and laws. They maintain and organize recordings from security cameras as they are sometimes used as evidence in police investigations. Some casinos use a catwalk over one-way mirrors located above the casino floor to augment electronic surveillance equipment. Surveillance agents occasionally leave the surveillance room and walk the casino floor.

All security officers must show good judgment and common sense, follow directions, testify accurately in court, and follow company policy and guidelines. In an emergency, they must be able to take charge and direct others to safety. In larger organizations, a security manager might oversee a group of security officers. In smaller organizations, however, a single worker may be solely responsible for all security.

Work environment. Most security guards and gaming surveillance officers spend considerable time on their feet, either assigned to a specific post or patrolling buildings and grounds. Guards may be stationed at a guard desk inside a building to monitor electronic security and surveillance devices or to check the credentials of people entering or leaving the premises. They also may be stationed at a guardhouse outside the entrance to a gated facility or community and may use a portable radio or cellular telephone to be in constant contact with a central station. The work usually is routine, but guards must be constantly alert for threats to themselves and the property they are protecting. Guards who work during the day may have a great deal of contact with other employees and the public. Gaming surveillance officers often work behind a bank of monitors controlling numerous cameras in a casino and thus can develop eyestrain.

Guards usually work shifts of 8 hours or longer for 40 hours per week and are often on call in case of an emergency. Some employers offer three shifts, and guards rotate to divide daytime, weekend, and holiday work equally. Guards usually eat on the job instead of taking a regular break away from the site. In 2006, about 15 percent of guards worked part time, and some held a second job as a guard to supplement their primary earnings.

Training, Other Qualifications, and Advancement

Generally, there are no specific education requirements for security guards, but employers usually prefer to fill armed guard positions with people who have at least a high school diploma. Gaming surveillance officers often need some education beyond high school. In most states, guards must be licensed.

Education and training. Many employers of unarmed guards do not have any specific educational requirements. For armed guards, employers usually prefer individuals who are high school graduates or who hold an equivalent certification.

Many employers give newly hired guards instruction before they start the job and provide on-the-job training. The amount of training guards receive varies. Training is more rigorous for armed guards because their employers are legally responsible for any use of force. Armed guards receive formal training in areas such as weapons retention and laws covering the use of force. They may be periodically tested in the use of firearms.

An increasing number of states are making ongoing training a legal requirement for retention of licensure. Guards may receive training in protection, public relations, report writing, crisis deterrence, first aid, and specialized training relevant to their particular assignment.

The American Society for Industrial Security International has written voluntary training guidelines that are intended to provide regulating bodies consistent minimum standards for the quality of security services. These guidelines recommend that security guards receive at least 48 hours of training within the first 100 days of employment. The guidelines also suggest that security guards be required to pass a written or performance examination covering topics such as sharing information with law enforcement, crime prevention, handling evidence, the use of force, court testimony, report writing, interpersonal and communication skills, and emergency response procedures. In addition, they recommend annual retraining and additional firearms training for armed officers.

Guards who are employed at establishments that place a heavy emphasis on security usually receive extensive formal training. For example, guards at nuclear power plants undergo several months of training before going on duty—and even then, they perform their tasks under close supervision for a significant period of time. They are taught to use firearms, administer first aid, operate alarm systems and electronic security equipment, and spot and deal with security problems.

Gaming surveillance officers and investigators usually need some training beyond high school but not usually a bachelor's degree. Several educational institutes offer certification programs. Classroom training usually is conducted in a casino-like atmosphere and includes the use of surveillance camera equipment. Previous security experience is a plus. Employers prefer either individuals with casino experience and significant knowledge of casino operations or those with law enforcement and investigation experience.

Licensure. Most states require that guards be licensed. To be licensed as a guard, individuals must usually be at least 18 years old, pass a background check, and complete classroom training in such subjects as property rights, emergency procedures, and detention of suspected criminals. Drug testing often is required and may be random and ongoing.

Guards who carry weapons must be licensed by the appropriate government authority, and some receive further certification as special police officers, allowing them to make limited types of arrests while on duty. Armed guard positions have more stringent background checks and entry requirements than those of unarmed guards.

Other qualifications. Most jobs require a driver's license. For positions as armed guards, employers often seek people who have had responsible experience in other occupations.

Rigorous hiring and screening programs consisting of background, criminal record, and fingerprint checks are becoming the norm in the occupation. Applicants are expected to have good character references, no serious police record, and good health. They should be mentally alert, emotionally stable, and physically fit to cope with emergencies. Guards who have frequent contact with the public should communicate well.

Like security guards, gaming surveillance officers and gaming investigators must have keen observation skills and excellent verbal and writing abilities to document violations or suspicious behavior. They also need to be physically fit and have quick reflexes because they sometimes must detain individuals until local law enforcement officials arrive.

Advancement. Compared with unarmed security guards, armed guards and special police usually enjoy higher earnings and benefits, greater job security, and more potential for advancement. Because many people do not stay long in this occupation, opportunities for advancement are good for those who make a career in security. Most large organizations use a military type of ranking that offers the possibility of advancement in both position and salary. Some guards may advance to supervisor or security manager positions. Guards with management skills may open their own contract security guard agencies. Guards can also move to an organization with more stringent security and higher pay.

Employment

Security guards and gaming surveillance officers held over 1 million jobs in 2006. More than half of all jobs for security guards were in investigation and security services, including guard and armored car services. These organizations provide security on a contract basis, assigning their guards to buildings and other sites as needed. Most other security officers were employed directly by educational services, hospitals, food services and drinking places, traveler accommodation (hotels), department stores, manufacturing firms, lessors of real estate (residential and nonresidential buildings), and governments. Guard jobs are found throughout the country, most commonly in metropolitan areas.

Gaming surveillance officers work primarily in gambling industries; traveler accommodation, which includes casino hotels; and local government. They are employed only in those states and on those Indian reservations where gambling is legal.

A significant number of law enforcement officers work as security guards when they are off duty, in order to supplement their incomes. Often working in uniform and with the official cars assigned to them, they add a high-profile security presence to the establishment with which they have contracted. At construction sites and apartment complexes, for example, their presence often deters crime. (Police and detectives are discussed elsewhere in this book.)

Job Outlook

Opportunities for security guards and gaming surveillance officers should be favorable. Numerous job openings will stem from employment growth, driven by the demand for increased security, and from the need to replace those who leave this large occupation each year.

Employment change. Employment of security guards is expected to grow by 17 percent between 2006 and 2016, which is faster than the average for all occupations. This occupation will have a very large number of new jobs arise, about 175,000 over the projections decade. Concern about crime, vandalism, and terrorism continues to increase the need for security. Demand for guards also will grow as private security firms increasingly perform duties—such as providing security at public events and in residential neighborhoods—that were formerly handled by police officers.

Employment of gaming surveillance officers is expected to grow by 34 percent between 2006 and 2016, which is much faster than

the average for all occupations. Casinos will continue to hire more surveillance officers as more states legalize gambling and as the number of casinos increases in states where gambling is already legal. In addition, casino security forces will employ more technically trained personnel as technology becomes increasingly important in thwarting casino cheating and theft.

Job prospects. Job prospects for security guards should be excellent because of growing demand for these workers and the need to replace experienced workers who leave the occupation. In addition to full-time job opportunities, the limited training requirements and flexible hours attract many people seeking part-time or second jobs. However, competition is expected for higher paying positions that require longer periods of training; these positions usually are found at facilities that require a high level of security, such as nuclear power plants or weapons installations. Job prospects for gaming surveillance officers should be good, but they will be better for those with experience in the gaming industry.

Earnings

Median annual wage-and-salary earnings of security guards were $21,530 in May 2006. The middle 50 percent earned between $17,620 and $27,430. The lowest 10 percent earned less than $15,030, and the highest 10 percent earned more than $35,840. Median annual earnings in the industries employing the largest numbers of security guards were

General medical and surgical hospitals $26,610
Elementary and secondary schools 26,290
Local government 24,950
Investigation, guard and armored car services 20,280

Gaming surveillance officers and gaming investigators had median annual wage-and-salary earnings of $27,130 in May 2006. The middle 50 percent earned between $21,600 and $35,970. The lowest 10 percent earned less than $18,720, and the highest 10 percent earned more than $45,940.

Related Occupations

Guards protect property, maintain security, and enforce regulations and standards of conduct in the establishments at which they work. Related security and protective service occupations include correctional officers, police and detectives, private detectives and investigators, and gaming services occupations.

Sources of Additional Information

Further information about work opportunities for guards is available from local security and guard firms and state employment service offices. Information about licensing requirements for guards may be obtained from the state licensing commission or the state police department. In states where local jurisdictions establish licensing

Projections data from the National Employment Matrix

Occupational Title	SOC Code	Employment, 2006	Projected employment, 2016	Change, 2006-16	
				Number	Percent
Security guards and gaming surveillance officers............................	33-9030	1,049,000	1,227,000	178,000	17
Gaming surveillance officers and gaming investigators	33-9031	8,700	12,000	2,900	34
Security guards..	33-9032	1,040,000	1,216,000	175,000	17

NOTE: Data in this table are rounded.

requirements, contact a local government authority such as the sheriff, county executive, or city manager.

Sheet Metal Workers

(O*NET 47-2211.00)

Significant Points

■ About 66 percent of sheet metal workers are found in the construction industry; around 21 percent are in manufacturing.

■ Workers learn through informal on-the-job training or formal apprenticeship programs.

■ Job opportunities in construction should be good, particularly for individuals who have apprenticeship training or who are certified welders; applicants for jobs in manufacturing may experience competition.

Nature of the Work

Sheet metal workers make, install, and maintain heating, ventilation, and air-conditioning duct systems; roofs; siding; rain gutters; downspouts; skylights; restaurant equipment; outdoor signs; railroad cars; tailgates; customized precision equipment; and many other products made from metal sheets. They also may work with fiberglass and plastic materials. Although some workers specialize in fabrication, installation, or maintenance, most do all three jobs. Sheet metal workers do both construction-related work and mass production of sheet metal products in manufacturing.

Sheet metal workers first study plans and specifications to determine the kind and quantity of materials they will need. They then measure, cut, bend, shape, and fasten pieces of sheet metal to make ductwork, countertops, and other custom products. In an increasing number of shops, sheet metal workers use computerized metalworking equipment. This enables them to perform their tasks more quickly and to experiment with different layouts to find the one that wastes the least material. They cut, drill, and form parts with computer-controlled saws, lasers, shears, and presses.

In shops without computerized equipment, and for products that cannot be made on such equipment, sheet metal workers make the required calculations and use tapes, rulers, and other measuring devices for layout work. They then cut or stamp the parts on machine tools.

Before assembling pieces, sheet metal workers check each part for accuracy using measuring instruments such as calipers and micrometers and, if necessary, finish pieces using hand, rotary, or squaring shears and hacksaws. After inspecting the pieces, workers fasten seams and joints together with welds, bolts, cement, rivets, solder, specially formed sheet metal drive clips, or other connecting devices. They then take the parts to the construction site, where they further assemble the pieces as they install them. These workers install ducts, pipes, and tubes by joining them end to end and hanging them with metal hangers secured to a ceiling or a wall. They also use shears, hammers, punches, and drills to make parts at the worksite or to alter parts made in the shop.

Some jobs are done completely at the jobsite. When installing a metal roof, for example, sheet metal workers usually measure and cut the roofing panels on site. They secure the first panel in place and interlock and fasten the grooved edge of the next panel into the grooved edge of the first. Then, they nail or weld the free edge of the panel to the structure. This two-step process is repeated for each additional panel. Finally, the workers fasten machine-made molding at joints, along corners, and around windows and doors for a neat, finished effect.

In addition to installation, some sheet metal workers specialize in testing, balancing, adjusting, and servicing existing air-conditioning and ventilation systems to make sure they are functioning properly and to improve their energy efficiency. Properly installed duct systems are a key component to heating, ventilation, and air-conditioning (HVAC) systems; sometimes duct installers are called *HVAC technicians*. A growing activity for sheet metal workers is building commissioning, which is a complete mechanical inspection of a building's HVAC, water, and lighting systems.

Sheet metal workers in manufacturing plants make sheet metal parts for products such as aircraft or industrial equipment. Although some of the fabrication techniques used in large-scale manufacturing are similar to those used in smaller shops, the work may be highly automated and repetitive. Sheet metal workers doing such work may be responsible for reprogramming the computer control systems of the equipment they operate.

Work environment. Sheet metal workers usually work a 40-hour week. Those who fabricate sheet metal products work in shops that are well-lighted and well-ventilated. However, they stand for long periods and lift heavy materials and finished pieces. Sheet metal workers must follow safety practices because working around high-speed machines can be dangerous. They also are subject to cuts from sharp metal, burns from soldering and welding, and falls from ladders and scaffolds. They are often required to wear safety glasses and must not wear jewelry or loose-fitting clothing that could easily be caught in a machine. They may work at a variety of different production stations to reduce the repetitiveness of the work.

Those performing installation work do considerable bending, lifting, standing, climbing, and squatting, sometimes in close quarters or awkward positions. Although duct systems and kitchen equipment are installed indoors, the installation of siding, roofs, and gutters involves much outdoor work, exposing sheet metal workers to various kinds of weather.

Training, Other Qualifications, and Advancement

Sheet metal workers learn their trade through both formal apprenticeships and informal on-the-job training programs. Formal apprenticeships are more likely to be found in construction.

Education and training. To become a skilled sheet metal construction worker usually takes between four and five years of both classroom and on-the-job training. While there are a number of different ways to obtain this training, generally the more formalized the training received by an individual, the more thoroughly skilled they become, and the more likely they are to be in demand by employers. For some, this training begins in a high school, where classes in English, algebra, geometry, physics, mechanical drawing and blueprint reading, and general shop are recommended.

After high school, there are a number of different ways to train. One way is to get a job with a contractor who will provide training on the job. Entry-level workers generally start as helpers, assisting more experienced workers. Most begin by carrying metal and cleaning up debris in a metal shop while they learn about materials and tools and their uses. Later, they learn to operate machines that bend or cut metal. In time, helpers go out on the jobsite to learn installation. Employers may send the employee to courses at a trade or vocational school or community college to receive further formal training. Helpers may be promoted to the journey level if they show the requisite knowledge and skills. Most sheet metal workers in large-scale manufacturing receive on-the-job training, with additional class work or in-house training as necessary. The training needed to become proficient in manufacturing takes less time than the training in construction.

Some employers, particularly large nonresidential construction contractors with union membership, offer formal apprenticeships. These programs combine paid on-the-job training with related classroom instruction. Usually, apprenticeship applicants must be at least 18 years old and meet local requirements. The length of the program, usually four to five years, varies with the apprentice's skill. Apprenticeship programs provide comprehensive instruction in both sheet metal fabrication and installation. They may be administered by local joint committees composed of the Sheet Metal Workers' International Association and local chapters of the Sheet Metal and Air-Conditioning Contractors National Association.

Sheet metal workers can choose one of many specialties. Workers can specialize in commercial and residential HVAC installation and maintenance, industrial welding and fabrication, exterior or architectural sheet metal installation, sign fabrication, and testing and balancing of building systems.

On the job, apprentices first receive safety training and then training in tasks that allow them to immediately begin work. They learn the basics of pattern layout and how to cut, bend, fabricate, and install sheet metal. They begin by learning to install and maintain basic ductwork and gradually advance to more difficult jobs, such as making more complex ducts, commercial kitchens, and decorative pieces. They also use materials such as fiberglass, plastics, and other nonmetallic materials. Workers often focus on a sheet metal specialty. In the classroom, apprentices learn drafting, plan and specification reading, trigonometry and geometry applicable to layout work, welding, the use of computerized equipment, and the principles of heating, air-conditioning, and ventilation systems. In addition, apprentices learn the relationship between sheet metal work and other construction work.

Other qualifications. Sheet metal workers need to be in good physical condition and have mechanical and mathematical aptitude and good reading skills. Good eye-hand coordination, spatial and form perception, and manual dexterity also are important. Courses in algebra, trigonometry, geometry, mechanical drawing, and shop provide a helpful background for learning the trade, as does related work experience obtained in the U.S. Armed Services.

It is important for experienced sheet metal workers to keep abreast of new technological developments, such as the use of computerized layout and laser-cutting machines. Workers often take additional training, provided by the union or by their employer, to improve existing skills or to acquire new ones.

Certification and advancement. Certifications in one of the specialties can be beneficial to workers. Certifications related to sheet metal specialties are offered by a wide variety of associations, some of which are listed in the sources of more information at the end of this statement. Those that complete registered apprenticeships are certified as journey workers, which can help to prove their skills to employers.

Sheet metal workers in construction may advance to supervisory jobs. Some of these workers take additional training in welding and do more specialized work. Workers who perform building and system testing are able to move into construction and building inspection. Others go into the contracting business for themselves. Because a sheet metal contractor must have a shop with equipment to fabricate products, this type of contracting business is more expensive to start than other types of construction contracting.

Sheet metal workers in manufacturing may advance to positions as supervisors or quality inspectors. Some of these workers may move into other management positions.

Employment

Sheet metal workers held about 189,000 jobs in 2006. About 66 percent of all sheet metal workers were in the construction industry, including 45 percent who worked for plumbing, heating, and air-conditioning contractors; most of the rest in construction worked for roofing and sheet metal contractors. Some worked for other special trade contractors and for general contractors engaged in residential and commercial building.

About 21 percent of all sheet metal workers were in manufacturing industries, such as the fabricated metal products, machinery, and aerospace products and parts industries. Some sheet metal workers work for the federal government.

Compared with workers in most construction craft occupations, relatively few sheet metal workers are self-employed.

Job Outlook

Average employment growth is projected. Job opportunities in construction should be good, particularly for individuals who have apprenticeship training or who are certified welders; applicants for jobs in manufacturing may experience competition.

Employment change.

Employment of sheet metal workers is expected to increase 7 percent between 2006 and 2016, about as fast as the average for all occupations. This reflects growth in the number of industrial, commercial, and residential structures being built. The need to install energy-efficient air-conditioning, heating, and ventilation systems in older buildings and to perform other types of renovation and maintenance work also should boost employment. In addition, the popularity of decorative sheet metal products and increased architectural restoration are expected to add to the demand for sheet metal workers.

Job prospects. Job opportunities are expected to be good for sheet metal workers in the construction industry, reflecting both employment growth and openings arising each year as experienced sheet metal workers leave the occupation. Opportunities should be particularly good for individuals who have apprenticeship training or who are certified welders. Applicants for jobs in manufacturing may experience competition because a number of manufacturing plants that employ sheet metal workers are moving to other countries and the plants that remain are becoming more productive.

Sheet metal workers in construction may experience periods of unemployment, particularly when construction projects end and economic conditions dampen construction activity. Nevertheless, employment of sheet metal workers is less sensitive to declines in new construction than is the employment of some other construction

Projections data from the National Employment Matrix

Occupational Title	SOC Code	Employment, 2006	Projected employment, 2016	Change, 2006-16	
				Number	Percent
Sheet metal workers	47-2211	189,000	201,000	13,000	7

NOTE: Data in this table are rounded.

workers, such as carpenters. Maintenance of existing equipment—which is less affected by economic fluctuations than is new construction—makes up a large part of the work done by sheet metal workers. Installation of new air-conditioning and heating systems in existing buildings continues during construction slumps, as individuals and businesses adopt more energy-efficient equipment to cut utility bills. In addition, a large proportion of sheet metal installation and maintenance is done indoors, so sheet metal workers usually lose less worktime due to bad weather than other construction workers.

Earnings

In May 2006, median hourly earnings of wage and salary sheet metal workers were $17.96. The middle 50 percent earned between $13.30 and $24.89. The lowest 10 percent of all sheet metal workers earned less than $10.36, and the highest 10 percent earned more than $32.30. The median hourly earnings of the largest industries employing sheet metal workers were

Building finishing contractors $18.84

Plumbing, heating, and air-conditioning
contractors 18.60

Roofing contractors 17.27

Architectural and structural metals manufacturing 16.60

Apprentices normally start at about 40 to 50 percent of the rate paid to experienced workers. As apprentices acquire more skills, they receive periodic pay increases until their pay approaches that of experienced workers. In addition, union workers in some areas receive supplemental wages from the union when they are on layoff or shortened work weeks.

Related Occupations

To fabricate and install sheet metal products, sheet metal workers combine metalworking skills and knowledge of construction materials and techniques. Other occupations in which workers lay out and fabricate metal products include assemblers and fabricators; machinists; machine setters, operators, and tenders—metal and plastic; and tool and die makers. Construction occupations requiring similar skills and knowledge include glaziers and heating, air-conditioning, and refrigeration mechanics and installers.

Sources of Additional Information

For more information about apprenticeships or other work opportunities, contact local sheet metal contractors or heating, refrigeration, and air-conditioning contractors; a local of the Sheet Metal Workers International Association; a local of the Sheet Metal and Air-Conditioning Contractors National Association; a local joint union-management apprenticeship committee; or the nearest office of your state employment service or apprenticeship agency. You can also find information on the registered apprenticeship system with links to state apprenticeship programs on the U.S. Department of Labor's Web site: http://www.doleta.gov/atels_bat. Apprenticeship

information is also available from the U.S. Department of Labor's toll free helpline: 1 (877) 872-5627.

For general and training information about sheet metal workers, contact

▸ International Training Institute for the Sheet Metal and Air-Conditioning Industry, 601 N. Fairfax St., Suite 240, Alexandria, VA 22314. Internet: http://www.sheetmetal-iti.org

▸ National Center for Construction Education and Research, P.O. Box 141104, Gainesville, FL 32614. Internet: http://www.nccer.org

▸ Sheet Metal and Air-Conditioning Contractors' National Association, 4201 Lafayette Center Dr., Chantilly, VA 20151. Internet: http://www.smacna.org

▸ Sheet Metal Workers International Association, 1750 New York Ave. NW, Washington, DC 20006. Internet: http://www.smwia.org

For general information on apprenticeships and how to get them, see the *Occupational Outlook Quarterly* article "Apprenticeships: Career training, credentials—and a paycheck in your pocket," online at http://www.bls.gov/opub/ooq/2002/summer/art01.pdf and in print at many libraries and career centers.

Social and Human Service Assistants

(O*NET 21-1093.00)

Significant Points

■ A bachelor's degree usually is not required for these jobs, but employers increasingly seek individuals with relevant work experience or education beyond high school.

■ Employment is projected to grow much faster than average for all occupations.

■ Job opportunities should be excellent, particularly for applicants with appropriate postsecondary education, but wages remain low.

Nature of the Work

Social and human service assistants help social workers, health care workers, and other professionals to provide services to people. Social and human service assistant is a generic term for workers with a wide array of job titles, including human service worker, case management aide, social work assistant, community support worker, mental health aide, community outreach worker, life skills counselor, or gerontology aide. They usually work under the direction of workers from a variety of fields, such as nursing, psychiatry, psychology, rehabilitative or physical therapy, or social work. The amount of responsibility and supervision they are given varies a great deal. Some have little direct supervision—they may run a group home, for example. Others work under close direction.

Social and human service assistants provide services to clients to help them improve their quality of life. They assess clients' needs, investigate their eligibility for benefits and services such as food stamps, Medicaid, or welfare, and help to obtain them. They also arrange for transportation and escorts, if necessary, and provide emotional support. Social and human service assistants monitor and keep case records on clients and report progress to supervisors and case managers.

Social and human service assistants play a variety of roles in a community. They may organize and lead group activities, assist clients in need of counseling or crisis intervention, or administer food banks or emergency fuel programs, for example. In halfway houses, group homes, and government-supported housing programs, they assist adults who need supervision with personal hygiene and daily living skills. They review clients' records, ensure that they take their medication, talk with family members, and confer with medical personnel and other caregivers to provide insight into clients' needs. Social and human service assistants also give emotional support and help clients become involved in community recreation programs and other activities.

In psychiatric hospitals, rehabilitation programs, and outpatient clinics, social and human service assistants work with psychiatrists, psychologists, social workers, and others to help clients master everyday living skills, communicate more effectively, and live well with others. They support the client's participation in a treatment plan, such as individual or group counseling or occupational therapy.

The work, while satisfying, can be emotionally draining. Understaffing and relatively low pay may add to the pressure.

Work environment. Working conditions of social and human service assistants vary. Some work in offices, clinics, and hospitals, while others work in group homes, shelters, sheltered workshops, and day programs. Traveling to see clients is also required for some jobs. Sometimes working with clients can be dangerous even though most agencies do everything they can to ensure their workers' safety. Most assistants work 40 hours a week; some work in the evening and on weekends.

Training, Other Qualifications, and Advancement

A bachelor's degree is not required for most jobs in this occupation, but employers increasingly seek individuals with relevant work experience or education beyond high school.

Education and training. Many employers prefer to hire people with some education beyond high school. Certificates or associate degrees in subjects such as human services, gerontology or one of the social or behavioral sciences meet many employers' requirements. Some jobs may require a bachelor's or master's degree in human services or a related field, such as counseling, rehabilitation, or social work.

Human services degree programs have a core curriculum that trains students to observe patients and record information, conduct patient interviews, implement treatment plans, employ problem-solving techniques, handle crisis intervention matters, and use proper case management and referral procedures. Many programs utilize field work to give students hands-on experience. General education courses in liberal arts, sciences, and the humanities also are part of most curriculums. Most programs also offer specialized courses related to addictions, gerontology, child protection, and other areas.

Many degree programs require completion of a supervised internship.

The level of education workers have often influence the kind of work they are assigned and the degree of responsibility that is given to them. For example, workers with no more than a high school education are likely to receive extensive on-the-job training to work in direct-care services, helping clients to fill out paperwork, for example. Workers with a college degree, however, might do supportive counseling, coordinate program activities, or manage a group home. Social and human service assistants with proven leadership ability, especially from paid or volunteer experience in social services, often have greater autonomy in their work. Regardless of the academic or work background of employees, most employers provide some form of in-service training to their employees such as seminars and workshops.

Other qualifications. These workers should have a strong desire to help others, effective communication skills, a sense of responsibility, and the ability to manage time effectively. Many human services jobs involve direct contact with people who are vulnerable to exploitation or mistreatment; so patience and understanding are also highly valued characteristics.

It is becoming more common for employers to require a criminal background check, and in some settings, workers may be required to have a valid driver's license.

Advancement. Formal education is almost always necessary for advancement. In general, advancement to case management, rehabilitation, or social work jobs requires a bachelor's or master's degree in human services, counseling, rehabilitation, social work, or a related field.

Employment

Social and human service assistants held about 339,000 jobs in 2006. Over 60 percent were employed in the health care and social assistance industries. Nearly 3 in 10 were employed by state and local governments, primarily in public welfare agencies and facilities for mentally disabled and developmentally challenged individuals.

Job Outlook

Employment of social and human service assistants is expected to grow by nearly 34 percent through 2016. Job prospects are expected to be excellent, particularly for applicants with appropriate postsecondary education.

Employment change. The number of social and human service assistants is projected to grow by nearly 34 percent between 2006 and 2016, which is much faster than the average for all occupations. This occupation will have a very large number of new jobs arise, about 114,000 over the projections decade. Faced with rapid growth in the demand for social and human services, many employers increasingly rely on social and human service assistants.

Demand for social services will expand with the growing elderly population, who are more likely to need adult day care, meal delivery programs, support during medical crises, and other services. In addition, more social and human service assistants will be needed to provide services to pregnant teenagers, people who are homeless, people who are mentally disabled or developmentally challenged, and people who are substance abusers.

Projections data from the National Employment Matrix

Occupational Title	SOC Code	Employment, 2006	Projected employment, 2016	Change, 2006-2016	
				Number	Percent
Social and human service assistants	21-1093	339,000	453,000	114,000	34

NOTE: Data in this table are rounded.

Job training programs are also expected to require additional social and human service assistants. As social welfare policies shift focus from benefit-based programs to work-based initiatives, there will be more demand for people to teach job skills to the people who are new to, or returning to, the workforce.

Residential care establishments should face increased pressures to respond to the needs of the mentally and physically disabled. The number of people who are disabled is increasing, and many need help to care for themselves. More community-based programs and supportive independent-living sites are expected to be established to house and assist the homeless and the mentally and physically disabled. Furthermore, as substance abusers are increasingly being sent to treatment programs instead of prison, employment of social and human service assistants in substance abuse treatment programs also will grow.

Opportunities are expected to be good in private social service agencies. Employment in private agencies will grow as state and local governments continue to contract out services to the private sector in an effort to cut costs. Also, some private agencies have been employing more social and human service assistants in place of social workers, who are more educated and more highly paid.

The number of jobs for social and human service assistants in local governments will grow but not as fast as employment for social and human service assistants in other industries. Employment in the public sector may fluctuate with the level of funding provided by state and local governments and with the number of services contracted out to private organizations.

Job prospects. Job prospects for social and human service assistants are expected to be excellent, particularly for individuals with appropriate education after high school. Job openings will come from job growth, but also from the need to replace workers who advance into new positions, retire, or leave the workforce for other reasons. There will be more competition for jobs in urban areas than in rural ones, but qualified applicants should have little difficulty finding employment.

Earnings

Median annual earnings of social and human service assistants were $25,580 in May 2006. The middle 50 percent earned between $20,350 and $32,440. The top 10 percent earned more than $40,780, while the lowest 10 percent earned less than $16,180.

Median annual earnings in the industries employing the largest numbers of social and human service assistants in May 2006 were

Local government	$30,510
State government	29,810
Individual and family services	24,490
Vocational rehabilitation services	22,530
Residential mental retardation, mental health and substance abuse facilities	22,380

Related Occupations

Workers in other occupations that require skills similar to those of social and human service assistants include social workers, clergy, counselors, child care workers; occupational therapist assistants and aides, physical therapist assistants and aides, and nursing, psychiatric, and home health aides.

Sources of Additional Information

For information on programs and careers in human services, contact

▶ Council for Standards in Human Services Education, PMB 703, 1050 Larrabee Avenue, Suite 104, Bellingham, WA 98225-7367. Internet: http://www.cshse.org

▶ National Organization for Human Services, 90 Madison Street, Suite 206, Denver, CO 80206. Internet: http://www.nationalhumanservices.org

Information on job openings may be available from state employment service offices or directly from city, county, or state departments of health, mental health and mental retardation, and human resources.

Surgical Technologists

(O*NET 29-2055.00)

Significant Points

■ Employment is expected to grow much faster than average.

■ Job opportunities will be best for technologists who are certified.

■ Training programs last 9 to 24 months and lead to a certificate, diploma, or associate degree.

■ Hospitals will continue to be the primary employer, although much faster employment growth is expected in other health care industries.

Nature of the Work

Surgical technologists, also called scrubs and surgical or operating room technicians, assist in surgical operations under the supervision of surgeons, registered nurses, or other surgical personnel. Surgical technologists are members of operating room teams, which most commonly include surgeons, anesthesiologists, and circulating nurses.

Before an operation, surgical technologists help prepare the operating room by setting up surgical instruments and equipment, sterile drapes, and sterile solutions. They assemble both sterile and nonsterile equipment, as well as check and adjust it to ensure it is working properly. Technologists also get patients ready for surgery by washing, shaving, and disinfecting incision sites. They transport patients to the operating room, help position them on the operating table, and cover them with sterile surgical drapes. Technologists also observe patients' vital signs, check charts, and help the surgical team put on sterile gowns and gloves.

During surgery, technologists pass instruments and other sterile supplies to surgeons and surgeon assistants. They may hold retractors, cut sutures, and help count sponges, needles, supplies, and instruments. Surgical technologists help prepare, care for, and dispose of specimens taken for laboratory analysis and help apply dressings. Some operate sterilizers, lights, or suction machines, and help operate diagnostic equipment.

After an operation, surgical technologists may help transfer patients to the recovery room and clean and restock the operating room.

Certified surgical technologists with additional specialized education or training also may act in the role of the surgical first assistant or circulator. The surgical first assistant, as defined by the American College of Surgeons (ACS), provides aid in exposure, hemostasis (controlling blood flow and stopping or preventing hemorrhage), and other technical functions under the surgeon's direction that help the surgeon carry out a safe operation. A circulating technologist is the "unsterile" member of the surgical team who interviews the patient before surgery; prepares the patient; helps with anesthesia; obtains and opens packages for the "sterile" people to remove the sterile contents during the procedure; keeps a written account of the surgical procedure; and answers the surgeon's questions about the patient during the surgery.

Work environment. Surgical technologists work in clean, well-lighted, cool environments. They must stand for long periods and remain alert during operations. At times, they may be exposed to communicable diseases and unpleasant sights, odors, and materials.

Most surgical technologists work a regular 40-hour week, although they may be on call or work nights, weekends, and holidays on a rotating basis.

Training, Other Qualifications, and Advancement

Training programs last nine to 24 months and lead to a certificate, diploma, or associate degree. Professional certification can help in getting jobs and promotions.

Education and training. Surgical technologists receive their training in formal programs offered by community and junior colleges, vocational schools, universities, hospitals, and the military. In 2006, the Commission on Accreditation of Allied Health Education Programs (CAAHEP) recognized more than 400 accredited training programs. Programs last from nine to 24 months and lead to a certificate, diploma, or associate degree. High school graduation normally is required for admission. Recommended high school courses include health, biology, chemistry, and mathematics.

Programs provide classroom education and supervised clinical experience. Students take courses in anatomy, physiology, microbiology, pharmacology, professional ethics, and medical terminology. Other topics covered include the care and safety of patients during surgery, sterile techniques, and surgical procedures. Students also

learn to sterilize instruments; prevent and control infection; and handle special drugs, solutions, supplies, and equipment.

Certification and other qualifications. Most employers prefer to hire certified technologists. Technologists may obtain voluntary professional certification from the Liaison Council on Certification for the Surgical Technologist by graduating from a CAAHEP-accredited program and passing a national certification examination. They may then use the Certified Surgical Technologist (CST) designation. Continuing education or reexamination is required to maintain certification, which must be renewed every four years.

Certification also may be obtained from the National Center for Competency Testing (NCCT). To qualify to take the exam, candidates follow one of three paths: complete an accredited training program; undergo a two-year hospital on-the-job training program; or acquire seven years of experience working in the field. After passing the exam, individuals may use the designation Tech in Surgery-Certified, TS-C (NCCT). This certification must be renewed every five years through either continuing education or reexamination.

Surgical technologists need manual dexterity to handle instruments quickly. They also must be conscientious, orderly, and emotionally stable to handle the demands of the operating room environment. Technologists must respond quickly and must be familiar with operating procedures in order to have instruments ready for surgeons without having to be told. They are expected to keep abreast of new developments in the field.

Advancement. Technologists advance by specializing in a particular area of surgery, such as neurosurgery or open heart surgery. They also may work as circulating technologists. With additional training, some technologists advance to first assistant. Some surgical technologists manage central supply departments in hospitals, or take positions with insurance companies, sterile supply services, and operating equipment firms.

Employment

Surgical technologists held about 86,000 jobs in 2006. About 70 percent of jobs for surgical technologists were in hospitals, mainly in operating and delivery rooms. Other jobs were in offices of physicians or dentists who perform outpatient surgery and in outpatient care centers, including ambulatory surgical centers. A few technologists, known as private scrubs, are employed directly by surgeons who have special surgical teams, like those for liver transplants.

Job Outlook

Employment of surgical technologists is expected to grow much faster than the average for all occupations. Job opportunities will be best for technologists who are certified.

Employment change. Employment of surgical technologists is expected to grow 24 percent between 2006 and 2016, much faster than the average for all occupations, as the volume of surgeries increases. The number of surgical procedures is expected to rise as the population grows and ages. Older people, including the baby

Projections data from the National Employment Matrix

Occupational Title	SOC Code	Employment, 2006	Projected employment, 2016	Change, 2006-2016	
				Number	Percent
Surgical technologists	29-2055	86,000	107,000	21,000	24

NOTE: Data in this table are rounded.

boom generation, who generally require more surgical procedures, will account for a larger portion of the general population. In addition, technological advances, such as fiber optics and laser technology, will permit an increasing number of new surgical procedures to be performed and also will allow surgical technologists to assist with a greater number of procedures.

Hospitals will continue to be the primary employer of surgical technologists, although much faster employment growth is expected in offices of physicians and in outpatient care centers, including ambulatory surgical centers.

Job prospects. Job opportunities will be best for technologists who are certified.

Earnings

Median annual earnings of wage-and-salary surgical technologists were $36,080 in May 2006. The middle 50 percent earned between $30,300 and $43,560. The lowest 10 percent earned less than $25,490, and the highest 10 percent earned more than $51,140. Median annual earnings in the industries employing the largest numbers of surgical technologists were

Offices of physicians	$37,300
Outpatient care centers	37,280
General medical and surgical hospitals	35,840
Offices of dentists	34,160

Benefits provided by most employers include paid vacation and sick leave, health, medical, vision, dental insurance and life insurance, and retirement program. A few employers also provide tuition reimbursement and child care benefits.

Related Occupations

Other health occupations requiring approximately 1 year of training after high school include dental assistants, licensed practical and licensed vocational nurses, clinical laboratory technologists and technicians, and medical assistants.

Sources of Additional Information

For additional information on a career as a surgical technologist and a list of CAAHEP-accredited programs, contact

▸ Association of Surgical Technologists, 6 West Dry Creek Circle, Suite 200, Littleton, CO 80120. Internet: http://www.ast.org

For information on becoming a Certified Surgical Technologist, contact

▸ Liaison Council on Certification for the Surgical Technologist, 6 West Dry Creek Circle, Suite 100, Littleton, CO 80120. Internet: http://www.lcc-st.org

For information on becoming a Tech in Surgery-Certified, contact

▸ National Center for Competency Testing, 7007 College Blvd., Suite 705, Overland Park, KS 66211.

Surveyors, Cartographers, Photogrammetrists, and Surveying and Mapping Technicians

(O*NET 17-1021.00, 17-1022.00, 17-3031.00, 17-3031.01, and 17-3031.02)

Significant Points

■ About 7 out of 10 jobs are in architectural, engineering, and related services.

■ Opportunities will be best for surveyors, cartographers, and photogrammetrists who have a bachelor's degree and strong technical skills.

■ Overall employment of surveyors, cartographers, photogrammetrists, and surveying technicians is expected to grow much faster than the average for all occupations through the year 2016.

Nature of the Work

Surveyors, cartographers, and photogrammetrists are responsible for measuring and mapping the Earth's surface. *Surveyors* establish official land, airspace, and water boundaries. They write descriptions of land for deeds, leases, and other legal documents; define airspace for airports; and take measurements of construction and mineral sites. Other surveyors provide data about the shape, contour, location, elevation, or dimension of land or land features. *Cartographers and photogrammetrists* collect, analyze, interpret, and map geographic information from surveys and from data and photographs collected using airplanes and satellites. *Surveying and mapping technicians* assist these professionals by collecting data in the field, making calculations, and helping with computer-aided drafting. Collectively, these occupations play key roles in the field of geospatial information.

Surveyors measure distances, directions, and angles between points and elevations of points, lines, and contours on, above, and below the Earth's surface. In the field, they select known survey reference points and determine the precise location of important features in the survey area using specialized equipment. Surveyors also research legal records, look for evidence of previous boundaries, and analyze data to determine the location of boundary lines. They are sometimes called to provide expert testimony in court about their work. Surveyors also record their results, verify the accuracy of data, and prepare plots, maps, and reports.

Some surveyors perform specialized functions closer to those of cartographers and photogrammetrists than to those of traditional surveyors. For example, *geodetic surveyors* use high-accuracy techniques, including satellite observations, to measure large areas of the earth's surface. *Geophysical prospecting surveyors* mark sites for subsurface exploration, usually to look for petroleum. *Marine or hydrographic surveyors* survey harbors, rivers, and other bodies of water to determine shorelines, the topography of the bottom, water depth, and other features.

Surveyors use the Global Positioning System (GPS) to locate reference points with a high degree of precision. To use this system, a surveyor places a satellite signal receiver—a small instrument mounted on a tripod—on a desired point, and another receiver on a point for which the geographic position is known. The receiver simultaneously collects information from several satellites to establish a precise position. The receiver also can be placed in a vehicle for tracing out road systems. Because receivers now come in different sizes and shapes, and because the cost of receivers has fallen, much more surveying work can be done with GPS. Surveyors then interpret and check the results produced by the new technology.

Field measurements are often taken by a survey party that gathers the information needed by the surveyor. A typical survey party consists of a party chief and one or more surveying technicians and helpers. The party chief, who may be either a surveyor or a senior surveying technician, leads day-to-day work activities. Surveying technicians assist the party chief by adjusting and operating surveying instruments, such as the total station, which measures and records angles and distances simultaneously. Surveying technicians or assistants position and hold the vertical rods, or targets, that the operator sights on to measure angles, distances, or elevations. They may hold measuring tapes if electronic distance-measuring equipment is not used. Surveying technicians compile notes, make sketches, and enter the data obtained from surveying instruments into computers either in the field or at the office. Survey parties also may include laborers or helpers who perform less-skilled duties, such as clearing brush from sight lines, driving stakes, or carrying equipment.

Photogrammetrists and cartographers measure, map, and chart the Earth's surface. Their work involves everything from performing geographical research and compiling data to producing maps. They collect, analyze, and interpret both spatial data—such as latitude, longitude, elevation, and distance—and nonspatial data—for example, population density, land-use patterns, annual precipitation levels, and demographic characteristics. Their maps may give both physical and social characteristics of the land. They prepare maps in either digital or graphic form, using information provided by geodetic surveys and remote sensing systems including aerial cameras, satellites, and LIDAR.

LIDAR—light-imaging detection and ranging—uses lasers attached to planes and other equipment to digitally map the topography of the Earth. It is often more accurate than traditional surveying methods and also can be used to collect other forms of data, such as the location and density of forests. Data developed by LIDAR can be used by surveyors, cartographers, and photogrammetrists to provide spatial information to specialists in geology, seismology, forestry, and construction, and other fields.

Geographic Information Systems (GIS) have become an integral tool for surveyors, cartographers and photogrammetrists, and surveying and mapping technicians. Workers use GIS to assemble, integrate, analyze, and display data about location in a digital format. They also use GIS to compile information from a variety of sources. GIS typically are used to make maps which combine information useful for environmental studies, geology, engineering, planning, business marketing, and other disciplines. As more of these systems are developed, many mapping specialists are being called *geographic information specialists*.

Work environment. Surveyors and surveying technicians usually work an 8-hour day, 5 days a week and may spend a lot of time outdoors. Sometimes, they work longer hours during the summer, when weather and light conditions are most suitable for fieldwork. Construction-related work may be limited during times of inclement weather.

Surveyors and technicians engage in active, sometimes strenuous, work. They often stand for long periods, walk considerable distances, and climb hills with heavy packs of instruments and other equipment. They also can be exposed to all types of weather. Traveling is sometimes part of the job, and land surveyors and technicians may commute long distances, stay away from home overnight, or temporarily relocate near a survey site. Surveyors also work indoors while planning surveys, searching court records for deed information, analyzing data, and preparing reports and maps.

Cartographers and photogrammetrists spend most of their time in offices using computers. However, certain jobs may require extensive field work to verify results and acquire data.

Training, Other Qualifications, and Advancement

Most surveyors, cartographers, and photogrammetrists have a bachelor's degree in surveying or a related field. Every state requires that surveyors be licensed.

Education and training. In the past, many people with little formal training started as members of survey crews and worked their way up to become licensed surveyors, but this has become increasingly difficult to do. Now, most surveyors need a bachelor's degree. A number of universities offer bachelor's degree programs in surveying, and many community colleges, technical institutes, and vocational schools offer one-, two-, and three-year programs in surveying or surveying technology.

Cartographers and photogrammetrists usually have a bachelor's degree in cartography, geography, surveying, engineering, forestry, computer science, or a physical science, although a few enter these positions after working as technicians. With the development of GIS, cartographers and photogrammetrists need more education and stronger technical skills—including more experience with computers—than in the past.

Most cartographic and photogrammetric technicians also have specialized postsecondary education. High school students interested in surveying and cartography should take courses in algebra, geometry, trigonometry, drafting, mechanical drawing, and computer science.

Licensure. All 50 states and all U.S. territories license surveyors. For licensure, most state licensing boards require that individuals pass a written examination given by the National Council of Examiners for Engineering and Surveying (NCEES). Most states also require surveyors to pass a written examination prepared by the state licensing board.

Licensing happens in stages. After passing a first exam, the Fundamentals of Surveying, most candidates work under the supervision of an experienced surveyor for four years and then for licensure take a second exam, the Principles and Practice of Surveyors.

Specific requirements for training and education vary among the states. An increasing number of states require a bachelor's degree in surveying or in a closely related field, such as civil engineering or forestry, regardless of the number of years of experience. Some states require the degree to be from a school accredited by the

Accreditation Board for Engineering and Technology. Many states also have a continuing education requirement.

Additionally a number of states require cartographers and photogrammetrists to be licensed as surveyors, and some states have specific licenses for photogrammetrists.

Other qualifications. Surveyors, cartographers, and photogrammetrists should be able to visualize objects, distances, sizes, and abstract forms. They must work with precision and accuracy because mistakes can be costly.

Members of a survey party must be in good physical condition because they work outdoors and often carry equipment over difficult terrain. They need good eyesight, coordination, and hearing to communicate verbally and using hand signals. Surveying is a cooperative operation, so good interpersonal skills and the ability to work as part of a team is important. Good office skills also are essential because surveyors must be able to research old deeds and other legal papers and prepare reports that document their work.

Certification and advancement. High school graduates with no formal training in surveying usually start as apprentices. Beginners with postsecondary school training in surveying usually can start as technicians or assistants. With on-the-job experience and formal training in surveying—either in an institutional program or from a correspondence school—workers may advance to senior survey technician, then to party chief. Depending on state licensing requirements, in some cases they may advance to licensed surveyor.

The National Society of Professional Surveyors, a member organization of the American Congress on Surveying and Mapping, has a voluntary certification program for surveying technicians. Technicians are certified at four levels requiring progressive amounts of experience and the passing of written examinations. Although not required for state licensure, many employers require certification for promotion to positions with greater responsibilities.

The American Society for Photogrammetry and Remote Sensing has voluntary certification programs for technicians and professionals in photogrammetry, remote sensing, and GIS. To qualify for these professional distinctions, individuals must meet work experience and training standards and pass a written examination. The professional recognition these certifications can help workers gain promotions.

Employment

Surveyors, cartographers, photogrammetrists, and surveying technicians held about 148,000 jobs in 2006. Employment was distributed by occupational specialty as follows:

Surveying and mapping technicians 76,000

Surveyors 60,000

Cartographers and photogrammetrists....................12,000

The architectural, engineering, and related services industry—including firms that provided surveying and mapping services to other industries on a contract basis—provided 7 out of 10 jobs for these workers. Federal, state, and local governmental agencies provided about 14 percent of these jobs. Major federal government employers are the U.S. Geological Survey (USGS), the Bureau of Land Management (BLM), the National Geodetic Survey, the National Geospatial Intelligence Agency, and the Army Corps of Engineers. Most surveyors in state and local government work for highway departments or urban planning and redevelopment agencies. Construction, mining and utility companies also employ surveyors, cartographers, photogrammetrists, and surveying technicians.

Job Outlook

Surveyors, cartographers, photogrammetrists, and surveying and mapping technicians should have favorable job prospects. These occupations should experience much faster than average employment growth.

Employment change. Overall employment of surveyors, cartographers, photogrammetrists, and surveying and mapping technicians is expected to increase by 21 percent from 2006 to 2016, which is much faster than the average for all occupations. Increasing demand for fast, accurate, and complete geographic information will be the main source of growth for these occupations.

An increasing number of firms are interested in geographic information and its applications. For example, GIS can be used to create maps and information used in emergency planning, security, marketing, urban planning, natural resource exploration, construction, and other applications. Also, the increased popularity of online mapping systems has created a higher demand for and awareness of geographic information among consumers.

Job prospects. In addition to openings from growth, job openings will continue to arise from the need to replace workers who transfer to other occupations or who leave the labor force altogether. Many of the workers in these occupations are approaching retirement age.

Opportunities for surveyors, cartographers, and photogrammetrists should remain concentrated in engineering, surveying, mapping, building inspection, and drafting services firms. However, employment may fluctuate from year to year with construction activity or with mapping needs for land and resource management.

Opportunities should be stronger for professional surveyors than for surveying and mapping technicians. Advancements in technology, such as total stations and GPS, have made surveying parties smaller than they once were. Additionally, cartographers, photogrammetrists, and technicians who produce more basic GIS data may face competition for jobs from offshore firms and contractors.

Projections data from the National Employment Matrix

Occupational Title	SOC Code	Employment, 2006	Projected employment, 2016	Change, 2006-2016	
				Number	Percent
Surveyors, cartographers, photogrammetrists, and surveying technicians..	—	148,000	179,000	31,000	21
Cartographers and photogrammetrists	17-1021	12,000	15,000	2,500	20
Surveyors	17-1022	60,000	74,000	14,000	24
Surveying and mapping technicians	17-3031	76,000	90,000	15,000	19

NOTE: Data in this table are rounded.

As technologies become more complex, opportunities will be best for surveyors, cartographers, and photogrammetrists who have a bachelor's degree and strong technical skills. Increasing demand for geographic data, as opposed to traditional surveying services, will mean better opportunities for cartographers and photogrammetrists who are involved in the development and use of geographic and land information systems.

Earnings

Median annual earnings of cartographers and photogrammetrists were $48,240 in May 2006. The middle 50 percent earned between $37,480 and $65,240. The lowest 10 percent earned less than $30,910 and the highest 10 percent earned more than $80,520.

Median annual earnings of surveyors were $48,290 in May 2006. The middle 50 percent earned between $35,720 and $63,990. The lowest 10 percent earned less than $26,690 and the highest 10 percent earned more than $79,910. Median annual earnings of surveyors employed in architectural, engineering, and related services were $47,570 in May 2006.

Median annual earnings of surveying and mapping technicians were $32,340 in May 2006. The middle 50 percent earned between $25,070 and $42,230. The lowest 10 percent earned less than $20,020, and the highest 10 percent earned more than $53,310. Median annual earnings of surveying and mapping technicians employed in architectural, engineering, and related services were $30,670 in May 2006, while those employed by local governments had median annual earnings of $37,550.

Related Occupations

Surveying is related to the work of civil engineers, architects, and landscape architects because an accurate survey is the first step in land development and construction projects. Cartographic and geodetic surveying are related to the work of environmental scientists and geoscientists, who study the earth's internal composition, surface, and atmosphere. Cartography also is related to the work of geographers and urban and regional planners, who study and decide how the earth's surface is being and may be used.

Sources of Additional Information

For career information on surveyors, cartographers, photogrammetrists, and surveying technicians, contact

▸ American Congress on Surveying and Mapping, Suite 403, 6 Montgomery Village Ave., Gaithersburg, MD 20879. Internet: http://www.acsm.net

Information about career opportunities, licensure requirements, and the surveying technician certification program is available from

▸ National Society of Professional Surveyors, Suite 403, 6 Montgomery Village Ave., Gaithersburg, MD 20879.

For information on a career as a geodetic surveyor, contact

▸ American Association of Geodetic Surveying (AAGS), Suite 403, 6 Montgomery Village Ave., Gaithersburg, MD 20879.

For career information on photogrammetrists, photogrammetric technicians, remote sensing scientists and image-based cartographers or geographic information system specialists, contact

▸ ASPRS: Imaging and Geospatial Information Society, 5410 Grosvenor Lane., Suite 210, Bethesda, MD 20814-2160. Internet: http://www.asprs.org

General information on careers in photogrammetry, mapping, and surveying is available from

▸ MAPPS: Management Association for Private Photogrammetric Surveyors, 1760 Reston Parkway, Suite 515, Reston, VA 20190. Internet: http://www.mapps.org

Information on about careers in remote sensing, photogrammetry, surveying, GIS, and other geography-related disciplines also is available from the Spring 2005 *Occupational Outlook Quarterly* article, "Geography Jobs", available online at http://www.bls.gov/opub/ooq/2005/spring/art01.pdf

Teachers—Preschool, Kindergarten, Elementary, Middle, and Secondary

(O*NET 25-2011.00, 25-2012.00, 25-2021.00, 25-2022.00, 25-2023.00, 25-2031.00, and 25-2032.00)

Significant Points

■ Public school teachers must be licensed, which typically requires a bachelor's degree and completion of an approved teacher education program.

■ Many states offer alternative licensing programs to attract people into teaching, especially for hard-to-fill positions.

■ Job prospects should be favorable; opportunities will vary by geographic area and subject taught.

Nature of the Work

Teachers play an important role in fostering the intellectual and social development of children during their formative years. The education that teachers impart plays a key role in determining the future prospects of their students. Whether in preschools or high schools or in private or public schools, teachers provide the tools and the environment for their students to develop into responsible adults.

Teachers act as facilitators or coaches, using classroom presentations or individual instruction to help students learn and apply concepts in subjects such as science, mathematics, or English. They plan, evaluate, and assign lessons; prepare, administer, and grade tests; listen to oral presentations; and maintain classroom discipline. Teachers observe and evaluate a student's performance and potential and increasingly are asked to use new assessment methods. For example, teachers may examine a portfolio of a student's artwork or writing in order to judge the student's overall progress. They then can provide additional assistance in areas in which a student needs help. Teachers also grade papers, prepare report cards, and meet with parents and school staff to discuss a student's academic progress or personal problems.

Many teachers use a "hands-on" approach that uses "props" or "manipulatives" to help children understand abstract concepts, solve problems, and develop critical thought processes. For example, they teach the concepts of numbers or of addition and subtraction by playing board games. As the children get older, teachers use more sophisticated materials, such as science apparatus, cameras, or computers. They also encourage collaboration in solving problems by having students work in groups to discuss and solve problems together. To be prepared for success later in life, students must be able to interact with others, adapt to new technology, and think through problems logically.

Preschool, kindergarten, and elementary school teachers play a vital role in the development of children. What children learn and experience during their early years can shape their views of themselves and the world and can affect their later success or failure in school, work, and their personal lives. Preschool, kindergarten, and elementary school teachers introduce children to mathematics, language, science, and social studies. They use games, music, artwork, films, books, computers, and other tools to teach basic skills.

Preschool children learn mainly through play and interactive activities. *Preschool teachers* capitalize on children's play to further language and vocabulary development (using storytelling, rhyming games, and acting games), improve social skills (having the children work together to build a neighborhood in a sandbox), and introduce scientific and mathematical concepts (showing the children how to balance and count blocks when building a bridge or how to mix colors when painting). Thus, a less structured approach, including small-group lessons, one-on-one instruction, and learning through creative activities such as art, dance, and music, is adopted to teach preschool children. Play and hands-on teaching also are used by *kindergarten teachers*, but academics begin to take priority in kindergarten classrooms. Letter recognition, phonics, numbers, and awareness of nature and science, introduced at the preschool level, are taught primarily in kindergarten.

Most *elementary school teachers* instruct one class of children in several subjects. In some schools, two or more teachers work as a team and are jointly responsible for a group of students in at least one subject. In other schools, a teacher may teach one special subject—usually music, art, reading, science, arithmetic, or physical education—to a number of classes. A small but growing number of teachers instruct multilevel classrooms, with students at several different learning levels.

Middle school teachers and *secondary school teachers* help students delve more deeply into subjects introduced in elementary school and expose them to more information about the world. Middle and secondary school teachers specialize in a specific subject, such as English, Spanish, mathematics, history, or biology. They also may teach subjects that are career oriented. *Vocational education teachers*, also referred to as career and technical or career-technology teachers, instruct and train students to work in a wide variety of fields, such as healthcare, business, auto repair, communications, and, increasingly, technology. They often teach courses that are in high demand by area employers, who may provide input into the curriculum and offer internships to students. Many vocational teachers play an active role in building and overseeing these partnerships. Additional responsibilities of middle and secondary school teachers may include career guidance and job placement, as well as follow-ups with students after graduation.

In addition to conducting classroom activities, teachers oversee study halls and homerooms, supervise extracurricular activities, and accompany students on field trips. They may identify students with physical or mental problems and refer the students to the proper authorities. Secondary school teachers occasionally assist students in choosing courses, colleges, and careers. Teachers also participate in education conferences and workshops.

Computers play an integral role in the education teachers provide. Resources such as educational software and the Internet expose students to a vast range of experiences and promote interactive learning. Through the Internet, students can communicate with other students anywhere in the world, allowing them to share experiences and differing viewpoints. Students also use the Internet for individual research projects and to gather information. Computers are used in other classroom activities as well, from solving math problems to learning English as a second language. Teachers also may use computers to record grades and perform other administrative and clerical duties. They must continually update their skills so that they can instruct and use the latest technology in the classroom.

Teachers often work with students from varied ethnic, racial, and religious backgrounds. With growing minority populations in most parts of the country, it is important for teachers to work effectively with a diverse student population. Accordingly, some schools offer training to help teachers enhance their awareness and understanding of different cultures. Teachers may also include multicultural programming in their lesson plans, to address the needs of all students, regardless of their cultural background.

In recent years, site-based management, which allows teachers and parents to participate actively in management decisions regarding school operations, has gained popularity. In many schools, teachers are increasingly involved in making decisions regarding the budget, personnel, textbooks, curriculum design, and teaching methods.

Work environment. Seeing students develop new skills and gain an appreciation of knowledge and learning can be very rewarding. However, teaching may be frustrating when one is dealing with unmotivated or disrespectful students. Occasionally, teachers must cope with unruly behavior and violence in the schools. Teachers may experience stress in dealing with large classes, heavy workloads, or old schools that are run down and lack many modern amenities. Accountability standards also may increase stress levels, with teachers expected to produce students who are able to exhibit satisfactory performance on standardized tests in core subjects. Many teachers, particularly in public schools, are also frustrated by the lack of control they have over what they are required to teach.

Teachers in private schools generally enjoy smaller class sizes and more control over establishing the curriculum and setting standards for performance and discipline. Their students also tend to be more motivated, since private schools can be selective in their admissions processes.

Teachers are sometimes isolated from their colleagues because they work alone in a classroom of students. However, some schools allow teachers to work in teams and with mentors to enhance their professional development.

Including school duties performed outside the classroom, many teachers work more than 40 hours a week. Part-time schedules are more common among preschool and kindergarten teachers. Although most school districts have gone to all-day kindergartens, some kindergarten teachers still teach two kindergarten classes a day. Most teachers work the traditional 10-month school year with a 2-month vacation during the summer. During the vacation break, those on the 10-month schedule may teach in summer sessions, take other jobs, travel, or pursue personal interests. Many enroll in college courses or workshops to continue their education. Teachers in districts with a year-round schedule typically work 8 weeks, are on vacation for 1 week, and have a 5-week midwinter break. Preschool teachers working in day care settings often work year round.

Most states have tenure laws that prevent public school teachers from being fired without just cause and due process. Teachers may obtain tenure after they have satisfactorily completed a probationary period of teaching, normally 3 years. Tenure does not absolutely guarantee a job, but it does provide some security.

Training, Other Qualifications, and Advancement

The traditional route to becoming a public school teacher involves completing a bachelor's degree from a teacher education program and then obtaining a license. However, most states now offer alternative routes to licensure for those who have a college degree in other fields. Private school teachers do not have to be licensed but still need a bachelor's degree. A bachelor's degree may not be needed by preschool teachers and vocational education teachers, who need experience in their field rather than a specific degree.

Education and training. Traditional education programs for kindergarten and elementary school teachers include courses designed specifically for those preparing to teach. These courses include mathematics, physical science, social science, music, art, and literature, as well as prescribed professional education courses, such as philosophy of education, psychology of learning, and teaching methods. Aspiring secondary school teachers most often major in the subject they plan to teach while also taking a program of study in teacher preparation. Many four-year colleges require students to wait until their sophomore year before applying for admission to teacher education programs. To maintain their accreditation, teacher education programs are now required to include classes in the use of computers and other technologies. Most programs require students to perform a student-teaching internship. Teacher education programs are accredited by the National Council for Accreditation of Teacher Education and the Teacher Education Accreditation Council. Graduation from an accredited program is not necessary to become a teacher, but it may make fulfilling licensure requirements easier.

Many states now offer professional development schools, which are partnerships between universities and elementary or secondary schools. Professional development schools merge theory with practice and allow the student to experience a year of teaching firsthand, under professional guidance. Students enter these one-year programs after completion of their bachelor's degree.

Licensure and certification. All 50 states and the District of Columbia require public school teachers to be licensed. Licensure is not required for teachers in most private schools. Usually licensure is granted by the state Board of Education or a licensure advisory committee. Teachers may be licensed to teach the early childhood grades (usually preschool through grade 3); the elementary grades (grades 1 through 6 or 8); the middle grades (grades 5 through 8); a secondary-education subject area (usually grades seven through 12); or a special subject, such as reading or music (usually grades kindergarten through 12).

Requirements for regular licenses to teach kindergarten through grade 12 vary by state. However, all states require general education teachers to have a bachelor's degree and to have completed an approved teacher training program with a prescribed number of subject and education credits, as well as supervised practice teaching. Some states also require technology training and the attainment of a minimum grade point average. A number of states require that

teachers obtain a master's degree in education within a specified period after they begin teaching.

Almost all states require applicants for a teacher's license to be tested for competency in basic skills, such as reading and writing, and in teaching. Almost all also require teachers to exhibit proficiency in their subject. Many school systems are presently moving toward implementing performance-based systems for licensure, which usually require teachers to demonstrate satisfactory teaching performance over an extended period in order to obtain a provisional license, in addition to passing an examination in their subject. Most states require teachers to complete a minimum number of hours of continuing education to renew their license. Many states have reciprocity agreements that make it easier for teachers licensed in one state to become licensed in another.

Licensing requirements for preschool teachers also vary by state. Requirements for public preschool teachers are generally more stringent than those for private preschool teachers. Some states require a bachelor's degree in early childhood education, while others require an associate's degree, and still others require certification by a nationally recognized authority. The Child Development Associate (CDA) credential, the most common type of certification, requires a mix of classroom training and experience working with children, along with an independent assessment of the teacher's competence.

Nearly all states now also offer alternative licensure programs for teachers who have a bachelor's degree in the subject they will teach, but who lack the necessary education courses required for a regular license. Many of these alternative licensure programs are designed to ease shortages of teachers of certain subjects, such as mathematics and science. Other programs provide teachers for urban and rural schools that have difficulty filling positions with teachers from traditional licensure programs. Alternative licensure programs are intended to attract people into teaching who do not fulfill traditional licensing standards, including recent college graduates who did not complete education programs and those changing from another career to teaching. In some programs, individuals begin teaching quickly under provisional licensure under the close supervision of experienced educators while taking education courses outside school hours. If they progress satisfactorily, they receive regular licensure after working for one or two years. In other programs, college graduates who do not meet licensure requirements take only those courses that they lack and then become licensed. This approach may take one or two semesters of full-time study. The coursework for alternative certification programs often leads to a master's degree. In extreme circumstances, when schools cannot attract enough qualified teachers to fill positions, states may issue emergency licenses to individuals who do not meet the requirements for a regular license that let them begin teaching immediately.

In many states, vocational teachers have many of the same licensure requirements as other teachers. However, knowledge and experience in a particular field are important, so some states will license vocational education teachers without a bachelor's degree, provided they can demonstrate expertise in their field. A minimum number of hours in education courses may also be required.

Private schools are generally exempt from meeting state licensing standards. For secondary school teacher jobs, they prefer candidates who have a bachelor's degree in the subject they intend to teach, or in childhood education for elementary school teachers. They seek candidates among recent college graduates as well as from those who have established careers in other fields.

© JIST Works

Other qualifications. In addition to being knowledgeable about the subjects they teach, teachers must have the ability to communicate, inspire trust and confidence, and motivate students, as well as understand the students' educational and emotional needs. Teachers must be able to recognize and respond to individual and cultural differences in students and employ different teaching methods that will result in higher student achievement. They should be organized, dependable, patient, and creative. Teachers also must be able to work cooperatively and communicate effectively with other teachers, support staff, parents, and members of the community. Private schools associated with religious institutions also desire candidates who share the values that are important to the institution.

Additional certifications and advancement. In some cases, teachers of kindergarten through high school may attain professional certification in order to demonstrate competency beyond that required for a license. The National Board for Professional Teaching Standards offers a voluntary national certification. To become nationally certified, experienced teachers must prove their aptitude by compiling a portfolio showing their work in the classroom and by passing a written assessment and evaluation of their teaching knowledge. Currently, teachers may become certified in a variety of areas, on the basis of the age of the students and, in some cases, the subject taught. For example, teachers may obtain a certificate for teaching English language arts to early adolescents (aged 11 to 15), or they may become certified as early childhood generalists. All states recognize national certification, and many states and school districts provide special benefits to teachers who earn certification. Benefits typically include higher salaries and reimbursement for continuing education and certification fees. In addition, many states allow nationally certified teachers to carry a license from one state to another.

With additional preparation, teachers may move into such positions as school librarians, reading specialists, instructional coordinators, or guidance counselors. Teachers may become administrators or supervisors, although the number of these positions is limited and competition for them can be intense. In some systems, highly qualified, experienced teachers can become senior or mentor teachers, with higher pay and additional responsibilities. They guide and assist less experienced teachers while keeping most of their own teaching responsibilities. Preschool teachers usually work their way up from assistant teacher, to teacher, to lead teacher—who may be responsible for the instruction of several classes—and, finally, to director of the center. Preschool teachers with a bachelor's degree frequently are qualified to teach kindergarten through grade 3 as well. Teaching at these higher grades often results in higher pay.

Employment

Preschool, kindergarten, elementary school, middle school, and secondary school teachers, except special education, held about 4.0 million jobs in 2006. Of the teachers in those jobs, about 1.5 million are elementary school teachers, 1.1 million are secondary school teachers, 673,000 are middle school teachers, 437,000 are preschool teachers, and 170,000 are kindergarten teachers. The vast majority work in elementary and secondary schools. Preschool teachers, except special education, are most often employed in child daycare services (59 percent), public and private educational services (16 percent), and religious organizations (15 percent). Employment of teachers is geographically distributed much the same as the population.

Job Outlook

Employment of preschool, kindergarten, elementary, middle, and secondary school teachers is projected to grow about as fast as average. Job prospects are expected to be favorable, with particularly good prospects for teachers in high-demand fields like math, science, and bilingual education, or in less desirable urban or rural school districts.

Employment change. Employment of school teachers is expected to grow by 12 percent between 2006 and 2016, about as fast as the average for all occupations. However, because of the size of the occupations in this group, this growth will create 479,000 additional teacher positions, more than all but a few occupations.

Through 2016, overall student enrollments in elementary, middle, and secondary schools—a key factor in the demand for teachers—are expected to rise more slowly than in the past as children of the baby boom generation leave the school system. This will cause employment of teachers from kindergarten through the secondary grades to grow as fast as the average. Projected enrollments will vary by region. Fast-growing states in the South and West—led by Nevada, Arizona, Texas, and Georgia—will experience the largest enrollment increases. Enrollments in the Midwest are expected to hold relatively steady, while those in the Northeast are expected to decline. Teachers who are geographically mobile and who obtain licensure in more than one subject should have a distinct advantage in finding a job.

The number of teachers employed is dependent on state and local expenditures for education and on the enactment of legislation to increase the quality and scope of public education. At the federal level, there has been a large increase in funding for education, particularly for the hiring of qualified teachers in lower income areas. Also, some states are instituting programs to improve early childhood education, such as offering full day kindergarten and universal preschool. These programs, along with projected higher enrollment growth for preschool age children, will create many new jobs for preschool teachers, which are expected to grow much faster than the average for all occupations.

Job prospects. Job opportunities for teachers over the next 10 years will vary from good to excellent, depending on the locality, grade level, and subject taught. Most job openings will result from the need to replace the large number of teachers who are expected to retire over the 2006–2016 period. Also, many beginning teachers decide to leave teaching for other careers after a year or two—especially those employed in poor, urban schools—creating additional job openings for teachers.

The job market for teachers also continues to vary by school location and by subject taught. Job prospects should be better in inner cities and rural areas than in suburban districts. Many inner cities—often characterized by overcrowded, ill-equipped schools and higher-than-average poverty rates—and rural areas—characterized by their remote location and relatively low salaries—have difficulty attracting and retaining enough teachers. Currently, many school districts have difficulty hiring qualified teachers in some subject areas—most often mathematics, science (especially chemistry and physics), bilingual education, and foreign languages. Increasing enrollments of minorities, coupled with a shortage of minority teachers, should cause efforts to recruit minority teachers to intensify. Also, the number of non-English-speaking students will continue to grow, creating demand for bilingual teachers and for those

Projections data from the National Employment Matrix

Occupational Title	SOC Code	Employment, 2006	Projected employment, 2016	Change, 2006-2016	
				Number	Percent
Teachers—preschool, kindergarten, elementary, middle, and secondary	—	3,954,000	4,433,000	479,000	12
Preschool and kindergarten teachers	25-2010	607,000	750,000	143,000	23
Preschool teachers, except special education	25-2011	437,000	552,000	115,000	26
Kindergarten teachers, except special education	25-2012	170,000	198,000	28,000	16
Elementary and middle school teachers	25-2020	2,214,000	2,496,000	282,000	13
Elementary school teachers, except special education	25-2021	1,540,000	1,749,000	209,000	14
Middle school teachers, except special and vocational education	25-2022	658,000	732,000	74,000	11
Vocational education teachers, middle school	25-2023	16,000	15,000	-800	-5
Secondary school teachers	25-2030	1,133,000	1,187,000	54,000	5
Secondary school teachers, except special and vocational education	25-2031	1,038,000	1,096,000	59,000	6
Vocational education teachers, secondary school	25-2032	96,000	91,000	-4,400	-5

NOTE: Data in this table are rounded.

who teach English as a second language. Qualified vocational teachers also are currently in demand in a variety of fields at both the middle school and secondary school levels. Specialties that have an adequate number of qualified teachers include general elementary education, physical education, and social studies.

The supply of teachers is expected to increase in response to reports of improved job prospects, better pay, more teacher involvement in school policy, and greater public interest in education. In addition, more teachers may be drawn from a reserve pool of career changers, substitute teachers, and teachers completing alternative certification programs. In recent years, the total number of bachelor's and master's degrees granted in education has been increasing slowly. But many states have implemented policies that will encourage even more students to become teachers because of a shortage of teachers in certain locations and in anticipation of the loss of a number of teachers to retirement.

Earnings

Median annual earnings of kindergarten, elementary, middle, and secondary school teachers ranged from $43,580 to $48,690 in May 2006; the lowest 10 percent earned $28,590 to $33,070; the top 10 percent earned $67,490 to $76,100. Median earnings for preschool teachers were $22,680.

According to the American Federation of Teachers, beginning teachers with a bachelor's degree earned an average of $31,753 in the 2004–05 school year. The estimated average salary of all public elementary and secondary school teachers in the 2004–05 school year was $47,602.

In 2006, more than half of all elementary, middle, and secondary school teachers belonged to unions—mainly the American Federation of Teachers and the National Education Association—that bargain with school systems over salaries, hours, and other terms and conditions of employment. Fewer preschool and kindergarten teachers were union members—about 17 percent in 2006.

Teachers can boost their earnings in a number of ways. In some schools, teachers receive extra pay for coaching sports and working with students in extracurricular activities. Getting a master's degree or national certification often results in a raise in pay, as does acting as a mentor. Some teachers earn extra income during the summer by

teaching summer school or performing other jobs in the school system. Although private school teachers generally earn less than public school teachers, they may be given other benefits, such as free or subsidized housing.

Related Occupations

Preschool, kindergarten, elementary school, middle school, and secondary school teaching requires a variety of skills and aptitudes, including a talent for working with children; organizational, administrative, and recordkeeping abilities; research and communication skills; the power to influence, motivate, and train others; patience; and creativity. Workers in other occupations requiring some of these aptitudes include teachers—postsecondary; counselors; teacher assistants; education administrators; librarians; childcare workers; public relations specialists; social workers; and athletes, coaches, umpires, and related workers.

Sources of Additional Information

Information on licensure or certification requirements and approved teacher training institutions is available from local school systems and state departments of education.

Information on teachers' unions and education-related issues may be obtained from the following sources:

▶ American Federation of Teachers, 555 New Jersey Ave. NW, Washington, DC 20001.

▶ National Education Association, 1201 16th St. NW, Washington, DC 20036.

A list of institutions with accredited teacher education programs can be obtained from

▶ National Council for Accreditation of Teacher Education, 2010 Massachusetts Ave. NW, Suite 500, Washington, DC 20036-1023. Internet: http://www.ncate.org

▶ Teacher Education Accreditation Council, Suite 300, One Dupont Circle, Washington, DC 20036. Internet: http://www.teac.org

Information on alternative certification programs can be obtained from

▶ National Center for Alternative Certification, 1901 Pennsylvania Ave NW, Suite 201, Washington, DC 20006. Internet: http://www.teach-now.org

Information on National Board Certification can be obtained from

▶ National Board for Professional Teaching Standards, 1525 Wilson Blvd., Suite 500, Arlington, VA 22209. Internet: http://www.nbpts.org

For information on vocational education and vocational education teachers, contact

▶ Association for Career and Technical Education, 1410 King St., Alexandria, VA 22314. Internet: http://www.acteonline.org

For information on careers in educating children and issues affecting preschool teachers, contact either of the following organizations:

▶ National Association for the Education of Young Children, 1509 16th St. NW, Washington, DC 20036. Internet: http://www.naeyc.org

▶ Council for Professional Recognition, 2460 16th St. NW, Washington, DC 20009-3575. Internet: http://www.cdacouncil.org

Teachers—Self-Enrichment Education

(O*NET 25-3021.00)

Significant Points

- Many self-enrichment teachers are self employed or work part time.

- Teachers should have knowledge and enthusiasm for their subject, but little formal training is required.

- Employment is projected to grow much faster than average, and job prospects should be favorable; opportunities may vary by subject taught.

Nature of the Work

Self-enrichment teachers provide instruction in a wide variety of subjects that students take for fun or self-improvement. Some teach a series of classes that provide students with useful life skills, such as cooking, personal finance, and time management. Others provide group instruction intended solely for recreation, such as photography, pottery, and painting. Many others provide one-on-one instruction in a variety of subjects, including dance, singing, or playing a musical instrument. Some teachers conduct courses on academic subjects, such as literature, foreign language, and history, in a non-academic setting. The classes self-enrichment teachers give seldom lead to a degree and attendance is voluntary, but dedicated, talented students sometimes go on to careers in the arts.

Self-enrichment teachers may have styles and methods of instruction that differ greatly. Most self-enrichment classes are relatively informal. Some classes, such as pottery or sewing, may be largely hands-on, with the instructor demonstrating methods or techniques for the class, observing students as they attempt to do it themselves, and pointing out mistakes to students and offering suggestions to improve techniques. Other classes, such as those involving financial planning or religion and spirituality, may center on lectures or might rely more heavily on group discussions. Self-enrichment teachers

may also teach classes offered through religious institutions, such as marriage preparation or classes in religion for children.

Many of the classes that self-enrichment educators teach are shorter in duration than classes taken for academic credit; some finish in 1 or 2 days or several weeks. These brief classes tend to be introductory in nature and generally focus on only one topic—for example, a cooking class that teaches students how to make bread. Some self-enrichment classes introduce children and youth to activities, such as piano or drama, and may be designed to last anywhere from 1 week to several months.

Many self-enrichment teachers provide one-on-one lessons to students. The instructor may only work with the student for an hour or two a week, but tells the student what to practice in the interim until the next lesson. Many instructors work with the same students on a weekly basis for years and derive satisfaction from observing them mature and gain expertise. The most talented students may go on to paid careers as craft artists, painters, sculptors, dancers, singers, or musicians.

All self-enrichment teachers must prepare lessons beforehand and stay current in their fields. Many self-enrichment teachers are self employed and provide instruction as a business. As such, they must collect any fees or tuition and keep records of students whose accounts are prepaid or in arrears. Although not a requirement for most types of classes, teachers may use computers and other modern technologies in their instruction or to maintain business records.

Work environment. Few self-enrichment education teachers are full-time salaried workers. Most either work part time or are self-employed. Some have several part-time teaching assignments, but it is most common for teachers to have a full-time job in another occupation, often related to the subject that they teach, in addition to their part-time teaching job. Although jobs in this occupation are primarily part time and pay is low, most teachers enjoy their work because it gives them the opportunity to share a subject they enjoy with others.

Many classes for adults are held in the evenings and on weekends to accommodate students who have a job or family responsibilities. Similarly, self-enrichment classes for children are usually held after school, on weekends, or during school vacations.

Students in self-enrichment programs attend by choice so they tend to be highly motivated and eager to learn. Students also often bring their own unique experiences to class, which can make teaching them rewarding and satisfying. Self-enrichment teachers must have a great deal of patience, however, particularly when working with young children.

Training, Other Qualifications, and Advancement

The main qualification for self-enrichment teachers is expertise in their subject area, but requirements vary greatly with the type of class taught and the place of employment.

Education and training. In general, there are few educational or training requirements for a job as a self-enrichment teacher beyond being an expert in the subject taught. To demonstrate expertise, however, self enrichment teachers may be required to have formal training in disciplines, such as art or music, where specific teacher training programs are available. Prospective dance teachers, for example, may complete programs that prepare them to teach many types of dance—from ballroom to ballet. Other employers may

Projections data from the National Employment Matrix

Occupational Title	SOC Code	Employment, 2006	Projected employment, 2016	Change, 2006-2016	
				Number	Percent
Self-enrichment education teachers	25-3021	261,000	322,000	60,000	23

NOTE: Data in this table are rounded.

require a portfolio of a teacher's work. For example, to secure a job teaching a photography course, an applicant often needs to show examples of previous work. Some self-enrichment teachers are trained educators or other professionals who teach enrichment classes in their spare time. In many self-enrichment fields, however, instructors are simply experienced in the field, and want to share that experience with others.

Other qualifications. In addition to knowledge of their subject, self-enrichment teachers should have good speaking skills and a talent for making the subject interesting. Patience and the ability to explain and instruct students at a basic level are important as well, particularly for teachers who work with children.

Advancement. Opportunities for advancement in this profession are limited. Some part-time teachers are able to move into full-time teaching positions or program administrator positions, such as coordinator or director. Experienced teachers may mentor new instructors.

Employment

Teachers of self-enrichment education held about 261,000 jobs in 2006. The largest numbers of teachers were employed by public and private educational institutions, religious organizations, and providers of social assistance and amusement and recreation services. More than 20 percent of workers were self employed.

Job Outlook

Employment of self-enrichment education teachers is expected to grow much faster than average, and job prospects should be favorable. A large number of job openings are expected due to job growth, the retirement of existing teachers, and because of those who leave their jobs for other reasons. New opportunities arise constantly because many jobs are short term and are often held as a second job.

Employment change. Employment of self-enrichment education teachers is expected to increase by 23 percent between 2006 and 2016, much faster than the average for all occupations. The need for self-enrichment teachers is expected to grow as more people embrace lifelong learning and as course offerings expand. Demand for self-enrichment education will also increase as a result of demographic changes. Retirees are one of the larger groups of participants in self-enrichment education because they have more time for classes. As members of the baby boom generation begin to retire, demand for self-enrichment education should grow. At the same time, the children of the baby boomers will be entering the age range of another large group of participants, young adults—who often are single and participate in self-enrichment classes for the social, as well as the educational, experience.

Job prospects. Job prospects should be favorable as increasing demand and high turnover creates many opportunities, but opportunities may vary as some fields have more prospective teachers than others. Opportunities should be best for teachers of subjects that are not easily researched on the Internet and those that benefit from

hands-on experiences, such as cooking, crafts, and the arts. Classes on self-improvement, personal finance, and computer and Internet-related subjects are also expected to be popular.

Earnings

Median hourly earnings of wage-and-salary self-enrichment teachers were $16.08 in May 2006. The middle 50 percent earned between $11.29 and $23.08. The lowest 10 percent earned less than $8.53, and the highest 10 percent earned more than $32.02. Self-enrichment teachers are generally paid by the hour or for each class that they teach. Earnings may also be tied to the number of students enrolled in the class.

Part-time instructors are usually paid for each class that they teach, and receive few benefits. Full-time teachers are generally paid a salary and may receive health insurance and other benefits.

Related Occupations

The work of self-enrichment teachers is closely related to that of other types of teachers, especially preschool, kindergarten, elementary school, middle school, and secondary school teachers. Self-enrichment teachers also teach a wide variety of subjects that may be related to the work done by those in many other occupations, such as dancers and choreographers; artists and related workers; musicians, singers, and related workers; recreation workers; and athletes, coaches, umpires, and related workers.

Sources of Additional Information

For information on employment of self-enrichment teachers, contact local schools, colleges, or companies that offer self-enrichment programs.

Tellers

(O*NET 43-3071.00)

Significant Points

- Tellers should enjoy working with the public, feel comfortable handling large amounts of money, and be discreet and trustworthy.

- About 1 out of 4 tellers work part time.

- Many job openings will arise from replacement needs because many tellers eventually leave for jobs in other occupations that offer higher pay or more responsibility.

- Employment of tellers is projected to grow as fast as the average; good job prospects are expected.

Nature of the Work

The teller is the worker most people associate with their bank. Among the responsibilities of tellers are cashing checks, accepting deposits and loan payments, and processing withdrawals. Tellers make up approximately one-fourth of bank employees and conduct most of a bank's routine transactions.

Prior to starting their shifts, tellers receive and count an amount of working cash for their drawers. A supervisor—usually the head teller—verifies this amount. Tellers disburse this cash during the day and are responsible for its safe and accurate handling. Before leaving, tellers count their cash on hand, list the currency received on a balance sheet making sure that the accounts balance, and sort checks and deposit slips. Over the course of a workday, tellers also may process numerous mail transactions. They also may sell savings bonds, accept payment for customers' utility bills and charge cards, process necessary paperwork for certificates of deposit, and sell travelers' checks. Some tellers specialize in handling foreign currencies or commercial or business accounts. Other tellers corroborate deposits and payments to automated teller machines (ATMs).

Being a teller requires a great deal of attention to detail. Before cashing a check, a teller must verify the date, the name of the bank, the identity of the person who is to receive payment, and the legality of the document. A teller also must make sure that the written and numerical amounts agree and that the account has sufficient funds to cover the check. The teller then must carefully count cash to avoid errors. Sometimes a customer withdraws money in the form of a cashier's check, which the teller prepares and verifies. When accepting a deposit, tellers must check the accuracy of the deposit slip before processing the transaction.

As banks begin to offer more and increasingly complex financial services, tellers are being trained to identify customers who might want to buy these services. This task requires them to learn about the various financial products and services the bank offers so that they can explain them to customers and refer interested customers to appropriate specialized sales personnel. In addition, tellers in many banks are being cross-trained to perform some of the functions of customer service representatives. (Customer service representatives are discussed separately in this book.)

Technology continues to play a large role in the job duties of all tellers. In most banks, for example, tellers use computer terminals to record deposits and withdrawals. These terminals often give them quick access to detailed information on customer accounts. Tellers can use this information to tailor the bank's services to fit a customer's needs or to recommend an appropriate bank product or service.

In most banks, head tellers manage teller operations. They set work schedules, ensure that the proper procedures are adhered to, and act as mentors to less experienced tellers. In addition, head tellers may perform the typical duties of a front-line teller, as needed, and may deal with the more difficult customer problems. They may access the vault, ensure that the correct cash balance is in the vault, and oversee large cash transactions.

Work environment. Tellers work in an office environment. They may experience eye and muscle strain, backaches, headaches, and repetitive motion injuries as a result of using computers every day. Tellers may have to sit for extended periods while reviewing detailed data.

Many tellers work regular business hours and a standard 40-hour week. Sometimes, they work evenings and weekends to accommodate extended bank hours. About 1 in 4 tellers worked part time.

Training, Other Qualifications, and Advancement

Most teller jobs require a high school diploma or higher degree. Tellers are usually trained on the job.

Education and training. Most tellers are required to have at least a high school diploma, but some have completed some college training or even a bachelor's degree in business, accounting, or liberal arts. Although a college degree is rarely required, graduates sometimes accept teller positions to get started in banking or in a particular company with the hope of eventually being promoted to managerial or other positions.

Once hired, tellers usually receive on-the-job training. Under the guidance of a supervisor or other senior worker, new employees learn company procedures. Some formal classroom training also may be necessary, such as training in specific computer software.

Other qualifications. Experience working in an office environment or in customer service, and particularly in cash-handling can be important for tellers. Regardless of experience, employers prefer workers who have good communication and customer service skills. Knowledge of word processing and spreadsheet software is also valuable.

Tellers should enjoy contact with the public. They must have a strong aptitude for numbers and feel comfortable handling large amounts of money. They should be discreet and trustworthy because they frequently come in contact with confidential material. Tellers also must be careful, orderly, and detail-oriented to avoid making errors and to recognize errors made by others.

Advancement. Tellers usually advance by taking on more duties and being promoted to head teller or to another supervisory job. Many banks and other employers fill supervisory and managerial positions by promoting individuals from within their organizations, so outstanding tellers who acquire additional skills, experience, and training improve their advancement opportunities. Tellers can prepare for jobs with better pay or more responsibility by taking courses offered by banking and financial institutes, colleges and universities, and private training institutions.

Employment

Tellers held about 608,000 jobs in 2006. The overwhelming majority of tellers worked in commercial banks, savings institutions, or credit unions. The remainder worked in a variety of other finance and other industries.

Job Outlook

Employment of tellers is expected to grow about as fast as the average for all occupations. Overall job prospects should be favorable due to the need to replace workers who retire or otherwise leave the occupation.

Employment change. Employment is projected to grow by 13 percent between 2006 and 2016, which is about as fast as the average for all occupations. To attract customers, banks are opening new branch offices in a variety of locations, such as grocery stores and shopping malls. Banks are also keeping their branches open longer during the day and on weekends. Both of these trends are expected to increase job opportunities for tellers, particularly those who work part time.

Projections data from the National Employment Matrix

Occupational Title	SOC Code	Employment, 2006	Projected employment, 2016	Change, 2006-16	
				Number	Percent
Tellers..	43-3071	608,000	689,000	82,000	13

NOTE: Data in this table are rounded.

Despite the improved outlook, automation and technology will continue to reduce the need for tellers who perform only routine transactions. For example, increased use of ATMs, debit cards, credit cards, and the direct deposit of pay and benefit checks have reduced the need for bank customers to interact with tellers for routine transactions. Electronic banking—conducted over the telephone or the Internet—also is spreading rapidly throughout the banking industry and will reduce the need for tellers in the long run.

Employment of tellers also is being affected by the increasing use of 24-hour telephone centers by many large banks. These centers allow a customer to interact with a bank representative at a distant location, either by telephone or by video terminal. Such centers usually are staffed by customer service representatives.

Job prospects. Job prospects for tellers are expected to be favorable. In addition to job openings expected from growth, most openings will arise from the need to replace the many tellers who transfer to other occupations—which is common for large occupations that normally require little formal education and offer relatively low pay. Prospects will be best for tellers with excellent customer service skills, knowledge about a variety of financial services, and the ability to sell those services.

Earnings

Salaries of tellers vary with experience, region of the country, size of city, and type and size of establishment. Median annual earnings of tellers were $22,140 in May 2006. The middle 50 percent earned between $19,300 and $25,880 a year. The lowest 10 percent earned less than $16,770, and the highest 10 percent earned more than $30,020 a year in May 2006.

Related Occupations

Tellers enter data into a computer, handle cash, and keep track of financial transactions. Other clerks who perform similar duties include bill and account collectors; billing and posting clerks and machine operators; bookkeeping, accounting, and auditing clerks; gaming cage workers; brokerage clerks; and credit authorizers, checkers, and clerks.

Sources of Additional Information

Information on employment opportunities for tellers is available from banks and other employers, local offices of the state employment service, and from

▸ Bank Administration Institute, 1 North Franklin St., Suite 1000, Chicago, IL 60606. Internet: http://www.bai.org

Truck Drivers and Driver/Sales Workers

(O*NET 53-3031.00, 53-3032.00, and 53-3033.00)

Significant Points

■ Overall job opportunities should be favorable.

■ Competition is expected for jobs offering the highest earnings or most favorable work schedules.

■ A commercial driver's license is required to operate large trucks.

Nature of the Work

Truck drivers are a constant presence on the nation's highways and interstates. They deliver everything from automobiles to canned food. Firms of all kinds rely on trucks to pick up and deliver goods because no other form of transportation can deliver goods door-to-door. Even though many goods travel at least part of their journey by ship, train, or airplane, almost everything is carried by trucks at some point.

Before leaving the terminal or warehouse, truck drivers check the fuel level and oil in their trucks. They also inspect the trucks to make sure that the brakes, windshield wipers, and lights are working and that a fire extinguisher, flares, and other safety equipment are aboard and in working order. Drivers make sure their cargo is secure and adjust the mirrors so that both sides of the truck are visible from the driver's seat. Drivers report equipment that is inoperable, missing, or loaded improperly to the dispatcher.

Drivers keep a log of their activities, as required by the U.S. Department of Transportation, to the condition of the truck, and the circumstances of any accidents.

Heavy truck and tractor-trailer drivers operate trucks or vans with a capacity of at least 26,000 pounds Gross Vehicle Weight (GVW). They transport goods including cars, livestock, and other materials in liquid, loose, or packaged form. Many routes are from city to city and cover long distances. Some companies use two drivers on very long runs—one drives while the other sleeps in a berth behind the cab. These "sleeper" runs can last for days, or even weeks. Trucks on sleeper runs typically stop only for fuel, food, loading, and unloading.

Some heavy truck and tractor-trailer drivers who have regular runs transport freight to the same city on a regular basis. Other drivers perform ad hoc runs because shippers request varying service to different cities every day.

Long-distance heavy truck and tractor-trailer drivers spend most of their working time behind the wheel but also may have to load or unload their cargo. This is especially common when drivers haul specialty cargo because they may be the only ones at the destination familiar with procedures or certified to handle the materials. Auto-transport drivers, for example, position cars on the trailers at the manufacturing plant and remove them at the dealerships. When picking up or delivering furniture, drivers of long-distance moving vans hire local workers to help them load or unload.

© JIST Works

Light or delivery services truck drivers operate vans and trucks weighing less than 26,000 pounds GVW. They pick up or deliver merchandise and packages within a specific area. This may include short "turnarounds" to deliver a shipment to a nearby city, pick up another loaded truck or van, and drive it back to their home base the same day. These services may require use of electronic delivery tracking systems to track the whereabouts of the merchandise or packages. Light or delivery services truck drivers usually load or unload the merchandise at the customer's place of business. They may have helpers if there are many deliveries to make during the day or if the load requires heavy moving. Typically, before the driver arrives for work, material handlers load the trucks and arrange items for ease of delivery. Customers must sign receipts for goods and pay drivers the balance due on the merchandise if there is a cash-on-delivery arrangement. At the end of the day, drivers turn in receipts, payments, records of deliveries made, and any reports on mechanical problems with their trucks.

A driver's responsibilities and assignments change according to the type of loads transported and their vehicle's size. The duration of runs depends on the types of cargo and the destinations. Local drivers may provide daily service for a specific route or region, while other drivers make longer, intercity and interstate deliveries. Interstate and intercity cargo tends to vary from job to job more than local cargo does.

Some local truck drivers have sales and customer service responsibilities. The primary responsibility of *driver/sales workers*, or *route drivers*, is to deliver and sell their firms' products over established routes or within an established territory. They sell goods such as food products, including restaurant takeout items, or pick up and deliver items such as laundry. Their response to customer complaints and requests can make the difference between a large order and a lost customer. Route drivers may also take orders and collect payments.

The duties of driver/sales workers vary according to their industry, the policies of their employer, and the emphasis placed on their sales responsibility. Most have wholesale routes that deliver to businesses and stores, rather than to homes. For example, wholesale bakery driver/sales workers deliver and arrange bread, cakes, rolls, and other baked goods on display racks in grocery stores. They estimate how many of each item to stock by paying close attention to what is selling. They may recommend changes in a store's order or encourage the manager to stock new bakery products. Laundries that rent linens, towels, work clothes, and other items employ driver/sales workers to visit businesses regularly to replace soiled laundry. Their duties also may include soliciting new customers along their sales route.

After completing their route, driver/sales workers place orders for their next deliveries based on product sales and customer requests.

Satellites and the Global Positioning System link many trucks with their company's headquarters. Troubleshooting information, directions, weather reports, and other important communications can be instantly relayed to the truck. Drivers can easily communicate with the dispatcher to discuss delivery schedules and what to do in the event of mechanical problems. The satellite link also allows the dispatcher to track the truck's location, fuel consumption, and engine performance. Some drivers also work with computerized inventory tracking equipment. It is important for the producer, warehouse, and customer to know their products' location at all times so they can maintain a high quality of service.

Work environment. Truck driving has become less physically demanding because most trucks now have more comfortable seats, better ventilation, and improved, ergonomically designed cabs. Although these changes make the work environment less taxing, driving for many hours at a stretch, loading and unloading cargo, and making many deliveries can be tiring. Local truck drivers, unlike long-distance drivers, usually return home in the evening. Some self-employed long-distance truck drivers who own and operate their trucks spend most of the year away from home.

The U.S. Department of Transportation governs work hours and other working conditions of truck drivers engaged in interstate commerce. A long-distance driver may drive for 11 hours and work for up to 14 hours—including driving and non-driving duties—after having 10 hours off-duty. A driver may not drive after having worked for 60 hours in the past 7 days or 70 hours in the past 8 days unless they have taken at least 34 consecutive hours off. Most drivers are required to document their time in a logbook. Many drivers, particularly on long runs, work close to the maximum time permitted because they typically are compensated according to the number of miles or hours they drive. Drivers on long runs face boredom, loneliness, and fatigue. Drivers often travel nights, holidays, and weekends to avoid traffic delays.

Local truck drivers frequently work 50 or more hours a week. Drivers who handle food for chain grocery stores, produce markets, or bakeries typically work long hours—starting late at night or early in the morning. Although most drivers have regular routes, some have different routes each day. Many local truck drivers, particularly driver/sales workers, load and unload their own trucks. This requires considerable lifting, carrying, and walking each day.

Training, Other Qualifications, and Advancement

A commercial driver's license (CDL) is required to drive large trucks and a regular driver's license is required to drive all other trucks. Training for the CDL is offered by many private and public vocational-technical schools. Many jobs driving smaller trucks require only brief on-the-job training.

Education and training. Taking driver-training courses is a good way to prepare for truck driving jobs and to obtain a commercial drivers license (CDL). High school courses in driver training and automotive mechanics also may be helpful. Many private and public vocational-technical schools offer tractor-trailer driver training programs. Students learn to maneuver large vehicles on crowded streets and in highway traffic. They also learn to inspect trucks and freight for compliance with regulations. Some states require prospective drivers to complete a training course in basic truck driving before getting their CDL.

Completion of a program does not guarantee a job. Some programs provide only a limited amount of actual driving experience. People interested in attending a driving school should check with local trucking companies to make sure the school's training is acceptable. The Professional Truck Driver Institute (PTDI), a nonprofit organization established by the trucking industry, manufacturers, and others, certifies driver-training courses at truck driver training schools that meet industry standards and Federal Highway Administration guidelines for training tractor-trailer drivers.

Training given to new drivers by employers is usually informal and may consist of only a few hours of instruction from an experienced driver, sometimes on the new employee's own time. New drivers may also ride with and observe experienced drivers before getting their own assignments. Drivers receive additional training to drive special types of trucks or handle hazardous materials. Some companies give one to two days of classroom instruction covering general duties, the operation and loading of a truck, company policies, and the preparation of delivery forms and company records. Driver/sales workers also receive training on the various types of products their company carries so that they can effectively answer questions about the products and more easily market them to their customers.

New drivers sometimes start on panel trucks or other small straight trucks. As they gain experience and show competent driving skills, new drivers may advance to larger, heavier trucks and finally to tractor-trailers.

Licensure. State and federal regulations govern the qualifications and standards for truck drivers. All drivers must comply with federal regulations and any state regulations that are in excess of those federal requirements. Truck drivers must have a driver's license issued by the state in which they live, and most employers require a clean driving record. Drivers of trucks designed to carry 26,000 pounds or more—including most tractor-trailers, as well as bigger straight trucks—must obtain a commercial driver's license. All truck drivers who operate trucks transporting hazardous materials must obtain a CDL, regardless of truck size. In order to receive the hazardous materials endorsement, a driver must be fingerprinted and submit to a criminal background check by the Transportation Security Administration. In many states, a regular driver's license is sufficient for driving light trucks and vans.

To qualify for a CDL, an applicant must have a clean driving record, pass a written test on rules and regulations, and demonstrate that they can operate a commercial truck safely. A national database permanently records all driving violations committed by those with a CDL. A state will check these records and deny a CDL to those who already have a license suspended or revoked in another state. Licensed drivers must accompany trainees until they get their own CDL. A person may not hold more than one license at a time and must surrender any other licenses when a CDL is issued. Information on how to apply for a CDL may be obtained from state motor vehicle administrations.

Many states allow those who are as young as 18 years old to drive trucks within their borders. To drive a commercial vehicle between states one must be at least 21 years of age, according to the Federal Motor Carrier Safety Regulations published by the U.S. Department of Transportation (U. S. DOT). Regulations also require drivers to pass a physical examination once every two years. Physical qualifications include good hearing, at least 20/40 vision with glasses or corrective lenses, and a 70-degree field of vision in each eye. Drivers may not be colorblind. Drivers must also be able to hear a forced whisper in one ear at not less than 5 feet, with a hearing aid if needed. Drivers must have normal use of arms and legs and normal blood pressure. People with epilepsy or diabetes controlled by insulin are not permitted to be interstate truck drivers.

Federal regulations also require employers to test their drivers for alcohol and drug use as a condition of employment and require periodic random tests of the drivers while they are on duty. Drivers may not use any controlled substances, unless prescribed by a licensed physician. A driver must not have been convicted of a felony involving the use of a motor vehicle or a crime involving drugs, driving under the influence of drugs or alcohol, refusing to submit to an alcohol test required by a state or its implied consent laws or regulations, leaving the scene of a crime, or causing a fatality through negligent operation of a motor vehicle. All drivers must be able to read and speak English well enough to read road signs, prepare reports, and communicate with law enforcement officers and the public.

Other qualifications. Many trucking companies have higher standards than those described here. Many firms require that drivers be at least 22 years old, be able to lift heavy objects, and have driven trucks for three to five years. Many prefer to hire high school graduates and require annual physical examinations. Companies have an economic incentive to hire less risky drivers, as good drivers use less fuel and cost less to insure.

Drivers must get along well with people because they often deal directly with customers. Employers seek driver/sales workers who speak well and have self-confidence, initiative, tact, and a neat appearance. Employers also look for responsible, self-motivated individuals who are able to work well with little supervision.

Advancement. Although most new truck drivers are assigned to regular driving jobs immediately, some start as extra drivers—substituting for regular drivers who are ill or on vacation. Extra drivers receive a regular assignment when an opening occurs.

Truck drivers can advance to driving runs that provide higher earnings, preferred schedules, or better working conditions. Local truck drivers may advance to driving heavy or specialized trucks or transfer to long-distance truck driving. Working for companies that also employ long-distance drivers is the best way to advance to these positions. Few truck drivers become dispatchers or managers.

Many long-distance truck drivers purchase trucks and go into business for themselves. Although some of these owner-operators are successful, others fail to cover expenses and go out of business. Owner-operators should have good business sense as well as truck driving experience. Courses in accounting, business, and business mathematics are helpful. Knowledge of truck mechanics can enable owner-operators to perform their own routine maintenance and minor repairs.

Employment

Truck drivers and driver/sales workers held about 3.4 million jobs in 2006. Of these workers, 445,000 were driver/sales workers and 2.9 million were truck drivers. Most truck drivers find employment in large metropolitan areas or along major interstate roadways where trucking, retail, and wholesale companies tend to have their distribution outlets. Some drivers work in rural areas, providing specialized services such as delivering newspapers to customers.

The truck transportation industry employed 26 percent of all truck drivers and driver/sales workers in the United States. Another 25 percent worked for companies engaged in wholesale or retail trade. The remaining truck drivers and driver/sales workers were distributed across many industries, including construction and manufacturing.

Around 9 percent of all truck drivers and driver/sales workers were self-employed. Of these, a significant number were owner-operators who either served a variety of businesses independently or leased their services and trucks to a trucking company.

Projections data from the National Employment Matrix

Occupational Title	SOC Code	Employment, 2006	Projected employment, 2016	Change, 2006-16	
				Number	Percent
Driver/sales workers and truck drivers..	53-3030	3,356,000	3,614,000	258,000	8
Driver/sales workers...	53-3031	445,000	421,000	-24,000	-5
Truck drivers, heavy and tractor-trailer..	53-3032	1,860,000	2,053,000	193,000	10
Truck drivers, light or delivery services.......................................	53-3033	1,051,000	1,140,000	89,000	8

NOTE: Data in this table are rounded.

Job Outlook

Overall job opportunities should be favorable for truck drivers, although opportunities may vary greatly in terms of earnings, weekly work hours, number of nights spent on the road, and quality of equipment. Competition is expected for jobs offering the highest earnings or most favorable work schedules. Average growth is expected.

Employment change. Overall employment of truck drivers and driver/sales workers is expected to increase by 8 percent over the 2006–2016 decade, which is about as fast as the average for all occupations, due to growth in the economy and in the amount of freight carried by truck. Because it is such a large occupation, truck drivers will have a very large number of new jobs arise, over 258,000 over the 2006–2016 period. Competing forms of freight transportation—rail, air, and ship transportation—require trucks to move the goods between ports, depots, airports, warehouses, retailers, and final consumers who are not connected to these other modes of transportation. Demand for long-distance drivers will remain strong because they can transport perishable and time-sensitive goods more effectively than alternate modes of transportation.

Job prospects. Job opportunities should be favorable for truck drivers. In addition to growth in demand for truck drivers, numerous job openings will occur as experienced drivers leave this large occupation to transfer to other fields of work, retire, or leave the labor force for other reasons. Jobs vary greatly in terms of earnings, weekly work hours, the number of nights spent on the road, and quality of equipment. There may be competition for the jobs with the highest earnings and most favorable work schedules. There will be more competition for jobs with local carriers than for those with long-distance carriers because of the more desirable working conditions of local carriers.

Job opportunities may vary from year to year since the output of the economy dictates the amount of freight to be moved. Companies tend to hire more drivers when the economy is strong and their services are in high demand. When the economy slows, employers hire fewer drivers or may lay off some drivers. Independent owner-operators are particularly vulnerable to slowdowns. Industries least likely to be affected by economic fluctuation, such as grocery stores, tend to be the most stable employers of truck drivers and driver/sales workers.

Earnings

Median hourly earnings of heavy truck and tractor-trailer drivers were $16.85 in May 2006. The middle 50 percent earned between $13.33 and $21.04 an hour. The lowest 10 percent earned less than $10.80, and the highest 10 percent earned more than $25.39 an hour. Median hourly earnings in the industries employing the largest numbers of heavy truck and tractor-trailer drivers in May 2006 were

General freight trucking	$18.38
Grocery and related product wholesalers	18.01
Specialized freight trucking	16.40
Cement and concrete product manufacturing	15.26
Other specialty trade contractors	14.94

Median hourly earnings of light or delivery services truck drivers were $12.17 in May 2006. The middle 50 percent earned between $9.31 and $16.16 an hour. The lowest 10 percent earned less than $7.47, and the highest 10 percent earned more than $21.23 an hour. Median hourly earnings in the industries employing the largest numbers of light or delivery services truck drivers in May 2006 were

Couriers	$17.80
General freight trucking	15.33
Grocery and related product wholesalers	12.84
Building material and supplies dealers	11.54
Automotive parts, accessories, and tire stores	8.38

Median hourly earnings of driver/sales workers, including commissions, were $9.99 in May 2006. The middle 50 percent earned between $7.12 and $15.00 an hour. The lowest 10 percent earned less than $6.19, and the highest 10 percent earned more than $20.30 an hour. Median hourly earnings in the industries employing the largest numbers of driver/sales workers in May 2006 were

Drycleaning and laundry services	$14.81
Direct selling establishments	13.72
Grocery and related product wholesalers	12.37
Full-service restaurants	7.11
Limited-service eating places	7.02

Local truck drivers tend to be paid by the hour, with extra pay for working overtime. Employers pay long-distance drivers primarily by the mile. The per-mile rate can vary greatly from employer to employer and may even depend on the type of cargo being hauled. Some long-distance drivers are paid a percent of each load's revenue. Typically, earnings increase with mileage driven, seniority, and the size and type of truck driven. Most driver/sales workers receive commissions based on their sales in addition to their hourly wages.

Most self-employed truck drivers are primarily engaged in long-distance hauling. Many truck drivers are members of the International Brotherhood of Teamsters. Some truck drivers employed by companies outside the trucking industry are members of unions representing the plant workers of the companies for which they work.

Related Occupations

Other driving occupations include ambulance drivers and attendants, except emergency medical technicians; bus drivers; and taxi

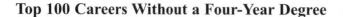

drivers and chauffeurs. Another occupation involving sales duties is sales representatives, wholesale and manufacturing.

Sources of Additional Information

Information on truck driver employment opportunities is available from local trucking companies and local offices of the state employment service.

Information on career opportunities in truck driving may be obtained from

▸ American Trucking Associations, Inc., 950 North Glebe Rd., Suite 210, Arlington, VA 22203. Internet: http://www.trucking.org

A list of certified tractor-trailer driver training courses may be obtained from

▸ Professional Truck Driver Institute, 2200 Mill Rd., Alexandria, VA 22314. Internet: http://www.ptdi.org

Information on union truck driving can be obtained from

▸ The International Brotherhood of Teamsters, 25 Louisiana Ave. NW, Washington, DC 20001.

Information on becoming a truck driver may be obtained from: http://www.gettrucking.com

Veterinary Technologists and Technicians

(O*NET 29-2056.00)

Significant Points

■ Animal lovers get satisfaction from this occupation, but aspects of the work can be unpleasant, physically and emotionally demanding, and sometimes dangerous.

■ Entrants generally complete a 2-year or 4-year veterinary technology program and must pass a state examination.

■ Employment is expected to grow much faster than average.

■ Overall job opportunities should be excellent; however, keen competition is expected for jobs in zoos and aquariums.

Nature of the Work

Owners of pets and other animals today expect state-of-the-art veterinary care. To provide this service, Veterinarians use the skills of veterinary technologists and technicians, who perform many of the same duties for a veterinarian that a nurse would for a physician, including routine laboratory and clinical procedures. Although specific job duties vary by employer, there often is little difference between the tasks carried out by technicians and by technologists, despite some differences in formal education and training. As a result, most workers in this occupation are called technicians.

Veterinary technologists and technicians typically conduct clinical work in a private practice under the supervision of a licensed veterinarian. They often perform various medical tests and treat and diagnose medical conditions and diseases in animals. For example, they may perform laboratory tests such as urinalysis and blood counts, assist with dental prophylaxis, prepare tissue samples, take blood samples, or assist Veterinarians in a variety of tests and analyses in which they often use various items of medical equipment, such as test tubes and diagnostic equipment. While most of these duties are performed in a laboratory setting, many are not. For example, some veterinary technicians obtain and record patients' case histories, expose and develop x rays and radiographs, and provide specialized nursing care. In addition, experienced veterinary technicians may discuss a pet's condition with its owners and train new clinic personnel. Veterinary technologists and technicians assisting small-animal practitioners usually care for companion animals, such as cats and dogs, but can perform a variety of duties with mice, rats, sheep, pigs, cattle, monkeys, birds, fish, and frogs. Very few veterinary technologists work in mixed animal practices where they care for both small companion animals and larger, nondomestic animals.

Besides working in private clinics and animal hospitals, veterinary technologists and technicians may work in research facilities, where they administer medications orally or topically, prepare samples for laboratory examinations, and record information on an animal's genealogy, diet, weight, medications, food intake, and clinical signs of pain and distress. Some may sterilize laboratory and surgical equipment and provide routine postoperative care. At research facilities, veterinary technologists typically work under the guidance of Veterinarians or physicians. Some veterinary technologists vaccinate newly admitted animals and occasionally may have to euthanize seriously ill, severely injured, or unwanted animals.

While the goal of most veterinary technologists and technicians is to promote animal health, some contribute to human health as well. Veterinary technologists occasionally assist Veterinarians in implementing research projects as they work with other scientists in medical-related fields such as gene therapy and cloning. Some find opportunities in biomedical research, wildlife medicine, the military, livestock management, or pharmaceutical sales.

Work environment. People who love animals get satisfaction from working with and helping them. However, some of the work may be unpleasant, physically and emotionally demanding, and sometimes dangerous. At times, veterinary technicians must clean cages and lift, hold, or restrain animals, risking exposure to bites or scratches. These workers must take precautions when treating animals with germicides or insecticides. The work setting can be noisy.

Veterinary technologists and technicians who witness abused animals or who euthanize unwanted, aged, or hopelessly injured animals may experience emotional stress. Those working for humane societies and animal shelters often deal with the public, some of whom might react with hostility to any implication that the owners are neglecting or abusing their pets. Such workers must maintain a calm and professional demeanor while they enforce the laws regarding animal care.

In some animal hospitals, research facilities, and animal shelters, a veterinary technician is on duty 24 hours a day, which means that some may work night shifts. Most full-time veterinary technologists and technicians work about 40 hours a week, although some work 50 or more hours a week.

Training, Other Qualifications, and Advancement

There are primarily two levels of education and training for entry to this occupation: a two-year program for veterinary technicians and a four-year program for veterinary technologists.

Education and training. Most entry-level veterinary technicians have a two-year associate degree from an American Veterinary Medical Association (AVMA)-accredited community college program in veterinary technology in which courses are taught in clinical and laboratory settings using live animals. About 16 colleges offer veterinary technology programs that are longer and that culminate in a four-year bachelor's degree in veterinary technology. These four-year colleges, in addition to some vocational schools, also offer two-year programs in laboratory animal science. Several schools offer distance learning.

In 2006, 131 veterinary technology programs in 44 states were accredited by the American Veterinary Medical Association (AVMA). Graduation from an AVMA-accredited veterinary technology program allows students to take the credentialing exam in any state in the country.

Persons interested in careers as veterinary technologists and technicians should take as many high school science, biology, and math courses as possible. Science courses taken beyond high school, in an associate or bachelor's degree program, should emphasize practical skills in a clinical or laboratory setting.

Technologists and technicians usually begin work as trainees in routine positions under the direct supervision of a veterinarian. Entry-level workers whose training or educational background encompasses extensive hands-on experience with a variety of laboratory equipment, including diagnostic and medical equipment, usually require a shorter period of on-the-job training.

Licensure and certification. Each state regulates veterinary technicians and technologists differently; however, all states require them to pass a credentialing exam following coursework. Passing the state exam assures the public that the technician or technologist has sufficient knowledge to work in a veterinary clinic or hospital. Candidates are tested for competency through an examination that includes oral, written, and practical portions and that is regulated by the state Board of Veterinary Examiners or the appropriate state agency. Depending on the state, candidates may become registered, licensed, or certified. Most states, however, use the National Veterinary Technician (NVT) exam. Prospects usually can have their passing scores transferred from one state to another, so long as both states use the same exam.

Employers recommend American Association for Laboratory Animal Science (AALAS) certification for those seeking employment in a research facility. AALAS offers certification for three levels of technician competence, with a focus on three principal areas—animal husbandry, facility management, and animal health and welfare. Those who wish to become certified must satisfy a combination of education and experience requirements prior to taking the AALAS examination. Work experience must be directly related to the maintenance, health, and well-being of laboratory animals and must be gained in a laboratory animal facility as defined by AALAS. Candidates who meet the necessary criteria can begin pursuing the desired certification on the basis of their qualifications. The lowest level of certification is Assistant Laboratory Animal Technician (ALAT), the second level is Laboratory Animal Technician (LAT), and the highest level of certification is Laboratory Animal Technologist (LATG). The AALAS examination consists of multiple-choice questions and is longer and more difficult for higher levels of certification, ranging from two hours and 120 multiple choice questions for the ALAT to three hours and 180 multiple choice questions for the LATG.

Other qualifications. As veterinary technologists and technicians often deal with pet owners, communication skills are very important. In addition, technologists and technicians should be able to work well with others, because teamwork with Veterinarians is common. Organizational ability and the ability to pay attention to detail also are important.

Advancement. As they gain experience, technologists and technicians take on more responsibility and carry out more assignments under only general veterinary supervision. Some eventually may become supervisors.

Employment

Veterinary technologists and technicians held about 71,000 jobs in 2006. About 91 percent worked in veterinary services. The remainder worked in boarding kennels, animal shelters, stables, grooming salons, zoos, state and private educational institutions, and local, state, and federal agencies.

Job Outlook

Excellent job opportunities will stem from the need to replace veterinary technologists and technicians who leave the occupation and from the limited output of qualified veterinary technicians from 2-year programs, which are not expected to meet the demand over the 2006–2016 period. Employment is expected to grow much faster than average.

Employment change. Employment of veterinary technologists and technicians is expected to grow 41 percent over the 2006–2016 projection period, which is much faster than the average for all occupations. Pet owners are becoming more affluent and more willing to pay for advanced veterinary care because many of them consider their pet to be part of the family. This growing affluence and view of pets will continue to increase the demand for veterinary care. The vast majority of veterinary technicians work at private clinical practice under Veterinarians. As the number of Veterinarians grows to meet the demand for veterinary care, so will the number of veterinary technicians needed to assist them.

The number of pet owners who take advantage of veterinary services for their pets—currently about 6 in 10—is expected to grow over the projection period, increasing employment opportunities. The availability of advanced veterinary services, such as preventive dental care and surgical procedures, also will provide opportunities for workers specializing in those areas as they will be needed to assist licensed Veterinarians. The rapidly growing number of cats kept as companion pets is expected to boost the demand for feline medicine and services. Further demand for these workers will stem from the desire to replace veterinary assistants with more highly skilled technicians and technologists in animal clinics and hospitals, shelters, boarding kennels, and humane societies.

Biomedical facilities, diagnostic laboratories, wildlife facilities, humane societies, animal control facilities, drug or food manufacturing companies, and food safety inspection facilities will provide additional jobs for veterinary technologists and technicians.

Projections data from the National Employment Matrix

Occupational Title	SOC Code	Employment, 2006	Projected employment, 2016	Change, 2006-2016	
				Number	Percent
Veterinary technologists and technicians	29-2056	71,000	100,000	29,000	41

NOTE: Data in this table are rounded.

However, keen competition is expected for veterinary technologist and technician jobs in zoos and aquariums, due to expected slow growth in facility capacity, low turnover among workers, the limited number of positions, and the fact that they work in zoos and aquariums attracts many candidates.

Job prospects. Excellent job opportunities are expected because of the relatively few veterinary technology graduates each year. The number of 2-year programs has recently grown to 131, but due to small class sizes, fewer than 3,000 graduates are anticipated each year, which is not expected to meet demand. Additionally, many veterinary technicians remain in the field for only 7 to 8 years, so the need to replace workers who leave the occupation each year also will produce many job opportunities.

Employment of veterinary technicians and technologists is relatively stable during periods of economic recession. Layoffs are less likely to occur among veterinary technologists and technicians than in some other occupations because animals will continue to require medical care.

Earnings

Median hourly earnings of veterinary technologists and technicians were $12.88 in May 2006. The middle 50 percent earned between $10.44 and $15.77. The bottom 10 percent earned less than $8.79, and the top 10 percent earned more than $18.68.

Related Occupations

Others who work extensively with animals include animal care and service workers, and veterinary assistants and laboratory animal caretakers. Like veterinary technologists and technicians, they must have patience and feel comfortable with animals. However, the level of training required for these occupations is less than that needed by veterinary technologists and technicians. Veterinarians, who need much more formal education, also work extensively with animals, preventing, diagnosing, and treating their diseases, disorders, and injuries.

Sources of Additional Information

For information on certification as a laboratory animal technician or technologist, contact

▶ American Association for Laboratory Animal Science, 9190 Crestwyn Hills Dr., Memphis, TN 38125. Internet: http://www.aalas.org

For information on careers in veterinary medicine and a listing of AVMA-accredited veterinary technology programs, contact

▶ American Veterinary Medical Association, 1931 N. Meacham Rd., Suite 100, Schaumburg, IL 60173-4360. Internet: http://www.avma.org

Water and Liquid Waste Treatment Plant and System Operators

(O*NET 51-8031.00)

Significant Points

■ Employment is concentrated in local government and private water, sewage, and other systems utilities.

■ Because of a large number of upcoming retirements and the difficulty of filling these positions, job opportunities will be excellent.

■ Completion of an associate degree or a 1-year certificate program increases an applicant's chances for employment and promotion.

Nature of the Work

Clean water is essential for everyday life. *Water treatment plant and system operators* treat water so that it is safe to drink. *Liquid waste treatment plant and system operators*, also known as wastewater treatment plant and system operators, remove harmful pollutants from domestic and industrial liquid waste so that it is safe to return to the environment.

Water is pumped from wells, rivers, streams, and reservoirs to water treatment plants, where it is treated and distributed to customers. Wastewater travels through customers' sewer pipes to wastewater treatment plants, where it is treated and either returned to streams, rivers, and oceans or reused for irrigation and landscaping. Operators in both types of plants control equipment and processes that remove or destroy harmful materials, chemicals, and microorganisms from the water. Operators also control pumps, valves, and other equipment that moves the water or wastewater through the various treatment processes, after which they dispose of the removed waste materials.

Operators read, interpret, and adjust meters and gauges to make sure that plant equipment and processes are working properly. Operators control chemical-feeding devices, take samples of the water or wastewater, perform chemical and biological laboratory analyses, and adjust the amounts of chemicals, such as chlorine, in the water. They employ a variety of instruments to sample and measure water quality, and they use common hand and power tools to make repairs to valves, pumps, and other equipment.

Water and wastewater treatment plant and system operators increasingly rely on computers to help monitor equipment, store the results of sampling, make process-control decisions, schedule and record maintenance activities, and produce reports. In some modern plants, operators also use computers to monitor automated systems and determine how to address problems.

Occasionally, operators must work during emergencies. A heavy rainstorm, for example, may cause large amounts of wastewater to flow into sewers, exceeding a plant's treatment capacity. Emergencies also can be caused by conditions inside a plant, such as chlorine gas leaks or oxygen deficiencies. To handle these conditions, operators are trained to make an emergency management response and use special safety equipment and procedures to protect public health and the facility. During these periods, operators may work under extreme pressure to correct problems as quickly as possible. Because working conditions may be dangerous, operators must be extremely cautious.

The specific duties of plant operators depend on the type and size of the plant. In smaller plants, one operator may control all of the machinery, perform tests, keep records, handle complaints, and perform repairs and maintenance. Operators in this type of plant may have to be on-call 24 hours a day in case of an emergency. In medium-sized plants, operators monitor the plant throughout the night by working in shifts. In large plants, operators may be more specialized and monitor only one process. They might work with chemists, engineers, laboratory technicians, mechanics, helpers, supervisors, and a superintendent.

Water quality standards are largely set by two major federal environmental statutes: the Safe Drinking Water Act, which specifies standards for drinking water, and the Clean Water Act, which regulates the discharge of pollutants. Industrial facilities that send their wastes to municipal treatment plants must meet certain minimum standards to ensure that the wastes have been adequately pretreated and will not damage municipal treatment facilities. Municipal water treatment plants also must meet stringent standards for drinking water. The list of contaminants regulated by these statutes has grown over time. As a result, plant operators must be familiar with the guidelines established by federal regulations and how they affect their plant. In addition, operators must be aware of any guidelines imposed by the state or locality in which the plant operates.

Work environment. Water and wastewater treatment plant and system operators work both indoors and outdoors and may be exposed to noise from machinery and to unpleasant odors. Operators' work is physically demanding and often is performed in unclean locations; they must pay close attention to safety procedures because of the presence of hazardous conditions, such as slippery walkways, dangerous gases, and malfunctioning equipment.

Plants operate 24 hours a day, 7 days a week. In small plants, operators may work during the day and be on-call in the evening, nights and weekends. Medium and large plants that require constant monitoring may employ workers in three 8-hour shifts. Because larger plants require constant monitoring, weekend and holiday work is generally required. Operators may be required to work overtime.

Training, Other Qualifications, and Advancement

Employers usually hire high school graduates who are trained on-the-job, and later become licensed. Education after high school improves job prospects.

Education and training. A high school diploma usually is required for an individual to become a water or wastewater treatment plant operator. The completion of an associate degree or a one-year certificate program in water quality and wastewater treatment technology increases an applicant's chances for employment and promotion

because plants are becoming more complex. The majority of such programs are offered by trade associations, and can be found throughout the country. These programs provide a good general knowledge of water and wastewater treatment processes, as well as basic preparation for becoming an operator. In some cases, a degree or certificate program can be substituted for experience, allowing a worker to become licensed at a higher level more quickly.

Trainees usually start as attendants or operators-in-training and learn their skills on the job under the direction of an experienced operator. They learn by observing and doing routine tasks such as recording meter readings, taking samples of wastewater and sludge, and performing simple maintenance and repair work on pumps, electric motors, valves, and other plant equipment. Larger treatment plants generally combine this on-the-job training with formal classroom or self-paced study programs.

Most state drinking water and water pollution control agencies offer courses to improve operators' skills and knowledge. The courses cover principles of treatment processes and process control, laboratory procedures, maintenance, management skills, collection systems, safety, chlorination, sedimentation, biological treatment, sludge treatment and disposal, and flow measurements. Some operators take correspondence courses on subjects related to water and wastewater treatment, and some employers pay part of the tuition for related college courses in science or engineering.

Licensure. The Safe Drinking Water Act Amendments of 1996, enforced by the U.S. Environmental Protection Agency, specify national minimum standards for certification of public water system operators. Operators must pass an examination certifying that they are capable of overseeing water treatment operations. Mandatory certification is implemented at the state level, and licensing requirements and standards vary widely depending on the state. There are generally three to four different levels of certification, depending on the operator's experience and training. Higher levels qualify the operator to oversee a wider variety of treatment processes. Although relocation may mean having to become certified in a new jurisdiction, many states accept other states' certifications.

Other qualifications. Water and wastewater treatment plant operators need mechanical aptitude and the ability to solve problems intuitively. They should also be competent in basic mathematics, chemistry, and biology. They must have the ability to apply data to formulas that determine treatment requirements, flow levels, and concentration levels. Some basic familiarity with computers also is necessary, as operators generally use them to record data. Some plants also use computer-controlled equipment and instrumentation.

Certification and advancement. In addition to mandatory certifications required by law, operators can earn voluntary certifications that demonstrate their skills and knowledge. The Association of Boards of Certification offers several levels and types of certification to people who pass exams and have sufficient education and experience.

As operators are promoted, they become responsible for more complex treatment processes. Some operators are promoted to plant supervisor or superintendent; others advance by transferring to a larger facility. Postsecondary training in water and wastewater treatment, coupled with increasingly responsible experience as an operator, may be sufficient to qualify a worker to become superintendent of a small plant, where a superintendent also serves as an operator. However, educational requirements are rising as larger, more complex treatment plants are built to meet new drinking water and water

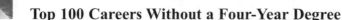

Projections data from the National Employment Matrix

Occupational Title	SOC Code	Employment, 2006	Projected employment, 2016	Change, 2006-16	
				Number	Percent
Water and liquid waste treatment plant and system operators	51-8031	111,000	126,000	15,000	14

NOTE: Data in this table are rounded.

pollution control standards. With each promotion, the operator must have greater knowledge of federal, state, and local regulations. Superintendents of large plants generally need an engineering or science degree.

A few operators get jobs as technicians with state drinking water or water pollution control agencies. In that capacity, they monitor and provide technical assistance to plants throughout the state. Vocational-technical school or community college training generally is preferred for technician jobs. Experienced operators may transfer to related jobs with industrial liquid waste treatment plants, water or liquid waste treatment equipment and chemical companies, engineering consulting firms, or vocational-technical schools.

Employment

Water and wastewater treatment plant and system operators held about 111,000 jobs in 2006. Almost 4 in 5 operators worked for local governments. Others worked primarily for private water, sewage, and other systems utilities and for private waste treatment and disposal and waste management services companies. Private firms are increasingly providing operation and management services to local governments on a contract basis.

Water and wastewater treatment plant and system operators were employed throughout the country, but most jobs were in larger towns and cities. Although nearly all operators worked full time, those in small towns may work only part time at the treatment plant, with the remainder of their time spent handling other municipal duties.

Job Outlook

Water and wastewater treatment plant and system operators jobs are expected to grow faster than the average for all occupations. Job opportunities should be excellent for qualified workers.

Employment change. Employment of water and wastewater treatment plant and system operators is expected to grow by 14 percent between 2006 and 2016, which is faster than the average for all occupations. An increasing population and the growth of the economy are expected to boost demand for water and wastewater treatment services. As new plants are constructed to meet this demand, new water and wastewater treatment plant and system operator new jobs will arise.

Local governments are the largest employers of water and wastewater treatment plant and system operators. Employment in privately owned facilities will grow faster, as federal certification requirements have increased utilities' reliance on private firms specializing in the operation and management of water and wastewater treatment facilities.

Job prospects. Job opportunities should be excellent because the retirement of the baby boomer generation will require that many operators with years of experience be replaced. Further, the number of applicants for these jobs is normally low, due primarily to the physically demanding and unappealing nature of some of the work. Opportunities should be best for persons with mechanical aptitude and problem solving skills.

Earnings

Median annual earnings of water and wastewater treatment plant and system operators were $36,070 in May 2006. The middle 50 percent earned between $28,120 and $45,190. The lowest 10 percent earned less than $21,860, and the highest 10 percent earned more than $55,120. Median annual earnings of water and liquid waste treatment plant and systems operators in May 2006 were $36,200 in local government and $34,180 in water, sewage, and other systems.

In addition to their annual salaries, water and wastewater treatment plant and system operators usually receive benefits that may include health and life insurance, a retirement plan, and educational reimbursement for job-related courses.

Related Occupations

Other workers whose main activity consists of operating a system of machinery to process or produce materials include chemical plant and system operators; gas plant operators; petroleum pump system operators, refinery operators, and gaugers; power plant operators, distributors, and dispatchers; and stationary engineers and boiler operators.

Sources of Additional Information

For information on employment opportunities, contact state or local water pollution control agencies, state water and liquid waste operator associations, state environmental training centers, or local offices of the state employment service.

For information on certification, contact

▸ Association of Boards of Certification, 208 Fifth St., Ames, IA 50010-6259. Internet: http://www.abccert.org

For educational information related to a career as a water or liquid waste treatment plant and system operator, contact

▸ American Water Works Association, 6666 West Quincy Ave., Denver, CO 80235. Internet: http://www.awwa.org

▸ National Rural Water Association, 2915 S. 13th St., Duncan, OK 73533. Internet: http://www.nrwa.org

▸ Water Environment Federation, 601 Wythe St., Alexandria, VA 22314-1994. Internet: http://www.wef.org

Water Transportation Occupations

(O*NET 53-5011.00, 53-5021.00, 53-5021.01, 53-5021.02, 53-5021.03, 53-5022.00, and 53-5031.00)

Significant Points

- Merchant mariners spend extended periods at sea.

- Entry, training, and educational requirements for many water transportation occupations are established and regulated by the U.S. Coast Guard.

- Faster-than-average growth and good job opportunities are expected.

Nature of the Work

The movement of huge amounts of cargo, as well as passengers, between nations and within our nation depends on workers in water transportation occupations, also known on commercial ships as merchant mariners. They operate and maintain deep-sea merchant ships, tugboats, towboats, ferries, dredges, offshore supply vessels, excursion vessels, and other waterborne craft on the oceans, the Great Lakes, rivers, canals, and other waterways, as well as in harbors.

Captains, mates, and pilots of water vessels command or supervise the operations of ships and water vessels, both within domestic waterways and on the deep sea. *Captains* or *masters* are in overall command of the operation of a vessel, and they supervise the work of all other officers and crew. Together with their department heads, captains ensure that proper procedures and safety practices are followed, check to make sure that machinery and equipment are in good working order, and oversee the loading and discharging of cargo or passengers. They also maintain logs and other records tracking the ships' movements, efforts at controlling pollution, and cargo and passengers carried.

Deck officers or *mates* direct the routine operation of the vessel for the captain during the shifts when they are on watch. On smaller vessels, there may be only one mate (called a *pilot* on some inland towing vessels), who alternates watches with the captain. The mate would assume command of the ship if the captain became incapacitated. When more than one mate is necessary aboard a ship, they typically are designated chief mate or first mate, second mate, third mate, etc. Mates also supervise and coordinate activities of the crew aboard the ship. Captains and mates determine the course and speed of the vessel, maneuvering to avoid hazards and continuously monitoring the vessel's position with charts and navigational aides. Captains and mates oversee crew members who steer the vessel, determine its location, operate engines, communicate with other vessels, perform maintenance, handle lines, and operate equipment on the vessel. They inspect the cargo holds during loading to ensure that the load is stowed according to specifications and regulations. Captains and mates also supervise crew members engaged in maintenance and the primary upkeep of the vessel.

Pilots guide ships in and out of harbors, through straits, and on rivers and other confined waterways where a familiarity with local water depths, winds, tides, currents, and hazards such as reefs and shoals are of prime importance. Pilots on river and canal vessels usually are regular crew members, like mates. Harbor pilots are generally independent contractors who accompany vessels while they enter or leave port. Harbor pilots may pilot many ships in a single day.

Ship engineers operate, maintain, and repair propulsion engines, boilers, generators, pumps, and other machinery. Merchant marine vessels usually have four engineering officers: A chief engineer and a first, second, and third assistant engineer. Assistant engineers stand periodic watches, overseeing the safe operation of engines and machinery.

Marine oilers and more experienced *qualified members of the engine department*, or QMEDs, assist the engineers to maintain the vessel in proper running order in the engine spaces below decks. These workers lubricate gears, shafts, bearings, and other moving parts of engines and motors; read pressure and temperature gauges; record data; and sometimes assist with repairs and adjust machinery.

Sailors or *deckhands* operate the vessel and its deck equipment under the direction of the ship's officers and keep the nonengineering areas in good condition. They stand watch, looking out for other vessels and obstructions in the ship's path, as well as for navigational aids such as buoys and lighthouses. They also steer the ship, measure water depth in shallow water, and maintain and operate deck equipment such as lifeboats, anchors, and cargo-handling gear. On vessels handling liquid cargo, mariners designated as *pumpmen* hook up hoses, operate pumps, and clean tanks; on tugboats or tow vessels, they tie barges together into tow units, inspect them periodically, and disconnect them when the destination is reached. When docking or departing, they handle lines. They also perform routine maintenance chores, such as repairing lines, chipping rust, and painting and cleaning decks or other areas. Experienced sailors are designated *able seamen* on oceangoing vessels, but may be called simply deckhands on inland waters; larger vessels usually have a *boatswain*, or *head seaman*.

A typical deep-sea merchant ship has a captain, three deck officers or mates, a chief engineer and three assistant engineers, plus six or more seamen, such as able seamen, oilers, QMEDs, and a cook. The size and service of the ship determine the number of crewmembers for a particular voyage. Small vessels operating in harbors, on rivers, or along the coast may have a crew comprising only a captain and one deckhand. On smaller vessels the cooking responsibilities usually fall under the deckhands' duties.

On larger coastal ships, the crew may include a captain, a mate or pilot, an engineer, and seven or eight seamen. Some ships may have special unlicensed positions for entry level apprentice trainees. Unlicensed positions on a large ship may include a full-time cook, an electrician, and machinery mechanics.

Motorboat operators operate small, motor-driven boats that carry six or fewer passengers on fishing charters. They also take depth soundings in turning basins and serve as liaisons between ships, between ship and shore, between harbors and beaches, or on area patrol.

Work environment. Water transportation workers' schedules vary based upon the type of ship and length of voyage. While on the water, crews are normally on duty for half of the day, 7 days a week.

Merchant mariners on survey and long distance cargo vessels can spend extended periods at sea. Most deep-sea mariners are hired for one or more voyages that last for several months; there is no job security after that. The length of time between voyages varies depending on job availability and personal preference.

Workers on supply vessels transport workers, supplies (water, drilling mud, fuel, and food), and equipment to oil and gas drilling platforms mostly in the Gulf of Mexico. Their voyages can last a few hours to a couple of weeks. As oil and gas exploration pushes into deeper waters, these trips take more time.

Workers on tugs and barges operate on the rivers, lakes, inland waterways, and along the coast. Most tugs have two crews and operate constantly. The crews will alternate, each working for 2-3 weeks and then taking 2-3 weeks off.

Many of those employed on Great Lakes ships work 60 days and have 30 days off, but do not work in the winter when the lakes are frozen. Others work steadily for a week or a month and then have an extended period off. Those on smaller vessels, such as tugs, supply boats and Great Lakes ships, are normally assigned to one vessel and have steady employment.

Workers on ferries transporting commuters work on weekdays in the morning and evening. Other ferries make frequent trips lasting a few hours. Ferries servicing vacation destinations often operate on seasonal schedules. Workers in harbors generally have year-round work. Work in harbors and on ferries is sought after because workers return home every day.

People holding water transportation jobs work in all kinds of weather, except when frozen waters make travel impossible. Although merchant mariners try to avoid severe storms while at sea, working in damp and cold conditions often is inevitable. While it is uncommon for vessels to suffer disasters such as fire, explosion, or a sinking, workers face the possibility that they may have to abandon their craft on short notice if it collides with other vessels or runs aground. They also risk injury or death from falling overboard and hazards associated with working with machinery, heavy loads, and dangerous cargo. However, modern safety management procedures, advanced emergency communications, and effective international rescue systems have greatly improved mariner safety.

Many companies are working to improve the living conditions on vessels to reduce employee turnover. Most of the nation's newest vessels are air conditioned, soundproofed to reduce machinery noise, and equipped with comfortable living quarters. Some companies have added improved entertainment systems and hired full-time cooks. These amenities lessen the difficulty of spending long periods away from home. Advances in communications, particularly e-mail, better link mariners to their families. Nevertheless, some mariners dislike the long periods away from home and the confinement aboard ship and consequently leave the occupation.

Training, Other Qualifications, and Advancement

Entry, training, and educational requirements for many water transportation occupations are established and regulated by the U.S. Coast Guard. Most officers and operators of commercially operated vessels must be licensed by the Coast Guard, which offers various kinds of licenses, depending on the position, body of water, and type of vessel. Individuals must be relicensed when they change the type of ship or the body of water they are on.

Education and training. Entry-level workers are classified as ordinary seamen or deckhands. Workers take some basic training, lasting a few days, in areas such as first aid and firefighting.

There are two paths of education and training for a deck officer or an engineer: applicants must either accumulate thousands of hours of experience while working as a deckhand, or graduate from the U.S. Merchant Marine Academy or another maritime academy. In both cases, applicants must pass a written examination. It is difficult to pass the examination without substantial formal schooling or independent study. The academies offer a four-year academic program leading to a bachelor-of-science degree, a license (issued only by the Coast Guard) as a third mate (deck officer) or third assistant engineer (engineering officer), and, if the person chooses, a commission as ensign in the U.S. Naval Reserve, Merchant Marine Reserve, or Coast Guard Reserve. With experience and additional training, third officers may qualify for higher rank. Generally officers on deep water vessels are academy graduates and those in supply boats, inland waterways, and rivers rose to their positions through years of experience.

Harbor pilot training usually consists of an extended apprenticeship with a towing company or a habor pilots' association. Entrants may be able seamen or licensed officers.

Licensure. Coast Guard licensing requirements vary by occupational specialty, type of vessel, and by body of water (river, inland waterway, Great Lakes, and oceans.) The requirements increase as the skill level of the occupational specialty increases and the size of the vessel increases.

Entry level seamen or deckhands on vessels operating in harbors or on rivers or other waterways do not need a license. All others working on larger, ocean-going vessels do need a license. To get the basic entry level license, workers must pass a drug screen, take a medical exam, and be U.S. citizens.

Workers on ocean-going or Great Lakes vessels need specialty licenses to work as engineering officers, or deck officers. On rivers or inland waterways, only the captain or anyone who steers the boat needs a license. For more information on licensing requirements see the Coast Guard's Web site listed in the sources of additional information. Radio operators are licensed by the Federal Communications Commission.

Other qualifications. Most positions require excellent health, good vision, and color perception. Good general physical condition is needed because many jobs require the ability to lift heavy objects, withstand heat and cold, stand or stoop for long periods of time, dexterity to maneuver through tight spaces, and good balance on uneven and wet surfaces and in rough water.

Advancement. Experience and passing exams are required to advance. Deckhands who wish to advance must decide whether they want to work in the wheelhouse or the engine room. They will then assist the engineers or deck officers. With experience, assistant engineers and deck offices can advance to become chief engineers or captains. On smaller boats, such as tugs, a captain may choose to become self-employed by buying a boat and working as an owner-operator.

Employment

Water transportation workers held more than 84,000 jobs in 2006. The total number who worked at some point in the year was significantly larger because many merchant marine officers and seamen worked only part of the year. The following tabulation shows employment in the occupations that make up this group:

Captains, mates, and pilots of water vessels 34,000

Sailors and marine oilers 33,000

Ship engineers 15,000

Motorboat operators 3,000

About 40 percent of all workers were employed in water transportation services. About 17 percent worked in inland water transportation—primarily the Mississippi River system—while the other 23 percent were employed in water transportation on the deep seas, along the coasts, and on the Great Lakes. Another 24 percent worked in establishments related to port and harbor operations, marine cargo handling, or navigational services to shipping. Governments employed 9 percent of all water transportation workers, many of whom worked on supply ships and are civilian mariners of the Navy Department's Military Sealift Command.

Job Outlook

Employment in water transportation occupations is projected to grow faster than average. Good job opportunities are expected.

Employment change. Employment in water transportation occupations is projected to grow 16 percent over the 2006–2016 period, faster than the average for all occupations. Job growth will stem from increasing tourism and growth in offshore oil and gas production. Employment will also increase in and around major port cities due to rapidly increasing international trade.

Employment in deep-sea shipping for American mariners is expected to remain stable. A fleet of deep-sea U.S.-flagged ships is considered vital to the nation's defense, so some receive federal support through a maritime security subsidy and other provisions in laws that limit certain federal cargoes to ships that fly the U.S. flag.

Employment growth also is expected in passenger cruise ships within U.S. waters. Vessels that operate between U.S. ports are required by law to be U.S.-flagged vessels. The staffing needs for several new U.S. flagged cruise ships that will travel to the Hawaiian Islands will create new opportunities for employment. In addition, increasing use of ferries to handle commuter traffic around major metropolitan areas should increase employment.

Some growth in water transportation occupations is projected in vessels operating in the Great Lakes and inland waterways. Growth will be driven by increasing demand for bulk products, such as coal, iron ore, petroleum, sand and gravel, grain, and chemicals. Since current pipelines cannot transport ethanol, some growth will come from shipping ethanol. Problems with congestion in the rail transportation system will increase demand for inland water transportation.

Job prospects. Good job opportunities will result from growth and the need to replace those leaving the occupation. Most water trans-

portation occupations require workers to be away from home for extended periods of time, causing some to leave these jobs.

Maritime academy graduates who have not found licensed shipboard jobs in the U.S. merchant marine find jobs in related industries. Many academy graduates are ensigns in the Naval or Coast Guard Reserve; some are selected or apply for active duty in those branches of the Service. Some find jobs as seamen on U.S.-flagged or foreign-flagged vessels, tugboats, and other watercraft or enter civilian jobs with the U.S. Navy or Coast Guard. Some take land-based jobs with shipping companies, marine insurance companies, manufacturers of boilers or related machinery, or other related jobs.

Earnings

Earnings vary widely with the particular water transportation position and the worker's experience. Earnings are higher than most other occupations with similar educational requirements for entry-level positions. While wages are lower for sailors than for mates and engineers, sailors' on-board experience is important for advancing into those higher paying positions. Workers are normally paid by the day. Since companies provide food and housing at sea and it is difficult to spend money while working, sailors are able to save a large portion of their pay.

Median annual wage-and-salary earnings of sailors and marine oilers were $30,630 in May 2006. The middle 50 percent earned between $23,790 and $39,380. The lowest 10 percent had earnings of less than $19,220, while the top 10 percent earned over $49,650.

Median annual wage-and-salary earnings of captains, mates, and pilots of water vessels were $53,430 in May 2006. The middle 50 percent earned between $38,880 and $69,570. The lowest 10 percent had earnings of less than $29,360, while the top 10 percent earned over $89,230. Annual pay for captains of larger vessels, such as container ships, oil tankers, or passenger ships may exceed $100,000, but only after many years of experience. Similarly, earnings of captains of tugboats are dependent on the port and the nature of the cargo.

Median annual wage-and-salary earnings of ship engineers were $54,820 in May 2006. The middle 50 percent earned between $41,190 and $74,360. The lowest 10 percent had earnings of less than $34,140, while the top 10 percent earned over $92,860.

Median annual wage-and-salary earnings of motorboat operators were $32,350 in May 2006. The middle 50 percent earned between $23,340 and $45,850. The lowest 10 percent had earnings of less than $17,270, while the top 10 percent earned over $55,170.

The rate of unionization for these workers is about 16 percent, higher than the average for all occupations. Unionization rates vary by region. In unionized areas, merchant marine officers and seamen, both veterans and beginners, are hired for voyages through union

Projections data from the National Employment Matrix

Occupational Title	SOC Code	Employment, 2006	Projected employment, 2016	Change, 2006-16	
				Number	Percent
Water transportation occupations	53-5000	84,000	98,000	14,000	16
Sailors and marine oilers	53-5011	33,000	38,000	5,200	16
Ship and boat captains and operators	53-5020	37,000	43,000	6,300	17
Captains, mates, and pilots of water vessels	53-5021	34,000	40,000	6,000	18
Motorboat operators	53-5022	3,000	3,300	300	11
Ship engineers	53-5031	15,000	17,000	2,100	14

NOTE: Data in this table are rounded.

hiring halls or directly by shipping companies. Hiring halls rank the candidates by the length of time the person has been out of work and fill open slots accordingly. Most major seaports have hiring halls.

Related Occupations

Workers in other occupations who make their living on the seas and coastal waters include fishers and fishing vessel operators and members of the Navy and the Coast Guard. Heavy vehicle and mobile equipment service technicians and mechanics perform work similar to shipboard engineers.

Sources of Additional Information

Information on a program called "Careers Afloat," which includes a substantial listing of training and employment information and contacts in the U.S., may be obtained through

▸ Maritime Administration, U.S. Department of Transportation, 400 7th St. SW, Room 7302, Washington, DC 20590. Internet: http://www.marad.dot.gov/acareerafloat

Information on merchant marine careers, training, and licensing requirements is available from

▸ U.S. Coast Guard National Maritime Center, 4200 Wilson Blvd., Suite 630, Arlington, VA 22203-1804. Internet: http://www.uscg.mil/stcw/index.htm

Information on careers with the Military Sealift Command can be found at

▸ Military Sealift Command, CIVMAR Support Center, 6353 Center Drive, Building 8, Suite 202, Norfolk, VA 23502. Internet: http://www.sealiftcommand.com

QUICK
JOB SEARCH
Seven Steps to Getting a Good Job in Less Time

The Complete Text of a Results-Oriented Minibook by Michael Farr

Millions of job seekers have found better jobs faster using the techniques in the *Quick Job Search*. So can you! The *Quick Job Search* covers the essential steps proven to cut job search time in half and is used widely by job search programs throughout North America. Topics include how to identify your key skills, define your ideal job, write a great resume quickly, use the most effective job search methods, get more interviews, and much more.

If you completed "Using the Job-Match Grid to Choose a Career" earlier in this book, the activities in this section will complement those efforts by helping you to define other skills you possess, focus your resume, and get a job quickly.

While it is a section in this book, the *Quick Job Search* is available from JIST Publishing as a separate booklet.

Quick Job Search Is Short, But It May Be All You Need

While *Quick Job Search* is short, it covers the basics on how to explore career options and conduct an effective job search. While these topics can seem complex, I have found some simple truths about looking for a job:

- If you are going to work, you might as well look for what you really want to do and are good at.

- If you are looking for a job, you might as well use techniques that will reduce the time it takes to find one—and that help you get a better job than you might otherwise.

That's what I emphasize in *Quick Job Search*.

Trust Me—Do the Worksheets. I know you will resist completing the worksheets. But trust me. They are worth your time. Doing them will give you a better sense of what you are good at, what you want to do, and how to go about getting it. You will also most likely get more interviews and present yourself better. Is this worth giving up a night of TV? Yes, I think so.

Once you finish this minibook and its activities, you will have spent more time planning your career than most people do. And you will know more than the average job seeker about finding a job.

Why Such a Short Book? I've taught job seeking skills for many years, and I've written longer and more detailed books than this one. Yet I have often been asked to tell someone, in a few minutes or hours, the most important things they should do in their career planning or job search. Instructors and counselors also ask the same question because they have only a short time to spend with folks they're trying to help. I've given this a lot of thought, and the seven topics in this book are the ones I think are most important to know.

This minibook is short enough to scan in a morning and conduct a more effective job search that afternoon. Granted, doing all the activities would take more time, but they will prepare you far better than scanning the book. Of course, you can learn more about all the topics it covers, but this minibook, *Quick Job Search,* may be all you need.

You can't just read about getting a job. The best way to get a job is to go out and get interviews! And the best way to get interviews is to make a job out of getting a job.

After many years of experience, I have identified just seven basic things you need to do that make a big difference in your job search. Each will be covered and expanded on in this minibook.

1. Identify your key skills.

2. Define your ideal job.

3. Learn the two most effective job search methods.

4. Create a superior resume and a portfolio.

5. Organize your time to get two interviews a day.

6. Dramatically improve your interviewing skills.

7. Follow up on all leads.

So, without further delay, let's get started!

 STEP 1: **Identify Your Key Skills and Develop a "Skills Language" to Describe Yourself**

One survey of employers found that about 90 percent of the people they interviewed might have the required job skills, but they could not describe those skills and thereby prove that they could do the job they sought. They could not answer the basic question "Why should I hire you?"

Knowing and describing your skills are essential to doing well in interviews. This same knowledge is important to help you decide what type of job you will enjoy and do well. For these reasons, I consider identifying your skills a necessary part of a successful career plan or job search.

The Three Types of Skills

Most people think of their skills as job-related skills, such as using a computer. But we all have other types of skills that are important for success on a job—and that are important to employers. The following triangle arranges skills in three groups, and I think that this is a very useful way to consider skills.

© JIST Works

Let's look at these three types of skills—self-management, transferable, and job-related—and identify those that are most important to you.

We all have thousands of skills. Consider the many skills required to do even a simple thing like ride a bike or bake a cake. But, of all the skills you have, employers want to know those key skills you have for the job they need done. You must clearly identify these key skills and then emphasize them in interviews.

Self-Management Skills

To begin identifying your skills, answer the question in the box that follows.

YOUR GOOD WORKER TRAITS

Write down three things about yourself that you think make you a good worker. Think about what an employer might like about you or the way you work.

1. _____

2. _____

3. _____

You just wrote down the most important things for an employer to know about you! They describe your basic personality and your ability to adapt to new environments. They are some of the most important skills to emphasize in interviews, yet most job seekers don't realize their importance—and don't mention them.

Review the Self-Management Skills Checklist that follows and put a check mark beside any skills you have. The key self-management skills listed first cover abilities that employers find particularly important. If one or more of the key self-management skills apply to you, mentioning them in interviews can help you greatly.

SELF-MANAGEMENT SKILLS CHECKLIST

Following are the key self-management skills that employers value highly. Place a check by those you already have.

❑ Have good attendance   ❑ Arrive on time

❑ Get work done on time   ❑ Get along with co-workers

❑ Am honest   ❑ Follow instructions

❑ Get along with supervisor   ❑ Am hard working/productive

(continued)

(continued)

Place a check by other self-management skills you have.

❏ Ambitious	❏ Discreet	❏ Helpful
❏ Mature	❏ Physically strong	❏ Sincere
❏ Assertive	❏ Eager	❏ Humble
❏ Methodical	❏ Practical	❏ Spontaneous
❏ Capable	❏ Efficient	❏ Humorous
❏ Modest	❏ Problem-solving	❏ Steady
❏ Cheerful	❏ Energetic	❏ Imaginative
❏ Motivated	❏ Proud of work	❏ Tactful
❏ Competent	❏ Enthusiastic	❏ Independent
❏ Natural	❏ Quick to learn	❏ Team player
❏ Conscientious	❏ Expressive	❏ Industrious
❏ Open-minded	❏ Reliable	❏ Tenacious
❏ Creative	❏ Flexible	❏ Informal
❏ Optimistic	❏ Resourceful	❏ Thrifty
❏ Culturally tolerant	❏ Formal	❏ Intelligent
❏ Original	❏ Responsible	❏ Trustworthy
❏ Decisive	❏ Friendly	❏ Intuitive
❏ Patient	❏ Results-oriented	❏ Versatile
❏ Dependable	❏ Good-natured	❏ Loyal
❏ Persistent	❏ Self-confident	❏ Well-organized

List the other self-management skills you have that have not been mentioned but you think are important to include.

_____

_____

_____

After you finish checking the list, circle the five skills you feel are most important and write them in the box that follows.

YOUR TOP FIVE SELF-MANAGEMENT SKILLS

1. _____

2. _____

3. _____

---

4. _____

5. _____

When thinking about their skills, some people find it helpful to complete the Essential Job Search Data Worksheet that starts on page 342. It organizes skills and accomplishments from previous jobs and other life experiences. Take a look at it and decide whether to complete it now or later.

Transferable Skills

We all have skills that can transfer from one job or career to another. For example, the ability to organize events could be used in a variety of jobs and may be essential for success in certain occupations. Your mission is to find a job that requires the skills you have and enjoy using.

It's not bragging if it's true. Using your new skills language may be uncomfortable at first, but employers need to learn about your skills. So practice saying positive things about the skills you have for the job. If you don't, who will?

TRANSFERABLE SKILLS CHECKLIST

Following are the key transferable skills that employers value highly. Place a check by those you already have. You may have used them in a previous job or in some nonwork setting.

❑ Managing money/budgets ❑ Using computers

❑ Speaking in public ❑ Meeting the public

❑ Managing people ❑ Writing well

❑ Organizing/managing projects ❑ Negotiating

❑ Meeting deadlines

Place a check by the skills you have for working with data.

❑ Analyzing data ❑ Observing/inspecting

❑ Counting/taking inventory ❑ Classifying data

❑ Auditing/checking for accuracy ❑ Paying attention to details

❑ Investigating ❑ Comparing/evaluating

❑ Budgeting ❑ Researching/locating information

❑ Keeping financial records ❑ Compiling/recording facts

❑ Calculating/computing ❑ Synthesizing

Place a check by the skills you have for working with people.

❑ Administering ❑ Being kind ❑ Being patient

❑ Counseling people ❑ Having insight ❑ Instructing others

❑ Being diplomatic ❑ Being outgoing ❑ Being pleasant

❑ Demonstrating ❑ Helping others ❑ Interviewing people

(continued)

© **JIST Works**

(continued)

❑ Being sensitive	❑ Being tactful	❑ Caring for others
❑ Listening	❑ Supervising	❑ Trusting
❑ Being sociable	❑ Being tough	❑ Coaching
❑ Persuading	❑ Tolerating	❑ Understanding
		❑ Confronting others

Place a check by your skills in working with words and ideas.

❑ Being articulate	❑ Being logical
❑ Creating new ideas	❑ Remembering information
❑ Being ingenious	❑ Communicating verbally
❑ Designing	❑ Speaking publicly
❑ Being inventive	❑ Corresponding with others
❑ Editing	❑ Writing clearly

Place a check by the leadership skills you have.

❑ Being competitive	❑ Having self-confidence
❑ Mediating problems	❑ Planning events
❑ Delegating	❑ Influencing others
❑ Motivating people	❑ Running meetings
❑ Directing others	❑ Making decisions
❑ Motivating yourself	❑ Solving problems
❑ Getting results	❑ Making explanations
❑ Negotiating agreements	❑ Taking risks

Place a check by your creative or artistic skills.

❑ Appreciating music	❑ Dancing
❑ Expressing yourself	❑ Playing instruments
❑ Being artistic	❑ Drawing
❑ Performing/acting	❑ Presenting artistic ideas

Place a check by your skills for working with things.

❑ Assembling things	❑ Operating tools/machines
❑ Driving or operating vehicles	❑ Constructing or repairing things
❑ Building things	

Add the other transferable skills you have that have not been mentioned but you think are important to include.

_____

_____

_____

When you are finished, circle the five transferable skills you feel are most important for you to use in your next job and list them below.

YOUR TOP FIVE TRANSFERABLE SKILLS

1. _____

2. _____

3. _____

4. _____

5. _____

Job-Related Skills

Job content or job-related skills are those you need to do a particular occupation. A carpenter, for example, needs to know how to use various tools. Before you select job-related skills to emphasize, you must first have a clear idea of the jobs you want. So let's put off developing your job-related skills list until you have defined the job you want—the topic that is covered next.

 # STEP 2: Define Your Ideal Job

Too many people look for a job without clearly knowing what they are looking for. Before you go out seeking a job, I suggest that you first define exactly what you want—not *just a job* but *the job*.

Most people think that a job objective is the same as a job title, but it isn't. You need to consider other elements of what makes a job satisfying for you. Then, later, you can decide what that job is called and what industry it might be in. You can compromise on what you consider your ideal job later if you need to.

EIGHT FACTORS TO CONSIDER IN DEFINING YOUR IDEAL JOB

As you try to define your ideal job, consider the following eight important questions. When you know what you want, your task then becomes finding a position that is as close to your ideal job as possible.

1. **What skills do you want to use?** From the skills lists in Step 1, select the top five skills that you enjoy using and most want to use in your next job.

   a. _____

   b. _____

   c. _____

   d. _____

   e. _____

(continued)

© JIST Works

(continued)

2. **What type of special knowledge do you have?** Perhaps you know how to fix radios, keep accounting records, or cook food. Write down the things you know from schooling, training, hobbies, family experiences, and other sources. One or more of these knowledge areas could make you a very special applicant in the right setting._____

_____

_____

3. **With what types of people do you prefer to work?** Do you like to work with competitive people, or do you prefer hardworking folks, creative personalities, relaxed people, or some other types?_____

_____

_____

4. **What type of work environment do you prefer?** Do you want to work inside, outside, in a quiet place, in a busy place, or in a clean or messy place; or do you want to have a window with a nice view? List the types of environments you prefer._____

_____

_____

5. **Where do you want your next job to be located—in what city or region?** If you are open to living and working anywhere, what would your ideal community be like? Near a bus line? Close to a childcare center?_____

_____

_____

6. **What benefits or income do you hope to have in your next job?** Many people will take less money or fewer benefits if they like a job in other ways—or if they need a job quickly to survive. Think about the minimum you would take as well as what you would eventually like to earn. Your next job will probably pay somewhere in between._____

_____

_____

7. **How much and what types of responsibility are you willing to accept?** Usually, the more money you want to make, the more responsibility you must accept. Do you want to work by yourself, be part of a group, or be in charge? If you want to be in charge, how many people are you willing to supervise?

_____

_____

_____

© **JIST Works**

8. **What values are important or have meaning to you?** Do you have important values you would prefer to include in considering the work you do? For example, some people want to work to help others, clean up the environment, build structures, make machines work, gain power or prestige, or care for animals or plants. Think about what is important to you and how you might include this in your next job._____

_____

_____

_____

Is It Possible to Find Your Ideal Job?

Can you find a job that meets all the criteria you just defined? Perhaps. Some people do. The harder you look, the more likely you are to find it. But you will likely need to compromise, so it is useful to know what is *most* important to include in your next job. Go back over your responses to the eight factors and mark a few of those that you would most like to have or include in your ideal job.

FACTORS I WANT IN MY IDEAL JOB

Write a brief description of your ideal job. Don't worry about a job title, or whether you have the experience, or other practical matters yet._____

_____

_____

_____

How Can You Explore Specific Job Titles and Industries?

You might find your ideal job in an occupation you haven't considered yet. And, even if you are sure of the occupation you want, it may be in an industry that is unfamiliar to you. This combination of occupation and industry forms the basis for your job search, and you should consider a variety of options.

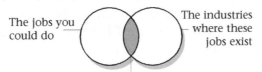

The jobs you could do | The industries where these jobs exist

Your ideal job exists in the overlap of those jobs that interest you most *and* in those industries that best meet your needs and interests!

There are thousands of job titles, and many jobs are highly specialized, employing just a few people. While one of these more specialized jobs may be just what you want, most work falls within more general job titles that employ large numbers of people.

REVIEW THE TOP JOBS IN THE WORKFORCE

The list of job titles that follows was based on a list developed by the U.S. Department of Labor. It contains 270 major jobs that employ about 90 percent of the U.S. workforce.

The job titles are organized within 16 major groupings called interest areas, presented in bold type. These groupings will help you quickly identify fields most likely to interest you. Job titles are presented in regular type within these groupings.

Begin with the interest areas that appeal to you most, and underline any job title that interests you. (Don't worry for now about whether you have the experience or credentials to do these jobs.) Then quickly review the remaining interest areas, underlining any job titles there that interest you. Note that some job titles are listed more than once because they fit into more than one interest area. When you have gone through all 16 interest areas, go back and circle the 5 to 10 job titles that interest you most. These are the ones you will want to research in more detail.

1. **Agriculture and Natural Resources:** Agricultural and Food Scientists; Agricultural Workers; Biological Scientists; Conservation Scientists and Foresters; Engineers; Farmers, Ranchers, and Agricultural Managers; Fishers and Fishing Vessel Operators; Forest, Conservation, and Logging Workers; Grounds Maintenance Workers; Material Moving Occupations; Pest Control Workers; Purchasing Managers, Buyers, and Purchasing Agents; Science Technicians.

2. **Architecture and Construction:** Architects, except Landscape and Naval; Boilermakers; Brickmasons, Blockmasons, and Stonemasons; Carpenters; Carpet, Floor, and Tile Installers and Finishers; Cement Masons, Concrete Finishers, Segmental Pavers, and Terrazzo Workers; Construction and Building Inspectors; Construction Equipment Operators; Construction Laborers; Construction Managers; Drafters; Drywall Installers, Ceiling Tile Installers, and Tapers; Electrical and Electronics Installers and Repairers; Electricians; Elevator Installers and Repairers; Glaziers; Hazardous Materials Removal Workers; Heating, Air-Conditioning, and Refrigeration Mechanics and Installers; Insulation Workers; Landscape Architects; Line Installers and Repairers; Maintenance and Repair Workers, General; Material Moving Occupations; Painters and Paperhangers; Pipelayers, Plumbers, Pipefitters, and Steamfitters; Plasterers and Stucco Masons; Roofers; Sheet Metal Workers; Structural and Reinforcing Iron and Metal Workers; Surveyors, Cartographers, Photogrammetrists, and Surveying and Mapping Technicians.

3. **Arts and Communication:** Actors, Producers, and Directors; Advertising, Marketing, Promotions, Public Relations, and Sales Managers; Air Traffic Controllers; Announcers; Artists and Related Workers; Barbers, Cosmetologists, and Other Personal Appearance Workers; Broadcast and Sound Engineering Technicians and Radio Operators; Commercial and Industrial Designers; Dancers and Choreographers; Dispatchers; Fashion Designers; Floral Designers; Graphic Designers; Interior Designers; Interpreters and Translators; Musicians, Singers, and Related Workers; News Analysts, Reporters, and Correspondents; Photographers; Public Relations Specialists; Television, Video, and Motion Picture Camera Operators and Editors; Writers and Editors.

4. **Business and Administration:** Accountants and Auditors; Administrative Services Managers; Billing and Posting Clerks and Machine Operators; Bookkeeping, Accounting, and Auditing Clerks; Brokerage Clerks; Budget Analysts; Communications Equipment Operators; Data Entry and Information Processing Workers; Engineering Technicians; File Clerks; Gaming Cage Workers; Human Resources Assistants, except Payroll and Timekeeping; Human Resources, Training, and Labor Relations Managers and

Specialists; Management Analysts; Meeting and Convention Planners; Meter Readers, Utilities; Office and Administrative Support Worker Supervisors and Managers; Office Clerks, General; Operations Research Analysts; Payroll and Timekeeping Clerks; Postal Service Workers; Procurement Clerks; Production, Planning, and Expediting Clerks; Secretaries and Administrative Assistants; Shipping, Receiving, and Traffic Clerks; Stock Clerks and Order Fillers; Top Executives; Weighers, Measurers, Checkers, and Samplers, Recordkeeping.

5. **Education and Training:** Archivists, Curators, and Museum Technicians; Counselors; Education Administrators; Fitness Workers; Health Educators; Instructional Coordinators; Librarians; Library Assistants, Clerical; Library Technicians; Teacher Assistants; Teachers—Adult Literacy and Remedial Education; Teachers—Postsecondary; Teachers—Preschool, Kindergarten, Elementary, Middle, and Secondary; Teachers—Self-Enrichment Education; Teachers—Special Education.

6. **Finance and Insurance:** Advertising Sales Agents; Appraisers and Assessors of Real Estate; Bill and Account Collectors; Claims Adjusters, Appraisers, Examiners, and Investigators; Cost Estimators; Credit Authorizers, Checkers, and Clerks; Financial Analysts and Personal Financial Advisors; Financial Managers; Insurance Sales Agents; Insurance Underwriters; Interviewers; Loan Officers; Market and Survey Researchers; Securities, Commodities, and Financial Services Sales Agents; Tellers.

7. **Government and Public Administration:** Agricultural Workers; Court Reporters; Fire Fighting Occupations; Inspectors, Testers, Sorters, Samplers, and Weighers; Occupational Health and Safety Specialists and Technicians; Police and Detectives; Science Technicians; Tax Examiners, Collectors, and Revenue Agents; Top Executives; Urban and Regional Planners.

8. **Health Science:** Agricultural Workers; Animal Care and Service Workers; Athletic Trainers; Audiologists; Cardiovascular Technologists and Technicians; Chiropractors; Clinical Laboratory Technologists and Technicians; Dental Assistants; Dental Hygienists; Dentists; Diagnostic Medical Sonographers; Dietitians and Nutritionists; Licensed Practical and Licensed Vocational Nurses; Massage Therapists; Medical and Health Services Managers; Medical Assistants; Medical Records and Health Information Technicians; Medical Transcriptionists; Nuclear Medicine Technologists; Nursing, Psychiatric, and Home Health Aides; Occupational Therapist Assistants and Aides; Occupational Therapists; Opticians, Dispensing; Optometrists; Pharmacists; Pharmacy Aides; Pharmacy Technicians; Physical Therapist Assistants and Aides; Physical Therapists; Physician Assistants; Physicians and Surgeons; Podiatrists; Radiation Therapists; Radiologic Technologists and Technicians; Recreational Therapists; Registered Nurses; Respiratory Therapists; Science Technicians; Speech-Language Pathologists; Surgical Technologists; Veterinarians; Veterinary Technologists and Technicians.

9. **Hospitality, Tourism, and Recreation:** Athletes, Coaches, Umpires, and Related Workers; Barbers, Cosmetologists, and Other Personal Appearance Workers; Building Cleaning Workers; Chefs, Cooks, and Food Preparation Workers; Flight Attendants; Food and Beverage Serving and Related Workers; Food Processing Occupations; Food Service Managers; Gaming Services Occupations; Hotel, Motel, and Resort Desk Clerks; Lodging Managers; Recreation Workers; Reservation and Transportation Ticket Agents and Travel Clerks; Travel Agents.

10. **Human Service:** Child Care Workers; Counselors; Interviewers; Personal and Home Care Aides; Probation Officers and Correctional Treatment Specialists; Psychologists; Social and Human Service Assistants; Social Workers.

(continued)

(continued)

11. **Information Technology:** Coin, Vending, and Amusement Machine Servicers and Repairers; Computer and Information Systems Managers; Computer Operators; Computer Programmers; Computer Scientists and Database Administrators; Computer Software Engineers; Computer Support Specialists and Systems Administrators; Computer Systems Analysts; Computer, Automated Teller, and Office Machine Repairers.

12. **Law and Public Safety:** Correctional Officers; Emergency Medical Technicians and Paramedics; Fire Fighting Occupations; Job Opportunities in the Armed Forces; Judges, Magistrates, and Other Judicial Workers; Lawyers; Paralegals and Legal Assistants; Police and Detectives; Private Detectives and Investigators; Science Technicians; Security Guards and Gaming Surveillance Officers.

13. **Manufacturing:** Agricultural Workers; Aircraft and Avionics Equipment Mechanics and Service Technicians; Assemblers and Fabricators; Automotive Body and Related Repairers; Automotive Service Technicians and Mechanics; Bookbinders and Bindery Workers; Computer Control Programmers and Operators; Desktop Publishers; Diesel Service Technicians and Mechanics; Electrical and Electronics Installers and Repairers; Electronic Home Entertainment Equipment Installers and Repairers; Food Processing Occupations; Heavy Vehicle and Mobile Equipment Service Technicians and Mechanics; Home Appliance Repairers; Industrial Machinery Mechanics and Maintenance Workers; Industrial Production Managers; Inspectors, Testers, Sorters, Samplers, and Weighers; Jewelers and Precious Stone and Metal Workers; Machine Setters, Operators, and Tenders—Metal and Plastic; Machinists; Material Moving Occupations; Medical, Dental, and Ophthalmic Laboratory Technicians; Millwrights; Painting and Coating Workers, except Construction and Maintenance; Photographic Process Workers and Processing Machine Operators; Power Plant Operators, Distributors, and Dispatchers; Precision Instrument and Equipment Repairers; Prepress Technicians and Workers; Printing Machine Operators; Radio and Telecommunications Equipment Installers and Repairers; Semiconductor Processors; Small Engine Mechanics; Stationary Engineers and Boiler Operators; Textile, Apparel, and Furnishings Occupations; Tool and Die Makers; Water and Liquid Waste Treatment Plant and System Operators; Water Transportation Occupations; Welding, Soldering, and Brazing Workers; Woodworkers.

14. **Retail and Wholesale Sales and Service:** Advertising, Marketing, Promotions, Public Relations, and Sales Managers; Cashiers; Counter and Rental Clerks; Customer Service Representatives; Demonstrators, Product Promoters, and Models; Funeral Directors; Order Clerks; Property, Real Estate, and Community Association Managers; Purchasing Managers, Buyers, and Purchasing Agents; Real Estate Brokers and Sales Agents; Receptionists and Information Clerks; Retail Salespersons; Sales Engineers; Sales Representatives, Wholesale and Manufacturing; Sales Worker Supervisors.

15. **Scientific Research, Engineering, and Mathematics:** Actuaries; Atmospheric Scientists; Biological Scientists; Chemists and Materials Scientists; Drafters; Economists; Engineering and Natural Sciences Managers; Engineering Technicians; Engineers; Environmental Scientists and Hydrologists; Geoscientists; Mathematicians; Medical Scientists; Photographers; Physicists and Astronomers; Psychologists; Science Technicians; Social Scientists, Other; Statisticians; Surveyors, Cartographers, Photogrammetrists, and Surveying and Mapping Technicians.

16. **Transportation, Distribution, and Logistics:** Aircraft Pilots and Flight Engineers; Bus Drivers; Cargo and Freight Agents; Couriers and Messengers; Material Moving Occupations; Postal Service Workers; Rail Transportation Occupations; Taxi Drivers and Chauffeurs; Truck Drivers and Driver/Sales Workers; Water Transportation Occupations.

> N
> o
> t
> e
>
> *You can find thorough descriptions for the job titles in the preceding list in the* Occupational Outlook Handbook, *written by the U.S. Department of Labor. Its descriptions include information on earnings, training and education needed to hold specific jobs, work environment, advancement opportunities, projected growth, and sources for additional information. Most libraries have this book.*
>
> *You also can find descriptions of these jobs on the Internet. Go to www.bls.gov/oco/.*
>
> *The* New Guide for Occupational Exploration, *Fourth Edition, also provides more information on the interest areas used in this list. This book is published by JIST Works and describes about 1,000 major jobs, arranged within groupings of related jobs.*
>
> *Finally, "A Short List of Additional Resources" at the end of this minibook gives you resources for more job information.*

CONSIDER MAJOR INDUSTRIES

What industry you work in is often as important as the career field. For example, some industries pay much better than others, and others may simply be more interesting to you. A book titled *40 Best Fields for Your Career* contains very helpful reviews for each of the major industries mentioned in the following list. Many libraries and bookstores carry this book, as well as the U.S. Department of Labor's *Career Guide to Industries*.

Underline industries that interest you, and then learn more about the opportunities they present. Jobs in most careers are available in a variety of industries, so consider what industries fit you best and focus your job search in these.

Agriculture and natural resources: Agriculture, forestry, and fishing; mining; oil and gas extraction.

Manufacturing, construction, and utilities: Aerospace product and parts manufacturing; chemical manufacturing, except drugs; computer and electronic product manufacturing; construction; food manufacturing; machinery manufacturing; motor vehicle and parts manufacturing; pharmaceutical and medicine manufacturing; printing; steel manufacturing; textile, textile products, and apparel manufacturing; utilities.

Trade: Automobile dealers, clothing, accessories, and general merchandise stores; grocery stores; wholesale trade.

Transportation: Air transportation; truck transportation and warehousing.

Information: Broadcasting; Internet service providers, Web search portals, and data processing services; motion picture and video industries; publishing, except software; software publishing; telecommunications.

Financial activities: Banking; insurance; securities, commodities, and other investments.

Professional and business services: Advertising and public relations; computer systems design and related services; employment services; management, scientific, and technical consulting services; scientific research and development services.

Education, health care, and social services: Child daycare services; educational services; health care; social assistance, except child care.

(continued)

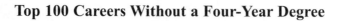
(continued)

> **Leisure and hospitality:** Art, entertainment, and recreation; food services and drinking places; hotels and other accommodations.
>
> **Government and advocacy, grantmaking, and civic organizations:** Advocacy, grantmaking, and civic organizations; federal government; state and local government, except education and health care.

THE TOP JOBS AND INDUSTRIES THAT INTEREST YOU

Go back over the lists of job titles and industries. For numbers 1 and 2 below, list the jobs that interest you most. Then select the industries that interest you most, and list them below in number 3. These are the jobs and industries you should research most carefully. Your ideal job is likely to be found in some combination of these jobs and industries, or in more specialized but related jobs and industries.

1. The five job titles that interest you most

   a._____

   b._____

   c._____

   d._____

   e._____

2. The five next most interesting job titles

   a._____

   b._____

   c._____

   d._____

   e._____

3. The industries that interest you most

   a._____

   b._____

   c._____

   d._____

   e._____

Is Self-Employment or Starting a Business an Option?

More than one in 10 workers are self-employed or own their own businesses. If these options interest you, consider them as well. Talk to people in similar roles to gather information and look for books and Web sites that provide information on options that are similar to those that interest you. A book titled *Best Jobs for the 21st*

Century (JIST Works) includes lists and descriptions of jobs with high percentages of self-employed. Also, the Small Business Administration's Web site at www.sba.gov is a good source of basic information on related topics.

SELF-EMPLOYMENT AREAS OF INTEREST

In the following space, write your current interest in self-employment or starting a business in an area related to your general job objective.

_____

_____

_____

Can You Identify Your Job-Related Skills Now That You've Defined Your Ideal Job?

Earlier, I suggested that you should first define the job you want and then identify key job-related skills you have that support your ability to do that job. These are the job-related skills to emphasize in interviews.

So, now that you have determined your ideal job, you can pinpoint the job-related skills it requires. If you haven't done so, complete the Essential Job Search Data Worksheet starting on page 342. Completing it will give you specific skills and accomplishments to highlight.

Yes, completing that worksheet requires time, but doing so will help you clearly define key skills to emphasize in interviews—when what you say matters so much. People who complete that worksheet will do better in their interviews than those who don't. After you complete the Essential Job Search Data Worksheet, you are ready to list your top five job-related skills.

> **Quip**
>
> **It's a hassle, but...** Completing the Essential Job Search Data Worksheet that starts on page 342 will help you define what you are good at—and remember examples of when you did things well. This information will help you define your ideal job and will be of great value in interviews. Look at the worksheet now, and promise to do it later today.

YOUR TOP FIVE JOB-RELATED SKILLS

List the top five job-related skills you think are most important. Include the job-related skills you have that you would most like to use in your next job.

1. _____

2. _____

3. _____

4. _____

5. _____

STEP 3: Use the Most Effective Methods to Find a Job in Less Time

Employer surveys have found that most employers don't advertise their job openings. They most often hire people they already know, people who find out about the jobs through word of mouth, or people who happen to be in the right place at the right time. Although luck plays a part in finding job openings, you can use the tips in this step to increase your luck.

Most job seekers don't know how ineffective some traditional job-hunting techniques tend to be. For example, the chart below shows that fewer than 15 percent of all job seekers get jobs from the newspaper want ads, most of which also appear online. Other traditional techniques include using public and private employment agencies, filling out paper and electronic applications, and mailing or e-mailing unsolicited resumes.

How people find jobs.

 This step covers a number of job search methods. Most of the material is presented as information, with a few interactive activities. While each topic is short and reasonably interesting, taking a break now and then will help you absorb it all.

Informal, nontraditional job-seeking methods have a much larger success rate. These methods are active rather than passive and include making direct contact with employers and networking.

Your job search objective. Almost everyone finds a job eventually, so your objective should be to find a good job in less time. The job search methods I emphasize in this minibook will help you do just that.

Get the Most Out of Less Effective Job Search Methods

The truth is that every job search method works for someone. But experience and research show that some methods are more effective than others are. Your task in the job search is to spend more of your time using more effective methods—and increase the effectiveness of all the methods you use.

So let's start by looking at some traditional job search methods and how you can increase their effectiveness. Only about one-third of all job seekers get their jobs using one of these methods, but you should still consider using them to some extent in your search. Later in the step, you'll read about the most effective methods, the ones you should devote the most time to in your search.

Newspaper and Internet Help Wanted Ads

Most jobs are never advertised, and fewer than 15 percent of all people get their jobs through the want ads. Everyone who reads the paper knows about these openings, so competition is fierce for the few advertised jobs.

The Internet also lists many job openings. But, as happens with newspaper ads, enormous numbers of people view these postings. Many job seekers make direct contact with employers via a company's Web site. Some people do get jobs through the bigger sites, so go ahead and apply. Just be sure to spend most of your time using more effective methods.

Filling Out Applications

Most employers require job seekers to complete an application form or an application online. Applications are designed to collect negative information, and employers use applications to screen people out. If, for example, your training or work history is not the best, you will often never get an interview, even if you can do the job.

Completing applications is a more effective approach for young and entry-level job seekers. The reason is that there is a shortage of workers for the relatively low-paying jobs typically sought by less-experienced job seekers. As a result, when trying to fill those positions, employers are more willing to accept a lack of experience or fewer job skills. Even so, you will get better results by filling out the application, if asked to do so, and then requesting an interview with the person in charge.

When you complete an application, make it neat and error-free, and do not include anything that could get you screened out. If necessary, leave a problem section blank. You can always explain situations in an interview.

Employment Agencies

There are three types of employment agencies. One is operated by the government and is free. The others, private employment agencies and temp agencies, are run as for-profit businesses and charge a fee to either you or an employer. Following are the advantages and disadvantages to using each.

The government employment service and One-Stop centers. Each state and province has a network of local offices to pay unemployment compensation, provide job leads, and offer other services—at no charge to you or to employers. The service's name varies by region. It may be called Job Service, Department of Labor, Unemployment Office, Workforce Development, or another name. Most of these offices are also online, and some require their users to sign up with a login and password to search for job leads and use other services on the Internet.

The Employment and Training Administration Web site at www.doleta.gov gives you information on the programs provided by the government employment service, plus links to other useful sites.

Visit your local office early in your job search. Find out whether you qualify for unemployment compensation and learn more about its services. Look into it—the price is right.

Private employment agencies. Private employment agencies are businesses that charge a fee either to you or to the employer who hires you. Fees can be from less than one month's pay to 15 percent or more of your annual salary. You will often see these agencies' ads in the help wanted section of the newspaper. Most have Web sites.

Be careful about using fee-based employment agencies. Recent research indicates that more people use and benefit from fee-based agencies than in the past. However, relatively few people who register with private agencies get a job through them.

If you use a private employment agency, ask for interviews with the employers who agree to pay the agency's fee. Do not sign an exclusive agreement or be pressured into accepting a job. Also, continue to actively look for your own leads. You can find these agencies in the phone book's yellow pages, and many state- or province-government Web sites offer lists of the private employment agencies in their states.

Temporary agencies. Temporary agencies offer jobs that last from several days to many months. They charge the employer an hourly fee, and then pay you a bit less and keep the difference. You pay no direct fee to the agency. Many private employment agencies now provide temporary jobs as well.

Temp agencies have grown rapidly for good reason. They provide employers with short-term help, and employers often use them to find people they might want to hire later. If the employers are dissatisfied, they can just ask the agency for different temp workers.

Temp agencies can help you survive between jobs and get experience in different work settings. Temp jobs provide a very good option while you look for long-term work, and you might get a job offer while working in a temp job. Holding a temporary job might even lead to a regular job with the same or a similar employer.

School and Other Employment Services

Only a small percentage of job seekers use school and other special employment services, probably because few job seekers have the service available to them. If you are a student or graduate, find out about any employment services at your school. Some schools provide free career counseling, resume-writing help, referrals to job openings, career interest tests, reference materials, Web sites listing job openings, and other services. Special career programs work with veterans, people with disabilities, welfare recipients, union members, professional groups, and many others. So check out these services and consider using them.

Mailing Versus Posting Resumes on the Internet

Many job search experts used to suggest that sending out lots of resumes was a great technique. That advice probably helped sell their resume books, but mailing resumes to people you do not know was never an effective approach. It very rarely works. A recent survey of 1,500 successful job seekers showed that only 2 percent found their positions through sending an unsolicited resume. The same is true for the Internet.

Although mailing your resume to strangers doesn't make much sense, posting it on the Internet might because

- It doesn't take much time.

- Many employers have the potential of finding your resume.

- You can post your resume on niche sites that attract only employers in your field.

- Your Internet resume is easily updated, allowing you to post your current accomplishments.

- You can easily link your resume to projects and Web sites that highlight your accomplishments.

Job searching on the Internet has its limitations, just like other methods. I'll cover resumes in more detail later and provide tips on using the Internet throughout this minibook.

Use the Two Job Search Methods That Work Best

The fact is that most jobs are not advertised, so how do *you* find them? The same way that about two-thirds of all job seekers do: networking with people you know (which I call making warm contacts) and directly contacting employers (which I call making cold contacts). Both of these methods are based on the job search rule you should know above all:

> **The Most Important Job Search Rule:** Don't wait until the job opens before contacting the employer!

Employers fill most jobs with people they meet before a job is formally open. The trick is to meet people who can hire you before a job is formally available. Instead of asking whether the employer has any jobs open, I suggest that you say, *"I realize you may not have any openings now, but I would still like to talk to you about the possibility of future openings."*

Most Effective Job Search Method 1: Develop a Network of Contacts in Five Easy Stages

Studies find that 40 percent of all people located their jobs through a lead provided by a friend, a relative, or an acquaintance. That makes the people you know your number one source of job leads—more effective than all the traditional methods combined! Developing and using your contacts is called *networking*, and here's how it works:

1. **Make lists of people you know.** Make a thorough list of anyone you are friendly with. Then make a separate list of all your relatives. These two lists alone often add up to 25 to 100 people or more. Next, think of other groups of people that you have something in common with, such as former co-workers or classmates, members of your social or sports groups, members of your professional association, former employers, neighbors, and other groups. You might not know many of these people personally or well, but most will help you if you ask them. An easy way to find networking contacts is to join an online networking site such as LinkedIn (www.linkedin.com).

2. **Contact each person in your list in a systematic way.** Obviously, some people will be more helpful than others, but any one of them might help you find a job lead.

3. **Present yourself well.** Begin with your friends and relatives. Call and tell them you are looking for a job and need their help. Be as clear as possible about the type of employment you want and the skills and qualifications you have. Look at the sample JIST Card and phone script later in this step for good presentation ideas.

4. **Ask your contacts for leads.** It is possible that your contacts will know of a job opening that interests you. If so, get the details and get right on it! More likely, however, they will not, so you should ask each person the Three Magic Networking Questions.

> **Quip**
>
> **Most jobs are never advertised because employers don't need to advertise or don't want to.** Employers trust people referred to them by someone they know far more than they trust strangers. And most jobs are filled by referrals and people that the employer knows, eliminating the need to advertise. So, your job search must involve more than looking at ads.

The Three Magic Networking Questions

- **Do you know of any openings for a person with my skills?**
  If the answer is "No" (which it usually is), then ask...

- **Do you know of someone else who might know of such an opening?** If your contact does, get that name and ask for another one.
  If he or she doesn't, ask...

(continued)

© **JIST Works**

(continued)

> ● **Do you know of anyone who might know of someone else who might know of a job opening?**
>
> *Another good way to ask this is "Do you know someone who knows lots of people?"* If all else fails, this will usually get you a name.

5. **Contact these referrals and ask them the same questions.** From each person you contact, try to get two names of other people you might contact. Doing this consistently can extend your network of acquaintances by hundreds of people. Eventually, one of these people will hire you or refer you to someone who will!

If you are persistent in following these five steps, networking might be the only job search method you need. It works.

Dialing for dollars. The phone can get you more interviews per hour than any other job search tool. But it won't work unless you use it actively.

The yellow pages in print and online provide the most complete, up-to-date listing of potential job search targets you can get. It organizes them into categories that are very useful for job seekers. Just find a category that interests you, call each listing, and then contact employers listed there. All it takes is a 30-second phone call. Ask to speak with the hiring authority.

Most Effective Job Search Method 2: Contact Employers Directly

It takes more courage, but making direct contact with employers is a very effective job search technique. I call these cold contacts because people you don't know in advance will need to warm up to your inquiries. Two basic techniques for making cold contacts follow.

Use the yellow pages to find potential employers. Begin by looking at the index in the front of your phone book's yellow pages. For each entry, ask yourself, *"Would an organization of this kind need a person with my skills?"* If you answer *"Yes,"* then that organization or business type is a possible target. You can also rate "Yes" entries based on your interest, writing a "1" next to those that seem very interesting, a "2" next to those that you are not sure of, and a "3" next to those that aren't interesting at all.

Next, select a type of organization that got a "Yes" response and turn to that section of the yellow pages. Call each organization listed there and ask to speak to the person who is most likely to hire or supervise you—typically the manager of the business or a department head—not the personnel or human resources manager. A sample telephone script is included later in this section to give you ideas about what to say.

You can easily adapt this approach for use on the Internet by using sites such as www.yellowpages.com to get contacts anywhere in the world, or you can find phone and e-mail contacts on an employer's own Web site.

Drop in without an appointment. Another effective cold contact method is to just walk into a business or organization that interests you and ask to speak to the person in charge. Although dropping in is particularly effective in small businesses, it also works surprisingly well in larger ones. Remember to ask for an interview even if there are no openings now. If your timing is inconvenient, ask for a better time to come back for an interview.

Most Jobs Are with Small Employers

Businesses and organizations with fewer than 250 employees employ about 72 percent of all U.S. workers. Small organizations are also the source for around 75 percent of the new jobs created each year. They are simply too important to overlook in your job search! Many of them don't have personnel departments, which makes direct contacts even easier and more effective.

Create a Powerful Job Search Tool—the JIST Card®

Look at the sample cards that follow—they are JIST Cards, and they get results. Computer printed or even neatly written on a 3-by-5–inch card, JIST Cards include the essential information employers want to know.

A JIST Card Is a Mini Resume

JIST Cards have been used by thousands of job search programs and millions of people. Employers like their direct and timesaving format, and they have been proven as an effective tool to get job leads. Attach one to your resume. Give them to friends, relatives, and other contacts and ask them to pass them along to others who might know of an opening. Enclose them in thank-you notes after interviews. Leave one with employers as a business card. However you get them in circulation, you may be surprised at how well they work.

You can easily create JIST Cards on a computer and print them on card stock you can buy at any office supply store. Or have a few hundred printed cheaply by a local quick print shop. While they are often done as 3-by-5 cards, they can be printed in any size or format.

Sandy Nolan

Position: General Office/Clerical

Cell phone: (512) 232-9213

Email: snolan@aol.com

More than two years of work experience plus one year of training in office practices. Type 55 wpm, trained in word processing, post general ledger, have good interpersonal skills, and get along with most people. Can meet deadlines and handle pressure well.

Willing to work any hours.

Organized, honest, reliable, and hardworking.

Richard Straightarrow   **Home: (602) 253-9678**
                                              Message: (602) 257-6643
                                              E-mail: RSS@email.cmm

Objective: Electronics installation, maintenance, and sales

Four years of work experience plus a two-year A.S. degree in Electronics Engineering Technology. Managed a $360,000/year business while going to school full time, with grades in the top 25%. Familiar with all major electronic diagnostic and repair equipment. Hands-on experience with medical, consumer, communication, and industrial electronics equipment and applications. Good problem-solving and communication skills. Customer service oriented.

Willing to do what it takes to get the job done.

Self-motivated, dependable, learn quickly.

© JIST Works

A JIST Card Can Lead to an Effective Phone Script

The phone is an essential job search tool that can get you more interviews per hour than any other job search tool. But the technique won't work unless you use it actively throughout your search. After you have created your JIST Card, you can use it as the basis for a phone script to make warm or cold calls. Revise your JIST Card content so that it sounds natural when spoken, and then edit it until you can read it out loud in about 30 seconds. The sample phone script that follows is based on the content of a JIST Card. Use it to help you modify your own JIST Card into a phone script.

Overcome phone phobia! Making cold calls takes guts, but most people can get one or more interviews an hour using cold calls. Start by calling people you know and people they refer you to. Then try calls to businesses that don't sound very interesting. As you get better, call more desirable targets.

"Hello. My name is Pam Nykanen. I am interested in a position in hotel management. I have four years' experience in sales, catering, and accounting with a 300-room hotel. I also have an associate degree in hotel management, plus one year of experience with the Brady Culinary Institute. During my employment, I helped double revenues from meetings and conferences and increased bar revenues by 46 percent. I have good problem-solving skills and am good with people. I am also well-organized, hard working, and detail-oriented. When may I come in for an interview?"

With your script in hand, make some practice calls to warm or cold contacts. If making cold calls, contact the person most likely to supervise you. Then present your script just as you practiced it—without stopping.

Although the sample script assumes that you are calling someone you don't know, you can change it to address warm contacts and referrals. Making cold calls takes courage but works very well for many who are willing to do it.

Use the Internet in Your Job Search

The Internet has limitations as a job search tool. While many have used it to get job leads, it has not worked well for far more. Too many assume they can simply add their resume to resume databases, and employers will line up to hire them. Just like the older approach of sending out lots of resumes, good things sometimes happen, but not often.

I recommend two points that apply to all job search methods, including using the Internet:

- It is unwise to rely on just one or two methods in conducting your job search.

- It is essential that you use an active rather than a passive approach in your job search.

Use More Than One Job Search Method

I encourage you to use the Internet in your job search, but I suggest that you use it along with other techniques. Use the same sorts of job search techniques online as you do offline, including contacting employers directly and building up a network of personal contacts that can help you with your search.

Tips to Increase Your Effectiveness in Internet Job Searches

The following tips can increase the effectiveness of using the Internet in your job search:

- **Be as specific as possible in the job you seek.** This is important in using any job search method, and it's even more important in using the Internet in your job search. The Internet is enormous, so it is essential to be as focused as possible in your search. Narrow your job title or titles to be as specific as possible. Limit your search to specific industries or areas of specialization. Locate and use specialized job banks in your area of interest.

- **Have reasonable expectations.** Success on the Internet is more likely if you understand its limitations and strengths. For example, employers trying to find someone with skills in high demand, such as nurses, are more likely to use the Internet to recruit job candidates.

- **Limit your geographic options.** If you don't want to move or would move only to certain areas, state this preference on your resume and restrict your search to those areas. Many Internet sites allow you to view or search for only those jobs that meet your location criteria.

- **Create an electronic resume.** With few exceptions, resumes submitted on the Internet end up as simple text files with no graphic elements. Employers search databases of many resumes for those that include key words or meet other searchable criteria. So create a simple text resume for Internet use and include words that are likely to be used by employers searching for someone with your abilities. (See Step 4 for more on creating an electronic resume.)

- **Get your resume into the major resume databases.** Most Internet employment sites let you add your resume for free and then charge employers to advertise openings or to search for candidates. Although adding your resume to these databases is not likely to result in job offers, doing so allows you to use your stored resume to easily apply for positions that are posted at these sites. These easy-to-use sites often provide all sorts of useful information for job seekers.

- **Make direct contacts.** Visit the Web sites of organizations that interest you and learn more about them. Many post openings, allow you to apply online, offer information on benefits and work environment, or even provide access to staff who can answer your questions. Even if they don't, you can always search the site or e-mail a request for the name of the person in charge of the work that interests you and then communicate with that person directly.

- **Network.** You can network online, too, finding names and e-mail addresses of potential employer contacts or of other people who might know someone with job openings. Look at and participate in interest groups, professional association sites, alumni sites, chat rooms, e-mail discussion lists, and employer sites—these are just some of the many creative ways to network and interact with people via the Internet.

Check Out Career-Specific Sites First

Thousands of Internet sites provide lists of job openings and information on careers or education. Many have links to other sites that they recommend. Service providers such as Yahoo! (www.yahoo.com) and the Microsoft Network (www.msn.com) have partnered with sites such as Careerbuilder.com to include career information and job listings plus links to other sites. Also check out www.jist.com. Three additional career-related sites are Riley Guide at www.rileyguide.com, Monster at www.monster.com, and Indeed, a job aggregator, at www.indeed.com.

 # STEP 4: Write a Simple Resume Now and a Better One Later

Sending out or e-mailing resumes and waiting for responses is not an effective job-seeking technique. But, many employers *will* ask you for a resume, and it can be a useful tool in your job search. I suggest that you begin with a simple resume you can complete quickly. I've seen too many people spend weeks working on a resume when they could have been out getting interviews instead. If you want a better resume, you can work on it on weekends and evenings. So let's begin with the basics.

Tips for Creating a Superior Resume

The following tips make sense for any resume format:

- **Write it yourself.** It's okay to look at other resumes for ideas, but write yours yourself. Doing so will force you to organize your thoughts and background.
- **Make it error-free.** One spelling or grammar error will create a negative impressionist (see what I mean?). Get someone else to review your final draft for any errors. Then review it again because these rascals have a way of slipping in.
- **Make it look good.** Poor copy quality, cheap paper, bad type quality, or anything else that creates a poor appearance will turn off employers to even the best resume content. Get professional help with design and printing if necessary. Many professional resume writers and even print shops offer writing and desktop design services if you need help.
- **Be brief, be relevant.** Many good resumes fit on one page, and few justify more than two. Include only the most important points. Use short sentences and action words. If it doesn't relate to and support the job objective, cut it!
- **Be honest.** Don't overstate your qualifications. If you end up getting a job you can't handle, who does it help? And a lie can result in your being fired later.
- **Be positive.** Emphasize your accomplishments and results. A resume is no place to be too humble or to display your faults.
- **Be specific.** Instead of saying, "I am good with people," say, "I supervised four people in the warehouse and increased productivity by 30 percent." Use numbers whenever possible, such as the number of people served, percentage of sales increase, or amount of dollars saved.

You should also know that everyone feels that he or she is a resume expert. Whatever you do, someone will tell you that it's wrong. Remember that a resume is simply a job search tool.

You should never delay or slow down your job search because your resume is not good enough. The best approach is to create a simple and acceptable resume as quickly as possible and then use it. As time permits, create a better one if you feel you must.

Avoid the resume pile. Resume experts often suggest that a dynamite resume will jump out of the pile. This is old-fashioned advice. It assumes that you are applying to large organizations and for advertised jobs. Today most jobs are with small employers and are not advertised. To avoid joining that stack of resumes in the first place, look for job openings that others overlook.

Writing Chronological Resumes

Most resumes use a chronological format where the most recent experience is listed first, followed by each previous job. This arrangement works fine for someone with work experience in several similar jobs, but not as well for those with limited experience or for career changers.

Look at the two resumes for Judith Jones that follow. Both use the chronological approach.

The first resume would work fine for most job search needs. It could be completed in about an hour.

Notice that the second one includes some improvements. The first resume is good, but most employers would like the additional positive information in the improved resume.

Basic Chronological Resume Example

Judith J. Jones

115 South Hawthorne Avenue
Chicago, Illinois 66204
tel: (312) 653-9217
email: jj@earthlink.com

JOB OBJECTIVE

A position in the office management, accounting, or administrative assistant area that enables me to grow professionally.

EDUCATION AND TRAINING

Acme Business College, Lincoln, IL
Graduate of a one-year business program.

John Adams High School, South Bend, IN
Diploma, business education.

U.S. Army
Financial procedures, accounting functions.

Other: Continuing-education classes and workshops in business communication, spreadsheet and database applications, scheduling systems, and customer relations.

EXPERIENCE

2006–present—Claims Processor, Blue Spear Insurance Co., Wilmette, IL. Process customer medical claims, develop management reports based on created spreadsheets and develop management reports based on those forms, exceed productivity goals.

2005–2006—Returned to school to upgrade business and computer skills. Completed courses in advanced accounting, spreadsheet and database programs, office management, human relations, and new office techniques.

2002–2005—E4, U.S. Army. Assigned to various stations as a specialist in finance operations. Promoted prior to honorable discharge.

2001–2002—Sandy's Boutique, Wilmette, IL. Responsible for counter sales, display design, cash register, and other tasks.

1999–2001—Held part-time and summer jobs throughout high school.

STRENGTHS AND SKILLS

Reliable, hardworking, and good with people. General ledger, accounts payable, and accounts receivable. Proficient in Microsoft Word, WordPerfect, Excel, and Outlook.

I give some tips you can use when you write your simple chronological resume. Use this resume as your guide.

Improved Chronological Resume Example

Judith J. Jones

115 South Hawthorne Avenue
Chicago, IL 66204

jj@earthlink.com
(312) 653-9217 (cell)

JOB OBJECTIVE

A position requiring excellent business management expertise in an office environment. Position should require a variety of skills, including office management, word processing, and spreadsheet and database application use.

EDUCATION AND TRAINING

Acme Business College, Lincoln, IL
Completed one-year program in **Professional Office Management.** Achieved GPA in top 30% of class. Courses included word processing, accounting theory and systems, advanced spreadsheet and database applications, graphics design, time management, and supervision.

John Adams High School, South Bend, IN
Graduated with emphasis on **business courses.** Earned excellent grades in all business topics and won top award for word-processing speed and accuracy.

Other: Continuing-education programs at own expense, including business communications, customer relations, computer applications, and sales techniques.

EXPERIENCE

2006–present—**Claims Processor, Blue Spear Insurance Company,** Wilmette, IL. Process 50 complex medical insurance claims per day, almost 20% above department average. Created a spreadsheet report process that decreased department labor costs by more than $30,000 a year. Received two merit raises for performance.

2005–2006—**Returned to business school to gain advanced office skills.**

2002–2005—**Finance Specialist (E4), U.S. Army.** Systematically processed more than 200 invoices per day from commercial vendors. Trained and supervised eight employees. Devised internal system allowing 15% increase in invoices processed with a decrease in personnel. Managed department with a budget equivalent of more than $350,000 a year. Honorable discharge.

2001–2002—**Sales Associate promoted to Assistant Manager, Sandy's Boutique,** Wilmette, IL. Made direct sales and supervised four employees. Managed daily cash balances and deposits, made purchasing and inventory decisions, and handled all management functions during owner's absence. Sales increased 26% and profits doubled during tenure.

1999–2001—**Held various part-time and summer jobs through high school while maintaining GPA 3.0/4.0.** Earned enough to pay all personal expenses, including car insurance. Learned to deal with customers, meet deadlines, work hard, and handle multiple priorities.

STRENGTHS AND SKILLS

Reliable, with strong work ethic. Excellent interpersonal, written, and oral communication and math skills. Accept supervision well, effectively supervise others, and work well as a team member. General ledger, accounts payable, and accounts receivable expertise. Proficient in Microsoft Word, Excel, PowerPoint, and Outlook; WordPerfect.

Tips for Writing a Simple Chronological Resume

Follow these tips as you write a basic chronological resume:

- **Name.** Use your formal name (not a nickname).

- **Address and contact information.** Avoid abbreviations in your address and include your ZIP code. If you may move, use a friend's address or include a forwarding address. Most employers will not write to you, so provide reliable phone numbers and other contact options. Always include your area code in your phone number because you never know where your resume might travel. Make sure that you have an answering machine or voice mail, and record a professional-sounding message. Include alternative ways to reach you, such as a cell phone and e-mail address.

- **Job objective.** You should almost always have one, even if it is general. Notice how Judith Jones keeps her options open with her broad job objective in her basic resume on page 327. Writing "secretary" or "clerical" might limit her from being considered for other jobs.

- **Education and training.** Include any training or education you've had that supports your job objective. If you did not finish a formal degree or program, list what you did complete and emphasize accomplishments. If your experience is not strong, add details here such as related courses and extracurricular activities. In the two examples, Judith Jones puts her business schooling in both the education and experience sections. Doing this fills a job gap and allows her to present her training as equal to work experience.

- **Previous experience.** Include the basics such as employer name, job title, dates employed, and responsibilities—but emphasize specific skills, results, accomplishments, superior performance, and so on.

- **Personal data.** Do not include irrelevant details such as height, weight, and marital status or a photo. Current laws do not allow an employer to base hiring decisions on these points. Providing this information can cause some employers to toss your resume. You can include information about hobbies or leisure activities in a special section that directly supports your job objective.

- **References.** Make sure that each reference will make nice comments about you and ask each to write a letter of recommendation that you can give to employers. You do not need to list your references on your resume. List them on a separate page and give it to employers who ask. If your references are particularly good, however, you can mention this somewhere—the last section is often a good place.

When you have a simple, errorless, and eye-pleasing resume, get on with your job search. There is no reason to delay! If you want to create a better resume in your spare time (evenings or weekends), use the name and contact information you currently have and improve the other sections of the resume.

Tips for an Improved Chronological Resume

Use these tips to improve your simple resume:

- **Job objective.** A poorly written job objective can limit the jobs an employer might consider you for. Think of the skills you have and the types of jobs you want to do; describe them in general terms. Instead of using a narrow job title such as "restaurant manager," you might write "manage a small to mid-sized business."

- **Education and training.** New graduates should emphasize their recent training and education more than those with a few years of related work experience would. A more detailed education and training section might include specific courses you took, and activities or accomplishments that support your job objective or reinforce your key skills. Include other details that reflect how hard you work, such as working your way through school or handling family responsibilities.

- **Skills and accomplishments.** Include those that support your ability to do well in the job you seek now. Even small details count. Maybe your attendance was perfect, you met a tight deadline, or you did the work of others during vacations. Be specific and include numbers—even if you have to estimate them. Judith's improved chronological resume example features more accomplishments and skills. Notice the impact of the numbers to reinforce results.

- **Job titles.** Past job titles may not accurately reflect what you did. For example, your job title may have been "cashier," but you also opened the store, trained new staff, and covered for the boss on vacations. Perhaps "head cashier and assistant manager" would be more accurate. Check with your previous employer if you are not sure.

(continued)

(continued)

- **Promotions.** If you were promoted or got good evaluations, say so—"cashier, promoted to assistant manager," for example. You can list a promotion to a more responsible job as a separate job if doing so results in a stronger resume.

- **Gaps in employment and other problem areas.** Employee turnover is expensive, so few employers want to hire people who won't stay or who won't work out. Gaps in employment, jobs held for short periods, or a lack of direction in the jobs you've held are all concerns for employers. So consider your situation and try to give an explanation of a problem area. Here are a few examples:

  2007—Continued my education at...   2006 to present—Self-employed as barn painter and...

  2007—Traveled extensively throughout...   2006—Took year off to have first child

  Use entire years to avoid displaying employment gaps you can't explain easily. If you had a few months of unemployment at the beginning of 2007 and then began a job in mid-2007, for example, you can list the job as "2007 to present."

Skip the negatives. Remember that a resume can get you screened out, but it is up to you to get the interview and the job. Cut out anything negative in your resume!

Writing Skills and Combination Resumes

The skills resume emphasizes your most important skills, supported by specific examples of how you have used them. This type of resume allows you to use any part of your life history to support your ability to do the job you want.

While skills resumes can be very effective, creating them requires more work. And some employers don't like them because they can hide a job seeker's faults (such as job gaps, lack of formal education, or little related work experience) better than can a chronological resume. Still, a skills resume may make sense for you.

Look over the sample resumes that follow for ideas. Notice that one resume includes elements of a skills *and* a chronological resume. This so-called combination resume makes sense if your previous job history or education and training are positive.

More Resume Examples

Find resume layout and presentation ideas in the four samples that follow.

A resume is not the most effective tool for getting interviews. A better approach is to make direct contact with those who hire or supervise people with your skills and ask them for an interview, even if no openings exist now. Then send a resume.

The chronological resume sample on page 331 focuses on accomplishments through the use of numbers. While Jon's resume does not say so, it is obvious that he works hard and that he gets results.

The skills resume on page 332 is for a recent high school graduate whose only work experience was at a school office!

The combination resume on page 333 emphasizes Grant's relevant education and transferable skills because he has little work experience in the field.

The electronic resume on page 334 is appropriate for scanning or e-mail submission. It has a plain format that is easily read by scanners. It also has lots of key words that increase its chances of being selected when an employer searches a database.

N o t e

Use the information from your completed Essential Job Search Data Worksheet to write your resume.

© **JIST Works**

The Chronological Resume to Emphasize Results

This simple chronological resume has few but carefully chosen words. It has an effective summary at the beginning, and every word supports his job objective.

Jon Feder

2140 Beach Road
Pompano Beach, Florida 20000

Phone: (222) 333-4444
E-mail: jfeder@com.com

Objective:	Management position in a major hotel
Summary of Experience:	Three years of experience in sales, catering banquet services, and guest relations in a 75-room hotel. Doubled sales revenues from conferences and meetings. Increased dining room and bar revenues by 40%. Won prestigious national and local awards for increased productivity and services.

He emphasizes results!

Experience:	Beachcomber Hotel, Pompano Beach, Florida
Assistant Manager
20XX to Present

Notice his use of numbers to increase the impact of the statements.

- Oversee a staff of 24, including dining room and bar, housekeeping, and public relations operations.
- Introduced new menus and increased dining room revenues by 40%. Awarded *Saveur* magazine's prestigious first place Hotel Cuisine award as a result of my selection of chefs.
- Attracted 58% more bar patrons by implementing Friday night Jazz at the Beach.

Beachcombers' Suites, Hollywood Beach, Florida
Sales and Public Relations
20XX to 20XX

Bullets here and above improve readability and emphasize key points.

- Doubled venues per month from weddings, conferences, and meetings.
- Chosen Chamber of Commerce Newcomer of the Year 20XX for the increase in business within the community.

Education:	Associate Degree in Hotel Management from Sullivan Technical Institute
Certificate in Travel Management from Phoenix University

While Jon had only a few years of related work experience, he used this resume to help him land a very responsible job in a large resort hotel.

The Skills Resume for Those with Limited Work Experience

In this skills resume, each skill directly supports the job objective of this recent high school graduate with very limited work experience.

Catalina A. Garcia
2340 N. Delaware Street · Denver, Colorado 81613
Home: (413) 643-2173 (Leave Message)
Cell phone: (413) 345-2189
E-mail: cagarcia@net.net

Note her key skills. →

Position Desired
Office assistant in a fast-paced business

Support for her key skills comes from her activities: school, clubs, and volunteer work.

Skills and Abilities

Communications
Excellent written and verbal presentation skills. Use proper grammar and have a good speaking voice.

Interpersonal
Able to get along well with all types of people. Accept supervision. Received positive evaluation from previous supervisors. ←

Flexible
Willing to try new things and am interested in improving efficiency on assigned tasks.

Notice the emphasis on adaptive skills. ←

Attention to Detail
Maintained confidential student records accurately and efficiently. Uploaded 500 student records in one day without errors. ↵

Hard Working
Worked 30 hours per week throughout high school and maintained above-average grades.

She makes good use of numbers.

← *This statement is very strong.*

Student Contact
Cordially dealt with as many as 150 students a day in Dean's office.

Dependable
Never absent or tardy in four years.

Awards
English Department Student of the Year, April 20XX
20XX Outstanding Student Newspaper, Newspaper Association of America

Education
Denver North High School. Took advanced English and communication classes. Member of student newspaper staff and FCCLA for four years. Graduated in top 30% of class.

Other
Girls' basketball team for four years. This taught me discipline, teamwork, how to follow instructions, and hard work. I am ambitious, outgoing, reliable, and willing to work.

Catalina's resume makes it clear that she is talented and hard working.

© JIST Works

The Combination Resume

Grant just finished computer programming school and has no work experience in the field. After listing the topics covered in the course, he summarized his employment experience, specifying that he earned promotions quickly. This would be attractive to any employer.

Grant Thomas

717 Carlin Court • Mendelein, IL 60000 • (555) 555-3333
E-mail: gthomas@com.com

Profile

- Outstanding student and tutor
- Winner of international computer software design competition three years
- Capable of being self-directed and independent, but also a team player
- Effective communicator, both orally and written
- Creative problem solver

Education and Training

M.S. in Software Engineering, Massachusetts Institute of Technology, Cambridge, MA
B.S. in Computer Engineering, California State University, Fullerton, CA
A rigorous education that focuses on topics such as

He includes important information that specifies topics he studied.

- Structure and interpretation of computer programs
- Circuits and electronics
- Signals and systems
- Computation structures
- Microelectronic devices and circuits
- Computer system engineering
- Computer language engineering
- Mathematics for computer science
- Analog electronics laboratory
- Digital systems laboratory

The work experiences support the job objective.

Highlights of Experience and Abilities

- Develop, create, and modify general computer applications software.
- Analyze user needs and develop software solutions.
- Confer with system analysts, computer programmers, and others.
- Modify existing software to correct errors.
- Coordinate software system installation and monitor equipment functioning to ensure specifications are met.
- Supervise work of programmers and technicians.
- Train customers and employees to use new and modified software.

Employment History

Software Specialist, First Rate Computers, Mendelein, IL 20XX – Present
- Technician and Customer and Employee Trainer throughout high school
- Promoted to software specialist and worked as a full-time telecommuting employee while completing the B.S. and M.S. degrees

References available on request

The Electronic Resume

```
William Brown
409 S. Maish Road
Phoenix, AZ 50000

Phone message: (300) 444-5567

E-mail: wbrown@email.com

OBJECTIVE

Store management career track in car audio store

===============================================================
SUMMARY OF SKILLS

Strategic planning, time management, team building,
leadership, problem solving, quality customer service,
conflict resolution, increasing productivity, confident,
outgoing, high performing, aggressive sales

===============================================================
EXPERIENCE

Total of three years in sales

* SHIFT SUPERVISOR, Tech World, Audio Department, Phoenix,
AZ, April 20XX to present: Promoted to Shift Supervisor of
nine salespeople in three months. Responsible for strategic
planning, time management, team building, leadership,
problem solving, quality customer service, conflict
resolution, and increasing productivity. Highest-selling
team for three years.

* AUDIO SALESPERSON, Tech World, Audio Department, Phoenix,
AZ, January 20XX to April 20XX: Arranged display, organized
stockroom, sales to customers, and tracked inventory.
Highest-selling staff member for three months.

===============================================================
EDUCATION AND TRAINING

Phoenix High School, top 40% of class

Additional training: Team Building, Franklin Time Management
seminar, Team Building seminar

===============================================================
OTHER

* Installed audio systems in 10 cars: family, friends, and
my own.

* Member of United States Autosound Association (USAA)
```

Because this electronic format is to be scanned or e-mailed, it has no bold, bullets, or italics.

The many key words ensure that the employers' computer searches will select this resume.

Note the results statements and numbers used below.

Use a Career Portfolio to Support Your Resume

Your resume is impressive, but there is another way that you can show prospective employers evidence of who you are and what you can do—a career portfolio.

What Is a Career Portfolio?

Unlike a resume, a career portfolio is a collection of documents that can include a variety of items. Here are some items you may want to place in your portfolio:

- Resume
- School transcripts
- Summary of skills
- Credentials, such as diplomas and certificates of recognition
- Reference letters from school officials and instructors, former employers, or co-workers
- List of accomplishments: Describe hobbies and interests that are not directly related to your job objective and are not included on your resume.
- Examples of your work: Depending on your situation, you can include samples of your art, photographs of a project, audiotapes, videotapes, images of Web pages you developed, and other media that can provide examples of your work.

Place each item on a separate page when you assemble your career portfolio.

Create a Digital Portfolio

A digital portfolio, also known as an electronic portfolio, contains all the information from your career portfolio in an electronic format. This material is then copied onto a CD-ROM or published on a Web site. With a digital portfolio, you can present your skills to a greater number of people than you can your paper career portfolio.

YOUR CAREER PORTFOLIO

On the following lines, list the items you want to include in your career portfolio. Think specifically of those items that show your skills, education, and personal accomplishments.

_____

_____

_____

_____

_____

_____

_____

_____

_____

_____

STEP 5: Redefine What Counts as an Interview, and Then Get Two a Day

The average job seeker gets about five interviews a month—fewer than two a week. Yet many job seekers use the methods in this *Quick Job Search* to get two interviews a day. Getting two interviews a day equals 10 a week and 40 a month. That's 800 percent more interviews than the average job seeker gets. Who do you think will get a job offer quicker?

However, getting two interviews a day is nearly impossible unless you redefine what counts as an interview. If you define an interview in a different way, getting two a day is quite possible.

> **The New Definition of an Interview:** Any face-to-face contact with someone who has the authority to hire or supervise a person with your skills—even if no opening exists at the time you talk with him or her.

If you use this new definition, it becomes *much* easier to get interviews. You can now interview with all sorts of potential employers, not just those who have job openings now. While most other job seekers look for advertised or actual openings, you can get interviews before a job opens up or before it is advertised and widely known. You will be considered for jobs that may soon be created but that others will not know about. And, of course, you can also interview for existing openings just as everyone else does.

Spending as much time as possible on your job search and setting a job search schedule are important parts of this step.

Make Your Search a Full-Time Job

Job seekers average fewer than 15 hours a week looking for work. On average, unemployment lasts three or more months, with some people out of work far longer (for example, older workers and higher earners). My many years of experience researching job seeking indicate that the more time you spend on your job search each week, the less time you will likely remain unemployed.

Of course, using the more effective job search methods presented in this minibook also helps. Many job search programs that teach job seekers my basic approach of using more effective methods and spending more time looking have proven that these seekers often find a job in half the average time. More importantly, many job seekers also find better jobs using these methods.

So, if you are unemployed and looking for a full-time job, you should plan to look on a full-time basis. It just makes sense to do so, although many do not, or they start out well but quickly get discouraged. Most job seekers simply don't have a structured plan—they have no idea what they are going to do next Thursday. The plan that follows will show you how to structure your job search like a job.

Decide How Much Time You Will Spend Looking for Work Each Week and Day

First and most importantly, decide how many hours you are willing to spend each week on your job search. You should spend a minimum of 25 hours a week on hard-core job search activities with no goofing around. The following worksheet walks you through a simple but effective process to set a job search schedule for each week.

PLAN YOUR JOB SEARCH WEEK

1. How many hours are you willing to spend each week looking for a job?_____

2. Which days of the week will you spend looking for a job?_____

3. How many hours will you look each day?_____

4. At what times will you begin and end your job search on each of these days?_____

_____

Create a Specific Daily Job Search Schedule

Having a specific daily schedule is essential because most job seekers find it hard to stay productive each day. The sample daily schedule that follows is the result of years of research into what schedule gets the best results. I tested many schedules in job search programs I ran, and this particular schedule worked best.

Consider using a schedule like this sample daily schedule. Why? Because it works.

A Sample Daily Schedule That Works

Time	Activity
7–8 a.m.	Get up, shower, dress, eat breakfast
8–8:15 a.m.	Organize work space, review schedule for today's interviews and promised follow-ups, check e-mail, update schedule as needed
8:15–9 a.m.	Review old leads for follow-up needed today; develop new leads from want ads, yellow pages, the Internet, warm contact lists, and other sources; complete daily contact list
9–10 a.m.	Make phone calls and set up interviews
10–10:15 a.m.	Take a break
10:15–11 a.m.	Make more phone calls, set up more interviews
11 a.m.–Noon	Send follow-up notes and do other office activities as needed
Noon–1 p.m.	Lunch break, relax
1–3 p.m.	Go on interviews, make cold contacts in the field
Evening	Read job search books, make calls to warm contacts not reachable during the day, work on a better resume, spend time with friends and family, exercise, relax

If you are not accustomed to using a daily schedule book or electronic planner, promise yourself to get a good one tomorrow. Choose one that allows for each day's plan on an hourly basis, plus daily to-do lists. Record your daily schedule in advance, and then add interviews as they come. Get used to carrying your planner with you and use it!

You can find a variety of computer programs or pocket-sized electronic schedulers to help organize your job search. If you don't use electronic tools, a simple schedule book and other paper systems will work just fine.

© JIST Works

STEP 6: Dramatically Improve Your Interviewing Skills

Interviews are where the job search action is. You have to get them; then you have to do well in them. According to surveys of employers, most job seekers do not effectively present the skills they have to do the job. Even worse, most job seekers can't answer one or more problem questions.

This lack of performance in interviews is one reason why employers will often hire a job seeker who does well in the interview over someone with better credentials. The good news is that you can do simple things to dramatically improve your interviewing skills. This section will emphasize interviewing tips and techniques that make the most difference.

Your First Impression May Be the Only One You Make

Some research suggests that if the interviewer forms a negative impression in the first five minutes of an interview, your chances of getting a job offer approach zero. I know from experience that many job seekers can create a lasting negative impression within seconds.

Tips for Interviewing

Because a positive first impression is so important, I share these suggestions to help you get off to a good start:

- **Make a good impression before you arrive.** Your resume, e-mails, applications, and other written correspondence create an impression before the interview, so make them professional and error-free.

- **Do some homework on the organization before you go.** You can often get information on a business and on industry trends from the Internet or a library.

- **Dress and groom the same way the interviewer is likely to be dressed—but cleaner!** Employer surveys find that almost half of all people's dress or grooming creates an initial negative impression. So this is a big problem. If necessary, get advice on your interviewing outfits from someone who dresses well. Pay close attention to your grooming, too—little things do count.

- **Be early.** Leave in plenty of time to be a few minutes early to an interview.

- **Be friendly and respectful with the receptionist.** Doing otherwise will often get back to the interviewer and result in a quick rejection.

- **Follow the interviewer's lead in the first few minutes.** It's often informal small talk but very important for that person to see how you interact. This is a good time to make a positive comment on the organization or even something you see in the office.

- **Understand that a traditional interview is not a friendly exchange.** In a traditional interview situation, there is a job opening, and you will be one of several applicants for it. In this setting, the employer's task is to eliminate all applicants but one. The interviewer's questions are designed to elicit information that can be used to screen you out. And your objective is to avoid getting screened out. It's hardly an open and honest interaction, is it?

  Setting up interviews before an opening exists eliminates the stress of a traditional interview. In pre-interviews, employers are not trying to screen you out, and you are not trying to keep them from finding out stuff about you. Having said that, knowing how to answer questions that might be asked in a traditional interview is good preparation for any interview you face.

- **Be prepared to answer the tough interview questions.** Your answers to a few key problem questions may determine whether you get a job offer. There are simply too many possible interview questions to cover one by one. Instead, 10 basic questions cover variations of most other interview questions. So, if you can learn to answer the Top 10 Problem Interview Questions well, you will know how to answer most others.

- **Be prepared for the most important interview question of all.** "Why should I hire you?" is the most important question of all to answer well. Do you have a convincing argument why someone should hire you over someone else? If you don't, you probably won't get that job you really want. So think carefully about why someone should hire you and practice your response. Then make sure you communicate this in the interview, even if the interviewer never asks the question in a clear way.

© JIST Works

Top 10 Problem Interview Questions

1. Why should I hire you?
2. Why don't you tell me about yourself?
3. What are your major strengths?
4. What are your major weaknesses?
5. What sort of pay do you expect to receive?
6. How does your previous experience relate to the jobs we have here?
7. What are your plans for the future?
8. What will your former employer (or references) say about you?
9. Why are you looking for this type of position, and why here?
10. Why don't you tell me about your personal situation?

Follow the Three-Step Process for Answering Interview Questions

I've developed a three-step process for answering interview questions. I know this might seem too simple, but the three-step process is easy to remember and can help you create a good answer to most interview questions. The technique has worked for thousands of people, so consider trying it.

1. **Understand what is really being asked.**

   Most questions are designed to find out about your self-management skills and personality, but interviewers are rarely this blunt. The employer's *real* question is often one or more of the following:

   - Can I depend on you?

   - Are you easy to get along with?

   - Are you a good worker?

   - Do you have the experience and training to do the job if we hire you?

   - Are you likely to stay on the job for a reasonable period of time and be productive?

   Ultimately, if you don't convince the employer that you will stay and be a good worker, it won't matter if you have the best credentials—he or she won't hire you.

2. **Answer the question briefly in a nondamaging way.** Present the facts of your particular work experience as advantages, not disadvantages. Many interview questions encourage you to provide negative information. One classic question I included in my list of Top 10 Problem Interview Questions was "What are your major weaknesses?" This is obviously a trick question, and many people are just not prepared for it.

   A good response is to mention something that is not very damaging, such as *"I have been told that I am a perfectionist, sometimes not delegating as effectively as I might."*

   But your answer is not complete until you continue with the next step.

3. **Answer the real question by presenting your related skills.** Base your answer on the key skills you have that support the job, and give examples to support these skills. For example, an employer might say to a recent graduate, *"We were looking for someone with more experience in this field. Why should we consider you?"* Here is one possible answer:

"I'm sure there are people who have more experience, but I do have more than six years of work experience, including three years of advanced training and hands-on experience using the latest methods and techniques. Because my training is recent, I am open to new ideas and am used to working hard and learning quickly."

In the previous example (about your need to delegate), a good skills statement might be

"I've been working on this problem and have learned to let my staff do more, making sure that they have good training and supervision. I've found that their performance improves, and it frees me up to do other things."

Whatever your situation, learn to answer questions that present you well. It's essential to communicate your skills during an interview, and the three-step process can help you answer problem questions and dramatically improve your responses. It works!

How to Earn a Thousand Dollars a Minute

What do you do when the employer asks, "How much money would it take to get you to join our company?"

Tips on Negotiating Pay

Remember these few essential tips when it comes time to negotiate your pay:

- **The Number 1 Salary Negotiation Rule: The person who names a specific amount first loses.**
- **The only time to negotiate is after you have been offered the job.** Employers want to know how much you want to be paid so that they can eliminate you from consideration. They figure if you want too much, you won't be happy with their job and won't stay. And if you will take too little, they may think you don't have enough experience. So never discuss your salary expectations until an employer offers you the job.
- **If pressed, speak in terms of wide pay ranges.** If you are pushed to reveal your pay expectations early in an interview, ask the interviewer what the normal pay range is for this job. Interviewers will often tell you, and you can say that you would consider offers in this range.

  If you are forced to be more specific, speak in terms of a wide pay range. If you figure that the company will likely pay from $25,000 to $29,000 a year, for example, say that you would consider "any fair offer in the mid- to upper-twenties." This statement covers the employer's range and goes a bit higher. If all else fails, tell the interviewer that you would consider any reasonable offer.

  For this tip to work, you must know in advance what the job is likely to pay. You can get this information by asking people who do similar work, or from a variety of books and Internet sources of career information.

- **If you want the job, you should say so.** This is no time to be playing games.
- **Don't say "no" too quickly.** Never, ever turn down a job offer during an interview! Instead, thank the interviewer for the offer and ask to consider the offer overnight. You can turn it down tomorrow, saying how much you appreciate the offer and asking to be considered for other jobs that pay better or whatever. And it is okay to ask for additional pay or other concessions. But if you simply can't accept the offer, say why and ask the interviewer to keep you in mind for future opportunities. You just never know.

STEP 7: Follow Up on All Job Leads

It's a fact: People who follow up with potential employers and with others in their network get jobs more quickly than those who do not.

Rules for Effective Follow-Up

Here are four rules to guide you in your job search:

- **Send a thank-you note or e-mail to every person who helps you in your job search.**
- **Send the note within 24 hours after speaking with the person.**
- **Enclose JIST Cards with thank-you notes and all other correspondence.**
- **Develop a system to keep following up with good contacts.**

Thank-You Notes Make a Difference

Although thank-you notes can be e-mailed, most people appreciate and are more impressed by a mailed note. Here are some tips about mailed thank-you notes that you can easily adapt to e-mail use:

- You can handwrite or type thank-you notes on quality paper and matching envelopes.

- Keep the notes simple, neat, and error-free.

- Make sure to include a few copies of your JIST Card in the envelope.

Here is an example of a simple thank-you note.

April 5, XXXX

Mr. Kijek,

Thanks so much for your willingness to see me next Wednesday at 9 a.m. I know that I am one of many who are interested in working with your organization. I appreciate the opportunity to meet you and learn more about the position.

I've enclosed a JIST Card that presents the basics of my skills for this job and will bring my resume to the interview. Please call me if you have any questions at all.

Sincerely,

Bruce Vernon

Use Job Lead Cards to Follow Up

If you use contact management software, use it to schedule follow-up activities. But the simple paper system I describe here can work very well or can be adapted for setting up your contact management software.

- Use a simple 3-by-5–inch card to record essential information about each person in your network.

- Buy a 3-by-5–inch card file box and tabs for each day of the month.

- File the cards under the date you want to contact the person.

- Follow through by contacting the person on that date.

> **Quip**
>
> The JibberJobber Web site (www.jibberjobber.com) provides online tools for tracking your contacts.

I've found that staying in touch with a good contact every other week can pay off big. Here's a sample card to give you ideas about creating your own.

```
ORGANIZATION: ___Mutual Health Insurance_____

CONTACT PERSON: __Anna Tomey_____    PHONE: __317-355-0216____

SOURCE OF LEAD: __Aunt Ruth_____

NOTES: __4/10 Called. Anna on vacation. Call back 4/15. 4/15 Interview set__

____4/20 at 1:30. 4/20 Anna showed me around. They use the same computers__

____we used in school! (Friendly people.) Sent thank-you note and JIST__

____Card, call back 5/1. 5/1 Second interview 5/8 at 9 a.m.!_____

_____

_____

_____
```

In Closing

This is a short book, but it may be all you need to get a better job in less time. I hope this will be true for you, and I wish you well in your search. Remember this: You won't get a job offer because someone knocks on your door and offers one. Job seeking does involve luck, but you are more likely to have good luck if you are out getting interviews.

I'll close this minibook with a few final tips:

- **Approach your job search as if it were a job itself.** Create and stick to a daily schedule, and spend at least 25 hours a week looking.

- **Follow up on each lead you generate and ask each contact for referrals.**

- **Set out each day to schedule at least two interviews.** Remember the new definition of an interview—an interview includes talking to potential employers who don't have an opening now.

- **Send out lots of thank-you notes and JIST Cards.**

- **When you want the job, tell the employer that you want it and why you should be hired over everyone else.**

Don't get discouraged. There are lots of jobs out there, and someone needs an employee with your skills—your job is to find that someone.

I wish you luck in your job search and in your life.

ESSENTIAL JOB SEARCH DATA WORKSHEET

Take some time to complete this worksheet carefully. It will help you write your resume and answer interview questions. You can also photocopy it and take it with you to help complete applications and as a reference throughout your job search. Use an erasable pen or pencil to allow for corrections. Whenever possible, emphasize skills and accomplishments that support your ability to do the job you want. Use extra sheets as needed.

Your name_____

Date completed_____

Job objective_____

Key Accomplishments

List three accomplishments that best prove your ability to do the kind of job you want.

1. _____

2. _____

3. _____

Education and Training

Name of high school(s) and specific years attended_____

Subjects related to job objective_____

_____

Related extracurricular activities/hobbies/leisure activities_____

_____

Accomplishments/things you did well_____

_____

Specific things you can do as a result_____

_____

Schools you attended after high school, specific years attended, and degrees/certificates earned_____

_____

Courses related to job objective_____

_____

Related extracurricular activities/hobbies/leisure activities_____

_____

Accomplishments/things you did well_____

_____

Specific things you can do as a result_____

_____

Other Training

Include formal or informal learning, workshops, military training, skills you learned on the job or from hobbies—anything that will help support your job objective. Include specific dates, certificates earned, or other details as needed._____

_____

(continued)

© JIST Works

(continued)

Work and Volunteer History

List your most recent job first, followed by each previous job. Military experience, unpaid or volunteer work, and work in a family business should be included here, too. If needed, use additional sheets to cover *all* significant paid or unpaid work experiences. Emphasize details that will help support your new job objective. Include numbers to support what you did: the number of people served over one or more years, number of transactions processed, percentage of sales increased, total inventory value you were responsible for, payroll of the staff you supervised, total budget responsible for, and so on. Emphasize results you achieved, using numbers to support them whenever possible. Mentioning these things on your resume and in an interview will help you get the job you want.

Job 1

Dates employed_____

Name of organization_____

Supervisor's name and job title_____

Address_____

Phone number/e-mail address/Web site_____

What did you accomplish and do well?_____

_____

Things you learned; skills you developed or used_____

_____

Raises, promotions, positive evaluations, awards_____

_____

Computer software, hardware, and other equipment you used_____

_____

Other details that might support your job objective_____

_____

Job 2

Dates employed_____

Name of organization_____

Supervisor's name and job title_____

Address_____

Phone number/e-mail address/Web site_____

What did you accomplish and do well?_____

_____

Things you learned; skills you developed or used_____

_____

© **JIST Works**

Raises, promotions, positive evaluations, awards _____

_____

Computer software, hardware, and other equipment you used _____

_____

Other details that might support your job objective _____

_____

Job 3

Dates employed _____

Name of organization _____

Supervisor's name and job title _____

Address _____

Phone number/e-mail address/Web site _____

What did you accomplish and do well? _____

_____

Things you learned; skills you developed or used _____

_____

Raises, promotions, positive evaluations, awards _____

_____

Computer software, hardware, and other equipment you used _____

_____

Other details that might support your job objective _____

_____

References

Think of people who know your work well and will be positive about your work and character. Past supervisors are best. Contact them and tell them what type of job you want and your qualifications, and ask what they will say about you if contacted by a potential employer. Some employers will not provide references by phone, so ask them for a letter of reference in advance. If a past employer may say negative things, negotiate what he or she will say or get written references from others you worked with there.

Reference name _____

Position or title _____

Relationship to you _____

Contact information (complete address, phone number, e-mail address) _____

(continued)

© JIST Works

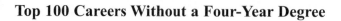

(continued)

Reference name_____

Position or title_____

Relationship to you_____

Contact information (complete address, phone number, e-mail address)_____

_____

Reference name_____

Position or title_____

Relationship to you_____

Contact information (complete address, phone number, e-mail address)_____

_____

A Short List of Additional Resources

Thousands of books and countless Internet sites provide information on career subjects. Space limitations do not permit me to describe the many good resources available, so I list here some of the most useful ones. Because this is my list, I've included books I've written or that JIST publishes. You should be able to find these and many other resources at libraries, bookstores, and Web bookselling sites.

Resume and Cover Letter Books

My books. *The Quick Resume & Cover Letter Book* is one of the top-selling resume books at various large bookstore chains. It is very simple to follow, is inexpensive, has good design, and has good sample resumes written by professional resume writers. For more in-depth but still quick help, check out my two books in the *Help in a Hurry* series: *Same-Day Resume* (with advice on creating a simple resume in an hour and a better one later) and *15-Minute Cover Letter,* co-authored with Louise Kursmark (offering sample cover letters and tips for writing them fast and effectively).

Other books published by JIST. The following titles include many sample resumes written by professional resume writers, as well as good advice: *Amazing Resumes* by Jim Bright and Joanne Earl; *Cover Letter Magic* by Wendy S. Enelow and Louise M. Kursmark; the entire *Expert Resumes* series by Enelow and Kursmark; *Federal Resume Guidebook* by Kathryn Kraemer Troutman; *Gallery of Best Resumes, Gallery of Best Cover Letters,* and other books by David F. Noble; and *Résumé Magic* by Susan Britton Whitcomb.

Job Search and Interviewing Books

My books. In addition to the books mentioned above, check out *Next-Day Job Interview* (quick tips for preparing for a job interview at the last minute). *The Very Quick Job Search* is a thorough book with detailed advice and a "quick" section of key tips you can finish in a few hours. *Getting the Job You Really Want* includes many activities and good career decision-making and job search advice.

Other books published by JIST. Titles include *Inside Secrets of Finding a Teaching Job* by Warner, Bryan, and Warner; *Insider's Guide to Finding a Job* by Wendy S. Enelow and Shelly Goldman; *Job Search Handbook for People with Disabilities* by Daniel J. Ryan; *Job Search Magic* and *Interview Magic* by Susan Britton Whitcomb; *Ultimate Job Search* by Richard H. Beatty; and *Over-40 Job Search Guide* by Gail Geary.

© **JIST Works**

Books with Information on Jobs

The primary reference books. The *Occupational Outlook Handbook* is the source of job titles listed in this book. Published by the U.S. Department of Labor and updated every other year, the *OOH* covers about 90 percent of the workforce. The *O*NET Dictionary of Occupational Titles* book has descriptions for almost 1,000 jobs based on the O*NET (Occupational Information Network) database developed by the Department of Labor. The *Enhanced Occupational Outlook Handbook* includes the *OOH* descriptions plus more than 7,000 additional descriptions of related jobs from the O*NET and other sources. The *New Guide for Occupational Exploration* allows you to explore major jobs based on your interests.

Other books published by JIST. Here are a few good books that include job descriptions and helpful details on career options: *Overnight Career Choice, Best Jobs for the 21st Century, 50 Best Jobs for Your Personality, 200 Best Jobs for College Graduates, 300 Best Jobs Without a Four-Year Degree, Salary Facts Handbook,* and *Health-Care CareerVision.*

Internet Resources

There are too many Web sites to list, but here are a few places you can start. A book by Anne Wolfinger titled *Best Career and Education Web Sites* gives unbiased reviews of the most helpful sites and ideas on how to use them. *Job Seeker's Online Goldmine,* by Janet Wall, lists the extensive free online job search tools from government and other sources. This book's job descriptions also include Internet addresses for related organizations. Be aware that some Web sites provide poor advice, so ask your librarian, instructor, or counselor for suggestions on those best for your needs.

Other Resources

Libraries. Most libraries have the books mentioned here, as well as many other resources. Most provide Internet access so that you can research online information. Ask the librarian for help finding what you need.

People. People who hold the jobs that interest you are one of the best career information sources. Ask them what they like and don't like about their work, how they got started, and the education or training needed. Most people are helpful and will give advice you can't get any other way.

Career Counseling. A good vocational counselor can help you explore career options. Take advantage of this service if it is available to you! Also consider a career-planning course or program, which will encourage you to be more thorough in your thinking.

Sample Resumes for Some of the Top Careers Without a Four-Year Degree

If you read the previous information, you know that I believe you should not depend on a resume alone in your job search. Even so, you will most likely need one, and you should have a good one.

Unlike some career authors, I do not preach that there is only one right way to do a resume. I encourage you to be an individual and to do what you think will work well for you. But I also know that some resumes are clearly better than others. The following pages contain some resumes that you can use as examples when preparing your own resume.

Each resume was written by a professional resume writer who is a member of one or more professional associations. These writers are highly qualified and hold various credentials. Most will provide help (for a fee) and welcome your contacting them (although this is not a personal endorsement).

The resumes appear in books published by JIST Works, including the following:

- *Expert Resumes for Computer and Web Jobs* by Wendy S. Enelow and Louise M. Kursmark
- *Gallery of Best Resumes for People Without a Four-Year Degree* by David F. Noble

Contact Information for Resume Contributors

The following professional resume writers contributed resumes to this section. Their names are listed in alphabetical order. Each entry indicates which resume that person contributed.

Janet L. Beckstrom
Word Crafter
1717 Montclair Ave.
Flint, MI 48503-2074
Toll-free: (800) 351-9818
Fax: (810) 232-9257
E-mail: wordcrafter@voyager.net
Member: CMI, PARW/CC
Certification: CPRW
Resume on page 357

Patricia Chapman
CareerPro-Naperville, Inc.
520 E. Ogden Ave., Suite 3
Naperville, IL 60563
Phone: (630) 983-8882
Toll-free: (866) 661-2269
Fax: (630) 983-9021
E-mail: pat@career2day.com
Web site: www.career2day.com
Member: CMI, PRWRA, NAFE
Certification: CRW
Resume on page 351

Michele Haffner
Advanced Resume Services
1314 W. Paradise Ct.
Glendale, WI 53209
Phone: (414) 247-1677
Fax: (414) 247-1808
E-mail:
michele@resumeservices.com
Web site: www.resumeservices.com
Certifications: CPRW, JCTC
Resume on page 350

Jan Holliday
Arbridge Communications
Harleysville, PA 19438
Phone: (215) 513-7420
Toll-free: (866) 513-7420
E-mail: info@arbridge.com
Web site: www.arbridge.com
Member: NRWA, CMI, IWA
Certifications: MA, NCRW, Certified Webmaster
Resume on pages 354–355

Melanie Noonan
Peripheral Pro, LLC
560 Lackawanna Ave.
West Paterson, NJ 07424
Phone: (973) 785-3011
Fax: (973) 256-6285
E-mail: PeriPro1@aol.com
Member: NRWA, PARW/CC
Certification: CPS
Resume on page 356

Diana Ramirez
Ramirez Consulting Services
Seatac, WA 98198
Phone: (206) 870-7366
Mobile: (253) 332-5521
E-mail:
ramirezconsulting@yahoo.com
Web site:
www.ramirezconsulting.us
Member: NRWA, NCDA, NAWW
Certifications: NCDA; Registered Counselor, Project Management, Human Resources Management
Resume on page 352

MeLisa Rogers
Ultimate Career
270 Live Oak Lane
Victoria, TX 77905
Toll-free: (866) 573-7863
Fax: (361) 574-8830
E-mail: success@ultimatecareer.biz
Web site: www.ultimatecareer.biz
Member: PARW/CC, SHRM, ASTD
Certifications: M.S. HRD, CPRW
Resume on page 358

Jane Roqueplot
JaneCo's Sensible Solutions
194 N. Oakland Ave.
Sharon, PA 16146
Phone: (724) 342-0100
Toll-free: (888) 526-3267
E-mail: jane@janecos.com
Web site: www.janecos.com
Member: CMI, NRWA, PRWRA, PARW/CC, AJST, NCDA
Certifications: CPBA, CWDP, CECC
Resume on page 349

Edward Turilli
Director, Career Development Center
Salve Regina University
100 Ochre Point Ave.
Newport, RI 02840
Anthem Resume & Career Services (ARCS)
918 Lafayette Road
North Kingstown, RI 02852
Phone: (401) 268-3020
Fax: (401) 341-2994
E-mail: turillie@salve.edu
Web site:
www.salve.edu/office_careerdev
Member: CMI, PARW/CC, NCDA, NACE, EACE, RICC
Certification: MA
Resume on page 353

Chefs, Cooks, and Food Preparation Workers

DONALD ARCHER
412 Old Castle Avenue • Sharon, Pennsylvania 16146 • 724-543-4671

"Co mpliments to the chef! This is the best prime rib I've ever eaten." — Ralph B
Monte Cello's, Sharon, PA

"Superb steak . . . cooked to perfection . . . excellent seasonings. My thanks to the chef."   — Actress
Debbie Reynolds
Radisson Hotel, Sharon, PA

Knowledgeable in:
- Food Preparation
- Menu Creation
- Inventory
- Ordering Supplies and Food
- Event Planning
- Serving 1–2,500
- Nutrition
- Sanitation
- Security
- Policies & Procedures
- Personnel Management
- Staff Training
- Record Keeping
- Preparation of Reports

EDUCATION

Culinary Arts
International Culinary Academy—Pittsburgh, Pennsylvania

Winner Institute of Arts & Sciences—Transfer, Pennsylvania

Food Competitions and Food Shows

Liberal Arts
Criminal Justice/
Pre-Law Course Work
Kent State University—Champion, Ohio

EXECUTIVE CHEF / PERSONAL CHEF / CATERING

- Select menu items with an eye toward quality, variety, availability of seasonal foods, popularity of past dishes and likely number of customers. Collaborate with owner(s) to plan menus to attract specific clientele.

- Estimate food consumption. Select and appropriately price menu items to cost-effectively use food and other supplies.

- Oversee food preparation and cooking, examining quality and portion sizes to ensure dishes are prepared and garnished correctly and in a timely manner.

- Proficient knowledge of computer programs, especially to create menus; analyze recipes to determine food, labor and overhead costs; and calculate prices for various dishes.

- Hardworking, self-motivated individual with proven record of responsibility. Equally effective working independently as well as in a team effort. Work well with a wide range of people at all levels; comfortable leading, collaborating or training.

- Able to view situations/issues in a positive way and propose solutions to streamline operations. Organized and detail-oriented. Identify and resolve challenges using available resources.

- Effective communicator. Monitor actions of employees to ensure health and safety standards are maintained. Represent an organization in a professional manner and appearance.

- Receptive to relocation.

EXPERIENCE

EXECUTIVE CHEF, Monte Cello's—*Sharon, Pennsylvania*
SOUS CHEF, Mr. D's Food Fair—*Brookfield, Ohio*
KITCHEN MANAGER, Sidetrack Inn—*Warren, Ohio*
STORE MANAGER, Pit Stop Pizza—*Cortland, Ohio*
GRILL AND SAUTÉ CHEF, Radisson Hotel—*Sharon, Pennsylvania*
PREP CHEF, Avalon Inn—*Howland, Ohio*
ASSISTANT MANAGER, Moovies, Inc.—*Cortland, Ohio*
PERSONAL SECURITY TECHNICIAN, Independent Contractor—
various locations

MILITARY

Military Police, 1984–1987, Honorable Discharge
United States Marine Corp.

© JIST Works

Computer Scientists and Database Administrators

DAVID SUZUKI

Email: davidsuzuki@yahoo.com

145 West Rosecliff Court
Saukville, WI 53080

Office: (414) 629-3676
Res: (262) 344-3449

TECHNICAL PROFILE

A dedicated and loyal systems professional with 20+ years of hands-on experience as a **database administrator and application developer.** Solid understanding of relational databases. Excellent design, coding, and testing skills. Strong oral and written communication abilities.

Databases:	DB2, Oracle, SQL
Languages:	COBOL, IBM/AS, Visual Basic
Operating Systems:	VM, UNIX, DOS, Windows 98 and XP
Third-Party Software:	COGNOS, Impromptu, Informatica, Microsoft Access

PROFESSIONAL EXPERIENCE

Midwest Staffing Inc., Milwaukee, WI   1984 to Present
  (A global employment services organization with annual sales in excess of $10 billion.)

LEAD DATABASE ADMINISTRATOR AND DEVELOPER
Lead mainframe and Oracle database administrator with 24/7 responsibility for performance, tuning, recovery, and planning. Use various utilities to transfer data to other platforms and build tables/indexes. Respond to end users' requests for information and resolve discrepancies in data reports. Research and interact with vendors in the purchase of third-party software. Train and supervise assistant DBAs. Write user manuals, operating procedures, and internal documentation.

Selected Database Development Projects and Achievements:

- Administer mission-critical payroll and billing database that bills $5+ million per week.
- Designed, developed, and implemented Oracle databank—a duplicate of the mainframe databank. End users now have greater access to data using desktop tools.
- Developed and maintain franchise fee billing application.
- Developed Central Billing consolidation application that bills $5 million per month.
- Researched and recommended purchase of ETL Informatica PowerMart utility. Data movement to the data repository, the Internet, and databases is now accomplished in one step. Previously, data movement involved large amounts of development time.
- Developed mainframe processes using the ESSCON Channel (high-speed data transfer) to move data from the mainframe to the AIX platform. Compared to the old method using Outbound, this has reduced data transfer time by at least 50%.
- Selected by management to train assistant database administrator. Assistant is now a reliable backup on mainframe-related database issues.

EDUCATION

Oracle and Oracle Tuning, Certificate Courses, University of Wisconsin—Milwaukee, 2003

Construction Laborers

Mark A. Benton

520 E. Ogden Avenue • Naperville, Illinois 06060 • 000–983–8882

PROFILE

Focus: Laborer position in the construction industry

Excel in troubleshooting and problem solving, readily understand instructions of a complicated nature, and respond to challenges with a "get the job done" attitude. Grasp client's requirements and management's needs quickly and apply appropriate actions to complete tasks in a timely manner. Constantly seeking new and more effective methods for performing professional duties. Working knowledge of Microsoft Windows and Word. Focused on personal and professional growth.

EXPERIENCE SUMMARY

- **Tradesman/Warehouseman/Laborer:** Light carpentry, painting, window preparations, frame building, shipping and receiving, loading of building supplies, use of various power tools and forklift operator.
- **Housekeeping Technician:** General housekeeping for one of the largest hotels in Chicago. Responsible for servicing up to 20 floors.
- **Building Services Technician:** General office cleaning, horizontal and vertical dusting, stripping/buffing of floors and restroom maintenance. Provided office security.
- **Security:** Ensured safe, clean and proper order of facility.
- **Administrative Support Technician:** Setup and maintenance of administrative files; answering and routing of phone calls; typing file labels, memos and letters using Microsoft Word. Copying and faxing documents, sorting incoming mail and preparing outgoing mail.

RELATED SKILLS

- Forklift Operator—Certified
- Computer Training and Enhancement
- Building Maintenance Services
- Equipment Maintenance Training

EMPLOYMENT HISTORY

Inventory/Receiving/Laborer, M&P Construction, Chicago, IL (02/01–Present)

Quality Control Coordinator, Teracotta Data Systems, Inc., Chicago, IL (04/99–02/01)

Laborer, Western and Block Construction, Chicago, IL (04/92–04/99)

Laborer, Buillion Construction/Cook County Hospital, Chicago, IL (01/89–04/92)

Housekeeper, Holiday Inn, Chicago, IL (03/86–01/89)

Warehouseman/Mover/Loader/Driver, We Move You, Chicago, IL (05/83–03/86)

Security, Your Answering Service, Bedford Park, IL (08/80–05/83)

EDUCATION

New Cycle Ministries, Inc., Chicago, Illinois. **Computer Training & Enhancement. 2004 Graduate**
Chicago High School, Chicago, Illinois. **1980 Graduate**

Dental Assistants

Carol A. Weiss
DENTAL ASSISTANT

62482 110th Avenue S., Federal Way, WA 99999   (000) 000-0000   email: cweiss@resume.com

PROFILE :

More than 15 years of Dental Assistant experience in meeting high infection-control standards, sterilizing and disinfecting instruments and equipment, preparing tray setup for dental procedures, and instructing patients on postoperative and general oral health care.

- ➢ **Supervised** two Dental Assistants.
- ➢ Trained in **product knowledge** (bonding, impression materials, and more).
- ➢ Experienced in working with all ages of people, from small children to senior citizens.
- ➢ **Managed office,** ensuring that it was organized, clean, fully stocked, and prepared daily.
- ➢ Worked in a **lab** within the same facility, making any shade changes or polishing of dentures, crowns, and bridge work.
- ➢ Caring, detailed-oriented, hard worker who has learned different state-of-the-art dentistry styles, **procedures, and techniques.** Always seeks ways to keep skills current.

SUMMARY OF QUALIFICATIONS:

- ▶ Root canal treatment
- ▶ Air particle machines
- ▶ Polishing of all fillings
- ▶ Soft and hard relines
- ▶ Rubber dam replacement

- ▶ Crown and bridge preparation and delivery
- ▶ Composite and amalgam fillings
- ▶ Denture and partial procedures
- ▶ Assisted with multiple extractions
- ▶ Took full-series radiographs and panolipse radiographs

OFFICE SKILLS:

- ▶ Windows, DOS, MS Office (Word, Excel, PowerPoint), word processing, spreadsheets, databases, Ex-Change+, Internet (Netscape, Explorer), email
- ▶ Typewriter, word processor, copier, calculator, fax machine, printers, multiline phone systems
- ▶ Records management, medical terminology, healthcare plan knowledge, billing codes

PROFESSIONAL EXPERIENCE:

Dr. Ronald McPherson, DDS—Federal Way, WA Dental Assistant	2001–Current
Dr. D. Maynard Debus, DDS—Federal Way, WA Dental Assistant	1999–2001
Dr. Larry W. Howard, DDS—Federal Way, WA Dental Assistant	1999 (temp)
Dr. Abel D. Sanchez, DDS—Federal Way, WA Dental Assistant	1979–1989

Licensed Practical and Licensed Vocational Nurses

Katherine E. Masterson

321 Nickerson Point Avenue
South Kingstown, RI 12121
(401) 444-4444

OBJECTIVE: A position as a Licensed Practical Nurse, utilizing 11 years of full-time, dedicated professional employment at the highest quality of nursing care.

- CAREER SUMMARY -

- Licensed Practical Nurse with 11 years of experience, including Cardiac Teaching and Pre-cardiac Catheterization
- Proven ability to meet the daily challenges of the nursing profession
- Work with the high standards and dedication expected of today's LPNs
- Received Highest LPN Service Award, two years

EDUCATION: **Community College of Rhode Island,** Lincoln, RI
Diploma as a Licensed Practical Nurse, July 1994
GPA: 3.8/4.0
Graduated third in a class of 88

Community College of Rhode Island, Warwick, RI
Liberal Arts Courses (leading to Registered Nurse Degree)

EXPERIENCE: **North County Memorial Hospital,** Cranston, RI
<u>Licensed Practical Nurse</u>, August 1998–Present
- Full-time staff member of the Coronary Care Unit
- Work in a team of three participants
- Maintain full awareness of monitored patients
- Care, assessment, charting, medicating, monitoring IV fluids/medications

North County Nursing and Subacute Unit, North Kingstown, RI
<u>Licensed Practical Nurse, Primary Care</u>, December 1994–1998
- Charge of nursing for 26 long-term and subacute residents
- Primary care nursing

LICENSES: Current Practical Nursing license #LPN 07542
CPR certification through November 2004

MEMBERSHIPS: Wickford Glen Condominium Association, President
Saint Paul's Parish Community Association
Rhode Island LPN Consortium, Secretary

VOLUNTEER: Annual Cancer Appeal Raffle ticket sales
Kent County Hospital Annual Appeal Phonathons
Toys for Tots Appeals

Excellent references will be furnished upon request

Office and Administrative Support Worker Supervisors and Managers

WENDY A. CARUTHERS

965 Old Bridge Lane
Lansdale, PA 00000

(555) 555-5555
wcaruthers@dotresume.com

OFFICE MANAGER

Bookkeeping
Human Resources Administration
General Operations

HIGHLIGHTS

Areas of Expertise

Bookkeeping: AP/AR, bank reconciliations, financial reports, payroll
HR Administration: 401(k) and medical benefits, employee manuals, training
General Operations: Office procedures, moves, startups, closings

Key Strengths

- Adept at handling multiple tasks in an organized manner.
- Proven ability to train and supervise staff.
- Experience working with vendors and building operations personnel.
- Sensitive to confidentiality of employee records and financial data.
- Excellent written and verbal communication skills.
- Proficient in Intuit QuickBooks Pro and MS Excel and Word; working knowledge of Microsoft Outlook, Windows 95/98/NT, and Internet Explorer.

EXPERIENCE

Office Manager
E-PRAXIS, INC., Blue Bell, PA (2000–2004)

Set up office procedures and bookkeeping system that accommodated growth of Internet startup from 10 to 40 employees. Developed orientation program and accompanying manual to quickly integrate new hires. Prepared monthly and annual financial reports for top management. Hired, trained, and supervised two administrative assistants.

Selected Accomplishments

- Managed two office moves with minimal inconvenience and downtime.
- Selected to assist with office closing—employee layoffs, contract terminations, and final audit.

WENDY A. CARUTHERS

page 2

EXPERIENCE
continued

Office Manager
EASTERN OFFICE SUPPLY, INC., Montgomeryville, PA (1997–1999)

Performed full-charge bookkeeping services and human resources administration for an independent office equipment dealership. Using QuickBooks Pro, prepared invoices, accounts payable, accounts receivable, bank reconciliations, financial statements, and payroll. Maintained confidential employee files and administered medical benefits and 401(k) program.

> *Selected Accomplishments*
> ♦ Increased efficiency by training staff in standard office procedures.
> ♦ Consistently received top ratings on performance evaluations.

Family Care and Home Management
(1994–1997)

Cared for two small children. Handled day-to-day household operations and acted as general contractor for building a home addition. Managed family finances in Quicken—established budget, paid bills, and balanced bank accounts. Prepared tax returns for three households using TurboTax.

Bookkeeper
CONCORDIA FABRICATIONS, INC., Telford, PA (1991–1994)

Prepared accounts payable/accounts receivable for manufacturing company with 50 employees. Maintained employee payroll and processed expense reports. Implemented conversion from manual to computerized bookkeeping system without disrupting normal operations.

Administrative Assistant
NEWMAN MEDICAL SUPPLY COMPANY, Quakertown, PA (1990–1991)

Assisted with broad range of bookkeeping functions, including bank reconciliations, accounts payable, accounts receivable, and payroll processing. Served as primary point of contact with vendors and building maintenance personnel.

EDUCATION

Courses in Word and Excel, Franklin Area Adult School, Morrisville, PA (1996–1997)

A.S., Accounting, Gateway Business College, Somerfield, PA (1990)

Teachers—Preschool, Kindergarten, Elementary, Middle, and Secondary

Heather Hammond

52 Lancaster Avenue
Newbold, AR 00000
(000) 000-0000
heatherhammond@email.com

QUALIFICATIONS

*More than 7 years of experience working in private preschool settings
with exposure to all childhood development stages*

Early Childhood Education Certificate, 1997
Willis County College

Certified in CPR and First Aid

TESTIMONIALS

"Heather has a natural talent for building immediate rapport with children. Her patience, confidence, and commitment make her a valuable member of our day care staff."
—Liz Kaufman, Director

"It is such a pleasure to work with Heather. She always stays calm, even in stressful moments with the children."
—Maryann Bradley, Teacher's Aide

"Kelsey loves you, and we can certainly tell she means the world to you. What we didn't realize was that you would bring out the musician in her."
—Linda and Greg Mills

"The following two words are simple but truly express our feelings for the fine job you did in helping Justin enjoy his first experience with academics. Thank you!!!"
—Sean and Deanna McFarland

"We came to you last year with our precious rosebud and have watched her bloom. We alerted you of her thorns, but you overcame most of them with your tender pruning and weeding."
—Annette and Frank DeMartino

"Thank you so much for all of your love and nurturing. Jolie loves coming to school every day, and I know you play the greatest role in her happiness."
—Janet Tremain

"Because of your gentle, kind and patient love for Rico, he has become more interested in learning. Thank you for keeping cool in the face of such great challenges."
—Consuelo and Pedro Cortez

"Thank you so very much for looking after our precious angel Adrianna. As a working mother, words can never express how thankful I am for your patience and guidance."
—Karen Fortner

"We, the parents of Kirit, wish to thank you from the bottom of our hearts for nurturing our child and expanding his horizons, opening his mind and heart in a caring and affectionate way."
—Pradeep and Naila Ashrani

PROFESSIONAL EXPERIENCE

SESAME STREET CHILDREN'S ACADEMY
Newbold, AR   1997–2004
Preschool Teacher
Promoted from Teacher's Aide after 1 year

✷ Taught 3 classes of 12 children each, ages 3–4, and supervised 2 teacher's aides.

✷ Used a variety of hands-on activities to instill an early love of learning in culturally diverse children.

✷ Created a safe, relaxed environment, which allowed the development of social and physical skills as well as creativity.

✷ Encouraged reading and writing through innovative alphabet games. By end of each school year, all children were able to print their names and orally spell them.

✷ Helped to build self-esteem by designating helpers and pairing shy children with assertive ones in play activities such as "Caterpillars and Butterflies."

✷ Contributed to a friendly, family-type work environment, sharing ideas with other teachers.

HOUSEHOLD OF MITCH AND DELIA BASCOMB
Newbold, AR   1994–1997
Nanny

✷ Assisted with educational and after-school activities for 3 children.

✷ Recommended by Mr. Bascomb for employment at Sesame Street Children's Academy.

© JIST Works

Tellers

Elizabeth J. Polawski

642 Deerfield Street   Kalamazoo, Michigan 49002   269-555-0086

Profile
- ❖ Ten years of financial institution experience; additional experience in retail management.
- ❖ Reputation for building relationships with members and providing top-notch member service. Equally outstanding relationships with colleagues, supervisors and management.
- ❖ Exemplify the organization's commitment to quality through "knowledgeable and concerned professionals."
- ❖ Highly motivated to meet new challenges by capitalizing on experience and skills.

Highlights of Employment

- ❖ Exceeded personal sales goals for 18 consecutive months. Frequently receive recognition from management for cross-selling and referrals.
- ❖ Selected by management as one of two instructors to train teller staff in use of new Quality computerized system.

Employment History

Grand Valley Credit Union • Kalamazoo, Michigan   1994–Present

Teller (full-time)
- Process member transactions, ensuring thoroughness, accuracy and the protection of the organization's funds. Consistently balance cash drawer.
- Provide all aspects of customer service. Respond to and resolve questions and concerns.
- Introduce products and services to members; handle sales and make appropriate referrals.

Highlights:
- Act as resource person after training in and transition to new computerized system.
- Conduct on-the-job teller training for new employees following the classroom component. Monitor and support trainees during transactions and interaction with members; polish trainees' technical and communication skills. Evaluate trainees and report to management.
- Serve on Marketing committee; previously sat on Steering and Lunchbox committees.

The Deb Shop • Battle Creek, Michigan   1993–1994

Assistant Store Manager
- Participated in all aspects of daily operations:
  - Opening/closing   - Merchandising
  - Cash handling and bank deposits   - Employee supervision
- Assisted customers with merchandise selection and processed purchases. Provided personalized customer service.

Training & Education
- ❖ LEAD program through CUNA (currently participating)
- ❖ Sales Plus and Service Plus programs
- ❖ General course work through Grand Valley Community College

"The most important single ingredient in the formula of success is knowing how to get along with people."
—Theodore Roosevelt

Truck Drivers and Driver/Sales Workers

Jason A. Zimmerman

2513 West Vista Lane   Miami, FL 33166   (cell) 786.522.9875   (home) 305.779.0036

> *Professional truck driver offers a winning combination to an organization that values stability, dependability, and timely deliveries*

- ❖ *3 Million Miles*
- ❖ *Multiple Safety Awards*
- ❖ *32 Years of Experience*

Single and Team Driver of the following rigs:

Vans	Step Deck	Reefers
Doubles	Flat Deck	Tankers

SAFETY AWARDS

SCHROEDER NATIONAL
6-Year Driver Safety Award
GREENWAY/LOADSTAR
5-Year Driver Safety Award
EAST POINT TRANSIT
800,000-Mile Driver Safety Award
SOUTHEAST EXPRESS
7-Year Driver Safety Award
PULMAN GROUP
2-Year Driver Safety Award

PROFESSIONAL EXPERIENCE

Nov 1996–Present
SCHROEDER NATIONAL
Richmond, Virginia
- Drive vans transporting general freight throughout the United States.
- Supervise the dock management of product: loading, unloading, and accounting.

Oct 1991–Oct 1996
GREENWAY/LOADSTAR
Buffalo, New York
- Drove single and double vans, flatbeds, and step decks transporting general freight throughout the United States.
- Supervised the dock management of product: loading, unloading, accounting, securing freight, and customer interaction.

Jan 1991–Oct 1991
GLOBAL MARINE
Charleston, South Carolina
- Drove specialized boat trailers transporting high-value yachts.
- Supervised the crane work and tie-down of the yachts.
- Coordinated delivery times with the customer.

1970–1991
**GLENDALE SHIPPING / REINOLD TRUCKING CO. / EAST POINT TRANSIT
INTERSTATE TRUCKING CO. / SOUTHEAST EXPRESS / COASTAL TRANSPORT
PULMAN GROUP**

Important Trends in Jobs and Industries

In putting this section together, my objective was to give you a quick review of major labor market trends. To accomplish this, I included three excellent articles that originally appeared in U.S. Department of Labor publications.

The first article is "Tomorrow's Jobs." It provides a superb—and short—review of the major trends that will affect your career in the years to come. Read it for ideas on selecting a career path for the long term.

The second article is "Employment Trends in Major Industries." While you may not have thought much about it, the industry you work in is just as important as your occupational choice. This great article will help you learn about major trends affecting various industries.

The third article, "Job Outlook for People Who Don't Have a Bachelor's Degree," discusses the large number of job openings for people without a four-year degree. It also covers high-paying jobs that do not require a four-year degree. The article can help you focus on promising careers in many industries.

Tomorrow's Jobs

Making informed career decisions requires reliable information about opportunities in the future. Opportunities result from the relationships between the population, the labor force, and the demand for goods and services.

Population ultimately limits the size of the labor force—individuals working or looking for work—which limits the goods and services that can be produced. Demand for various goods and services is largely responsible for employment in the industries providing them. Employment opportunities, in turn, result from demand for skills needed within specific industries. Opportunities for medical assistants and other healthcare occupations, for example, have surged in response to rapid growth in demand for health services.

Examining the past and present and projecting changes in these relationships are the foundation of the Occupational Outlook Program. This chapter presents highlights of the Bureau of Labor Statistics' projections of the labor force and occupational and industry employment that can help guide your career plans.

Population

Population trends affect employment opportunities in a number of ways. Changes in population influence the demand for goods and services. For example, a growing and aging population has increased the demand for health services. Equally important, population changes produce corresponding changes in the size and demographic composition of the labor force.

The U.S. civilian noninstitutional population is expected to increase by 21.8 million over the 2006–2016 period (Chart 1). The 2006–2016 rate of growth is slower than the growth rate over the 1986–1996 and 1996–2006 periods—9 percent, 11 percent, and 13 percent, respectively. Continued growth, however, will mean more consumers of goods and services, spurring demand for workers in a wide range of occupations and industries. The effects of population growth on various occupations will differ. The differences are partially accounted for by the age distribution of the future population.

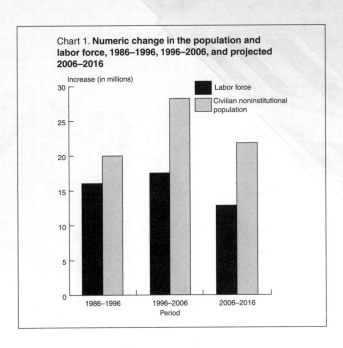

Chart 1. **Numeric change in the population and labor force, 1986–1996, 1996–2006, and projected 2006–2016**

As the baby boomers continue to age, the 55-to-64 age group will increase by 30.3 percent or 9.5 million persons, more than any other group. The 35-to-44 age group will decrease by 5.5 percent, reflecting a slowed birth rate following the baby boom generation, while the youth population, aged 16 to 24, will decline 1.1 percent over the 2006–2016 period.

Minorities and immigrants will constitute a larger share of the U.S. population in 2016. The numbers of Asians and people of Hispanic origin are projected to continue to grow much faster than other racial and ethnic groups.

Labor Force

Population is the single most important factor in determining the size and composition of the labor force—people either working or looking for work. The civilian labor force is projected to increase by 12.8 million, or 8.5 percent, to 164.2 million over the 2006–2016 period.

The U.S. workforce will become more diverse by 2016. White, non-Hispanic persons will continue to make up a decreasing share of the labor force, falling from 69.1 percent in 2006 to 64.6 percent in 2016 (Chart 2). However, despite relatively slow growth, white non-Hispanics will remain the overwhelming majority of the labor force. Hispanics are projected to be the fastest-growing ethnic group, growing by 29.9 percent. By 2016, Hispanics will continue to constitute an increasing proportion of the labor force, growing from 13.7 percent to 16.4 percent. Asians are projected to account for an increasing share of the labor force by 2016, growing from 4.4 to 5.3 percent. Blacks will also increase their share of the labor force, growing from 11.4 percent to 12.3 percent.

The numbers of men and women in the labor force will grow, but the number of women will grow at a slightly faster rate than the number of men. The male labor force is projected to grow by 8.0 percent from 2006 to 2016, compared with 8.9 percent for women, down from 12.7 and 13.4 percent, respectively, from 1996 to 2006. As a result, men's share of the labor force is expected to decrease from 53.7 to 53.4 percent, while women's share is expected to increase from 46.3 to 46.6 percent.

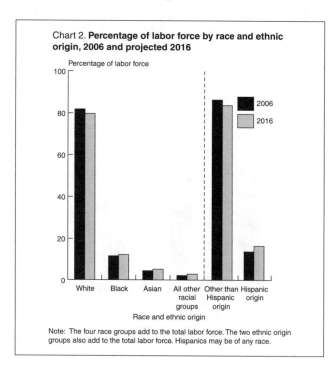

Chart 2. **Percentage of labor force by race and ethnic origin, 2006 and projected 2016**

Note: The four race groups add to the total labor force. The two ethnic origin groups also add to the total labor force. Hispanics may be of any race.

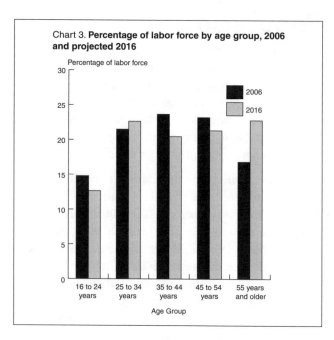

Chart 3. **Percentage of labor force by age group, 2006 and projected 2016**

The youth labor force, aged 16 to 24, is expected to decrease its share of the labor force to 12.7 percent by 2016. The primary working age group, between 25 and 54 years old, is projected to decline from 68.4 percent of the labor force in 2006 to 64.6 percent by 2016. Workers 55 and older, on the other hand, are projected to leap from 16.8 percent to 22.7 percent of the labor force between 2006 and 2016 (Chart 3). The aging of the baby boom generation will cause not only an increase in the percentage of workers in the oldest age category, but a decrease in the percentage of younger workers.

Employment

Total employment is expected to increase from 150.6 million in 2006 to 166.2 million in 2016, or by 10 percent. The 15.6 million jobs that will be added by 2016 will not be evenly distributed across major industrial and occupational groups. Changes in consumer demand, technology, and many other factors will contribute to the continually changing employment structure in the U.S. economy.

The following two sections examine projected employment change from industrial and occupational perspectives. The industrial profile is discussed in terms of primary wage and salary employment. Primary employment excludes secondary jobs for those who hold multiple jobs. The exception is employment in agriculture, which includes self-employed and unpaid family workers in addition to wage and salary workers.

The occupational profile is viewed in terms of total employment—including primary and secondary jobs for wage and salary, self-employed, and unpaid family workers. Of the roughly 150 million jobs in the U.S. economy in 2006, wage and salary workers accounted for 138.3 million, self-employed workers accounted for 12.2 million, and unpaid family workers accounted for about 130,000. Secondary employment accounted for 1.8 million jobs. Self-employed workers held nearly 9 out of 10 secondary jobs and wage and salary workers held most of the remainder.

Industry

Service-providing industries. The long-term shift from goods-producing to service-providing employment is expected to continue. Service-providing industries are expected to account for approximately 15.7 million new wage and salary jobs generated over the 2006–2016 period (Chart 4), while goods-producing industries will see overall job loss.

Education and health services. This industry supersector is projected to grow by 18.8 percent and add more jobs, nearly 5.5 million, than any other industry supersector. More than 3 out of every 10 new jobs created in the U.S. economy will be in either the healthcare and social assistance or public and private educational services sectors.

Health care and social assistance—including public and private hospitals, nursing and residential care facilities, and individual and family services—will grow by 25.4 percent and add 4 million new jobs. Employment growth will be driven by increasing demand for health care and social assistance because of an aging population and longer life expectancies. Also, as more women enter the labor force, demand for childcare services is expected to grow.

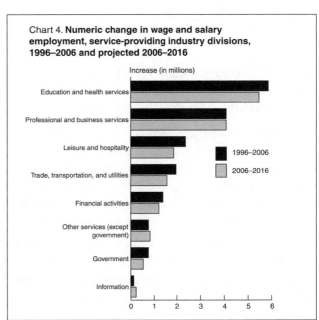

Chart 4. **Numeric change in wage and salary employment, service-providing industry divisions, 1996–2006 and projected 2006–2016**

Public and private educational services will grow by 10.7 percent and add 1.4 million new jobs through 2016. Rising student enrollments at all levels of education will create demand for educational services.

Professional and business services. This industry supersector, which includes some of the fastest-growing industries in the U.S. economy, will grow by 23.3 percent and add 4.1 million new jobs.

Employment in administrative and support and waste management and remediation services will grow by 20.3 percent and add 1.7 million new jobs to the economy by 2016. The largest industry growth in this sector will be enjoyed by employment services, which will be responsible for 692,000 new jobs, or more than 40 percent of all new jobs in administrative and support and waste management and remediation services. Employment services ranks second among industries with the most new employment opportunities in the nation and is expected to have a growth rate that is faster than the average for all industries. This will be due to the need for seasonal and temporary workers and for highly specialized human resources services.

Employment in professional, scientific, and technical services will grow by 28.8 percent and add 2.1 million new jobs by 2016. Employment in computer systems design and related services will grow by 38.3 percent and add nearly one-fourth of all new jobs in professional, scientific, and technical services. Employment growth will be driven by the increasing reliance of businesses on information technology and the continuing importance of maintaining system and network security. Management, scientific, and technical consulting services also will grow at a staggering 78 percent and account for another third of growth in this supersector. Demand for these services will be spurred by the increased use of new technology and computer software and the growing complexity of business.

Management of companies and enterprises will grow by 14.9 percent and add 270,000 new jobs.

Information. Employment in the information supersector is expected to increase by 6.9 percent, adding 212,000 jobs by 2016. Information contains some of the fast-growing computer-related industries such as software publishing, Internet publishing and broadcasting, and wireless telecommunication carriers. Employment in these industries is expected to grow by 32 percent, 44.1 percent, and 40.9 percent, respectively. The information supersector also includes motion picture production; broadcasting; and newspaper, periodical, book, and directory publishing. Increased demand for telecommunications services, cable service, high-speed Internet connections, and software will fuel job growth among these industries.

Leisure and hospitality. Overall employment will grow by 14.3 percent. Arts, entertainment, and recreation will grow by 30.9 percent and add 595,000 new jobs by 2016. Most of these new job openings, 79 percent, will be in the amusement, gambling, and recreation sector. Job growth will stem from public participation in arts, entertainment, and recreation activities, reflecting increasing incomes, leisure time, and awareness of the health benefits of physical fitness.

Accommodation and food services is expected to grow by 11.4 percent and add 1.3 million new jobs through 2016. Job growth will be concentrated in food services and drinking places, reflecting increases in population, dual-income families, and the convenience of many new food establishments.

Trade, transportation, and utilities. Overall employment in this industry supersector will grow by 6 percent between 2006 and 2016. Transportation and warehousing is expected to increase by 496,000 jobs, or by 11.1 percent, through 2016. Truck transportation will grow by 11 percent, adding 158,000 new jobs, while rail transportation is projected to decline. The warehousing and storage sector is projected to grow rapidly at 23.5 percent, adding 150,000 jobs. Demand for truck transportation and warehousing services will expand as many manufacturers concentrate on their core competencies and contract out their product transportation and storage functions.

Employment in retail trade is expected to increase by 4.5 percent. Despite slower-than-average growth, this industry will add almost 700,000 new jobs over the 2006–2016 period, growing from 15.3 million employees to 16 million. While consumers will continue to demand more goods, consolidation among grocery stores and department stores will temper growth. Wholesale trade is expected to increase by 7.3 percent, growing from 5.9 million to 6.3 million jobs.

Employment in utilities is projected to decrease by 5.7 percent through 2016. Despite increased output, employment in electric power generation, transmission, and distribution and natural gas distribution is expected to decline through 2016 because of improved technology that increases worker productivity. However, employment in water, sewage, and other systems is expected to increase 18.7 percent by 2016. Jobs are not easily eliminated by technological gains in this industry because water treatment and waste disposal are very labor-intensive activities.

Financial activities. Employment is projected to grow 14.4 percent over the 2006–2016 period. Real estate and rental and leasing is expected to grow by 18 percent and add 392,000 jobs by 2016. Growth will be due, in part, to increased demand for housing as the population grows. The fastest-growing industry in the real estate and rental and leasing services sector will be activities related to real estate, such as property management and real estate appraisal, which will grow by 29 percent—remnants of the housing boom that pervaded much of the first half of the decade.

Finance and insurance are expected to add 815,000 jobs, an increase of 13.2 percent, by 2016. Employment in securities, commodity contracts, and other financial investments and related activities is expected to grow 46 percent by 2016, reflecting the increased number of baby boomers in their peak savings years, the growth of tax-favorable retirement plans, and the globalization of the securities markets. Employment in credit intermediation and related services, including banks, will grow by 8.2 percent and add almost one-third of all new jobs within finance and insurance. Insurance carriers and related activities are expected to grow by 7.4 percent and add 172,000 new jobs by 2016. The number of jobs within agencies, brokerages, and other insurance-related activities is expected to grow about 15.4 percent. Growth will stem from the needs of an increasing population and new insurance products on the market.

Government. Between 2006 and 2016, government employment, not including employment in public education and hospitals, is expected to increase by 4.8 percent, from 10.8 million to 11.3 million jobs. Growth in government employment will be fueled by an increased demand for pubic safety, but dampened by budgetary constraints and outsourcing of government jobs to the private sector. State and local governments, excluding education and hospitals, are expected to grow by 7.7 percent as a result of the continued shift of responsibilities from the federal government to state and local governments. Federal government employment, including the Postal Service, is expected to decrease by 3.8 percent.

Other services (except government and private households). Employment will grow by 14.9 percent. About 2 out of every 5 new jobs in this supersector will be in religious organizations, which are expected to grow by 18.9 percent. Automotive repair and maintenance (as opposed to mechanical/electrical and body repair and maintenance) will be the fastest-growing industry at 40.7 percent, reflecting demand for quick maintenance services for the increasing number of automobiles on the nation's roads. Also included among other services are business, professional, labor, political, and similar organizations, which are expected to increase by 13.6 percent and add 68,000 new jobs. This industry includes homeowner, tenant, and property owner associations.

Goods-producing industries. Employment in the goods-producing industries has been relatively stagnant since the early 1980s. Overall, this sector is expected to decline 3.3 percent over the 2006–2016 period. Although employment is expected to decline overall, projected growth among goods-producing industries varies considerably (Chart 5).

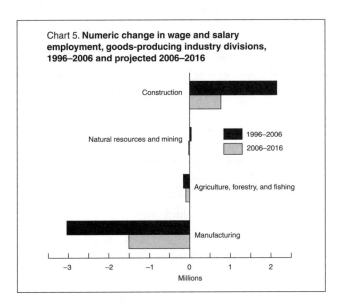

Chart 5. **Numeric change in wage and salary employment, goods-producing industry divisions, 1996–2006 and projected 2006–2016**

Construction. Employment in construction is expected to increase by 10.2 percent, from 7.7 million to 8.5 million. Demand for commercial construction and an increase in road, bridge, and tunnel construction will account for the bulk of job growth in this supersector.

Manufacturing. While overall employment in this supersector will decline by 10.6 percent or 1.5 million jobs, employment in a few detailed manufacturing industries will increase. For example, employment in pharmaceutical and medicine manufacturing is expected to grow by 23.8 percent and add 69,000 new jobs by 2016. However, productivity gains, job automation, and international competition will adversely affect employment in most manufacturing industries. Employment in household appliance manufacturing is expected to decline by 25.8 percent and lose 21,000 jobs over the decade. Similarly, employment in machinery manufacturing, apparel manufacturing, and computer and electronic product manufacturing will decline by 146,000, 129,000, and 157,000 jobs, respectively.

Agriculture, forestry, fishing, and hunting. Overall employment in agriculture, forestry, fishing, and hunting is expected to decrease by 2.8 percent. Employment is expected to continue to decline due to rising costs of production, increasing consolidation, and more imports of food and lumber. The only industry within this supersector expected to grow is support activities for agriculture and forestry, which includes farm labor contractors and farm management services. This industry is expected to grow by 10.5 percent and add 12,000 new jobs. Crop production will see the largest job loss, with 98,000 fewer jobs in 2016 than in 2006.

Mining. Employment in mining is expected to decrease 1.6 percent, or by some 10,000 jobs, by 2016. Employment in support activities for mining will be responsible for most of the employment decline in this industry, seeing a loss of 17,000 jobs. Other mining industries, such as coal mining and metal ore mining, are expected to see little or no change or a small increase in employment. Employment stagnation in these industries is attributable mainly to technology gains that boost worker productivity and strict environmental regulations.

Occupation

Expansion of service-providing industries is expected to continue, creating demand for many occupations. However, projected job growth varies among major occupational groups (Chart 6).

Professional and related occupations. These occupations include a wide variety of skilled professions. Professional and related occupations will be one of the two fastest-growing major occupational groups and will add the most new jobs. Over the 2006–2016 period, a 16.7 percent increase in the number of professional and related jobs is projected, which translates into nearly 5 million new jobs. Professional and related workers perform a wide variety of duties and are employed throughout private industry and government. Almost three-quarters of the job growth will come from three groups of professional occupations—computer and mathematical occupations; healthcare practitioners and technical occupations; and education, training, and library occupations—which together will add 3.5 million jobs.

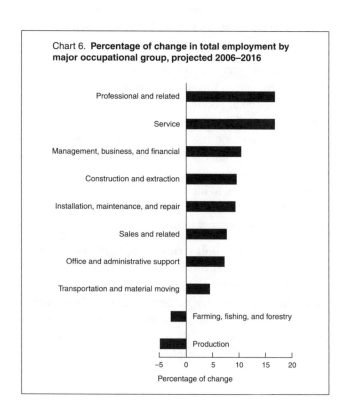

Chart 6. **Percentage of change in total employment by major occupational group, projected 2006–2016**

Service occupations. Duties of service workers range from fighting fires to cooking meals. Employment in service occupations is projected to increase by 4.8 million, or 16.7 percent, the second-largest numerical gain and tied with professional and related occupations for the fastest rate of growth among the major occupational groups. Food preparation and serving related occupations are expected to add the most jobs among the service occupations, 1.4 million, by 2016. However, healthcare support occupations and personal care and service occupations are expected to grow the fastest, at 26.8 percent and 22 percent, respectively. Combined, these two occupational groups will account for 2.1 million new jobs.

Management, business, and financial occupations. Workers in management, business, and financial occupations plan and direct the activities of business, government, and other organizations. Their employment is expected to increase by 1.6 million, or 10.4 percent, by 2016. Among management occupations, the numbers of social and community service managers and gaming managers will grow the fastest, by 24.7 percent and 24.4 percent, respectively. Construction managers will add the most new jobs—77,000—by 2016. Farmers and ranchers are the only workers whose numbers are expected to see a large decline, losing 90,000 jobs. Among business and financial occupations, accountants and auditors and all other business operation specialists will add the most jobs, 444,000 combined. Financial analysts and personal financial advisors will be the fastest-growing occupations in this group, with growth rates of 33.8 percent and 41 percent, respectively.

Construction and extraction occupations. Construction and extraction workers build new residential and commercial buildings and also work in mines, quarries, and oil and gas fields. Employment of these workers is expected to grow 9.5 percent, adding 785,000 new jobs. Construction trades and related workers will account for nearly 4 out of 5 of these new jobs, or 622,000, by 2016. Minor declines in extraction occupations will reflect overall employment stagnation in the mining and oil and gas extraction industries.

Installation, maintenance, and repair occupations. Workers in installation, maintenance, and repair occupations install new equipment and maintain and repair older equipment. These occupations will add 550,000 jobs by 2016, growing by 9.3 percent. Automotive service technicians and mechanics and general maintenance and repair workers will account for close to half of all new installation, maintenance, and repair jobs. The fastest growth rate will be among locksmiths and safe repairers, an occupation that is expected to grow 22.1 percent over the 2006–2016 period.

Transportation and material moving occupations. Transportation and material moving workers transport people and materials by land, sea, or air. Employment of these workers should increase by 4.5 percent, accounting for 462,000 new jobs by 2016. Among transportation occupations, motor vehicle operators will add the most jobs, 368,000. Material moving occupations will decline slightly, 0.5 percent, losing 25,000 jobs.

Sales and related occupations. Sales and related workers solicit goods and services to businesses and consumers. Sales and related occupations are expected to add 1.2 million new jobs by 2016, growing by 7.6 percent. Retail salespersons will contribute the most to this growth by adding 557,000 new jobs.

Office and administrative support occupations. Office and administrative support workers perform the day-to-day activities of the office, such as preparing and filing documents, dealing with the public, and distributing information. Employment in these occupations is expected to grow by 7.2 percent, adding 1.7 million new jobs by 2016. Customer service representatives will add the most new jobs, 545,000, while stock clerks and order fillers are expected to see the largest employment decline among all occupations, losing 131,000 jobs.

Farming, fishing, and forestry occupations. Farming, fishing, and forestry workers cultivate plants, breed and raise livestock, and catch animals. These occupations will decline 2.8 percent and lose 29,000 jobs by 2016. Agricultural workers, including farmworkers and laborers, will account for nearly three out of four lost jobs in this group. The number of fishing and hunting workers is expected to decline by 16.2 percent, while the number of forest, conservation, and logging workers is expected to decline by 1.4 percent.

Production occupations. Production workers are employed mainly in manufacturing, where they assemble goods and operate plants. Production occupations are expected to decline by 4.9 percent, losing 528,000 jobs by 2016. Some jobs will be created in production occupations, mostly in food processing and woodworking. Metal workers and plastic workers; assemblers and fabricators; textile, apparel, and furnishings occupations; and other production workers will account for most of the job loss among production occupations.

Among all occupations in the economy, healthcare occupations are expected to make up 7 of the 20 fastest-growing occupations, the largest proportion of any occupational group (Chart 7). These seven healthcare occupations, in addition to exhibiting high growth rates, will add nearly 750,000 new jobs between 2006 and 2016. Other occupational groups that have more than one occupation in the 20 fastest-growing occupations are computer occupations, personal care and service occupations, community and social services occupations, and business and financial operations occupations. High growth rates among occupations in the top 20 fastest-growing occupations reflect projected rapid growth in the healthcare and social assistance industries and the professional, scientific, and technical services industries.

The 20 occupations listed in Chart 8 will account for more than one-third of all new jobs, 6.6 million combined, over the 2006–2016 period. The occupations with the largest numerical increases cover a wider range of occupational categories than do those occupations with the fastest growth rates. Health occupations will account for some of these increases in employment, as will occupations in education, sales, and food service. Occupations in office and administrative services will grow by 1.7 million jobs, one-fourth of the job growth among the 20 occupations with the largest job growth. Many of the occupations listed below are very large and will create more new jobs than will those with high growth rates. Only 3 out of the 20 fastest-growing occupations—home health aides, personal and home care aides, and computer software application engineers—also are projected to be among the 20 occupations with the largest numerical increases in employment.

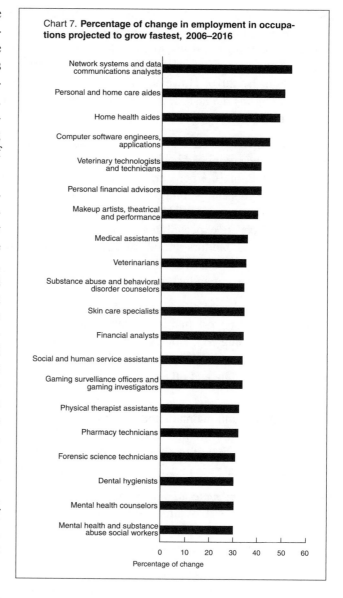

Chart 7. **Percentage of change in employment in occupations projected to grow fastest, 2006–2016**

Declining occupational employment stems from declining industry employment, technological advances, changes in business practices, and other factors. For example, installation of self-checkouts and other forms of automation will increase productivity and are expected to contribute to a decline of 118,000 cashiers over the 2006–2016 period (Chart 9). Fourteen of the 20 occupations with the largest numerical decreases are either production occupations or office and administrative support occupations, which are affected by increasing plant and factory automation and the implementation of office technology that reduces the need for these workers. The difference between the office and administrative occupations that are expected to experience the largest declines and those that are expected to see the largest increases is the extent to which job functions can be easily automated or performed by other work-

© JIST Works

ers. For instance, the duties of executive secretaries and administrative assistants involve a great deal of personal interaction that cannot be automated, while the duties of file clerks—adding, locating, and removing business records—can be automated or performed by other workers.

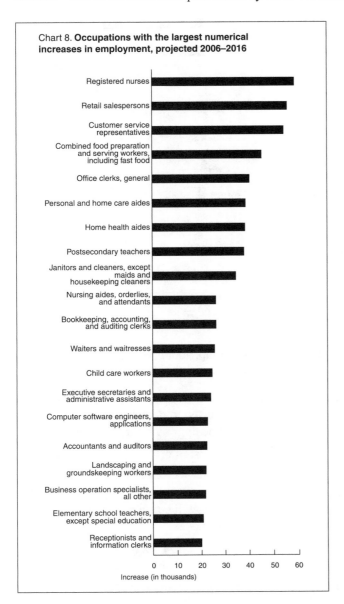

Chart 8. **Occupations with the largest numerical increases in employment, projected 2006–2016**

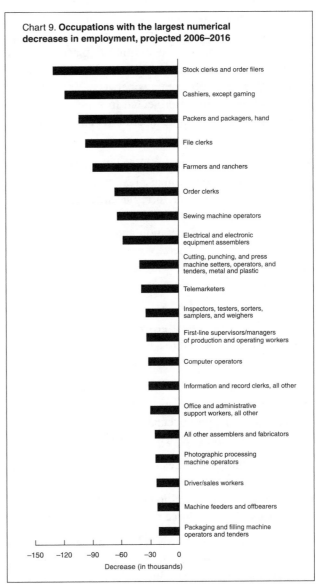

Chart 9. **Occupations with the largest numerical decreases in employment, projected 2006–2016**

Education and Training

For 12 of the 20 fastest-growing occupations, an associate degree or higher is the most significant level of postsecondary education or training. On-the-job training is the most significant level of postsecondary education or training for another 6 of the 20 fastest-growing occupations. In contrast, on-the-job training is the most significant level of postsecondary education or training for 12 of the 20 occupations with the largest numerical increases, while 6 of these 20 occupations have an associate degree or higher as the most significant level of postsecondary education or training. On-the-job training is the most significant level of postsecondary education or training for 19 of the 20 occupations with the largest numerical decreases.

Total Job Openings

Job openings stem from both employment growth and replacement needs (Chart 10). Replacement needs arise as workers leave occupations. Some transfer to other occupations while others retire, return to school, or quit to assume household responsibilities. Replacement needs are projected to account for 68 percent of the approximately 50 million job openings between 2006 and 2016. Thus, even occupations projected to experience slower-than-average growth or to decline in employment still may offer many job openings.

Service occupations are projected to have the largest number of total job openings, 12.2 million, and 60 percent of those will be due to replacement needs. A large number of replacements will be necessary as young workers leave food preparation and service occupations. Replacement needs generally are greatest in the largest occupations and in those with relatively low pay or limited training requirements.

Professional and related occupations are projected to be one of the two fastest-growing major occupational groups and are expected to add more jobs than any other major occupational group, about 5 million, by 2016. However, the majority of job openings are expected to come from more than 6 million replacements.

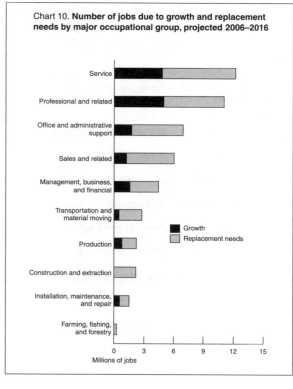

Chart 10. **Number of jobs due to growth and replacement needs by major occupational group, projected 2006–2016**

Office automation will significantly affect many individual office and administrative support occupations. While these occupations are projected to grow about as fast as average, some are projected to decline rapidly. Office and administrative support occupations are projected to create 6.9 million total job openings over the 2006–2016 period, ranking third behind service occupations and professional and related occupations.

Farming, fishing, and forestry occupations and production occupations should offer job opportunities despite overall declines in employment. These occupations will lose 29,000 and 528,000 jobs, respectively, but are expected to provide more than 2.4 million total job openings. Job openings among these groups will be solely due to the replacement needs of a workforce that is exhibiting high levels of retirement and job turnover.

Editor's Note: "Tomorrow's Jobs," with minor changes, came from the *Occupational Outlook Handbook* and was written by the U.S. Department of Labor staff. Much of this section uses 2006 data, the most recent available at press time. By the time it is carefully collected and analyzed, data used by the U.S. Department of Labor is typically several years old. Because market trends tend to be gradual, this delay does not affect the material's usefulness.

Employment Trends in Major Industries

The U.S. economy can be broken down into numerous industries, each with its own set of characteristics. The Department of Labor has identified 45 industries that account for three-quarters of all workers. This section provides an overview of these industries and the economy as a whole.

Nature of the Industry

Industries are defined by the processes they use to produce goods and services. Workers in the United States produce and provide a wide variety of products and services and, as a result, the types of industries in the U.S. economy range widely—from agriculture, forestry, and fishing to aerospace manufacturing. Each industry has a unique combination of occupations, production techniques, inputs and outputs, and business characteristics. Understanding the nature of industries that interest you is important because it is this unique combination that determines working conditions, educational requirements, and the job outlook.

Industries consist of many different places of work, called establishments. Establishments are physical locations in which people work, such as the branch office of a bank, a gasoline service station, a school, a department store, or a plant that manufactures machinery. Establishments range from large factories and corporate office complexes employing thousands of workers to small community stores, restaurants, professional offices, and service businesses employing only a few workers. Establishments should not be confused with companies or corporations, which are legal entities. Thus, a company or corporation may have a single establishment or more than one establishment. Establishments that use the same or similar processes to produce goods or services are organized together into industries. Industries are, in turn, organized together into industry groups such as Information and Trade. These are further organized into industry subsectors and then ultimately into industry sectors. For the purposes of labor market analysis, the Bureau of Labor Statistics organizes industry sectors into industry supersectors. A company or corporation could own establishments classified in more than one industry, industry sector, or even industry supersector.

Each industry subsector is made up of a number of industry groups, which are, as mentioned, determined by differences in production processes. An easily recognized example of these distinctions is in the food manufacturing subsector, which is made up of industry groups that produce meat products, preserved fruits and vegetables, bakery items, and dairy products, among others. Each of these industry groups requires workers with varying skills and employs unique production techniques. Another example of these distinctions is found in utilities, which employs workers in establishments that provide electricity, natural gas, and water.

There were almost 8.8 million private business establishments in the United States in 2006. Business establishments in the United States are predominantly small; 60.4 percent of all establishments employed fewer than 5 workers in

March 2006. However, the medium-sized to large establishments employ a greater proportion of all workers. For example, establishments that employed 50 or more workers accounted for only 4.7 percent of all establishments, yet employed 56.5 percent of all workers. The large establishments—those with more than 500 workers—accounted for only 0.2 percent of all establishments, but employed 17.1 percent of all workers. Table 1 presents the percent distribution of employment according to establishment size.

The average size of these establishments varies widely across industries. Most establishments in the construction, wholesale trade, retail trade, finance and insurance, real estate and rental and leasing, and professional, scientific, and technical services industries are small, averaging fewer than 20 employees per establishment. However, wide differences within industries can exist. Hospitals, for example, employ an average of 542.7 workers, while physicians' offices employ an average of 10.3. Similarly, although there is an average of 14.7 employees per establishment for all of retail trade, department stores employ an average of 130.3 people but jewelry stores employ an average of only 5.9.

Establishment size can play a role in the characteristics of each job. Large establishments generally offer workers greater occupational mobility and advancement potential, whereas small establishments may provide their employees with broader experience by requiring them to assume a wider range of responsibilities. Also, small establishments are distributed throughout the nation—every locality has a few small businesses. Large establishments, in contrast, employ more workers and are less common, but they play a much more prominent role in the economies of the areas in which they are located.

Table 1. Percent distribution of establishments and employment in all private industries by establishment size, March 2006

Establishment size (number of workers)	Percent of establishments	Percent of employment
Total	100.0	100.0
1 to 4	60.4	6.8
5 to 9	16.5	8.3
10 to 19	10.9	11.2
20 to 49	7.6	17.3
50 to 99	2.6	13.4
100 to 249	1.5	16.6
250 to 499	0.4	9.4
500 to 999	0.1	6.7
1,000 or more	0.1	10.4

Working Conditions

Just as the goods and services produced in each industry are different, working conditions vary significantly among industries. In some industries, the work setting is quiet, temperature-controlled, and virtually hazard-free, while other industries are characterized by noisy, uncomfortable, and sometimes dangerous work environments. Some industries require long workweeks and shift work, but standard 40-hour workweeks are common in many other industries. In still other industries, a lot of the jobs can be seasonal, requiring long hours during busy periods and abbreviated schedules during slower months. Production processes, establishment size, and the physical location of work usually determine these varying conditions.

One of the most telling indicators of working conditions is an industry's injury and illness rate. Overexertion, being struck by an object, and falls on the same level, are among the most common incidents causing work-related injury or illness. In 2006, approximately 4.1 million nonfatal injuries and illnesses were reported throughout private industry. Among major industry divisions, manufacturing had the highest rate of injury and illness—6.0 cases for every 100 full time workers—while financial activities had the lowest rate—1.5 cases. About 5,703 work-related fatalities were reported in 2006; the most common events resulting in fatal injuries were transportation incidents, contact with objects and equipment, assaults and violent acts, and falls.

Work schedules are another important reflection of working conditions, and the operational requirements of each industry lead to large differences in hours worked and in part-time versus full-time status. In food services and drinking places, for example, fully 36.5 percent of employees worked part time in 2006 compared with only 2.0 percent in motor vehicles and motor vehicle equipment manufacturing. Table 2 presents industries having relatively high and low percentages of part-time workers.

Table 2. Part-time workers as a percent of total employment, selected industries, 2006

Industry	Percent part-time
All industries	15.4
Many part-time workers	
Food services and drinking places	36.5
Grocery stores	31.9
Clothing, accessories, and general merchandise stores	36.4
Arts, entertainment, and recreation	27.2
Child day care services	26.1
Motion picture and video industries	23.6
Social assistance, except child day care	23.6
Few part-time workers	
Mining	2.6
Computer and electronic product manufacturing	2.4
Pharmaceutical and medicine manufacturing	2.4
Steel manufacturing	2.1
Motor vehicle and parts manufacturing	2.0
Utilities	1.8
Aerospace product and parts manufacturing	1.8

The low proportion of part-time workers in some manufacturing industries often reflects the continuous nature of the production processes that makes it difficult to adapt the volume of production to short-term fluctuations in product demand. Once these processes are begun, it is costly to halt them; machinery must be tended and materials must be moved continuously. For example, the chemical manufacturing industry produces many different chemical products through controlled chemical reactions. These processes require chemical operators to monitor and adjust the flow of materials into and out of the line of production. Because production may continue 24 hours a day, 7 days a week under the watchful eyes of chemical operators who work in shifts, full-time workers are more likely to be employed. Retail trade and service industries, on the other hand, have seasonal cycles marked by various events that affect the hours worked, such as school openings or important holidays. During busy times of the year, longer hours are common, whereas slack periods lead to cutbacks in work hours and shorter workweeks. Jobs in these industries are generally appealing to students and others who desire flexible, part-time schedules.

Employment

The total number of jobs in the United States in 2006 was 150.6 million. This included 12.2 million self-employed workers, 130,000 unpaid workers in family businesses, and 138.3 million wage and salary jobs—including primary and secondary job holders. The total number of jobs is projected to increase to 166.2 million by 2016, and wage and salary jobs are projected to account for almost 153.3 million of them.

As shown in table 3, wage and salary jobs are the vast majority of all jobs, but they are not evenly divided among the various industries. Education, health, and social services had the largest number of jobs in 2006 with almost 29.1 million. The trade supersector was the second largest, with about 21.2 million jobs, followed by professional and business services with 17.6 million jobs in 2006. Manufacturing accounted for roughly 14.2 million jobs in the United States in 2006. Among the industries covered in the *Career Guide*, wage and salary employment ranged from only 154,300 in steel manufacturing to more than 13.6 million in health care. The three largest industries—education services, health care, and food services and drinking places—together accounted for 38.5 million jobs, more than one-quarter of the nation's wage and salary employment.

Table 3. Wage and salary employment in industries covered in the *Career Guide*, 2006 and projected change, 2006–2016 (Employment in thousands)

Industry	2006		2016		2006–2016	
	Employment	Percent distribution	Employment	Percent distribution	Percent change	Employment change
All industries	138,310	100.0	153,262	100.0	10.8	14,951
Natural resources, construction, and utilities	10,076	7.3	10,710	7.0	6.3	634
Agriculture, forestry, and fishing	1,220	0.9	1,114	0.7	-8.6	-105
Construction	7,689	5.6	8,470	5.5	10.2	781
Mining	619	0.4	609	0.4	-1.6	-10
Utilities	548	0.4	518	0.3	-5.7	-31
Manufacturing	14,197	10.3	12,695	8.3	-10.6	-1,503
Aerospace product and parts manufacturing	472	0.3	497	0.3	5.4	25
Chemical manufacturing, except drugs	576	0.4	486	0.3	-15.7	-90
Computer and electronic product manufacturing	1,316	1.0	1,159	0.8	-12.0	-157
Food manufacturing	1,484	1.1	1,489	1.0	0.3	5
Machinery manufacturing	1,192	0.9	1,045	0.7	-12.3	-146
Motor vehicle and parts manufacturing	1,070	0.8	918	0.6	-14.3	-153
Pharmaceutical and medicine manufacturing	292	0.2	362	0.2	23.7	69
Printing	636	0.5	497	0.3	-21.8	-138
Steel manufacturing	154	0.1	116	0.1	-25.1	-39
Textile, textile product, and apparel manufacturing	595	0.4	385	0.3	-35.4	-211
Trade	21,217	15.3	22,332	14.6	5.3	1,115
Automobile dealers	1,247	0.9	1,388	0.9	11.3	141
Clothing, accessory, and general merchandise stores	4,352	3.1	4,676	3.1	7.5	324
Grocery stores	2,463	1.8	2,479	1.6	0.7	16
Wholesale trade	5,898	4.3	6,326	4.1	7.3	428
Transportation and warehousing	4,466	3.2	4,962	3.2	11.1	496
Air transportation	486	0.4	522	0.3	7.3	35
Truck transportation and warehousing	2,074	1.5	2,381	1.6	14.8	307

Industry	2006		2016		2006–2016	
	Employment	Percent distribution	Employment	Percent distribution	Percent change	Employment change
Information	3,055	2.2	3,267	2.1	6.9	212
Broadcasting	331	0.2	362	0.2	9.3	31
Motion picture and video industries	357	0.3	396	0.3	10.9	39
Publishing, except software	660	0.5	611	0.4	-7.5	-49
Software publishers	243	0.2	321	0.2	32.0	78
Telecommunications	973	0.7	1,022	0.7	5.0	48
Internet services providers, web search portals, and data processing services	383	0.3	437	0.3	14.0	54
Financial activities	8,363	6.0	9,570	6.2	14.4	1,207
Banking	1,825	1.3	1,898	1.2	4.0	74
Insurance	2,316	1.7	2,488	1.6	7.4	172
Securities, commodities, and other investments	816	0.6	1,192	0.8	46.1	376
Professional and business services	17,552	12.7	21,644	14.1	23.3	4,092
Advertising and public relations services	458	0.3	520	0.3	13.6	62
Computer systems design and related services	1,278	0.9	1,768	1.2	38.3	489
Employment services	3,657	2.6	4,348	2.8	18.9	692
Management, scientific, and technical consulting services	921	0.7	1,639	1.1	77.9	718
Scientific research and development services	593	0.4	649	0.4	9.4	56
Education, health, and social services	29,082	21.0	34,543	22.5	18.8	5,461
Child day care services	807	0.6	1,078	0.7	33.7	272
Educational services	13,152	9.5	14,564	9.5	10.7	1,412
Health services	13,621	9.8	16,576	10.8	21.7	2,954
Social assistance, except child day care	1,502	1.1	2,326	1.5	54.8	823
Leisure and hospitality	13,143	9.5	15,016	9.8	14.2	1,873
Arts, entertainment, and recreation	1,927	1.4	2,522	1.6	30.9	595
Food services and drinking places	9,383	6.8	10,407	6.8	10.9	1,024
Hotels and other accommodations	1,833	1.3	2,088	1.4	13.9	254
Government and advocacy, grantmaking, and civic organizations	11,210	8.1	11,895	7.8	6.1	685
Advocacy, grantmaking, and civic organizations	1,234	0.9	1,392	0.9	12.8	158
Federal Government	1,958	1.4	1,868	1.2	-4.6	-90
State and local government, except education and health	8,018	5.8	8,634	5.6	7.7	617

NOTE: May not add to totals due to omission of industries not covered.

Although workers of all ages are employed in each industry, certain industries tend to possess workers of distinct age groups. For the previously mentioned reasons, retail trade employs a relatively high proportion of younger workers to fill part-time and temporary positions. The manufacturing sector, on the other hand, has a relatively high median age because many jobs in the sector require a number of years to learn and perfect specialized skills that do not easily transfer to other industries. Also, manufacturing employment has been declining, providing fewer opportunities for younger workers to get jobs. As a result, more than one-fourth of the workers in retail trade were 24 years of age or younger in 2006, compared with only 8.1 percent of workers in manufacturing. Table 4 contrasts the age distribution of workers in all industries with the distributions in five very different industries.

Table 4. Percent distribution of wage and salary workers by age group, selected industries, 2006

Industry	Age group			
	16 to 24	25 to 44	45 to 64	65 and older
All industries	14	45	37	4
Computer systems design and related services	5	63	30	2
Educational services	9	42	45	4
Food services and drinking places	43	38	17	2
Telecommunications	8	53	37	2
Utilities	4	42	54	1

Employment in some industries is concentrated in one region of the country. Such industries often are located near a source of raw or unfinished materials upon which the industry relies. For example, oil and gas extraction jobs are concentrated in Texas, Louisiana, and Oklahoma; many textile mills and products manufacturing jobs are found in North Carolina, South Carolina, and Georgia; and a significant proportion of motor vehicle manufacturing jobs are located in Michigan and Ohio. On the other hand, some industries—such as grocery stores and educational services—have jobs distributed throughout the nation, reflecting the general population density.

Occupations in the Industry

The occupations found in each industry depend on the types of services provided or goods produced. For example, because construction companies require skilled trades workers to build and renovate buildings, these companies employ large numbers of carpenters, electricians, plumbers, painters, and sheet metal workers. Other occupations common to construction include construction equipment operators and mechanics, installers, and repairers. Retail trade, on the other hand, displays and sells manufactured goods to consumers. As a result, retail trade employs numerous retail salespersons and other workers, including more than three-fourths of all cashiers. Table 5 shows the industry sectors and the occupational groups that predominate in each.

Table 5. Industry sectors and their largest occupational group, 2006

Industry sector	Largest occupational group	Percent of industry wage and salary jobs
Agriculture, forestry, fishing, and hunting	Farming, fishing, and forestry occupations	58.3
Mining	Construction and extraction occupations	37.8
Construction	Construction and extraction occupations	66.8
Manufacturing	Production occupations	52.5
Wholesale trade	Sales and related occupations	26.3
Retail trade	Sales and related occupations	54.1
Transportation and warehousing	Transportation and material moving occupations	59.8
Utilities	Installation, maintenance, and repair occupations	27.1
Information	Professional and related occupations	33.3
Finance and insurance	Office and administrative support occupations	49.8
Real estate and rental and leasing	Sales and related occupations	24.5
Professional, scientific, and technical services	Professional and related occupations	45.0

Industry sector	Largest occupational group	Percent of industry wage and salary jobs
Management of companies and enterprises	Management, business, and financial occupations	33.1
Administrative and support and waste management and remediation services	Service occupations	31.4
Educational services, public and private	Professional and related occupations	67.4
Health care and social assistance	Professional and related occupations	43.3
Arts, entertainment, and recreation	Service occupations	58.8
Accommodation and food services	Service occupations	86.6
Government	Service occupations	25.0

The occupational distribution clearly is influenced by the structure of its industries, yet there are many occupations, such as general managers or secretaries, that are found in all industries. In fact, some of the largest occupations in the U.S. economy are dispersed across many industries. For example, the group of professional and related occupations is among the largest in the nation while also experiencing the fastest growth rate. (See table 6.) Other large occupational groups include service occupations; office and administrative support occupations; sales and related occupations; and management, business, and financial occupations.

Table 6. Total employment and projected change by broad occupational group, 2006–2016 (Employment in thousands)

Occupational group	Employment, 2006	Percent change, 2006–2016
Total, all occupations	150,620	10.4
Professional and related occupations	29,819	16.7
Service occupations	28,950	16.7
Office and administrative support occupations	24,344	7.2
Sales and related occupations	15,985	7.6
Management, business, and financial occupations	15,397	10.4
Production occupations	10,675	-4.9
Transportation and material moving occupations	10,233	4.5
Construction and extraction occupations	8,295	9.5
Installation, maintenance, and repair occupations	5,883	9.3
Farming, fishing, and forestry occupations	1,039	-2.8

Training and Advancement

Workers prepare for employment in many ways, but the most fundamental form of job training in the United States is a high school education. Better than 88 percent of the nation's workforce possessed a high school diploma or its equivalent in 2006. However, many occupations require more training, so growing numbers of workers pursue additional training or education after high school. In 2006, 28.7 percent of the nation's workforce reported having completed some college or an associate degree as their highest level of education, while an additional 30.2 percent continued in their studies and attained a bachelor's or higher degree. In addition to these types of formal education, other sources of qualifying training include formal company-provided training, apprenticeships, informal on-the-job training, correspondence courses, Armed Forces vocational training, and non–work-related training.

The unique combination of training required to succeed in each industry is determined largely by the industry's production process and the mix of occupations it requires. For example, manufacturing employs many machine operators who generally need little formal education after high school, but sometimes complete considerable on-the-job training. In contrast, educational services employs many types of teachers, most of whom require a bachelor's or higher degree. Training requirements by industry sector are shown in table 7.

© **JIST Works**

Table 7. Percent distribution of workers by highest grade completed or degree received, by industry sector, 2006

Industy sector	High school diploma or less	Some college or associate degree	Bachelor's or higher degree
All industries	41.1	28.7	30.2
Agriculture, forestry, fishing, and hunting	62.3	22.0	15.8
Mining	58.8	24.9	16.3
Construction	64.5	24.2	11.3
Manufacturing	50.7	25.6	23.6
Wholesale trade	43.0	29.3	27.8
Retail trade	50.8	32.1	17.1
Transportation and warehousing	52.3	32.1	15.7
Utilities	39.3	34.4	26.3
Information	25.6	31.6	42.8
Finance and insurance	22.7	31.0	46.3
Real estate and rental and leasing	33.6	32.5	33.9
Professional, scientific, and technical services	13.4	24.6	61.9
Administrative and support and waste management services	53.9	28.3	17.9
Educational services	17.3	19.2	63.5
Health care and social assistance	29.8	34.6	35.5
Arts, entertainment, and recreation	39.5	32.1	28.3
Accommodation and food services	61.3	27.8	10.9

Persons with no more than a high school diploma accounted for about 64.5 percent of all workers in construction; 62.3 percent in agriculture, forestry, fishing, and hunting; 61.3 percent in accommodation and food services; 58.8 percent in mining; 53.9 percent in administrative and support and waste management services; and 52.3 in transportation and warehousing. On the other hand, those who had acquired a bachelor's or higher degree accounted for 63.6 percent of all workers in private educational services; 61.9 percent in professional, scientific, and technical services; 46.3 percent in finance and insurance; and 42.8 percent in information.

Education and training also are important factors in the variety of advancement paths found in different industries. Each industry has some unique advancement paths, but workers who complete additional on-the-job training or education generally help their chances of being promoted. In much of the manufacturing sector, for example, production workers who receive training in management and computer skills increase their likelihood of being promoted to supervisory positions. Other factors that impact advancement and that may figure prominently in industries include the size of the establishments, institutionalized career tracks, and the mix of occupations. As a result, persons who seek jobs in particular industries should be aware of how these advancement paths and other factors may later shape their careers.

Earnings

Like other characteristics, earnings differ by industry, the result of a highly complicated process that reflects a number of factors. For example, earnings may vary due to the nature of occupations in the industry, average hours worked, geographical location, workers' average age, educational requirements, profits, and the degree of union representation of the workforce. In general, wages are highest in metropolitan areas to compensate for the higher cost of living. Also, as would be expected, industries that employ a large proportion of unskilled minimum-wage or part-time workers tend to have lower earnings.

The difference in earnings between software publishers and the food services and drinking places industries illustrates how various characteristics of industries can result in great differences in earnings. In software publishers, earnings of all wage and salary workers averaged $1,444 a week in 2006, while in food services and drinking places, earnings of all wage and salary workers averaged only $215 weekly. The difference is large primarily because software publishing establishments employ more highly skilled, full-time workers, while food services and drinking places employ many lower skilled workers on a part-time basis. In addition, most workers in software publishing are paid an annual salary, while many workers in food services and drinking places are paid an hourly wage, but many are able to supplement their low hourly wage rate with money they receive as tips. Table 8 highlights the industries with the highest and lowest average weekly earnings.

Table 8. Average weekly earnings of production or nonsupervisory workers on private nonfarm payrolls, selected industries, 2006

Industry	Earnings
All industries	$568
Industries with high earnings	
Software publishers	1,444
Computer systems design and related services	1,265
Scientific research and development services	1,136
Utilities	1,136
Aerospace product and parts manufacturing	1,153
Securities, commodities, and other investments	1,055
Industries with low earnings	
Employment services	453
Grocery stores	328
Arts, entertainment, and recreation	332
Hotels and other accommodations	353
Child day care services	316
Food services and drinking places	215

Employee benefits, once a minor addition to wages and salaries, continue to grow in diversity and cost. In addition to traditional benefits—paid vacations, life and health insurance, and pensions—many employers now offer various benefits to accommodate the needs of a changing labor force. Such benefits sometimes include childcare, employee assistance programs that provide counseling for personal problems, and wellness programs that encourage exercise, stress management, and self-improvement. Benefits vary among occupational groups, full- and part-time workers, public and private sector workers, regions, unionized and nonunionized workers, and small and large establishments. Data indicate that full-time workers and those in medium-sized and large establishments—those with 100 or more workers—usually receive better benefits than do part-time workers and those in smaller establishments.

Union representation of the workforce varies widely by industry, and it also may play a role in determining earnings and benefits. In 2006, about 13.2 percent of workers throughout the nation were union members or covered by union contracts. As table 9 demonstrates, union affiliation of workers varies widely by industry. 51.6 percent of the workers in air transportation were union members, the highest rate of all the industries, followed by 37.6 percent in educational services, and 34.4 percent in public administration. Industries with the lowest unionization rate include computer systems design and related services, 1.7 percent; food services and drinking places, 1.5 percent; and Internet service providers, web search portals, and data processing services and software publishing, both with virtually no union workers.

Table 9. Union members and other workers covered by union contracts as a percent of total employment, selected industries, 2006

Industry	Percent union members or covered by union contract
All industries	13.2
Industries with high unionization rates	
Air transportation	51.6
Educational services	37.6
Public administration	34.4
Utilities	31.9
Industries with low unionization rates	
Computer systems design and related services	1.7
Food services and drinking places	1.5
Internet service providers, web search portals, and data processing services	0.0
Software publishing	0.0

Outlook

Total wage and salary employment in the United States is projected to increase by about 10.8 percent over the 2006–2016 period. Employment growth, however, is only one source of job openings. The total number of openings in any industry also depends on the industry's current employment level and its need to replace workers who leave their jobs. Throughout the economy, replacement needs will create more job openings than will employment growth. Employment size is a major determinant of job openings—larger industries generally have larger numbers of workers who must be replaced and provide more openings. The occupational composition of an industry is another factor. Industries with high concentrations of professional, technical, and other jobs that require more formal education—occupations in which workers tend to leave their jobs less frequently—generally have fewer openings resulting from replacement needs. On the other hand, more replacement openings generally occur in industries with high concentrations of service, laborer, and other jobs that require little formal education and have lower wages because workers in these jobs are more likely to leave their occupations.

Employment growth is determined largely by changes in the demand for the goods and services provided by an industry, worker productivity, and foreign competition. Each industry is affected by a different set of variables that determines the number and composition of jobs that will be available. Even within an industry, employment may grow at different rates in different occupations. For example, changes in technology, production methods, and business practices in an industry might eliminate some jobs, while creating others. Some industries may be growing rapidly overall, yet opportunities for workers in occupations within those industries could be stagnant or even declining because they are adversely affected by technological change. Similarly, employment of some occupations may be declining in the economy as a whole, yet may be increasing in a rapidly growing industry.

As shown earlier in table 3, employment growth rates over the next decade will vary widely among industries. Natural resources, construction, and utilities are primarily expected to grow due to growth in construction, offsetting job declines in agriculture, mining, and utilities. Growth in construction employment will stem from new factory construction as existing facilities are modernized; from new school construction, reflecting growth in the school-age population; and from infrastructure improvements, such as road and bridge construction. Employment in agriculture, forestry, and fishing should continue to decrease with consolidation of farm land, increasing worker productivity, and depletion of wild fish stocks. Employment in mining is expected to decline due to the use of new laborsaving technology and with the continued reliance on foreign sources of energy.

Employment in manufacturing is expected to decline overall with some growth in selected manufacturing industries. Employment declines are expected in chemical manufacturing, except drugs; computer and electronic product manufacturing; machinery manufacturing; motor vehicle and parts manufacturing; printing; steel manufacturing; and textile, textile product, and apparel manufacturing. Textile, textile product, and apparel manufacturing is projected to lose about 211,000 jobs over the 2006–2016 period—more than any other manufacturing industry—due primarily to increasing imports replacing domestic products.

Employment gains are expected in some manufacturing industries. Small employment gains in food manufacturing are expected, as a growing and ever more diverse population increases the demand for manufactured food products. Employment growth in pharmaceutical and medicine manufacturing is expected as sales of pharmaceuticals increase with growth in the population, particularly among the elderly, and with the introduction of new medicines to the market. Both food and pharmaceutical and medicine manufacturing also have growing export markets. Aerospace product and parts manufacturing is expected to have modest employment increases as well.

Growth in overall employment will result primarily from growth in service-providing industries over the 2006–2016 period, almost all of which are expected to have increasing employment. Job growth is expected to be led by health care and educational services, with large numbers of new jobs also in food services and drinking places; social assistance, except child day care; management, scientific, and technical consulting services; employment services, state and local government, except education and health care; arts entertainment, and recreation; computer systems design and related services; and wholesale trade. When combined, these sectors will account for nearly two-thirds of all new wage and salary jobs across the nation. Employment growth is expected in many other service-providing industries, but they will result in far fewer numbers of new jobs.

Health care will account for the most new wage and salary jobs, almost 3.0 million over the 2006–2016 period. Population growth, advances in medical technologies that increase the number of treatable diseases, and a growing share of the population in older age groups will drive employment growth. General medical and surgical hospitals, public and private—the largest health care industry group—is expected to account for about 691,000 of these new jobs.

Educational services is expected to grow by 10.7 percent over the 2006–2016 period, adding about 1.4 million new jobs. A growing emphasis on improving education and making it available to more children and young adults will be the primary factors contributing to employment growth. Employment growth is expected at all levels of education, particularly at the postsecondary level, as children of the baby boomers continue to reach college age, and as more adults pursue continuing education to enhance or update their skills.

Employment in the nation's fastest growing industry—management, scientific, and technical consulting services— is expected to increase by almost 78 percent, adding another 718,000 jobs over the 2006–2016 period. Projected job growth can be attributed primarily to economic growth and to the continuing complexity of business. A growing number of businesses means increased demand for advice in all areas of business operations and planning.

The food services and drinking places industry is expected to add more than 1.0 million new jobs over the 2006–2016 projection period. Increases in population, dual-income families, and dining sophistication will contribute to job growth. In addition, the increasing diversity of the population will contribute to job growth in food services and drinking places that offer a wider variety of ethnic foods and drinks.

Almost 617,000 new jobs are expected to arise in state and local government, except education and health care, growth of almost 8 percent over the 2006–2016 period. Job growth will result primarily from growth in the population and its demand for public services. Additional job growth will result as state and local governments continue to receive greater responsibility from the federal government for administering federally funded programs.

Wholesale trade is expected to add more than 428,000 new jobs over the coming decade, reflecting growth both in trade and in the overall economy. Most new jobs will be for sales representatives at the wholesale and manufacturing levels. However, industry consolidation and the growth of electronic commerce using the Internet are expected to limit job growth to 7.3 percent over the 2006–2016 period, less than the 10.8 percent projected for all industries.

Continual changes in the economy have far-reaching and complex effects on employment in industries. Job seekers should be aware of these changes, keeping alert for developments that can affect job opportunities in industries and the variety of occupations that are found in each industry.

Editor's Note: The preceding article was adapted from the Career Guide to Industries, *a publication of the U.S. Department of Labor. A book titled* 40 Best Fields for Your Career *(JIST Publishing) includes information from the* Career Guide to Industries *plus useful "best fields" lists and other helpful insights.*

© JIST Works

Job Outlook for People Who Don't Have a Bachelor's Degree

You have skills. You have knowledge. And you can have a good career—regardless of whether you have a bachelor's degree. According to U.S. Bureau of Labor Statistics (BLS) projections, millions of job openings will be available between 2006 and 2016 for people who don't have a bachelor's degree. And many of these job openings will be in high-paying occupations.

A bachelor's degree brings many benefits, but it is not the only route to a job. In fact, most jobs are filled by workers who do not have a degree, and BLS does not expect that to change. Between 2002 and 2012, job openings for workers who are entering an occupation for the first time and who don't have a bachelor's degree are expected to total roughly 40 million. That's almost six times the number of job openings expected for workers who have a bachelor's degree.

Many of these jobs will require some training after high school. That could mean enrolling in vocational classes at a technical school, taking a few college courses, training on the job in an apprenticeship program, or getting an associate degree.

But which occupations should you train for? Which are expected to offer the best prospects? Read on to learn about the occupations that are projected to have the most openings for people who do not have a bachelor's degree and about high-demand occupations that pay well. Next, learn more about career fields—including construction, healthcare, education, and computer work—that are expected to provide good opportunities for new workers. Accompanying tables identify projected openings and 2006 earnings for occupations in each of these career fields.

The data in this article are estimates. They are based on the education levels of current workers and on projections of future job growth. Additionally, the results assume that future workers will have education levels similar to those of current workers. The data provided throughout the article, along with the resources listed at the end, can help you decide how to pursue a career that interests you.

Openings and Where They Will Be

Between 2006 and 2016, BLS expects about 50 million job openings to be filled. Of this total, about 40 million openings are projected to be filled by workers who do not have a bachelor's degree and who are entering an occupation for the first time. About 19 million of these openings are expected to be held by workers who have a high school diploma or less education. Another 13 million openings are expected for workers who have some college education or an associate degree but do not have a bachelor's degree.

Job openings are expected in every type of occupation. But some occupations and career fields will have more job openings and better earnings than others.

Occupations with Potential

Two main factors determine whether an occupation will have many job openings for workers entering an occupation. One factor is how many workers leave the occupation permanently. Large occupations—that is, occupations in which many jobs exist nationwide—have more workers and, therefore, also usually have more workers who leave the occupation and create openings. Occupations with few training requirements or low earnings also often have more workers who leave. And occupations with many older workers usually provide more openings because of retirements.

Another factor affecting job openings is job growth. Some occupations gain new positions faster than others, providing more openings for workers who seek to enter the occupation.

The occupations that are expected to need the most new workers between 2006 and 2016 employ workers with widely varying levels of education. Many openings are expected in occupations that people can enter right after high school. But openings in other occupations, especially higher-paying ones, often attract people who have additional training or education. People without training also enter these occupations, but they often start out earning less while they train on the job.

Occupations with the most openings. Chart 1 shows the occupations that are projected to have the most job openings between 2006 and 2016 for people who have less education than a bachelor's degree. Most of these occupations involve working with the public.

You can enter most of the occupations shown in the chart if you have a high school diploma or less education. Workers often qualify for jobs after less than 1 month of on-the-job training. But five of the occupations—truck drivers; customer service representatives; executive secretaries and administrative assistants; bookkeeping, accounting, and auditing clerks; and registered nurses—usually require more training. These are also the highest-paying occupations on the chart.

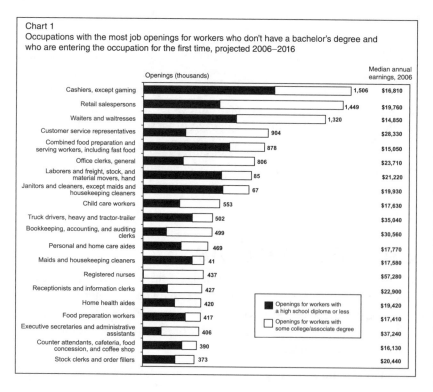

Chart 1
Occupations with the most job openings for workers who don't have a bachelor's degree and who are entering the occupation for the first time, projected 2006–2016

Occupation	Openings (thousands)	Median annual earnings, 2006
Cashiers, except gaming	1,506	$16,810
Retail salespersons	1,449	$19,760
Waiters and waitresses	1,320	$14,850
Customer service representatives	904	$28,330
Combined food preparation and serving workers, including fast food	878	$15,050
Office clerks, general	806	$23,710
Laborers and freight, stock, and material movers, hand	85	$21,220
Janitors and cleaners, except maids and housekeeping cleaners	67	$19,930
Child care workers	553	$17,630
Truck drivers, heavy and tractor-trailer	502	$35,040
Bookkeeping, accounting, and auditing clerks	499	$30,560
Personal and home care aides	469	$17,770
Maids and housekeeping cleaners	41	$17,580
Registered nurses	437	$57,280
Receptionists and information clerks	427	$22,900
Home health aides	420	$19,420
Food preparation workers	417	$17,410
Executive secretaries and administrative assistants	406	$37,240
Counter attendants, cafeteria, food concession, and coffee shop	390	$16,130
Stock clerks and order fillers	373	$20,440

■ Openings for workers with a high school diploma or less
□ Openings for workers with some college/associate degree

Truck drivers usually need 1 month to 1 year of training on the job; some attend vocational schools to learn the basics of commercial driving. Customer service representatives, who also often receive 1 month to 1 year of training, usually start their jobs by observing experienced workers. Executive secretaries and administrative assistants may acquire their skills from work experience in clerical and secretarial jobs. Bookkeeping and related clerks usually receive on-the-job training but may also need formal classes in specific software applications. Registered nurses, unlike the other occupations in the chart, almost always have some college training. About two-fifths of registered nurses over age 25 have an associate degree or have taken some college courses, and nearly all of the rest have a bachelor's degree.

Chart 1 also gives the occupations' 2006 median earnings. (Median earnings show that half of the workers in the occupation earned more than that amount and half earned less.) All but four of the occupations had median earnings below $30,400, the median for workers in 2006.

But median earnings don't show the wide variation in pay that exists in some occupations. For example, earnings for some customer service representatives, such as those who provide help for complex computer problems, are significantly higher than the median. But these same workers are usually highly skilled and have several months of on-the-job training; some also have a bachelor's degree.

Occupations with high earnings and lots of openings. According to BLS

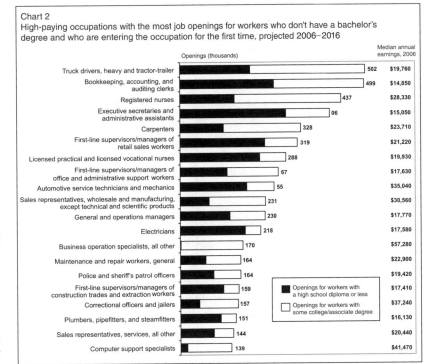

Chart 2
High-paying occupations with the most job openings for workers who don't have a bachelor's degree and who are entering the occupation for the first time, projected 2006–2016

Openings (thousands)		Median annual earnings, 2006
Truck drivers, heavy and tractor-trailer	502	$19,760
Bookkeeping, accounting, and auditing clerks	499	$14,850
Registered nurses	437	$28,330
Executive secretaries and administrative assistants	06	$15,050
Carpenters	328	$23,710
First-line supervisors/managers of retail sales workers	319	$21,220
Licensed practical and licensed vocational nurses	288	$19,930
First-line supervisors/managers of office and administrative support workers	67	$17,630
Automotive service technicians and mechanics	55	$35,040
Sales representatives, wholesale and manufacturing, except technical and scientific products	231	$30,560
General and operations managers	230	$17,770
Electricians	218	$17,580
Business operation specialists, all other	170	$57,280
Maintenance and repair workers, general	164	$22,900
Police and sheriff's patrol officers	164	$19,420
First-line supervisors/managers of construction trades and extraction workers	159	$17,410
Correctional officers and jailers	157	$37,240
Plumbers, pipefitters, and steamfitters	151	$16,130
Sales representatives, services, all other	144	$20,440
Computer support specialists	139	$41,470

■ Openings for workers with a high school diploma or less
□ Openings for workers with some college/associate degree

data, about 285 of the occupations expected to provide openings for high school graduates also had higher-than-average median earnings in 2006. Chart 2 shows the high-paying occupations that are expected to have the most job openings for workers who don't have a bachelor's degree. Workers in all of these occupations have technical skills or supervisory responsibilities. And all of the occupations usually employ workers who complete moderate- or long-term on-the-job training, college courses, or vocational classes.

Several of the occupations in the chart relate to construction or mechanical repair. Some of these occupations require physical strength, but many, such as electricians, do not. Completing a formal apprenticeship can increase your chances of getting a job in these occupations. Studying algebra and taking vocational classes in high school can also help you qualify.

Another way to a high-paying career is to work toward becoming a supervisor. Many high school graduates transfer to managerial occupations as they gain experience. According to some studies, having formal training or taking college courses can increase the chances of becoming a supervisor.

Competing with college workers. Some of the occupations shown in the charts are expected to provide jobs to workers who have a bachelor's degree, as well as to workers who do not have one. When an occupation has workers who have different levels of education, the workers with more education are often better able to compete for jobs. This is particularly true if the occupation requires complicated math, science, writing, or other academic skills.

If you do not have a bachelor's degree and are competing with people who do, you can increase your competitiveness in a number of ways. These include gaining work or volunteer experience, taking high school or college classes that relate to an occupation, and completing a certification.

Additionally, consider contacting your state's labor market information office to learn about work, volunteer, education, and training opportunities. You can also find out which training programs have high placement rates and which occupations are most in demand in your area.

Table 1
Selected office and administrative support occupations

Occupations	Net openings for workers without bachelor's degree, projected 2006–2016	Median annual earnings, 2006	Most significant source of education or training	Percent of workers aged 25 to 44 with…		
				High school diploma or less	Some college/ associate degree	Bachelor's or graduate degree
Office clerks, general	990,800	$23,710	Short-term on-the-job training	36%	45%	19%
Customer service representatives	1,158,400	28,330	Moderate-term on-the-job training	34	44	22
Bookkeeping, accounting, and auditing clerks	594,300	30,560	Moderate-term on-the-job training	34	50	16
Executive secretaries and administrative assistants*	496,680	37,240	Work experience in a related occupation	33	49	18
Receptionists and information clerks	488,820	22,900	Short-term on-the-job training	42	46	13
Stock clerks and order fillers	404,620	20,440	Short-term on-the-job training	63	29	8
Tellers	347,450	22,140	Short-term on-the-job training	39	45	16
Secretaries, except legal, medical, and executive*	331,300	27,450	Moderate-term on-the-job training	33	49	18
Shipping, receiving, and traffic clerks	212,560	26,070	Short-term on-the-job training	64	30	6
Bill and account collectors	165,110	29,050	Short-term on-the-job training	38	48	13

*BLS does not have reliable education data for different types of secretaries; all secretaries were categorized as a group.

Career Fields with Promise

Opportunities abound in almost every career field. The information that follows gives an overview of the expected job openings and common educational requirements for occupations in six widely varying fields. Career fields with the most expected openings are discussed first.

The accompanying tables show occupations that are expected to have many openings over the 2006–2016 decade. The tables also show 2006 earnings, along with the percentage of current workers aged 25 to 44 who have a high school diploma or less, some college courses or an associate degree, or a bachelor's or graduate degree. College courses or degrees may or may not relate to the occupation.

Also listed is the specific type of training, such as on-the-job training, a vocational certificate, or an associate degree, that BLS analysts deemed most significant in the occupation.

Office and administrative support. People who like business and teamwork should expect to find many opportunities in office and administrative support occupations. Between 2006 and 2016, these occupations are projected to provide several million openings for workers who do not have a bachelor's degree. Many of these openings, such as those for stock clerks, usually require little training after high school. (See table 1.) Summer jobs or high school classes in English, typing, and computer-related subjects can pave the way.

Other occupations, such as customer service representatives, often require on-the-job training. Many office workers also take college courses to hone their skills, earn certifications, and increase their opportunity for advancement.

Health care. For workers who have an interest in science and in helping people, health-care occupations are expected to provide some of the most plentiful and highest-paying career opportunities. Overall, health-care occupations are projected to provide more than 10 million job openings between 2006 and 2016 for workers who don't have a bachelor's degree. Many of these openings are expected to result from fast growth. Table 2 lists 10 of the health-care occupations with high earnings in 2006 and a large number of expected openings over the 2006–2016 decade.

Table 2
Selected health-care occupations

Occupations	Net openings for workers without bachelor's degree, projected 2006–2016	Median annual earnings, 2006	Most significant source of education or training	Percent of workers aged 25 to 44 with...		
				High school diploma or less	Some college/ associate degree	Bachelor's or graduate degree
Home health aides	454,080	$19,420	Short-term on-the-job training	55%	37%	7%
Registered nurses	437,345	57,280	Associate degree	1	43	56
Nursing aides, orderlies, and attendants	393,150	22,180	Postsecondary vocational award	55	37	7
Licensed practical and licensed vocational nurses	309,220	36,550	Postsecondary vocational award	21	72	7
Medical assistants*	199,400	26,290	Moderate-term on-the-job training	31	59	10
Pharmacy technicians*	178,400	25,630	Moderate-term on-the-job training	27	57	16
Dental assistants	130,290	30,220	Moderate-term on-the-job training	34	58	9
Medical records and health information technicians	76,190	28,030	Associate degree	37	51	12
Emergency medical technicians and paramedics	61,600	27,070	Postsecondary vocational award	18	68	14
Dental hygienists	54,727	62,800	Associate degree	3	64	33

*Education data for this occupation come from the larger occupational group of which it is a part.

As the table shows, training varies widely within most of these occupations. For example, the most significant source of preparation for nursing aides and home health aides is less than 1 month of on-the-job training. But a large number of aides have taken college courses—either to qualify for certifications or to prepare for other, higher-paying health-care occupations. Some aides may have college coursework unrelated to their job.

In part because the skills they need are becoming more complex, health-care workers are getting more training. Often, this extra education pays off. Although many dental assistants train on the job, for example, about 25 percent of these workers aged 25 and over have an associate degree. And median earnings of dental assistants who have an associate degree are about 10 percent higher than the earnings of those who have a high school diploma or less.

For some health-care occupations, BLS analysts were able to draw conclusions about the level of competition that future job seekers might face. Analysts gathered anecdotal evidence and other data, including information on the number of people who have recently completed training programs. Analysts concluded that over the 2006–2016 decade, there could be excellent opportunities in the following health-care occupations:

★ Dental assistants

★ Dental hygienists

★ Clinical laboratory technologists and technicians

★ Nursing, psychiatric, and home health aides

★ Registered nurses

These occupations usually employ people who have some on-the-job training or education after high school.

Construction. An interest in building things can lead to a career with prospects. More than 1.5 million job openings are projected for workers entering construction occupations between 2006 and 2016. And most of these occupations pay more than the average for all occupations.

There are many types of construction occupations. Some require outdoor work, others don't; some involve a high level of mathematics, others require math skills that are more basic. Many workers in construction occupations start as apprentices, taking vocational classes and getting paid for on-the-job training. Some workers receive college credit for the vocational classes they take.

Table 3
Selected construction occupations

Occupations	Net openings for workers without bachelor's degree, projected 2006–2016	Median annual earnings, 2006	Most significant source of education or training	Percent of workers aged 25 to 44 with…		
				High school diploma or less	Some college/ associate degree	Bachelor's or graduate degree
Carpenters	347,800	$36,550	Long-term on-the-job training	73%	22%	6%
Electricians*	233,920	43,610	Long-term on-the-job training	51	42	7
Construction laborers	227,220	26,320	Moderate-term on-the-job training	79	17	5
First-line supervisors/managers of construction trades and extraction workers	177,760	53,850	Work experience in a related occupation	60	30	10
Plumbers, pipefitters, and steamfitters	156,830	42,770	Long-term on-the-job training	68	29	4
Painters, construction and maintenance	136,710	31,190	Moderate-term on-the-job training	76	17	6
Operating engineers and other construction equipment operators*	117,670	36,890	Moderate-term on-the-job training	78	20	3
Cement masons and concrete finishers	89,390	32,650	Moderate-term on-the-job training	86	12	2
Sheet metal workers	58,540	37,360	Long-term on-the-job training	63	32	4
Roofers	58,140	32,260	Moderate-term on-the-job training	86	11	3

*BLS does not have reliable education data for this occupation specifically; data for related occupations were used.

Table 3 shows the 10 construction occupations expected to have the most job openings over the 2006–2016 decade. In 2006, all of these occupations had median earnings that were above the average for all occupations.

For three of the occupations in the table—carpenters; plumbers, pipefitters, and steamfitters; and roofers—BLS analysts concluded that the job openings could outnumber jobseekers in some years and in some places. Prospects are considered excellent. BLS analysts also concluded that two other construction occupations—insulation workers and brickmasons, blockmasons, and stonemasons—are expected to provide good opportunities.

Police and other protective service. Workers who keep the public safe from crime, natural disasters, and fire are projected to be in high demand. Between 2006 and 2016, protective service occupations are expected to provide about 1 million job openings for workers who don't have a bachelor's degree. As table 4 shows, most of these openings are projected to be in three occupations: security guards, police and sheriff's patrol officers, and correctional officers and jailers.

Table 4
Selected protective service occupations

Occupations	Net openings for workers without bachelor's degree, projected 2006–2016	Median annual earnings, 2006	Most significant source of education or training	Percent of workers aged 25 to 44 with…		
				High school diploma or less	Some college/ associate degree	Bachelor's or graduate degree
Security guards*	386,560	$21,530	Short-term on-the-job training	46%	42%	13%
Correctional officers and jailers*	175,500	35,760	Moderate-term on-the-job training	40	49	11
Police and sheriff's patrol officers*	163,585	47,460	Long-term on-the-job training	16	52	33
Fire fighters	142,030	41,190	Long-term on-the-job training	23	59	18
Lifeguards, ski patrol, and other recreational protective service workers*	72,712	17,160	Short-term on-the-job training	35	34	31
First-line supervisors/ managers of police and detectives	25,174	69,310	Work experience in a related occupation	18	49	33
First-line supervisors/ managers of fire fighting and prevention workers	22,440	62,900	Work experience in a related occupation	18	64	17
Crossing guards	21,260	21,060	Short-term on-the-job training	67	28	5
Detectives and criminal investigators	19,029	58,260	Work experience in a related occupation	10	35	54
First-line supervisors/ managers of correctional officers	11,821	52,580	Work experience in a related occupation	26	49	25

*BLS does not have reliable education data for this occupation specifically; data for related occupations were used.

Security guards can usually qualify for their jobs if they have a high school diploma or less. Once employed, security guards often receive some on-the-job training. Armed guards need training and licensure. Guards working in specialized fields, such as nuclear power plant security, receive extensive formal training after being hired and usually earn more than other guards. Correctional officers also train on the job, but they usually train longer and are paid more than security guards. In some states, correctional officers receive months of training and instruction, often while attending academies.

Police and sheriff's patrol officers train on the job in police academies, and many take classes in criminal justice after high school and before entering the academy. Bachelor's degrees are becoming more common among police and can make it easier to advance, but skills and character are often more important than education. Employers' requirements depend on geographic location and job type.

Education and child care. Career opportunities in schools and day-care centers will continue to be plentiful. More than 1 million openings are expected in this field between 2006 and 2016 for workers who don't have a bachelor's degree. Within these occupations, workers have wide ranges of training and education. Teacher assistants, who are expected to have the most job openings among occupations in this group, are often required to have an associate degree or to pass an exam. But many others train on the job, especially if their work involves supervising children rather than helping with instruction.

Preschool teachers and child-care workers often have an associate degree, too. But the degree is not always required for workers in these two occupations; instead, workers earn an associate or bachelor's degree to learn skills and increase their advancement opportunities. A common strategy is to take courses that lead to certifications and later apply the courses toward a 2- or 4-year degree or both.

Computer. Explosive growth in information technology is expected to create many openings for people who like working with computers. Openings in computer-related occupations for workers who don't have a bachelor's degree are expected to total about 1.4 million between 2006 and 2016. Industry certifications and computer experience are particularly important in this field, in part because many college graduates also compete for these jobs.

According to industry experts, people who don't have a bachelor's degree may find it easiest to enter the following computer occupations: computer support specialists, network and computer systems administrators, and certain types of network systems and data communications analysts.

The computer support specialist occupation is projected to provide the most openings for people without a bachelor's degree. Specialists who don't have a 4-year degree increase their marketability by earning certifications or getting computer experience while they are in school or are working in other jobs.

Network and computer systems administrators include workers at every educational level. Many administrators who don't have a degree begin their careers as computer support specialists, switching to more highly paid administrator jobs after they gain computer experience.

Webmasters, computer security professionals, and Local Area Network (LAN) support staff are also expected to be in high demand. These workers are part of the occupation of network systems and data communications analysts. Many of these workers have a bachelor's degree, but others substitute coursework, experience, or certifications.

Workers in each of these computer occupations had above-average earnings in 2006. But workers who have a bachelor's degree are included in those earnings figures; earnings might be lower for workers who have less education.

How These Numbers Were Developed

Measuring job outlook by education is complicated, and there are many ways to do it. This analysis used expected job openings as a way to measure outlook because the number of job openings helps to determine how easy it will be for workers to enter an occupation. The analysis used survey data as an objective way to separate openings by education level.

Like any analysis based on projections and estimates, however, this one has limitations. Understanding these limitations allows people to better use the results.

© **JIST Works**

Methods Used

To determine job prospects, BLS analysts started by projecting the total number of job openings available between 2006 and 2016 for workers entering an occupation for the first time. Next, analysts estimated how many of those openings would be filled by workers who do not have a bachelor's degree and how many openings would be in high-paying occupations.

Job openings. Job openings come from two sources: the need to fill newly created positions and the need to replace workers who leave an occupation permanently.

To estimate the number of openings that will come from newly created positions, analysts projected how much each occupation would grow or decline between 2006 and 2016. There are many reasons that the number of jobs in an occupation might change. Sometimes, the demand for a certain type of good or service increases—for example, when an aging population creates the need for more healthcare services and, as a result, more healthcare technicians. The way a good or service is provided also can create the need for more jobs in an occupation, such as when library technicians gain jobs faster than librarians do because employment of technicians is considered to be more cost effective.

Many occupations that employ people who do not have a bachelor's degree are projected to gain jobs rapidly. In fact, for 9 of the 10 fastest-growing occupations, a bachelor's degree is not the most significant source of training. The occupation projected to be the fastest-growing of all occupations over the 2006–2016 decade, retail salesperson, usually employs people who train on the job.

The need to replace workers who leave an occupation permanently is expected to provide more openings than job growth will. To estimate how many workers will need to be replaced during the 2006–2016 decade, analysts studied past trends in each occupation and the ages of current workers. In some occupations, workers usually stay for many years. In others, people tend to leave more quickly. These considerations affect replacement needs.

Openings by education. After analysts projected the total number of job openings in each occupation, they estimated how many of those openings would be filled by workers who fall into one of three different education levels: a high school diploma or less, some college or an associate degree, or a bachelor's or graduate degree.

Analysts determined which levels of education were significant in each occupation by looking at the education levels of current workers as reported in 2002, 2003, and 2004 Current Population Survey data. If at least 20 percent of workers had a particular level of education, that level was deemed significant. Expected job openings were divided among each of the significant education levels according to how common that education level was for workers in the occupation.

For example, chemical technicians include workers who have each of the three levels of education: About 30 percent of technicians have a high school diploma or less, about 32 percent have completed some college or an associate degree, and about 37 percent have a bachelor's or graduate degree. Therefore, the expected openings for chemical technicians were divided among these categories using the corresponding percentages. The openings for workers who had less than a bachelor's degree were added to the total.

In addition to describing the three educational attainment categories, this article discusses specific education and training requirements for some occupations. These discussions are based on occupational analyses conducted for the *Occupational Outlook Handbook.*

Openings by earnings. The earnings data in this article are from the BLS Occupational Employment Statistics survey. The survey reflects the 2006 earnings of all workers without regard to education level or experience. Also, the survey does not include self-employed workers.

Limitations of the Data

To measure total job openings and openings by education level, BLS analysts needed to make some assumptions about the future. First, analysts assumed that the education levels in each occupation would remain roughly the same over the 2006–2016 decade. In reality, the educational characteristics of some occupations change over time. Many occupations—such as registered nurses and police officers—have shown a gradual increase in the education levels of their workers.

Analysts also ignored education levels that were uncommon in an occupation; as stated previously, at least 20 percent of workers in an occupation had to have a given level of education for it to be considered significant. So, for example, even though 19 percent of current massage therapists have a high school diploma or less, none of that occupation's future openings were slated for workers with that level of education.

Another limitation of this study is that it focuses on the number of job openings expected in an occupation. Job openings give only a partial view of the prospects that workers can expect. The number of people who will compete for those openings is also important. For most occupations, BLS analysts do not have enough information about the future supply of workers to analyze the competition for jobs.

Finally, the accuracy of this study is limited by its use of survey data. Surveys are always subject to some error because not every worker is counted and because the information gathered is sometimes incorrect. In addition, many of the occupations studied here could not be counted with enough statistical accuracy because the number of workers surveyed was too small. In those cases, analysts substituted the education levels of similar occupations or groups of occupations that had larger numbers of workers.

Despite the assumptions and limitations of this analysis, there is evidence that counting future job openings using the method described here produces accurate results. When existing jobs are separated into educational categories using this method, the results closely match current numbers.

For More Information

To learn more about the occupations described here and about the hundreds of other occupations expected to provide openings for workers who don't have a bachelor's degree, see the 2008–2009 *Occupational Outlook Handbook,* available in many libraries and career centers and online at www.bls.gov/oco. The *Handbook* describes the job outlook, education and training requirements, and job duties of 270 occupations.

Another BLS publication, the 2008–2009 *Occupational Projections and Training Data bulletin,* explains in detail the methods used in this study and lists the projected job openings and worker education levels for every occupation studied by the BLS Office of Occupational Statistics and Employment Projections. The bulletin is available online at www.bls.gov/emp/optd/home.htm and is for sale by calling the Superintendent of Documents toll-free at (866) 512-1800.

To help workers prepare for a career, the U.S. Department of Education offers information about financial aid for people attending 2-year colleges, 4-year colleges, and vocational schools. Call the financial aid hotline toll-free at (800) 4FED-AID (433-3243); write the Federal Student Aid Information Center, P.O. Box 84, Washington, DC 20044-0084; or visit online at www.studentaid.ed.gov.

Studying potential job openings is only a starting point when deciding on a career. Many other considerations are important, including individual skills and interests, personal circumstances, and the needs of local employers. To explore these and other factors in your career decision, visit state labor market information offices and career centers. Information is available online at www.servicelocator.org or by calling the U.S. Department of Labor's toll-free helpline, (877) US2-JOBS (872-5627).

Opportunities are as varied as the workers who seek them. And when it comes to training, finding what is best for you is one of the surest routes to reward.

From the **Occupational Outlook Quarterly** *by the U.S. Department of Labor. Written by Roger Moncarz and Olivia Crosby, economists in the Office of Occupational Statistics and Employment Projections. Adapted with updated economic data.*

Index